DOOMED AT THE START

TEXAS A&M UNIVERSITY

MILITARY HISTORY SERIES

24

DOOMED
AT THE START

American Pursuit Pilots in the Philippines, 1941-1942

WILLIAM H. BARTSCH

FOREWORD BY HERBERT ELLIS

TEXAS A&M UNIVERSITY PRESS
College Station

Library of Congress Cataloging-in-Publication Data

Bartsch, William H., 1933–
    Doomed at the start : American pursuit pilots in the Philippines,
1941–1942 / William H. Bartsch ; foreword by Herbert Ellis. — 1st
ed.
      p.   cm. — (Texas A&M University military history series ;
no. 24)
    Includes bibliographical references and index.
    ISBN 0-89096-492-0 (alk. paper)
    1. World War, 1939–1945—Aerial operations, American.   2. World
War, 1939–1945—Campaigns—Philippines.   3. United States. Army.
Air Corps. Pursuit Group, 24th—History.   4. World War, 1939–1945—
Regimental histories—United States.   I. Title.   II. Series.
D790.B35   1992
940.54'5973—dc20   91-34307
                                                           CIP

To the officers and men of the 24th Pursuit Group,
living and dead

. . . One gets a bit disgusted when he lays his life on the line
for our lousy, out-of-date Air Corps. . . .
Well, we all hope [war] comes soon, because
we are doomed at the start.

2ND LT. MAX LOUK,
20th Pursuit Squadron,
Clark Field, Philippines,
to his sister,
November 23, 1941

Contents

Illustrations

Maps

Foreword

This history is the end product of Bill Bartsch's childhood interest in the pursuit squadrons that fought in the Philippines in the opening days of World War II. These squadrons of the 24th Pursuit Group were part of the small contingent of the U.S. Army Air Corps stationed in the Philippines when the Japanese Empire plunged the United States into a war for which the U.S. was, as usual, unprepared.

Following a re-awakening of his childhood obsession with the Philippines campaign in the 1970s, he began a search for information on the Army Air Corps in the Philippines; he found there was very little available, and there was certainly nothing anywhere near definitive. He began to feel as though the activities of our small Army Air Corps might be fast becoming a lost page in history.

Since it was then thirty-four years after the event, Bill concluded that if such a work was to be produced, he'd have to do it himself. On that note he went about collecting every scrap of information he could find. By the time he wrote to me in 1978, he had already amassed an impressive amount of raw information and knowledge of the subject.

After we began corresponding, he complained that the information available was inadequate, confusing, and contradictory. He said he found the Japanese records invariably at odds with the American version, and "I suspect more reliable in some cases . . . , [and that] . . . even the participants can't be sure what happened, or if they are sure, each one has a different interpretation."

There are several causes for these inconsistencies. The main cause is, without doubt, the confusion that existed at the time. Confusion is a given in war. And it doesn't just happen; it is contrived. Once started, it feeds on itself.

Twenty-five centuries ago, the great Chinese General Sun Tzu Wu wrote, "All warfare is based on deception." The ability to deceive and confuse is one of the most effective weapons of war. Each side uses every stratagem it can devise to confuse the opponent as to capabilities and intent. The success rate is high.

It is, of course, rare for any two people to come away from any dramatic incident with the same story. When the dramatic incident consists of being on the wrong end of an air raid, the number of divergent accounts of the incident is in direct proportion to the number of people in the target area. And besides, it is very difficult to get a good panoramic or objective view of the event from the bottom of a foxhole.

Then there is the terrible destruction of war, which transforms the familiar into the unfamiliar, and which in turn causes disorientation. The individual's sense of permanence and stability is lost; he finds himself in a world turned upside down. Anyone caught up in this contrived maelstrom is very likely to have a distorted viewpoint of what happened, and when he attempts to reconstruct an event some thirty-five or more years later, the passage of time does little to ensure accuracy.

This story of the experiences of the officers and soldiers of the 24th Pursuit Group during the short-lived first Philippine campaign represents the author's reconciliation of contradictory personal accounts provided him through narratives, correspondence, and interviews of individuals who were there. Despite his frequent frustrations in trying to reconstruct what happened in the Philippine campaign, the author persevered in his thirteen-year research right up to the day he submitted his manuscript for publication. He has been indefatigable in his efforts to uncover every scrap of information. He has gone over source material time and again in order to establish or disprove their authenticity. In the end he has produced a record that is probably more inclusive, and more accurate, than any other work on the same subject, and it is closer to the truth than most of the fragments of information with which he had to work. In short, our author has done his homework.

Although this is a story of defeat, it is well worth the reading. There is an old saying, "The victor learns nothing; only the defeated make any effort to learn from their mistakes." This volume contains enough lessons for a college course in *how not to*. Lesson one: there is no second place in a war.

Herbert Ellis
Former Commanding Officer
3rd Pursuit Squadron

Preface

I was nine years old when daily radio and newspaper reports of the heroic defense of our outnumbered forces on Luzon and Bataan against the cruel Japanese flooded my impressionable head. MacArthur was my hero, and Bataan and Corregidor were magic names of faraway places where a life-and-death struggle of good against evil was being waged. Then after the Second World War was over, I gave little thought to the Philippines campaign as I proceeded on with a normal life as a youth, then a grown man. But at the age of about thirty-five, a resurgence of interest in the Pacific War and the Philippines campaign in particular began to intrude into my daily routine—was it an early stage of nostalgia for childhood days?

I found myself searching libraries for books on the Pacific War and the Philippines campaign, eager to see if the accounts of the fighting corresponded to my childhood memories. I especially wanted to read stories on the air heroes of that campaign—Buzz Wagner, Colin Kelly, Grant Mahony, "Shorty" Wheless—names made famous during my childhood. But I found relatively little to satisfy my craving. True, there was Walter D. Edmonds's *They Fought with What They Had*, but it cut off the account of Philippines air operations at December 31, 1941, and thus excluded the Bataan period. Allison Ind's wartime narrative *Bataan: The Judgment Seat* did cover the story of the air force in the Philippines through mid-March, 1942, but the book struck me as propagandistic and straining too much for literary effect.

I began to wonder—if the full, true story of our pilots in the Philippines campaign has not yet been told, might I consider filling the void myself? I had written much in the field of development economics—my profession—so could I perhaps take up the writing of history too?

But where would I find the sources I would need to write such a history? I had heard that relatively little of MacArthur's records had survived the fall of the Philippines, but perhaps I could go to the surviving participants themselves for their stories and piece together an account. But where to find them? And would they be willing to share their experiences with me, an outsider, who was not a professional writer and could not work more than part-time on the project?

In 1976 I succeeded in locating two surviving pilots of the 24th Pursuit Group—George Armstrong and John Brownewell—who proved to be so supportive of the project that I fully committed myself. I also decided to limit my coverage of the aerial operations in the Philippines to that of the pursuit pilots, for it seemed to me that their story in itself was of enough interest to merit telling at book length. Little by little, I established contact not only with other surviving pilots of the group but also with key enlisted men—"Cowboy" Wright of the 17th Pursuit, Jim Brown of the 20th Pursuit, and Tom Gage of the 34th Pursuit—who shared my enthusiasm in reconstructing the history of the group's pursuit squadrons. Each day's mail brought written and taped narratives the participants had prepared at my request, letters with answers to my detailed questions, photos, and, in some cases, even copies of diaries. A picture was developing of the wartime experiences of 24th Pursuit Group officers and enlisted men in the Philippines campaign.

By the early 1980s I had succeeded in locating and gaining the support of most of the surviving pilots and many of the enlisted men and non-flying officers. I decided to expand my search to include the relatives of those who died in the campaign or who survived but were since deceased. I thought that brothers, sisters, aged parents, and children may have retained items relating to their deceased relative that could help add to the story. After identifying the hometowns of individual pilots, I searched through telephone books and city directories to spot possible relatives with the same names. Using this method, I succeeded in many cases in locating relatives. Most were amazed that someone should be inquiring after a long-deceased family member. Where such a search method did not yield results, I tried writing to hometown newspapers and even to postmasters for leads on where to find relatives. So many people were remarkably cooperative.

By various means I gradually came into contact with surviving family members, most of whom were pleased to help with the project. Invariably, the pilots had written home in the prewar period to relate events and express their feelings, and now I was lent their letters, from which I extracted useful information that in the end would permit me to write the chapters of the book covering the prewar period.

In piecing together accounts of wartime incidents, I not surprisingly found that the memories of the participants often confused dates and places, as well as details of events, particularly those in which they did not participate directly themselves. In an effort to straighten out personal accounts, I turned to whatever records I had located—including a cache of U.S. Army Forces in the Far East (USAFFE) papers at the Mac-Arthur Memorial in Norfolk that were not known to exist until some years ago. There were also the diaries of participants as well as Japanese wartime records and accounts. Among the latter the official Japanese war history volumes on the Philippines campaign proved vital, but also important were intercepted Japanese naval messages, war diaries of participating Japanese Navy units, and the memories of many surviving Japanese Zero and bomber pilots from the Japanese navy who had participated in the campaign and whom I had located via go-betweens so essential in Japan for such purposes.

Early on, I had decided that this story would be written from the viewpoint of the participants—the pilots, nonflying officers, and enlisted men—not that of the "brass." I have tried to tell the story through their experiences, their feelings, their incomplete understanding of what was happening around them as their world disintegrated in the face of the relentless Japanese offensive. This is meant to be a *human* story, not one focusing on details of aerial victories or technical characteristics of the aircraft flown.

From the outset of this project, the participants urged me to give an honest and accurate account of what happened, "warts and all," not a Hollywood-style rendition. Over the course of the thirteen years of researching and writing this story, I have unearthed much information that is not flattering to the Air Corps leadership or, in some cases, to individual participants but have included it in the interest of historical accuracy. In most cases, the mistakes made or the less-than-heroic acts committed simply represent differing human reactions to the stress and terror of war. While certain individuals covered in the account, as well as surviving relatives of some of the deceased participants, may feel offended, I hope they will understand that my intention has not been to embarrass or degrade anyone but rather to be faithful to my mandate to tell it like it was.

Acknowledgments

Without the unstinting support I received from the surviving pilots and enlisted men who lived this story, I could not have completed this ambitious project. Lt. Cols. (USAF, Ret.) George H. Armstrong and John L. Brownewell expressed enthusiasm for this enterprise from the start and over the next thirteen years supported it to the maximum of their abilities, additionally providing the invaluable endorsement I needed to gain the support of the other pilots and the enlisted men of the 24th Pursuit Group. Over the years as I proved my commitment to the story through persistent efforts to locate reliable information, other survivors of the Philippine campaign in increasing numbers devoted time to answering detailed questions posed in my letters and in many cases prepared written and taped narratives for me.

It is difficult to single out individuals, but because of their particularly sustained and time-consuming efforts I must mention my gratitude to a few of them. These include, in addition to George Armstrong and John Brownewell, their 17th Pursuit squadron mates Dave Obert (recently deceased), John Posten, Bill Rowe, "Red" Sheppard, and the late "Cowboy" Wright. Among the 3rd Pursuiters I wish to thank especially Herb Ellis, whose long letters and prodigious memory were instrumental in clarifying events, as well as Hank Thorne and the late Andy Krieger. Joe Moore, Lloyd Stinson, and Jim Brown of the 20th Pursuit stayed with me over the whole lifetime of this project to ensure that I had as accurate a picture as possible of the operations of their squadron. Two of only three surviving pilots of the 21st Pursuit, Sam Grashio and Gus Williams, early on gave their full support to my efforts to present an accurate account of the experiences of their squadron. For the history of the 34th Pursuit, I relied mainly on the memories of "Shorty" Crosland, Frankie Bryant, Stewart Robb, and Tom Gage, who from the beginning supported the project wholeheartedly. For an inside view of the activities of 24th Group's

Headquarters Squadron, the former CO, Maj. Gen. (USAF, Ret.) Benny Putnam, gave me his recollection of operations, while from the enlisted man's standpoint, Jesse White provided me a colorful and detailed narrative of events as he recalled them.

For entrusting their personal diaries of wartime experiences to me, I am particularly grateful to Dave Obert, Bill Rowe, the late Randy Keator, John Geer, Bill Powell, and Don Steele. I am equally indebted to Martha Gies for providing me a copy of the wartime diary of her late father, Carl Parker Gies, and to Michael Raudenbush for a copy of the diary of his late father, Bill Hennon.

The relatives of many of the pursuit pilots killed during the campaign or who died before the initiation of this project kindly lent me letters and photos sent home in the prewar period by the pilots. In this connection, I would like to thank the families of A. W. Balfanz, Jerry Brezina, Carl Gies, Wilson Glover, Bill Hennon, Forrest Hobrecht, Ben Irvin, Arthur Knackstedt, Lawrence Lodin, Max Louk, Morgan McCowan, Grant Mahony, Don Miller, Percy Ramsey, Charles Sneed, and Varian Kiefer White, as well as the wife of Andy Krieger, who made his letters available to me during his fatal illness. Edie Neri also transcribed for me historical items from the letters her husband, Frank, had sent her following her repatriation to the United States in May, 1941.

On the Japanese side, I am grateful to Hideki Shingo, the flying commander of the Tainan *kokutai,* who declined to write his own book on his wartime experiences but unfailingly provided me with answers to my numerous questions about the operations of his unit in the Philippines campaign. It is my deep regret that he died before this project was completed.

A great number of institutions responded to my requests for records of the campaign. I particularly wish to thank John Taylor, Will Mahony, and Charles Shaughnessy of the National Archives for their help with materials through the gestation period of this project. James Boone at the MacArthur Memorial identified and photocopied records from memorial archives relating to air operations and beach defense on Bataan that were among the most important sources for this story. Richard Sommers at the U.S. Army Military History Institute at Carlisle Barracks, Pennsylvania, provided me access to the institute's collections on the Philippines campaign during my visit there, including the Louis Morton materials used for his 1953 classic, *The Fall of the Philippines.* Similarly, I would like to acknowledge the assistance of Martin Gordon of the Historical Division, Corps of Engineers, Quantico, Virginia, who put the yet uncataloged papers of the late Brig. Gen. Hugh Casey, comprising the invaluable 1941–42 records of USAFFE engineer operations, at my disposal. I am also grateful to Col. William Ryan and the staff of the American

Battle Monuments Commission in Washington, D.C., for their unfailing responses to my frequent requests for information on the deaths of officers and enlisted men of the 24th Pursuit Group.

Finally, I would like to apologize to my long-suffering wife, Lila, who thought this project and its constant demand on my time would never come to an end.

Part One
PHILIPPINES BUILDUP

Secretary of Navy Frank Knox was adamant: the United States would defend its ward the Philippine Commonwealth against any attack. When reminded by reporters at the Washington press conference that some military analysts had expressed doubt that the islands, seven thousand miles distant from the United States, could be held against a full-scale Japanese invasion, he replied crisply, "We can defend anything."

It was October 23, 1940, and the Far Eastern situation looked grim. With the collapse of the Netherlands and France and the prospect that Britain would go down in defeat soon too, their possessions in East Asia looked ripe for the picking by an increasingly expansionist Japan. Indeed, three months earlier, Japan had forced the Vichy government of France to accept the presence of Japanese bases in northern Indochina. Then in late September it had signed a tripartite pact with Germany and Italy, making clear its intentions to force a division of American forces between the Atlantic and Pacific oceans and thus to limit the possibilities for American responses to further Japanese excursions in the western Pacific basin.

Knox could not admit it, but the public commitment to defend the distant Philippines was more rhetoric than reality. The 1922 Limitation of Arms Conference proscribed any defensive improvements of the Philippines. The secret War Plan Orange-3 provided only for the small American garrison to hold the approaches to the Manila Bay area until the Pacific Fleet could come to its rescue—six months later. Implicitly, the United States had accepted the likelihood that it would lose its main Pacific possession in the event of war with Japan.

Still, the United States could not let the Philippines go by default to Japan. It would embark on a limited reinforcement of its meager forces there. The day of Knox's pronouncement, the War Department announced to the press that two pursuit squadrons—the 17th from Selfridge Field and the 20th from Hamilton Field—were being ordered transferred to the Philippines to bolster the islands' aerial defenses. To equip the squadrons, forty (later increased to fifty-seven) Republic EP-1 fighters, an export model of the Air Corps's Seversky P-35, were being taken over from a Swedish contract for diversion to the Philippines.

In May, 1940, immediately after he took over command of the Philippine Department, an integral part of the U.S. Army, Maj. Gen. George Grunert began complaining to the War Department about the sorry state of defenses in the Philippines—in particular, the air defenses. How could he be expected to repel possible aerial and naval attacks with his small force of 1934-vintage B-10 bombers and 1933-model P-26A pursuit aircraft that had been dumped on the Philippine Department after they had outlived their usefulness elsewhere? While he was pleased to hear of the addition of the two pursuit squadrons and P-35 fighters in response to his earlier request, this was not enough. In the coming months, he bombarded the War Department with further requests for air defense: an air warning system, funds to construct more airfields, two additional pursuit squadrons and one more bombardment squadron, and pursuit aircraft more modern than the P-35.

In March, 1941, thirty-one new P-40B Tomahawk pursuit aircraft were consigned to Grunert, and the following month eighteen B-18 bombers were ordered transferred to him from Hawaii. Then, in an organizational upgrading of his air units, the Philippine Department Air Force was established in early May, with Brig. Gen. Henry Clagett as its commander, the first Air Corps general officer to be assigned to the Philippines.

The War Department's reinforcements were still far below Grunert's stated requirements, but he was told that U.S. defense commitments in men and matériel were expanding elsewhere too beyond its capacity to fulfill them all adequately. Grunert would simply have to be patient. This was cold comfort to the Philippine Department commander, who knew that his "air force" was only a token force and would not be able to stand up against even a mildly determined and ill-equipped foe.

The next aggressive act of the Japanese completely changed

the situation of the Philippines' defense. On July 24, a powerful invasion force disembarked in southern Indochina, where it seized air and naval bases. Japan was now within striking distance of the Dutch East Indies and Malaya.

In retaliation for this hostile act, perceived as a direct threat to peace, President Roosevelt two days later ordered all Japanese assets in the United States frozen. At the same time, the U.S. government reorganized defensive forces in the Philippines by ordering all units of the American and Filipino armies put under a single operational command—USAFFE. Former chief of staff of the U.S. Army Douglas MacArthur, since 1935 serving as the chief military adviser to the commonwealth government, was called to active service as a major general to command the USAFFE. Funds were also to be provided for the mobilization of the Philippine Army. A few days later, Army Chief of Staff George Marshall told his staff that it was the policy of the United States to defend the Philippines—and this time the country would be backing it up with actions. The Philippines were to be given the highest priority for all military equipment.

In mid-August, MacArthur was informed that the 200th Coast Artillery (AA) Regiment and the 194th Tank Battalion were being assigned to his command. For his aerial defenses, he was being shipped fifty new P-40Es. When the War Department asked MacArthur how many additional air force squadrons could be operated from existing fields at that time, at the end of three months, and after six months, MacArthur was not modest in his response. At present he could use ten more pursuit, seven more medium bombardment, and three heavy bombardment squadrons. In three months he could handle three more heavy bombardment squadrons, and in six months three additional pursuit, two more medium bombardment, and four extra heavy bombardment squadrons. Still, this level of reinforcements was considerably less than his air chief, General Clagett, would be requesting a month later in a memo to MacArthur. On the basis of Clagett's analysis, the newly designated Air Force, USAFFE, would need twenty-seven squadrons of pursuit aircraft, thirty squadrons of heavy bombers, and eighteen squadrons of light bombers, on the assumption that the Japanese had one thousand bombers on Formosa for attacking the Philippines. But lack of airfields would be a stumbling block to such an expansion: fifty-six would be needed, against some ten existing at the time.

Reinforcement of the Philippines with the new four-engine B-17 Flying Fortress particularly intrigued planners at the War Department. The threat posed to Japanese bases on Formosa and even the Japanese mainland itself from such long-range heavy bombers was being regarded as a means to discourage further Japanese expansion and possible entry into the war. With the safe arrival at Clark Field of nine B-17s flown across the Pacific in mid-September, MacArthur was given priority for all B-17s as they came off the production lines. In October, twenty-six more B-17s would be winging their way to the Philippines from California, with thirty-three more scheduled for December, fifty-one for January, and forty-six in February.

Following the establishment in mid-September of the 24th Pursuit Group from the three pursuit squadrons of the old 4th Composite Group, a second group was assigned at the beginning of October to the Philippines—the 35th Pursuit Group. An additional 50 P-40Es were being shipped to equip the new group, and by December 31 MacArthur was scheduled to have a total of 240 P-40Es for his projected interceptor command.

In addition to heavy bombers and pursuit aircraft, Mac-Arthur was being transferred a group of A-24 dive-bombers— the 27th Bomb Group (Light)—as a defense against Japanese invasion forces. It was expected, however, that its fifty-two aircraft would arrive only after the group's personnel, who were to arrive in Manila in mid-November.

The massive buildup of the Philippines' air defenses now called for an upgrading of MacArthur's air force organization. Highly regarded Maj. Gen. Lewis Brereton was being transferred from the States to take command of the newly designated Far East Air Force (FEAF), the main combat components of which would be the 5th Bomber Command and the 5th Interceptor Command. MacArthur was particularly pleased following Brereton's arrival on November 4. Brereton had brought with him a copy of the new Rainbow-5 war plan, which now confirmed that the defense of the Philippines was not to be limited to the Manila Bay area but rather to be extended to cover all the islands of the commonwealth, in response to Mac-Arthur's persuasive arguments the past months for an expansion of his mandate. The new plan even included a reference to the mounting of air raids against Japanese forces and installations within tactical range of his air force. MacArthur now ordered his subordinate commands to meet any invader on the beaches, which were to be held at all costs.

Disturbing news reached the USAFFE on November 28th. The long negotiations with Japanese representatives in Washington had resulted in failure. Hostile action was expected at any time. MacArthur immediately put all his forces on "readiness" status. His component commands, including the FEAF, issued detailed instructions to their subordinate units for preparation for all eventualities. MacArthur was skeptical that the Japanese would attack his command, however. In a meeting on December 6 with Adm. Thomas Hart, commander in chief of the Manila-based U.S. Asiatic Fleet, and visiting Vice Adm. Tom Phillips, British Royal Navy commander at Singapore, MacArthur indicated he would need four more months to complete his buildup but expressed his belief that "the inability of an enemy to launch his air attacks on these islands is our greatest security . . . the inability of the enemy to bring not only air but mechanized and motorized elements leaves me with a sense of complete security" ("Report of Conference, December 6, 1941," in Admiral Hart Personal Papers, Series 1, Item 12).

Brereton did not share MacArthur's assessment of the situation. A few days earlier he had shifted half his force of thirty-five B-17s to Del Monte on Mindanao, beyond the range of any Japanese bombers on Formosa. He expected war at any moment.

1. "GOD, IT'S A RECKLESS, CAREFREE LIFE WE HAVE IN THE AIR"

1 As the creaking World War I transport *Etolin* slowly headed into Manila Bay, 2nd Lt. Dave Obert and twenty-three other brand new flying school graduates of the class of 40-H at Kelly Field were on the deck to get their first views of their new home, the Philippine Islands. It was the morning of Monday, February 10, 1941, and they were taking up their new assignments to the army's Philippine Department at Nichols Field, just south of Manila.

Obert, a twenty-two-year-old farmboy from Apache, Oklahoma, who had worked his way through the University of Oklahoma for three and one half years before entering army flying school, was the only one of his Kelly Field class assigned to the Philippines who had not asked for it; he had put in for March Field. At 6'½", too tall by Kelly Field standards to apply for pursuit, Obert had been recommended for bombardment, against his preference. When squadron assignments were given out on the *Etolin* en route to the Philippines, however, he was happy to find that he had been picked for the 17th Pursuit Squadron, which was receiving its first pilot reinforcements since its arrival two months earlier from Selfridge Field. Assigned with Obert to the 17th were George "Ed" Kiser (Somerset, Kentucky), Jack Dale (Willoughby, Ohio), Nathaniel "Cy" Blanton (Shawnee, Oklahoma), and Joe Kruzel (Wilkes-Barre, Pennsylvania).

Six other "newies" were posted to the 20th Pursuit: Martin Connelly (Syracuse, New York), Frank Ansley (Niagara Falls, New York), Bob Duncan (Dallas, Texas), Edwin Gilmore (Highland Park, Michigan), Morgan McCowan (Leoti, Kansas), and James "Buck" Weaver (Freeport, Illinois). Assigned along with the 17th Pursuit to the 4th Composite Group, the 20th Pursuit Squadron had arrived in the Philippines from Hamilton Field, California, on November 23, 1940, twelve days ahead of the 17th.

Five other 40-H graduates were sent to the 3rd Pursuit, which before arrival of the 17th and 20th was the only pursuit squadron in the 4th Composite Group, to which it had been assigned since 1919. Two of the

Dave Obert, later of the 17th Pursuit Squadron, as a flying cadet at Kelly Field, October, 1940. *Courtesy National Archives*

squadron's newies were from Ohio—Don Steele from Akron and John Griffith from Cincinnati—while Andy Krieger hailed from Salamanca, New York; his best friend, George Ellstrom, from Sellersville, Pennsylvania; and Doug Levee, from Stillwater, Oklahoma.

Krieger was enthusiastic about his choice of assignment after only a few days in the islands. The Philippines was "the most wonderful country I have ever seen from a great many aspects . . . a veritable paradise for the Army," he wrote his widowed father, a colonel in the regular army. Krieger had decided on a military career after completing three years at Cornell University and had applied for flight training; he wanted to make his father proud of him. He was particularly pleased to be assigned to the 3rd Pursuit, where "all the officers are swell fellows." His commanding officer, William A. R. "Robbie" Robertson, was "a great sport" and "not unreasonable with us, as some COs are prone to be." By the beginning of March, Krieger had already put in about twenty hours on the squadron's venerable Boeing P-26As, with which the 3rd Pursuit had been equipped since 1937. Exhilarated by the experience, the novice military pilot informed his father, "I have decided that pursuit is the only thing for me."

For flying school classmate Doug Levee, any possibility of a career in pursuit had ended ten days earlier. At 8:00 A.M. on February 21, he had taken a P-26A up in his checkout flight along with Don Steele. During the scheduled one-hour hop, Levee separated from Steele and headed south of Manila. Planning on a little daredevil flying in his "Peashooter," he tried to fly upside down only fifty feet off the ground to impress the Filipino sugar mill workers at Calamba, Laguna Province, thirty miles southeast of Manila. He became disoriented, however, misjudged his position, and flew into the ground. He was killed instantly.

By the end of March, fifty-two of the fifty-seven Seversky P-35As that had been taken over by the Army Air Corps from a Swedish contract and sent to the Philippines had been received by the depot at Nichols Field and were assigned to the three pursuit squadrons. For the first time, there were more P-35As in commission than P-26As—forty-two against twenty-two. With only forty-eight flying officers in the three squadrons, it was now possible to assign P-35As to individual pilots. To Andy Krieger, it was a "nice feeling to have such an expensive, capable piece of machinery all your own, to do with as you like." He was delighted with its handling characteristics: "You sit there with 1,200 horsepower in your lap and a feather in your back."

The other pilots shared Krieger's pleasure with the P-35A. It was comfortable, stable, very strong, easy to control, and it could take off in less than 400 feet and land with 871 feet. On the negative side, it did have a tendency to ground-loop if not watched carefully in the landing roll. It was also difficult to get the tail down on landing; the engine was mounted too far forward, which caused a weight distribution problem. But because of its stability, responsiveness, and excellent visibility, the pilots found the P-35A an ideal machine for formation flying. With each

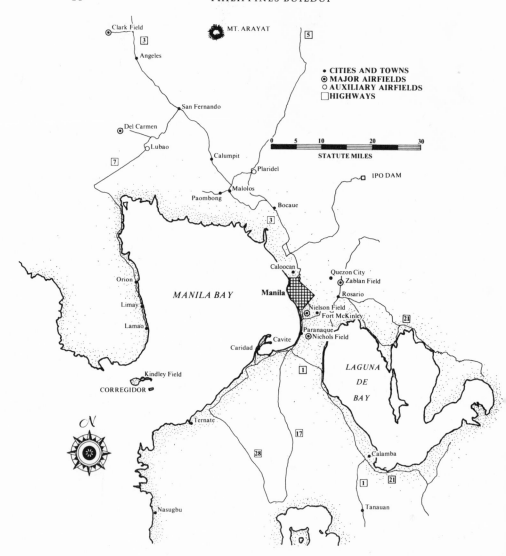

Map 1.   Manila Area

squadron now assigned an adequate number of pilots, such formation flying became the principal flying activity. The pilots flew three-ship Vs,
with nine planes in a formation, usually in a staggered position to allow
rapid turning of the entire formation, an exercise comparable to close
order drill in the infantry. Such formations were used for aerial reviews
and other show purposes.

2 On Sunday, May 4, an eighteen-ship formation of P-26As was ordered out to meet the Boeing 314 flying boat coming in that day. This flight of the "China Clipper" was something special for the pursuit pilots; a brigadier general was on board—Henry B. Clagett, who would be taking over army air operations in the Philippines. Andy Krieger and the others from the three pursuit squadrons had a difficult time giving the clipper "a good buzz" because it was traveling as fast as their obsolete pursuit planes. But finally the "Peashooters" clustered around the immense flying boat while escorting it into Manila. They looked "like flies" to Krieger.

Two days later, Clagett took over his new position as commanding general of the Philippine Department Air Force, established that day. His chief of staff was Col. Harold H. George, who had arrived with Clagett on the Clipper and who had been serving under Clagett at Selfridge Field. A short, dark-faced man of forty-eight years with a quick smile and penetrating dark eyes, "Pursuit" George—to differentiate him from the other Harold George in the Air Corps, "Bomber" George—had been popular with the pilots at Selfridge, largely because he was a former pursuit pilot himself, having flown in World War I. Having served under him at Selfridge, William "Red" Sheppard, who had come out with the 17th Pursuit in December, 1940, was sure that Colonel George would make "a real flying outfit" out of the raw material under his command.

In his first personnel decisions upon taking up his assignment, Clagett promoted the COs of the 17th and 20th pursuit squadrons—Majs. Kirtley J. Gregg and Orrin Grover—to the command and operations officer positions, respectively, of the 4th Composite Group. First Lt. Boyd "Buzz" Wagner, the senior ranking officer of the squadron, at twenty-four years of age only slightly older than most of his squadron mates and a "hot shot" pilot, moved up as CO of the 17th Pursuit. Assuming command of the 20th Pursuit was 1st Lt. Joseph H. Moore, like Wagner nearly a contemporary of his pilots—at twenty-seven years of age—and the ranking officer in the squadron. A 38-B flying school graduate from Spartanburg, South Carolina, Moore had already shown natural leadership qualities that would eventually carry him to the highest ranks of the air force. To complete the wholesale changes in the command of the pursuit squadrons, it was announced that "Robby" Robertson would be leaving the 3rd Pursuit on May 14 for a new assignment in the United States. Replacing him would be thirty-four-year old Maj. William H. Maverick, of the well-known Maverick family of Texas, who held the Army Air Corps record for hits scored on a sleeve target.

3 At nine o'clock on the morning of May 8 a huge crowd was headed down to Pier 7 in Manila Bay again. The USAT *Washington* had just docked with another group of reinforcements for the Philippine Department. In-

P-35A of Buzz Wagner, CO of the 17th Pursuit Squadron, at Nichols Field, spring, 1941. Note the distinctive snow owl insignia of the squadron and the two fuselage stripes of the squadron commander. *Courtesy Carlton Edsall*

cluded among the passengers were thirty-nine graduates of army flying schools—class 41-B—who were being transferred to the Philippines. Disembarking amid cheers and band music, the latest batch of newies was taken immediately by the officers assigned to them to the Army and Navy Club, where a big all-day reception was being put on for them and for the wives of other officers who would be departing for the United States on the USAT *Republic* and the USAT *Washington*.

Each of the pursuit squadrons was assigned eight of the 41-B pilots. Among those assigned to the 20th Pursuit were Carl Parker Gies, Max Louk, and Erwin Crellin, who had decided to share a house. Gies, a native of Salem, Oregon, and older than the others at twenty-six years, had never intended to be a flier but had taken an Air Corps exam as a lark with some university classmates and had passed it. Louk, at twenty-two years the baby of the group, and Crellin, the most popular of the three with the ladies, were both from Kansas. Two of the newies assigned to the 17th Pursuit were Minnesotans—Lawrence Kermit Lodin from Minneapolis and William J. Hennon from Mound. Hennon had decided to link up with four other 41-Bs going to the 17th, including John Posten from Atlantic Highlands, New Jersey, and Bill Rowe from Lynn, Massachusetts, to rent a house right across the road from Nichols Field.

By mid-May, the newies had commenced their training program, starting out with their squadrons' North American A-27 two-place ship, then putting in ten to fifteen hours in the P-26A before graduating to the P-35A. After some fifty hours in the P-35A, the rookie pilots of the 20th Pursuit would begin transition to the Curtiss P-40B. A shipment of thirty-one of the fast new fighters had arrived on May 17 and were uncrated and assembled by the Air Depot. The 20th Pursuit received twenty-five of them.

Although the 20th Pursuit was to be totally reequipped with the new P-40s, the other pursuit squadrons were to receive two each, in order to become acquainted with them before the arrival of P-40Es. Third Pursuiters Andy Krieger and Frank Neri, a 40-D flying school graduate who had come over with the 20th Pursuit in November, 1940, were pleased with the characteristics of the new fighter, which was "equipped with all the latest improvements, including armor plate and bullet-proof gas tanks."

The pilots' initial favorable reaction turned to derision when it was discovered that the P-40Bs had been shipped without the Prestone coolant required for their liquid-cooled engines. Since the depot had warned that to run up the engines for a few seconds without Prestone would ruin them beyond repair, the P-40Bs after assembly were being lined up at Nichols and left standing idle. The Philippines pilots had modern pursuit aircraft for the first time but were unable to fly them.

4 On the morning of Tuesday, June 24, another U.S. Army transport pulled into Pier 7 in Manila Bay. Among the disembarking passengers on the *President Pierce* were ninety-six fresh graduates of flying school—sixty-eight from the class of 41-C and twenty-eight from 41-D. The 41-D contingent was literally just out of school. The pilots had completed their advanced flying class at Stockton Field, California, and were commissioned second lieutenants on May 30, only one week before the *Pierce* sailed from San Francisco.

The arrival of the *Pierce* caught the Philippine Department unprepared. Because of security precautions observed by the transport, it had maintained radio silence during the voyage and thus had not informed the department of its time of arrival. Despite the lack of preparations, the newies were taken immediately to the Army and Navy Club for an impromptu welcoming party given by the squadrons to which they were being assigned. The 3rd Pursuit was getting twenty-two of the new pilots, the 17th Pursuit was assigned twenty-one, and the 20th Pursuit received twenty. In one stroke, the pilot strength of each squadron was doubled.

Unlike their predecessors, however, the pursuit squadrons' newies would not be looking for accommodations in the Nichols Field area after

Pilots of the 20th Pursuit Squadron at Nichols Field, mid-May, 1941. *Left to right, front row:* Varian White, Carl Gies, John Valkenaar, Max Louk, Erwin Crellin, Harrison Hughes, and John Geer; *second row:* Marshall Anderson, Tex Marble, Ozzie Lunde, Joe Moore, Bill Cummings, Charley Sneed, Fred Armstrong, and Edwin Gilmore; *back row:* Morgan McCowan, Martin Connelly, Robert Duncan, Buck Weaver, and Eugene Shevlin. *Courtesy George H. Armstrong, Lt. Col. USAF (Ret.)*

the party. They were informed that all tactical squadrons at Nichols were being ordered to Clark Field to the north by the end of the month so that a major construction program could be carried out at Nichols, largely to overcome a flooding problem. Rain had flooded the 17th Pursuit's men out of their tent camp and obliged the squadron during the past two weeks to park their airplanes outside so the men could live in the hangars instead. The landing field, which was submerged during the rainy season, was to be properly drained and lengthened, and a second, concrete runway was to be built in anticipation of five pursuit squadrons being assigned to the field. Additional barracks and officers quarters were also to be built.

As soon as the party was over, the newies—most of whom had gotten "plastered" during the excitement of their first hours in their new post—were loaded onto ten army trucks for the eighty-five-mile drive north over narrow, congested roads to Clark Field and adjoining Fort Stotsenburg, where all Clark-based officers were accommodated.

Most of the 41-B pilots (now no longer newies) were getting in their final hours in the P-35A before leaving Nichols. Kermit Lodin, who had found the P-35A "a bit complicated" at first, had now become very familiar with it and was enjoying himself immensely flying it. As he wrote to his parents on June 27, "Things that used to scare me when I was in the only plane in the sky, we now do in six-plane formation: loops, Immelman turns and half rolls. Our leaders attack every other squadron on the island in formations of six or couples. God, it's a reckless, carefree life we have in the air. All rules followed in flying schools are abandoned here."

Following the letup of the heavy rain of the past days, the Nichols-based squadrons headed north. On the morning of July 2, the pilots of the 3rd and 20th pursuit squadrons began shuttling their aircraft to Clark. The 3rd Pursuit transferred all its aircraft in commission—twelve P-35As and seven P-26As. By the end of the day, the 20th Pursuiters had shifted all fourteen P-35As and six P-26As, but none of their twenty-five P-40Bs— the Prestone for them still had not arrived. The 17th Pursuit was assigned to Iba, on the west coast of Luzon, for gunnery training and by late afternoon moved its flyable thirteen P-35As and seven P-26As from Nichols to the field. But the squadron's twenty-one newies at Clark Field were left uninformed when they would be moved to Iba.

5 At Clark Field in early July, the 3rd and 20th Pursuit squadrons were commencing their training program for the forty-two newies assigned to the two squadrons. As in the case of the previous newcomers, the 41-C and 41-D trainees would be starting with three to four hours in the A-27, then would be moving up to the P-26A for about twelve hours' flying time, followed by graduation to the P-35A. By mid-July the 41-B pilots of the 3rd and 20th pursuit squadrons had put in their required fifty hours in the P-35A and thus completed their own training program. For the 20th Pursuiters, however, there was still the transition work in their P-40Bs to be done. By the end of the first week of July, the Prestone had arrived and the planes were finally moving up to Clark.

Over at Iba, thirty-seven miles to the west, the twenty-one newies of the 17th Pursuit had arrived from Clark but were unable to start their training program until July 8 because of incessant rain caused by a typhoon. Finally, they were split up into training flights of seven pilots each, with two senior pilots as instructors in each flight. Forrest Hobrecht, a former actor from Dallas, Texas, and at twenty-seven the oldest pilot in the 17th, found that he was going to have to unlearn a lot of his flying habits taught at Stockton Field. Flying as the trainee in the squadron's A-27, he was told to forget all the safety precautions he had learned in

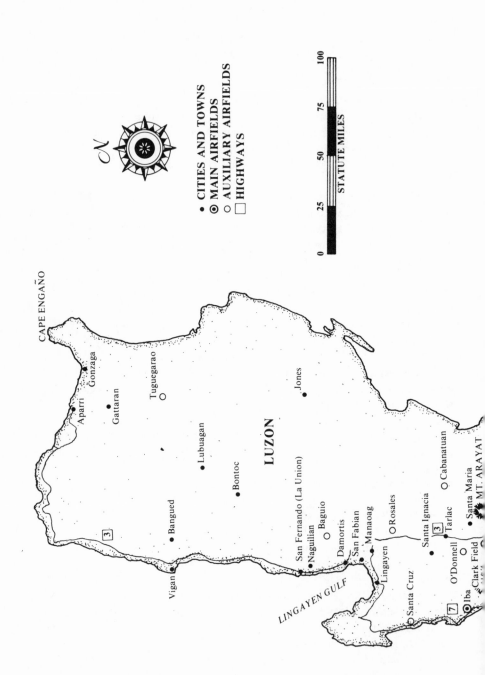

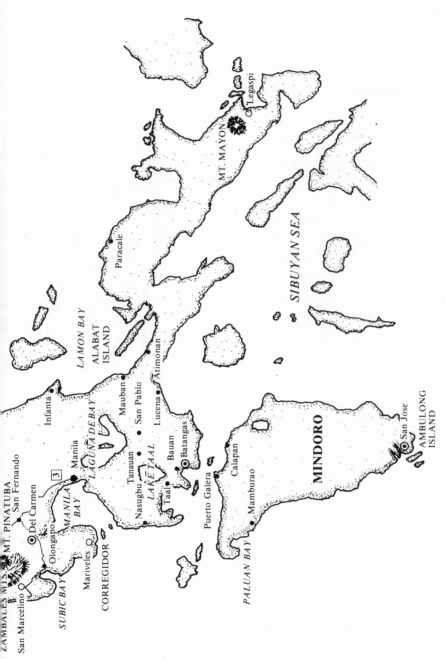

Map 2. Luzon and Mindoro

P-35A no. 41-17439 after it was nosed up at Clark Field on July 2, 1941, by 3rd Pursuit
CO Maj. Billy Maverick. *Courtesy Fred Roberts, Col USAF (Ret.)*

flying school, since he was supposed to know the rudiments of flying now.
By the time of his second hop in the two-seat attack plane, a version of
the Texan trainer, he had succeeded in overcoming his initial nervousness.

Outside of flying when weather permitted, there was not much to do
at the isolated Philippine Army post. Except for an occasional game of
poker, the pilots turned in at 8:00 P.M. every night. There was the possibility of swimming in the China Sea, of course, but the water was "rough
and dirty," in the view of one of the newies.

6 Within three weeks following their shift to Clark Field, 3rd Pursuit
pilots were compiling an unenviable record of accidents, all in P-35As.
Commanding officer Billy Maverick started off the string, ground-looping
at Clark on July 2. Five days later, Ray Gehrig, one of the original 40-A
pilots of the 17th Pursuit, since transferred to the 3rd, ground-looped another at Nichols. On July 10, 41-B flying school graduate Bob Newman
wrecked his P-35A in a landing at Clark. Newie Ed Smith suffered a freak
accident at Clark on July 18 when the exhaust ring and firewall of his

A P-35A of the 17th Pursuit comes in for a puddle landing at Iba, summer, 1941. *Courtesy William M. Rowe, Lt. Col. USAF (Ret.)*

P-35A blew out and the .50-caliber ammunition in the right wing gun exploded. The worst incident, though, occurred on July 23, when newie Charley Sheeley went into a spin over Paombong, Bulacan, and was unable to recover. Fortunately the Pueblo, Colorado, native was able to parachute in time. His P-35A hit a rice paddy and buried itself so deeply that it could not be found by a crew sent out to look for it. The loss of the five P-35As was eased somewhat for the 3rd Pursuit with the transfer in July of a like number of the aircraft from the 20th Pursuit, which was gradually disposing of its Severskys as it switched to the P-40Bs. By the end of the month it had twenty-two P-35As, of which fourteen were in commission.

At Iba, the 17th Pursuit was also undergoing a spate of accidents that was pushing Buzz Wagner's patience to the limit. On July 29, newie Grant Manley nosed up one of the squadron's three remaining P-26As when he hit the brakes too hard while taxiing.[1] "Oldie" Maurice Hughett, a 41-B flying school graduate, incurred Wagner's wrath when he landed one of the squadron's two A-27s with his wheels up the same day. Then the following day, newie Jim Ross ground-looped a P-35A. Wagner summarily grounded all three pilots.

On August 18, Forrest Hobrecht's nerves were tested to the limit. Heavy rains had forced his training flight down at the tiny airstrip at Santa Cruz, thirty miles north of Iba that day. After failing to get a reply to a wire sent to Iba for instructions, flight leader "Ed" Kiser opted to try to make it back to Iba despite the terrible weather. After the worst flight Hobrecht had ever experienced, hugging the coast at about one hundred feet altitude and unable to see anything under conditions "a thousand times worse than driving an auto in a storm without a windshield wiper," he and the others reached Iba. Visibility was about one-quarter mile and the ceiling two hundred feet.

Hobrecht waited as the others tried to land. The frantic trainees kept overshooting the field in their landing attempts, striving to come in two at a time but not seeing each other. One lowered his flaps instead of his wheels and nearly dove into the ocean. Finally, one made it in safely, and another landed behind him, just missing nosing up. Then Kiser set his P-35A down "pretty easy," but midway down the field he veered right and hit a large pool of water. The tail of his ship began easing up in the air, then suddenly shot up as the Seversky went over on its nose, somersaulted fifteen feet in the air, and landed on its back. It took a good ten minutes to extricate Kiser from the wreck. The plane's rudder was pushed all the way forward to the canopy, and the pilot was hanging upside down, the top of his head in water and mud. But aside from a few scratches, he was uninjured.

Overhead, the remainder of the flight was kept circling for some twenty minutes after the accident, which obstructed the middle of the field. Finally, the pilots received permission to land, and all worked their way around the wreck. Hobrecht made his best landing ever, using only one-half the field and a very narrow strip on the edge, to the praise of his squadron mates. But he was still upset. He felt it was a mistake to have put all their lives in the hands of one officer. It turned out that Wagner had wired them to stay at Santa Cruz overnight, but the message was received only after the precipitous decision by Kiser to leave.

2. "ALL THE FLYING CHARACTERISTICS OF A STREAMLINED SAFE"

1 At Clark Field on the evening of August 26, 1941, a party was held for Maj. Kirtley J. Gregg, the commanding officer of the 4th Composite Group and former CO of the 17th Pursuit Squadron. Gregg was being transferred to the A-4 staff position of the recently created Air Force, USAFFE, successor to the Philippine Department Air Force. Succeeding Gregg as 4th Group CO was his operations officer, Maj. Orrin Grover. The group operations position now went to Maj. Billy Maverick, the 3rd Pursuit's commanding officer. Completing the chain reaction of command changes was the appointment of 1st Lt. Benny Putnam, one of the original 20th Pursuit pilots transferred to the Philippines in November, 1940, as CO of the 3rd Pursuit.

On taking over the 3rd Pursuit, Putnam immediately introduced his own ideas of how the squadron should be run. The main change was to cut down the number of flights from six to three, but with the same total number of pilots in them. There were to be no more training flights; the newies were now expected to fly with the three combat flights.

Unlike Putnam, the 20th Pursuit's CO, Joe Moore, had not integrated his newies into the squadron's combat flights. The 20th still had three combat flights of six P-40Bs each for the eighteen most senior pilots plus separate training flights. On September 11, C Flight's veterans made a flight almost to 27,000 feet in their P-40Bs, using oxygen and setting a record for the Philippines. From that height they could see the entire island of Luzon.

Five days later, an important organizational change was made in the Air Force, USAFFE. On September 16, 1941, General MacArthur's General Orders No. 1 established the 24th Pursuit Group (Interceptor), comprising the 3rd, 17th, and 20th pursuit squadrons hived off from the 4th Composite Group, plus a newly designated Headquarters Squadron. On October 1 the new group was activated under the command of Maj. Orrin Grover, transferred from his 4th Composite Group responsibilities.

The pursuit pilots were happy to be divorced from the bombers, which remained in the reduced 4th Composite Group, and to have pursuit officers tell them how to fly pursuit for a change. No longer would the Clark Field commanding officer be grounding pursuit pilots for "dangerous takeoff" when they chandelled off the field; the CO had never understood that such a 180-degree climbing turn was safe in a pursuit plane.

2 At Iba the newies of the 17th Pursuit commenced their gunnery training in the first week of September by shooting at ground targets. Each pilot was assigned one of the 6'×10' paper targets lined up in an isolated spot at the south end of the field, with unobstructed approaches by air and unobstructed areas behind the targets so he could pull up out of his dive and continue to fly a circular pattern. When the pilot was about 90 degrees from the target, he banked sharply and dove until the 6'×6' scoring area of the target was very sharp in his gunsight. He would then give it a short burst, pull out of the dive in a steep climbing turn to avoid the pilot following behind, and go around again for another round. Although it seemed easy in theory, Forrest Hobrecht found that "it's hard as the devil to dive at from 250 to 300 feet and make that sight stay on a little target."

Squadron Operations Officer Willie Feallock led the more senior pilots in new configuration practices. Flying in two- instead of three-ship elements, the wingman could cross back and forth on the element leader during turns and maintain proper distance without changes in power setting. The wingman did not need to concentrate on keeping his eyes on his leader only a few feet away as in three-ship elements and could instead look for targets or threats, as could the element leader as well. The widely spaced ships would be more difficult for an enemy to attack except to pick off the "tail-end Charlie." None of the 17th Pursuiters doubted that the two-ship element was the best configuration for air-to-air combat, as proved by RAF experience.

At Clark Field, Joe Moore had started his 20th Pursuit oldies in night flying practice in late September. Takeoffs were scheduled at the same time as those of the 3rd Pursuit at the other end of the field—4:30 A.M.— and the practice lasted until 6:00, allowing the pilots to land at sunrise. The veteran pilots were now also flying reconnaissance missions for the first time in their P-40Bs.

On Monday, October 13, tragedy struck the squadron. Moore was leading a flight of nine P-40Bs in maneuvers, mock strafing the infantry near Manila. While flying in very tight formation at over 300 MPH, "Buck" Weaver, the squadron adjutant, momentarily got out of position. In trying to return to his slot, he inadvertently flew under Max Louk's P-40, hitting Louk's wing. The two planes' wings locked, and Weaver's ship was thrown into Louk's propeller, which cut into Weaver's canopy. With his plane in a dive, Weaver did not bail out until he was only fifty feet off the ground, not enough time for him to open his chute. Louk was able to land his damaged plane and was unhurt.

Near Iba on the same day a 17th Pursuiter almost met the same fate as Weaver. Allison Strauss, a 40-A oldie, was leading B Flight in formation flying in the P-35As. When Strauss called for reforming into two-ship configurations from the three-ship elements they were flying, Joe Kruzel, a 40-H pilot recently transferred back to the 17th Pursuit, "came barreling into position," but too close to Bill Hennon's plane before easing back on the throttle. Kruzel's prop cut the rear fuselage and tail off Hennon's ship just behind the cockpit. Almost knocked unconscious by the force of the collision, Hennon failed to react as the front section of his severed aircraft went spinning earthward. Finally, he pushed his canopy back and jumped. His chute opened at once, and he landed in an open field. Nearby, the remains of the forward fuselage burned after they hit the ground and exploded. After returning to Iba field, Hennon was remarkably relaxed about the near-fatal accident. The only comment he had to offer his squadron mates was that he had lost a shoe in the jump.

3 The 17th Pursuit's oldies and newies alike were excited at the prospect of checking out the squadron's new P-40Es. At the Philippine Air Depot at Nichols, fifty P-40Es that had come into Manila on September 29 were uncrated and assembled for delivery to the 3rd and 17th pursuit squadrons. The 17th was to receive the first twenty-five following its return to Nichols from gunnery training at Iba on October 17. Since the 3rd Pursuit would be shifted from Clark to Iba for its turn in gunnery practice immediately afterward, it would not be receiving its twenty-five P-40Es until sometime into its gunnery training program. While waiting for the week to ten days for the depot to test the new aircraft and install the six .50-caliber guns in the wings, many of the airmen went over to the depot to look over the new ships.

On October 27, Wilson Glover, of class 41-C, took one up for his checkout flight. He was pleased to find that it was much easier to land than the P-35A, but the seven feet of nose made it impossible for him to see what was in front of him while taking off and landing. The Nichols control tower had to help him by radio. Forrest Hobrecht also found during his checkout flight the next day that the P-40E was not difficult to handle and landed "easier than anything I've ever flown."

Not all the initial flights in the new ship went so smoothly for the squadron. On October 23, while flying between Clark and Nichols, twenty-two-year-old Elmer "Bud" Powell, a 41-B from University City, Missouri, experienced motor failure. Too far away from Clark to return there, and with neither the altitude nor the range to reach an emergency field, Powell opted to set his aircraft down on the narrow black ribbon of Highway 3 below him. He managed to land on an empty stretch just north of the town of Calumpit and was rolling along the highway at a fast clip when a big, lumbering bus came into view. Instinctively, the terrified pilot kicked the left rudder hard, gunned the engine to give more pull for a turnout, and hurtled off the road in a ground loop. His plane was a total wreck, but Powell climbed out with hardly a scratch on him and walked to the nearest telephone.

Exactly one week later, another oldie also experienced failure of the P-40E's liquid-cooled Allison engine. On a routine flight over Nichols, 40-H graduate Jack Dale was at 400 feet when his engine quit over the field. Trying to glide the ship in, Dale kept the nose too high and stalled, spinning in from 100 feet. The impact of the crash in a swamp between Nichols Field and Pasay cemetery was so great that the fuselage was severed from the rest of the aircraft and flipped over with the pilot under it. An enlisted man nearby who saw the crash rushed to the site and extricated the unconscious pilot, his skull fractured, spleen ruptured, and face cut on the gunsight. Although Dale regained consciousness on the way to Sternberg Hospital, doctors rated his condition as serious. "Nobody that saw the accident would have given a nickel for the life of the pilot," squadron mate Larry Lodin observed, but in the second day of Dale's scheduled seven-day hospital stay, the brash, boisterous pilot was already trying to get out.

4 Following the departure of the 3rd Pursuit to Iba on October 18, the 20th was now the only pursuit squadron left at Clark Field. The 41-C and 41-D pilots were now being checked out in the squadron's P-40Bs, while the oldies were continuing night flying practice and devoting increasing time to interception and mock combat maneuvers. With the death of "Buck" Weaver on October 13 and the transfer of Bill Cummings, one of the original 20th Pursuiters assigned to the Philippines, the squadron's 41-B pilots were rapidly gaining seniority. Max Louk was now designated by Joe Moore as an element leader in Louk's combat flight, the first of the 41-B pilots in the squadron to be advanced to that position. Two of the competition—John Geer and John Valkenaar—had recently been transferred to bombardment, reducing the number of 41-B pilots in the squadron to six.

Another of the 41-B pilots was in bad odor with Moore and his squadron mates. As his flight was coming in to land at Clark, Erwin Crellin was ignoring radioed warnings about following too closely behind Moore. When the two P-40Bs touched down, Crellin was obliged to hit his brakes hard to avoid ramming Moore's ship just ahead of him, which forced Crellin's P-40B over on its back. Although the pilot was not hurt, his $50,000 aircraft was totally wrecked.

Also training at Clark now were ten brand new flying school graduates in the class of 41-G from Luke Field who had arrived on the *Tasker H. Bliss* on October 23. They were attached to Headquarters Squadron of the 24th Group for their training before being assigned to the three tactical pursuit squadrons of the group. The other pursuit pilots could not understand why the War Department would be sending more totally inexperienced flying school graduates to the Philippines as war clouds were looming increasingly over the islands.

5 In the early afternoon of Tuesday, November 4, the inhabitants of Manila were treated to a spectacular sight. Strung out in a line in V formation of three aircraft each, forty-two P-40s and P-35As of the three pursuit squadrons roared low over the city, then headed east to meet a PanAm clipper bringing in the new commanding general of the USAFFE Air Force. Maj. Gen. Lewis H. Brereton. The B-17s and B-18s from Clark Field first spotted the flying boat over the Polillo Islands; the pursuit ships were flying under the overcast and missed it. When they did link up with the clipper, the pursuit pilots put on a show, doing rolls upside down near the big ship and disporting themselves immensely trying to scare the clipper pilots.

Four days after Brereton's arrival the 3rd Pursuit had finally received its full allotment of twenty-five P-40Es. The pilots' initial reactions to the new ship were mixed. After five hours in the P-40E, Andy Krieger rated them as "pretty good—at least they are not antiquated—outmoded but not obsolete. . . . It is very fast and heavily armed, although it could handle easier," he wrote his father. At any rate, Krieger felt it would be able to outperform the German ME 109—"the most advanced type we shall meet over here"—except at high altitude.[1]

After having slow-timed a number of the squadron's new P-40Es in order to break in their engines, Squadron Operations Officer Herb Ellis held much less positive views on the performance characteristics of the aircraft than did Krieger. The Allison V-1710-39 engine was an improvement over the P-40B's V-1710-33, but at 1,150 horsepower it was still grossly underpowered for the E model's heavier airframe. With "all the flying characteristics of a streamlined safe," the P-40E, in Ellis's judgment, could not be expected to function satisfactorily in its interceptor role with the 24th Pursuit Group.

Although the 3rd Pursuit now had its quota of P-40Es, they would not be used for gunnery training. Target firing from the six guns would result in a heavy expenditure of scarce .50-caliber ammunition. Rather, gunnery practice would continue in the P-35As, using the ship's two .30-caliber nose guns. When gunnery training was completed, the P-35As would be turned over to the Philippine Army Air Corps in exchange for more P-40Es

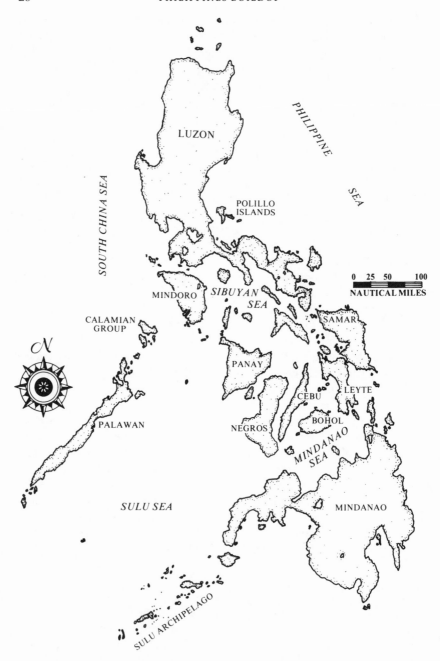

Map 3.   The Philippines

expected to arrive soon. Already, a "1" had been painted in front of the group aircraft number of the P-35As to indicate that they were no longer tactical airplanes.

The 3rd Pursuit was now operating under yet another new squadron commander, Benny Putnam had been replaced on October 2 by Capt. William K. "Hoot" Horrigan following damage to many of the P-35As in a flying incident that day. Then at the end of the month, 1st Lt. Hank Thorne was transferred from the Nichols Field Depot to Iba to take over command, with Horrigan moving to a staff position with the USAFFE Air Force. A native of Waco, Texas, Thorne had enlisted in the army as a private following high school graduation and was subsequently commissioned a second lieutenant in the Air Corps upon completing flying school. Although he had not attended college, the twenty-eight-year-old CO had an impressive vocabulary, was well read, and spoke authoritatively but at ease. Andy Krieger, for one, thought Thorne was just the right officer to command the squadron.

With the squadron now operating twenty-five P-40Es and eighteen P-35As, Thorne found himself short of crew chiefs among his enlisted men. To remedy the situation, he assigned half of his pilots to work as crew chiefs, pending the arrival of additional aircraft mechanics being sent the squadron. Some of the officers were also assigned as armorers, for these were in short supply, too. The .50-caliber guns for the P-40Es were only now arriving at Iba, and with little equipment for installing them in the wings, the men were working flat out clearing the guns of the Cosmoline in which they were packed before mounting them.

6 In response to Major General Brereton's new training schedule issued on November 6, which increased working hours of his air force to the maximum and required at least 40 percent of all flight training to be in night operations, the 17th Pursuit was putting in considerable time in its new P-40Es. The three combat flights of twelve pilots each, following Wagner's reorganization of the squadron in early November, were now practicing night flying from 4:30 to 6:00 in the morning, then flying formation from 7:30 till noon, trying to find out as much as possible about the formation ability of the P-40E.

By the third week of November, there had been two more crashes in the squadron's P-40Es, both a result of carelessness on the part of 41-D newies. On November 18, Ed Erickson damaged one through pilot error, but the plane could be repaired. Then a few days later Truett Majors veered too far to the right on takeoff from Nichols and caught his right wing under the propeller of another P-40E that was being run up by one of the mechanics. The prop sheared off four feet of Majors's wing, causing the ship to cartwheel to the right. On the first flip, the prop and nose section broke off. After several more cartwheels, the P-40E came to rest on the east edge of the field, a complete wreck. Laughing as he climbed out of the cockpit—the only intact piece of the plane—Majors exclaimed, "Boy, that was close!" He did not have a scratch on him.

To "Red" Sheppard, now a veteran pilot of the 17th, the root cause of all the accidents of the newies assigned to the 24th Group was poor training in flying school, a result in turn of the fact that their instructors were themselves just recently graduated from flying school. Over at Clark Field, Sheppard's flying school classmate and fellow 17th Pursuiter Russ Church shared Sheppard's sentiments. Assigned by Major Grover, the 24th Group's CO, to help train the recently arrived 41-G newies, he was fed up with their carelessness and undeveloped flying abilities. In two days, three of the little group of ten trainees had managed to wipe out a like number of P-35As that had been turned over to them by the 17th Pursuit. On November 11, Billy Tom Akins collided over Candaba, twenty-two miles southeast of Clark Field, with his best friend, Fred Siler. Both pilots bailed out and were unhurt. The next day, Paul Racicot wrecked another at Clark; "pilot error" was given as the cause.

At the 20th Pursuit's operations area at Clark, Joe Moore was satisfied with the progress his pilots were making in their training program—night flying in formation and mock interceptions. But there was one important aspect of their training that was sorely lacking: gunnery practice. Indeed, none of the pilots had yet fired the P-40Bs' .30- and .50-caliber guns. It was not that Moore was not trying. He had repeatedly called attention to the fact that the guns of the P-40B had never been fired but was told that gunnery training for the 20th would have to wait until the 3rd Pursuit had finished its training at Iba, expected in early December. In the meantime, in response to his expressed concern whether the nose .50s of his P-40Bs would fire properly between the three-bladed prop, he was given permission to test-fire the .50s of one P-40B with fifty rounds of ammunition; no more .50-caliber rounds could be spared, for it was in too short supply.

3. "WE ARE DOOMED AT THE START"

1 In ninety-degree heat—high for that time of the year—a crowd had formed at Pier 7 in Manila late on the morning of Thursday, November 20, to welcome yet another ship coming in with troops and equipment for the Philippines' accelerated defense buildup. This time it was the army transport *President Coolidge* with a load of new "fly-boys" and supporting enlisted men. Unlike previous Air Corps arrivals over the past nine months, these pilots were not untrained reinforcements for squadrons serving in the Philippines but rather were experienced pilots of the 27th Bombardment Group (Light) from Savannah, Georgia, and the 35th Pursuit Group from Hamilton Field, California. General MacArthur's insistent requests for additional Air Corps units were paying off.

For 2nd Lt. Jack Hall of the 35th Group's 34th Pursuit Squadron, the scene was familiar. Only fifteen months earlier he had spent six weeks on holiday in Manila visiting his sister Lucy Hall Chiles, who was married to an officer serving in the 57th Infantry, Philippine Scouts. An inveterate sightseer, the twenty-five-year-old native of Liberty, Missouri, had worked his way over to the Philippines as a seaman on a Danish cargo ship in the summer of 1940 following the award of his M.A. degree in merchandising from New York University in June. During his 1940 sojourn, Hall had spent some time at Nichols Field, where he became friendly with many of the pursuit pilots there. Uncertain about his career plans, then and there he made his decision; he was going to learn to fly and serve in the Army Air Corps. On return to the United States, he had enlisted in the Air Corps in the fall of 1940 and been selected for flying school. Graduating from Kelly Field in the 41-C class, the extroverted, immensely popular Hall was then assigned to the 34th Pursuit Squadron.

With Hall were fourteen other pilots of his squadron, only half the number being assigned to the Philippines. The sister 21st Pursuit Squadron had also been sent out at only half-strength in pilots: thirteen. With the international situation deteriorating rapidly, the War Department had decided to ship the two squadrons in a hurry; the rest of the pilots would be following on a later transport, along with the group's Headquarters Squadron and the 70th Pursuit Squadron.[1] At the time of sailing from San Francisco, personnel of the two squadrons did not know their destination; they knew only that the code name for their new post was "Plum." Some of the pilots thought they were being assigned to Trinidad in South America. Only after they departed the United States were they informed they were being transferred to the Philippines.

Unlike arrangements for arriving pilots during calmer times, the 35th Group arrivals were not whisked off to the Army and Navy Club for a welcoming party. Instead, mess sergeants of the two pursuit squadrons set up field kitchens right on the docks and served a lunch of hot dogs and sauerkraut. After downing their meal (which was in sharp contrast to the cuisine they enjoyed as first-class passengers on the *Coolidge* during the nineteen-day voyage from San Francisco), officers and enlisted men alike were unceremoniously transported to Nichols Field, where the two squadrons were being assigned for the time. They were being attached to the 24th Pursuit Group until the rest of the personnel of the 35th Pursuit Group arrived.

When the enlisted men of the two pursuit squadrons were off-loaded from their trucks in front of their future accommodations at the Nichols base, they did a double-take at the five-man squad tents. Nichols certainly was not Hamilton Field. The officers were more fortunate; they were put into the Reyes Court complex of houses near the field.

If the personnel of the two squadrons were less than enthusiastic about living conditions at their new post, they were even less so about the equipment they would be expected to operate. Commanding Officers William "Ed" Dyess of the 21st and Sam Marett of the 34th had been informed on departing Hamilton Field, California, that fifty P-40Es would be provided the two squadrons on arrival at their destination, but they found that none earmarked for them had yet reached the Philippines. Pending the receipt of the P-40Es, they were to be given the P-35A discards of the 24th Pursuit Group—pursuit planes they had never flown before.

2 On Wednesday, November 26, the 17th Pursuit Squadron, now sharing the field with the 21st and 34th, turned over all its remaining P-35As to the two newly arrived squadrons. The 34th, which had now received its orders to a new field, was given some twelve to fifteen, which left only a few for the 21st Pursuit. Since it would be remaining at Nichols, the 21st would be assigned the 3rd Pursuit's P-35As as soon as that squadron was finished with its gunnery training at Iba.

Looking over their new aircraft, the pilots and mechanics of the two squadrons were appalled at their condition. It was bad enough to be given such obsolete equipment, but these birds were worn-out, too. The heavy

P-35As of the 17th Pursuit at Iba in August, 1941, show the effects of weather on their water-based camouflage paint. *Courtesy William R. "Cowboy" Wright*

demand on the machines by the 17th's newies during their gunnery period at Iba had run up the engine time to beyond the point required for an engine change. And the .30-caliber nose guns were in bad shape from excessive firing on the gunnery range.

That evening, the 34th's three ground officers and 218 enlisted men began moving out of Nichols Field to the squadron's new post at Del Carmen Field, fifteen miles due south of Clark Field. The trucks loaded with the squadron's personnel inched their way all night under blackout conditions the tortuous sixty miles northwest from Manila, with rough maps the only guide for the drivers. Passing through the innumerable small villages along the way, the smell of "smoke, sweat, and stink" assailed the men's nostrils. Arriving at the new field at dawn, the men found that the base camp was at the edge of a sugarcane field. The area was already occupied by a company of the 803rd Aviation Engineers, which had leveled the 3,600-foot pulverized loam strip and was now busy smoothing it. Pooped out from the sleepless trip, the 34th's personnel happily accepted the engineers' invitation to join them for breakfast. After breakfast, the men pitched tents and set up the squadron's field equipment at the primitive site.

That afternoon, they gathered at the strip to greet the arrival of their pilots. One by one, the 34th Pursuiters touched down on the field safely in their old, weathered P-35As, but suddenly six of them flipped their planes over in ground loops. Never having flown the P-35 before, they were providing a dramatic demonstration of the tricky landing characteristics of the Severskys. When one of the last arriving pilots collided with a parked P-35A in a ground loop, Sam Marett turned "completely purple." The erring aviator was in his CO's doghouse for days after the accident.

During the next days, the squadron's men busied themselves in making their own Lewis gun emplacements and revetments around the field, with some help from the 803rd Engineers. For running water and latrine needs, they were obliged to use a nearby river. Some water was also being hauled seven miles to the field by tank truck.

Still at Nichols Field under relatively more comfortable conditions, the 21st Pursuit was also trying to familiarize itself with the few P-35As it had received. None of its pilots had ever flown the P-35 either. While the squadron's mechanics were trying to keep the aircraft's engines in running condition, Sgt. Al Sly and the other armorers were struggling to get the ships' .30- and .50-caliber guns in satisfactory working order. They had been poorly maintained the past six weeks following the completion of the 17th's gunnery training at Iba; the 21st's armorers had to dismantle, clean, then reinstall them.

But the squadron would not be operating the P-35A for long. A cargo of twenty-four crated P-40Es had come into Manila by freighter on November 25, the first part of the shipment of the new aircraft promised the 35th Group.[2] Some of the squadron's mechanics were at the depot, along with a few of the 34th's who had remained behind, all eagerly helping depot personnel uncrate and assemble the aircraft in order to speed up delivery to their squadrons. In order to flesh out the pilot strength of the squadron pending the arrival of the rest of the 21st Pursuit's officers, six pilots from the 3rd, 17th, and 20th pursuit were assigned to the 21st, bringing the total of its pilots to nineteen.

3 At Iba, on Thursday, November 27—Thanksgiving Day—half the officers and men of the 3rd Pursuit were enjoying the holiday, on leave from their work at the field, lying on the beach or wandering around in Iba town, when the peace was suddenly disturbed at 8:00 P.M. The squadron's officer of the day and 1st Sgt. Wyman Langland came barreling into town in their jeep and over the jeep's loudspeaker ordered the squadron's personnel to report back to the field immediately. Assembled in the barracks area, the personnel of the 3rd Pursuit were informed the reason for the unexpected order. A formation of unidentified planes had been picked up flying at high altitude over central Luzon, and all USAFFE forces were going on alert.

Evidently the "bogies" had been detected by the Christmas tree–like apparatus that a Signal Corps detachment was operating between the barracks building and the beach. Since its installation the last week of October, the equipment had been the subject of speculation by the squadron; it was very hush-hush, and the pilots were not allowed in the associated operations truck to see how it worked. They did know, however, that it was some sort of device that could spot approaching aircraft at great distance.[3]

Hank Thorne ordered all the squadron's P-40Es and P-35As dispersed around the field. The 3rd Pursuit's commanding officer then assigned the senior pilots to two combat flights of P-40s. A full load of .50-caliber ammunition was stacked alongside each of the P-40Es, the green boxes left open for immediate loading by the squadron's armorers. Gas tanks were filled, and gun blast tubes installed. Ready to take off on thirty minutes' notice, Frank Neri and the other eleven oldies waited for an order to intercept hostile aircraft. But the evening wore on with no developments. Finally, they curled up under the wings of their planes for some shut-eye. At 7:30 the next morning, Neri was wakened and told to take the squadron's A-27 down to Nichols to pick up the mail. No Japanese war threat would be allowed to stop the squadron's mail from getting through.

At 4:30 P.M. that day, the alert was called off. But now the squadron was ordered on "readiness" status instead, along with all other units of the Far East Air Force. Like the other air bases, Iba was to be on a twenty-four-hour operating basis, base air defense preparations were to be made, pursuit planes were to be readied for defending central Luzon, and all combat aircraft were to be armed. The FEAF was now on a war footing.[4] The readiness order came just as gunnery training for the newies of the 3rd Pursuit was completed. The squadron's P-35As were now no longer needed.

Late in the morning of Sunday, November 30, a twin-engine Douglas C-39 transport landed at Iba. The Nichols Field operations officer and former 3rd Pursuiter Grant Mahony was bringing in some seventeen pilots of the 17th Pursuit to pick up the 3rd's surplus P-35As and fly them back to Nichols for use by the 21st Pursuit.[5] Four of the old birds were held back by Thorne to serve as squadron hacks.

4 At Nichols Field, the 17th and 21st pursuit squadrons were in readiness status too, following Brereton's order of November 28. All the 17th's pilots were on one-hour's notice to take off in their combat-loaded P-40Es and intercept in the event of a Japanese attack. All flying was suspended while they waited. For Dave Obert, the readiness order had thrown his personal plans into a hat. The young Oklahoman got married on November 30, as planned several months earlier, but now his hoped-for ten-day honeymoon trip was down the drain. Exceptionally, Buzz Wagner was allowing him to go on leave for that period, but Obert had to make himself

Grant Mahony of the 3rd Pursuit (left) and 1st Sgt. Wyman Langland at Nichols Field in the spring of 1941. *Courtesy Edith R. Krieger*

available for instant recall by telephone, which meant spending his honeymoon at his apartment near the Army and Navy Club, a ten-minute drive to Nichols Field.

Before the readiness order, the 17th had been scheduled to be moved to Del Monte on Mindanao, but now with tension with Japan at its peak, transfer plans were put on hold. "About twice a day we go tearing around for air raid drill," Forrest Hobrecht wrote his parents. All-night blackouts of the Manila area were frequent, too.

Tragedy struck the squadron on November 27, the day before the readiness order had gone into effect. Newie Grant Manley had taken off from Nichols in a P-40 E at 4:00 A.M. for the usual two-hour night flying practice, but when he had not returned by 7:00 A.M., Hobrecht, as airdrome officer of the day, sent the 17th Pursuit and 2nd Observation squadrons out to search for him. The Philippine Constabulary, however, eventually found him. He had crashed at Paombong, Bulacan Province, twenty-five miles northwest of Nichols Field. The P-40E was badly smashed up, its engine half-buried in the swampy ground. Inside the wreckage, the constabulary found only Manley's dismembered right arm and left leg.

Eyewitnesses to the crash said that the plane exploded in the air about 5:00 A.M., then crashed to earth, though the pilot examining the wreckage was more inclined to believe that it nose-dived and exploded upon hitting the ground. Hobrecht, Larry Lodin, and other squadron mates were convinced that the plane blew up when Manley lit a cigarette and ignited gasoline vapors in the cockpit, released by the P-40's fuel system, which was known to be faulty. The pilots had orders never to smoke in the P-40s, but Manley had been ignoring them; he had told his squadron mates at lunch one day that he did it all the time.

Manley's crash was the sixth accident in a P-40E for the squadron, but only its first fatality. Although the last four crashes were caused by pilot errors, even the highly experienced oldies of the 17th were skittish about taking off during the readiness period in combat-loaded P-40Es with their extra 1,800 pounds of .50-caliber ammunition. After bringing one back, flight leader Johnny Brownewell told 39-A flying school classmate George Armstrong that "his knees were still shaking"; he had just barely got the ship off Nichols Field and had real difficulty in handling it in the air.

5 At Clark Field, all training flights were now suspended. The ten 41-G newies attached to Headquarters Squadron had reported to their assigned tactical squadrons. They had managed to get some eight to ten hours in on the P-40B after having finished up with the P-35A before their training program had come to an abrupt end. When Joe Moore received the readiness order on November 28, he immediately terminated all training, including the night formation flying practices in which his 20th Pursuit had recently been concentrating, had his P-40Bs fully loaded with ammunition for combat, and maintained a state of readiness for any eventuality. It still worried him, though, that his pilots had yet to fire their guns in the P-40B.

Like many of the pilots in the other pursuit squadrons, Max Louk was becoming increasingly skeptical of the combat capabilities of the P-40. Eleven days earlier, he and eleven other pilots of the 20th Pursuit flew a practice mission to "attack" a flight of B-17s heading toward Clark at 25,000 feet. Heavily encumbered with oxygen masks, life vests, and parachutes, Louk and his squadron mates pulled their P-40Bs up to 30,000 feet. Spotting the four-engine bombers below them, they dove and ran a successful interception, but then the huge bombers simply sped away from the P-40Bs.

Louk knew from talking to the pilots of the 17th and 3rd pursuit squadrons that the latest E model of the P-40 that they were flying was not really an improvement over the B, and he was bitter. Writing his sister in late November, he unburdened himself. "They say that we are getting the latest equipment, but we who are here flying it know that it is no good. Our planes—the latest P-40s—are not good enough to fight with! Someone in Washington said, 'They are the best' and so we have them. The English don't want our pursuit, they want bombers. . . . You know, Dee, one gets a bit disgusted when he lays his life on the line for our lousy, out-of-date Air Corps."

And what did Louk think of the likelihood of war with Japan? "Well, we all hope it comes soon, because we are doomed at the start."

For the 21st Pursuit Squadron at Nichols Field, Thursday, December 4, was a red-letter day; the squadron was beginning to receive newly assembled P-40Es from the depot. The same day, it happily turned its P-35As over to the 34th Pursuit Squadron at Del Carmen.

The news that the 21st Pursuit was being given the whole shipment of twenty-four P-40Es that was being assembled put officers and enlisted men of the 34th Pursuit in a foul mood. After all, they had as much time at Hamilton Field in P-40s as did their sister squadron. To most, it looked like a question of who was more senior or who had more influence with the brass of the Far East Air Force—Sam Marett or Ed Dyess. On that basis, it was no contest—Dyess was senior and impressed everyone he met as one of the most outstanding young officers of the Air Corps. The 34th would just have to wait for the second half of the P-40E shipment to come in. Unknown to all, it was at that moment at sea on the freighter *Blomfontein*, scheduled to reach Manila on January 4. In addition to the eighteen P-40Es in crates on the *Blomfontein*, another twenty were on board the freighter *Ludington*, due in Manila about January 10.[6]

4. "YOU ARE NOT NECESSARILY
A SUICIDE SQUADRON"

1 At Clark Field on December 1, the 20th Pursuit was still on readiness status. Each evening since the November 28 order, Joe Moore had sent eight of his senior pilots to the flight line to spend the night next to their combat-loaded P-40Bs, ready for takeoff on short notice. With flying suspended and trips off the base forbidden, the 20th Pursuit's pilots had time on their hands. They talked among themselves about their situation and combat tactics they should use in the event of war. All were particularly concerned about their lack of training in night interception.

Equally disturbed over the inexperience of his pilots in night interception, Moore decided to reinstate training flights to overcome this weakness in their capabilities. He proposed a plan for "intercepting" a B-18 of the 28th Bombardment Squadron at Clark, in coordination with the 200th Coast Artillery's antiaircraft searchlights, to Maj. Orrin Grover, CO of the 24th Pursuit Group. Grover approved Moore's proposal but decided to extend it to the 3rd and 17th pursuit squadrons as well. He scheduled the night training for the first week of December, to start at 4:00 A.M. on December 2. In order to minimize risk to the group's P-40s during this period of extreme international tension, the night practices would be mounted two hours before dawn so the pilots could land in the first rays of daylight, as had been the practice during previous night training exercises. Each squadron's commanding officer would select his six most experienced pilots to participate in the hazardous training.

On Tuesday morning, December 2, a combined flight of 24th Group Headquarters Squadron and the 20th Pursuit Squadron led off the night interception exercise. Major Grover himself headed the flight. He had selected his former 20th Pursuit stalwarts to join him—Bill Cummings, Ozzie Lunde, and Benny Putnam—along with Joe Moore and Charley Sneed, the 20th Pursuit's most senior pilots. Wingtip lights turned on for safety's sake, the six P-40Bs took off in the darkness and formed up in well-spaced two-ship elements as they began their search for the lone

B-18. Soon the lead element of the flight spotted the twin-engine bomber, illuminated by searchlights as it flew south to north over Clark. Grover made a stern approach with his wingman, then when fairly close turned off and radioed the next pair that he was clear and they should proceed to attack; he then got back in position behind the third element. As the bomber continued to fly an oval pattern, reversing its direction when it reached the north and south ends of the area outside the reach of the searchlights, each of the three elements of P-40s, flying just outside the oval, came in to "attack." This procedure was repeated until the first light, when all the aircraft came in to land. At breakfast, the pursuit pilots critiqued the exercise.

On Thursday, December 4, the third morning of the exercise, things did not go according to plan. Moore and his wingman, Cummings, were just turning back on the track of the B-18, returning behind the third element. After leveling off and watching the bomber ahead of them bathed in the searchlight glare, they suddenly noticed what looked like a P-35 with wingtip lights on in a steep bank flying hell-for-leather right between them and the B-18. Moore radioed Cummings to watch for it, but no one saw it again. Later, at breakfast, the six pilots discussed the incident and concluded the "P-35" must have been from one of the other squadrons, trying to harass them. But when Grover contacted the other squadrons, he found out that none of their planes had been up that morning. Could it have been Japanese?

At Iba, Hank Thorne had been awakened in the small hours of the morning by the commanding officer of the air warning detachment operating the radar unit there, Lt. Charlton Wimer. Did Thorne know if there were any American planes flying offshore? The SCR-270B unit had just picked up aircraft flying south along the coastline of western Luzon. The 3rd Pursuit's CO was quite sure there were no American planes out flying off the coast at that hour and asked Wimer to notify him the next time he picked up a series of plots on his oscilloscope. When Thorne checked later that morning with Grover's headquarters at Clark and with FEAF Headquarters at Nielson Field in Manila, he received confirmation that there were no friendly aircraft in that vicinity during the night.

The next morning, just after midnight on December 5, Wimer again wakened Thorne. He was picking up aircraft plots again. The two officers ran downstairs and out the barracks building over to the site of the radar operation. Sure enough, some kind of airplanes were on the scope, about fifty miles offshore and flying south.

Thorne decided to check out the bogies himself. After making hurried arrangements with the 3rd's radio ground station for vectoring him, he rushed over to his waiting P-40E and took off for the China Sea, determined to identify the mystery aircraft. As he was outbound, he was instructed over the radio to turn more to the left; the bogies were making good speed. But at about twenty-five miles out, he lost radio contact with Iba. The moon was almost full, but there were cumulus clouds that restricted Thorne's visibility. After milling about for a half hour and not spotting anything, the frustrated pilot returned to Iba. Checking with Wimer again, Thorne was informed that the bogies had continued south to the Bataan/Corregidor area, then turned around and headed back north.

After only a few hours' sleep, Thorne was up again, this time to lead a six-plane flight of his squadron over to Clark. It was the turn of the 3rd Pursuit for the Clark night interception practice. Arriving over Clark about 4:30 A.M., Thorne contacted ground control at the field by radio and climbed with the others to 10,000 feet. There they remained in the northwest quadrant, circling and waiting for the B-18 to appear from the north and be illuminated by the searchlights.

About 4:50 A.M. Thorne noticed aircraft navigation lights well below him, in the vicinity of Mount Arayat to the east. This was strange; there was not supposed to be any other aircraft around. Thorne called Bob Hanson, leading the third two-ship element, and told him to go down and identify the plane. But then the mystery plane turned off its navigation lights. Hanson and his wingman dropped out of the flight and headed down toward the spot where the plane had been seen but could find no trace of it in the dark. After Hanson returned to the formation, the flight continued its night interception practice with the B-18, which by then had shown up. When Thorne and the other 3rd Pursuiters landed at Clark at daylight, they went over to 24th Group Headquarters Squadron mess for breakfast. Several of the pilots were talking about the incident when Major Grover, who had just come in, overheard the conversation and joined them. Grover then told them of the similar experience of the flight he had led the previous morning.

Reacting to this latest incident, Grover called Colonel George at 5th Interception Command at Nielson Field, as he had done the day before. The information came as no surprise to George; the Iba radar unit had also been calling in reports to him the past few days about tracks off the Luzon coast. But now intruders had been visually identified for two days running. He decided to ask MacArthur's chief of staff, Brigadier General Sutherland, for authority to intercept the bogies the next time they appeared. When Colonel George got back to Grover later in the day, he had new orders for the 24th Group: if they ran into bogies off the shore of Luzon, they should act defensively, but if the intruders were over Luzon airspace, they should attack. MacArthur had given the green light for the next escalation of hostile relations with Japan.

The 17th Pursuit Squadron took its turn for the next night's interception practice—4:30 to 6:30 A.M. on December 6. Grover ordered its CO,

Buzz Wagner, to arm fully the squadron's six participating P-40Es to make them ready for combat with the snooper if it should show up again over Clark. This was not going to be the usual B-18 cum searchlight practice; any bogies encountered would be forced down or, if they tried to elude Wagner's flight, shot down.

For this possible first combat mission of the 24th Pursuit Group, Wagner selected five of his most proficient pilots: Johnny Brownewell, Willie Feallock, Russ Church, Red Sheppard, and Bill Hennon. But in fact the assignment proved anticlimactic. No snooper showed up over Clark this time. After spending the two hours "chasing stars," Wagner's flight headed back to its Nichols base. At Iba, Thorne had a flight of six P-40Es on standby all that night for a possible interception. He also had received orders to shoot down any snooper if it flew within Philippine territorial limits. But the Iba radar did not pick up any plots.

2 At Nichols Field, in midmorning of December 6, the pilots of the 17th and 21st pursuit squadrons were summoned for a meeting at the base theater. As they entered the long room and sat down on benches and chairs, the short, broad-shouldered chief of staff of the 5th Interceptor Command watched his men in silence.

Then, after the last pilot had taken his seat, Colonel George, standing with his arms folded, looked into the faces of each of the sixty-odd aviators and announced, "Men, you are not a suicide squadron yet, but you are damned close to it. There will be war with Japan in a few days. It may come in a matter of hours." Tensely, the young pilots then listened to Colonel George's estimate of the number of Japanese aircraft on Formosa and on aircraft carriers ready to descend on the Philippines. Then he gave them his estimate of the number of pursuit needed to defend the islands against such a force—five to eight groups. "Yes," he concluded, "you men know how many planes we can get in the air. Well, that's the job you will be facing within a very short time."

As the pilots walked back to the field after the brief meeting, no one doubted the seriousness of the situation. One was less pessimistic than the others, however. Sam Grashio, one of the 21st Pursuit's 41-C Kelly Field flying school graduates, bet his CO, Ed Dyess, ten pesos that there would be no war.

Later that morning, Colonel George was at Clark Field to give the same message to the officers of the other pursuit squadrons. From Iba came the senior pilots of the 3rd Pursuit in their P-40Es. All the pilots of the 34th Pursuit at Del Carmen flew up in their venerable P-35As. Also attending were the officers of the home base 24th Group Headquarters and Headquarters Squadron and Moore's 20th Pursuit Squadron. They all crowded into one of the rooms of the Officers Club set aside for special functions. Colonel George repeated his assessment of the situation that

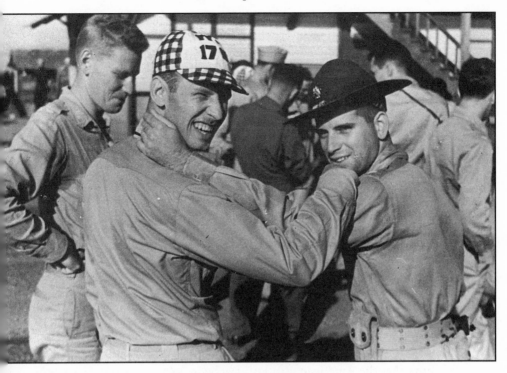

Left to right: Red Sheppard, John Brownewell, and Jack Dale, 17th Pursuit pilots, clown it up upon their arrival at Iba in July, 1941. Baseball caps like that worn by Brownewell, issued to all the pilots of the 17th, added to the esprit of the squadron. *Courtesy George H. Armstrong, Lt. Col. USAF (Ret.)*

he had given at Nichols earlier in the day. He added that a great Japanese fleet was drifting slowly south along the western reaches of the South China Sea, destination unknown.[1] Each pilot was told to file a will in his squadron's safe within the next few days. Terminating the brief meeting, Colonel George shocked the pilots with a repeat of his Nichols Field summation of their situation: "You are not necessarily a suicide squadron, but you are Goddamn near it!"

3 When the 24th Group's pilots had returned to their respective bases after the tense meetings, they reflected on their situation. In terms of the numbers they would be facing, they would certainly be at a disadvantage if the Japanese struck now, before further expected aircraft reinforcements—A-24 dive-bombers and P-40Es—reached them. Japanese airfields on Formosa, however, from where any land-based attack would come, were over five hundred miles to the north. While their great number of bombers could cover that distance and return easily, was not cen-

tral Luzon beyond the range of Formosa-based fighters that would be needed to escort them? But what about fighters based on carriers? No one knew anything about the location of Japanese carriers and their possible role in an attack on the Philippines.

Colonel George had emphasized the hopelessly disproportionate numbers that they would be facing, but what about the advantages they would have in terms of quality of flying personnel and aircraft? They had heard so often that Japanese pilots could not dogfight because they were all nearsighted and their glasses would fall off. Even if their vision was all right, their nervous systems could not take the violent acrobatics of combat flying. And what would the Japanese be flying? Five-year-old stuff with fixed landing gears and underpowered engines. They had all seen War Department Field Manual 30-38, *Identification of Japanese Aircraft*, that had been distributed to the Philippine Department Air Force in May. The Japanese operational bombers—the Army Type 97 and Navy Type 96— were slow and unarmored, duck soup for the P-40. Most felt the fighter they would most likely face would be the Nakajima Type 97, armed with only two .30-caliber machine guns. True, there was a page on a new Japanese fighter cited as "Fighter 100 (Also called Zero Type)." The manual did not include a photo or silhouettes as it did for the other Japanese aircraft, "only some ridiculous performance figures and claims for its extreme maneuverability" that led Willie Feallock of the 17th Pursuit to think that the American military attache in Tokyo, who must have provided the information, "had been drinking too much sake."

Against such opposition, most of the pilots figured they had the advantage. They were clearly more physically and emotionally suited for combat flying, and their P-40Es were the most modern pursuit aircraft in operation in the U.S. Air Force at the time. But Max Louk and some of the others had serious reservations about their P-40s. As the 20th Pursuit's interception of the B-17s three weeks earlier had shown, the P-40 could not keep up with a fast bomber at high altitude; indeed, its performance above 18,000 feet was sluggish at best.[2] Furthermore, its slow rate of climb when combat-loaded threw into question its effectiveness as an interceptor. And no one knew for sure if the P-40's guns would work when needed. With only one or two exceptions, they had not yet been fired by the pilots. The shortage of .50-caliber ammunition in the Far East Air Force was too acute to allow test-firing in the P-40Bs and Es—there was reportedly only enough to load their guns two times.[3]

But whatever the odds against them, the 165 pilots of the 24th Pursuit Group (including those of the attached 35th Group) were tired of the readiness status of the past eight days. On constant standby to take off for combat, their nerves were taut. Why did Japan not attack, so they could get on with it, for better or for worse?

4 In the small hours of Sunday, December 7, 1941, Buzz Wagner took his six-ship flight up to Clark Field again for the sixth B-18/searchlight interception practice as well as to wait for any Japanese intruders that might show up that morning. Once more, the exercise ended with no sign of any bogies, and the pilots returned to Nichols Field.

Since the readiness order had gone into effect nine days earlier, Wagner had cut down the size of each of the 17th's three flights from twelve to six pilots, selecting the most experienced and capable of his squadron strength of forty-one pilots.[4] In practice, this group comprised his most senior eighteen pilots, excluding 39-A oldie George Armstrong, who was on detachment service at Clark in a nonflying job. Each flight was organized into two-ship elements, a decided improvement in combat conditions over the old three-plane "show formation" element. Thanks to the capable and demanding instruction of Squadron Operations Officer Willie Feallock during practices in the P-35As from July through October, the 17th's pilots were all skilled in flying basic two-ship maneuvers.

Much to the regret of Red Sheppard and many of the other senior pilots, however, the squadron had not spent any significant time in developing combat tactics. At Iba with their P-35As, the 17th had done all the fun things—mock dogfighting, low flying, acrobatics, and close-formation flying—but had not once practiced interceptions against real or simulated bombers with or without escorts, their main tactical responsibility in the group. There had been no interception practice with the newly received P-40Es at Nichols either; most of November had been spent in trying to learn to handle their difficult steeds, then learning to fly them in formation, before all training was suspended on November 28 by the readiness order. The only bomber interception training they had received was during the past two nights, when only a few senior pilots had the opportunity to participate in the night interception practice against the B-18 at Clark.

With the loss of Grant Manley's ship ten days earlier, the squadron was down to twenty-one of its original twenty-five P-40Es, and two of these had suffered accidents in November (Erickson's and one by newie Jerry Brezina) and were only now back in service. This was cutting it rather close for operations—the strength specified by the Table of Organization and Equipment (T.O. and E.) for a pursuit squadron was twenty-five aircraft for daily eighteen-ship availability, the seven additional being counted on to fill in for those out of commission, undergoing major repairs after accidents, or away on cross-country missions.

The six .50-caliber guns of each of the squadron's P-40Es had been bore-sighted, but except for those of the CO's ship, none had been test-fired. But there was another big question mark about the likely effectiveness of the P-40s' guns in a combat situation. When the aircraft were received in mid-October, the squadron's armorers were ordered by the depot to plug the inlet of all the hydraulic gun charger valves, making the hydraulic gun charging system inoperative. A technical order of Wright Field Maintenance Command accompanying the shipment of the fifty P-40Es had spelled out the details of this required operation. The order would remain in effect until receipt of further instructions. Although the reason for disconnecting the hydraulic gun charging system was not given in the Wright Field order, the armorers had heard that the problem was that the P-40's landing gear, flaps, and guns were on the same hydraulic system, with different valves. Evidently in charging the guns, the rubber hoses to the guns often broke, resulting in a loss of hydraulic pressure necessary to operate the associated landing gear and flaps.

Deactivating the P-40E's hydraulic gun system meant that each plane would need to have its guns charged manually before takeoff, one at a time, from under the wings with a cable. With such a crude method, the 17th Pursuit's armorers were worried about the impossibility of clearing jammed guns in the air when the pilots were engaged in combat; the pilots would have to return to the field and have them cleared on the ground by the armorers.

Although they complied with the Wright Field order, the armorers were not convinced of the need to deactivate the gun charging system and decided to check it themselves. After mounting one of the P-40Es on special wing stands, they unplugged the gun charger valves, then charged the guns hydraulically and ran the wheels up and down. For three days they operated the system without the hoses rupturing; the hydraulic system functioned perfectly. The 17th Pursuit reported the favorable results of their test to the depot but could not get it to rescind the Wright Field order, and with no subsequent instructions from Wright Field to allow operation again of the hydraulic gun charging mechanism, the squadron's armorers were obliged to maintain the primitive manual gun charging procedures.[5]

5 Down at one end of Nichols Field, the 21st Pursuit Squadron had dispersed its P-40Es in the woods at the edge of the field on the orders of its CO, Ed Dyess, following his return from the pilots' meeting with Colonel George the day before. Around each of the planes, the squadron's armorers had stacked wooden boxes full of .50-caliber ammunition. The aircraft were ready for combat on short notice. Following delivery of ten of the P-40Es on December 4, the 21st had received another ten on December 6, with two more scheduled to be turned over to the squadron on December 8.[6] None of the new aircraft had been flown more than two hours.

The armorers of the 21st had made their aircrafts' hydraulic gun charging systems inoperative by plugging the valves, in accordance with the Wright Field technical order.[7] A bigger, filthier job was boiling the thick, greasy Cosmoline off the .50-caliber guns following their removal from the packing crates. After the guns were cleaned, they were installed in the wings and boresighted.

In addition to the thirteen original 21st Pursuit pilots who had arrived seventeen days earlier, the squadron now had five pilots from the other squadrons temporarily serving with it, including 41-B flying school graduates Bob Newman from the 3rd Pursuit and John Vogel from the 17th, and 41-C and 41-D newies Charles "Junior" Burris and Bob Krantz from the 17th. Ten of the originally assigned thirteen pilots were very recent flying school graduates in the classes of 41-C, -D, -E, and -F; however, unlike their classmates shipped to the Philippines shortly after completing their training, these newies had been assigned to Hamilton Field, where they had gained experience in flying the earlier models of the P-40. Thus, they were not intimidated by its handling characteristics.

All five of the squadron's 41-C pilots had gone through Kelly Field together. The liveliest of the bunch was twenty-three year-old Sam Grashio, from Spokane, Washington, who had enlisted in the Army Air Corps after completing the minimum two years of college required by the Air Corps, at Gonzaga University. Like many other youths of his generation, he had been obsessed with the excitement of aviation in the 1930s. His only ambition had been to become a pilot. Two of Grashio's 41-C squadron mates were college graduates from the deep South. Twenty-three-year-old Joe Cole, from Kingstree, South Carolina, had received his B.S. degree from the Citadel in June, 1940, before entering flying school. Lloyd Allen Coleman—known as "L. A." to his peers—at twenty-six was one year older than his CO, Ed Dyess. A native of Doddsville, Mississippi, he had graduated from the University of Mississippi in June, 1938, with a B.S. degree in chemistry.

Next to I. B. "Jack" Donalson, a 41-F graduate of Kelly Field, 41-E Stockton Field graduates Johnny McCown and Gus Williams were the most junior of the squadron's pilots. They were also best friends. Born on a ranch near Globe, Arizona, twenty-four-year-old Williams completed three years of engineering in junior college in Phoenix and a semester at the University of Arizona in Tucson before being taken ill for a year. After recuperating, he took the CAA flight training program, where he logged thirty hours of flight time before eventually entering Air Corps flight training in November, 1940. If war was coming, Williams preferred to be a pilot. One of the squadron's three oldies—40-G Kelly Field graduate Ben Irvin—was another of the squadron's southerners, hailing from Washington, Georgia. Although he was only twenty-three years old, he had already gained unusual flying experience in addition to his Hamilton Field service, having been assigned in England three months in the summer of 1941 as an American observer with the RAF.

All the 21st Pursuiters had developed admiration and respect for their CO, Ed Dyess, who had taken over command of the squadron at Hamilton Field in mid-1941. A graduate of John Tarleton Agricultural College, the tall Albany, Texas, son of a judge possessed a natural, easy charm and leadership capabilities that were evident during his college days and then at Kelly Field, where he graduated in the class of 37-C at the age of twenty-one. The most skillful pilot of the 21st, Dyess was now demonstrating his training abilities with the junior-level pilots of his squadron.

6 At Iba, ninety miles to the northwest of Nichols, a six-ship flight of combat-loaded P-40Es had been ready again on the early morning of Sunday, December 7, for immediate takeoff if any Japanese should make a return visit offshore. As was the case the morning before, however, no snoopers were picked up by the Iba radar unit.

Following the November 28 readiness order, CO Hank Thorne had reorganized his 3rd Pursuit into three combat flights of six aircraft each, with A Flight under Thorne, B Flight led by Ed Woolery, and C Flight by Herb Ellis. Each flight was composed of three two-ship elements. The nine element leader positions were filled by the flight leaders and the six most senior pilots of the squadron, 40-A and 40-D oldies. The nine wingmen were drawn from the 40-H and 41-B pilots. As Wagner had done with the 17th Pursuit, Thorne was going with his most senior pilots.

The 3rd had another similarity to the 17th: it had not spent enough time in combat tactics training either, in the view of Ellis and other senior pilots. As for the 17th, the transition from the P-35A to the P-40E had occupied the squadron's senior pilots most of November, leaving little opportunity for them to develop any interception capability in their new ships, even if interception practice had been proposed. During the earlier, less stressful period at Clark while flying their P-35As, only a few interception practices against simulated enemy bombers had been scheduled, and they had proven dismal failures.

With the loss of only one P-40E in an accident, the 3rd Pursuit had a complement of twenty-four of the pursuit ships, of which eighteen were maintained at all times in commission and six as spares. It had also retained four of its old P-35As and a single A-27.

During the first week of December, the armament section of the squadron was working twenty-four hours a day to complete the installation in the P-40Es of the .50-caliber guns, which had arrived considerably after the aircraft had been delivered to Iba. The squadron newies were working side-by-side with the enlisted men armorers, clearing the Cosmoline off the guns and installing and boresighting them. Not having received any technical instructions on procedures for installing and boresighting the guns, S. Sgt. Walter Engstrom devised a "Rube Goldberg" operation to accomplish the job. By the end of the day, Sunday, December 7, guns had been installed in all the squadron's P-40Es, and the last four were being boresighted. In accordance with the Wright Field technical order, the armorers of the 3rd Pursuit had plugged the valves of the hydraulic gun charging mechanisms of their P-40Es, too. The pilots were not very happy about having to depend on manually charging their ships' guns on the ground. None had yet test-fired the guns, either.

Another problem involving operations with the P-40Es was the non-availability at Iba of adapters required to transfer oxygen from the high-pressure tanks in which it was stored to the P-40E's low-pressure system. This meant that the 3rd's pilots would not have oxygen available to them and thus would not be able to fly their P-40Es above 15,000 feet for more than a few minutes.

In addition to the difficulties he faced in trying to maintain an effective interception capability, Hank Thorne was also burdened with the responsibility of providing a ground defense for the exposed field. He was obliged to park the squadron's planes right along the landing strip, unable to provide any dispersal because there was no additional space available. Native landowners at Iba had refused to allow the Far East Air Force to use their adjoining land for such purpose. No revetments had been constructed to protect the aircraft from aerial attack, for sandbags were in short supply. Indeed, there was no effective way to camouflage the planes, for that matter.

For antiaircraft defense, the squadron had been supplied twelve .30-caliber Lewis guns of World War I vintage. Gun positions around the base were prepared by the men, "each to his own inventiveness." T. Sgt. "Woody" McBride developed his position, at the north end of the runway, by cutting out the ends of fifty-five-gallon gasoline drums, filling them with sand, and sandbagging in between. Two emplacements held his group of ten men and their two Lewis guns, which as in other emplacements were each mounted on galvanized steel pipe driven into the ground.

In addition to the Lewis gun positions, some foxholes had been dug on the beach side of the base. Empty fifty-five-gallon drums were lowered in upright position into the shallow holes and arranged in a circle, then sand was piled on the outside of the exposed parts of the drums. No one really knew what proper foxholes looked like or how they should be dug, but it was felt these improvised structures would serve the purpose.

Iba's defense mainly depended on its SCR-270B radar unit, the only one installed and operational in the Philippines by December 7. It had already proven its effectiveness during the past ten days, detecting snooping Japanese aircraft coming down the west coast of Luzon. The unit con-

sisted of an operations van housed in a tent some one hundred yards behind the squadron's barracks building on the beach side and a power van
and antenna trailer twenty yards away in another tent. The 3rd Pursuit's
personnel by now knew that the setup was a detection device, but except
for CO Thorne, no one had been allowed to see it in operation.

On the evening of December 7, the officers and men of the 3rd Pursuit
were prepared for any eventuality. Thorne had formed a special six-ship
alert flight that evening, its pilots to sleep near the radar installation.
The other twelve members of the three regular combat flights were preparing to bed down by their P-40Es on the flight line, their ships in tactical readiness. In each Lewis gun pit, an enlisted man was on guard duty,
scheduled for relief at 6:00 A.M.

7 At Clark Field, the antiaircraft defense situation was better than
at Iba or any other FEAF field. Located at strategic positions around the
field and adjoining Fort Stotsenburg were a mobile battalion of 3-inch
and a battalion of 37-mm antiaircraft guns of the 200th Coastal Artillery
regiment, charged with defense of Clark and Fort Stotsenburg. To protect
its twenty-three P-40Bs, the 20th Pursuit, with the help of the resident
Headquarters Company of the 803rd Aviation Engineers, in late November had constructed V-shaped revetments on the north and west perimeters of the field from empty fifty-five-gallon gasoline drums filled with
sand and stacked two high, facing in all directions. All but Joe Moore's
plane were sheltered in these scattered revetments; his was parked across
the road from the squadron's operations shack for quick access by Moore
in the event of a scramble order. Near it was also parked the P-40B of
the 24th Group's commanding officer, Maj. Orrin Grover.

All around the revetments, squadron operations shack, barracks, and
other structures at Clark, V-trenches and foxholes had been dug by the
803rd Engineers. Each side of the V-trenches was six to eight feet long,
and some were five feet deep. To keep the trenches from caving in, they
were revetted with woven bamboo, and the top one and a half to two feet
were faced with boards. Visiting U.S. Army officers passing through the
Philippines after having served with British forces in North Africa had
impressed upon the Clark Field commanding officer the effectiveness
of such trenches in protecting personnel from even close hits by bombs.

Unlike the other pursuit squadron commanders, Moore had divided
his pilot strength into two sections of eighteen pilots each for flying the
eighteen aircraft kept in tactical readiness, and he planned to alternate
the two sections on all missions. He reasoned that this arrangement was
better for ensuring adequate rest and also for maintaining morale than
forming a combat echelon of the top eighteen pilots of his squadron. Moore
led one section, while the squadron's next most senior pilot, Charley
"Mort" Sneed, since late November appointed squadron operations offi-

cer, led the other. After the considerable combat tactics training of the past two months in their P-40Bs, Moore regarded each section—comprising three six-ship flights each in two-ship elements—as about equal in capability.

Although the squadron's P-40Bs were not scheduled for an engine change until they reached 250 hours' flying time, the Allison 1710-33s had proven short-lived, lasting only 75 to 125 hours. In November a shipment of new engines for all the P-40Bs had arrived from the States. By working fourteen to sixteen hours a day, S. Sgt. Ken Stanford, Sgt. Bill Joy, and Pfc Jim Brown had managed to install new power plants in all the squadron's twenty-three P-40Bs by December 7.

That Sunday evening, all five remaining members of the squadron's 41-B flying school class decided to go to the movie at Clark Field. Each had been promoted by Moore to element leader—Parker Gies, Max Louk, and Harrison Hughes in Moore's Section 1, and Kiefer White and Erwin Crellin in Sneed's Section 2. White and Crellin were on the alert that evening, but it was decided it would be only a one-hour alert this time, to allow them to go to the show. Attending the show was just a poor alternative to what they had originally planned for the weekend: to go into Manila to attend an "elaborate officers' party" being given for General Brereton. It would have been the occasion of Gies's first date since he had arrived in the Philippines seven months earlier. But the readiness order was still in effect, confining all Clark Field officers to the base.

8 Just south of Clark, the 34th Pursuit Squadron was also confined to its base, a primitive area, compared to Clark, in terms of the facilities available. Officers and men alike were living under crude circumstances near their still-incomplete airstrip.

The past week the fifteen pilots of the 34th plus the pilots attached from other pursuit squadrons had been flying daily patrols of sixty miles between Clark Field to the north and Nichols Field to the south while waiting for the inevitable word of a Japanese attack. Operations from Del Carmen field were difficult at best; the dust on the field was a good six inches deep, obscuring the vision of the pilots during takeoffs and landings. It was the dry season in the Philippines. In an effort to keep the dust down, the 803rd Aviation Engineers were sprinkling the field with molasses, using a tank truck.

Following the transfer of the 21st Pursuit's aircraft on December 4, the squadron now had twenty-two P-35As at the field. All were overdue for an engine change, but no new engines were available. The squadron's mechanics were obliged to do the best they could to keep the worn-out aircraft in commission, a task not made any easier by the pervasive dust.

Squadron CO Sam Marett had ordered his men to put in long hours and hard work the first week of December to get gun positions dug and

Left to right: Carl Gies, Max Louk, Erwin Crellin, and Varian White with a P-40B of their 20th Pursuit Squadron at Clark Field, August, 1941. *Courtesy Dorothy W. Tilforth*

plane revetments prepared while also maintaining twenty-four-hour guard duty. Six gun pits had been completed, six feet deep and four feet in diameter, in the center of each was embedded a steel pipe on which a Lewis .30-caliber machine gun had been mounted. The 34th's adjutant, Lt. John Jennings, also had twelve 30-06 Springfield rifles to issue, but he did not know which of the squadron's 218 enlisted men should receive them. The six Lewis guns and the rifles were the sum total of the field's defense.

Marett's severe work program had caused much grumbling among the enlisted men. Then, on the afternoon of December 6, just back from hearing Colonel George's speech at Clark, he held a meeting with all the personnel of the squadron to explain why he was driving them so hard. With a grave expression on his face, he informed his charges that war was imminent; there was a large Japanese bomber force on the southern tip of Formosa, a bare three hundred miles north of them, and its only plausible objective was the Philippines. For a half minute Marett's words were met with complete silence. Then, in a calm and authoritative voice, the 34th's CO reminded all that they had been thoroughly trained for this eventuality. He expected them to carry on in the same competent manner they had shown so far.

To Marett's men, this performance only confirmed their high regard for the leadership abilities of their CO. Such esteem was not generated by his physical appearance, though. A native of New Braunfels, Texas, Marett was a rather small man, with dark and pocked facial features. He always seemed to the men to be bitter about something, perhaps attributable to his Air Corps experiences as a "mustang"—an enlisted man who had been awarded an officer's commission. He had made first lieutenant and had been assigned as commanding officer of the 34th just before the squadron's departure for the Philippines.

Next in seniority to Marett—a 38-B flying school graduate of Kelly Field—was 1st Lt. Ben S. Brown, from Hawkinsville, Georgia, a dark and swarthy man of relatively short stature, too, who had completed flying school in the class of 40-D. The third oldie of the squadron was 41-A graduate Don Pagel, a twenty-five year old from Aurora, Illinois, who had been a star halfback on his high school football team.

Three of the squadron's six 41-C pilots were from Missouri: Jack Hall, Bill Baker, and Art Knackstedt. Although he did not drink or smoke, Hall was already living up to his reputation as the life of the party. The same age as Hall, Knackstedt had worked in his uncle's dairy farm after graduating from a two-year junior college but had decided in September, 1940, to enlist in the Air Corps. Baker also had enlisted in 1940 after completing college and getting married. Twenty-four-year-old Larry McDaniel, another of the squadron's 41-C pilots and a native of Jackson, North Carolina, also entered the Air Corps directly from college. A fifth 41-C flying school graduate was the squadron's lone Californian, Stewart Robb, twenty-three years old, a native of Bakersfield who had started flying at the age of sixteen. He already had three hundred hours' flying time when he entered army flying school in late 1940 after graduating in aeronautics from California Polytechnic in San Luis Obispo earlier that year.

All four of the squadron's 41-D pilots were from Texas. Best friends Don "Shorty" Crosland and Frankie Bryant had attended North Texas State Teachers College and gone through Stockton Field flying school together, then joined the 34th Pursuit at Hamilton Field, California, at the same time. At twenty-six years of age, the same age as Marett, Crosland was short but fast and had starred on his high school basketball team. The baby of the squadron at twenty-two years, Bryant had completed two years of college on a football scholarship, then decided to join the Air Corps with Crosland in 1940. Claude Paulger, from Lubbock, Texas, had been a premed student when he dropped out to enlist.

On the evening of December 7, Marett put his pilots through a surprise night alert, as he had told them the day before he might do at any time. The quiet of the rural setting was suddenly broken by the racket of the starter shotgun shells as they exploded in the P-35As and the old engines caught. Then, after running the engines up for a few minutes, the pilots shut them down. They were as ready as they could be for what awaited them.

9 Just after midnight on the evening of December 7/8, the radar operator in the SCR-270B tent at Iba noted blips on his scope again, indicating aircraft about 115 miles northwest of Iba. He informed Lieutenant Wimer and radioed the Air Warning Service at Nielson Field in Manila.[8] When Wimer woke Hank Thorne to give him the news, the 3rd Pursuit's CO gave the word to wake the rest of the squadron. The squadron's bugle boy was so excited that he could scarcely blow, succeeding in getting out only one sour blast in the barracks building. Then someone outside shouted, "Hang it out the window and let the wind blow it!" In the tension of the moment, the wisecrack elicited a good laugh.

As the SCR-270B's scope showed the blips continuing southeast toward Corregidor, Thorne put his interception plan into operation. He had been ordered by FEAF Headquarters to have a flight of six P-40Es on alert this evening to intercept any intruders; all other pursuit aircraft were grounded, to avoid any confusion. The five other pilots of Thorne's alert flight, who had been sleeping by the radar installation, were now at their aircraft, whose engines had been kept warmed up by their crew chiefs. Within five minutes, Thorne led his flight off the field in a cloud of dust, with orders to shoot down any intruders over Philippine air space.

Mindful of the radio communications problem he had experienced three nights earlier, Thorne had arranged this time that radio calls be transmitted to the flight in Morse code in longer-range high frequency radio after voice transmission faded five to ten miles out. Thorne had picked Gerry Keenan to fly as third element leader this night, replacing Herb Ellis, so Keenan could receive information from the 3rd Pursuit's radio station on the position of the bogies; Keenan had gone to signal school and was a qualified radio operator, fluent in Morse code.

On the ground at Iba, the twelve pilots of the two other flights, on readiness status, milled excitedly around, from time to time checking in the radar scope tent to follow the blips. In the 3rd Pursuit's radio station, near the radar site, 1st Lt. Jim Donegan was at the key, radioing the course of the bogies and compass readings in Morse code.

Now some forty miles offshore, Thorne was leading his flight through several local rain squalls; visibility was very poor. When the 3rd Pursuiters reached 4,000 feet, they ran into bright moonlight above a layer of broken clouds. Still climbing and headed south on a course Donegan indicated on the radio should bring them into contact with the bogies, they encountered another thin layer of scattered clouds at 9,000 feet. But voice transmission had faded, and soon Keenan could no longer pick up any Morse code messages.[9] The flight had broken up into two-ship elements, each flying staggered at different altitudes, searching for the elusive intruders.

In the 3rd Pursuit's radio shack, Donegan continued sending direction indications to Keenan, but he was receiving no acknowledgments. Crowding around the scope in the radar tent, Herb Ellis, Frank Neri, and other pilots of the three combat flights watched the two sets of blips converge — those of the P-40s heading south and the bogies flying southeast. Then the tracks merged about four miles west of Corregidor, and someone yelled, "Contact enemy!" Everyone thought the interception had been made, but then after about one minute, the bogies broke out of the confused mass of blips and reversed course, heading back out to sea on a reciprocal course, and the 3rd Pursuit blips headed back north to Iba.

After flying at different altitudes in a vain search for the bogies, with no radio calls to guide them, Thorne had decided to turn around and was bringing his flight back to Iba. As they approached the field, they could see its outline in the darkness; all the cars and trucks of the squadron had been lined up at the edge of the field with their lights turned on to illuminate the strip. Ellis and the others had figured correctly that this crude arrangement would provide better lighting than the portable string of lights installed at the field, which provided only very dull light that could hardly be seen from the air. The six P-40Es touched down without incident. It was the first night landing at Iba for the 3rd Pursuit Squadron.

To a disappointed group of squadron mates, Thorne explained that they had not intercepted the bogies—not even at the point where the blips had converged on the radar scope. Apparently all three elements of the flight, although flying staggered at different altitudes, had passed below the high-flying Japanese at the contact point.[10] Exhausted from their frustrating experience, Thorne and the pilots of his flight turned in to get what little sleep they could before the night was finished. The first FEAF attempt at ground-controlled interception in a potential combat situation had failed.

Over at Clark Field, a little while after midnight, the field siren had sounded, then the phones at the 20th Pursuit's officer quarters at Fort Stotsenburg rang; Joe Moore was ordering all his pilots to the 24th Group's operations hangar on the line at the field. Parker Gies and the other 41-B pilots had just gotten to sleep after having attended the picture show and slinging the bull a while before turning in. Now they hurriedly dressed again and headed over to Clark. When they were all assembled in the operations hangar, Major Grover explained why they had been called out; the Iba radio direction finder had plotted a large formation of bogies proceeding down the west coast of Luzon, heading toward Manila. After his brief explanation, Grover ordered the thirty-six pilots of Sections 1 and

2 of Moore's 20th Pursuit to report to the line and go on standby status. From 1:30 to 2:30, the sleepy officers remained near the planes, then finally Moore's Section 1 was allowed to go back to its quarters for rest. Sneed's Section 2 would remain on readiness.

Back in bed at Fort Stotsenburg, Parker Gies "felt pretty safe" with "our elaborate QA-1 [ground-to-air radio communications] or aircraft spotting system." With the Iba radar, they could know "the approach, speed, course, and number of enemy aircraft from the time they reached the island." Furthermore, the 20th Pursuit had worked tactical problems with B-18s and B-17s and had been able to intercept them. After the failure of their intercept attempt at Iba that night, however, the pilots of the 3rd Pursuit had a different view than Gies's. Their SCR-270B could not indicate altitude, a critical weakness for any ground-controlled interception. Even if the radar could have provided such information, Iba's ground-to-air radio communications had been proven totally unreliable as a means to vector the pilots to the target. And the interception capabilities of the P-40 against high-flying bombers? Even Gies's own housemate Max Louk had forcibly expressed his views on that subject.

Part Two
THE FATAL DECEMBER EIGHTH

At his penthouse in the Manila Hotel, the sleep of Lt. Gen. Douglas MacArthur, commanding general of U.S. Army Forces in the Far East, was disturbed at 3:55 on the night of December 7/8; a message from Adm. Thomas Hart, his navy counterpart, had been received by one of the USAFFE duty officers at MacArthur's quarters, informing of an attack on Pearl Harbor by Japanese naval aircraft at 2:35 Manila time. Japan had initiated hostilities against the United States. By 5:00 A.M., MacArthur's USAFFE staff was assembled at its headquarters, No. 1 Calle Victoria in the walled city of Manila. A state of war between the United States and Japan had been confirmed by Washington. At 5:15 all USAFFE posts were notified of the outbreak of hostilities.

When MacArthur's chief of staff, Brig. Gen. Richard Sutherland, called Maj. Gen. Lewis Brereton, commanding general of the Far East Air Force, the news came as no surprise to MacArthur's top air force officer. Brereton even expected a Japanese attack on the Philippines any time after daylight. At 7:15, Brereton reported in to USAFFE headquarters to request permission of MacArthur for initiating offensive action immediately against Japanese air bases on Formosa with his Clark-based B-17s. But MacArthur was in conference. Sutherland told Brereton to go ahead with preparations, but he would need to wait for MacArthur's approval before launching any attack against the Japanese. The USAFFE's role for the time being was defensive.

Sutherland's position was in accordance with the "full alert" radiogram received from the War Department in Washington on November 28, stipulating that "if hostilities cannot be avoided, the U.S. desires that Japan commit the first overt act." Evidently Sutherland did not consider the attack on Pearl Harbor as an overt act in terms of the USAFFE's *Philippines* defense responsibilities; the Philippines was a commonwealth, not a part of U.S. territory. Yet USAFFE had been informed at 6:15 A.M. that the city of Davao on Mindanao had been attacked by Japanese aircraft at dawn. Did this not constitute an overt act against the Philippines?

In response to a renewed request by Brereton for authorization for an attack on Formosa, Sutherland phoned him at 8:50 to say, "Hold off bombing Formosa for the present." Brereton was not to load his B-17s with bombs. Sutherland also told Brereton not to call USAFFE again on this matter; he would be informed when any new decision was taken by MacArthur. But when Brereton received word at 9:23 that Camp John Hay in Baguio and Tuguegarao in northern Luzon had just been bombed by Japanese aircraft, he ignored Sutherland's instructions and at 10:00 called again. He informed MacArthur's chief of staff that Japanese aircraft were operating over Luzon, but Sutherland already had received a report himself at 9:05 of the Baguio bombing. Nevertheless, Sutherland reiterated that all aircraft were to be held in reserve; "the present attitude was strictly defensive." Irritated with USAFFE's unbending and unreasonable stance, Brereton warned Sutherland that if Clark Field were taken out, the FEAF would not be able to operate offensively.

With confirmation at 9:47 of the Davao airport attack and at 9:58 of the bombing of Baguio and Tuguegarao, MacArthur finally accepted that overt acts had been committed against his Philippines command. At 10:14 MacArthur telephoned Brereton, authorizing him to take offensive action as he saw fit. In response, Brereton indicated that he was waiting for reports of a B-17 reconnaissance over Formosa that he had sent out earlier, but recon report or no, he would attack Japanese air bases on Formosa late that afternoon. Brereton then completed plans for two squadrons of B-17s to attack known airdromes on southern Formosa "at the latest daylight hour that visibility will permit." At 11:56, in response to a call from Sutherland, Brereton briefed the chief of staff on the air situation since he had last contacted USAFFE and confirmed his intentions to bomb Formosan fields in late afternoon.

But at 11:37 a report had come in to FEAF from the Iba radar station that ten minutes earlier a flight of enemy planes had been detected seventy miles off Lingayen Gulf and headed south. In response, Air Warning at Nielson Field sent a teletype message to 24th Pursuit Group operations at Clark Field, warning of the incoming force. As the Air Warning and 5th Interceptor Command officers continued to follow this flight and a second spotted flying down Lingayen Gulf on a line to Clark Field, they became increasingly agitated. About 12:20, Capt. "Bud" Sprague, the 5th Interceptor Command's operations officer, drafted another message for Clark, ordering the 24th Group to intercept the Clark-bound flight, and took it to the teletype room for transmission to Major Grover.

Evidently confused by conflicting messages being received from many directions, Grover took no action on Sprague's message after it was received on his teletype machine in the 24th Group's operations hangar. But now it was too late; overhead, twenty-six Mitsubishi G3M2 "Nell" twin-engine bombers of the 1st *kokutai* (Naval Air Group), followed immediately by twenty-seven Mitsubishi G4M1 "Betty" bombers of the Takao *kokutai*, had begun dropping their loads of twelve 132-pound bombs at 12:35. Their attack was virtually flawless, smothering the Clark base with over six hundred bombs.

Once the pattern bombing run was completed, thirty-four escorting Mitsubishi A6M2 Zeros of the Tainan *kokutai*, in repeated strafing runs during the next twenty-two minutes, came down low to pour 20- and 7.7-mm fire into the hapless P-40s and B-17s caught on the ground.

Yet when the Tainan *kokutai* Zeros finally left at 1:00 P.M., it was still not over for the Clark base. Another force of fifty-one Zeros from the 3rd *kokutai*, including a detachment from the Tainan *kokutai*, arrived over the field to pick out remaining targets of opportunity. Their devastating work completed, at 1:15 P.M. they headed north for the return trip to Formosa.

The second group of Zeros had just finished shooting up Iba Field. Another attack force from Formosa, composed of fifty-three G4M1s of the Takao and Kanoya *kokutai* and the fifty-one Zeros had arrived over Iba at between 12:40 and 12:44. After the G4M1s had dropped 486 bombs of 132 pounds and 26 of 550 pounds on the tiny field and its installations, the Zeros proceeded to strafe the remaining targets.

5. "HARD TO BELIEVE THERE WAS ACTUALLY A WAR IN PROGRESS"

1 At 4:00 A.M. on Monday, December 8, 1941, the ringing of the telephone awakened newly married 2nd Lt. Dave Obert at his residence near Nichols Field. As he went to answer it, he thought, "It's another false alarm." The call was an order for the 17th Pursuit Squadron to report to the field immediately. Obert quickly dressed, and as he left, he told his wife of eight days that it was just another practice alert; he would be back for breakfast. But when he reached Nichols ten minutes later, he found his fellow 17th Pursuiters in a state of excitement; *Hawaii had been bombed.* Obert could not believe the report. "It's just another rumor," he told himself. How could Japanese bombers reach Hawaii?

Over at the office of the 20th Air Base Group, Buzz Wagner talked to its CO, Maj. Billy Maverick, about the situation. The 17th Pursuit's CO had been ordered to lead a mission but had not received further instructions. Reporting back to the 17th Pursuit's operations area, Wagner assigned pilots to the three six-plane flights, based on his assessment of his pilots' combat capabilities and experience. Willie Feallock would lead one flight, while Johnny Brownewell and Wagner himself would lead the other two. As usual, the squadron's 40-A oldies, Russ Church, Walt Coss, Red Sheppard, and Allison Strauss, would fly as element leaders.[1] It was still dark when Wagner and his designated pilots climbed into their P-40Es and began taxiing them to the east end of the new concrete runway, their takeoff position at Nichols. Then they turned off their engines and waited for takeoff orders over their radios. Behind Wagner was his wingman, Cy Blanton, followed in third position by Dave Obert, who would be the only 40-H element leader on the mission. None of the pilots was in uniform.

At the end of the other runway at Nichols, Ed Dyess and the others of his 21st Pursuit were also in their P-40Es, none with over three hours on its engine, waiting for radio orders to take off. But no instruction was forthcoming. After a few minutes, the pilots cut their engines (the Allisons overheated quickly), got out of their cockpits, and sat under the wings of their aircraft.

The 21st Pursuiters were a tired bunch. They had first been roused about 2:30 A.M. by the squadron's officer of the day, L. A. Coleman, and told to report immediately to the 21st's operations tent at Nichols. Gus Williams and his 41-E classmate Johnny McCown were particularly bleary-eyed as they climbed out of their beds; they had had a late night on the town. When they reported for duty, Dyess had simply told them that there was an emergency. He did not explain that the reason for the order was that bogies had been picked up on the Iba radar, heading in the direction of Manila. Then, ten minutes later, he told his pilots to go back to their quarters. Only two hours later, Coleman was back, banging on their doors again. This time he shouted that Pearl Harbor had been attacked. Assembled once more in the dim glow of a blacked-out gas lantern, the pilots had the report confirmed by Dyess. To all, it was simply incomprehensible.

At Clark Field, the news of the Pearl Harbor attack had first been picked up by the 20th Pursuit Squadron's cook, Pvt. Harry Seiff. On an early shift, he had been listening to music from Manila on his Zenith Trans-Oceanic radio when the program was interrupted with the startling announcement. Excitedly, Seiff woke the enlisted men and spread the word.

Between 4:30 and 5:00 A.M., Joe Moore ordered the eighteen pilots of his own Section 1 to the flight line from their Fort Stotsenburg quarters. Outside the squadron's operations shack on the line, Moore confirmed the Pearl Harbor report. Still in their P-40Bs, ready to take off on a moment's notice, Charley Sneed's Section 2 of eighteen pilots waited for orders. Moore and the others of his section took off their ties. Most of them were relieved that the long period of waiting was over. For the next two hours, they remained on the flight line, listening to radio reports of the Pearl Harbor attack. Then, about 7:00 A.M., Moore told them to go back to their quarters and get some sleep. They would be relieving Section 2 at 10:00 A.M.

Fighting drowsiness, Sneed's pilots on the line at Clark Field continued to wait for the takeoff order. If it was still dark, the signal would be a Very gun flare; if daylight, a red flag would be run up the flagpole at the squadron operations shack. All had been briefed earlier to charge their guns and fire a practice round once airborne to make sure the weapons worked. None of the pilots had yet fired the two .50-caliber nose guns or the four .30-caliber wing guns.

Just south of Clark, at Del Carmen, news of the Pearl Harbor attack did not reach the 34th Pursuit Squadron until about 8:00, when a radio message was received from 24th Pursuit Group headquarters at Clark. Marett immediately put his squadron on combat alert—pilots in their P-35As, ready for takeoff.

20th Pursuit pilots in front of the squadron operations shack at Clark Field, summer, 1941. *Left to right:* Bob Duncan, Milt Woodside, and Edwin Gilmore. *Courtesy Lloyd Stinson, Col. USAF (Ret.)*

At Iba, the officers of the 3rd Pursuit were in the mess hall at 6:00 A.M. for breakfast. CO Hank Thorne and the other five pilots in his flight had gotten only two hours' sleep after the failed interception of the early morning hours. The other twelve pilots of the three combat flights were also drowsy, having slept fitfully by their planes that night. Then someone snapped on the radio to get the news. Don Bell in Manila was reporting an attack on Pearl Harbor. The pilots could not believe their ears.

After receiving orders from group headquarters at Clark, Thorne called the whole squadron together outside the barracks building. He told his men that the United States would probably be declaring war on Japan and that they could expect an attack on the Philippines sometime during the day. The 3rd Pursuit was being ordered on full combat status. On Thorne's orders, Assistant Operations Officer Andy Krieger assigned the eighteen ranking pilots of the squadron to the eighteen P-40Es in tactical commission. Then Thorne led the five pilots of his A Flight to their aircraft, situated at the south end of the three-thousand-foot strip. Squadron Operations Officer Ed Woolery took the men of his B flight to the north end of the field, where their six P-40Es awaited them. Squadron Adjutant Herb Ellis walked with the five pilots of his C flight to their P-40Es, situated off the midpoint of the strip. Then all climbed into their cockpits, ready for instant takeoff in their combat-loaded aircraft. The weather was perfect; comparatively dry, with cloudless, crystal-clear skies. The temperature was cool and comfortable. Visibility was exceptionally good; the mountains to the east of Iba, the Zambales range, stood out in bold relief.

2 In the cockpit of his P-40E at Nichols Field, Dave Obert had watched the sun come up as a big red ball and was now beginning to feel pretty warm on his back. He had confirmation of the Pearl Harbor attack. He knew that this time he would be going up for the real thing. Nearby, the junior pilots of the squadron assembled at the field were as nervous as the more senior ones waiting to take off. To Steve Crosby, from Greenwood, Mississippi, the usual rumble of traffic on nearby Rizal Avenue "made it hard to believe there was actually a war in progress"; there was an air of unreality to the situation.

Finally, about 8:00 o'clock, the anxious 17th Pursuiters received the order to take off. The Iba radar had picked up planes about thirty miles off the coast of Luzon, heading south in the direction of Clark Field. The 17th was to intercept them over Tarlac, twenty-one miles north of Clark. As the eighteen heavily loaded P-40Es roared down the length of the runway and began to climb, twisting their wheels sidewise in drawing them into the wings, Obert was feeling pessimistic about the chances of a successful interception. He was reflecting on the miserable results in recent practice interceptions of high-flying bombers.

At Clark Field, Charley Sneed and his Section 2 pilots saw the red flag being run up on the pole near the 20th Pursuit's operations shack. It was 8:15 A.M. After taxiing their combat-loaded P-40Bs out to the sod field, they ran up their Allison engines and went into their takeoff rolls, barely missing B-17 bombers also trying to get airborne before the Japanese reached the field. As they climbed to their assigned altitude of 15,000 feet, oxygen masks hooked up, they received their orders over the radio: patrol in the vicinity of Tarlac and intercept an incoming flight of Japanese aircraft when it reached that area.

Major Grover apparently wanted to take no chances that the Japanese planes would get through to Clark; he had assigned both the 17th and the 20th pursuit squadrons to block them at the same point. Now the CO of the 24th Pursuit Group ordered the 34th Pursuit at Del Carmen to patrol over Clark Field. The squadron's P-35As should intercept any Japanese that broke through the two patrols of P-40s to the north.

3 At about 8:45, the eighteen P-40Es of the 17th Pursuit reached the Tarlac area and began circling at 12,000 to 15,000 feet, waiting for the incoming Japanese aircraft. But the minutes were ticking by with no sight yet of the enemy. Then suddenly Buzz Wagner spotted them—two large planes coming in from the north. Immediately, Wagner yelled, "Prepare

First Lt. Charley Sneed with his P-40B no. 53 (later numbered 48) at Clark Field, summer, 1941. *Courtesy Mrs. Nora Sneed Sparks*

to attack!" over the radio and led his six-ship flight into a sharp, diving turn. Right behind Wagner's two-ship element, Dave Obert was closely following his commander, his heart in his throat and "pounding like a sledgehammer." His mouth was so dry that he was nearly choking. But outwardly he was never calmer in his whole life.

On Wagner's turn, his wingman, Cy Blanton, became separated from him. For a moment, Obert was tempted to get lost on purpose, but he continued on down with the rest of the flight. Approaching the two "Japanese" bombers, they saw they were B-17s instead. Having worked himself up so much, Obert experienced deep disappointment that the bombers had not been enemy after all. He wanted to let off steam by doing some shooting. While test-firing his six .50s earlier for the first time, he had been surprised at the tremendous vibration they had made in his ship.

Returning to their patrol altitude to join the others, Wagner's flight continued covering the Tarlac area with the other two flights, but there was no sign of the enemy. Now, after some two and a half hours in the air, the pilots were getting low on gas. Wagner decided to head back to Clark to land. Apparently the Japanese had changed their plans about bombing the field. Patrolling to the east of the 17th Pursuit, Charley

Sneed's eighteen P-40Bs had not seen any incoming Japanese aircraft either, though at one time they were radioed that the enemy were getting closer.[2] Their fuel running low, they also now headed back to Clark.

4 At Iba, the pilots of the 3rd Pursuit were becoming increasingly bored around 10:00, sitting in their cockpits and waiting for a takeoff order that never came. Frank Neri then started to play with the receiver on his plane's radio. As he ran across other frequencies, he was startled to hear reports of Baguio being bombed, Aparri was under attack, Tuguegarao was also hit. Some of the other 3rd Pursuiters were picking up the reports on their radios, too.

Under the cloudless sky, the pilots were getting too warm. Thorne issued instructions for them to remain on alert, but to do so sitting under the wings of their P-40s. Happy to escape the sun's rays, Neri and the others climbed out of their cockpits and made themselves comfortable under the wings, sitting on their parachutes, where they joined their crew chiefs. Shortly afterward, the squadron mess sergeant brought out sandwiches and cold drinks for the pilots and crew chiefs.

Later in the morning, Thorne made a tour of the flight line. As he approached C Flight at midfield, Herb Ellis called to him and suggested he say something memorable on the occasion of this great historical event, such as, "Damn the torpedos, take to the hills!" Ellis was maintaining his reputation as the squadron wag.

5 At about eleven o'clock, the 17th and 20th pursuit squadrons came in to land at Clark Field. The pilots of the visiting 17th taxied their P-40Es over to the front of hangars 1 and 2, where they parked their ships, wingtip to wingtip, for refueling. Charley Sneed led the 20th Pursuit's ships back to their usual perimeter location, in their revetted positions, also for regassing.

When the pilots of the two squadrons reported in at 24th Group's operations hangar, they were given some shocking news; while they were airborne, Baguio and Tuguegarao north of their patrol area had been bombed by two flights of Japanese planes. What had happened?

Dave Obert thought that he had the answer, at least for the nearer Baguio attack group: the Japanese must have spotted the P-40s waiting for them seventy miles to the south and decided to turn off and unload on the summer capital of the Philippines instead. Parker Gies of the 20th Pursuit expressed another possibility: both groups had aborted their missions after being warned of the P-40s by fifth columnists operating secret radio stations in the area. Unknown to the pilots, both assumptions were wrong.[3]

6.   "TALLY HO — CLARK FIELD"

1 After they had been informed of the bad news on landing at Clark, the pilots of the 17th and 20th pursuit squadrons dispersed. Buzz Wagner's men were directed to the mess hall of the 20th Pursuit's enlisted men for a late breakfast/early lunch. None of the visitors had eaten anything yet this eventful day. Seated at the table covered with a cheerful oilcloth, they dug into the greasy porkchops that were served them. Outside, in front of Hangars 1 and 2 where they were parked in a long line, wingtip to wingtip, their eighteen P-40Es were being refueled.

Tired from a sleepless night and a fruitless morning search, the eighteen pilots of Charley Sneed's Section 2 of the 20th Pursuit headed for their quarters at Fort Stotsenburg for rest. The squadron's assistant operations officer, Lloyd Stinson, was too tense to relax, however, and instead returned to the flight line at Clark after only taking a shower at his quarters. There he watched as squadron maintenance men pumped gas and added oxygen in each of the P-40Bs dispersed around the north and west perimeters of the field. They were being readied for the next mission, to be flown by the eighteen pilots of the squadron's Section 1, headed by the CO, Joe Moore.

Except for Moore's own plane, the squadron's P-40Bs were parked in blast-proof revetments. In order to be ready for takeoff in the lead position, Moore had ordered that his own plane be parked in the open across the road from the 20th Pursuit's operations shack, on the southwest section of the field. In this way he could stay on the operations shack's phone to 24th Group operations for instructions until the last minute.

After their early lunch, the 17th Pursuit pilots walked over to the 24th Group's operations hangar for further instructions. There they found squadron mate George Armstrong occupied with nonflying matters. The week before Armstrong had been requested by the 24th Group CO, Major Grover, for temporary duty at Clark to help Grover with communications problems.

Clark Field Communications Center was located in the group hangar, the locus of all message traffic between the Air Warning Service at Niel-son Field in Manila and Clark Field, as well as between airborne aircraft and the center. At the back end of the hangar, a teletype machine had been set up in the group operations area, protected by sandbags all around and across the top. Across from operations was the "war room," where a plotting board had been installed—a table on which a map of the Clark Field area had been placed, with big circles around the field's location indicating a maximum line of penetration at which hostile aircraft would have to be intercepted.

Up on the wall of the operations area of the hangar was a loudspeaker connected to an SCR-197 radio communications trailer positioned just outside the hangar. All voice messages between the SCR-197 and airborne aircraft were amplified by the loudspeaker for all to hear in the vicinity of the operations complex. Field telephones were also installed to con-nect the operations room and in SCR-197.

Things were now beginning to get hectic for Armstrong and the 24th Group Headquarters staff and men in the operations area. Air Warning at Nielson was relaying often differing telephone and telegraph reports it was receiving from towns in northern Luzon of aircraft heading south. Armstrong and the others were trying to sort them out and plot them on the board. Then at about 11:40, a teletype message was received from Air Warning: a flight of enemy planes, number unknown, headed south about seventy miles west of Lingayen Gulf at 11:27 A.M., had been picked up by the SCR-270B radar at Iba.

Grover and his staff decided to act on the Iba message; there was no doubt about the veracity of this report. The Japanese flight must be heading for Manila. In the best position to stop them were the eighteen P-40s of the 3rd Pursuit at Iba. Immediately, Grover gave orders for the SCR-197 to radio Thorne at Iba to get his aircraft airborne and to wait over Iba at 15,000 feet for the Japanese.

Five minutes later, another teletype message came in; Air Warning was now reporting another flight of planes heading south, this one directly over Lingayen Gulf.[1] That would put the Japanese only some one hun-dred miles north of Clark Field. Since the P-40s of the 17th and 20th pur-suit squadrons outside were not yet completely refueled and serviced, Grover was left with the 34th Pursuit at nearby Del Carmen with eigh-teen P-35s and the 21st Pursuit at Nichols Field with eighteen P-40Es for immediate protection of Clark Field. Grover then issued orders via the SCR-197 for the 34th and the 21st to take off and cover Clark.[2]

2 At Iba, the eighteen pilots of the 3rd Pursuit were still sitting under the wings of their aircraft, waiting for orders to take off, when finally the signal was flashed from the control tower in midfield. Their CO, Hank Thorne, had just received a radio message from Grover at Clark: "Point

Iba, 15,000 feet," and had passed the takeoff order to 1st Lt. Jim Donegan, assigned to the control tower this day.

At 11:45 A.M. Thorne climbed into his P-40E at the southeast end of the field and began taxiing to the center of the narrow strip, where he was joined by his wingman taxiing behind him. On the opposite side of the field, second element leader Bob Hanson was also taxiing to the center, third in takeoff position, followed by his wingman and the third element leader, Gerry Keenan, and his wingman.[3] A Flight would take off to the north, into a slight wind blowing north to south.

By the time the last aircraft in Thorne's flight had lifted off, the sod field was almost obscured by a giant cloud of dust. At the north end of the strip, Ed Woolery, leader of B Flight, could not see the south end of the field in the dust. Perhaps for this reason, he elected to take off from his position instead of taxiing down through the dust to the south end for a takeoff to the north, as Thorne had done. Woolery taxied to the center of the strip at his north end, his wingman, Andy Krieger, behind him. On the other side, Ray Gehrig moved his P-40E to the center mark too as Woolery roared downfield. Behind Gehrig was his wingman, "Hawk" Root. Third element leader Don Steele and his wingman, Ship Daniel (the only squadron newie assigned to fly this day), brought up the rear.

At midfield on the western side, C Flight leader Herb Ellis, seated in the cockpit of his P-40E with its engine running, was expecting to see Woolery taxi past him on his way to the south end of the field, when the next thing he knew, an aircraft went past him, clearing the field on a takeoff to the south, followed by five others in succession. In further-diminished visibility, Ellis began to taxi his plane through the heavy dust to the south end of the field, preparatory to a takeoff into the wind, as Thorne had done. It was now five minutes since he had fired up his engine following the takeoff signal from the tower. On reaching the south end of the field and turning around to face downfield, however, Ellis was surprised to find himself alone. Where were the other five of his flight?

His engine now beginning to get too hot, Ellis decided to take off and pick up the rest of his flight over the field. After climbing to about 1,000 feet, he circled the field, waiting for the rest of his flight to take off and join him. Looking down, his assumption proved correct; his wingman, Bill Powell, had taxied to the north end of the field and was taking off to the south. Unknown to Ellis, Powell had figured that Ellis had erred in taking off to the north and chose to ignore his flight leader's decision and take off to the south instead. Following behind Powell were the second element leader Fred Roberts and his wingman, George Ellstrom,[4] then third element leader Frank Neri and his wingman, "Chubby" Allen.

As one of the errant members of his flight cleared the field, Ellis dove across in front of him to allow him to join up, but he did not, and before

Ellis could circle back, Ellis lost sight of him against the mountains and could not spot any of the other four following their takeoffs. Ellis continued to circle for a few more minutes, then gave up and began to climb to his assigned altitude of 15,000 feet on what was a beautiful, crystal-clear day.

Disoriented by the conflicting takeoff directions of the squadron, Bill Powell shortly after takeoff realized that he had lost his leader and decided to join up with the second-element leader, Fred Roberts, who had apparently lost his wingman in the confused situation. As the four remnants of C Flight continued to climb, they ran into the six P-40s of Woolery's B Flight, also climbing, and linked up with them. A few minutes later, they interrupted their ascent; several of the pilots had picked up a radio call from 24th Group operations at Clark that ordered them to head for Manila instead.[5] At 6,000 feet, Woolery turned to lead the ten-ship flight southeast to Manila.

3   At Nichols Field, the thirteen pilots of the 21st Pursuit and the five attached pilots from the 3rd and the 17th had climbed out of the cockpits of the 21st's P-40Es at 11:00 A.M. in response to Dyess's call for them to report to the operations tent. There was a tub of Coca Cola ready for them, as well as olives and sandwiches. Then at about 11:45, the phone rang and Dyess went to answer it. When he returned, he told his pilots that Nichols base had received a radio call for the 21st: "Tally Ho, Clark Field."

Taking off immediately in response to the orders, Dyess led the 12 P-40Es of his A and B flights in a climb for altitude. Bob Clark's C Flight was delayed in takeoff by five minutes, however, because several of the brand new planes were experiencing minor engine difficulties.[6]

When C Flight finally did get airborne, the pilots were unable to find the rest of the squadron. Separated from the others, Clark decided to take the flight to Laguna de Bay, the huge lake just five miles southwest of Nichols Field, in order to test their guns. Over the lake, the pilots fired their six .50-caliber guns for the first time with short bursts into the water. But then Clark and his wingman, Jimmy May, radioed the others in the flight that their engines, which they had not yet finished slow-timing, were throwing oil on the windshield—too much to be able to see. They were reluctantly obliged to abort the mission and return to Nichols.

Shortly after takeoff, Dyess radioed 24th Group operations that he was taking the squadron up to 24,000 feet and heading north for Clark, as ordered. But when he and the other pilots of his A and B flights were just north of Manila, Dyess received a radio message ordering the squadron back to a point over Manila Bay midway between Corregidor and Cavite. They were to intercept Japanese bombers apparently expected to swing into Manila Bay from the west to attack Manila.[7]

Still over Laguna de Bay at low altitude, the remaining four pilots of C Flight regrouped, with Sam Grashio as their leader. Not having picked up the radio call from group, Grashio, with Gus Williams on his wing, and Joe Cole, with Johnny McCown as his wingman, headed north toward Clark in a steady climb, ignorant of the changed orders for the squadron.[8]

4 About the same time Grashio began to head north, Ed Woolery was approaching Manila at the head of his B Flight and the four hangers-on from the splintered "C" flight. At 12:10 they had been spotted at 6,000 feet by watchers at Caridad, ten miles southwest of Manila, and their presence had been reported to the 16th Naval District at Manila—"nationality unknown."[9] Only some twelve miles south of them, but over 10,000 feet higher, twelve P-40s of Ed Dyess' 21st Pursuit were beginning their patrol over the southern part of Manila Bay, unseen by Woolery's group.

Hoping to pick up instructions over Manila, the 3rd Pursuiters circled over Manila Bay for a short period, but could not get anything on their radios, tuned on the standard 4495-kc frequency assigned to the 24th Group for all air-to-air and air-to-ground communication. Then, suddenly, Andy Krieger heard a lot of yelling over the radio: "Tally Ho, Clark Field! Tally Ho, Clark Field! All Pursuit to Clark! Messerschmitts over Clark!"[10] Immediately, Krieger and the rest of Woolery's B Flight, followed by the remnant of C Flight, headed north posthaste—all except Don Steele and Ship Daniel, that is. These two easygoing "tail-end Charlies" of the ten-plane group had continued past Manila in the direction of Alabat Island instead of circling the area. They had not heard the frantic call for help from Clark Field over their radios but now headed in the direction of their group as it started northward from Manila. Not realizing the gravity of the situation, they dawdled behind the others and soon fell thirty miles behind the speeding formation.

5 In the 24th Group's operations hangar at Clark just about 12:00 noon, the CO of the 17th Pursuit, Buzz Wagner, and the leaders of his B and C flights, Willie Feallock and Johnny Brownewell, were anxiously watching more teletype messages coming in from Air Warning, each indicating the progress of the Japanese flights off the west coast of Luzon and heading south. The last one had reported aircraft just forty miles from Iba, and now no more seemed to be coming. Restlessly, the three senior pilots of the 17th now looked to Grover for some decision. The 24th Group CO "was taking an awfully long time to make up his mind." Doubting whether the 3rd Pursuit could successfully intercept the Japanese over Iba, he had switched its orders to cover the Manila area—the obvious target—and had also changed the 21st's patrol to Manila Bay from its original Clark destination.

Finally, at 12:15 P.M., Grover gave the 17th its takeoff orders; it was to patrol the Manila Bay area at 18,000 feet and intercept any Japanese bombers approaching from the west. Wagner passed the orders to the fifteen pilots waiting outside the hangar, and all ran to their P40Es, parked in a long row in front of hangars 1 and 2 and all now completely refueled and serviced.

Dave Obert, in third position for takeoff, followed Wagner and Cy Blanton as they rolled down the sod runway in their ships, but the engine of his P-40 started missing. Realizing he would not be able to get off, the distressed Oklahoman braked and turned, heading back to the line, where he would have a mechanic check the Allison engine. Back at the line, however, he changed his mind and decided to give it another try. Pushing the throttle into override position, Obert barely succeeded in getting airborne. With the engine still acting up, he managed to catch up with the formation, his engine putting out enough power to keep up with the others.

Also experiencing difficulties in taking off was B Flight leader Feallock. In the rush to get airborne, he had flooded his engine, as had his wingman. Feallock waved the rest of his flight off; the two of them would catch up with the others after the whole squadron had taken off. Minutes later, the two got their engines running and headed for Manila in a high-speed climb.

Back in the 24th Group's hangar, another teletyped message had come in about 12:20 P.M. from Air Warning at Nielson. This one had been sent by Colonel George and his operations officer, Capt. "Bud" Sprague. It was an order to intercept Japanese aircraft approaching Clark Field.[11]

The only squadron available to Grover now was the 20th Pursuit.[12] After their eighteen P-40Bs had been refueled, the pilots of Section 1 of the squadron had been put on alert and were now sitting in their cockpits, anxiously awaiting takeoff orders. Sandwiches and water had been sent out to them by their CO. Under the wings of the aircraft, the ground crews had positioned themselves to avoid the burning midday sun.

Seated in the cockpit of Joe Moore's aircraft was his crew chief. Moore himself was in the 20th Pursuit's operations shack, two hundred yards from the group hangar. Glued to the telephone, he, like his pilots, restlessly awaited takeoff orders from Grover. When he had earlier bicycled over to the group hangar for instructions, he had been told that as soon as the conflicting reports coming in could be sorted out, the 20th Pursuit would be scrambled. It was now 12:30. Still Grover was holding the 20th Pursuit on the ground.

6 Overhead, eight P-40s had just arrived from the Manila area: Ed Woolery's flight minus Steele and Daniel plus the four of C Flight. They had flown at high speed to Clark in response to the "Tally Ho" call. But where were the Japanese planes? They circled around for a few minutes. Then Andy Krieger spotted two aircraft above him and pointed them out

to Woolery. The two 3rd Pursuiters went into a climbing turn, chandelling onto the tails of the two planes, but quickly identified them as P-40s.[13]

The call to fly to Clark was obviously a false alarm, Krieger concluded. And nothing was coming over their radios from group operations below them. Woolery now decided to lead his group back to Iba for new orders and refueling.

About this time, four other P-40s appeared over Clark, at considerably higher altitude than Woolery's group. Sam Grashio had brought the remnant of the 21st Pursuit's C Flight to Clark in a steady climb from Manila. Everything seemed peaceful to Grashio and the others. It was a beautiful day, without a cloud in the sky. After circling over Clark for a few minutes, they spotted a flight of single-engined aircraft off to the west of Clark, heading west toward the China Sea. Assuming they were P-40s from A and B flights of his squadron that he figured had flown to Clark ahead of his C flight, according to original orders, Grashio excitedly now took after them with his flight mates behind them.

As Grashio gained on them, he could see that they were indeed other P-40s, but that there were just six of them, only half the number of Dyess's formation. "Which squadron are they from?" Grashio wondered, as he, Williams, Cole, and McCown closed in on them to identify them from their 24th Group tail numbers.

The pilots of Ed Woolery's group heading back to Iba had not noticed the four P-40s approaching them from the rear at their own altitude. Woolery's formation was down to six planes now; Roberts and Powell were no longer with them. They had separated from the others after reaching Clark Field and were now some miles behind Woolery, also heading back to Iba. It was now 12:35 P.M.

7. "GOOD GOD ALMIGHTY—YONDER THEY COME"

1 Sgt. Bill Jones of the 20th Pursuit Squadron was standing near the operators in the SCR-197 radio communications trailer of the 24th Pursuit Group, parked behind the group's hangar at Clark Field, as a message was being received at 12:30 in Morse code from the 3rd Pursuit Squadron's radio at Iba. In transcription, the message was reporting a flight of large aircraft approaching Iba from the west. Suddenly, the Iba operator switched to voice transmission, which surprised Jones; that was a breach of security regulations. Excitedly, in his anxiety to be sure the message got through, the Iba operator repeated the message, describing the flight of aircraft; then abruptly he went silent. With no responsibility for the radio operations of the trailer, though he frequently visited it while some of the squadron's radiomen under him were being trained on the SCR-197, Jones now headed for the 20th Pursuit's mess hall for lunch.

Over at the 20th Pursuit's operations shack, some fifty yards from the mess hall, Joe Moore at 12:35 was still awaiting orders from group to scramble his pilots. Suddenly he was startled by the cry of one of the 20th's crew chiefs standing near the operations shack: "Good God almighty—yonder they come!" Moore looked up and saw a long column of planes, very high, flying in a V of Vs. They looked very small to him; he thought they must be fighter planes from a carrier. Hurriedly, he ordered the squadron's red flag run up on the pole outside the operations shack as the signal for takeoff, then ran toward his waiting P-40B, yelling, "Wind her up!" to his crew chief.

Behind Moore's plane was Randy Keator's, parked in number 2 position for takeoff, with Keator standing next to it. Edwin Gilmore was already in the cockpit of his aircraft, ready for takeoff in the number 3 position, near the other three P-40Bs of A Flight, parked near the operations shack. Spread out in the squadron's dispersal area were the planes of B and C flights, their pilots waiting for the takeoff order.

When he heard the crew chief's cry, 2nd Lt. Jack Gates of Charley Sneed's Section 2 came out the door of the operations shack to see what was going on. Looking up at the formation of twin-engine planes, flying very high in the cloudless sky, now almost directly overhead, Gates began to count them—exactly fifty-four.[1] They were coming in two waves from the northwest in a perfect V of Vs formation, carrying them in a straight line over Clark.

Breaking off his dangerous observation, Gates headed for a large L-shaped trench some thirty feet away and jumped in. The other pilots of Section 2 and most of the enlisted men of the squadron who were not crew chiefs on the line piled into Gates's trench and another one near it.

As soon as Sgt. Bill King of the 20th Pursuit spotted the planes, he fired his pistol three times in the air as a raid warning, then got on the phone in the operations shack to group operations. First Lt. Benny Putnam, the CO of Headquarters Squadron, answered, and King told him to sound the air raid alarm; Japanese planes were approaching. Holding King on the line, Putnam passed the message to Major Grover. But Grover asked Putnam, "How does he know they are Japanese planes?" King then yelled to Putnam, "We don't have so Goddamn many!"

Just then, someone burst into the group hangar, shouting that many bombers were high overhead. Putnam and Bill Cummings, group operations officer, ran out the door at the back of the hangar and looked up just as bombs were falling.

With the air raid siren sounding, Putnam and Cummings sprang for the nearest slit trench and jumped in, with George Armstrong just behind. But Grover opted to remain behind in the hangar, seeking protection in the sandbagged area.

2 Not even taking time to buckle on his parachute, Joe Moore started his takeoff roll after taxiing out fifty feet to the turf runway. Behind him, his wingman, Randy Keator, was giving his engine full throttle for takeoff, followed by Edwin Gilmore, the second element leader. The P-40Bs of Lts. Dan Blass and Max Louk and Louk's wingman, engines running, were in position behind Gilmore for takeoff too.

From their positions at the north and west ends of Clark Field, the twelve pilots of B and C flights were now starting up their engines, preparing for takeoff, one after the other. Out of sight of the warning flag C Flight had been alerted by 2nd Lt. Lloyd Stinson, who drove over to the pilots in his automobile moments earlier.

As Moore, Keator, and Gilmore cleared the ground on their west-to-east takeoff and began retracting their wheels, bombs followed them down the field. Gilmore's plane experienced heavy turbulence when the first ones detonated on Clark Field. Moore turned to the left, and Keator formed up on him. As they headed back toward the west in a high-speed climb, both pilots looked down at Clark and saw that the field they had just left was now smothered in the flames and smoke of bursting bombs.

Unseen by Moore and Keator, Dan Blass was about to become airborne behind Gilmore when fragments from the blanket of bombs falling on Clark shredded both his tires. The 41-C newie from LeCompte, Louisiana, promptly jumped out of his immobilized aircraft and sprinted the one hundred yards to the trenches near the squadron's operations shack.

Behind Blass's ship, right at the end of the runway, Max Louk's P-40B was hit by an incendiary bomb just seconds before it finished its takeoff roll. His ship blazing, Louk frantically tried to force open his canopy, but it was stuck in position. Now he pulled the emergency release, but still the canopy remained jammed in its tracks. Trapped in his cockpit, the twenty-two-year-old Kansan was soon consumed by the flames.

Over on the north side of the field, 1st Lt. Fred Armstrong, a 40-D oldie from Indianapolis, had taxied out of his position and was preparing to lead his B Flight in a takeoff diagonally across the open field to get it airborne as quickly as possible. Then two bombs exploded, one on each side of him. The one on the right he heard, but not the one on his left, which hit very near the rear of his P-40B. Momentarily knocked unconscious by the concussion, Armstrong came to with his head down by his knees, flames coming up from the cockpit floor. Still dazed, he extricated himself from the cockpit, jumped down onto the wing root, then slid to the ground. On his hands and knees, he crawled through a wide area of burning fuel under his plane to get beyond the ring of fire — severely burning his face, hands, and knees.

Third in position for takeoff in Armstrong's flight, Parker Gies had buckled his chute and belt and started the motor up when the first bombs hit only twenty feet in front of his P-40B, riddling it with shrapnel and shutting down the engine. In a state of shock, Gies unbuckled his belt and got out of the stricken ship in a hurry. Just as the second wave of the bombers unloaded on the field, the Oregonian dove into a V trench some fifty feet away, along with Cpl. Robert Corkery, his crew chief. Gies felt lucky; if those first bombs had been incendiaries, he would have burned alive in the plane.

After 2nd Lt. Jim Fossey, a 41-C newie from Buffalo, Oklahoma, had taxied to the edge of the runway and was holding for takeoff, he saw the chain of explosions progressing across the field. Kicking his rudder and releasing his brakes, Fossey began taxiing to the right toward the last big explosions, but away from the apparent line of progression. His plane rocked violently for a moment, as smoke and dust enveloped the area. Keeping his engine running at ground speed and riding the brake, Fossey began taxiing away from the fires and smoke on his left to head toward the west, where he had spotted a clear area. But a crew chief was waving frantically at him to cut his engine and get out. When Fossey climbed out, he saw a large hole in his left wing and gasoline, which fortunately

Max Louk of the 20th Pursuit checks out an obsolescent P-26A at Clark Field, June, 1941. *Courtesy Jane B. Terry*

had not ignited, pouring from a hole in the fuselage immediately behind the cockpit. The terrified pilot lay prone on the ground for a moment but then realized that the cogan grass was burning, as were several planes nearby. Climbing back into his plane, he generated the inertia starter, started the engine, and taxied the plane further to the west to a denuded parking area. Then he got out and ran toward a ditch near the parked cars on the field.

Directly behind Fossey's P-40B, 2nd Lt. Lloyd Mulcahy, a 41-G newie only three months out of flying school, had started taxiing for takeoff from his revetment when only one hundred feet out, one of the shower of bombs hit directly on his plane, killing him in his cockpit instantly. Called "Tod" by his fellow 20th Pursuiters, the twenty-two-year-old native of Tulare, California, popular for his terrific sense of humor, had married his college sweetheart just before being shipped out to the Philippines with his classmates in November.

Also killed in his cockpit by a direct bomb hit was 41-C newie Jesse Luker, from Porterville, California. Like Mulcahy, he had been taxiing out for takeoff when his P-40B was struck. Two other pilots in Moore's

Section 1 were casualties in the takeoff attempt during the bombing. Guy Iversen, a 41-D from Cedar Falls, Iowa, and Max Halverson, a 41-G from Salt Lake City, Utah, were both badly burned when their P-40Bs caught fire from incendiary hits near their revetments.

Behind the 24th Group's operations hangar, radio operators in the SCR-197 communications trailer had been frantically calling in the clear for help from moments before the first bombs fell. Despite the bombing, they were sticking to their posts.

3 Overhead, at 10,000 feet, Sam Grashio and the three others of the 21st Pursuit's C Flight were about to link up with the six P-40s of Ed Woolery's group heading west to Iba when suddenly Grashio's radio blared out, "All pursuit to Clark Field! All pursuit to Clark Field! Enemy bombers overhead!"[2] The radio operator's voice was getting more and more excited, almost hysterical. Then in their headsets Grashio and the others heard bombs exploding.

As Grashio immediately wheeled his flight around to go back to Clark Field in response to the radio call, he was surprised to see that the other group of six P-40s, still unidentified to him, was continuing on its westerly course. Why did they not turn too? He concluded that the pilots must not have picked up the frantic order on their radios. The moment they turned in the direction of Clark, Grashio and the others were shocked to see a rising pillar of smoke over the field. Approaching Clark at 13,000 feet, they could even make out the red fires in it.

Over Iba, thirty-seven miles to the west, still circling at 15,000 feet, Hank Thorne had also heard the call from Clark that Grashio had picked up. The radio operator was yelling, "Many bombers Clark Field! Many bombers Clark Field!." The call ended with, "Go get 'em!" Thorne turned his A Flight to the east on a course that would take it over the Zambales Mountains, whence it would go into a gentle descent to 12,000 feet the rest of the way to Clark. But one of his men did not join up with him. Gerry Keenan, his third-element leader, had separated from the others when he spotted a "Messerschmitt" over Iba at his altitude of 15,000 feet and had gone after it (see chapter 8).[3]

About sixteen miles southeast of Clark, two other errant 3rd Pursuiters were headed for the field at 8,000 feet.[4] Suddenly, Don Steele and Ship Daniel heard someone yell, "Tally Ho!" over their radios. Another voice screamed that Clark Field was being blown up. That was enough for the two previously lighthearted aviators. Daniel "came scooting under" Steele's wing, and they excitedly raced for Clark Field.

4 On the ground at Clark, a bomb had hit the road near the slit trench in which Benny Putnam and Bill Cummings had just sought protection, caving the trench in on them. Blood was gushing all over Putnam from a decapitated enlisted man who had been next to him in the trench, causing Putnam to think that he had been hit, too. As Putnam and Cummings extricated themselves, uninjured, they spotted a pair of legs and a bottom sticking out of the collapsed trench. Cummings pulled the hapless half-buried individual out by his belt, and he turned out to be George Armstrong. The 17th Pursuiter had dived into the trench headfirst a moment before the bomb had exploded. With burning gasoline from a yellow fuel truck only twenty feet away draining into the trench, the three shaken officers took off for another trench some one hundred yards away and jumped in, just before the second wave of bombers began unloading.

Nearby, 1st Lt. Ross Huguet of Headquarters Squadron was trying to drive his car away from the area of attack, but when the bombing "got too hot for him," he stopped the car, opened the door, and rolled out. At that moment, he was hit in the leg with a piece of shrapnel that would later cost him the limb. His car did not suffer even a scratch.

Inside the 20th Pursuit's operations shack, Lloyd Stinson was reaching for his helmet when the bombs started detonating on the field. He dropped to the floor and rolled under a cot. The bombs kept getting closer and closer, then one hit five feet on one side of the shack, and the next one five feet on the other side. Fragments from the two bombs sprayed through the shack, tearing holes in Stinson's trousers and taking off the end of his right shoe, a piece of metal burying itself in his big toe.

Just outside the shack, many of the 20th Pursuit's officers and men were huddling at the bottom of the two large L-shaped trenches recently dug on each side of the shack to provide them protection from a bombing attack. Terrified, Pfc Glenn Bowers and 2nd Lt. Jack Gates listened as the explosions became louder and louder, the ground around them trembling, then jumping, until the bombs passed over to the other side. The air was filled with buzzes and plops as pieces of shrapnel whizzed and struck the earth and sizzled with heat. Never again would anyone who was at Clark Field this day refer to the trenches as Maitland's Folly, so named after the previous commanding officer of Clark Field, who had ordered them dug months earlier.

Halfway on his run to the 20th Pursuit's trenches from the armament hangar of the base, Pfc Jim Brown had seen the first bombs explode on a direct line with him. Just as he jumped into a half-dug foxhole, a bomb detonated behind him, covering him completely with dirt except for his head, right shoulder, and arm. He then heard an old World War I sergeant yell, "Gas!" but Brown knew it was only the acrid smell of bursting bombs. As soon as the first wave of bombers had passed, Brown wriggled free from the loose dirt, climbed out, and headed for his assigned trench. Moments before the bombs of the second wave began ripping up the field, he jumped in, joining his squadron mates.

And then, as abruptly as it had begun, the bombing was over.

Lloyd Stinson (*foreground*) and Jim Fossey of the 20th Pursuit Squadron fly in their P-35As over Clark in the summer of 1941. *Courtesy Lloyd Stinson, Col. USAF (Ret.)*

Jack Gates climbed out of his trench and started looking for those who needed help. Thick yellow-brown dust and smoke blocked his view. The air reeked of cordite. Even the long cogan grass covering the area was burning. At the 20th Pursuit's parking area for its planes, 150 feet away, Gates and another man from the squadron found someone lying on his back, looking straight up to the sky, lifeless but without a mark on him. Turning the man over, they found a huge wound in the middle of his back. Apparently he had been hit by a large piece of shrapnel while running for cover.

Out on the field, several of the pursuit pilots of Moore's section who had not been injured in the bombing attempted to take off again in the few P-40Bs that had survived the attack. All around them, planes were on fire, and the cogan grass was burning, making the field an inferno of fire and black smoke.

Parker Gies climbed into one of the undamaged P-40Bs, started the engine up, and began to taxi fast into takeoff position, but then he hit a bomb crater. At the same moment, Gies saw low-flying planes shooting across the field — strafers. Immediately the Oregonian cut the switch, jumped out of his ship, and ran back to his trench in midfield, accompanied by his crew chief, Corporal Corkery.

Still continuing in his takeoff roll, squadron mate Jim Drake, a 41-D newie from Dallas, Texas, had managed to avoid holes in the pockmarked field and was now near the end of the runway when a strafer caught him. He was killed instantly, and his plane was set afire.

In groups of nine, the Japanese swept across the field from every direction out of shallow dives, continuously circling in criss-crossing string formations. At a range of about 100 yards, and as low as 30 feet, they poured their devastating fire into man and machine alike.

Running back to the trenches, the officers and men of the 20th Pursuit hunkered down again as the cannon and machine-gun fire hit all around them, splintering the top boards of the trenches. Buried under his steel helmet and squatting as low as he could get, Gates never once looked out of the trench.

Fortunately for the squadron personnel, a slight breeze was blowing dense black smoke across the two trenches, partly obscuring their occupants from the view of the Japanese pilots. The smoke was coming from Major Grover's P-40B, which, parked near Moore's, had been hit during the bombing raid and was now burning fiercely. Also contributing smoke was Stinson's car, parked near the operations shack.

In his trench, Jim Brown was not taking the attack lying down. He had braced himself against the north wall of the trench and was firing his rifle at the low-flying planes as they passed overhead in their north-south strafing runs. Chain-smoking "Luckies," Brown was applying duck-shooting principles learned as a teenager back home, firing one round after another at the silver planes.

In the SCR-197 communications van behind the group hangar, cannon and machine gun fire from the strafers had damaged the transmitting and receiving equipment, knocking the radio station off the air. Then, while the strafers fired at him continuously, one of the pursuit pilots hitched a truck to the van and towed it out to the road behind the hangar and into the woods. In order to get the van under the trees, the men assigned to it tore down the guy wires holding up the antennae.

5 When Don Steele and Ship Daniel arrived over Clark Field from the southeast at about 12:39, they were appalled at the sight 8,000 feet below. "There was beautiful Clark Field, all in flames . . . every building on the airdrome was on fire, forming a total of one of the largest fires I have ever seen . . . large columns of smoke rising to 18,000 feet . . . sleek and shining B-17s that we were so proud of and had just been received from the States were all sitting on the ground, blazing," Steele recorded

in his diary that evening. The two 3rd Pursuiters saw the bomber force above them, retiring to the north "in a beautiful formation," and single-engine planes just starting diving attacks on the antiaircraft and gun emplacements below as ack-ack fire filled the sky. Then they spotted two strafers flying a "beautiful" two-ship formation and working over a B-18. They decided to go down after the Japanese. But before they could reach their targets, they were cut off by a flight of six of the enemy pursuit aircraft that had been sitting above them in the sun. Steele later recorded: "They came down at us, head-on. Golly, what a feeling! My throat got dry and my breath short. But we tore into them, nevertheless."

One of the Japanese singled out Steele, but fortunately for Steele, the Japanese pilot in his head-on approach was a bit too far to the left. Cannon fire ripped into Steele's left wing, shearing away the entire wing tip from the aileron out, while the fuselage absorbed all the 7.7-mm fire. The noise of the cannon fire on the wing was "terrific," as if it were being hit by a sledgehammer. Steele's arm was grazed by a bullet or a piece of metal that came through the fuselage, causing a small gash about six inches long on the forearm.

For a second, Steele thought the two planes were going to crash head-on, but then the Japanese pilot pulled off to one side at the very last moment, missing a collision by inches. Although only one of the P-40E's six .50-caliber guns was working, and only five or six rounds hit the Japanese, the Zero was belching smoke as it passed by. Steele followed it down to about 3,000 feet, where it went into a spin and finally crashed into the mountains. Steele and Daniel then gave chase to the rest of the Japanese fighters but could not catch them. With only some fifteen minutes' gas left in their tanks, they headed for Iba. It was about 12:56.[5]

6 Arriving over Clark from the west about the same time Steele and Daniel reached the base from the southeast, Sam Grashio and his wingman, Gus Williams, circled around and around above the smoke. They had become separated from Joe Cole and his wingman, Johnny McCown. Down below, Grashio and Williams could make out Japanese planes darting in and out of the smoke across the field. Trying to get up the courage to go down after the strafers, the two hesitant youth then saw one of the Japanese emerge only about 3,000 to 4,000 feet below them. Committing themselves, they started down after the enemy for the first combat of their lives. Lining up the Japanese in his gunsight, Grashio poured .50-caliber fire from his wing guns into his adversary. Smoking, the Zero fell off.

Williams had sighted a group of nine planes approaching them some 1,500 feet below just before the 21st Pursuiters attacked the lone Japanese. As they passed under Williams, he tipped his wing to see what markings they had on their wings. They were red meatballs.

Going into a tight diving turn to get behind them, Williams and Grashio got off a couple of bursts at the tail end of the Japanese flight. But only two-thirds of the way through the Americans' turn, the two lead Zeros had already completed a tight climbing turn and were now firing at only one hundred yards' distance on Grashio and Williams. When he saw tracers going by both sides of his canopy, Williams yelled to Grashio over the radio, "Let's get out of here!" As Grashio veered sharply to the left, one of the two Japanese fired an explosive 20-mm cannon shot through Grashio's left wing and cartridge can, causing his P-40E to shudder momentarily. In a desperate bid to elude his pursuer, Grashio went into a steep dive through the smoke over Clark Field. When he pulled out of his power dive at treetop level just west of Clark, Grashio was relieved to find his brand new ship responding so well. Looking back, he saw that the Zeros were still chasing him but were now falling farther and farther behind as he headed for Nichols, their fire increasingly wide of the mark.

Having split from his element leader, Williams turned his P-40E upside down, pushed the throttle forward, and headed straight for the ground. When he pulled out of his dive over the tree tops, he found he was clocking over 500 MPH. His pursuer had broken off his attack at 1,500 feet, unable to match the diving speed of the heavier plane.

A shaken Williams found the sky still full of the fantastically maneuverable mystery planes. Figuring he would never make it back to altitude for another diving attack, he elected to head back to Nichols instead.

After becoming separated from Grashio and Williams, Joe Cole and his wingman, Johnny McCown, also attacked the low-flying strafers, then got into a dogfight with Zeros at a higher altitude. But after a few minutes of all-out combat flying, the engine of Cole's brand-new P-40E started throwing oil on the windshield. Only partly able to see, Cole headed back to Nichols, leaving McCown to continue the fight.

7 Some miles behind Woolery's group of six P-40s returning to Iba, Fred Roberts and his wingman, Bill Powell, were over the mountain pass between Clark and Iba, two-thirds of the way back to their base, at about 12:40.[6] They had picked up no calls on their radios. Then they happened to look behind them and saw a huge column of black smoke rising from Clark Field.

Roberts was well known in the 3rd Pursuit for his independent ways. Now he needed only a split second to make a decision. Banking around, he headed flat out for Clark, Powell following on his wing. When they reached Clark at about 12:46, they spotted some other P-40s and joined up with them.[7] Below, they could see strafers shooting up the field.

Roberts led Powell in a two-ship dive. Powell figured that they had five Japanese below them "cold turkey" as he and Roberts positioned themselves to fire on the strafers' tails. But Roberts found that only one of his six .50s was firing, and a second later, when Powell pressed the trigger, *none* of his guns would fire.

Now things began to get hot for the two Americans. As they hung on the tails of the Japanese in front, others flying in an angled Lufberry (a closed circular flight formation to protect each others' tails) behind the P-40s began firing on them.[8] In the excitement of first combat, it had not occurred to Powell that someone would try to shoot him down, and now he was fighting for his life. Desperately working his gun switches, trying to get his .50s to fire, Powell realized that he was helpless and had better break off combat before it was too late. As he headed back to Iba, he thought he would get his guns fixed back on the field and then return to the fight.

The Zero behind Roberts had knocked holes in his wings and had shot out the cables at his feet. Pieces of shrapnel had torn into his leg. Roberts also decided he had pushed his luck far enough and opted to break off combat. He rolled his P-40E over on its back, dived away from the Japanese, and headed back toward Iba. Total combat time for Roberts and Powell had only been some three minutes. It was now about 12:49.[9] Minutes later, as Powell flew westward through the pass in the Zambales Mountains between Clark and Iba, he noticed another P-40 flying in the same direction to one side and below him. He recognized the plane as that of Roberts.

8 Just about the time that Roberts and Powell reached Clark after aborting their return to Iba, five P-40s of Hank Thorne's A Flight appeared over the field, but at a higher altitude—12,000 feet—after a ten-minute flight from Iba.[10] Thorne was appalled at the sight below. The entire area seemed to be burning. Huge pillars of black smoke from the gasoline storage area behind the hangars towered up, reaching almost to his altitude.

But he saw no airplanes. At 12,000 feet, his view obscured by the smoke over the field, he did not notice the Japanese strafers on the deck and the few P-40s engaging them in combat. By this time, the high-flying bombers had passed out of sight to the south. Then, on the flight's radio frequency, he heard an urgent call from one of the pursuit pilots: "Many bombers, Iba!"[11] In quick response, Thorne now turned his flight on a reciprocal heading and started to climb for a return to Iba. He now found, however, that his flight had been reduced to three P-40s; Vern Ireland and Gordon Benson had become separated from the other three and remained over Clark.[12]

9 Just south of Clark Field, at Del Carmen, the 34th Pursuit Squadron's clerk, Sgt. Tom Gage, was excited. One of the squadron's cooks, E. J. Batson, had just told him that he had heard on his shortwave radio that Pearl Harbor had been attacked. Stepping out of the orderly tent, Gage looked north in the direction of Clark and saw the sky full of black dots.

His first reaction was, "My God, look at the enemy planes—there are thousands of them!" In a few moments, however, he was able to distinguish between antiaircraft bursts and the much smaller dots that were the bombers flying in formation. Gage then ran across the square of the base camp to the tent of the squadron's adjutant, 1st Lt. Jack Jennings, to report what Batson had told him about Pearl Harbor. But Jennings, whose style of behavior was quite formal, wanted to know if Gage had an official report on the alleged attack. Angrily, Gage retorted, "Goddamn it, Lieutenant, look out the back of your tent—Clark Field is going up in smoke!"

Down on the squadron's flight line, there was no doubt that war had come. After having returned about 11:00 A.M. from their morning patrol over Clark, the 34th Pursuit's pilots had been waiting in vain for another order from Clark Field to take off.[13] Now, as they saw the columns of smoke rising over Clark and heard the bombs hitting the field, they would not need any notification that the Japanese had finally attacked. Sam Marett, their CO, ordered all planes to take off and intercept the enemy over Clark; to hell with waiting for orders to materialize from group! Marett and his wingman, 2nd Lt. Frankie Bryant, led sixteen well-worn P-35As down the dirt strip, stirring up clouds of thick dust.[14]

Only 500 feet off the ground, Marett and Bryant were suddenly jumped by two Japanese fighters diving out of the overcast at 6,000 feet, coming from the direction of Clark. Stewart Robb, who had just taken off from Del Carmen as the leader of the third flight of P-35As, thought they were A-27s but immediately realized otherwise when he saw tracer fire coming from their nose guns. Reacting instantly to the burst of fire from behind, Bryant turned his plane on its back and pulled back on the stick, then almost collided with one of the other P-35As just taking off. Although Bryant's plane had taken some hits, it was not seriously damaged. To Bryant, this was a miracle; "a blind man could have shot us down" in their helpless position, he reflected years later.

Right behind Bryant, best friend "Shorty" Crosland, climbing and now at about 300 feet after takeoff, turned into Bryant's tormentor and fired two long bursts into the Zero. In the tight turn, however, Crosland's ship stalled out. At that moment, Bryant caught the nimble Japanese in his gunsight and pressed the trigger button, but the guns would not fire.

After their frustrating encounter with the strange new Japanese planes, Bryant and Crosland climbed to rejoin the rest of their squadron, which was continuing on to Clark Field. But Sam Marett was no longer leading them. When he discovered that his guns were not working either, he dropped out and headed back to Del Carmen. First Lt. Ben Brown was now leading the mission. With no oxygen equipment to allow the pilots to go higher, Brown was holding the formation down to 8,000 feet.

Approaching Clark Field at the base of the overcast, the 34th Pursuiters ran into six Zeros. The Japanese were "very aggressive and cocky" and came right into the Americans. Brown made a 90-degree pass at a two-ship element, his fire missing the lead ship but scoring with a deflection shot on the wingman.

Despite outnumbering their adversaries by over two to one, the 34th Pursuiters quickly realized that they were at a clear disadvantage in the swirling dogfight. The Zeros were outperforming the obsolete, engine-worn P-35As in every maneuver except dives. The fire from the Japanese 20- and 7.7-mm guns was also more effective than that from the P-35As' two .50-caliber and two .30-caliber guns, many of which were not working. The combat inexperience of the Americans was also further tilting the balance in favor of the Japanese.

Stewart Robb received a terrifying lesson of the Japanese superiority in man and machine. In a concentrated attack on one of the Zeros—itself firing at a P-35A in front of it—Robb was getting good hits and drawing smoke and flame from its engine, when suddenly, Robb's windshield disappeared before his eyes. Too intent on his target, he had not noticed another Japanese who had slipped up behind him. Robb immediately made a tight vertical turn to the right but drew a stream of fire almost the entire length of his wing. Overshooting the lumbering P-35A, the Zero pilot went into a loop. Robb was still in his tight turn when the Japanese completed his loop and caught the hapless American, ripping his ship with cannon and machine-gun fire "from stem to stern." Injured in the face and arms from shattered plexiglas and fragments, his engine shot out, Robb spun out of the tight turn. Fortunately the Zero did not follow him. Shaken but still alive, he headed back to Del Carmen.

Unable to hold the P-35A in the landing roll, Robb did a ground loop, but without dragging the wing or damaging it further. But his ship was already boneyard-bound. Robb counted twenty-five to thirty machine-gun hits in the wings and fuselage, from the prop hub every eighteen inches all the way to the rudder. There were also two 20-mm cannon holes in the wings, and the right tire was blown out.

By some miracle, none of the 34th Pursuiters was shot down in this their initial combat experience.

10 At 12:50 P.M., the minesweeper *Lark* in Manila Bay was reporting to the 16th Naval District that it had sighted seventeen enemy planes over the bay. These "enemies" were actually the P-40Es of the 17th Pursuit, which had now reached their patrol position after takeoff from Clark at 12:15 P.M. Circling over Manila Bay, they awaited the Japanese bombers that were supposed to be on the way in from the west. About eight minutes before they had reached the Manila area, the pilots found they were no longer receiving calls from QA-1, the 24th Group's ground control station at Clark that was directing their flight by voice transmission.

But Dave Obert for one thought nothing of it, "because we knew from past experience that it might easily break down and be unable to transmit for a while."[15]

A little to the east of the 17th's patrol position, over the Cavite area, the twelve P-40Es of A and B flights of the 21st Pursuit were also patrolling. Like the 17th Pursuit planes, they had been identified as enemy and had been fired on by U.S. Navy gunners at the Cavite base.

8. "LOOK AT THE PRETTY FORMATION OF B-17s"

1 At Iba at 12:20, the radar crew was still monitoring the flight of Japanese planes heading down the South China Sea, now some fifty miles to the northwest of the base. Near the SCR-270B's oscilloscope, Cpl. "Skeedie" Gillett of the 3rd Pursuit, a member of the seven-man radio crew in the combined radio/radar tent reinforced with wooden sides, was again being visited by his close friend, Pfc Orville Roland, who was busy digging a hole and sandbagging a Lewis gun position outside the tent. Seeing the blips on the radar screen moving closer and closer to Iba made Roland increasingly anxious. How were they really going to defend the place against a heavy bombing attack with the few machine guns they had?

Eating ham sandwiches in their gun emplacement at the north end of the field, S. Sgt. "Woody" McBride and his crew of nine were ready for whatever fate should send their way. McBride and his men had dug pits on either side of the gasoline drum emplacement. Cpl. Eric Schramm had been put in charge of the Lewis guns of one of the pits, and Cpl. Claire Cross the other. Just that morning, the regular crew of four men had been augmented by six when a couple of crew chiefs, two men from operations and armament, a cook, and a Filipino houseboy had come to McBride and asked for places in the pits. The cook was not proving of much use—he was drunk—but McBride used him to bring sandwiches to the emplacement from the mess hall.

Second Lt. Glenn Cave, one of the squadron's newies with no assigned function that day, was standing near the radar tent when another newie, hearing the drone of the planes overhead, called out, "Look at the pretty formation of B-17s." Glancing skyward, Cave reacted immediately: "You're crazy—there aren't that many B-17s in the Philippines!" Then the bombs started exploding on the field, the first that Cave had ever heard in his life. Terrified, the twenty-two-year-old native of Santa Ana, California, started running toward the beach in search of cover. Spotting a round foxhole dug earlier on the beach by the squadron's men, Cave dove in, landing on the shallow bottom, only the depth of a gasoline drum and a mere six feet in diameter. "Scared to death," he tried to put his whole body under his World War I helmet as the explosions bracketed his sanctuary.

In the sandbagged communications tent, WO John McBeath and S. Sgts. Kelly Davis and Floyd Grow were on duty with Skeedie Gillett and one of the four radio trainees. Grow had just returned with sandwiches from the mess hall, and Davis was busy taking a message from Manila on the squadron's SCR-191 radio. Then they heard bomb explosions walking down the runway toward them. Grow hit the dirt, just as a bomb exploded outside the tent. His earphones still on, Davis was blown thirty feet away, the debris of the tent and sandbags all around him. Picking himself up, the dazed radio operator ran to the beach, accompanied by McBeath and Grow, and crawled under a nipa shack.

Pvt. Hardy Bradley and another radio trainee had left the radio tent some ten minutes earlier, headed for the squadron mess. Trudging along, dog-tired from digging trenches and worked up with fear and excitement that they would soon be at war, they met another radio trainee, Pvt. Harry Terrill, and Cpl. Cecil Bird. Then one of the little group stopped the others and asked if they heard planes droning. Looking up, they saw the sky filled with shining objects fluttering down. As they came closer, an ominous whistling sound could be heard. The four men immediately turned and started running toward trenches a good two hundred yards away. Then Bradley's ears were filled with a thunderous explosion, and he was lifted into the air and slammed facedown into the ground. He heard shrapnel zinging through the air, then something hot and sharp hit his elbow. No sooner had he jumped to his feet than another blast flattened him again. Crawling on his hands and knees, he reached the edge of a large crater some twenty feet away and dropped six feet to the bottom, landing on hot and sizzling pieces of shrapnel. Suddenly, someone rolled in on top of him; it was Bradley's buddy Terrill, unhurt but as dirty and scared to death as he was.

Over in the mess hall, Sgt. Herb Tyson was eating with a crowd of other men of the squadron when someone yelled, "Get out of the mess hall; here they come!" Everyone jumped up from their chairs and grabbed their helmets, which were stacked on a table. Fumbling through the pile, Tyson could not find his. Finally, only one was left, so he took it and ran out the door. Looking up, he saw the Japanese formation and the bombs glinting in the sun, then headed in the direction of his Lewis gun position. About halfway between the mess hall and the emplacement, the bombs started exploding on the area. Spotting a large garbage pit just across the fence from where he was standing, Tyson made a dive into it. At the bottom he joined several other men of the squadron who earlier had opted for the smelly but functional sanctuary.

At "Woody" McBride's gun emplacement just off the north end of the runway, a 1941 Ford coupe had pulled up with three officers of the squadron. Second Lt. Shelton E. Avant, from Tennessee Colony, Texas, the 3rd Pursuit's nonflying ground defense officer, was making the rounds of the Lewis gun positions with 2nd Lts. John "Casa" O'Connell from Chicago and Robert "Jim" Hinson from Lufkin, Texas, two newie pilots of the squadron. Avant and O'Connell got out of the car, and O'Connell started walking toward McBride's position. Then O'Connell stopped, looked up, and remarked, "Golly, look at the planes up there. They must be navy planes coming in." O'Connell's misidentification of the aircraft became apparent seconds later as the first of the bombs began falling in a pattern from north to south across the field. The surprised youth started to run for the gun emplacement, but he never made it; shrapnel from an explosion tore the back of his head off.

Avant had also been hit by shrapnel and was "bleeding like a sieve" when McBride and his men pulled him to the shelter of the gun emplacement. Still conscious, the young officer was calling for first aid, but there was no place to take him. Inside the car, Hinson grabbed his helmet, put it on his head, and remained sitting on the seat, even as the Ford jumped from near-misses.

2 Some 15,000 feet overhead, Herb Ellis was circling in search of the missing pilots of his C Flight. The sky was beautifully clear and visibility unlimited, but there was no sign of any other planes. Then, suddenly, he spotted a P-40 on the opposite side of the wide circular track he was flying. Assuming it was one of his flight, Ellis continued to fly at a low angle of bank, wagging his wings in a sign for the other aircraft to join up. After completing another full circle, Ellis noticed that the other pilot was now banking more sharply to the right and was taking up a course that would allow him to line up with Ellis. As he watched the approach of the pilot, now only some four hundred yards away, Ellis observed smoke pouring back from his wings. A split second later, the realization flashed through Ellis's head: "That stupid bastard is shooting at me!"

Without hesitation, Ellis rolled his P-40E over into a split S and pulled back hard on the stick to get into a vertical position as quickly as possible. The fire of the other P-40 had been passing harmlessly by him, since the ship was lined up directly behind Ellis, but Ellis did not intend to remain a sitting duck for another confused 3rd Pursuiter who had obviously taken him for a Japanese. Screaming down in a steep dive, Ellis held the stick steady until the P-40 had reached a low altitude, then finally started the pullout. Blacking out as intended, he held the pullout to the point at which he could come out of it with a slight relaxation of the stick. Screeching southward across Iba strip, he leveled out just at treetop level, the landscape a green blur. A glance at his airspeed indicator showed that he was still doing over 500 MPH. Ellis looked back but saw nothing; he had shaken his adversary.

Now what? Should he land and try to find out what the hell was going on? No, he still had plenty of fuel left. While mulling over the situation, Ellis began a climb in a slow spiral directly over the field. Reaching 5,000 feet after a few minutes, Ellis was just crossing the field again, doing one of the slow circles, when he noticed something flashing by. Catching the glint of the sun again out of the corner of his eye, he realized what it was—just another tropical rain shower. But wait a minute—a shower without a single cloud in the sky? Looking up to see what was going on, Ellis was shocked to find the largest formation of aircraft he had ever seen. They were directly overhead, and there he was, right in the middle of a train of falling bombs.

Now he understood; it was the sun glinting off the bombs that had caught his eye. And the bright silver underbellies of the twin-engine bombers sparkled from the rays of the sun reflecting off the ocean. The Japanese bombers were formed in two great Vs of three-ship Vs, moving slowly north to south. To Ellis, they looked like a great set of corporal's chevrons. The second V was following immediately behind the first, each of twenty-seven planes. They appeared to be at about 25,000 feet, far above Ellis. As he watched, the formation began a gentle turn to the southwest, their brief mission of destruction completed. The bombers on the outside began to fall behind the others, being so far from the pivot point of the turn that they were unable to keep up. No longer mesmerized by the scene above him, Ellis continued his climb, maintaining the same relative position behind the Japanese formation. He was going to try to intercept them, despite the odds against success.

A few minutes before the bombs began raining down on Iba, Ed Woolery and the other five pilots of his B Flight and of Ellis's C Flight had returned over Iba from their 11:45 patrol that had taken them to Manila, then Clark Field. As they approached the field, Frank Neri, leader of the third element of C Flight, had called Iba tower for instructions and got a reply, "Do not land, enemy planes overhead!" Whether they heard the warning or not, the four pilots of B Flight were low on fuel and began their descent, while Neri and his wingman, Dana "Chubby" Allen, remained high. Woolery's wingman, Andy Krieger, descended only to 5,000 feet, however, where he began circling the field to provide top cover for the others. Things seemed fishy to him; he had noticed a freighter and a PT boat "going like hell" down the coastline, the PT boat "zigzagging like mad."

On final approach, flaps in full down position, Woolery cleared the fence at the south end of the field and touched down in a three-point landing just as bombs began exploding at the far end of the field. As his P-40E continued to roll north on the strip and the explosions marched down the field toward him, a bomb hit just behind him and blew the tail off his aircraft. Without hesitation, Woolery jumped out of the wrecked plane, its nose to the sky and propeller still turning, and headed for McBride's nearby gun position.

Behind Woolery in the landing pattern, Ray Gehrig, leader of the flight's second element, was leveling off when the first stick of bombs hit at the far end of the strip. Going to full combat RPM, Gehrig pulled away and went into a climb. Minutes later, circling back over the field, he found it covered in a mass of smoke.

Gehrig's wingman, Richard "Hawk" Root, from Buena Vista, Colorado, was less fortunate. Aborting his landing, he began to apply power, as had Gehrig in front of him, but as he was about to clear the north end of the strip, his plane was hit by shrapnel and crashed nearby, killing him instantly.[1]

Neri and his wingman, Allen, decided to check out a little boat a couple of miles off the coast of Iba. A few minutes later they were skimming back over the water toward the base. Going over Iba at low altitude, Neri was startled when the field blew up in front of him, forcing him to fly through debris from the barracks thrown up from the hits. Clearing the explosions, he realized that he had become separated from Allen. Alone, he began a slow climb for altitude. He would try to intercept the bombers that had destroyed his field and were now heading southwest.

In the meantime, Andy Krieger was also climbing to attack the bombers after having seen the explosions on the field. Switching to full combat RPM at 5,000 feet, he soon overheated his Allison engine and had to level off at 12,000 feet to let the engine cool off with a reduced power setting. Looking up, he was discouraged to see that even at that altitude, the bombers were still high above him. Looking down, he saw what appeared to be P-35As circling the field. Assuming they were trying to land, Krieger wondered why the fools could not see that the field had been bombed. Then it occurred to him that perhaps they were Japanese planes. After descending to get a better look at the aircraft, Krieger still couldn't make them out. They did not resemble anything that Intelligence had told them to expect or that he had seen in the War Department manual on identification of Japanese aircraft. Then he saw the red *hinomaru* on the wings; they were Japanese, all right. The light gray ships were circling the field and strafing in a beautiful right-hand traffic pattern.

All alone against nine adversaries, Krieger suddenly felt very insignificant. In an attempt to even the odds, he started to call, "All pursuit to Iba!" over his radio. But just at that moment another call came booming through his receiver: "All pursuit to Clark!"[2] Looking over in the direction of Clark, Krieger saw a huge pillar of smoke that appeared to be over 20,000 feet high. Figuring anyone seeing that would realize that Clark needed help, he called, "All 3rd Pursuit to Iba!"

Krieger now boldly plunged into the *buntai* (a nine-ship unit of a *kokutai*) of Zeros below him but found he could not get his gunsights on the planes when they were in firing range, as they were too low to pass under. Then he decided to penetrate right into their traffic pattern. Entering between two of the Japanese, he began firing at the Zero directly in front of him. Tracers from the Zero behind him were whizzing past as he scored hits with his .50-caliber guns and the Japanese pilot's ship began to smoke. But when Krieger looked back, he saw three of the nimble fighters "throwing everything at me but the kitchen sink." Deciding that discretion was the better part of valor, Krieger broke away in a vertical climb from the Japanese formation. Fortunately for the combat-inexperienced American, the Zeros maintained their strafing run instead of chasing the intruding P-40, which, unknown to Krieger, was no match for a Zero in a climb.

Low on gas, Krieger called over his radio for instructions on where to land. Picking up his call, his CO, Hank Thorne, radioed Krieger to head for Rosales, the squadron's auxiliary field fifty-eight miles to the northeast.

3 Still climbing in his effort to intercept the withdrawing Japanese bombers, Herb Ellis was finding out that it would be impossible to close the great distance between him and his adversaries. He was now well out over the China Sea. During the fruitless chase, he had been able to count the number of bombers: twenty-seven in the first echelon, but only twenty-six in the second.[3] When he reached 17,000 feet, he realized that he should not go much higher without oxygen, of which he had no supply in his P-40E. His unsupercharged Allison engine also needed oxygen at that altitude and was beginning to become sluggish. Ellis was also beginning to think about his dwindling fuel supply and questioned the wisdom of running out of gas over the China Sea. Finally making up his mind on a course of action, Ellis turned his ship around and began heading back to Iba. He was far out; even at his high altitude, the horizon stood out boldly in the crystal-clear sky, and the Zambales Province coast was a long way behind it. After what seemed to Ellis like an eternity (but was more probably about six minutes), he finally got close enough to see the beach coming toward him under the nose of his P-40. A great pall of black, greasy-looking smoke hung over the area.

As Ellis drew closer to Iba, he could make out aircraft flying low in a right-hand traffic pattern around the field. That made no sense; the squadron always used a left-hand pattern regardless of whether its aircraft were preparing to land to the north or to the south. As he came in from the south at 15,000 feet, he could make out the big red-orange circles on the wings of the circling planes and realized what was happening. They were Japanese, and they had set up a right-hand traffic pattern, moving north off the coast and parallel to the landing strip and then making a 180-degree turn to the south. They were strafing the field on the north-to-south run.

Ellis decided to join the Japanese on the offshore leg of their traffic pattern, in a left-hand pattern outside their own. After rechecking his gun loading and turning on the firing switch, he went into a long, steep dive. With a rapid rate of closure, he came in over the top of one of the Zeros then leveled out behind another at about 500 feet.[4] Remembering that the usual tendency in going into battle the first time was to open fire too soon, Ellis held his fire until he was so close that the short bursts of his tracers were going down both sides of the fuselage of the Japanese, ricocheting off the wing roots. Waiting until the last second, he then pitched his P-40 under the Zero. As soon as he was clear, he pulled the P-40 up to the left in a chandelle and got into position to make a second run.

On the second pass, Ellis followed the same procedure, but the speed differential was not as great. Again, he pitched under the Zero; this tactic prevented the opponent from seeing him, as he would have if Ellis had pulled up instead. Even though fewer of his .50-caliber guns were working this time, his fire was proving effective. The target was relatively motionless, making no effort to take evasive action.

Only two of Ellis's guns fired on the third pass, and during the fourth run, nothing at all happened when he pressed the trigger. At this juncture, he pulled out of the Japanese formation and began to climb in a circle, keeping a lookout for any Japanese set to intercept him. But all the Zeros continued on their strafing run below him. Not during any of the runs had the Japanese fired on him or broken their pattern to chase him. In the shallow water offshore and in line with the traffic pattern, Ellis counted five downed Japanese aircraft.[5]

Now as he climbed, Ellis kept pressing the trigger switch, but to no avail. He was sure he had not expended all his ammunition, so it must be a case of a jammed firing mechanism. What to do now? Landing at Iba was certainly out of the question. Since he had enough fuel left, he decided to head for Clark.

As he zigzagged eastward through the mountain pass east of Iba at about 1:05 P.M., ever alert to the possibility of an attack on his ship, Ellis "never felt quite so alone" in all his life, "to say nothing of being scared." Leaving the pass behind and now out over the great central plain of Luzon, Ellis was dismayed to see the great cloud of smoke hanging over the area of Clark Field.

4 Frank Neri had managed to get up to 18,000 feet, his P-40E inching

Japanese Zero pilots of the 3rd *kokutai* taking off from Takao, Formosa, on December 8, 1941, to launch the initial attack against the Philippines. *Courtesy Tamotsu Yokoyama, Maj. Gen. Japan Air Self-Defense Force (Ret.)*

up at only some 800 feet a minute in the rarefied air, but he could see that the Japanese bombers withdrawing to the south were still a good 5,000 feet above him. Running low on fuel and unable to remain at that altitude without oxygen, Neri, as had Ellis, decided to break off his interception. Descending 8,000 feet, he began calling over the radio on the 3rd Pursuit's frequency, "Anybody around?" Then on his receiver he picked up a response. Gerry Keenan, his best friend, asked, "Where are you?"

Neri responded: "I'm over Pinatuba at 8,000 feet. I'll wait for you. Where will you be coming from?"

"I'll be coming from the south," Keenan replied. The third element leader of Thorne's splintered A Flight had been milling around the Iba area and beyond ever since becoming separated about 12:35 from Thorne and the others patrolling over Iba at 15,000 feet. And the "Messerschmitt 109" Keenan had intercepted over Iba just before the field had been bombed was the P-40 of his own squadron mate, Ellis.

As Neri circled around over 5,800-foot Mount Pinatuba, waiting for his friend to join him, he noticed vibrations in his P-40. Checking his indicators for possible sticking valves, he found the engine to be in fine condition. And the gun selector switches were all off.

Then Neri spotted three aircraft approaching and called out, "Hey, Gerry, is that you?"

"Yeah," replied Keenan.

"But who you got with you?"

"Nobody."

"Oops—you've got two Nips on your tail, Gerry!"

Now Neri started wondering: "If Gerry didn't realize he had Japs on his tail, maybe I've got them too." He looked back, and "sure enough, there one was" on his tail.[6] Those blinking lights he now saw would explain his plane's vibrations: hits from the Zero's guns.

Neri immediately put his ship into a dive, straight down. Then he started into a climbing turn to shake the Zero off his tail and allow him to see from the circle what he was up against, a maneuver he had practiced many times in the past. But as he came up in the oblique loop one-fourth of the way, he looked back and saw the Japanese pilot cutting inside of him. He thought, "Neri, this ain't no place for you!" Opting for some low-lying clouds, he plunged his P-40 into them.

When he came out of the cloud bank, he found he had eluded the Zero on his tail but was headed toward another one. Neri immediately pressed the gun trigger switch, but the Zero disappeared into another cloud. Looking around, the 3rd Pursuiter was relieved to find the sky free of Japanese aircraft. But his buddy Gerry Keenan was nowhere to be seen either. Neri decided to head for Clark and check out the situation there.

5 At about 12:58, Fred Roberts and Bill Powell of Ellis's splintered C flight were just arriving over Iba from Clark Field, having escaped further damage from the Zeros there. Below, they saw their home field in flames and Japanese aircraft still strafing ground targets. Roberts immediately took after one of the strafers in a diving attack and started firing on his tail, although only two of his guns were working. Trying to stay in the tight turn of the nimble single-seater, Roberts was hit by another behind him.[7] His P-40E now smoking and down to ten gallons of gas, Roberts decided to head out to sea to beach his ship, but as close to shore as possible; there was no place left to bring it in on what remained of Iba Field. Diving the P-40 at 120 MPH, Roberts misjudged his approach— too high—and hit the water, and his plane nosed down about 150 yards offshore.

Watching Roberts's crash landing from shore, S. Sgt. Al Bland and two other men of the squadron ran to the shoreline and plunged into the water. After swimming out a few minutes in the shallow water, they arrived at the aircraft, stepped up on the wings, and reached into the open cockpit. Undoing the seat belt of the dazed aviator, they helped him climb out of the plane and supported him as he made his way to shore, plowing through the water fairly steadily despite his experience.

While Roberts was engaged in combat, Powell was circling Iba, no guns working, "watching the fun." Then he spotted a Zero taking after him from the sea. Naively deciding to climb away from the Japanese pursuit and head for the auxiliary field at Lingayen, fifty-eight miles to the north, Powell switched his Allison to a military power setting and "didn't pay much attention to that fellow." After he had turned 180 degrees to get headed in the right direction and had straightened out, Powell looked back. "There that bird was, right on my tail!" Reacting quickly, Powell "opened her wide-open, to the firewall," getting an indicated air speed of 300 MPH. After a few minutes, Powell noticed that he was gradually losing his pursuer, but not before the Japanese had scored a few hits on his ship.

6 Only about a minute after Roberts and Powell had reached Iba from Clark, about 12:59, Hank Thorne and the two remaining pilots of his A Flight were approaching Iba from the south at 15,000 feet after leaving Clark. Below them, the sight of their burning, smoking field, pockmarked from the Japanese pattern bombing, sickened them. After searching the sky for signs of the Japanese bombers, Thorne spotted two waves flying on a northerly course over the field. They were far above Thorne's group, at about 23,000 feet[8] but Thorne and the two others began a power climb to intercept. After about nine minutes, the heavy, slow-climbing P-40s managed to reach 21,000 feet, but they were still 2,000 feet below the Japanese.[9] The Allison engines were operating very poorly in the rarefied air. Thorne had developed a bad headache from lack of oxygen at the high altitude and was becoming concerned that the other two might pass out from anoxia. And their fuel was running low, rapidly being consumed in the power climb.

Some twenty miles north of Iba, just out over the China Sea, Thorne decided to break off the interception attempt. Leading the others in a turn to the northeast and reducing altitude, Thorne called out on his radio for all 3rd Pursuit pilots to proceed to Rosales and land. Suddenly, a loud and angry voice boomed into Thorne's earphones, "Go to hell, you Japanese bastards!" A confused and frustrated "Chubby" Allen, Frank Neri's wingman, who had become separated from Neri over Iba at the time the field was bombed, was reacting to what he believed was a decoy call by one of the Zero pilots.[10]

7 When the Zeros began their low-level strafing of what was left of Iba Field after the bombers had made their devastating pass over the tiny area at 12:44, Cpl. Claire Cross of "Woody" McBride's gun emplacement was ready for them. Behind his .30-caliber Lewis gun in one of the two pits, he poured a steady stream of fire into the line of Zeros after they turned right at the north end of the field and began their north-south strafing run. McBride saw a piece of one of the Zeros fly off from the fire. But after Cross switched to a second drum of ammunition, he could get

off only a couple of rounds at a time, then had to clear the gun manually before it would fire. Sand and dust stirred up from the bombing had gotten into the drum, causing the gun — intended for aerial combat, not ground defense — to jam. The Zeros were flying so close to the emplacement that the men felt they could have gotten better results if they had thrown rocks at the strafers instead.

In the other gun pit, McBride was hunkered down at the side of the sand-filled gas drums with the wounded Shelton Avant when a second wave of twenty-seven bombers flew south to north over the field. Suddenly McBride hollered in pain, hit by something in his left hip that "burned like fury."[11] Hearing the scream, Cpl. Eric Schramm, the Lewis gun operator in the pit, yelled, "My God, they've got Mac!"

Blood was oozing out of Avant's body from "what looked like a thousand holes." As McBride's men began to put him onto a cot to carry him off the field, they were joined by Ed Woolery, whose P-40 had been hit as he was landing twenty minutes earlier. Together they carried the mortally wounded officer to a nearby coconut grove.

Near the emplacement, Jim Hinson opened the door of Avant's car as soon as the strafing ceased, intending to get over to the gun pits. But he had been severely hit by bomb fragments in the left leg, right thigh, and the arch of the foot, and he fell on his face as soon as he tried to take his first step with the broken leg. Sprawled on the ground, Hinson reached for his helmet, which had fallen off, and noticed that it had a hole in it, punched from the inside out; a shell or fragment piece had penetrated it between the liner band and the edge while he had been sitting in the car.

Near the mess hall area of the field, Herb Tyson and the other occupants of the garbage pit that had provided them cover during the bombing had done their best to avoid becoming strafing victims. The pit was so large that they had to follow the Zeros in their strafing pattern and change sides of the pit to be out of the firing line of the Japanese.

Minutes earlier, a direct hit during the bombing run had destroyed the kitchen at the end of the mess hall. The squadron's popular Filipino cook, who had been with them for seven years, had burned to death in the icebox, where he had taken refuge during the bombing. And 2nd Lt. Andy Webb, a 41-C newie from Forest, Mississippi, had been killed while trying to get the kitchen staff to safety.

Lying on the ground in a shallow crater near the burning radio shack was 2nd Lt. Bart Passanante, who had been blown off his feet by an exploding bomb. There was no blood, but his right leg pained him and felt broken. While he surveyed the scene of destruction around him, he noticed that one corner of the radio shack was starting to fall and that he was in its line of fall. "Oh, oh, there goes my back!" Passanante thought. Then the 3 × 4 piece of wood fell directly across his back, but it did not hurt; the crater in which he was lying was deep enough to save him from a broken back. Lying pinned to the ground, blood beginning to ooze through the pants on his right leg, he suddenly heard the stitching sound of machine gun fire. Then he noticed a cement cistern, about one and a half feet high and ten feet in diameter, behind him. With a burst of strength, Passanante pulled his broken leg after him and snaked his way over to the cistern on the opposite side from the direction of strafing, propping his back up against the side of the cistern, and with his head below the level of the structure.

As the Zeros made one strafing run after another down the alley, Passanante began to feel hot from the midday sun beating down on him. Trying to get cool, he rubbed the sweat off his completely bald head, shaved just that morning. When the strafers had finished their deadly work, the wounded officer lay back in the shade of the cistern cover. Then he heard the sound of running and yelled for help. Two enlisted men stopped and stared at him, froze, then replied, "We'll be right back, don't move!" Unknown to Passanante at the time, the men thought the top of his head had been blown off; he had smeared blood all over his bald pate in rubbing his head.

Over in the beach area, Sgt. Kelly Davis had not enjoyed immunity from the fire of the strafing Zeros as had Passanante. When the first strafer came heading down the beach, the Japanese pilot spotted the hapless radio operator and began firing his 7.7-mm nose guns. With sand spitting up all around him, Davis dove into the beach, feeling the thump of the fire as it went past him. But he was not hit.

Huddled in a nearby foxhole on the beach, Glenn Cave had escaped injury during the bombing. But when he saw what appeared to be P-35s coming in his direction, then noticed red lights blinking from them and bullets hitting the sand near him, he froze, transfixed. He followed the line of nine single-engine aircraft as they strafed the field from north to south. They were so low he could almost count the rivets in the bottom of their fuselages from the safety of the foxhole. Then he heard the deep rumble of bombers coming back, flying south to north this time. After the bombers had cleared the field, the Japanese Zeros were back for another strafing run, but a few minutes later, it was all over. Cave checked his watch; it was now 1:05 P.M.[12]

9. "I WONDER WHAT MY CHANCES ARE OF MAKING IT ALL THE WAY TO THE END"

1 Climbing at full throttle after their takeoff from Clark at 12:35, Joe Moore, Randy Keator, and Edwin Gilmore were headed in a westerly direction intended to bring them into contact with the outbound Japanese bombers that had unloaded on their base. At about 21,000 feet, the leading two of the three P-40Bs leveled off some thirty miles west of Clark Field. Keator was now about 100 feet below and 1,200 feet behind Moore on his right. Gilmore, still climbing, was trailing about 2,500 feet behind and 3,000 feet below Moore.

It was now 1:10 P.M. Suddenly, Moore noticed a flight of planes at his altitude, rapidly approaching him from the right. Thinking they were P-40s from Iba, Moore began wagging his wings in a signal for them to join up with his flight. The planes closed rapidly. When they were about even with Moore's right wing, in a tight formation of Vs, they went into a diving turn to their right. Then Moore saw that there were nine of them and that there was a "big fried egg" on their wings. Seemingly oblivious to Moore, the Japanese planes went after Keator and Gilmore below him. Reacting quickly to the advantage presented him, Moore went into a hard 180-degree diving turn, ending up just behind and above the Japanese. As he closed with the nearest one, he fired and then continued in his dive, with only some of his guns working.

Below Moore, Keator also had turned tightly to the right and now found himself face-to-face with the lead plane of the V column. Firing the machine guns of his P-40B for the first time ever, Keator saw his tracers striking the Japanese plane's engine and canopy. Suddenly the Zero exploded, the Keator flew right through the debris.[1] The vibration of his cockpit that the guns caused was a new sensation for Keator and sent cold chills down his spine; he thought the Zero was shooting him to pieces. As he started to pull up after making his successful pass, he looked back and saw a Zero just getting him lined up in its sights, closing in fast on his tail. Instinctively, Keator pushed the control stick forward, pitching his

P-40 into a near vertical dive. His head hit the canopy and his feet left the rudder pedals; he then realized that in the panic of the takeoff, he had forgotten to fasten his seat belt and shoulder harness. Holding the stick forward until he had enough speed to pull away from his pursuer, Keator then pulled back hard on the stick and blacked out completely. When he regained consciousness, he found himself in a steep climb and the Zero gone from his tail.

After leveling off and fastening his seat belt, Keator began looking around for the Zeros. A few thousand feet below his altitude of 19,000 feet, he spotted Moore diving on a Zero's tail, but a Zero was on Moore's tail, too. Coming to his commanding officer's rescue, Keator dove on the second Zero, causing the Japanese to break off his attack. As the nimble Zero went into a right climbing turn, Keator closed fast on it, following the plane around in a circle, watching his tracers ripping into it. But the more maneuverable Zero continued in a tighter turn until Keator had to break off or go into a stall. Losing sight of his adversary, Keator went into another diving turn, then returned to the scene of the combat in a fast climb. He found himself completely alone, however; Moore, Gilmore, and the Zeros had disappeared. Below, Keator saw three planes burning on the ground.

Joe Moore had gotten in a second firing pass from behind and above at the Zeros before a three-plane element broke "like a covey of quail" and went after him with a vengeance. Trying to shake the Zeros off his tail, his head swinging from side to side, he jerked the oxygen mask off his face in annoyance. Employing some of his favorite escape tricks that had always succeeded in shaking P-40s off his tail in practices, Moore still could not elude the persistent Zeros. Showers of tracers flashed past his plane, appearing to be arcing into his cockpit but missing. After what seemed to Moore like an eternity, he dove for the ground and outran his pursuers.

Considerably below Moore and Keator, Gilmore had found himself the object of the Zeros' attack at the outset of the dogfight. As his two squadron mates had done, Gilmore turned sharply to his right to intercept them. But when one got on his tail right away, firing tracers past him, Gilmore immediately went into a diving turn to the left. After his P-40 had built up sufficient speed, Gilmore pulled it up sharply to the right, blacking out temporarily. Looking back, he saw that he had evaded his pursuers. With the sky clear of aircraft, Gilmore set out for Del Carmen field; he figured Clark would be too cratered to land on.

The dogfight over, Keator climbed to 22,000 feet and started back for Clark. Before reaching his home field, he spotted a plane heading south, flying on top of a solid bank of cloud at about 5,000 feet. From his altitude, Keator could not make out if it was Japanese or not and decided to go down and take a look. Waiting until the plane passed underneath him, Keator dove out of the sun, approaching the aircraft from the rear. Recognizing the red *hinomarus* on the wings, Keator opened up on the unsuspecting pilot. Curiously, the Zero did not take any evasive action as Keator leveled out behind it and fired at close range, his tracers striking the tail and canopy. Almost immediately, the plane started to burn, slowly rolling upside down and entering the clouds inverted.

2 About five minutes after the P-40Bs had intercepted the nine Zeros west of Clark, a lone P-40E came over the field from the direction of Iba. The pilot was 1st Lt. Herb Ellis, leader of the 3rd Pursuit's C Flight, still separated from his pilots. His guns not working, "scared to death" after his harrowing experience over Iba ten minutes earlier, he had headed for Clark in the hope of finding a place to land. His hopes faded when on entering the great central plain of Luzon after passing through the Zambales Range, he saw a great pall of smoke that almost completely obscured his view of Clark Field.

Approaching Clark from the west, Ellis noted that the black smoke from the field was drifting to the south and that by flying to the north of Clark, he was able to keep most of the field in sight. He headed for a large cumulus cloud that he had spotted just east of Clark and turned to a southerly heading when he reached it. By keeping the cloud on his left, Ellis figured he would be able to reduce the area he had to watch for Japanese aircraft to the hemisphere on his right.

Ellis had just barely turned to his new heading when he saw black puffs of smoke about fifty to one hundred yards ahead and to the right, a little below his altitude. It was immediately obvious to him what they were; the Clark Field antiaircraft boys were firing at him. Reacting immediately to lessons learned in practices, Ellis pitched his P-40E violently downward and out of the line of fire, then leveled out at what he regarded as a safe altitude — 5,000 feet. Back in his earlier position in relation to the cumulus cloud, Ellis again continued to keep a sharp lookout to the right of his aircraft. But when he glanced to his left to make a cursory, and seemingly unnecessary, check for Japanese planes, he was shocked to find flaming tracers "about the size of baseballs" coming straight at him, then curving in behind his cockpit. A Zero, diving through the cloud, had by pure chance come out only some hundred yards away and at a 90-degree angle to Ellis's plane. By the time Ellis realized what was happening, the Japanese had already put a long burst into the P-40's fuel tank behind Ellis's seat and into the rear fuselage and was now starting to turn to follow Ellis's line of flight.

Resisting the natural inclination to pull back on his stick and turn into his opponent, Ellis immediately pitched his plane down, out of the Zero's line of fire and went into a steep dive. Although his own self-

Herb Ellis, later of the 3rd Pursuit Squadron, as a flying school cadet at Kelly Field in August, 1939. *Courtesy National Archives*

confidence was gone, he still had confidence in his plane; the P-40 could outrun any aircraft in the world in a dive. Still with plenty of altitude, Ellis held the plane in the dive for some time. In a few seconds, though, he began to smell the unmistakable odor of burning paint. He looked all around but could see nothing that would account for the smell; visibility to the rear was very limited in a P-40. But as the smell persisted, Ellis decided to crank open his canopy to get a better look behind. The entire tail end of his P-40 was enveloped in flames, leaving a trail at least two hundred yards long.

Ellis knew there was only one thing to do in such a situation—bail out. But glancing at his airspeed indicator, he saw he was going too fast in the dive to jump. To kill off speed and level out, Ellis pulled back on the stick. It came back easily; there was no pressure. But nothing happened; his plane continued in the same dive angle. Then he realized that the horizontal control surfaces of fabric must have burned away. Ellis immediately pulled his canopy back and started to get out of the plane. But as soon as he got his head and shoulders out of the cockpit, the rush of the wind jammed him against the crash pad and the forward edge of the open canopy, blocking his efforts. In desperation, Ellis began trying to wriggle his body out by elbowing his way against the open canopy and the edge of the cockpit. Finally, he managed to get far enough out that the wind caught him and pulled him out. He ducked his head to avoid being hit by the horizontal stabilizer of the tail, but nevertheless the stabilizer caught him in the small of his back. Then he was caught behind the knees by the stabilizer, which banged his head.

Now everything began to occur in slow motion to Ellis. He felt very hot, then very cold. As he spun through the air, everything became a whirling kaleidoscope of green, blue, and brown colors. Then he realized that he had better pull his rip cord. The parachute opened immediately. At that moment, Ellis recalled that as a flying cadet at Randolph Field he had been told by the instructor during his parachute training that only five pilots in the Air Corps had bailed out under 250 feet and survived. Would he be the sixth, he wondered?

Looking up, Ellis noticed an aircraft at some distance above him and in the direction from which he had come, in a slight turning dive. Then its wings leveled out and the pilot started a long dive toward Ellis. Convinced that he was about to be strafed, Ellis began to climb up the risers on the left side of his parachute harness until the parachute was turned halfway inside out and spilled most of its air, putting him nearly in a free-fall.

Just then, Ellis caught sight of a P-40, flying out of nowhere, moving from right to left toward the diving Zero. Breaking off his head-on approach to Ellis, the Japanese pilot went into a sharp dive to the right. The firing of the P-40's machine guns resounded in Ellis' ears.[2]

Ellis held the left-hand risers until he could see the ground rushing up at him, then let go. The parachute blossomed out again immediately. Ellis swung forward, then back, and hit the ground on the next forward swing, standing. "Now there are six," he thought as soon as he touched the ground.

Ellis found that he had landed in one of a number of dry rice paddies around him. Very carefully, still experiencing everything in slow motion, he bundled up his chute and started to walk toward a road that ran off to the south.

3 Some twenty-eight miles north-northwest of Clark Field, at Santa Ignacia, another drama was unfolding at the same time as Ellis was going through his ordeal. Col. Richard C. Mallonee, senior American instructor of the 21st Field Artillery Regiment, 21st Division, Phillipine Army, had detected the hum of airplane motors high in the sky over his position. Then, for the first time, he heard the sound of machine gun fire. Looking up, he saw several Japanese planes working over a lone P-40. The American plane suddenly burst into flames and fell "like a rock." The pilot had bailed out and was floating to earth, very slowly. It looked like the pilot would land near the 21st Division's command post, so Mallonee and others with him continued to watch the enemy planes flying northward until they were out of sight.

Shortly afterward, a Filipino boy on a calesa pony dashed in to the command post. He had found the aviator sitting on his chute, dazed and needing help. There was no road leading to the location, about two and a half miles away, so Mallonee sent a doctor and litter bearers with the boy. About two hours later, they returned with Lt. George Ellstrom, who had taken off from Iba with the others of Ellis's C Flight at 11:45 that morning.

It was clear to Mallonee that Ellstrom was suffering from shock. Although Ellstrom complained of severe stomach pains, Mallonee could not see any wounds on him except brush burns on his shoulders. His watch had stopped, shattered, at 1:20 P.M. Mallonee then took a statement from Ellstrom. The luckless pilot said that he was on a routine reconnaissance over the Zambales, having taken off from Iba. He knew that war had started but did not know there were any enemy planes nearer than Japan and had not seen any hostile planes until he was surrounded by Zeros. He kept repeating, "We were tricked." On the way to the hospital, he died.

Evidently, Ellstrom had become separated from the others of Ellis's C Flight on takeoff from Iba that morning and was left behind when the others flew down to Manila. His position as Fred Roberts's wingman had been taken by Bill Powell when Powell failed to link up with his element leader, Herb Ellis. Ellstrom must have flown around for about an hour in the general area of Zambales after having been left behind. It was his bad luck that he happened to be over the rendezvous point of the Tainan *kokutai*'s Zeros for their return trip to Taiwan just at the moment the flying commander of the Japanese group and his two wingmen had reached the area after their attack on Clark. The three Zeros were surprised to find a lone P-40 approaching the point from their rear, but they quickly shot it down.[3]

4 At about 1:05 P.M. a lone, shot-up P-40E appeared over Iba from the east. Don Steele was returning to his home field after his perilous combat with Zeros over Clark. Steele could see no aircraft anywhere, but the base was in flames, and the landing strip was pocked with bomb craters. He also incorrectly thought he saw a Japanese destroyer offshore shelling the field. To Steele, it was "strictly an unhealthy place to be." Deciding against trying to land at Iba, but with fuel getting low, Steele had to find a place to set his P-40 down soon. Turning to the south, he soon noted a dried-up riverbed a few miles out, in the direction of San Marcelino, thirty miles further south, and opted for a landing there.

Somehow, Steele managed to put the plane down in one piece on the unlikely landing site. Climbing out of the "old junk heap," he looked his steed over. He could not believe how it could have flown in its condition. Later he recalled, "Right then and there, I thanked the Curtiss company for building such a sturdy airplane." Steele managed to roll the P-40 into some trees, out of sight. Then he saw someone coming out of the bushes. It turned out to be his squadron mate Lt. Gordon "Squirrely" Benson! By a strange coincidence, Benson had also landed in the riverbed and rolled his P-40 into the bushes. Steele was delighted to find Benson with him. Together, they now set out on foot in the direction of San Marcelino.

Unknown to Steele, his wingman, Ship Daniel, had not been far behind him as Steele approached Iba. He was also looking for a place to land his P-40E, which had all six .50-caliber guns jammed. Dismayed at the condition of Iba Field, but too low on gas to make it to Rosales or any other field he knew of, Daniel figured it was Iba or nothing. Avoiding bomb craters, he managed to bring the warbird to a halt on the field, where he was met by Glenn Cave. Daniel then decided to try to take off in one of the squadron's spare P-40s immediately; his own plane was too damaged to fly again.[4] Daniel was lucky; of the five P-40s remaining, one was still in flying condition after the Japanese attack. A sixth one had been flown out earlier by Ed Woolery after his original plane had been destroyed on landing at Iba and he had taken cover during the bombing and strafing attack.

Daniel and Cave, his 41-C flying school classmate from Kelly Field, worked out an arrangement for Daniel to take off from Iba in the spare P-40. Minutes later, Cave was standing in a bomb crater in the middle of the field, waving a torn sheet to signal to Daniel that he had to clear the field by that point; beyond were craters. Developing maximum power in the Allison engine, Daniel's P-40 screamed down the southern end of the field and lifted off after using up only 1,200 feet of the strip. Then he headed it north.

5 At Lingayen, fifty-eight miles north of Iba, another P-40E was descending for a landing about 1:13 P.M. after an eleven-minute dash from Iba at 330 MPH. The pilot, Bill Powell, had managed to outrun a Zero in level flight.[5] Coming in to land on the field, which was actually a Philippine Army parade ground area rather than an airstrip, Powell put his wheels down and hit the sandy ground at 140 MPH, the hottest landing he had ever made. With the help of the sand and good braking, he succeeded in stopping the Warhawk before it ran off the tiny parade ground and just as it ran out of gas. He heaved a sigh of relief after getting the P-40 hidden among some palm trees with the help of a few Philippine Army troops stationed nearby.

6 Also fifty-eight miles from Iba, but more to the east, Andy Krieger was bringing his P-40E down safely at Rosales at 1:20 P.M. As he taxied back up the primitive strip, his gas ran out. Six minutes earlier, passing high over Santa Ignacia on his Iba-Rosales route, Krieger had spotted three Zeros below him but had declined the opportunity for an easy attack because of his dangerously low fuel. Unknown to him, he had been looking at the Tainan *kokutai shotai* that in a moment would be the cause of death of his flying school classmate and best friend, George Ellstrom. When Krieger climbed out of his plane, he found that his commanding officer, Hank Thorne, was already there, as were several others of the 3rd Pursuit, including Bob Hanson and Howard Hardegree.[6] They had parked their P-40s in dispersed positions around the 2,500-foot strip and had started to service them.

Some minutes later, at about 1:30 P.M., the pilots looked up when they heard a plane approaching the field. It was another P-40, just clearing the trees, its flaps and wheels down. It hit the ground and slowed down quickly; the left tire was flat. Everyone at the field ran over to meet the pilot, who turned out to be Frank Neri. He had headed to Rosales after circling Clark Field, fifty miles to the south, but found it too damaged to land on. His gas gauge on empty, he had barely made it into Rosales.[7] Examining Neri's P-40, the other pilots at Rosales were amazed Neri had made it back safely. The left tire had been ripped to shreds, the aileron and left wingtip were badly damaged, and there were holes in the propeller. The most hair-raising hits, however, had been made in a long stitch all the way down the right side of the fuselage, with just a break for the cockpit area. Looking at the neat line of 7.7-mm holes, Neri for the first time felt fear. Neri and the others pushed the sieved P-40 under a tree off the strip. His was the only one that was not flyable of those that had landed at Rosales.

Then they heard another plane coming low over the field. It was a P-40,

Best friends Andy Krieger (left) and George Ellstrom in front of a P-35A of their 3rd Pursuit Squadron at Nichols Field, spring, 1941. *Courtesy Edith R. Krieger*

too, but the pilot just buzzed the strip and then headed south in the direction of Manila.

7 At Nichols Field, Sam Grashio of the 21st Pursuit had landed after his close scrape with Zeros over Clark. Approaching Manila in his shot-up P-40E, he had radioed Nichols tower for advice and had been told to climb to 8,000 feet over an uninhabited area. Then wheels and flaps down, he found he had no trouble coming in safely. As Grashio pulled himself

out of the cockpit and dropped to the ground, S. Sgt. Byron Gibson met him and hugged him joyfully. The warm-hearted, emotional officer was very popular with the squadron's enlisted men.

Grashio found that Gus Williams and Johnny McCown, who had shared the terrifying experience with Grashio over Clark, were back safely, too. They all were met on landing by Ed Dyess, who had returned much earlier after leading the fruitless patrol of A and B flights over Manila Bay. Grashio was still very excited about his experience. The right aileron of his P-40 had been nearly shot off, and the wing had a hole "you could throw a hat through." "By God," he exclaimed, "they ain't shooting spitballs, are they!" As the planes—except Grashio's, which was beyond repair—were being serviced, the pilots went over to Dyess's tent, where cokes were in the tubs and olives and sandwiches had been put out for them.

A few minutes after Grashio landed, another P-40E approached the field and came in, this one with only three gallons of gas left in its tanks. The pilot was Lt. Ray Gehrig of Woolery's B Flight. Having escaped the Zeros at Iba, Gehrig first headed for Clark, but when he found it "a smoke-covered mess," and with his fuel getting lower and lower, he decided Nichols might be the best bet for a place to put down safely. It was a good choice.

Shortly afterward, Gehrig was joined by his flight leader, Ed Woolery, who had buzzed Rosales earlier with intentions of landing there but had decided to head for Nichols instead, since he had enough gas. Gehrig and the others were excited to hear of Woolery's brush with death on landing at Iba and his escape from the heavily damaged field in another P-40.

8 Up at Del Carmen, the pilots of the 34th Pursuit had somehow brought their P-35s back after the one-sided encounter on the way to Clark with the Japanese mystery planes, subsequently identified as Zeros. Amazingly, none of the worn-out, slow American pursuit planes had been shot down, but all were damaged. Second Lt. Stewart Robb had made a deadstick landing—a landing made with the propeller stopped—wheels down, but with both tires flat.

Some of the pilots were terrified by their experience. After landing, 2nd Lt. Jim Henry vowed never to go up again in a P-35 against the Zero. On the ground, the pilots learned that the two Zeros that had jumped them shortly after takeoff had afterward made a short strafing attack on the field, though with little damage inflicted.[8] It was warning enough, however, for the CO of the 34th to order the men to strike their tents and disperse. In the meantime, Lt. Edwin Gilmore of the 20th Pursuit, who had earlier evaded Zeros pursuing him over Clark, brought his P-40B in for a landing on the Del Carmen strip.

9 About the time Gilmore was landing at Del Carmen, his squadron mate Randy Keator was approaching Clark Field, fifteen miles due north,

and trying to contact the control tower for landing instructions. He received no reply by either radio or light signal. Following procedures for emergency landings, Keator lowered his altitude to 1,000 feet and came in slowly, wheels down, from the east. Dense black smoke was rising from burning aircraft, oil tanks, and debris on the field. He could not find a strip of land wide enough to land on that was not cratered, so he went around again. After two more tries, he finally was able to put his P-40B down safely between several burning B-17s at the extremity of the field.

The exhausted pilot climbed out of his plane and jumped onto the deserted field. Then heads slowly began appearing out of slit trenches nearby. When everyone realized that it was a friendly plane that had landed, they rushed over to Keator and asked if his plane had been hit. He replied that he did not think so. Surprised, one of the men exclaimed, "Well, our antiaircraft gunners were firing at you with every available gun the whole time you were circling the field!" A few more chills went up and down Keator's spine.

A few minutes later, Joe Moore was also circling the field at low altitude, likewise finding no place to land that was not cratered. Finally, after having circled twice, he decided to put down on the 2,000-foot extension strip close to the 19th Bombardment Group area, near where Keator had landed earlier, despite its pocked condition.

The other pilots of the 20th Pursuit at Clark were surprised to find their commanding officer safe and sound. Randy Keator had told them that Moore had been shot down. Keator had assumed that one of the three crashed, burning planes he had seen on the ground during his combat west of Clark was Moore's. The last Keator had seen of his CO, Moore was diving straight down with the Zeros on his tail.

Shaken by the day's experiences, Keator wondered, "If this is an example of what war is like and it is only the first day, I wonder what my chances are of making it all the way to the end?"

At about 3:00 P.M., the eighteen P-40Es of the 17th Pursuit Squadron came in to land at Nichols. All were practically out of gas after having patrolled almost two and a half hours over Manila Bay. The pilots had seen no enemy aircraft of any kind. Reporting in to the operations office of the squadron, they received some shocking news. About twenty minutes after they had taken off from Clark Field and headed south to their assigned patrol area, the base had been practically destroyed. The radio station had been hit, which explained why the 17th had not received any messages from QA-1. They had circled Manila Bay almost within sight of Clark Field all during the raid and known nothing of it.[9] Then they also heard that Iba had been hit, too, and the 3rd Pursuit there had been nearly wiped out.

The pilots of the 17th Pursuit were a "tired and bewildered bunch" as they stood around the operations office, hearing the news. "We had been flying all day and had seen nothing, yet disaster had struck all around us," Dave Obert wrote that evening in his diary. "And what next?", the dispirited young men wondered. The 17th and the 21st were now the only fully equipped pursuit squadrons left to defend the Philippines.

10. "THERE AIN'T NO MORE 24TH PURSUIT GROUP"

1 At Rosales, the 3rd Pursuit's designated secondary airfield one hundred miles north-northwest of Nichols. Hank Thorne and the other pilots of the squadron's splintered A, B, and C flights were busy in midafternoon removing the five-foot barbed-wire fence that rimmed the 2,500-foot strip so that they could take off with the remaining flyable P-40Es they had flown in earlier that afternoon. The fence had been erected by the custodian of the field, an American sugarcane grower, to prevent his carabao from wandering onto the field. There was plenty of aviation gasoline at Rosales — ten thousand gallons had been stored there — but no fuel servicing pump. How could they fill the empty tanks of the four P-40Es? Thorne decided to go into town and beg, borrow, or steal enough funnels and five-gallon cans to permit manual servicing of their planes.

Commandeering the first vehicle that passed on the road, the 3rd Pursuit's CO rode into the small town and managed to locate enough funnels and gas cans to do the job. While there, he also telegraphed FEAF Headquarters at Nielson Field that he had four P-40Es and one B-18 able to fly as soon as they were serviced and would await instructions.[1]

Back at Rosales Field, Thorne joined his pilots in the time-consuming and arduous task of manually gassing up the planes. First, they had to load the fifty-five gallon drums, each of which weighed some three hundred pounds, on the back of a truck at the fuel dump, then drive the truck to the vicinity of the planes, pour the gasoline from the drums into the five-gallon cans, and finally, pour the gas from the cans through a funnel into the gas tanks of the planes.

Twenty-five miles to the northwest of Rosales, Bill Powell of C Flight had his own troubles. After he had gotten his P-40 hidden among the palm trees off the beach at Lingayen with the help of men from the Philippine Army division there, he found two American lieutenants assigned to the division and showed them his plane. They were surprised to see holes in it, for things had been very quiet for them up there, and they hardly knew there was a war going on. A technical sergeant was located who was familiar with .50-caliber guns. After being shown how to get to the guns in the wings, he diagnosed the problem—a sticking or improperly installed solenoid—and repaired them. But Powell still had a gas and oil problem, and a check of the area confirmed that there was none there suitable for his plane. The two lieutenants then took Powell to their mess, where he had a good meal of fried chicken. He also accepted the offer of their bunks but was unable to nap, worked up as he was over the day's events.

Later in the afternoon, the 3rd Pursuiter, increasingly anxious to get back to his squadron, decided to make a trip over to Rosales, where he knew he could get gas and oil and perhaps some information. The American colonel in charge of the division, however, did not see why Powell should be in such a hurry and refused to help in providing him transportation to Rosales. "One plane or pilot more or less won't make any difference," he argued. But one of the lieutenants was of a different mind and helped Powell commandeer a car in Lingayen town for the short trip to Rosales.

South of Iba Field, Don Steele of B Flight and Gordon Benson of A Flight walked to a camp of the 31st Infantry Regiment near San Marcelino after leaving their fuelless P-40s in the riverbed south of the town. But their request for gas or transportation fell on deaf ears; the officer in charge of the camp told them that he was "too busy to bother with Air Corps." Setting out on foot again, the two hungry and frustrated aviators now saw a typical Filipino truck rattling along the provincial road and decided to commandeer it. Stopping the driver, they pulled out their .45s and told the terrified native they would shoot him on the spot if he did not drive them to Olongapo, the American naval base some twenty miles south of San Marcelino. In Olongapo, they located a drum of gasoline and loaded it for the return trip to their P-40Es but then decided to wait until the morning before setting out again. The post commander had invited them to stay at his quarters, where they were "fed and plied with liquor." Navy hospitality was certainly superior to that of the army. They also finally got a radio message through to Thorne, advising him where they were.

2 At Clark Field, where Randy Keator and Joe Moore had landed in early afternoon, fuel dumps and planes were burning, and heavy smoke lay over the entire field. Keator thought there was not a square yard that had not been raked with cannon or machine gun fire. Everyone he saw seemed dazed from the shock of the bombing and strafing. Moore assembled his surviving officers and men at the 20th Pursuit's operations area for a check on casualties. The operations shack had been burned down, and all the automobiles parked nearby had been destroyed by machine gun fire and flames, but no one who had taken refuge in the two L-shaped trenches had been killed or even injured, though several bombs had hit

within fifty feet of them. But out on the field, it was a different story. All of the squadron's twenty-three P-40Bs — except the three that had gotten airborne — had been destroyed or made inoperative by the attack. Those that had not been hit by the bombs had been set ablaze by the strafers.

Moore now had the gruesome job of identifying the bodies of the pilots killed in the squadron's takeoff attempt. They were strung out on a line near their wrecked aircraft. The distraught CO confirmed the charred remains of one as Max Louk; also there were the bodies of Jesse Luker, Tod Mulcahy, and Jim Drake. With three others badly burned — Armstrong, Iversen, and Halverson — Moore's Section 1 of eighteen pilots had suffered 40 percent pilot casualties. Among the other officers of the squadron there had been only one casualty; Lloyd Stinson in Charley Sneed's Section 2 had been only slightly wounded. Of the squadron's enlisted men, five were dead and six were wounded, some 7 percent of the total of 163.[2] Without the shelter provided by the L-shaped trenches, the losses among the men and the officers on the ground that day would have been much higher.

Parker Gies, who had barely escaped with his life, was awed by the accuracy of the Japanese bombing. Not one of the bombs had hit more than two hundred feet outside any border of the field.[3] And the pilots had been told that the Japanese "couldn't hit their hats." Gies wondered if they had stolen the U.S. Army Air Corps' vaunted Norden bombsight or perfected a better one. And what about the reports of the ineptitude of their fighter pilots and the inferior equipment they flew? Moore and Keator put an end to such stories that afternoon as they described their hair-raising experiences in combat with the Zeros.

Before, it had been unthinkable for them to run away from a dogfight. They had been trained to lock horns and the best man get on the other's tail. But with tracer fire streaming past their cockpits in a seemingly solid wall, Moore and Keator had quickly learned to adopt the best method of combat with Zeros: dive, then turn around and come back.

The squadron's wounded had earlier been taken to the hospital at Fort Stotsenburg, adjacent to Clark Field. Badly burned, Fred Armstrong was now waiting his turn in the operating room. Elsewhere in the hospital, a doctor had removed a bomb splinter from Lloyd Stinson's foot. Much against Stinson's wishes, the doctor was holding him at the hospital because of the wound, minor as it was.

In the squadron's operations area, most of the personnel of the 20th Pursuit were making preparations for evacuating Clark Field. Late that afternoon, Joe Moore led his dispirited charges, carrying blankets, web belt equipment, and gas masks, to a well-covered area in the jungle some four miles south of the field, where they were to establish a base camp. A few men were left behind to service and rearm any P-40s that should come into Clark later that day.

Over at the operations area of the 24th Pursuit Group's Headquarters Squadron, 1st Lt. Benny Putnam had assembled the 230 men under his command and was moving them to a new site, a bivouac area about three miles from Clark. On the way, Pfc Jesse White and a few others stopped by an abandoned barracks to pick up a change of clothes and take a shower. Unexpectedly, Putnam burst into the shower area and screamed at them to get out—the Japanese could be back any minute. At that moment, however, the Japanese did not worry White as much as the filth on his body; he had rolled into a sewer during the bombing attack and had wondered when he would ever be able to wash himself.

3 Still in a state of shock from banging his head on the tail of his P-40 after bailing out, Herb Ellis was walking back toward Clark Field when he was picked up by a soldier driving a vehicle. Delivered to the base operations building on the line, Ellis searched for an officer for information. He finally located one, a major whom he did not know, but who evidently was Maj. Lee Johnson, adjutant general of Clark Field. As Ellis recalled years later: "He was very busy with a whole desk full of papers. He let me cool my heels. Finally, he looked up and asked me what I wanted. For some unknown reason, he was very surly. I told him who I was and that I had been shot down and was looking for the headquarters of the 24th Pursuit Group. He paused for a long time. Then he said, 'There ain't no more 24th Pursuit Group,' and returned to his paper work. I had obviously been dismissed." Leaving the building, Ellis wandered off, trying to find someone he knew. From time to time, he ran into a few people at the nearly deserted base, but they had never heard of the 24th Pursuit Group.

Clark Field was a shambles. Nearly everything that could burn had either done so or was still burning. The corrugated iron hangars were slightly pumpkin-shaped now. Bombs had penetrated the roofs of the hangars and detonated on contact with the concrete floors, tearing thousands of small holes in the corrugated iron. From the inside, the hangars look to Ellis "like planetariums with star-studded skies." Not yet inured to "gutted towns and destroyed equipment," Ellis was appalled at the destruction.

Continuing his wanderings, Ellis stumbled onto an antiaircraft machine gun platoon. The sergeant in charge saw to it that Ellis got something to eat and drink. After the meal, the two talked and Ellis told the sergeant that he had served with the 62nd Coast Artillery (Anti-Aircraft) and was in fact a master gunner of artillery. Hearing this, the sergeant informed Ellis that the second lieutenant in charge of his platoon had been hit during the bombing of Clark and suggested that Ellis take his place as platoon commander. Since Ellis was completely unattached at the moment, he accepted the offer.

Aerial view of Clark Field in August, 1941. *Courtesy Dorothy W. Tilforth*

4 When Fred Roberts reached the shore at Iba about 1:15 P.M. after being rescued from his ditched P-40E in the water, a scene of panic and chaos greeted him. The barracks building and the gas truck were on fire. The field was completely pockmarked with bomb craters. From the adjacent barrio, also on fire, came the shrieks of wounded and terrified Filipinos and the squeals of their pigs. Realizing that he was the ranking officer on the field, Roberts attempted to take charge of the situation as best he could under the circumstances.

Medics from the 3rd Pursuit Squadron and other men were already attending to the wounded under the supervision of the squadron's medical officer, Lt. Frank Lloyd Richardson. The bespectacled doctor was working heroically to save the wounded, but with practically no medical supplies (the squadron dispensary had been destroyed in the attack), it was a tough job. Afterward, the wounded were taken to the small provincial hospital in Iba town, an empty building with no staff or medicine, where they were spread out on the floor to await transportation to Sternberg Hospital in Manila.

Some six to eight of the squadron's dead had also been taken to the hospital building. Roberts now began the task of making up a list of the casualties. The distressing job of identifying the dead was made difficult by the fact that many of the officers and men were not wearing their dogtags, and their bodies had been destroyed beyond the possibility of positive identification.

At the coconut grove near S. Sgt. "Woody" McBride's machine gun emplacement, Richardson had tried to save 2nd Lt. Shelton Avant, but the wounded man had lost too much blood. Already dead on the field were Lts. "Casa" O'Connell, Andy Webb, and "Hawk" Root. Of the squadron's 148 enlisted men, Roberts determined that 11 had been killed in the attack.[4]

First Lt. Jim Donegan, from Paterson, New Jersey, one of the senior pilots of the squadron, had an amazing escape from death. During the whole attack he was in the little crow's nest that served as the squadron's radio tower, twenty feet above the ground. Although he had been hit several times by the strafers, including receiving a bullet through the ankle, he escaped mortal injury. Three other officers—Bart Passanante, John Hylton, and Jim Boone—had also been wounded, albeit under less dramatic circumstances.[5]

Early that afternoon reports of Japanese landings just off the coast began to circulate among the demoralized men of the squadron. Terrified, most of those who could manage to walk took off for the jungle behind Iba. No one was in charge of them; the squadron's first sergeant was so panic-stricken he could not give an order or even talk. By the time darkness enveloped the area, with no sign of a Japanese landing, the men began to regain their composure and returned to the field.

Roberts had commandeered a Philippine bus in Iba town, and Richardson was loading the injured on it for evacuation to Manila's Sternberg Hospital. To make enough room for all the wounded men as well as some Iba natives who had also been hurt during the attack, the men had ripped out the seats. Packed together on the floor of the open-sided bus, they now set out to the south on what would prove a rough and tiring journey by way of San Marcelino.

While the wounded were being loaded on the bus, an enlisted man had run up to Glenn Cave and the men near him and excitedly announced that the Japanese were landing off the coast of Iba. A fresh sense of panic came over Cave's group. The young officer spontaneously decided to get off the coast as fast as possible and began rounding up men to join him for a hike to Clark Field across the Zambales Mountains to the east. With no food, proper clothes, equipment, or information on conditions, Cave and twenty-nine enlisted men started out in darkness along the trail leading to the mountains.

In the meantime, Roberts was organizing the rest of the squadron's personnel for evacuation to Manila on other commandeered vehicles. It was midnight before the little convoy proceeded out of Iba and headed south over the same route that the bus of wounded had taken earlier in the day.

5 At Nichols Field at 5:30 P.M., orders had gone out for the 17th and 21st pursuit squadrons to move their aircraft to Clark Field. The FEAF brass had figured that Nichols would be hit by the Japanese next, probably that night, and they did not want to lose any more of their P-40s. "Bud" Sprague, the operations officer of the 5th Interceptor Command at nearby Nielson Field, had flown a reconnaissance mission to Clark at 4:30 and reported to FEAF Headquarters that it would still be possible to land light planes on the field there.

Immediately after the order was received, the pilots of the two squadrons began taking off, one by one; there was to be no formation on this mass exodus. Leading the group of thirty-six P-40s were the eighteen of the 21st Pursuit, with the eighteen of the 17th Pursuit bringing up the rear. Three of the 17th's twenty-one P-40Es required minor repairs after the two patrols of the day and remained behind with their pilots: Obert, Blanton, and Kruzel. Ed Dyess also left behind a number of the 21st's P-40Es that were out of commission, including those of Cole, Clark, and May, whose engines had been throwing oil while over Clark Field, as well as Grashio's, which had been shot up beyond repair.

As the 21st Pursuit pilots approached Clark Field in the fading light of late afternoon, they saw the towering pillars of smoke rising from the base and wondered how they were going to be able to land. Everything in sight was burning, and the whole field was covered with wrecked aircraft and bomb craters. But the few men on the ground had marked the holes for them, and Dyess spotted an auxiliary strip intact enough to land on, though it appeared to the 21st's CO as "little better than a country road."[6] When Dyess's P-40E touched down and rolled to a halt, he stirred up blinding clouds of dust. The cogan grass cover of the strip had been burned off during the attack, leaving the soft, dry surface exposed. For safety's sake, the pilots of the 21st took several minutes each before attempting to land in order to allow the dust to settle somewhat before coming in.

Overhead, Buzz Wagner and his 17th Pursuit pilots were getting restless as they waited their turn to land. It was beginning to get dark. Figuring it would be a long time before his squadron would be able to land with the procedures being followed, Wagner radioed his squadron mates and told them to follow him to Del Carmen Field. On arrival at Del Carmen, the 17th's pilots found that landing conditions there were no better than at Clark; the field was covered with several inches of pure dust. As at Clark, the pilots had to come in one at a time and allow two to three minutes between landings for the dust to settle. Only one of the 17th's pilots was missing—John Posten. He had not picked up Wagner's radio call (his radio was malfunctioning) and had inadvertently landed with Dyess's squadron at Clark.

When the 17th Pursuiters parked their P-40Es and climbed out, they were roundly greeted by the pilots of the 34th Pursuit based there. Also on the field was Edwin Gilmore of the 20th Pursuit, who had landed at Del Carmen in the early afternoon after his narrow escape from the Zeros over Clark.

When Sam Grashio climbed out of his P-40E after landing at Clark, he was struck with how deserted everything appeared to be at the base. Near a pile of smoking debris, he saw something that made him feel sick —a helmet with a hole in it and a piece of bone in the hole. Wandering over the field, Posten was equally disturbed at the sight: "automobiles, trucks, and planes wrecked and burning all over the place." Some of the dead were still lying where they had fallen, including a whole B-17 crew next to its burning plane. Every few minutes, Posten jumped at the sound of exploding ammunition.

Searching for men to service their P-40Es, the pilots of the 21st Pursuit located an old master sergeant who after a while was able to round up enough men for the job. Then the 21st Pursuiters walked over to the hangar of 24th Group operations. But no one except a lone soldier was there; they were told that group operations had moved into a jungle location near the field. When they finally found the new operations area and reported in to Major Grover, they were given their orders: be ready early next morning to provide cover for B-17s that would be coming up from Del Monte on Mindanao.

6 Up at Rosales, the awaited orders from FEAF Headquarters—in a telegram—had finally arrived as the sun was setting. Hank Thorne was directed to transfer the four flyable P-40s on the field to Nichols without delay. Evidently the FEAF brass had changed their minds about the likelihood of Nichols being hit next by the Japanese. After turning over responsibilities for activities at Rosales to Frank Neri, whose plane was unflyable, Thorne took off right after dark with Bob Hanson, Andy Krieger, and Howard Hardegree. Left behind with Neri were two other 3rd Pursuiters who were to fly to Nichols early the next morning.[7]

When the quartet arrived over Nichols, they were unable to contact the control tower to ask for field, runway, or obstruction lights to be turned on. Since they all knew Nichols Field very well, they decided to try to land without any field lights. Lining up on the single narrow runway left open, they headed in. Thorne and Hanson were unable to get their ships' landing lights on and approached in pitch darkness. As he touched down, Hanson ground-looped, damaging his P-40E's left wing and propeller. The others touched down safely and taxied over to the hangar, where they turned their planes over to ground crew members of the 17th Pursuit for servicing and dispersal.

As soon as he got to a telephone at Nichols, Thorne called FEAF Headquarters at nearby Nielson to report in. Colonel George wanted to know what losses the 3rd Pursuit had suffered, but Thorne had only an incomplete picture, having been separated from most of his pilots this fateful day. To Colonel George's repeated question about the state of Iba as an operational field, Thorne explained, "You might as well try to land in a quarry."

After the call, Thorne checked in with Major Maverick, a former CO of the 3rd Pursuit and now CO of the 20th Air Base Group at Nichols. Maverick was delighted to see Thorne; he had believed the entire 3rd Pursuit had been wiped out, from the reports he had received. Thorne was also now reunited with Ray Gehrig and Ed Woolery of his B Flight, who had landed separately that afternoon at Nichols. Gehrig had come into Nichols with only one gallon of gas left after barely escaping from Iba and flying over Clark in a vain hope of landing there. Woolery told Thorne that he had buzzed Rosales that afternoon after Neri had landed there.

Thorne and the others tried to piece together what had happened to the eighteen pilots of the squadron who had taken off from Iba that morning. It was a difficult task, since all three flights had become splintered during the day's ordeal. In Woolery's B Flight, Woolery knew that "Hawk" Root, Gehrig's wingman, had been killed in attempting to land at Iba, and Daniel had landed at Rosales. As for Daniel's leader, Don Steele, he had phoned Thorne from Olongapo that he and "Squirrely" Benson, in Thorne's A Flight, were all right. But Vern Ireland in A Flight had been reported as dead by Clark Field; he had been shot down and killed when he crashed into nearby Mount Arayat. In Herb Ellis's C Flight there were reports from Clark that Ellis himself had been shot down but had bailed out safely and that George Ellstrom had been killed in his chute. But there was no news about Bill Powell, Fred Roberts, or "Chubby" Allen.

It would be days before Thorne got the final tally of losses of pilots and aircraft of his 3rd Pursuit. Ireland, Root, and Ellstrom had been killed, but none of the other fifteen pilots up that day had been killed or wounded, despite stories that the 3rd Pursuit had been wiped out. However, thirteen of the squadron's twenty-four P-40Es were lost, including five of the six in C Flight.[8]

About 8:30 that night, Maverick, Thorne, and the other 3rd Pursuiters headed over to Nichols Field Post Exchange for some supper. Thorne and his pilots had eaten nothing since those late morning sandwiches at Iba. A half hour later, just beginning their meal, they heard a "terrific blast" outside the PX. Thorne and Woolery instantly dived to the floor. Finding themselves completely alone, the others having fled out of the building, they picked themselves up, ran outside, then dived headlong into a ditch. There they crouched in the mud, waiting for the next bombs to hit. But it was quiet. A few minutes later, they heard a group of soldiers running along the road above them.

Climbing back up to the road, Thorne and Woolery asked the next passerby if the bombing was over. They were told that there had been no bombing; the noise they heard was the Nichols Field saluting cannon, which was now serving as the air raid warning for the field. Feeling very sheepish, Thorne and Woolery walked to Thorne's house near Nichols Field, where Thorne's Filipino houseboy prepared a plate of sandwiches for them.

7 Back at Rosales, Bill Powell had arrived from Lingayen after dark in his commandeered car on his mission to get gas for his P-40 on the beach at Lingayen. There he met Frank Neri and the other two pilots who had been left behind by Thorne. Neri told Powell that the others would be flying out of Rosales for Nichols early the next morning. Figuring the skies would be full of Japanese the next day, Powell told Neri he would be back before daylight to join them; it would be too risky to fly alone. After Neri put a truck at his disposal, loaded with two fifty-five gallon drums of aviation gas and cans of oil, Powell set out for the forty-mile return trip to Lingayen.

8 On the night of the first day of war in the Philippines, the officers and men of the 24th Pursuit Group were trying to sleep under rude circumstances, far from their familiar quarters. The only exception was the personnel of the 34th Pursuit, still at their Del Carmen base.

While the 34th Pursuit was relatively comfortable, their unexpected guests, the pilots of the 17th Pursuit, were obliged to spend the night in a gully at the site of the Del Carmen airfield after eating a couple of hot dogs for dinner. For John Brownewell, it was "probably the most uncomfortable night of my life, under a big, heavy engine cover on a night that for the Philippines was unusually cold."

At Clark, the pilots of the 21st Pursuit had finished a cold meal of pork, beans, bread, blackberry jam, and coffee before spreading themselves out on the ground in the jungle back of the field in the hope of getting some sleep before their early morning mission.

Four miles south of Clark, the pilots and most of the enlisted men of the 20th Pursuit, lying down in some underbrush on both sides of a dirt road, their blankets pulled over themselves, were trying to sleep too. But sleep would not come to Randy Keator; he was still thinking about the two or three men he had killed that day. Even though they were Japanese, it still bothered him.

At Nichols Field, the enlisted men of the 17th Pursuit had evacuated their new barracks at 6:00 P.M. as earlier ordered. They had taken only a few clothes items and toilet articles with them to their designated sleeping area, the gun positions surrounding the field. One who had not gone was T. Sgt. Bill "Cowboy" Wright. He had been asked by the line chief of the squadron to stay in the hangar area for the night. Looking at the concrete runway next to the hangars with the moon shining down on it, Wright figured that it was not the best place to be if the Japanese came in for a night raid. With T. Sgt. Carlton Edsall, he took off for about a mile and a half to the southeast of the field to bed down on the ground for the night.

No one was trying to sleep at Iba; it was completely deserted. On the bumpy road from Iba to Manila, the wounded of the 3rd Pursuit were trying to sleep on the floor of their commandeered bus, being driven under blackout conditions. Far behind the bus, Fred Roberts's group would be reaching San Marcelino, only 35 miles into the 135-mile trip to its Nichols Field destination, by about 2:00 A.M. In worse shape was Glenn Cave's group, already exhausted in its effort to reach Clark Field by foot—35 miles distant from Iba as the crow flies—on ill-marked trails and over the Zambales Mountains.

Also out on the road this night was Bill Powell. In defiance of the total blackout then in force, he was driving his truck with the lights on. Several times he had nearly been shot as he crossed bridges and went through towns and barrios where patrols were enforcing the blackout. Finally, at about 11:00 P.M., he arrived back at Lingayen, his precious cargo of gas and oil intact.

Part Three
LAST DAYS ON LUZON

MacArthur's Far East Air Force had suffered a fatal blow on December 8. At Clark, half of his force of thirty-five B-17s were now burning wreckage, alongside the twisted remains of twenty P-40 pursuits. At Iba, the vital radar station had been destroyed, along with seven P-40s caught on the field. Six others had been shot down or damaged beyond repair. Of MacArthur's ninety-two operational P-40s at day's start, only fifty-eight remained flyable after the two-pronged attack. His air warning capability shattered, his interceptor and bomber forces deeply pared back, Brereton would no longer need to think about offensive operations against Japanese bases on Formosa. Just deploying his depleted resources for the defense of Luzon would prove challenge enough for his command.

Scarcely fourteen hours after their devastating aerial attack, which was the overture to the Philippines campaign, the Japanese Naval Air Force was back again, this time over the Manila area. As the personnel of Nichols Field tried to catch some sleep after a false alarm two hours earlier, the alarm went off again at 3:15 A.M. on December 9, and minutes later seven twin-engine "Nell" bombers began unloading on the base. The damage to facilities and loss of life were not great, but USAFFE forces now knew they were in for a continuous aerial onslaught by their relentless foe. All during December 9, MacArthur's men nervously awaited a second major attack from the air, but no Japanese aircraft made an appearance this day; unknown to the defenders, heavy fog over the Formosan airfields had forced the Japanese to cancel the day's ambitious plans.

By early the next morning, bad news from another direction was relayed to MacArthur: the Japanese were landing

troops on northern Luzon, at Aparri and Vigan. The two landing parties were small, however, and were believed to be a
feint to lure USAFFE into dispersing its forces prior to a main
landing. Consequently, MacArthur decided not to offer ground
opposition, though he mounted aerial attacks, which proved
of limited effectiveness.

There was nothing minor about the force from the air that
descended on the Manila and Del Carmen areas between 12:45
and 1:00 P.M. that day. In two attack groups, the Japanese sent
fifty-two Zeros and eighty-one "Betty" and "Nell" bombers to
wipe out Nichols and Del Carmen fields as well as the Cavite
Navy Yard, just south of Manila. In the Manila area, antiaircraft fire could not reach the high-flying bombers, and the defending P-40s were caught flying low by the Zeros, while the
P-35As at Del Carmen were parked like sitting ducks on the
ground. When the Japanese headed back to Formosa, they left
Cavite in shambles and a decimated 24th Pursuit Group.

Later that day, MacArthur radioed the War Department in
Washington that "the enemy has an overwhelming preponder-
ance of air strength. If he continues his thrust, he cannot fail
to reduce our air force to destruction through attrition."

Two days later, on December 12, Japanese troops landed
again on Luzon, this time at Legaspi on the southern tip of
the island. Once again, the landing party was small—about
twenty-five hundred men—and met only light opposition.

By the time of the Legaspi landing, MacArthur had reached
a painful decision. With no reconnaissance capability left
from his 2nd Observation Squadron, whose aircraft had been
destroyed during the first days of the campaign, he was left
with no other option than to use his dwindling pursuit force
exclusively in that role. He was sensitive to the likely adverse
effect on his pilots' morale, but reconnaissance to report Japanese ground movements on Luzon was vitally required. Reluctantly, he informed the War Department of his decision to conserve his P-40s for reconnaissance, reporting, "Pilots have been
ordered to avoid direct combat."

MacArthur needed aerial reinforcements immediately. Aircraft carriers would be the most expeditious means by which
to bring the two hundred pursuit aircraft and fifty dive-bombers
they required, according to Far East Air Force chief Brereton.
In response to MacArthur's radiograms of December 13 and
14 to this effect, the War Department underlined the adverse
consequences on transportation capabilities occasioned by

the heavy naval losses but promised to rush the reinforcements by an unmentioned means.

One week later, MacArthur was informed that pursuit and dive-bombers on their way to Australia, including a contingent originally shipped to the Philippines before war's outbreak and subsequently diverted to Australia, were to be transferred to him. Brereton was counting on their arrival around the first week of January. But the War Department was letting the question of how to get them to the Philippines from Australia depend on strategic conditions in the area.

MacArthur was soon preoccupied with the most serious threat yet to his command: a force of over forty-three thousand Japanese troops landed in Lingayen Gulf the early morning of December 22 from some eighty transports. This was clearly the main show. Against ineffective resistance, the Japanese during the next two days made rapid advances down Luzon, reaching just north of the Agno River, some fifteen miles south of Lingayen Gulf.

And then on the morning of December 24, news of yet another landing, this one at three points along Lamon Bay, only sixty miles southwest of Manila, reached MacArthur's command. The Japanese plan was obviously to attack Manila from the north and the south, with the seven-thousand-man force in the south linking up with the Lingayen group. Against the dispersed USAFFE forces in the south, the Japanese once again made rapid advances following a virtually unopposed landing.

A day before the Lamon Bay landings, MacArthur decided that in view of the failure of his forces to hold the Japanese at the Lingayen beaches and of the enemy's rapid advances, he would have to put War Plan Orange-3 into effect. This defensive prewar plan, rejected by MacArthur when he had taken command of USAFFE in July, 1941, called for the withdrawal of American and Filipino forces from Luzon into Bataan, the small peninsula appendage of southwestern Luzon. MacArthur's faith in the fighting ability of his Filipino forces had proven misplaced.

On the evening of December 23 and morning of December 24, the units of MacArthur's command were notified that "WPO-3 is in effect." Then at 11:00 A.M. on December 24, MacArthur announced the decision to his headquarters staff that they were to evacuate to the fortified island of Corregidor in Manila Bay with him that evening. In a meeting that day with Brereton, MacArthur accepted his air chief's request of the day

before to move the headquarters of the Far East Air Force south
to Java in the Dutch East Indies, where he would set up an
advanced operations base from which he would support defense of the Philippines, including the securing of bases on
Mindanao. Brereton's remaining operational units were to join
the general evacuation into Bataan.

MacArthur's ground forces in northern and southern Luzon
were to withdraw in phased stages. The South Luzon Force,
under Maj. Gen. George Parker, would shift west and north
along successive defense lines through Manila and cross the
Calumpit Bridge leading into Bataan by January 8. Lt. Gen.
Jonathan Wainwright's North Luzon Force was to move south
into five delaying positions, the distance between which could
be covered in one night's march each, beginning at D-1, ten
miles south of Lingayen Bay, and ending at D-5, just north of
Clark Field. It would hold at D-5 until Parker's forces had been
able to slip behind the northern force into San Fernando and
thence into Bataan.

On the evening of December 24, the withdrawal of ground
forces began and continued all through the night. The movements were generally orderly and well organized. But for the
officers and men of the squadrons of the Far East Air Force,
who were not involved in the defensive holding operations and
who had simply been ordered, "Go to Bataan," it was chaos.
With Brereton no longer in command and a confused leadership situation among the remaining brass of the FEAF, individual units assembled their personnel and tried to make their
way into Bataan as best they could.

At Nichols Field, air force units left so fast that great quan-
tities of equipment and other matériel were left behind. The
air force detachment at San Marcelino, on the west coast of
Luzon, was so panicked when it was told it had twenty-four
hours to leave that it cleared out in seventeen minutes instead,
leaving everything behind, including food. At Clark Field, the
orders to move out were given by excited officers, "who made
it sound as if the Japanese were just down the road" instead
of a good fifty-five miles to the north.

With the departure south of the remaining B-17s days earlier, the Far East Air Force was now reduced to the status of
an aerial reconnaissance unit in support of Bataan ground operations. On Christmas Day, MacArthur's expectations of
aerial reinforcements to upgrade the rump outfit to an effec-

tive combat force were thrown into doubt with word from the War Department that plans for ferrying P-40s in Australia to the Philippines were "jeopardized": the relentless Japanese advance southward was now threatening the stepping-stone airfields on Borneo in the Dutch East Indies that the short-ranged pursuit required for refueling purposes.

11. "WE WERE AFRAID TO STAY VERY LONG IN ONE SPOT"

1 On the beach at Lingayen, Bill Powell was filling the tanks of his P-40 late in the evening of December 8 with the gas he had brought back from Rosales. By 1:00 A.M., the plane was gassed and ready to go. Still keyed up from the events of the past twenty-four hours, Powell had decided to take advantage of the excellent visibility afforded by the bright moon and fly immediately to Rosales to join his mates there, instead of waiting until early morning.

As Powell warmed up his ship, he noticed that his hydraulic pressure was low and that he could not maintain pressure in the system. However, since his tail wheel was still down, he concluded that he had a bullet nick in a line and was losing pressure but could take off and get down again OK. As the P-40 started rolling for the takeoff, the sandy field was causing a bad drag on the wheels. Powell began to wonder whether he would be able to get up enough speed to lift off the short field.

"Well, the problem was definitely settled for me a moment later," Powell recorded in his wartime diary, "I was up to 80 miles an hour and beginning to bounce a little in the sand when I hit a soft, sandy chuckhole with my right wheel and it politely and disastrously folded up. The results were obvious. I slid down the rest of the field on my belly, . . . ending up in a slight ditch at the side of the field, very much startled and very much shaken but otherwise unhurt except in feelings and pride. I was pretty mad and disgruntled because I wanted so much to fly my plane in undamaged and ready to get back in the fight."

Fearing fire, Powell hurriedly climbed out of his wrecked plane. While surveying the damage, he was greeted by his lieutenant friend of the previous day, who had shown up in a car. "He was surprised and I even suspect a little disappointed in not being a rescuing hero. However, he was pretty glad to see me alive after tearing up the field in the manner I did." As the two young officers were discussing the situation, an orderly from the colonel came rushing up with an order to "put that damned plane back where I got it."

A survey of the P-40's condition indicated that the six .50-caliber guns, the radio, and 1,400 rounds of ammunition were undamaged. Powell immediately offered the whole lot to his friend to make use of as he so desired. "I knew they could use the guns in the beach defense, and the radio equipment was better than any they had—just a field set."

The reaction of the colonel to the offer was predictable. He ordered the lieutenant "to leave it where it was, he didn't need any damn Air Corps equipment to run his war!" Fed up with the whole business, Powell accompanied his friend back to the bunk area and turned in for the rest of the night.

2 Over at Clark Field, the sleep of the pilots of the 20th and 21st pursuit squadrons was interrupted around 2:00 A.M. by the unsynchronized drone, a sort of "on and off" pulsating sound, of the engines of enemy bombers overhead. Hearing them heading south in the direction of Manila, Randy Keator knew they were going to hit Nichols Field, as yet untouched by the Japanese pilots.

Fifteen miles south, at Del Carmen, Buzz Wagner had received orders from Major Grover at Clark Field to get a six-ship flight up immediately to intercept the Japanese. With some skepticism about the feasibility of the mission (the 17th had practiced night interceptions only a few times in early December), Wagner gave the job to Willie Feallock. After rounding up the five pilots he wanted to participate in the interception with him, Feallock informed them of the assignment. Each was to taxi up to the takeoff point on the field, line himself up on the light at the end of the runway, and take off individually, allowing time for the dust stirred up by the preceding plane to settle. One by one, Feallock, followed by his wingman, 41-D newie Jim Rowland, then element leader Walt Coss roared down the field and lifted off safely.

Coss's wingman, Larry Lodin, prepared for takeoff in the number 4 spot. He was still under nervous strain; he had returned to Nichols after taking off for Clark with the rest of the squadron the afternoon before, suffering from a case of war jitters.[1] Straining to pick up the light to serve as his guide for lining up his P-40 for the takeoff roll, Lodin now spotted it; unknown to him, however, he was lining up on the wing light of the P-40 of Red Sheppard, who was waiting to the left in front of Lodin at the edge of the runway to turn into the strip and take off behind him. In his anxiety, Lodin had not allowed enough time for the cloud of dust stirred up by Coss to settle before attempting to take off. Veering some 30 degrees to the left in its takeoff roll, Lodin's P-40 collided with the wing of Sheppard's ship in the taxiway, somersaulted, grazed the P-40 of

Maurice Hughett, waiting behind Sheppard for takeoff, and immediately caught fire.

Observing the ill-fated takeoff at the field, Lodin's housemate Bill Rowe and several others from the 17th and 34th pursuit squadrons rushed over to the accident site to try to pull Lodin from the flaming wreckage, but it was no use: the intensity of the heat and the exploding ammunition from Lodin's guns made it impossible to get near. The 17th had suffered its first World War II casualty.

Overhead, Feallock, Rowland, and Coss, flying without lights of any kind, soon became separated from each other. Alone in the dark over central Luzon, they spent several hours milling about, searching in vain for the Japanese bombers. Then, their fuel supply dwindling, they headed back to Del Carmen. But now they faced the problem of getting their planes down in the darkness. Their only guide was the tiny runway lights that had war hoods on them, making it virtually impossible to see them unless the pilots were below 300 feet. After descending to low altitude, they picked up the slits of light from the field in making their landing approach and held their P-40s in a pronounced skid to keep the lights in view. Despite the difficulty, all three managed to get down safely.

3 At Nichols Field, the air raid siren had gone off around 1:30 A.M. with the first warning of the approaching Japanese, and all personnel had gone to their posts. But a half hour later, the "all clear" sounded, and they all went back to bed. Another false alarm!

Hank Thorne and the other pilots of the 3rd Pursuit had been in bed only about forty-five minutes when the air raid siren went off again. This time everyone at the base could hear the droning of the engines of the aircraft coming from the west. Then at 3:15 A.M., the bombs started to hit Nichols.

In response to the Nichols Field air raid warning cannon, Thorne "leaped out of bed, grabbed my tin hat, pistol belt, gas mask, and tore out the door, dived across the road and skidded to a stop on my tummy in a little ditch." But when Capt. Dick Fellows and Lt. Jack Batchelor, who had also been in his house, kept going past him, Thorne got up and ran after them, then collided with a tennis backstop of chicken wire. "I was so confused that I backed up about ten feet and charged full tilt at it again. After carefully running around one end of the backstop, I joined Dick and Jack and we ran on up toward the north end of the field," he recalled six years later in a report of his Philippine experiences.

Back at Nichols, men of the 27th Materiel Squadron were firing their .30-caliber Lewis machine guns at the high-flying Japanese from seven emplacements scattered around the perimeter of the field. Their tracers cut through the night sky "like Roman candles" in a beautiful display, but to absolutely no effect: at over 16,000 feet, the Japanese were out of range.

The first string of 132-pound bombs crashed into the veterinary hospital, one corner of the Bachelor Officers Quarters (BOQ), and a corner of the number 4 hangar at Nichols. Fire burst out in the quarters and the hangar. Andy Krieger and others were pressed into service to help the fire department fight the blazes.

Two P-40s had taken off from Nichols at 3:30 to try to intercept the Japanese bombers but failed to make contact. As they returned to the field, one of the 27th Materiel Squadron's Lewis machine gun operators opened up on them. The firing continued until the 27th's CO rushed over to the gun emplacement and put a stop to it.

After the night raid, Nichols Field officers assessed the extent of the damage. Two officers in the BOQ, as well as a private, had been killed, and fifteen men had been wounded. Number 4 hangar was destroyed, and one B-18 and an O-52 damaged. Despite the relatively light losses, the nerves of all at Nichols were on edge from this initial experience of being bombed and the lack of sleep.

4 It was still dark at Clark Field when Major Grover and Ed Dyess went around waking up the pilots of Dyess's 21st Pursuit as they lay stretched out on the ground.[2] Grover briefed them on their mission: to cover the expected landing of B-17s heading up from Del Monte base on Mindanao and their takeoffs for an attack on Formosa. The FEAF brass were taking no chances of their precious B-17s being hit on the ground again.

Concerned about the dusty conditions on the field, Dyess instructed his pilots on the procedures to be followed on takeoffs. They were to watch him carefully when he took off in the lead and follow his route exactly after having taxied into position, lined themselves up properly, and allowed a few minutes for the dust to settle. After Dyess made a perfect takeoff, his wingman, followed by Sam Grashio in third position, lined themselves up correctly, waited for the dust to clear, then lifted off the field without incident.

In fourth position, Bob Clark pressed hard on his brakes and added power to full throttle, then released the brakes and began his takeoff roll —but too soon; the dust stirred up by Grashio's P-40 had not yet settled. Disoriented in the dark and dust, he was heading off the edge of the runway without realizing it.

Dyess overhead and the pilots behind Clark saw what was happening and yelled frantically to Clark over their radios, but to no avail. Continuing on his disastrous course, he crashed into a B-17 parked off to the side of the field. As the P-40E hit the big bomber, "there was a sudden flash of light, a violent explosion, and a hail of bullets all over the area as flaming gasoline from the B-17's ruptured tanks set off the six loaded .50-caliber guns." Clark had no chance of surviving the conflagration.

Next in line for takeoff, John Posten, still flying with the 21st Pursuit, was shaken by the "horrible sight." Lining himself up carefully after the dust had settled, he stayed clear of the site of Clark's fatal accident as he thundered down the field and lifted off.

Even when they carefully followed Dyess's instructions, the 21st's pilots found they were taking off under terrifying conditions. As soon as his P-40 started moving down the field, Charley Burris in sixth position behind Posten realized that he was making a blind takeoff. "There was no horizon at all, just blackness all around me, and I was committed to the takeoff," he recalled years later. When he happened to look straight up and saw stars, he immediately understood the situation—the dust stirred up by Posten's ship was totally obscuring his view. Using a star as his guide, he made the takeoff looking almost straight up. As he cleared the field, he grazed the treetops.

Further back, Jack Donalson also took off blind, without even the benefit of a star to guide him. Applying full throttle, he gunned his P-40 down the strip "without even the slightest idea where I would end up." He was lucky and did not hit anything.

Less fortunate were three other 21st Pursuiters. L. A. Coleman taxied into a bomb crater and wiped out his P-40. Johnny McCown managed to take off successfully, but his brand new Allison engine conked out at 100 feet; the subsequent crash into trees tore his P-40 apart, but he escaped without serious injury. Another pilot wrecked his ship when he got off course in the takeoff and struck a field light.[3]

Sam Grashio almost met a fate similar to McCown's. After getting airborne and reaching 7,000 feet, his engine suddenly started cutting in and out and losing power. As his P-40 continued to lose altitude, Grashio anxiously tried to identify the problem and keep his composure. Gradually, he regained control of his ship, though it could not maintain flying speed. He would have to come in and try to land back at Clark. He knew there was a certain identification procedure for landing at Clark, but this was an emergency situation. Coming in from an unexpected direction, he was now fired on by the 200th Coast Artillery gunners protecting the base. Even when he wagged his wings and put his wheels down, they continued to shoot at the excited pilot. None scored a hit on his P-40, however, and he managed to touch down safely in the darkness, no mean feat in itself.

Overhead, most of the pilots who had succeeded in taking off and reaching their assigned altitude (except Burris and Donalson, who had failed to link up) were now patrolling in the early-morning light over Clark Field, waiting for the arrival of the B-17s from Mindanao. But as they continued circling around, their engines throttled back, they started to wonder what had happened to the Flying Fortresses.[4] Then, beginning to get low on gas after two hours' patrolling, Dyess led them north to Rosales for a landing.

5 At 5:45 that morning, Hank Thorne had gone over to the new base command post off the east side of Nichols Field and telephoned Colonel George at 5th Interceptor Command Headquarters at Nielson Field for orders. Earlier, having given up any further attempt at sleep that evening, he had notified the P-40 pilots at Nichols to stand by one hour before daylight, as per Colonel George's previous instructions to him. Thorne's new orders were to maintain an air alert over Nichols Field all day. Colonel George had little confidence in the effectiveness of the air warning system and did not want Nichols bombed again in a surprise attack. Major Maverick, responsible for the field's air defense, earlier had tried to convince George to move the planes at Nichols to safer locations, but his request had been rejected by the FEAF brass.

To guard against surprise attacks by Zeros while his P-40s were taking off or landing, Thorne decided to divide his strength of eight pilots and planes in half in order to provide alternating covering patrols. The relief flight taking off was to be protected by the alert flight, and the alert flight was to wait before landing until the relieving flight had gained sufficient altitude to be in a position to protect the alert flight's landing.

Starting at dawn that day, Thorne and Cy Blanton of the 17th Pursuit, who had been left behind at Nichols the day before when his squadron moved to Del Carmen, took turns leading the two flights on their patrols. Assigned to the flights were 3rd Pursuiters Bob Hanson, Andy Krieger, Ray Gehrig, Ed Woolery, and Howard Hardegree.

Dave Obert was also temporarily based at Nichols. Like Blanton, he had been left behind pending completion of a checkup on his P-40. He had not been at the field when Thorne assigned the Nichols pilots to the two flights. When he reported in to the operations hangar at Nichols early that morning, he was told that a flight had just taken off to patrol over Nichols, but that there was another P-40 on the field available if he wished to join them: the one that Hanson had damaged when he flew in from Rosales the evening before, which was now operational again.

Obert climbed into the P-40 and took off, hoping to find the flight patrolling over Nichols. After climbing to 17,000 feet, he searched for the others, but could not locate them. Circling the area for hours until his gas was nearly exhausted, the disappointed pilot came in to land at Nichols.

Obert was surprised to find that all the Nichols Field personnel seemed to have vanished except for a single enlisted man who ran up to him as he was parking the P-40. He told Obert that Major Maverick wanted him to get his P-40 off the ground before it was bombed: Nichols was expecting another raid.

The excited pilot told the enlisted man to get the gas truck to the plane so that it could be refueled. When the soldier told Obert that the driver was gone and he could not drive, Obert jumped out, ran across the field, got in the truck, and headed for the plane, "all the while cursing the inefficiency of the army" and expecting to be bombed any minute. But when Obert arrived back at the P-40, he found a few mechanics "who had come out of the bushes and holes," ready to help him service the plane.

As soon as he could, Obert took off and began circling over the field again, this time at 15,000 feet. He saw no planes in the air, either Japanese or American. Then, becoming more and more bored with the aimless patrolling, Obert decided to do some acrobatics. After performing a series of loops, slow rolls, and other maneuvers, he started into a big barrel roll. Then, when he happened to glance behind him, his blood froze: there were four planes bearing down on him.

They looked like P-40s, but the way they were coming at him, Obert did not know what to think. "Don't shoot, it's Obert!" he now shouted over his radio. The next moment, the planes pulled off, and Obert fell in with them. They *were* other P-40s. The relieved Oklahoman swore to himself that from then on, he was going to pay attention and try to look around him everywhere at the same time: this was serious business. For the rest of the three-and-a-half-hour patrol, Obert remained with his new companions, then came in to land with them.

Back safely on the ground, Obert talked with the 3rd Pursuiters about the disastrous events at Iba and Clark the day before. Don Steele and "Squirrely" Benson were at Nichols now too, having brought their P-40Es in that morning from their San Marcelino resting place. Ship Daniel had also flown in from Rosales in the morning. Then a little later in the afternoon Obert greeted his own squadron mates, who had just landed at Nichols after an early afternoon patrol over Del Carmen. They had taken off from Del Carmen at 7:00 A.M. and patrolled the area south of Clark, then landed at Clark. At 1:00 P.M., they had taken off again for the Del Carmen patrol.

After refueling at Nichols, Buzz Wagner led his squadron back to Clark, minus Bill Rowe, who had slightly damaged his wing tip in landing at Nichols.[5] Taking his place on the return flight to Clark was Cy Blanton, who had now been relieved by Thorne from flying the Nichols patrols.

Arriving at Nichols just in time to participate in the last patrol of the day, at 5:00 P.M., was Bill Powell. He had commandeered a car and driver at Lingayen and been driven all the way to Manila via Clark Field. After dismissing his driver, he had found his CO, Hank Thorne, and other 3rd Pursuiters in an improvised air raid shelter on the other side of the field.

6 When Buzz Wagner and his squadron mates arrived back at Clark in the late afternoon, they were informed by Major Grover that the 17th and 20th pursuits would henceforth have their P-40s pooled and share flying them. The 20th Pursuit got the better deal in this arrangement, as they had only three P-40s in commission after the disastrous events of the day before.

Shortly after the 17th Pursuit arrived back at Clark, Willie Feallock, who had been left behind in the morning takeoff from Del Carmen, came in too, in an old P-35A of the 34th Pursuit. He had become restless at Del Carmen, waiting for the completion of the repair of his P-40, and decided to fly up to 24th Group Headquarters at Clark to check out the situation there. As he taxied his P-35A in the fading light around the bomb craters and past the wrecked planes to a corner of the field between the hangars and the BOQ, he was moved by the utter desolation everywhere. When he shut off his engine, complete stillness enveloped him. Across the field, in the last of the twilight, he could make out a small figure of a soldier coming toward him, his gun on his shoulder. Then a truck drove up to him and picked him up for the ride over to group headquarters in the jungle. After talking with Grover's staff about the situation, Feallock declined their offer to spend the evening in the woods and headed back to the officer quarters instead for a shower and a proper bed.

7 Late in the afternoon at Del Carmen, the 34th Pursuit received orders to move their P-35As to San Marcelino, a newly completed strip thirty miles due west on the China Sea coast. The FEAF brass reasoned that the Del Carmen field was due for a raid from the Japanese, who had discovered it the day before, whereas San Marcelino was believed to be still unknown to them.

Earlier that day, the understrength squadron had received two pilots from the 20th Pursuit at Clark, which had a pilot surplus after the destruction of almost all of its P-40Bs. Ed Houseman, a 41-C flying school graduate from Philadelphia, Pennsylvania, and Billy Tom Akins, a 41-G newie from Hillsboro, Texas, were selected by Joe Moore for transfer to the 34th.

On approaching San Marcelino at dusk, the 34th's pilots noticed another group of planes, big ones, flying in a southerly direction at about 2,000 feet, but they could not identify them in the fading light. Then, suddenly, antiaircraft fire started streaming up from the ground at them, and the P-35A formation broke up, "like leaves scattered by the winds." The mystery planes continued flying straight ahead, but the P-35As made a left turn in an easterly direction around the mountain and headed for the big planes again. When they were within range of each other, each side opened fire. To Frankie Bryant in one of the P-35As, it was like "a 4th of July fireworks." But when the 34th Pursuiters saw that the seven big planes were coming in for a landing at San Marcelino, they followed suit, each group subjected to further ground fire. Hampered by poor visibility in the descending darkness and the dust stirred up on the dirt field, as well as anxious to get down as quickly as possible before being hit by the trigger-happy Filipino troops, Bryant missed the runway and went into a foxhole, wrecking his landing gear.

On the ground, the 34th Pursuit's pilots soon learned that the other planes were B-17s and got together with their crews. Each group was hungry and tired, but the base could offer them nothing. Indeed, the so-called field had no installations whatsoever, and no water supply. There was only a single small truck on the sand-swept field.

Pooling their financial resources, the crews of the B-17s and the P-35 pilots collected enough money to buy some bread and other food items in San Marcelino town, four miles away. Then a group of them set out in the truck about 7:30 P.M. for the town. At 11:30, the group returned, but empty-handed. They had gotten lost four times before finding San Marcelino, and when they finally found the right place, there was a complete blackout in effect. Repeated knocking on the doors of the town's bakery and grocery store failed to elicit a response. Evidently the owners were afraid there would be reprisals from the Japanese believed nearby if they helped the Americans. That night the B-17 crews slept in their spacious planes, but the pursuit pilots had no place to sleep except on the floor of unfinished wooden barracks, using their gas masks as pillows, and on empty stomachs.

The pilots of the sister 21st Pursuit Squadron also spent the night at an unfamiliar field after having flown on patrol all day. Ed Dyess had brought them into Rosales, the 3rd Pursuit's designated alternative field. "We were afraid to stay very long in one spot," John Posten recorded in his diary that night at Rosales.

Despite the many air raid alarms—all false—the Japanese had not struck them this day, for some unknown reason. The Americans knew, however, that they would be back soon.[6]

12. "I'LL BE KILLED IN THE FIRST DOGFIGHT I GET IN"

1 Somewhat before 2:00 A.M. on Wednesday, December 10, 1941, Nichols Field Base Operations Officer Grant Mahony received a call from Major Grover at Clark. The CO of the 24th Pursuit Group had a job for him. Capt. "Bud" Sprague, operations officer of the 5th Interceptor Command at Nichols Field, on behalf of Colonel George had ordered Grover to have one of his P-40s at Nichols reconnoiter the Vigan–San Fernando area on the west coast of central Luzon for any activity of vessels and to report the number and size of any spotted. Reports had been coming in of a Japanese surface force off the coast near Vigan, but the Far East Air Force needed aerial confirmation.

Grover knew that the only pilots at Nichols qualified for the recon where Mahony and his former squadron mate and buddy Bob Hanson. The two knew the islands better than any of the other pursuit pilots in the FEAF because of their frequent cross-country flying before the war. Grover opted for Mahony.

At 2:10 A.M., the restless Mahony, now finally getting the action he craved during his Philippines tour, roared down the Nichols runway in his P-40E and headed north. Not hampered by the darkness, he navigated his ship into the Vigan area without problem and in spite of the poor visibility was able to make out the ships off the coast—six transports, supported by one cruiser and ten destroyers. But as Mahony approached Nichols Field with the critical news, antiaircraft fire from the field suddenly struck his ship, critically damaging it. Mahony was obliged to bail out in the pitch darkness.

On the ground, Bob Hanson, waiting for the return of his friend, saw what had happened. An antiaircraft position operated by Filipino troops had fired on the P-40 without bothering to identify it as friend or foe. Enraged, Hanson picked up a gun the moment they started firing at Mahony and ran toward the Filipinos, shouting all the way. Fortunately for the Filipinos, Mahony was not injured in his jump. The two pursuit pilots headed over to Nichols Base, from where Mahony telephoned in his recon report at 5:13 to Col. Francis Brady, chief of staff of General Brereton, at FEAF Headquarters.

Brady was relieved to hear from Mahony. He had called USAFFE Headquarters at 4:45 A.M. and informed them that Mahony must have been lost on the mission, since there had been no word from him and he would have been out of gas by then. Now at 5:30 Brady had the happier task of relaying Mahony's report to USAFFE, which was anxiously awaiting the news of the recon.

Fifteen minutes after USAFFE Headquarters received Mahony's report, it ordered the FEAF to attack the Japanese landing with all available force. In quick response, Clark-based B-17s of the 19th Bomb Group and P-40s of the 24th Pursuit Group took off on separate strike missions just before dawn.

Getting the nod for the P-40 mission was the 17th Pursuit Squadron. Following the pooling of the aircraft of the 17th and 20th pursuits, Buzz Wagner and Joe Moore had flipped to determine which squadron would fly the first mission under the arrangement for alternating missions. Wagner had won the flip. The 17th's CO selected John Brownewell and Al Strauss to lead the two six-ship flights in a strafing attack. But following takeoff, Brownewell found that his six .50-caliber guns were inoperative after he tried to test-fire them, and he was obliged to return to Clark. Jack Dale took over his flight.

Flying with only the small fuselage lights of the P-40s and the exhaust fires from their engines, the pilots entered a solid layer of overcast shortly after takeoff and began to spread apart from each other. When Dale and Strauss arrived over the Vigan area at 7:15 that morning, they found that their flights were splintered.

One who had become separated was Cy Blanton. When he began his descent through broken clouds over what he calculated to be the Vigan area, the sun had risen, allowing him to see that he was directly over several destroyers and a large cruiser in the center. Blanton lined himself up for a strafing attack on the cruiser. As his .50-caliber tracers hit the steel deck of the warship, they ricocheted in all directions, causing the crew to scatter wildly, but not inflicting much damage.

Concentrating his attack on another ship, Walt Coss and the three others in his flight, all in line astern, made repeated strafing passes in dives out of the sun. The Japanese warship was towing a raft on which a machine gun was mounted. On each pass, the Japanese gunner would fire at the P-40s. Coss doubted his efforts were successful; only one of his guns was firing. Also experiencing difficulties with his guns was Jack Dale. All six worked on the first and second passes, but only four on the third pass. None of Bill Hennon's guns were working.

With diminishing offensive capability and Japanese antiaircraft fire becoming heavier, Dale and Strauss at about 8:00 A.M. broke off the two flights' attacks and headed back to Clark Field, returning safely back with little damage inflicted on their ships. For leading his flight in the attack, Dale was recommended by MacArthur's staff for award of the Distinguished Flying Cross. Heroes were desperately needed in these times of bad news in the Philippines campaign.[1]

2 At about 8:30 A.M., twelve P-35As of the 34th Pursuit Squadron were struggling to take off from the Del Carmen strip for the second strafing attack by the 24th Group on the Japanese ships at Vigan. This was the maximum number of P-35As the squadron could muster for the mission, and all were in bad condition. A thirteenth—Claude Paulger's ship—was expected to participate too, but its engine refused to turn over, forcing Paulger to drop out.

Earlier that morning, the 34th's pilots had brought the flyable P-35As back from their overnight stay at San Marcelino field on the west coast of Luzon. On landing back at Del Carmen, Jack Hall had taxied into a hole, bending a blade of his ship's propeller. Undaunted, several of his squadron mates pushed the P-35A out of the hole and straightened the prop with a rock, rendering it fit for the morning's mission.

Now as they tried to get airborne, thick dust once again was causing problems, requiring several minutes' break between individual takeoffs. Finally, all twelve managed to get off and assemble overhead, with CO Sam Marett leading the first flight of six ships and Ben Brown the second flight of an equal number as top cover. But when they arrived over Vigan at 9:30, Marett had only five planes left in his flight and Brown three; the other four had to return to Del Carmen with engine trouble. Then, just after they reached the target area, the motor of the P-35A of Brown's wingman, Ed Houseman, failed. Houseman parachuted out, but the loss of his ship cut the force down to only seven P-35As.

As Brown and his new wingman dove to strafe the Japanese landing party, Marett and his wingman, "Shorty" Crosland, led the other three of their flight down to 100 feet in echelon to take on what they believed was a 10,000-ton transport but was in actuality a 630-ton minesweeper. Attacking below deck level, Marett's ship was suddenly rocked by an explosion from the stern of the minesweeper, which blew off its right wing and sent the CO's plane crashing into the water.[2]

With debris from the explosion flying everywhere, Crosland pulled up as soon as he could. Then all the P-35As scattered as the Japanese warships began circling and firing at them. Crosland climbed to about 5,000 feet to look things over. He could see a cruiser directly below firing at him, very close to where the minesweeper had sunk. He turned and went straight down and fired on the ship, then pulled up and strafed small boats that were landing troops. Pulling up once more and realizing that he was about out of ammunition, Crosland set course for Del Carmen.

In the meantime, Jack Hall and Don Pagel were pouring fire into two of the transports and set them ablaze. Ben Brown attacked a third transport but, on pulling up, experienced engine problems and set out for Del Carmen too, followed by the others.[3]

3 Before the P-35As of the 34th Pursuit had taken off from Del Carmen for their Vigan mission, one of the pilots of the 17th Pursuit left behind at Del Carmen after the disastrous night interception mission of December 8/9 received word that he should join his squadron in its attack mission on the Japanese landing at Vigan. Around 9:00 A.M. "Red" Sheppard climbed into his newly repaired P-40E, grazed in Lodin's crash, and headed down the dusty strip. Pointing his ship in the direction of Vigan, Sheppard scanned the sky for a sight of his squadron mates but could see no sign of any aircraft. Unknown to him, they had already returned to Clark after completing their mission. As he approached Vigan, Sheppard was unexpectedly joined by another P-40, which took up a position on his wing. Sheppard could not make out who the pilot was but was glad to have the company.[4] Then, three miles inland from the Luzon coast near Vigan, Sheppard and the other pilot spotted three twin-engined Japanese bombers in front of them at about their altitude of 15,000 feet.[5] "I felt like an experienced big game hunter who'd caught up with three tigers," Sheppard later recalled. In his first pass at the unsuspecting Japanese, Sheppard held the gun trigger down as he swept past the bombers from the rear but saw that fire was coming from only two of his six guns. Swinging around for another rear attack, Sheppard, now alone, poured more .50-caliber fire into the bombers during a second, then a third pass. Pieces of the bombers were beginning to fall off as the 17th Pursuiter scored effective hits.

But the Japanese were firing back too, from the ventral gun position, and Sheppard was "collecting a lot of lead" during his passes. Then he noticed that his coolant temperature warning light had gone on. The Prestone cooling system had been hit. Realizing that his ship was doomed, Sheppard now began looking for a suitable place on which to land or over which to bail out. In the distance, he noticed that the two bombers he had hit had dropped out of formation, smoking heavily, and were losing altitude. An engine on one of them was out.[6]

Trying to get as far away from the Japanese beachhead at Vigan as possible to avoid possible capture, Sheppard nursed the stricken P-40E up the river valley toward Bangued, his engine throttled back but still running. A few minutes later, the Allison engine burst into flames, whereupon Sheppard pushed the canopy open, rolled the ship over on its back, unfastened his seat belt, pushed the stick a bit, and let himself fall out. His parachute blossomed out, and he fell into a big thornbush, uninjured. Not far away, he saw his plane crash into some storage huts close to a barrio, triggering a huge fire. Sheppard gathered up his chute and walked a few hundred feet to a road, where he joined some Filipinos. Together, they flagged down a passing truck, which took them into the town of Bangued. Arriving at the home of Major Capayas of the Philippine Constabulary, Sheppard was surprised to meet another American pilot, Ed Houseman, who told Sheppard that he also had bailed out, during the 34th Pursuit's mission over Vigan.

4 At Clark Field, following the return at about 8:45 A.M. of the 17th Pursuit pilots from their early morning strike at Vigan, the twelve P-40s were being refueled and rearmed. Joe Moore was assigning pilots from his 20th Pursuit to the P-40s for the second Vigan attack mission under the rotation system he and Buzz Wagner had worked out earlier. Moore would lead this mission.

Moore's designated wingman, Randy Keator, was feeling apprehensive. Like his squadron mates, he had never been in the cockpit of a P-40E in his life. The night before, he had examined the interior of one of them for the first time, illuminating the inside with the help of a small flashlight. Later, he had been awakened along with other 20th Pursuiters and driven from the jungle camp to the field for a quick briefing on the characteristics of the E model. Keator learned that the P-40E was much heavier than the P-40B.[7] The instrumentation was also arranged differently.

Despite his nervousness over flying the E model, Keator had no trouble as he lifted off from Clark behind his squadron commander. In third place Edwin Gilmore, flying in Jack Dale's plane, was having problems seeing things through the dust thrown up by Moore and Keator. Taxiing into position, Gilmore failed to notice a bomb crater in front of him. One of his wheels fell into the hole, causing his ship to fall to the side. Once the propeller hit the ground, it stopped turning. Scratch one P-40 from the mission.

Overhead, Keator had pulled up through the heavy overcast above Clark Field. But where were the others? Not a single plane was in sight. Unknown to Keator, the others were in a similar fix. They all became separated after takeoff and flew the mission in individual sorties.

As Keator arrived over the target area, he spotted the invasion fleet off the coast. He picked out "a big, fat transport" anchored near the shore. After circling into the sun, he put his heavy ship into a power dive. At some distance from his target, Keator began pouring .50-caliber fire into the ship and happily watched his tracers "bouncing all over the deck." But only two of his guns were working, and then as he reached the transport, one of those jammed, too. Concentrating too hard through his gunsight, Keator barely missed flying through the transport's mast. Clearing the ship, he held the P-40E down low, barely above the water, to avoid the antiaircraft fire bursting just above him. Once out of range of the guns, he began to pull up, then spotted a group of single-engined Japanese fighters diving on him from about 8,000 feet.[8] Keator applied maximum RPM; he was going to outrun the Japanese on his homeward trip. Performing well at such low altitude, his Allison engine soon carried him along at over 400 MPH for the next few minutes, and his attackers were soon left behind.

Standing on the sidelines near the edge of the woods off of Clark Field, Edwin Gilmore and several other pilots were watching as Moore, Keator, and the other 20th Pursuiters were landing about 11:15 A.M. after completing the Vigan mission. The dust was thick and rising fifteen to twenty feet in the air as the P-40Es rolled down the strip. Then Gilmore noticed that one of the P-40s was leveling off too high as it came in and was dropping in a stall. Gilmore realized that the pilot, unused to flying the heavier E model, did not understand that he had to bring it in a little faster and lower than a B model. Attempting to recover, the pilot began applying maximum power, but it was too late. The plane hit the ground and swerved 45 degrees to the left, putting it on a direct collision course with Gilmore and the others, who now fell prostrate to the ground.

Further down the field, near the tree line, Cy Blanton of the 17th was talking to Glen Alder of the 20th when the two pilots turned in the direction of shouts. "Staring them in the face" was the nose of a P-40 hurtling toward them. Blanton and Alder hit the ground instantly as the out-of-control pursuit ship continued on its trajectory and crashed into the trees. Blanton got up and rushed to the wreckage to try to rescue the pilot; 20th Pursuiter Jim Fossey and some others were already there with an axe and a fire extinguisher, working to free him. But the rescue effort was to no avail; the pilot was already dead, his head crushed in by the electric gunsight. It was Morgan "Sorg" McCowan, Gilmore's housemate.

After walking out of the trees and brush, Blanton saw Alder standing at the edge of the field. The 39-B oldie from Los Angeles, California, appeared quite dazed and asked what had happened. Blood was trickling out of his left ear. In the crash, a tree limb had evidently fallen on his head, and a piece had pierced his ear. Blanton took his friend by the arm and guided him to a command car that had just driven up to take any injured persons to the hospital. Then Blanton noticed a sergeant lying facedown in a pool of blood on the ground, near where they had been standing at the time of the accident.[9] Blanton called out for help, and someone helped get the sergeant into the car too. As they headed to Fort Stotsenburg hospital nearby, Blanton noticed that Alder could sit up, but the sergeant was unconscious and was having trouble breathing from all the mud in his nose and mouth. Blanton cleared the mud and also put a handkerchief on his head, where blood was oozing out. Evidently the propeller of the P-40 had struck him in the head, and part of his crown had been torn away.

When the car passed the Clark Field dispensary, it stopped so that Maj. Emmett "Doc" Lentz, the base surgeon, could examine the two. Lentz took charge of Alder and sent the car on to Fort Stotsenburg with the sergeant, a more serious case. When they arrived at the hospital, a nurse told Blanton and the driver to take the sergeant immediately to the head of a line waiting for emergency treatment. Moments later the nurse returned and told Blanton to take him away: he was already dead.

On the way back to Clark Field, Blanton stopped at the dispensary to see how Alder was doing. "Doc" Lentz gave him the unexpected, shocking news that Alder was dead too. It was not as minor a problem as the doctor had originally thought.

5 Down at Del Carmen, five P-35As of the 34th Pursuit that had survived the Vigan mission landed before noon. Since there were no revetments on the field, the planes were lined up side by side on one side of the dirt strip with those that did not make the mission. Standing nearby, "Shorty" Crosland and the other pilots of the squadron were in a somber mood following the loss of their commanding officer.

The sixth survivor of the Vigan mission, 2nd Lt. Bill Coleman, landed at Clark instead. There he bumped into squadron mate Frankie Bryant, who had flown over to Clark from San Marcelino in a B-17 early that morning and thus had missed the Vigan mission. Then at about 12:28, the Clark Field air raid siren went off, and the two out-of-place 34th Pursuiters hurried over to Coleman's P-35A. Bryant climbed into the plane's baggage compartment, and a few minutes later, Coleman raced down the dusty field for the takeoff, bound for the home Del Carmen field nearby. Just after takeoff, Coleman passed an unnerving message to Bryant: there were Zeros on their tail. They made it to the field successfully, where, after touching down, Bryant pushed open the baggage compartment door on the side of the ship and jumped out, flattening himself in the dust near Coleman, who had taken similar defensive action.

From their emplacement, the operators of the six Lewis machine guns on each side of the field now opened fire in unison at some eighteen Zeros that had followed Coleman in from Clark and were now making a strafing run from the southeast.[10] But four of the old guns jammed on their first burst of .30-caliber fire. Low and close, the Japanese picked out easy targets on the strip, the sitting duck P-35As and the squadron's gas trailer tanker, as pilots and ground crews alike scurried across the field to take shelter under the trees.

Over in the woods, the pilots and ground crews were soon joined by other squadron mates from the base camp, which was also being shot up by the Zeros. Lying flat on the ground, squadron clerk S. Sgt. Tom Gage, with his assistant, Cpl. Robert V. Reynolds, and Pfc Dermitt R. Toycen could not see anything, but they "could sure hear"; the spent slugs were buzzing around. One clanged off Reynolds's helmet. When Ben Brown nearby stood up to look, he was immediately pulled down by some of the other officers. Sgt. Tom Blaylock also tried to look out from his shelter, a pup tent set up over the head of a ravine, but the others pulled him down and made him keep his head down. The Japanese were strafing everywhere around the Del Carmen base now.

T. Sgt. Bill Cott and his radio crew were in the 34th's radio shack, yelling "Mayday" on the 24th Group's frequency to anyone who might be listening. The shack was partly underground, providing an effective sanctuary from the murderous fire of the marauding Zeros.

At Clark, about fifteen minutes earlier, orders had gone out to get all aircraft on the field into the air; a Japanese force was reported heading in.[11] In the wild scramble to get airborne in the P-40s, the pilots of the 17th, 20th, and 21st pursuit fought for the possession of each plane. Many of the P-40s were taken up without adequate gas, ammunition, or pilots' equipment.

Chaos ruled supreme. One of the ships, piloted by Bob Newman, on detachment to the 21st Pursuit from the 3rd Pursuit, plowed into a B-17 when Newman became disoriented in the dust storm stirred up by two P-40s taking off ahead of him. In the collision, the B-17's wing was torn off just outboard of the number 1 engine and its back broken just behind the main entrance door. Shaken but unbelievably uninjured (there was no fire or explosion), Newman released his safety belt and took off across the dust to the edge of the field.

Weaving a P-40E around the bomb craters and through the thick dust, Newman's CO, Ed Dyess, suddenly realized that he had forgotten his goggles, helmet, and even his parachute. Then, emerging into the dazzling sunlight after breaking through the overcast following takeoff, he found his ship was almost touching another P-40E. The other pilot was Buzz Wagner, who was "laughing like a hyena" over the close call.

When Edwin Gilmore in his P-40E had gotten on top of the heavy overcast blanketing Clark, he spotted another P-40 on his right and joined up on his wing: it was Al Strauss of the 17th Pursuit. Minutes later, a call came over Gilmore's radio: "Tally Ho, Del Carmen! Tally Ho, Del Carmen!" Gilmore had picked up Cott's distress signal.

As Strauss and Gilmore approached Del Carmen, they noticed two Zeros above the overcast, preparing for a strafing run on the base. Gilmore signaled that he would take the one on the left. Diving down from 2,000 feet to get on his adversary's tail, he opened fire with his six .50-

caliber wing guns. After only one burst, however, his guns quit. He now tried the hydraulic gun charger, but to no avail; unfamiliar with the E model, Gilmore did not know the chargers had been disconnected. For a second, he considered ramming the Zero's tail but then noticed black smoke coming from his enemy's engine. Figuring that he must have hit the Zero with his single burst, he now pulled up into the overcast. With no guns working, he did not want to hang around to see if the Zero crashed.

Also having trouble with his guns was Jack Dale, who had picked up the "Tally Ho" call from Del Carmen too. Before reaching the field, he had cleared the guns on his P-40E at about 10,000 feet to warm them up, and four of the six fired at that time. But now, closing from one hundred and fifty down to twenty yards on the tail of one of the strafers, Dale pressed the trigger and *all* guns failed. Cursing, the frustrated pilot broke off and headed for Nichols Field to have the guns cleared by hand.

Fortunately, the guns of Parker Gies's P-40E were working perfectly. He had arrived over Del Carmen with 20th Pursuit squadron mate Henry Rancke in response to the same distress call. Diving down through the overcast into a group of strafers, Gies poured fire into one of them and sent it smoking to the ground. When Gies rejoined Rancke, they immediately came under the attack of three other Zeros. Undaunted, Gies turned into them and set one afire while dispersing the other two. Although his P-40E was badly damaged, he still managed to fly it back to Clark.

On the ground at Del Carmen, "Shorty" Crosland had seen two P-40s diving on the Zeros near the end of their twenty-one-minute strafing attack. One of the Zeros went down off the end of the field. After the raid, Crosland and the others found the wreck of the Zero with the pilot's body still in it.[12]

For the pilots of the 34th Pursuit, it was the end of flying as a squadron. Of the fifteen P-35As that were on the field at the time of the Japanese attack, seven were destroyed by the strafers, and three were badly damaged, leaving only five survivors, all out of commission.[13] Fortunately, however, there had been no loss of life among the squadron's personnel. Later that afternoon, Ben Brown, who had assumed command of the squadron on Marett's death, ordered the 34th's personnel, except for a skeleton ground and communications crew, to evacuate the field for the nearby sugar central of Del Carmen. Heavy of spirit, officers and men alike struck out on foot across the grass and cane for their destination.

6 During the scramble from Clark at 12:30, Dyess and many of the others picked up a call on their radios from 24th Group Headquarters at Clark, reporting that the Japanese bombers had passed over Clark without attacking and were apparently on their way to Manila instead. The pilots were ordered to intercept them there.

Also responding to the group's radioed order, John Posten was halfway to Manila when he ran into Zeros. Despite being scared in this his first combat experience, he entered into a dogfight with one of them. But after his right tire, gas tank, both wings, and the tail had been riddled by the Japanese in the one-sided encounter, Posten decided to break off combat and went into a steep dive from 15,000 feet. Then, by flying back up into a cloud bank, he finally succeeded in shaking off two Zeros that were on his tail and headed back to Clark Field.

Unlike Posten, Dyess had not encountered any Zeros as he approached Manila. He could make out bombers high up, unloading on the dock area. Deciding to warm up his six .50-caliber guns, Dyess pressed the trigger. Nothing happened. A second try resulted in only a "discouraging click." Then, after a fruitless third try, he gave up and headed down to land at an auxiliary field near Manila to have his guns cleared and recharged on the ground.

Two 20th Pursuiters who had headed for the Manila area too were lucky to have escaped with their lives following disastrous encounters with Zeros. Milton Woodside, a 41-C flying school graduate from Charlotte, North Carolina, was flying without ammunition in Buzz Wagner's P-40E after the frenzied takeoff from Clark. Some twenty miles northeast of Manila, near the Ipo Dam, he was jumped from behind by Zeros. His instrument panel shattered in the attack, he put his ship in a dive and jumped out, coming to earth near the town of Bocaue, Bulacan Province. In similar circumstances, Kiefer White, one of the 41-B flying school graduates, was not watching behind himself when he was hit by a Zero from that quarter. When his Allison engine conked out and began to burn, he opted to bail out. He hit the ground hard but was not hurt.

7 At Nichols Field, Bill Powell was just sitting down for lunch in the tent mess hall on the north side of the field with his CO, Hank Thorne, and five other 3rd Pursuiters, including Howard Hardegree and Ship Daniel. It was 12:40. Their relief flight under Grant Mahony had taken off minutes earlier in their seven P-40Es. Thorne was still maintaining a patrol over Manila at all times, since they could not trust the air warning system.

Powell's flight had landed just before noon after being unable to refuel at Rosales, since there still was no gasoline pump there. Early in the morning, the pilots had patrolled over Clark Field at 18,000 feet for forty-five minutes, in expectation of a Japanese attack that never materialized.

At some 6,000 to 8,000 feet over Nichols, Willie Feallock was beginning to take his flight down for a landing. Feallock's group had covered the earlier landing of Powell's flight and now the takeoff of Mahony's relief flight. Suddenly, their radios crackled, "Cavite being attacked by airplanes at low altitude!" Looking over toward the naval base, Feallock and the others saw a swarm of Zeros. With not enough gas for ten minutes of combat and already in landing configuration, Feallock radioed the tower at Nichols for instructions. Should they attack with what little fuel they had, at the price of their aircraft, or try to make for some nearby strip and conserve their planes? The tower radioed back for Feallock to use his own judgment. Feallock and the others elected to attack.

Swinging around in a climb, Feallock now went after a string of three Zeros at low altitude, five miles off his right wing over Zablan, on the outskirts of Manila. The Japanese were circling as if to strafe.

Retracting his landing gear, Feallock hoped his six guns were now operative. Earlier, he had turned on his cockpit heater to thaw the heating tubes leading to the butts of his guns, which had frozen at 20,000 feet.

Closing fast from the west behind the Zeros, Feallock "drew a fine bead" on one of them and pressed his gun trigger, but nothing happened. Then the Zero pilot saw Feallock and turned into him. Shocked, Feallock watched the Zero apparently turn 180 degrees in its own length. After two turns with the Japanese pilot, with machine gun and cannon fire coming at him and past the cockpit, Feallock realized the Zero's rate of turn was far superior to his own. He now opted for a straight chase over the Fort McKinley and Nichols Field antiaircraft units, hoping that the .50-caliber guns in the pits there could knock off his pursuer.

When he was down to less than 100 feet, pulling seventy-five inches of mercury, indicating about 360 MPH, "jinking through trees, houses, anything to be a tough target," Feallock heard the rattle of machine gun slugs on the armor plate of his P-40E and the duller noise of 20-mm cannon shells exploding on the rear of the fuselage. His control surfaces were now beginning to get mushy, and the engine was running rough. Then a few moments later, he noticed a burning smell as his ship began to smoke. Time to jump, but not at 50 feet altitude! Pulling his stricken ship up to 200 feet, Feallock rolled back the canopy. When it immediately filled with flames, he closed the canopy and unbuckled his shoulder straps. Then at some 500–800 feet altitude, Feallock reopened the canopy and jumped over the side. With the ground coming up "terribly fast," his chute started to open. Moments later, Feallock hit the ground hard, in a field in Rosario, Pasig, eight miles west of Manila, spraining both ankles. Sixty feet away, the wreckage of his ship was burning, detonating his .50-caliber ammunition.

While Feallock tangled with the three Zeros near Zablan, another pilot in his flight, Andy Krieger, was facing problems of his own. Early on he calculated that his flight was outnumbered by the Zeros three to one.[14] Under such conditions, Krieger decided to fire arbitrarily on any aircraft crossing his gunsight. As he recorded in his wartime narrative:

I finally got a good shot at one and saw him stagger and fall off just as my own ship was hit astern. I half-rolled and looked at my tail—it had a large shell hole through it and I remember wondering why it stayed on. An Immelmann turn threw the Nip off, and when I rolled out, had two of them dead in my sight.

Just as I was about to pull the trigger, my engine quit—out of gas. I dove quickly, but the two clamped right on my tail. They hit my tail again as I banked, and the ship rolled onto its back and started to spin. But I got it out, somehow—will never know how, because I was too low to get out of an inverted spin, and was sure my time had come.

When I recovered, I just barely touched the water of a little creek. My engine was running in fits and starts, using the last of my gasoline, so I began to run at ground level, wide open, with the two Zeros still on my tail, peppering away.

I gave them such a ride as they won't forget for a while, taking them up and down ravines, between houses and trees, but they were pretty careful and didn't hit anything. I hit a couple of treetops with my wings, but thank God our airplanes are built to take it, and the wings stayed on.

The metal on my fuselage and wings was peeling forward from the volume of their fire, and the noise of their cannon shells bursting on my armor plate was deafening.

Well, it wasn't long before that airplane wasn't good anymore. When the engine quit entirely, I suddenly remembered that good old life insurance strapped to the seat, so pulled up until she stalled, and jumped.

I was about 500 feet high and couldn't pull the ripcord until about 100 because they were shooting at me as I fell. But she opened very fast and I lit without a jounce.

Krieger had come to earth at Barrio Pasacola, Caloocan, Rizal Province, just north of Manila.

Another member of Feallock's flight, Ray Gehrig, was attacked by three of the Zeros from above, with none of his P-40E's guns working. Tracers were going by the cockpit, then an explosion to the left of his head blew out his canopy and most of his instruments. Gehrig went into a tight turn and in a moment entered some clouds. As he recalled years later, "I discovered I was bleeding in several places, and using the scattered to broken cloud deck, started for Del Carmen field to the north. But before I got there, I saw Zeros strafing there." Gehrig then headed east to a small civilian field at Plaridel, twenty-five miles southeast of Del Carmen. As he remembered, "I almost got there, was cranking my gear down by hand (hydraulic system shot out) when the engine quit. Hit a mango tree about three feet in diameter and ended up against the gunsight with my face—broken cheekbone and upper jaw."

A fourth pilot in Feallock's ill-fated flight, Bill Rowe, was leading an

Bill Rowe, 17th Pursuit, on the wing of his P-35A at Iba, summer, 1941. *Courtesy William M. Rowe, Lt. Col. USAF (Ret.)*

element of the 21st Pursuit following takeoff from Nichols but soon dropped down to join Feallock and Krieger at 10,000 feet to patrol the Nichols area. After several hours patrolling, it was about 12:45 when he noticed a large formation of bombers far above them, heading in toward Manila and Cavite. While watching them and getting ready to head down with the others for refueling at Nichols, Rowe suddenly found himself in the unwelcome company of a flock of Japanese pursuit aircraft. One of the Zeros immediately got on his tail, but the 17th Pursuiter was able to shake it off after a steep dive. But after maneuvering several more minutes with his nimble opponents, who were outturning him every time, and with gas getting too low, Rowe, like Gehrig, elected to head for Del Carmen Field.

Nearing the field, Rowe called in for a landing but was told the field was being strafed, so he flew on to nearby Clark Field. Then he ran out of gasoline in one tank and had just switched to another when he looked over his wing. Tracer fire was going by. Two silver Zeros had come up from behind and were shooting at him. Reacting immediately, Rowe went into a half roll and dove straight down at top speed, then pulled out. He had shaken off his pursuers. In an agitated nervous state, he almost fired on another P-40 while approaching Clark for a landing, then cut off a B-17 as it was landing. Safely back on the ground, Rowe climbed into a truck and headed for the 20th Pursuit's base camp in the jungle.

8 Gus Williams, one of the 21st Pursuit's pilots who had been flying with Rowe at the beginning of the patrol over Nichols, was also coming in to land at Nichols at 12:40, his gas gauges registering almost empty. But as Williams turned on the base leg, the Nichols tower called over his receiver, "There are aircraft strafing at the end of the field!" To Williams the call seemed strange—he saw no aircraft near the field. He went ahead on the base leg and turned on his final approach. But as he set the wheels of his P-40E down prior to landing, Williams noticed single-engined planes strafing hangars and aircraft at the far end of the field. It was too late to abort his landing, however. Rolling to a stop, he hurriedly made a turn off the runway onto the golf course where the 21st used to park its aircraft and fairly close to a tree that he hoped would provide him some protection.

Williams knew his life depended on getting out of the plane and under cover as fast as possible. In his haste, he forgot to cut the ignition off and tried to climb out of the cockpit with his canteen, .45-caliber pistol, and parachute still on, which only slowed his exit from the aircraft. Running toward a pile of sandbags, he had to circle them three times before he could find an opening. But when he heard the drone of twin-engine bombers in V formation above Nichols, he figured his shelter was not ideal and ran towards a building at the base about one hundred feet away.[15]

Crawling under the building, the terrified Arizonan began digging a hole with a metal helmet. He was soon joined by several others who began digging with helmets too.

Another 21st Pursuiter who had been flying with Williams also made a hurried landing, but at another field and with more disastrous results for his aircraft. Running out of gas, and with Nichols and Del Carmen under strafing attack, John Burns had decided to head for Maniquis Field, a Philippine Army Air Force base sixty miles due north of Manila, near Cabanatuan. On approaching, he found the field covered with obstacles and buzzed it so the Filipinos would remove them. But in his anxious state of mind, and his gas tanks empty, the Akron, Ohio, native came in before the field was cleared and crash-landed right through the drums. Burns was unhurt, but his P-40E was a total wreck.

Yet another P-40E lost from the ill-fated patrol group over Nichols was piloted by Gordon "Squirrely" Benson. Pursued by two Zeros, the 3rd Pursuiter, like Feallock, led his antagonists low across Nichols Field during the strafing attack as men of the 27th Materiel Squadron fired on them. But Benson's aircraft was already ablaze and moments later crashed into Manila Bay just a half mile opposite the 27th Squadron's position. Benson managed to get out safely, unhurt.

9 The relief flight led by Grant Mahony that had taken off from Nichols about 12:35 had just gotten the wheels of their seven P-40Es up and were at about 2,000-feet altitude when they were hit by the flock of Zeros that minutes earlier had attacked Feallock's flight. The Americans were taken completely by surprise.

As the flight splintered, Don Steele found that two of the Zeros had tacked on to his tail. As Steele recorded in his diary:

> We went around and around, gradually losing altitude, the two of them taking turns shooting at me. I could hear the 20 mm [shells] striking the armor plate behind me, and expected each one in turn to finally break through. I kept sliding further and further forward in my seat. It sounded like someone hitting the back in with a sledge hammer. Most of the shots were angle shots coming from about 210 degrees.
>
> I finally managed to get into some clouds that were about 1,000 feet high over Manila. One Zero followed me in, and the other one turned and went back just before we went into the clouds. We lost sight of each other while in the clouds, and I made a 45-degree turn to the left.
>
> When I came out, the Zero was just ahead and below me, to the right. He was rocking his wings frantically and trying to find me, looking below him all the time, and flying fairly straight.
>
> I skidded over on to his tail and gave him one burst, and he completely disintegrated. The air was filled with flying wheels, cowling, and scraps of airplane. He rolled over half on his back and crashed into the shore of Laguna de Bay, just east of Nichols Field.

Steele now headed due north, climbing up to 15,000 feet, and returned to Manila. Then he saw twelve twin-engine bombers above him at 20,000 feet, with an escort of about twenty-five Zeros about 2,000 feet above them, heading northwest. Approaching Nichols Field, the 3rd Pursuiter saw that the base was on fire and could not make out any aircraft on the ground. Deciding against landing there under such conditions, he headed south and put down at the Philippine Army Air Force base at Batangas, fifty-five miles due south of Nichols.

Steele was surprised to find another P-40 on the field. It turned out to be the ship of Earl Stone of the 17th Pursuit, who was another member of Feallock's ill-fated flight. Stone had been in combat with the Zeros too and had opted to get down at Batangas, a field not subject to the attack of the marauding Zeros that afternoon.

Of Steele's seven-ship flight, he, Mahony, Bob Hanson, and "Dub" Balfanz had managed to get their P-40s down safely, but the other three members had less fortunate experiences. Wilson Glover's P-40E was hit in the instrument panel by a 20-mm shell. When his electrical system and guns were subsequently knocked out and his engine started overheating, Glover headed north for Clark Field. But eighteen miles short of his destination, over San Fernando, he was forced to bail out. He hit the ground safely and was picked up by Filipinos, who tended him.

Jim Phillips, a 41-C flying school classmate and 17th Pursuit squadron mate of Glover, was hot on the tails of two Zeros that had been attacking two PBY Catalina flying boats that had taken off from Sangley Point at the Cavite naval base just south of Manila. But then a Zero latched on Phillips's tail as he headed back over Sangley Point. As the two adversaries passed over the Marine antiaircraft battalion at the Cavite base, the Marines opened up on the Zero with 3-inch fire but hit Phillips's P-40 instead. His ship fatally stricken, Phillips bailed out over Manila Bay, where he was picked up by the navy.

Squadron mate Forrest Hobrecht was down low over Nichols Field during the strafing raid of 12:40 to 12:45, shortly after his takeoff, a Zero on his tail. When about three-fourths the way across the field, 20-mm shells from the Zero set his P-40E on fire. In his attempt to bail out, he hit the stabilizer and fell to the ground in Barrio Navarro, about three miles east of Nichols, his chute unopened. Filipino police found his lifeless body near the ship. Just before taking off from Nichols, Hobrecht had remarked to a friend (probably "Dub" Balfanz), "I'll be killed in the first dogfight I get in." It was an ironic fate for the meticulously careful pilot, who had not been keen to fly pursuit in the first place.

10 At Barrio Pasacola, Caloocan, on the north side of Nichols Field and Manila, Andy Krieger was contemplating his luck in surviving his low-level bailout when he abruptly found himself face-to-face with sev-

Flying school classmates "Dub" Balfanz (*left*) and Forrest Hobrecht with their 17th Pursuit P-35As at Iba, summer, 1941. *Courtesy Alfred P. Hobrecht, Col. USA (Ret.)*

eral Filipino farmers armed with bolos, pitchforks, and various kinds of antiquated firearms. They thought he was one of the Japanese and intended to express their displeasure with Japan's aggression against their homeland. But when it became clear that Krieger was one of their country's heroic defenders, they became overjoyed and could not show their appreciation enough. They took him to their village of nipa huts, where about a hundred natives crowded around him, offering him presents. To avoid offending them, Krieger downed two half-pint bottles of "some kind of native rotgut" proffered him. It was fiery, but in his state of shock from his nearly fatal flying accident, he did not feel a thing. Then a Filipino captain of the Philippine Constabulary took Krieger to his home nearby, where they each had a couple of bottles of beer.

When General Francisco, chief of the constabulary, showed up in a big Buick with a motorcycle escort, Krieger was given a car and escort of his own for a ride to the constabulary barracks in Quezon City. There he had a round with each of what seemed like dozens of Filipino officers.

They had all witnessed Krieger's dogfight over Quezon City and he was now quite a celebrity (and quite inebriated).

11 In a less festive mood that afternoon were the brass of the Far East Air Force and USAFFE Headquarters. Of the fifty-one P-40s available for operations at the start of the day,[16] only twenty-eight were now left, including six requiring repairs, a loss of twenty-three.[17] Taking into consideration that ten P-35As has also been destroyed or heavily damaged on December 10 (with only five now remaining), the loss of thirty-three pursuit aircraft this day was almost as great as the loss of thirty-five on December 8.

If the pursuit pilots were not convinced after the December 8 events, they were now: it was impossible to turn with a Zero in combat. Miraculously, only one (Hobrecht) had lost his life.[18] But many were no longer prepared to go up in a P-40 against a Zero.[19]

It was bad enough to have to dogfight with the Zero in such an aerodynamically inferior aircraft. In addition, the pilots invariably found themselves having to take off to intercept with only a few minutes' notice of an incoming attack because of the absence of any functioning air warning system. As Grant Mahony complained, "The first warning any of us on the ground would get that Japs were in the vicinity would come when we saw them diving over the hills shooting at us." And when the pilots did not suffer from an altitude disadvantage and were pressing home an attack, many or all of their .50-caliber guns were often inoperative—they were jammed, because of either ammunition feeding problems or the residue of cold-hardened Cosmoline left around the breech block. The pilots were helpless to remedy the situation in the air. The guns had to be cleared and recharged on the ground.[20]

With over 70 percent of its aircraft destroyed after only three days of the campaign, the 24th Pursuit Group now had a heavy surplus of pilots in relation to planes. A decision was made to reserve the remaining aircraft for the most senior and experienced pilots of the group. The others were assigned to nonflying duties in communications, transportation, and other ground support activities of the USAFFE.

13. "EVERYTHING ALL RIGHT. HAVE A SAFE JOB"

1 Shortly after daybreak on Thursday, December 11, lone P-40s began taking off from Clark, Nichols, and Nielson fields on reconnaissance missions that would extend throughout the whole day. Reports of rapid progress of Japanese landing forces at Vigan and also now at Aparri, on the northern coast of Luzon, had created an urgent need for such reconnaissance flights to report any further landings and monitor the enemy's movements. Since the O-46s and O-52s of the 2nd Observation Squadron were all now either destroyed or damaged, the task had fallen to the pursuit pilots.

The pursuiters were not thrilled with their new assignment, and when they learned that they were also being ordered by USAFFE Headquarters to "avoid direct combat," they were even more resentful. All P-40 missions were to be assigned by FEAF Headquarters only, in response to USAFFE Headquarters orders. The reason given was that with the number of P-40s now reduced to twenty-two only (ten at Nichols and twelve at Clark) it was necessary to "conserve them to the maximum."

The first pilot back from the morning recon missions was Grant Mahony. After landing at Nielson at 7:25 A.M., he reported negative Japanese activity on his recon of southwest Luzon and the west coast of Mindoro to the south. Forty-five minutes later, his buddy Bob Hanson reported in on his mission covering the thirty miles north of Lingayen Gulf down to Subic Bay: no Japanese vessels observed in that area either.

The hot spots of Aparri and Vigan were being given priority attention in reconnaissance flights from Clark Field. At 9:30 George Armstrong was instructed to send a P-40 to the Aparri area to secure information on the type and location of Japanese vessels and transports in the water between Cape Engaño and Aparri. Ordered to fly at high altitude and avoid combat, the P-40 pilot selected for the mission took off at 10:47. One hour later, another pilot in from his recon of Vigan reported seeing five small transports and one large one as well as a naval vessel (believed to be a battleship) and three destroyers.

The surveillance of the Japanese landings at Aparri and Vigan continued into the afternoon. At 2:25 P.M. a mission was ordered to reconnoiter
Aparri again. Instructions were given to use only experienced pilots on
recon missions. When Russel Church landed at 7:05 that evening after
a reconnaissance of Vigan, he reported spotting six transports and ten
small and three larger naval craft, with the overcast reaching up to 16,000
feet. One hour before midnight, FEAF Headquarters ordered new missions from Clark Field at daybreak to cover the Aparri and Vigan areas
again.

2 At Nichols Field, the pilots flying recon missions were living under
better conditions than their counterparts at Clark. Compared with the
Clark pilots, roughing it in their camp in the jungle, they were "fairly
sleek and clean," in Don Steele's view, and were eating well at the Army
and Navy Club in Manila.

For the enlisted men and planeless officers of his 3rd Pursuit Squadron, the past few days had been traumatic. The day before, disorganized
groups of the 3rd Pursuit who had evacuated Iba Field on December 8
under chaotic conditions began straggling into Nichols Field. Many arrived just as Nichols was being subjected to the midday bombing and
strafing attack of December 10. It was Iba all over again for the men, who
had not yet recovered from their earlier ordeal there.

For those who had walked over the mountains and gotten lost, it would
be several days before they arrived at Nichols, shoeless and completely
beaten in spirit. For S. Sgt. Floyd Grow, led barefoot through the mountains with several others by Negrito tribesmen, it proved to be a five-day
ordeal.

At the Knights of Columbus canteen in downtown Manila on December 10, Fr. Forbes Monaghan, an American Jesuit professor of philosophy
at the Ateneo de Manila, was trying to comfort a group of the squadron's
enlisted men, "mere boys of 18 or 20," who had arrived in Manila that
day from Iba, "ragged, hungry, and demoralized." As Father Monaghan
talked to them, "the siren of a police car sounded on the street outside.
A look of panic came over their faces and they leaped for a corner in which
to hide. When I reassured them, they sat down, trembling, but their faces
never lost the set crazed look that had been on them since I first entered
the canteen." After telling them stories to ease their anxiety, Father Monaghan went back to his college "to get them socks, underwear, tooth-
brushes, and other necessities which the broken-down supply system could
not furnish them at the time." But when he returned, they were gone.

The men had reported in at Nichols Field to their CO, Hank Thorne,
who was now arranging for their needs as best he could under the circumstances. They now joined remnants of the 17th Pursuit's enlisted men,
who shared their C rations with the men of their sister squadron. Then

they were issued gabardine flight suits, the only clothing available to wear, but at least an improvement over the tattered apparel they had worn on the trek from Iba. All needed to take a bath, but the only water available near them was a carabao wallow, and they had to stand in line to wait their turns in the muddy water.

Although they were not shell-shocked, the 17th Pursuit's enlisted men were not much better off in living conditions than were the 3rd Pursuit men. The officer in charge of the men, 1st Lt. Ridgley Hall, the 17th Pursuit's adjutant, had moved the men into the woods some two miles south of Nichols Field after the December 10 attack on Nichols. Sleeping there under rude conditions, they were also being rained on almost every night. At that distance from the field, it was also "just impossible" for them to carry out any effective maintenance of the aircraft at Nichols.

The day before, Dave Obert had taken upon himself supervision of the aircraft maintenance work at Nichols. It was not his job, but Hall just did not understand what had to be done or how to do it. The first sergeant, Joe King, told Obert that despite his efforts, he could not get the mechanics to stay at the field and do the maintenance work required; they were scared of bombing attacks following the December 8/9 night raid on Nichols. Obert had spent most of the morning of December 10 rounding up the crews and getting them back to work. He found that as long as he stayed there with them, he could keep them at work. On December 11, he was "still trying to push the maintenance work on the planes and get the squadron's ground crews organized."

To add to the problems, Major General Brereton, commanding general of the FEAF, ordered that every man available in the Nichols area be armed and placed in readiness to combat any paratroop attack. He had heard a report that Japanese paratroopers had landed further north on Luzon and expected a repeat performance in the Nichols area. "All that day," Obert recorded in his diary, "the vicinity of Nichols sounded like a battlefield; everyone seemed to want to test his rifle or machine gun every little while, and the rattle of small arms could be heard continually." But no Japanese appeared.

The next day, December 12, the 3rd Pursuit was ordered by FEAF Headquarters to move into de la Salle College, in Manila, where the squadron could be gotten together again and organized. At the same time, the enlisted men of the 21st Pursuit, who had remained behind at Nichols Field when most of the pilots had gone up to Clark, were also ordered to the college. Many of the 21st's men had scattered in terror after the December 10 bombing and strafing of Nichols, but now all would be reunited. There they would be joined by the pilots of their squadron, who were being transferred without their planes back to Manila from Clark.

Before he moved to his new quarters at de la Salle College that day,

Don Steele managed to solve his transportation needs. Spotting a "big, red 1941 Packard convertible with red leather upholstery," Steele "convinced" the local owner to give it to him, though the man "was not too happy about the exchange, as I had nothing to offer." At any rate, the owner "saw my point of view after a while and I promised him that he would get it back, but did not give him any definite time as to when to expect it."

Dave Obert found that he was also to move that day. He had been ordered up to Clark Field with a few of the other 17th Pursuiters at Nichols to join the others at Clark. For the newly married pilot, it was a tough order to obey. That morning at the Army and Navy Club, Dorothy Obert was holding back tears as her husband, lump in his throat and straining to keep his voice from quivering, was trying to cheer her up after giving her the unwelcome news. All during the long rainy trip to Clark in a truck that afternoon, Obert wondered if he would ever get back to Manila.

3 At the 20th Pursuit's jungle camp off Clark Field the morning of December 12, the pursuit pilots were excitedly listening to the account of Buzz Wagner, who landed at 10:00 and was reporting on the results of his "reconnaissance" of the Aparri area. He had quite a story to tell.

The 17th Pursuit's commanding officer had taken off from Clark at 6:15 that morning. Running into heavy overcast at 5,000 feet, he turned on the oxygen and climbed over it at 16,000 feet. Dead reckoning for about two hundred miles, he let his P-40 down on instruments and broke through the overcast at 8,000 feet, an estimated ten minutes north of Aparri, "almost on top of two Japanese destroyers," about one mile north of the mouth of the river at Aparri. As Wagner recounted:

> Almost at once they threw a heavy barrage up around me and I turned nose-down and dived within a few feet of the water, avoiding their A.A., and swung inland several miles. I knew that I was approaching Aparri airport but flying into the sun I couldn't see clearly.
>
> Suddenly tracer fire tore by me from overhead, and instinctively I did a steep chandelle into the sun. Looking back, I saw two Japanese pursuit behind me and three more overhead, low-wing fixed landing gear single seaters, so I pulled nose-up and continued to climb directly into the sun at full throttle and low pitch. Now the two Nippos who fired on me lost me. I went into a half barrel roll onto their tails from my upper position and attacked them from the rear. They were in close formation and both burst into flames almost simultaneously, the fliers going down with their planes.
>
> Then for the first time I realized that I was right over their airport. Almost directly below me was a runway and on it twelve enemy pursuit planes. I made two passes at the field, strafing the grounded planes as I swept over. I saw five of them burst into flames.
>
> Just as I was pulling up from my second pass, I saw that three pursuits above had seen me and were pouring down on me. I dropped an

Buzz Wagner on the beach at Iba, summer, 1941. *Courtesy Ada E. Childers*

empty belly tank for greater speed and dived close to the ground, making it difficult for them to see me, then gave it the needle and easily
outdistanced them.

I had filled my assignment, and as gas was getting low, headed for
home. The last I saw of the field was two long columns of black smoke.

For his exploit, Wagner received lavish praise in Major Grover's official report on the incident, including his completing the assigned task
of observing Japanese vessels offshore. MacArthur's chief of staff, Brigadier General Sutherland, was informed at 10:30 by Brereton's chief of staff,
Colonel Brady, that "12 aircraft on Aparri field were raked by a reconnaissance with good effect."[1] Strictly speaking, Wagner had not violated
the USAFFE order in taking on the Japanese interceptors, since he had not
sought combat; rather, he was defending himself from attack, which was
permitted. His strafing attack, however, was outside this authorization.

Publicity in the United States on this and subsequent daring attacks
made "Buzz" Wagner the best-known pursuit pilot in the Philippines campaign and a national hero. All who knew him in the Philippines agreed
that he was a genius with a plane who could "do anything with it." As
Andy Krieger of the 3rd Pursuit maintained a few years later, "When Wagner went out, he knew he'd be all right, because there was not another
man on earth who could fly like him."

Wagner's feat was not the only example of daring flying on December 12. At 6:40 that morning, USAFFE Headquarters was informed that Japanese warships had landed troops at 5:00 at Legaspi, in southeastern Luzon.[2] To oppose this third incursion of the Japanese on Philippine soil, Sutherland and Brady in late morning discussed a bombing attack by B-17s, but for some reason it did not materialize. In the event, two P-40 pilots at Nichols Field were ordered to attack the Japanese at Legaspi. They were to dive-bomb the Legaspi-Manila railroad terminus and thus, it was hoped, slow the enemy's progress north to Manila.

That afternoon Grant Mahony and Bob Hanson took off on the mission, clearly one of a combat nature. Hanson's P-40 was not equipped with bomb racks, so he was given the responsibility for flying cover for Mahony while the latter bombed the railroad. Arriving over Legaspi, Mahony bombed and strafed the target area in several passes as Hanson guarded him overhead. Then he radioed Hanson, "I've dropped all my bombs and am ready to go home. My ammunition is all gone so you'd better not come down—I can't cover you."

But Hanson radioed back, "Wait a minute, Grunt, you're not going to have all the fun!" Diving down through thick antiaircraft fire, Hanson first strafed the newly occupied airstrip, wrecking equipment and scattering troops, then attacked transports and small boats unloading troops, flying so close the Japanese on the boat were obliged to jump into the water. Next he shot down a large four-engine flying boat trying to take off under cover of fire from an escorting destroyer. Then with his remaining ammunition, Hanson went after another destroyer, putting one of its antiaircraft guns out of commission. On the way home, the two jubilant Californians sang "On Westlake" and "Hail to You, Vallejo Junior High" over their radios, "loud enough for everyone in the Far East to hear us." Back at Nichols, Mahony and Hanson were praised for their feat. But they were also criticized for blaring out those school songs over their radios. The two answered that since they were not giving out any military information, why not broadcast their songs?

At a 4:15 P.M. meeting with Sutherland, Brereton was not quite fully informative when he told MacArthur's chief of staff that the Air Corps had "reconnoitered" Legaspi that afternoon. This was the same stance taken by the FEAF in its report to USAFFE G-2 at 4:00 P.M. Apparently the Mahony/Hanson mission had not been cleared with USAFFE Headquarters, and perhaps not even with FEAF Headquarters. But MacArthur needed heroes. Hanson was subsequently awarded the Distinguished Flying Cross for the mission and Mahony the Distinguished Service Cross for this and earlier exploits. After the mission, in typical fashion for him, Mahony cabled his mother in Vallejo, California: "Everything all right. Have a safe job."

4 When Dave Obert and the other Nichols-based 17th Pursuit pilots arrived at Clark Field late in the afternoon of December 12, they found that all the personnel of the field had moved back into the jungle to escape air raids. They reported in at the "20th's camp," named after the original occupants, the 20th Pursuit Squadron. It was sited about three miles from Clark Field in the jungle on both sides of the old Spanish Trail leading across Mount Pinatuba to the China Sea.

Reunited with the rest of the pilots of their squadron, Obert and the others heard of the really scary raid on Clark that morning. At about 10:30, eighteen twin-engine bombers had descended below the heavy overcast obscuring the base and had unloaded at only 900 feet.

Bill Rowe, Joe McClellan, and Wilson Glover were over at the Officers Club at nearby Fort Stotsenburg for a haircut and a shave when they heard the bombers overhead. Springing out of the barber shop, they ran up the road and hid in a culvert, McClellan and Rowe in one end and Glover in the other. The sound of the bombs exploding and the antiaircraft fire was terrific. Rowe had never been more scared in his life. When the raid was over, fifteen minutes later, the three 17th Pursuiters found out that the bombers had hit near Clark Field but not close to them; it just felt like they were in the target area.

Dropped at such a low altitude, many of the bombs had failed to go off. One of the duds had landed in a trench among a group of enlisted men, scaring the daylights out of them. After the raid, demolition crews went out to set off the unexploded bombs. Reverberations rocked the base every few minutes.

At the 20th's camp, Obert was not too impressed with the living accommodations; they were mainly of bamboo poles to hold up vines covered with banana leaves as a roof, a bed of leaves, and G.I. blankets or a cot. He was told that it rained every morning, leaving the pilots soaked in their leaking shelters. For washing and bathing, there was a stream of fresh water nearby.

Six of the pooled pilots of the 17th and 20th pursuit squadrons were ready for missions at all times during their twenty-four hour alert call. They would get up early in the morning and walk down to 24th Group Headquarters, located in an old farmhouse in the woods north of Clark. There they would pass the morning in the hope that if a recon were ordered, they would be selected to fly it. To Obert, there seemed to be no plan for the future. At least, no one seemed to have any idea.

The enlisted men of the 20th Pursuit were also living in the 20th camp area, trying to make their rude accommodations as livable as possible. Sgt. Bill Joy and Pfc Jim Brown had fashioned "rather comfortable" quarters with shelter halves and blankets. As Brown recalls. "We had only to crawl out of bed and dip some water from the adjacent creek to wash.

Pilots of the 17th and 20th pursuit squadrons in the jungle near Clark Field, December 11, 1941. *Left to right, seated:* Buzz Wagner, Russel Church, Bill Hennon, Dan Blass, Percy Ramsey, and Fred Browne (on ground); *standing, front row:* unknown, John Posten, Jack Dale, John Vogel, Carl Gies, unknown, unknown, unknown, Bud Powell (with back to tree), and unknown; *back row:* unknown, Willis Culp, unknown, unknown, Silas Wolf, Jack Gates, and Tom Patrick. *Photograph by Carl Mydans; copyright © Life Magazine*

Our World War I helmets were used as wash basins. Our drinking water source was Lister bags in the field kitchen area."

The work of the squadron's enlisted men was to keep Clark's P-40s in repair, under the guidance of 2nd Lt. Harrison "Spec" Hughes, the squadron's engineering officer, one of its 41-B flying school contingent. Every morning, the men were awakened at dawn by CWO Bill Heller, who would bellow in his foghorn voice, "Daylight in the swamp — hit the deck!" After a quick breakfast, the men were loaded on trucks and hauled to the repair area, which was in a wooded area on the east edge of the flying field, well camouflaged with netting.

During their "long, bone-wearing" stints, Jim Brown and the other mechanics of the 20th Pursuit dragged damaged aircraft from the field into the woods and then hunted spare parts from other wrecks on the field. Many planes were assembled by using two or three wrecks to make one good plane. Two of the squadron's P-40Bs were rebuilt this way, giving Clark five P-40Bs in service at the time. As Brown noted years later, "The jury-rigged repair work would have resulted in a court-martial of every mechanic in the squadron if it had been done in peacetime." But now there was no alternative. Most of the spare parts and service equipment of the squadron had been wiped out by the Japanese in the first attack on the field.

The salvage work was equally exhausting for the men of the group's Headquarters Squadron, sited in the woods south of the field. Working a twelve- to sixteen-hour day, Pfc Jesse White and the other maintenance men of the squadron toiled under the blazing sun salvaging aircraft parts and rebuilding P-40 wrecks, "the sweat pouring off our bodies, drenching our clothing and swishing in our shoes, while the dust from the runway turned to mud on our faces. We resembled mud balls with two eyes peeping out," White recalls. Trudging back to their bivouac area at the end of their day, the men usually slipped by the deserted sawali barracks of the 19th Bomb Group for a shower.

The squadron's line chief, Clarence Hatzer, and flight chief, Bill Miller, "were everywhere, supervising, inspecting and working with us as we put the pieces together. We cannibalized every wrecked P-40 on the base for spare parts. We found one P-40 intact, a half-mile from the end of the runway in a cane field. No one knew how it got there. We assumed that the pilot had tried to take off during the December 8 bombing and had run out of fuel on takeoff, as the tanks were empty.[3] We towed it back to the runway and soon had it back in commission."

Despite the best efforts of the mechanics of both squadrons to get as many planes into operation as possible, maintenance work suffered with the dawn-to-dusk use of the aircraft. Thus Cy Blanton, on a recon one day in a P-40 that the day before had incurred damage that had gone unnoticed, had to get back on the ground as fast as he could immediately following takeoff when the liquid-cooled Allison heated far beyond its limit, smoke and steam streaming out of the engine.

Despite frequent Japanese air attacks on Clark, the repair camp of the 20th Pursuit in the woods, with its airplanes, tools, and personnel, went unnoticed by the raiders. To Jim Brown, this was surprising, since "the dust was so thick it turned the trees brown and new green camouflage on the camp's netting stood out like 'Rudolph's Red Nose.'" Apparently the Japanese were preoccupied with the fleet of paper decoy planes the engineers had built on wooden posts, with propellers that actually turned in the wind, along with the planes left in the "boneyard." The decoy planes were rebuilt after each raid. The boneyard planes would take repeated strafing without burning, as they had been drained of all gas and oil before being assigned to the scrap pile.[4]

5 Down at Del Carmen field, some of the 34th Pursuit's enlisted men were also busy keeping decoys on the field to occupy Japanese bombers and strafers. Ben Brown had ordered his men to patch up the P-35As disabled in the December 10 raid and position them on a make-believe take-off line on the strip.[5] Wood dummy P-35As were also constructed and added to the others. During the next few days, Japanese Army and Navy bombers and fighters would work over the decoys during intensive raids and return with glowing reports of the numbers of planes destroyed.

Another target for the Japanese aircraft was two sugar railway tank cars used earlier to transport molasses from the sugar refinery to the airstrip, where it was sprinkled to keep the pervasive dust down. The tank cars were parked on a siding near the runway, filled with the liquid molasses mixture. On December 13, a strafing Zero made a pass at what the pilot must have assumed were fuel tankers, firing tracers into the tanks and then pulling up, obviously waiting for the explosion. When nothing happened, the pilot made another pass, but still with no effect. Likely giving up in disgust, he never knew that he had saturated the surrounding ground with molasses.

More worrisome to most of the enlisted men of the 34th Pursuit, living away from the field in the sugar central area, were the five-hundred-pound bombs scattered all through the scrub brush near them. The bombs had been intended for the use of the A-24 single-engined bombers of the 27th Bomb Group that were to have been based at Del Carmen but never reached the Philippines. Although the ordnance people had assured the men that they could not explode if hit during the frequent Japanese air attacks, many of the men were skeptical.

Except for the twenty or so men left at the field, there was little work for either officers or men of the virtually planeless 34th Pursuit during this period. The men in the sugar central guarded the entrance to the town. At the field the antiaircraft gun and communications dugout was manned, and a ground crew was alerted to service any planes that might land and to keep the decoys in good condition and in position on the field.

6 At 6:00 A.M. on December 13, 1st Lts. Marshall Anderson and Walt Coss lifted their P-40s off the Clark strip on the first reconnaissance missions of the day. The two pilots had spent the night sleeping in their chutes under a pile of lumber outside the operations shack near Clark Field to be ready for their daybreak missions. They did not get much sleep, since it rained some during the evening and the lumber pile leaked.

Anderson was headed to Vigan, while Coss's mission was to Aparri, where he was supposed to look for shipping, road traffic, and any military activity on this the fourth day of the Japanese landing. It was also the day after "Buzz" Wagner had stirred up the hornet's nest of Japanese fighters based there.

After climbing to altitude, Coss ran into an overcast over northern Luzon. As did Wagner under similar circumstances the day before, Coss flew above it and out to sea twenty to thirty miles north of Aparri, then turned back south and dropped down into the overcast. As he recalled years later,

> Every few minutes I'd drop out of the bottom of the overcast, take a look around, and then climb back into the clouds. I got a good look at the airfield and roads and thought I had a pretty safe system. That is, until I unexpectedly ran out of the overcast and into the clear, right in front of and below two Japs. They must have been tracking me, but I don't know how.
>
> I saw two aircraft, but only one fired.[6] He didn't have to do much but pull the trigger. I went into a dive but at about 1,000 feet the engine quit and started throwing out smoke. I rolled over on my back, pushed the stick forward, and opened the safety belt. The altimeter read 800 feet when I left, but I delayed opening the chute until about 200 feet. I was right over the middle of the Cagayan River and several miles north of the town of Gattaran.
>
> After I landed in the river, one of the Japs strafed me four or five times.[7] Fortunately I was able to rid myself of the chute and the bright yellow life vest I was wearing. I threw the vest into the middle of the floating chute and dove for the river bottom. After each pass, I'd come to the surface and watch the Jap climb away. He finally headed back to the airfield and I swam out of the river on the west side.

After the 17th Pursuiter got out of the river, he was assisted by local natives, who provided him with food, clothing, guides, and a .25-caliber automatic pistol to replace the .45 Colt that had torn loose from his belt during the jump. Then he set out on foot in the direction of Clark.

Marshall Anderson's recon mission turned out much less traumatic. After landing safely back at Clark, the 20th Pursuiter phoned in to USAFFE Headquarters at 9:25 A.M. with his report of Japanese activities on the coast from Vigan to Lingayen Gulf and down to Iba. He had seen two transports at Vigan, but "nothing else of interest."

7 One hour after Anderson's report was phoned to USAFFE Headquarters, another came in on the results of a recon to Legaspi. The pilot had spotted ships off of Legaspi and in Poliqui Bay that he identified as a carrier, a cruiser, two destroyers, and seven unknown.[8] But USAFFE wanted more information on this force and the progress of the Japanese

landings at Legaspi. At 11:40, FEAF Headquarters ordered another reconnaissance mission by P-40s from Nichols.

The call for the mission went once more to that indomitable pair, Grant Mahony and Bob Hanson, at their quarters at Paranaque near Nichols that they shared with Andy Krieger. FEAF wanted one or both of them to go down to Legaspi again. Hanson yelled over to Mahony, "Let's get going, Grunt!" But then he took back his words. His buddy had been on a mission the night before after returning from the Legaspi bombing mission in the afternoon and was pretty tired. As Mahony climbed out of bed, Hanson said, "Oh, no you don't. You go back to bed. Krieger will go with me."

When Hanson and Krieger arrived in their car at the Nichols Field gate around 12:30, they were informed that there was an alert on; enemy bombers were expected momentarily. The air raid siren had sounded about fifteen minutes earlier, but they had not paid much attention to it. Now they continued out to the field; a raid was the furthest thing from their minds.

As they turned into Nichols Field, Hanson remarked, "Well, I hope we get off the ground before they get here." Everyone was running for shelter at the entrance to Nichols. Then a guard stopped their car and told them they had better go back because the Japanese were coming over. Krieger and Hanson turned around and started for the beach, a couple of blocks away. Then Krieger looked up and saw them, about fifty-four in the first wave. They were at the bomb release line. The two 3rd Pursuiters jumped out of the car and ran to a concrete wall beside the road and lay down next to it.

The target was Nichols Field, but the bombs were missing and falling one block west, which was right where the two pilots were hunkering down. On the first salvo, Hanson was hit. Krieger saw the blood coming from his arm and thought a fragment had just hit him there and broken his arm, causing him to faint. But when Krieger grabbed his arm at the pressure point in the armpit, he saw that the fragment had gone right through his chest too. While the second wave came over and dropped its load, Krieger sat by Hanson and tried to revive him, but it was no use. Hanson died without regaining consciousness.

The second salvo was falling in the same area as the first, and shrapnel was flying all around Krieger, but he hardly noticed it. Krieger took Hanson's helmet and scooped out a shallow trench, which partially protected him. The third wave came over and dropped its bombs, and then it was all over.

Krieger felt numb all over. He had prayed hard and thought his time had come for sure. The concrete wall was absolutely riddled. The houses in the vicinity were sieves, and some had been knocked down. All the trees were splintered. It looked like there were a good fifty craters within one hundred feet of where they had been lying.[9] Krieger wanted to put Hanson in the car and take him to the morgue, but one of the tires was blown out, and there was no jack. He noticed several holes through vital parts too, including the engine. Finally, a military truck came and picked him up.

Despite his crushing experience, Krieger still had to go fly the Legaspi mission.[10] "It was kind of hard, and I was all shot," he recorded in his wartime narrative. That night, after his return, Krieger went out and got drunk.

Also undergoing a traumatic experience as a result of the inaccuracy of the Japanese bomber pilots this day was Krieger's squadron mate Don Steele. He had watched the raid from the roof of a house of a friend he was visiting at the time. Seeing that many of the bombs had fallen on Barrio Baclaren adjacent to Nichols Field, Steele and squadron mates Gordon Benson and Jim Field drove over to the scene to offer their help to the Filipino inhabitants. Arriving some ten minutes before the ambulances, the pilots witnessed a scene of carnage all around them. "Everywhere people were screaming and hollering and we started to pull them out and lay them on the road," he recorded in his diary that evening. All of them had been hit by shrapnel. It appeared that they had just stood and watched the bombing, rather than take shelter.

The first person Steele tried to pick up was a woman whose head and shoulders were sticking out from under an upturned table, plaster piled on top of it. Steele tipped the table back and found that the lower half of the woman's body was completely blown away. "This did not make me feel any too good, and Lt. Field promptly left the scene and went and lay down on the seat of the car," Steele wrote that night. He and Benson managed to control their feelings, however, and moved everyone they could who was "still making a noise" up the road.

Nearby, at adjoining Paranaque, 2nd Lt. Joe Cole of the 21st Pursuit, who with most of the other pilots of his squadron had arrived at Manila from Clark during the raid, was going through what remained of his old house. He managed to extricate most of his clothes and headed into Manila to arrange for their storage.

8 At 4:30 P.M. on Sunday, December 14, the Japanese at their newly established base at Legaspi were surprised to find themselves under attack by a lone P-40. On his way back to Nichols from a cross-country mission to Mindanao, Grant Mahony had decided to return via Legaspi to take a look at the situation there. He knew that FEAF Headquarters would be interested in any fresh information on Japanese activities he might be able to bring back. And with the death of his best friend, Bob

Hanson, the day before, the war against the Japanese had become a personal vendetta for him.

Diving from 13,000 feet, Mahony spotted the radio shack formerly operated by U.S. forces and raked it with .50-caliber fire. From the tiny structure, Japanese came streaming out and fled down the slope into foxholes. As soon as he had begun his dive, antiaircraft guns "began winking little lights" at him from over in the corner of the Legaspi airstrip. As he turned away, the guns kept firing at him.

Diving down again to swing over the trees, Mahony spotted a number of Mitsubishi G4M "Betty" bombers and Zero fighters, plus a transport resembling a Lockheed, parked at one end of the field.[11] "I thought: *This is mine,*" Mahony recounted to a war correspondent two months later. Here was the challenge the worked-up Californian had been waiting for since the war began, and an opportunity to avenge Hanson's death. But just before he put his stick over to go for them, he took a quick look up just to be sure everything was all right.

"Everything was *not* all right. There were four Zeros standing straight up and down, falling on my tail as perpendicular as raindrops," as he described the situation to the war correspondent. "I swung over toward the parked bombers and fighters, leading the reception committee out of the line of their dive. We reached a place over the aircraft about the same time, and everybody was shooting: the Japs at me and I at the Mitsubishis and fighters. I don't know whose bullets did more damage to the [parked] aircraft. But they hardly touched me."[12]

Mahony then headed over to Mount Mayon, the volcano just five miles to the northwest of Legaspi town. The Zeros were still chasing him. "They could do everything better and faster than I could and I thought I was a goner." Mahony decided to try to confuse his opponents by playing "ring around a rosy." As he flew around the eight-thousand-foot, conelike Mount Mayon, the Japanese split into two and circled around the mountain in opposite directions. "They got so confused guessing which was themselves and which was me" that Mahony on the second go-around managed to slip down to treetop level and make a getaway through the valleys back to Nichols.

9 At de la Salle College in Manila on the afternoon of December 15, all the enlisted men of the 21st Pursuit, plus Joe Cole and three other officers of the squadron, were piling into buses for a trip to a new field the Japanese did not know about. That morning, FEAF Headquarters had ordered their transfer to the new fighter strip being constructed at Barrio Prado, off the road seven miles west of Lubao—a small town thirty-five miles northwest of Manila. The field was now reportedly ready for operations. Except for their CO, Ed Dyess, who would be going to the Lubao field too, the other officers of the 21st Pursuit not assigned to the secret

field, including Sam Grashio and Gus Williams, received new assignments to nonflying duties and were being detailed elsewhere.

After the 21st Pursuit had moved out of de la Salle College for its new assignment, the enlisted men of the 17th Pursuit moved in, ending their period of roughing it in the bivouac area of Fort McKinley reservation. At the college, they now bedded down in the gymnasium. With the men of the 3rd Pursuit and a few other Air Corps units staying there too, there were now 350 enlisted men at de la Salle College on the morning of December 16, 1941, under the supervision of a few Air Corps second lieutenants.

10 At Clark Field the night before, there had been a big party at the Fort Stotsenburg Officers Club held by the pilots of the 17th and 20th pursuit squadrons. From their camp in the jungle nearby, the pilots had discovered in recent days that the club was still open, despite the regular Japanese bombing attacks on adjacent Clark Field, and they had virtually turned it into a pilots' lounge.

For this party, the pilots had invited the nurses at Fort Stotsenburg hospital and had 1,500 cases of beer available to relieve any inhibitions. However, there were about fifteen pilots fighting for the attention of each nurse. Still, 2nd Lt. Erwin Crellin, one of the 41-B contingent of the 20th Pursuit, had managed to "sew up" one of them, Sally Blaine, to the apparent envy of his classmate Parker Gies.

Less cheerful at the party was "Spec" Hughes, the 20th's engineering officer. He was mad because no one would go down with him to the line and help him with maintaining Clark's dwindling supply of P-40s. But Gies rationalized that most of the pilots "would only be in the way. Don't know a thing about it."

Joe Moore and Buzz Wagner had more serious matters on their minds that evening than beer drinking and fighting over nurses. They were getting ready to flip a coin for an important mission at daybreak. On a morning reconnaisssance that day, Russel Church of the 17th Pursuit had spotted twenty-nine Japanese pursuit planes on the field at Vigan.[13] Reacting quickly, Major Grover decided—without checking with FEAF Headquarters at McKinley—to send two P-40s up to bomb and strafe them the next morning. Moore and Wagner each wanted to lead the mission. If Wagner won the toss, he would take Church as his wingman, while if Moore won, Keator would fly his wing, as he had done the first day of the war. The two commanding officers flipped, and Wagner won.

At 5:50 on the morning of December 16, with each P-40 carrying six instantaneous-fuse thirty-pound fragmentation bombs under its wings, Wagner and Church took off for the Vigan mission. Joining them was Allison Strauss, who was to fly top cover for them. Arriving over Vigan, they were met by intense Japanese antiaircraft fire. While Strauss remained up at 15,000 feet, Wagner went into a dive, followed a half mile behind by Church. Below them, at the west end of the field, were parked some twenty-five pursuit planes, a Douglas-type transport, and five other types of aircraft.

At 2,500 feet over the motionless Japanese ships, Wagner released his bombs, scoring several direct hits. But when Church went into his diving approach, the Japanese guns were ready for him and scored a hit on his plane's nose, which burst into flames. Looking back for Church after he had pulled out of his dive, Wagner saw that the whole belly of Church's P-40 was in flames. Over the radio, Wagner ordered Church to turn back and bail out. But Church did not turn back. He dipped the nose of his blazing ship toward the target, going down "like a hellbent fireball," then flattened out over the target. Wagner saw every bomb fall squarely among the grounded planes, a "perfectly executed attack."

As Wagner recalled the experience months later, "For seconds it almost seemed that Russel would be able to gain control. The ship still held its course, still flaming, and then it suddenly rocked wildly and plunged sideways to earth. Its gas tank exploded at the same time the plane hit the ground. . . . I know that Church knew he was facing certain death when he decided to remain with the mission."

Sweeping back over the field, Wagner was joined by Strauss in one strafing pass after another on the still motionless Japanese aircraft. Just as Wagner started yet another strafing run, a "Nate" managed to get off the ground. Although Wagner spotted the fixed-landing-gear fighter, the Japanese was half-hidden from Wagner's sight by his own wing. Flipping his P-40 on its back only feet above the ground for a clear view, Wagner got the Nate in his sights, then righted his plane and throttled back to let the Japanese pursuit build up speed. A burst from Wagner's .50-caliber guns sent the Japanese into the ground.

With his ammunition exhausted and gas low, Wagner signaled Strauss, and the two headed back to Clark. Behind them, they left an estimated ten Japanese aircraft on fire or shattered on the airfield and a fuel tank on fire.[14]

Joe Moore, who had lost the flip for the Vigan assignment, flew a mission to Aparri instead, with Marshall Anderson (rather than Randy Keator) as his wingman, also carrying wing bombs. The compass of Moore's P-40 went out, however, and he ended up way off course and had to abort the mission.

Although they regretted the loss of the popular Church, the other pilots of the group at Clark were cheered to hear the results of the Vigan attack. It was a good morale booster.[15] But FEAF Headquarters did not share their enthusiasm on hearing a few hours after the return of Wagner and Strauss of the unauthorized mission. At 12:20 P.M., Major General

Brereton called Major Grover at Clark and directed him to execute only missions ordered by FEAF Headquarters except in dire emergency and to furnish a report on the Vigan attack. Grover had clearly violated the order of December 10 barring direct combat and requiring FEAF approval of all 24th Group missions. Although the mission was flown in violation of USAFFE and FEAF orders, Wagner and Church on MacArthur's recommendation were awarded Distinguished Service Crosses four days later for their exploit.

14. "NOBODY BUT A LOW-RANKING FIRST LIEUTENANT WOULD BE DUMB ENOUGH TO STAY ON THAT FIELD"

1 At Nichols Field late in the evening of December 17/18, Grant Mahony was preparing for what would prove to be his last mission in the Philippines campaign. He had been ordered to fly the C-39 transport at Nichols Field south to Australia, ferrying pilots of the 24th Pursuit Group and the planeless 27th Bomb Group. In addition to the C-39, two B-18 bombers were assigned to the mission. A total of twenty pilots from the 27th Bomb Group and three from the 24th Pursuit Group would be flying out this evening. The 27th pilots would pick up Douglas A-24 dive-bombers that had now finally arrived in Australia for their use and fly them back to the Philippines over the ferry route set up for this purpose. Similarly, Mahony, Gerry Keenan, and Allison Strauss would lead back flights of the P-40s that had arrived with the A-24s in Australia.

After flying school classmates Keenan and Strauss had joined several of the 27th Bomb pilots in the transport, Mahony roared down the Nichols runway in the pitch darkness and headed south for his first stop, Del Monte on Mindanao. Following closely behind him were the two B-18s. It was 3:45 A.M.

2 While MacArthur was losing, albeit only temporarily, three of his most experienced pursuit pilots this evening, another believed lost after being shot down a week earlier had reported in at Clark that afternoon. Not much worse for the experience, "Red" Sheppard described his jungle trek to the other pursuit pilots around him at the 20th's camp. He and Ed Houseman had spent the first night at a Filipino major's house at Bangued, where they learned that the Japanese had cut off the coast road leading south, by which the pilots intended to return to Clark. The next morning they set out for the central valley of northern Luzon through rugged mountains. Over the next days, they hiked some sixty miles during daylight over wild mountain wilderness all the way to Lubuagan, on the central road to Baguio, feet aching and legs attacked by big leeches in the streams.

Emerging at Lubuagan, on the central north-south road, they hiked for an additional twelve miles, then caught transportation "over the most hair-raising mountain roads imaginable" to Bontoc, then on to Baguio, where they arrived on the evening of December 16. On the next day they managed a ride back to Clark Field, arriving one week after their bail-outs over the Vigan area.

Having spent a good deal of time traveling and hunting in the islands since his arrival in the Philippines a year earlier, Sheppard was not both-ered by the prodigious distances they covered by foot during the day. Houseman, however, a Philadelphia city boy, was nervous about the wild country they traversed and about its inhabitants. The two pilots were crossing the territory of five of the old head-hunting tribes, all carrying heavy spears and axes to use on any Japanese they met. Since Sheppard regarded the experience as a kind of sport and Houseman as a "pretty bad show," the two did not communicate very well during their trek.

On the day Sheppard and Houseman arrived back at Clark safely, Shep-pard's flying school classmate Walt Coss was four days into his own hike through the jungle from the north coast of Luzon and heading south after having been shot down over Aparri on his recon mission of December 13. On the evening of December 15, Coss had managed to send a report on his December 13 reconnaissance mission to Major Grover at Clark, re-porting having seen some twenty thousand Japanese troops landing from eight transports at Aparri and Gonzaga.[1] "Am trying to reach Baguio be-fore my feet give out," he concluded his message. Finally reaching Baguio on December 18, two days after Sheppard and Houseman, Coss was able to hitch a ride into Clark with an army ground officer, arriving on De-cember 20.

3 On December 16, Buzz Wagner called four of his 17th Pursuiters to the 24th Group headquarters off of Clark Field. In the bamboo shack, he expressed his displeasure with the administrative situation at Nichols, where all the enlisted men of his squadron had been left under three ad-ministrative officers following the shift of most of the squadron's pilots to Clark days before. Now he wanted John Brownewell to go down to Nichols to take temporary command and ensure that maintenance work was properly done at both Nichols and Nielson fields. Ordered to join Brownewell were Dave Obert, Steve Crosby, and Earl Stone.

Dave Obert was particularly pleased with this turn of events, as he wanted to be back in Manila to be with his bride of two weeks. Steve Crosby also welcomed the move, for he and the others assigned the task would now be the only pilots based permanently at Nichols; the 21st Pur-suit was being moved to Lubao and the 3rd Pursuit to a new field at Tanauan.

At eight o'clock the next morning, Brownewell, accompanied by Crosby,

Obert, and Stone, reported in to Capt. "Bud" Sprague, operations officer of the 5th Interceptor Command (now moved with the rest of the FEAF from Nielson to Fort McKinley) for a briefing on his new responsibility. They were told in no uncertain terms that "things, including maintenance and camouflage of planes, were so bad that they must improve." Obert was given half the maintenance crews from his 17th Pursuit and told to get things in order at Nichols. Stone was given the same job at Nielson.

Reporting for duty at Nichols, Obert first made an inspection of each plane still at the field. He found that they were all in bad shape. They had been flown almost continuously since the war started, and no work had been done on them during that period. Plunging wholeheartedly into his assignment, the young Oklahoman set himself the goal of getting the planes in even better shape than under prewar conditions, despite the adverse conditions under which maintenance now had to be carried out, since now "the pilots really had to depend on the perfect operation of every part of the plane."

Brownewell's investigation of the personnel situation of the 17th Pursuit revealed equally unsatisfactory conditions. The senior administrative officer of the squadron, 1st Lt. Ridgley Hall, had been so apprehensive after the December 10 bombing of Nichols that he had moved his command post over a mile from where the men were camped, in the direction of Fort McKinley. In Brownewell's view, the squadron's three administrative officers "were less than useless" in organizing the men, as they were "scared to death" and projected their feelings throughout the squadron. Fortunately, however, the squadron's senior noncoms, WO Jack Day, 1st Sgt. Joe King, and M. Sgts. Doak Geren and Carlton Edsall, were holding the men together as best they could.

At 1:00 P.M. the next day, Obert was deep into his maintenance work when the Nichols Field air raid warning sounded. Instead of taking cover, he remained on the field, figuring he could wait until the planes actually arrived and head for shelter before they reached bombing position. But Obert had miscalculated. They were already overhead. It was too late to get off the field, and he "couldn't find a hole anywhere." Then he spotted a small patch of weeds nearby and wormed himself into a slight depression in the patch. "There I lay, wringing wet with sweat, my heart pounding away."

Moments later he heard a whistling, hissing sound above, the first time he had ever heard a bomb falling. When he heard what sounded like hundreds more falling, the terrified officer burrowed his nose into the ground and thought, "This must be the end." The first one hit several hundred feet away and went off with a terrific explosion. Then the others hit all around him, but none very close.

Master armorer Jack Day of the 17th Pursuit and his crew working on the .50-caliber machine guns of a P-40B in a Nichols Field hangar, spring, 1941. *Courtesy Richard Damm*

After a few seconds of quiet, Obert pulled his nose out of the dirt and ventured a look. But there were the bombers returning again. Back he went to his patch, and in a few seconds more bombs were falling. This time the first one hit close enough to make the ground shudder under him, "and this time I felt certain my time had come." Then another bomb exploded, and he was still alive. Moments later the raid was over.[2]

4 In charge of Nielson Field, five miles north of Nichols, was 1st Lt. Jim McAfee of the planeless 27th Bomb Group. McAfee had been given the job on December 14, when FEAF Headquarters abandoned the exposed field for the safety of Fort McKinley. As McAfee recorded in his diary the day of his assigment, "I guess they figure that nobody but a low-ranking 1st Lieutenant would be dumb enough to stay on that field — it's going to be bombed to hell."[3]

McAfee had been given ninety men to run the field, including M. Sgt. Carlton Edsall and others of the 17th Pursuit transferred from Nichols for this purpose. To help him carry out his assignment, he was also assigned three young officers, "but two of them are useless and scared to death. I don't blame them."

Brereton wanted to use Nielson Field for courier and reconnaissance missions by a few pursuit planes to be stationed there. The problem for McAfee was to hide them from the view of the Japanese marauders. Despite the efforts of McAfee and his men to camouflage the P-40s and P-35s on the field there during the first days of his Nielson assignment, they achieved only partial success.

Criticism of his work by higher-ups made him angry. As he recorded in his diary, "Everyone drives by outside the field and they're too damned scared to stop, so they go on to some safe place with a phone and call me up and give me hell for not hiding the planes any better. They thought they could see one. Hell, you can't make them invisible!"

Obstructions had also been put on the field to guard against any Japanese surprise paratrooper landing attempt. But the barriers also made it "damned hard" for visiting P-40s to set down, as in the case of Don Steele's effort to land on December 15.

When the three officers originally assigned McAfee had been replaced on December 15 by three others from the 27th Group, plus Earl Stone from the 17th Pursuit, who was put in charge of maintenance as from December 17, the situation at Nielson improved. Concealed revetments were built for the planes that kept them from Japanese view from the air.[4] General Brereton was able to report to General Sutherland on the morning of December 17 that there were three P-40s at Nielson "well-spotted for reconnaissance." Two days later there were two P-35s and two P-40s stationed at the field.

5 At Nichols on the morning of December 18, Hank Thorne was ordered to take seven of his 3rd Pursuit officers and all his enlisted men and depart Nichols for the little town of Tanauan, some forty miles by road southwest of Manila. There they would camouflage the auxiliary field near the town and build revetments for aircraft.

Thorne informed his officers in the deepest secrecy. As Don Steele recorded in his diary that day, "Thorne keeps taking the boys off in a corner and whispering in their ears." Only five minutes before departure were they informed of the actual destination. Thorne was still sensitive after being criticized the day before by Brereton's chief of staff for his squadron's being "loose-lipped about military information . . . during their trips into Manila after hours" and was taking no chances on the news of this hush-hush move getting out. The officers were also instructed to remove all identifying Air Corps insignia from their uniforms and to give a false name for their destination to the Filipino drivers of the trucks that would transport them. The trucks were to move at odd intervals, so as not to appear to be a convoy.

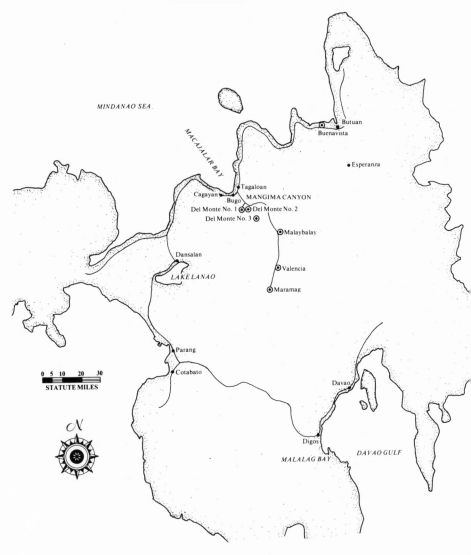

Map 4.   Mindanao

After arrival at Tanauan a few hours later, they were shown the airdrome to be camouflaged, which was a rectangular area about one and a half miles long and a mile wide. At dark, by which time the move was completed, the enlisted men were dispersed to various houses around town in groups of four and six, while the eight officers managed to take over an unfurnished house of their own.

6 At 9:00 A.M. on Saturday, December 20, John Brownewell came down to Nichols Field to see Dave Obert. Brownewell had just returned from a meeting at FEAF Headquarters at Fort McKinley and informed Obert that Brownewell had been ordered immediately to Del Monte. Obert would be taking over Brownewell's job and keeping his maintenance responsibility too. At the meeting at McKinley, Brownewell had been told that General Sutherland wanted FEAF Headquarters to provide a pilot to fly reconnaissance for Brigadier General Sharp, commanding general of the Visayas-Mindanao Force.[5] Could Brownewell suggest a suitable pilot for the assignment? Replying that he had only three pilots with him at Nichols and Nielson, all "very young and inexperienced," Brownewell volunteered to take the job himself. His offer accepted, Brownewell was told to leave immediately for Del Monte.

Expecting the mission to be one of a few days' duration only, Brownewell packed a few toilet articles. After giving Obert his new assignment, he then went to the Air Depot, in the process of moving to Quezon City, northeast of Manila, and drew a brand-new P-40E. Its guns had not yet even been test-fired. At 1:00 P.M., not even bothering to eat lunch, he took off for his new assignment.

After a flight of over five hundred miles, Brownewell arrived over Del Monte in late afternoon but ran into an unexpected welcoming committee. As he made his first swing over Del Monte No. 1 field, someone fired three shots from a .30-caliber Springfield at him, then the rest of the men picked up the shooting, including machine gunners in the pits off to the side of the field. Inexperienced enough to keep right on trying to get in to the field despite the barrage, and low on gas, Brownewell now tried everything to look friendly. He let down his flaps at 500 feet and jiggled his wings, but nothing did any good. Fortunately, the gunners were all shooting well behind his P-40. Finally, after Brownewell had been flying about fifteen minutes around the field, some of the 5th Air Base Group officers in charge of the Del Monte base drove down and put a stop to the shooting.

On landing, the 17th Pursuiter inspected his plane and found just two .30-caliber holes in it. Then he immediately flew the P-40 over to the narrow Dalirig fighter strip eight miles from Del Monte No. 1 and alongside Tagoloan Canyon, camouflaged his ship, and reported in to Col. Ray Elsmore, commanding officer of the Del Monte base.

The men of the 5th Air Base Group were jumpy and trigger-happy as a result of having been attacked by Japanese aircraft for the first time the previous afternoon. Before 4:00 P.M. on December 19, three B-18 bombers had landed, one of which brought Brigadier General Clagett, just relieved of command of the 5th Interceptor Command, to Del Monte on his way to Australia. Hidden under coconut leaves were four B-17s, the last ones based in the Philippines and scheduled to leave for Australia that night. As Elsmore was showing Clagett the base's underground shelter and some slit trenches at the end of the number 1 runway at 4:10 P.M., four Zeros came in, skimming the tops of the surrounding pineapple fields. Unobserved by lookouts on the hills, they flew from east to west across the field and opened fire with tracers and 20-mm cannon shells before anyone even knew they were approaching. One of the three B-18s out in the open now went up in flames. Two of the B-17s, though hit, were not damaged. Also unscathed were Elsmore and Clagett, who were piled on one another in the shallow trench into which they had jumped.[6]

7 About an hour before dark on Friday, December 19, 24th Pursuit Group operations at Clark had received a phone call from FEAF Headquarters at McKinley. Brereton wanted pilots to move nine of the twelve P-40s in commission immediately from Clark to San Marcelino, ostensibly for inspection and daytime maintenance of the aircraft.

In a FEAF staff conference at 10:00 that morning, Brereton had expressed his displeasure at the failure to disperse the remaining twenty-three P-40s and nine P-35s in commission on Luzon in accordance with his policy on that subject. He was irritated to learn that most of the pursuit ships were still at Clark, despite daily raids on the field.[7] He agreed with Bud Sprague that it was not desirable to use the new, secret airdromes (such as at Lubao) until the arrival of expected air reinforcements but wanted the Clark pursuit dispersed at once to one of the three candidate fields: San Marcelino, Del Carmen, or Nichols. San Marcelino, thirty miles southwest of Clark, was judged the best choice.

After nine pilots were selected for the transfer operation, "Red" Sheppard led seven of them off, including John Posten, Cy Blanton, Jim Rowland, and Ed Erickson, just as darkness was setting in. All were apprehensive about a night landing on a field they had never seen before. The ninth pilot selected for the mission, Jim Phillips, had been partying all afternoon at Clark and took off late, by himself. Unable to find the others, he elected to return to Clark, but he came in wrong, tried to turn too close to the ground, cracked up, and injured himself. He was rushed to Fort Stotsenburg hospital. The remaining eight pilots had to get down at San Marcelino without benefit of any field lighting. Misjudging his landing approach, Rowland dropped in from fifteen to twenty feet and broke his landing gear, effectively washing out his P-40.

The initial irritation of the pilots with the rationale of this move turned to anger the next day when they discovered that there were no facilities or arrangements made for any work to be done on their seven remaining aircraft. San Marcelino did not have maintenance tools of any description. And the living conditions there were worse than at Clark Field, Posten complained in his diary that evening. "All we had to eat was a chunk of beef that I think was half-rotten and a cup of bitter coffee!" In Blanton's opinion, the messing facilities were filthy. "Why every man there didn't have dysentery is a mystery," he commented later.

One hour before dark on Sunday, December 21, orders were received to return to Clark Field immediately. The only work that had been done on the P-40s during the three days there was what some of the enlisted men at the field could do with the few hand tools that had been brought in by truck from Clark. Except for the daily run-up by the pilot, several of the P-40s had not even been touched during their stay at San Marcelino.

In twilight, the pilots took off in the seven P-40s for the return trip, landing safely some fifteen minutes later. Jim Rowland, who had wiped out his P-40 in landing at San Marcelino, managed to fly back to Clark with the others in a P-35A left on the field by the 34th Pursuit; it had a bent propeller and one landing gear strut replaced by a 2 × 4.

8 At the secret Lubao Field, where the 21st Pursuit had arrived on the evening of December 15, work on completion of the strip had now been achieved, including construction of revetments. The squadron's enlisted men, attired in old denims and straw hats, had joined forces with the 71st Engineering Battalion (Philippine Army), in charge of the construction, and four hundred Filipino laborers in a round-the-clock effort. Ed Dyess had been informed by FEAF Headquarters that the Lubao field would be ready for pursuit operations on December 14,[8] but on his inspection trip on the afternoon of December 15, the 21st's CO found that this was not the case.

The biggest problem now facing Dyess and his work force was the camouflaging of the field. It was being built in Pampanga Province, seven miles west of Lubao town, just off the main road from Lubao leading into Bataan, over which heavy traffic passed. Colonel George himself had picked the site during one of his searches in the Bataan-Pampanga area for suitable airfield sites from which his few pursuit could operate a step ahead of the advancing Japanese forces.

Dyess hit upon an ingenious solution to the camouflaging problem. The 3,600-foot northwest/southeast runway would be divided down the middle, with one half of the 180-foot width left standing in growing cane and the cane of the other half cut down. The second half would then be covered with windrows of dead cane, which from the air looked like it had been cut during harvesting and left to rot. The dead cane would be swept to the side by the men to allow the aircraft to take off on this half of the field. After takeoff, the planes' wheel tracks would be brushed out, and the cane put back on the field.

But how to camouflage the planes—expected to arrive soon—and their revetments and parking strips? Here a very involved procedure was devised. Parking strips were constructed at right angle to the airstrip, with revetments dug into the ground wide and deep enough for the plane and sandbagged to a depth of five feet. At each corner of a revetment, a bamboo pole was erected, with chicken wire stretching across the top of the poles over each revetment and adjoining the wire of the other revetments down the length of the field. Put through the wire mesh were short top sections of cane that had been freshly cut and notched, their tops level with the tops of the live cane across the field. These top sections were changed every two or three days to keep the cane sections fresh over the revetments and parking strip areas.

In front of each of the twelve revetments, each 40' × 20', a line of bamboo cups about two feet in length and two feet apart was emplaced in the soil. Sugar cane sections were then stuck into these cups carefully so that their tops also matched the height of the live cane growing on the other half of the field. These walls of cane could then be pulled out in a moment to allow a plane in a revetment to run onto the field. From the air, Lubao field on completion was indistinguishable from a cane field that was partly harvested. Neither directly nor at an angle overhead could an aircraft be detected in its revetment.

Life for the enlisted men of the squadron during the construction period at Lubao had been rough. Living in portable nipa shacks they built and put out on the field, they sweltered in the heat and humidity during the day and were bitten by mosquitoes unmercifully at night, as well as bothered by rats. However, the meal situation was not bad. The squadron's trucks were driven back and forth to Manila for all the food and other supplies needed during the 21st's stay at the field.

For the officers and senior noncoms, a large house was located eight miles west of the field, off the road leading to Dinalupihan and Bataan, in Barrio San Benito. Situated on top of a high hill, the house had been acquired in 1940 by the local landowning family from Benedictine Fathers and included a chapel and sixteen rooms. When the Americans moved in, the Filipino family moved to a small building in the compound near the house.

9 At Tanauan, the other new secret airfield site, the 3rd Pursuit Squadron had begun work on the morning of December 19. Some three thousand Filipino laborers were hired and equipped by the engineers with picks, shovels, and all the equipment needed. All that day, under the supervision of the officers and men of the squadron, they worked in construc-

tion of twelve revetments for P-40s and four revetments for B-17s, all made of thrown-up earth and bamboo frame, about two hundred yards away from the field, under a thick cover of trees.[9]

Don Steele was in charge of one thousand of the native workers. He was having a difficult time getting any production out of them, as they were only "half-heartedly" shoveling dirt, with no idea for what purpose. Some would sign in and then "go behind a tree and sleep for the balance of the day," he recorded in his diary.

One crew of the Filipino laborers was assigned to make a portable native village of bamboo, to be moved to the center of the runway and laid out to resemble a native settlement, then moved off when the runway was to be used. Around the houses, postholes were dug, into which freshly chopped trees were stuck every few days and removed when planes would need to pass. However, Thorne was skeptical that this camouflage effort would fool the Japanese pilots, as no native village was normally located out in an open area when there were areas of thick trees where they could build their shacks.

During the next few days, as work progressed, single Japanese observation planes often would fly overhead. The men of the squadron would shout, "Take cover!" and throw themselves on the ground in any nearby ditch or foxhole and lie still. Even though the native supervisors would blow whistles, however, the Filipino workers would form a crowd around the prone men, laughing and pointing at the crazy Americans. Realizing that large groups of people could attract the attention of the plane overhead and invite a strafing attack, the 3rd Pursuit men would shout at the natives to go away, but they would only continue to laugh and stand over the men. Fortunately, the observation planes did not check out the scene below.

Despite such incidents, the men were in excellent spirits as they went about their tasks. Each day an officer would drive in to Manila to pick up the mail and any supplies the squadron wanted, "plus a good stock of rumors." The officers had managed to scrounge six dozen bottles of pale Pilsen beer, a ten-gallon can, and ice, and would sit around at night drinking beer, listening to the radio, and exchanging ideas on what would happen next in this war.

10 Back at FEAF Headquarters at Fort McKinley, Brereton was considering easing the restriction on pursuit ships engaging in combat. Lt. Gen. Jonathan Wainwright had radioed MacArthur for air action against Japanese troops assembling just outside Vigan on December 19 and beginning to move south on Route 3 toward Lingayen. Although the commander of the North Luzon Force was informed that afternoon that "nothing was available," the FEAF was under pressure to take some positive action to help him.

That afternoon, Steve Crosby, who had been helping Obert run Nichols Field, was ordered to go over to Nielson Field to pick up a P-35A and ferry it to Clark for a mission. After hedgehopping all the way to Clark, Crosby landed safely and was joined by five other P-35As already there. All six planes were then loaded with six thirty-pound fragmentation bombs under the wings. The pilots, including three from the 34th Pursuit, were informed that they were to fly an attack mission the next morning against a concentration of Japanese troops. The mission was apparently in response to Wainwright's request for an air strike against the Vigan landing force.

Following takeoff in the dark on December 20, the flight leader of the little attack force brought the pilots at dawn right over the target: a schoolhouse just east of Route 3 where the Japanese had bivouacked the previous evening. The six P-35As then turned east toward the mountains, gained altitude, and peeled off in a string. Crosby saw the machine gun burst of the plane in front of him go just over the target, so he tripped his guns and when he saw the tracers going home, released his bombs and pulled out. After dropping their bombs, the pilots circled and made several strafing passes at the Japanese, "who were running to and fro like ants from a broken hive." The mission successfully accomplished, the elated airmen, pleased to be back in combat, headed home to Clark and landed without incident.

The day's excitement was not yet over for Crosby. On his way back to Manila in the afternoon, flying just under a thin overcast at about 9,000 feet, Crosby's thoughts were far from war. Suddenly, he noticed tracer fire passing by his P-35. Angry with himself for being so careless not to be keeping an eye out for hostile aircraft, he now reacted sharply by dropping ten degrees of flaps and pulling up sharply into a quick loop, "almost putting me into position on the surprised Jap's tail."

In his concentration to follow the weaving Army Nakajima "Nate" in front of him, Crosby failed to notice the other Japanese pursuit on his tail. Fire from its 7.7-mm nose guns shattered Crosby's instrument panel to bits, punctured his fuel and oil lines, and "caused a bright tongue of flame to blow back into the cockpit." Only then did he realize that he was also very close to the ground; he had no alternative but to get out of the doomed aircraft immediately.[10] He released the canopy, unfastened his safety belt, rolled the stabilizer all the way forward, did a half roll, and turned loose. He pulled the rip cord, and his chute caught. He swung once, then hit the ground with a jolt that knocked him out.

Coming to later, he found himself surrounded by a group of curious Filipinos. After checking himself for any broken bones and finding none, the shaken-up 17th Pursuiter made his way to the highway, where he caught a ride back into Manila before dark.

As a follow-up to FEAF's response to Wainwright's request that led to Crosby's mission, FEAF Headquarters made arrangements on the afternoon of December 20 to send an Air Corps officer to Wainwright's North Luzon Force to act as liaison officer between the ground forces and the FEAF. First Lt. Tom Gerrity of the 27th Bomb Group was selected for the job and was briefed "as to what information is required before an air operation can be directed to assist ground troops."

Evidently the USAFFE had decided to lift its ban on offensive actions by pursuit pilots in view of the deteriorating ground defense situation. Earlier that day, Brereton had discussed with Colonel George the possibility of intercepting Japanese bombers. Brereton wanted to know how many pursuit ships George could get in the air and what his probable losses would be. In addition, Brereton asked if there would be sufficient pursuit left after such an attack to perform the necessary reconnaissance and for delaying actions. On the afternoon of the next day, December 21, FEAF Headquarters was discussing with Major Grover "the possibilities of using P-40s for dive-bombing and strafing attacks on hostile airdromes in Luzon." Clearly, the FEAF was planning to go over to the offensive again, despite its meager supply of pursuit ships.

11 A serious situation was developing in which the new policy of the USAFFE and the FEAF would need to be applied. Reports had been coming in to USAFFE Headquarters since December 18 of the movement of a hostile convoy toward Luzon. Was this the main Japanese invasion force, expected for weeks? Parker Gies of the 20th Pursuit got the answer at 12:30 A.M. on December 22 at Clark when he was awakened as the First Sergeant of the squadron went about calling for all enlisted men to report with their rifles. The Japanese were landing in force at Lingayen Gulf, only seventy miles to the north, and parachute troops were expected at dawn.[11]

The young Oregonian was unable to get back to sleep with all the excitement. At any rate, at 3:00 A.M., he and seven other pilots of the squadron—Joe Moore, Erwin Crellin, Kiefer White, Bob Duncan, Randy Keator, Percy Ramsey, and Jim Fossey—were called to go on a strafing party against the Japanese at Lingayen. The eight 20th Pursuiters reported in at the 24th Group's command post and then went down to the line. Since the squadron had only six P-40s in commission, they drew to see who would not go. Duncan and Fossey were the losers (or winners?).

The 17th Pursuit also had six P-40s in commission at Clark, including four with wing bombs attached. Steve Crosby had flown one of them to Clark the day before; it was the remaining P-40 at Nichols being used for patrol missions. Buzz Wagner now assigned pilots to the six P-40s. In addition to himself, he picked Crosby, Red Sheppard, George "Ed" Kiser, Bill Hennon, and Walt Wilcox. With Wagner in the lead, the twelve-plane strike group roared off the field in the darkness at 5:45, an hour before dawn.

According to Gies, it was "the worst take-off ever dreamed of. Pitch black. Field solid dust. No lights. Strange planes." But he managed to pull the heavy P-40E over the end of the fence at the field's edge. Immediately after takeoff, the pilots ran into a solid overcast extending all the way up to 10,000 feet. To Gies, it was a "wonder we weren't all killed." Because of the complete lack of visibility, all the pilots had to go over to instruments.

Wagner and his wingman, Bill Hennon, kept circling the field, trying to form up with the rest of the flight, but in the pitch darkness, they could not find the others. Finally, after about an hour circling in vain, they headed up to Lingayen together.

Arriving over Lingayen at about 7:15, Wagner and Hennon first noticed several flashes from USAFFE artillery aimed at some eight Japanese naval vessels, including a cruiser. Proceeding up the beach of Lingayen, they then spotted some eighty to ninety transports in a long line extending four or five miles north from the town of Agoo. Half of the transports were about one-half mile offshore, with the other half in a parallel line three miles offshore. Close to shore were three lines of small boats and barges that had apparently already discharged troops of the landing force.

Wagner now peeled off, followed by Hennon. Each P-40E carried six thirty-pound fragmentation bombs under the wings. Hennon aimed his bombs at a group of boats offshore and troops on the beach. In a fairly steep dive, he released in salvo at about 1,500 feet. He could not see where his bombs hit, but he did notice that Wagner's had hit on the water's edge very near the landing barges. After pulling up, Hennon circled and came in very low over the troops on the beach. They were all flattened out and were firing back with their rifles as Hennon proceeded to pour .50-caliber fire into them. The young Minnesotan circled around again and made several more passes at the troops at 30-feet altitude.

During the strafing, Hennon had lost sight of Wagner. Now Japanese pursuit aircraft, army "Nates," were after him. Chased by some seven of them, Hennon climbed and headed into a cloud. When he came out, he found there were even more of them above him, at about 6,000 feet. Undaunted, Hennon made one more pass at the troops, then headed into the mountains to the east, with "Nates" all about him. He managed to get under the clouds and headed down a valley to central Luzon and Clark.

While Hennon had encountered antiaircraft fire only once, as he flew over the transports in trying to elude the "Nates," Wagner met extremely heavy antiaircraft fire from both the beach and the ships. After strafing the cruiser and a minesweeper, the 17th's CO was jumped by the "Nates." In the unequal contest, the Japanese pursuit riddled Wagner's cowling.

More damaging, 7.7-mm fire shattered his windshield. One shell hit his left shoulder, and glass splinters and pieces of metal cut his face and both eyes. But now "Ed" Kiser and Walt Wilcox had joined up with their CO and were guiding him back, his vision reduced by his eye injury.

Except for Wagner and Hennon, the 17th's pilots had all arrived individually over Lingayen. Steve Crosby had been impressed by the sight of a huge fleet of transports and warships below him as he cleared the last row of palms on the beach at Damortis. Linking up with some of the others, Crosby first strafed the barges, then made pass after pass at the ships until he exhausted his .50-caliber ammunition.

The sixth 17th Pursuiter on the mission, Red Sheppard, had gone after the cargo and transport vessels after arriving over Lingayen alone. After setting a transport afire, he found that a "Nate" had latched onto his tail, firing tracers at him. However, by maneuvering in steep dives, high G-turns, and "a sloppy Immelmann" into the overcast, Sheppard managed to shake him.

Returning over the scene near the southern end of the bay, Sheppard now spotted what he believed to be a destroyer and expended the remainder of his ammunition on it in steep diving passes in the face of heavy antiaircraft fire. By this time, however, his Allison engine was in overheat, with pressure troubles on all liquids because of hits scored earlier by the "Nate," so he now climbed back into the cloud cover in preparation for the return trip to Clark.

Of the six 20th Pursuiters on the mission, only Moore, Gies, and White managed to reach Lingayen. Gies dove through the overcast and came out over a "battleship and a destroyer," into the face of "terrific" antiaircraft fire. After one pass, he went back into the clouds and then came down on the transports near the shore. But after two strafing passes, he found that few of his six .50s were working.

Despite his eye injuries, Wagner managed to bring his P-40E safely back to Clark. After landing, he was taken to the 20th's camp, where squadron medical officer Johnny Rizzolo took the bigger pieces of the glass shards out of his eyes, then sent him over to Fort Stotsenburg hospital. Wagner's flying days in the Philippines were over.

Sheppard's plane was the only other one damaged on the mission, although Hennon's had several holes in the wings. On approach to Clark, Sheppard's engine failed, forcing him to land dead stick. Upon examination, some two hundred holes were counted in his P-40E; it never flew again.

Although Gies's P-40E had taken no hits, the whole experience of the mission had unnerved the 20th Pursuiter. "I was so sick with nervousness and fright I couldn't eat dinner," he confided to his diary at the end of the day.

When Randy Keator earlier had tried to land at Clark after aborting the mission, he found it closed in by ground fog, so headed south to Nichols to land. He arrived there at 7:30 A.M., almost out of gas, and began taxiing down the runway with Dave Obert riding on his wing to guide him to a revetment. "Suddenly, bombs started falling around us," Keator recorded in his diary. "I quickly cut the throttle and bailed out." Keator had forgotten to disconnect his oxygen mask hose in his haste to get out of his plane. Stretched out to its full length from the cockpit to the ground, it broke, the loose end slapping Keator so hard on the side of his head that he thought he had been hit by shrapnel.

Both Keator and Obert ended up in a slight depression on the edge of the runway, where they remained while the bombers passed overhead at an estimated 15,000 feet. Everyone on the field was firing at the Japanese with anything they could find, a useless exercise, the two pilots felt.

After the attack, Keator now got back into the P-40E and started taxiing it again to a revetment. But before the two young aviators could push it into the revetment, the bombers made another pass across the field. This time the bombs fell very close but missed them again.[12]

Keator's problems for the day were not over yet. After taking off for Clark later that afternoon, he found that his landing gear would not come down as he came in to land. The emergency landing system of his P-40E was in working order, however, and he managed to land safely. That evening, reflecting on his day's experiences, Keator recorded in his diary, "I figure if I had nine lives to start with, I must have used up five or six of them today!"

12 After the bombing attack on Nichols was over, Dave Obert took off on a previously scheduled recon to the Legaspi area in a P-40E. Arriving over Legaspi, where the Japanese had landed twelve days earlier, he saw no activity of any kind except two Zeros circling the field. Before diving on the Zeros, Obert first checked his guns by squeezing the trigger. None fired. Relieved that he had tested them before entering into combat that could have turned out disastrously for him, Obert aborted the attack and turned for the return to Nichols.

That same day, December 22, Obert became acting commander of the 17th Pursuit again because of an accident suffered by Maurice Hughett, who had taken over from Obert on December 20. Coming in to land in a P-40 at Nielson Field on return from a recon mission he had flown earlier that day from Nielson, Hughett apparently did not notice the barricades on the east-west runway in the dusk and plowed through an accumulation of footlockers and other obstacles that had been placed a week earlier on the strip. The P-40's wheels collapsed, and all the guns started to fire. The plane was wrecked, but Hughett was only slightly injured, though sufficiently to have to turn command over to Obert.

Still in charge of Nielson operations, Jim McAfee witnessed yet another crash on his field the following day. Approaching for a landing on the barricaded runway, "Dub" Balfanz, another 17th Pursuiter, also crashed through the obstacles. His plane "all torn to hell," Balfanz climbed out of the wreck and told the flabbergasted McAfee, "The Japs can land on this runway."

13 Down at Tanauan, the 3rd Pursuit had now finished building revetments and camouflaging the field. The squadron was anxiously awaiting the arrival of six B-17s due in the early morning of December 23. Thorne had been so informed the morning of December 22 by Maj. Billy Maverick, commanding officer of the 20th Air Base Group at Nichols. They were to be serviced, camouflaged, and maintained for a short period.

Early that evening, assisted by a matériel squadron, the 3rd Pursuit distributed the supplies of gasoline, oil, oxygen, pumps, and ammunition it had received by motor vehicle and train that afternoon to each of the six camouflaged locations that had been built for the B-17s. Thorne had also arranged to have eighteen carabao with ropes to stand by in the morning to help move the B-17s from the field to their locations.

That evening, Don Steele and the rest of the squadron slept out near the field. Steele, who had picked out a tree for shelter, had no blanket and spent "a perfectly miserable night" in the chilly air. On the morning of December 23, "we started the day with no breakfast, no news, and no airplanes." By 6:00 P.M., still no B-17s had arrived, so the 3rd Pursuiters went back to their camp, sorely disappointed. Later that evening, Thorne was informed that the plans for the B-17s had been changed and that they would not be landing at Tanauan, though they might come in at a later date.[13]

15. "IT LOOKED LIKE A SMALL DUNKIRK"

1 Late in the morning of December 24, Joe Moore was asking for four volunteers at the 20th Pursuit's camp off of Clark Field. FEAF Headquarters had been informed of a new Japanese landing near Mauban, on Lamon Bay, some sixty miles southwest of Manila, and it had decided to oppose it with four P-35As and four P-40s, all from Clark. Marshall Anderson volunteered to lead the flight of the P-35As, selected to attack the Japanese first. They had originally been assigned to strafe tanks to the north but were now diverted for this more urgent matter. Also volunteering were Anderson's squadron mates Tex Marble and Bill Carter, plus LaMar Gillett of the 17th Pursuit. The four P-35As were hidden behind Clark Field in an area of trees. Each had an inch of dust on the outside and a quarter of an inch inside. None had functioning radios.

After getting the P-35As in operational condition, the pilots taxied out onto Clark Field and took off.[1] At about noon they arrived over the Mauban area, where they went down below the overcast for strafing attacks on Japanese shipping and the troops on the shore. Suddenly, several Zeros broke through the overcast and engaged the P-35As.[2] In the ensuing dogfight, one of the Zeros was shot down with no loss to the Americans.[3] Anderson's P-35A was so shot up, however, that he barely managed to limp into Nichols Field, where he crash-landed.

His tail section and fuselage shot up, Gillett headed back to Clark by dead reckoning, accompanied by Marble and Carter. Over Angeles, they went into the approved traffic pattern but were still fired on by the antiaircraft defense of the field. When they finally managed to get down, they found no one was on the field to meet them. They had no choice but to set out on foot for the 20th's camp, deep into the woods.

At about 1:00 P.M., while the P-35As were heading back, four P-40s from Clark arrived over the Lamon Bay area in the second stage of the day's aerial opposition to the Japanese landings. Unlike the P-35As, they were equipped with fragmentation bombs. In repeated attacks, they bombed and strafed the Japanese vessels and the landing party. The P-40 piloted by Jim Rowland of the 17th Pursuit was hit in the gas tank. Leaking gas, Rowland made it back only as far as Laguna de Bay, where he made a water landing in the lake. Uninjured, he managed to swim to shore as his aircraft headed for the bottom.

2 About noon on December 24 Dave Obert, now relieved as acting CO of the 17th Pursuit at Nichols, received startling orders: the squadron was to start packing and get things ready to move on six hours notice to Bataan peninsula. Although Obert had not been informed, MacArthur was putting War Plan Orange-3 into effect, with all his forces to be moved to Bataan for a last-ditch resistance until the arrival of reinforcements. Colonel George, appointed CO of the 5th Interceptor Command on Clagett's evacuation the week before, would be taking over command of what remained of the Far East Air Force. Brereton was to move his command to Australia, taking the remaining B-17s and their flight crews of the 19th Bomb Group with him.

Obert immediately started his men gathering up all the technical supplies and mechanics' equipment they could find so that the squadron would be able to operate adequately when it reached its new base, Pilar Field on Bataan. But then another order came in: Obert was to evacuate Nichols Field *immediately* and go to the port area. A boat would be waiting at Pier 7 to transport them to Bataan. What the squadron could not take on the vessel was to be destroyed.

Regarding this new order "a little unusual," Obert decided to drive back to FEAF Headquarters at Fort McKinley "to see what was up." On entering the building, he saw "confusion everywhere." Everyone was rushing around packing their equipment or burning papers. Most of the FEAF's offices had already been vacated, and the remaining "highly excitable" officers did not want to talk to the young second lieutenant.

Obert finally succeeded in getting instructions: all flyable aircraft at Nichols were to take off immediately for Lubao. All others were to be destroyed by the engineers at the field that evening. Obert asked permission to keep the few men working on two P-40s undergoing repair until their work was finished so that the planes could be flown out the next morning, but the answer was no. He was to move all his men out as soon as possible.

When Obert returned to Nichols Field, he informed M. Sgt. "Cowboy" Wright and his crew, in the process of replacing an engine in a P-40 that had been damaged in combat, of Headquarters' decision. Although the men needed only two or three more hours to finish the job, Obert had to tell them to pack their tools and clothing and board trucks that would take them to the dock area for the trip to Bataan. At about 4:00 in the afternoon, all the flyable aircraft at Nichols—three P-35As and a few P-40s—took off for Lubao Field.[4]

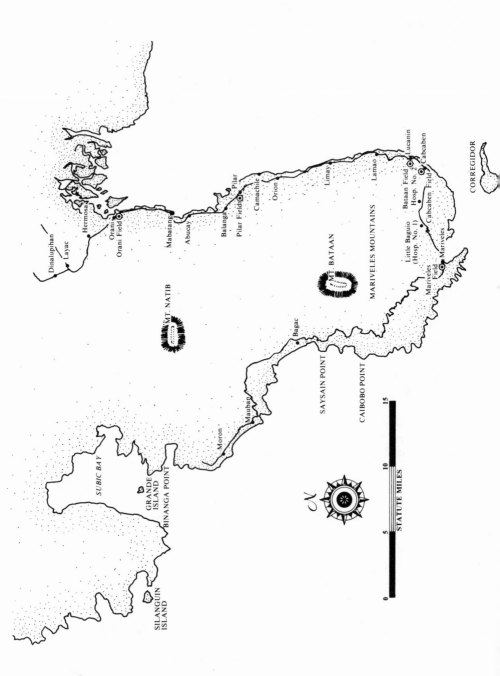

By the time that Obert and Steve Crosby, who was helping him, had finished loading the trucks with all the enlisted men and the equipment they would need at the new field for the move, the engineers were placing demolition charges in the concrete runways preparatory to blowing them up and were setting fire to the thousands of gallons of gasoline stores.[5] Smoke from Nichols was now rolling skyward all around the area. To Obert, it "seemed to be the end of everything." Nichols had been his home station ever since his arrival in the Philippines ten months earlier, and now it was being destroyed. The gravity of the situation was beginning to sink in. What could they expect next?

By five o'clock, the trucks were at Pier 7. The men were ready to load their equipment on the SS *Legaspi*, an interisland steamer that would take them and the matériel to Bataan. After the ship was loaded for its short trip, Obert and Crosby headed back for Nichols for a last look, but not before Obert had stopped off in Manila to tell his wife he would probably be leaving for Bataan that evening.

Back at Nichols, Obert happened to think of an ammunition dump that he had checked out the day before. Looking at it again now, abandoned by the Ordnance Department, the young officer made a split decision: he would get a truck and load on all the .50-caliber ammunition he could get into the vehicle to take to Bataan for use by his squadron. After finding a suitable 2½-ton truck, he, Crosby, and Maurice Hughett backed it up to the dump and proceeded to haul boxes of ammunition onto the truck, an estimated thirty thousand rounds in all.

After completing the loading job, the three adventurous 17th Pursuiters had another idea: why not get some more trucks and load them up with rations and other supplies the squadron could use on Bataan and take the convoy out the next morning? This action would be in violation of the orders Obert had received earlier in the day and could result in severe punishment, but they felt it was worth the risk.

After locating five trucks that had been abandoned by other units leaving by boat for Bataan, Obert, Hughett, Crosby, and a few other 17th Pursuiters who had remained behind drove over to the port area quartermaster warehouse to pick up their cargoes. A captain there insisted on a requisition order before agreeing to allow the trucks to be loaded. Naturally, the 17th Pursuiters could not produce such an order, but Acting CO Hughett, backing up his argument with a .45, got the captain's approval when he accepted the captain's request to sign for everything taken.

Obert now split off from the others and headed back home for the night. On arrival, his wife gave him some bad news: she had just been laid off her job at the Military Intelligence Department, as it was moving to Bataan too but could not take any civilian employees along. Manila was to be declared an open city, however, so Obert should not worry about her. That night, they packed what few things Obert felt he would need and stayed up all night talking and trying to make plans for the long separation.

2 For the 3rd Pursuit, forty miles south of Nichols at Tanauan, the word to evacuate came at 3:00 P.M. that day, when 1st Lt. Robert Wray landed in an A-27 from Nichols Field. Without even turning off the engine, he handed Herb Ellis some secret orders that, when decoded, gave detailed instructions on the manner of evacuating Tanauan. A train was to come to pick them up and take them to Manila.

All that morning, Don Steele had noticed American tanks going by the airstrip, headed for Manila. Until the message from Wray was received, Steele had imagined that they were going north to help in the fighting on northern Luzon. Now he figured that FEAF Headquarters "must have forgotten about us and then suddenly remembered about us being down here!"

The squadron CO, Hank Thorne, now dispatched one of his pilots as liaison with the headquarters of the Southern Luzon Force, which was only about one mile north of Tanauan. He was to send an immediate warning if it was necessary to depart before hearing further from the FEAF. A few hours later, in early evening, the liaison officer called Thorne and advised him it would be wise to leave Tanauan that same evening.

Although the Japanese troops that had landed at Lamon Bay very early that morning were in actuality still over twenty-five miles away, the story quickly spread among the squadron's personnel that they were only three miles from the airstrip. The news "threw us all into a bit of tumult," Steele recorded in his diary. "We took axes and chopped holes in all the gasoline drums we had there." Since the train from Manila had not showed up, several details of men went out to find transportation in addition to what the squadron already had, so that they could move into Manila that night.[6]

During the next few hours, not only the 3rd Pursuit but also the other army units in Tanauan at the time combed the area, commandeering every vehicle available. By nine o'clock that evening, the squadron's men had succeeded in assembling enough transport means to get them to Manila. "I imagine that we cleared the town out of everything that had a motor and went," Steele wrote that evening in his diary, "because we had everything from sports roadsters to old vegetable trucks." Also included were commercial dump trucks, buses, panel trucks, and four Air Corps tugs (resembling the type that pull airline baggage), which carried only three passengers each besides the driver. There were about twenty-five vehicles in all, as well as plenty of rope, "as we knew some of the cars would not last the run into Manila," Steele recorded. For Thorne, "A more motley congregation of vehicles would be difficult to imagine."

Thorne had planned to ride in his sedan, the official car, and bring up the rear. However, he was obliged to dispatch it with the driver in an effort to catch up with the four tugs, whose drivers had misunderstood instructions and had left prior to the departure of the main body, set for ten o'clock. A half hour later, with no return of his car, Thorne began wondering if the driver had also misunderstood and did not realize he was supposed to return and pick him up.

Figuring it would be wisest to start walking and catch him along the road on his return trip, or at least be further north when daylight came, Thorne and Lt. Jim Duck now set out by foot. After forty-five minutes, they met the driver of the car on the road, who reported that he had been unable to catch up with the tugs. Thorne and Duck climbed into the sedan and joined the rest of the convoy. Up ahead, Fred Roberts was driving one of the tugs. Since they had no windshield, and thus allowed more direct observation of the road, the tugs could be driven under the blackout conditions faster than the rest of the vehicles in the convoy.

4   At about three o'clock on the afternoon of December 24, a message from Colonel George was received at Clark Field, ordering eight pursuit pilots there to report in to his headquarters by 5:00 P.M. with their flying equipment for a special mission. Those picked by Colonel George were Joe Kruzel, Cy Blanton, Walt Coss, Jack Dale, and Jim Rowland of the 17th Pursuit and Edwin Gilmore, Carl Gies, and Randy Keator from the 20th Pursuit. Hurriedly collecting their gear, six of the selected pilots (Dale and Rowland could not be located) piled into Joe Moore's station wagon and were transported to Manila by Moore's driver.[7] On the way, they passed about twenty-five light tanks heading north toward the battlefront.

When they reached FEAF Headquarters at Fort McKinley, they found it largely deserted but did meet two other pilots who had also been selected for the mission, Frank Neri and Jim Alsobrook of the 3rd Pursuit, bringing the number to ten. They were surprised to find that Colonel George had left for Bataan but were informed by his operations officer, Capt. Bud Sprague, that their mission was to fly to Australia and to lead flights of P-40s back to the Philippines. Unfortunately, however, the two twin-engined Beech 18s that were to take the pursuiters to Australia had been assigned instead to staff officers of the FEAF for their own evacuation.[8] This news bitterly disappointed the young airmen. Sprague then told them that they might as well go down to Pier 7 and join the crowd of Air Corps personnel going over to Bataan in a steamer. Maybe other means could be found later to get them to Australia in fulfillment of their orders.

5   At 4:00 P.M., while the Australia-bound pursuit pilots had been packing at Clark for the trip down to McKinley, another message was received at Clark by telephone. All personnel at the air base were to be evacuated

Jim Alsobrook, 3rd Pursuit Squadron, checking out a P-40E just received at Iba, November, 1941. *Courtesy William J. Staser*

immediately to Bataan. All Clark's storage warehouses and its PX were now thrown open to anyone who wanted to take supplies to Bataan. Equipment, ordnance, and anything else too heavy to be moved to Bataan was to be burned. Many of the officers and men of the 20th Pursuit had their own priority on items to take to Bataan: the whiskey stock at the Officers Club at Fort Stotsenburg. But when they had collected their haul at Clark prior to moving out, the squadron medic, "Doc" Johnny Rizzolo, with the approval of Joe Moore, moved in and confiscated the whole stock. As Rizzolo methodically was breaking one bottle after another, the men were pleading with him to reconsider; they might need the whiskey for medicinal purposes on Bataan. They finally prevailed on the popular, affable doctor, and the loading of the remaining bottles began.

Pilots at Clark were assigned to fly out all aircraft in commission to the new Lubao airfield. Joe Moore detailed his second in command, 1st Lt. Charley Sneed, to lead the flight to the secret field.

When 2nd Lt. Lloyd Stinson of the 20th Pursuit reached the P-40 that he had been assigned to fly out, parked under some trees at the north end of Clark, he found that someone had smeared brown grease all over the propeller to prevent any reflections from the sun. His first thought was, "When the engine starts, all that grease is going to end up on my windshield and I won't be able to see out." With no rags or towels at hand, Stinson now took off his shirt and began wiping the grease off the propeller. In a few minutes, he was a mess. To add to his frustrations, he could not get the Allison engine to start, despite repeated attempts; it had not been run up for several days. In disgust, Stinson climbed out of the balky aircraft and jumped up on one of the trucks evacuating the squadron personnel late that afternoon.

Several other aircraft at Clark could not be started either and were left on the ground as the remaining group of about fifteen flyable planes, a mixed group mainly of P-40Es and P-40Bs, but also a few P-35As and an A-27, took to the air at 4:30 P.M.[9] For the next two hours, Sneed and the others searched for the Lubao field, but without success. Dyess's men had succeeded only too well in camouflaging it. Finally, gas running low, the formation proceeded to Nielson Field to refuel and seek further information on the exact whereabouts of the elusive field.

Flying the first time in the heavier E model of the P-40, fully armed to boot, 2nd Lt. Jim Fossey of the 20th Pursuit brought the plane in too slow for the landing. Giving it the gun to go around again, the torque held him in a turn to the left, leading the helpless pilot right to the hangar near the runway. A moment later, Fossey crashed through the wall of the hangar. Extricating himself from the wreck, the terrified Oklahoman ran through a side door seconds before the plane and hangar burst into flames. A staff car picked Fossey up and sped him to Sternberg Hospital in Manila. He escaped with only head lacerations from banging his forehead into the electric gunsight.

After receiving instructions on how to locate Lubao Field, the remaining pilots now took off without incident for their destination. But after another fruitless search of two hours, the frustrated young men finally landed at Del Carmen field for the night.

Back at Clark Field, the enlisted men and the remaining planeless pilots of the 20th Pursuit, as well as Gillett and Posten of the 17th, were loading all their service gear onto trucks for the evacuation. Tool kits, field generators, spare machine guns, parts, and ammunition were being taken. Nearby, 1st Lt. Benny Putnam, CO of Headquarters Squadron of the 24th Pursuit Group, was supervising the loading of his squadron's trucks. Foodstuffs, hospital and medical supplies, and weapons and ammunition were thrown aboard. Even an entire pig farm was being evacuated.

Neither squadron had any of its own vehicles left at Clark; all had been destroyed in the Japanese bombing and strafing attacks of the past two weeks. By the time they were ready to move out, however, they had assembled a pool of trucks and buses commandeered from the local civilian community. More fortunate were LaMar Gillett, Jack Gates, and three other pilots, who were offered a ride by John Posten in his old Chrysler automobile. At 7:30 P.M., under the command of Joe Moore, the convoy of vehicles began to move out, leaving behind it smouldering supplies and equipment the evacuating personnel could not take with them.

6 Down at Pier 7 in Manila's port area, most of the enlisted men of the 17th Pursuit were assembled shortly after 7:00 P.M. for boarding the SS *Legaspi* for the trip over to Bataan. Those evacuated from Nichols had now been joined by the group that had been working at Nielson Field. Fires from the Nichols area provided all the illumination they needed to load and board the interisland steamer. By 11:00 P.M., embarkation was completed, and the *Legaspi* pulled out for its forty mile crossing of Manila Bay for Mariveles, on the southern tip of Bataan.

Also on board the *Legaspi* were eight of the ten pursuit pilots who were supposed to have gone that evening on the two Beech 18s to Australia. Andy Krieger of the 3rd Pursuit had boarded too, along with a number of Air Corps "casuals" whom he had been ordered to take charge of by a senior officer who recognized him at the pier. Sam Grashio and Leo Golden of the 21st Pursuit, looking for a way to get to Bataan, had slipped aboard the ship just before it departed.

For Dave Obert and Steve Crosby, the night's work was only beginning. After seeing the 17th Pursuit's enlisted men off, they spent the rest of the night with the squadron's transportation section of enlisted men in loading trucks with ammunition, guns, food, and clothing for the overland move to Bataan. Not until 3:00 A.M. did the convoy of ten trucks move out on the road, going west and then south to Pilar.

Late that night, approaching Manila from the south in a commandeered Japanese school bus, Don Steele and twenty-two enlisted men of the 3rd Pursuit Squadron evacuating Tanauan could see the reflection of large fires on the skyline. About fifteen miles outside the city, they stopped and asked a native what was causing the fires they saw. In broken English, he told them that Japanese bombers had been raiding Manila all night. That made everyone really nervous. They had already imagined that the Japanese from the Lamon Bay force were following right behind them.

When Steele's bus got within five miles of Nichols Field, "there was a terrific explosion, with flames shooting up to about 100 feet in the air." Then someone in the back of the bus yelled, "Raid!" and Steele, sitting on the step of the only door, "was promptly used as a door mat by twenty-two pairs of GI shoes evacuating the bus!" While it only took about fifteen seconds to empty the bus, it was twenty minutes before the men could be reboarded, as they all had taken to the bushes.

After several repeats of this incident among the vehicles, the 3rd Pursuit Squadron's convoy was stopped a few miles short of Nichols Field, and a scouting party went ahead. Hank Thorne in his fast sedan would check out the situation and report back to his men. He did not want them to drive into the middle of a bombing raid. When Thorne returned a short while later, he had calming news. The engineers at Nichols were dynamiting the one-hundred-drum gasoline dumps that dotted the area between Nichols and Fort McKinley. This explained the noise and flames. Then he distributed several baskets of warm bread he had picked up from a local shop. By this time, the convoy had pretty much broken down. Most of the vehicles that were still operating under their own power were towing two or three other vehicles behind them.

At 3:00 A.M., when the convoy finally reached its destination, de la Salle College, where the squadron had stayed prior to their move to Tanauan, the exhausted men flopped down on the hard cement floors and slept. Thorne tried in vain to contact someone at FEAF Headquarters at McKinley. He did find out later, however, that a train had been sent down to Tanauan by the FEAF to evacuate the squadron but on arrival late that night found that the squadron had already gone.

In another convoy proceeding without lights south from Clark Field, the enlisted men and many officers of the 20th Pursuit were making slow but steady progress toward their Bataan destination. On their way, they met other convoys from Manila, Cavite, McKinley, and Olongapo, also inching their way toward Bataan. The roads were littered with wrecked cars and trucks. To 2nd Lt. John Posten of the 17th Pursuit, traveling in the 20th Pursuit's group in his ancient Chrysler with five others cramped in the car, "It looked like a small Dunkirk." About halfway to Bataan, the Chrysler broke down. After pushing it off the road, Posten and his passengers caught a ride with an army truck in another convoy. The 20th's convoy rolled until about midnight, by which time everyone was exhausted. It pulled off the road near a small village, and everyone flopped on the hard ground for a few hours' sleep.

Also dead tired were the pilots from Clark Field who had spent all afternoon searching for the Lubao strip from the air in their assorted aircraft. After having landed at Del Carmen that evening, they went over to the Del Monte sugar company and had a very good supper, then slept in the quarters at the estate taken over by the 34th Pursuit. The 34th was still awaiting its orders to evacuate into Bataan.

Not with the others from Clark Field, however, was their flight leader, Charley Sneed. He was out on the road, trying to locate Lubao Field in a command car. This time he succeeded in finding it and was sure he could guide his pilots in the next morning.

7 Early on the morning of Christmas Day, Hank Thorne sent an officer of his 3rd Pursuit Squadron down to the Manila port area to locate a means of getting personnel of the squadron over to Bataan. At about

6:00 A.M., the officer called back and informed Thorne he had been successful.

When the men awoke from their uncomfortable night at de la Salle
College, they were informed they would be moving out that day. The
priests at the college distributed Christmas boxes to each man that morning, a reflection of their kindness toward the squadron.

Reaching Pier 7 after leaving the college at about 10:00 A.M., the men
were immediately put to work loading the 100-foot interisland steamer
Antonia for the trip across to Lamao, their destination on the east coast
of Bataan. There was no Filipino labor available to help them, and time
was of the essence, so the men worked frantically alone to finish the job
as quickly as possible. In addition to the material the squadron had brought
up from Tanauan, large stores of army supplies found on the pier were
loaded on the boat, including about 500,000 rounds of .50-caliber aircraft
ammunition, about fifty .50-caliber aircraft machine guns in their crates,
a half dozen of .30-caliber M-1903 rifles, a large stock of canned food,
some tentage, and part of the equipment that belonged to the Air Depot.

By noon, the men had almost completed loading the *Antonia*, Thorne
then decided to clear the port area in expectation of the daily Japanese
attack at lunchtime. Just when he had gotten the officers and the NCOs
together, someone yelled, "There they come!" High overhead, they saw
two flights of nine Japanese bombers each. Within seconds, the men
cleared the dock for cover. One of the squadron's officers astutely quipped,
"They will never be able to destroy the 3rd Pursuit Squadron—they don't
make enough bombs to cover the area that the 3rd does."

From their various bombproof vantage points, the officers and men of
the squadron watched the Japanese bombers, circling high over Manila,
unload on the port area. This was the Manila that had been declared an
open city.

Two of Thorne's officers were not with him. Don Steele and Dana
"Chubby" Allen had sneaked away from the others just before Thorne had
assembled everyone and worked their way over to the Army and Navy
Club "for our final meal." They had had a swim in the club's pool and
were taking a shower when they heard bombs exploding nearby in the
port area. As Steele recorded in his diary that day, "We lay on the floor
of the shower room like a couple of mummies, watching the windows
rattle, and hoping the next one wouldn't have our name on it." When the
explosions stopped, the two young officers hurriedly dressed, "stepped over
a couple of colonels who were still playing safe," and went upstairs for
their Christmas dinner. At a cost of 5 pesos each ($2.50), "we ate the best
of everything and topped it off with some good imported wine."

Crouched on the curb of a street in the Luneta Park area of Manila,
Hank Thorne and the rest of the squadron were dining under less favor-

able conditions, wolfing down Christmas turkey and the trimmings, including mince pies, that 1st Lt. Ed Woolery and several other of the officers had brought over from de la Salle College by borrowed truck. Their meal finished, Thorne's group walked back to Pier 7 at about two o'clock, where Steele and Allen had now returned too. After sweating out another visit of two hours by a few Japanese planes circling over the piers at very low altitude, but not bombing, the squadron finished loading supplies and finally boarded the *Antonia* and departed for Lamao at 4:00 P.M.

Near Lubao Field, just northeast of the entrance to Bataan peninsula, Ed Dyess and his 21st Pursuit Squadron were celebrating Christmas at a hacienda about ten miles from the field with the Clark Field pilots, who had finally located the secret strip that morning. The squadron was consuming roast turkey, canned cranberry sauce, plenty of vegetables, plum pudding, coffee, "and a few drops of holiday cheer," all brought in earlier from Manila on special trips during the evacuation period.

All the Clark pilots had set their aircraft down safely on the dirt strip after taking off from Del Carmen at dawn except 1st Lt. Tex Marble of the 20th Pursuit. He had hit a soft spot on the field, slammed on the brakes, "bounded in the air in a complete somersault," and landed the P-40 on its nose, wrecking the plane. His only injury, however, was from the impact of his head on the unpadded gunsight of the E model, leaving a "V for Victory" cut on his forehead and sending him to Sternberg Hospital in Manila.

When the three hundred Filipinos still working on the field witnessed Marble's spectacular crash, they ran wildly onto the runway, "like so many chickens," and were directly in the path of the other planes coming in to land. To Dyess, it looked like a mass tragedy was at hand. Spontaneously, the 21st Pursuit's CO ran toward them, "yelling like a wild Indian and firing my automatic." Terrified of the bullets whining just over their heads, the laborers cleared the field for a cane patch in seconds.

Ten miles southwest of Lubao, on a strip at Dinalupihan the 803rd Aviation Engineers were rushing to completion, another P-40 came to grief about six hours after Marble's crash on the Lubao field. Second Lt. Glenn Cave of the 3rd Pursuit had been searching for a strip on Bataan he had been told would be easy to find when he saw a field under construction below him and assumed it was his destination. He buzzed the strip to let the engineers know he wanted to land, and they moved the equipment off the runway. When the P-40 hit the ground, the landing gear folded, and the plane skidded along the ground, tearing up its tail, wing tips, and belly before finally coming to a halt.

Shaken but uninjured, the young Californian quickly jumped out of the wreck, not knowing if it was going to catch fire or not. When a few engineers approached, Cave told them to drag the plane off to the side of the field and take what they wanted, because it would not be possible to repair it. Then he took his parachute and the maintenance logs of the plane and walked out to the road heading south, where he caught a ride into Bataan on a truck carrying bombs.

To Cave, the whole business had been ridiculous from the start. As a surplus pilot of the 3rd Pursuit following the Iba attack of December 8, he had been detached to the Signal Corps's Message Center in the Walled City. On Christmas morning, he was ordered to report to FEAF Headquarters at Fort McKinley, as a pursuit pilot was needed to fly a P-40 out of Nichols, and Cave was the only one around.

Arriving at Nichols, in burned-out condition after the previous evening's destructive activities, he was told to fly the P-40, the last one at Nichols,[10] to a field "on Bataan," but with no further guidance and without benefit of charts, maps, or communications. He had to hurry, as the engineers were getting ready to blow up the last operational runway with dynamite charges.

After taking off about noon, Cave tried to test-fire the guns and found them inoperative. Then he noticed formations of Japanese bombers high above him, coming in to Manila from the west, and began wondering about his chances to make it to Bataan. Flying on a northwest course, a short while later he thought he had found his field, but this one was actually just north of Bataan. But what more could be expected from an anxious and inexperienced twenty-two-year old, forced to fly for the first time in war to an unknown field without any navigation aids?

Cave was not the only pursuit pilot feeling misused by the brass this Christmas Day. Carl Gies and the other seven pilots who had been ordered to Australia the day before, after arriving at Mariveles at 9:30 A.M., spent the whole day under chaotic conditions, driving up and down the peninsula looking in vain for Colonel George. After a Christmas dinner of army canned rations, the frustrated youth, now joined by Jim Rowland, who had also been picked for the Australia mission, slept on the docks at Mariveles, ignoring an air raid in the middle of the night on the port town.

The enlisted men of the 17th Pursuit had also disembarked from the *Legaspi* at Mariveles at 9:30. After the squadron's equipment and supplies were unloaded, the men faced the problem of finding their new operations area of Pilar, halfway up the east coast of Bataan, some 16 miles away as the crow flies. With no transport available, some of the men decided to set out by foot.

Headed in the opposite direction, Dave Obert and Steve Crosby had left the new Pilar base in a truck to try and locate the squadron's men. Reaching the vicinity of Mariveles in early afternoon, they ran into the small group, straggling north on the highway, loaded them on the truck,

Wrecked P-35As at Nichols Field in January, 1942. *Courtesy National Archives*

and continued into Mariveles, where they found the rest of the squadron's personnel, "lost, sleepy, hungry, and bewildered."

After first telling Lt. Ridgley Hall, the squadron adjutant, to keep the men together, Obert drove back to the Pilar campsite, had the trucks unloaded that he had brought in from Manila that morning, and sent them down to Mariveles to pick up the men and their equipment. That afternoon, the reunited squadron personnel camped in a grove near Pilar and thought this might be their new location. A little before dark, they were ordered to a new site a little over a mile south of Pilar. It did not look like a suitable place; there was no cover except for a few hedges.

A few officers of the 17th were missing. Arriving about 4:00 P.M. on Bataan, John Posten and LaMar Gillett, after a few hours rest, were now looking for the 17th Pursuit, but no one seemed to know where they belonged or where anyone else was. After spending all day trying to find their squadron, they gave up and settled in for the night after a C rations

Christmas dinner. Obert had had better luck that afternoon in his own search for the 24th Group's CO, Maj. Orrin Grover. When his camp was located, Obert received orders to get the Pilar airstrip ready as soon as possible for operations.

Bivouacked only two miles north in the area of Balanga on Christmas Day were the officers and men of the 20th Pursuit. Here in a bamboo brake the squadron was recuperating from the previous night's experience of sleeping on the ground. Lt. Lloyd Stinson was still uncomfortable, though; dust and dirt had stuck to his greasy uniform during the night and he looked a mess.

After finishing off a Christmas dinner of baked ham, candied yam, asparagus tips, and a canned peach half, the men were looking forward to a bit of holiday cheer from the whiskey they had stashed away when they had evacuated Clark. Unfortunately, Joe Moore discovered their intentions before the men could get to it, and he "hit the ceiling." The agreement had been for it to be used for medicinal purposes only. Eventually, however, he softened his stance and allowed each man to have "a couple of snorts." But the rest of the precious liquid was now ordered to be destroyed. Moore figured he had enough problems without having to put up with an inebriated bunch of men. That evening, the men set up a bar on the tailgate of a squadron truck, dispensed the shots, and sang Christmas carols before turning in for the night.

Some twenty-two miles to the north, at Del Carmen, the officers and men of the 34th Pursuit also had enjoyed a fine Christmas dinner, the last decent meal they would have in the Philippines campaign. Earlier in the day, the squadron had finally received its evacuation orders: it was to take up operations at a dirt strip near the village of Orani, at the northern tip of Bataan. They had decided it would not be wise to travel on the road in daytime, and besides they did not wish to pass up the invitation of the Spreckles Sugar Company's people there to have Christmas dinner in the company's luxurious dining hall. Nothing had been spared for the men's enjoyment; all the imported food, beer, and liquor they could put away was made available to them. At midnight, the "true spirit of Christmas reigned" as the squadron departed Del Carmen field in trucks for their new destination, some eight miles north of the 20th's campsite at Balanga.

Before abandoning the field, however, there was the matter of destroying all equipment that could not be moved, and this included the squadron's remaining P-35As that were out of commission. After an officer showed them how, Pfcs Glen Flesher and Ivan Foster put tracers in their .45s and fired them into the gas tanks of the P-35As, which immediately burst into flames. Foster, still "drunk as a skunk" after having spent too much time at the Spreckles Sugar Company's bar, fired his tracer too close to his plane: the explosion singed his face and hair.

Nearby, S. Sgts. Alonzo Lawrence and Elbert Coleman and Pfc Dave Oestreich were agonizing over their order to destroy two of the FEAF's rapidly dwindling supply of P-40s that were also on the field. Although one had an unusable engine, the other, damaged by Larry Lodin's P-40E on December 9, suffered only a bent propeller and a hairline crack on the nose. With time and parts, it could have been salvaged. But time had run out. Coleman, with a heavy heart, fired tracers into the first P-40E from a .30-caliber Lewis machine gun and watched it burn in the black night. Then the three men pulled the other P-40E off the field, took the fuel tank caps off, stuck some rags partially in the openings, soaked them with gas, and set the plane afire with a match. For Oestreich, it was the hardest thing he ever had to do in his life.

Early on the morning of December 25, General MacArthur, who had now moved his headquarters to Corregidor, received a sour Christmas present from the War Department in Washington. By radiogram 879, he was informed that

IN VIEW OF YOUR MESSAGE RELATIVE TO FUTURE TACTICAL OPERATIONS ON LUZON, IT NOW APPEARS THAT THE PLANS FOR REACHING YOU WITH PURSUIT PLANES ARE JEOPARDIZED. STOP. YOUR DAY TO DAY SITUATION AND THAT OF BORNEO WILL DETERMINE WHAT CAN BE DONE AT ANY MOMENT BUT THE WAR DEPARTMENT WILL PRESS IN EVERY WAY FOR THE DEVELOPMENT OF A STRONG UNITED STATES AIR POWER IN THE FAR EAST BASED ON AUSTRALIA. . . .

Not only was the possibility eliminated of pursuit reinforcement by carrier, but now the War Department was being pessimistic over the chances of flying P-40s base-by-base up to the Philippines too, in view of the Japanese threat to the Dutch East Indies to the south.[11]

Over on Bataan, however, Colonel George, now commanding what was left of the FEAF in the Philippines, was going ahead with his plans to send pilots down to Australia to pick up P-40s. On December 26, he showed up at Mariveles, where Carl Gies and the other nine pursuiters designated for the Australia mission were staying, and told them to stand by, because the mission "may yet go through." The pilots then moved to Colonel George's camp to be ready for the flight south if and when it should materialize.

Every single additional P-40 Colonel George could mobilize at this stage would be vital for the success of his operations from Bataan. On this score, he was receiving unexpected help from Lt. Dick Fellows and the other officers and men of the Philippine Air Depot in Quezon City, just outside Manila. They had disobeyed Brereton's orders of December 24 to evacuate the depot and destroy all equipment, determined as they were to finish assembling and repairing four P-40Es that required only a few days to make them operational. In addition to the one that Pete Warden flew into Nichols on December 24, two others were expected to be ready for transfer to Bataan on December 27, and the fourth one ready for movement on January 1.

Part Four
EARLY BATAAN OPERATIONS

By January 2, the American and Filipino troops of the North and South Luzon forces had successfully withdrawn from both ends of Luzon and joined up at San Fernando, Pampanga, their designated rendezvous point for the evacuation into Bataan. That same day, Japanese troops marched into Manila, one week after MacArthur had declared it an open city to avoid needless destruction of the capital.

Just south of San Fernando, Lieutenant General Wainwright now established a ten-mile-long defense line between Guagua and Porac, guarding the entrance into Bataan. Under heavy assault by the Japanese from January 2, the Guagua-Porac line was abandoned by January 5 and a new one established some nine miles to the south. But just as the new line was secured, Wainwright issued orders for the withdrawal into Bataan through Layac Junction, to begin at dark on January 5.

By 2:00 A.M. on January 6, the last of USAFFE units had cleared the junction and were now in Bataan. The Japanese had lost the opportunity to cut off the retreat of the American and Filipino forces, which fought a successful delaying action all the way. But the withdrawal had cost Wainwright 12,000 of his 28,000-man North Luzon Force, mostly through desertion of Filipino soldiers. Major General Parker had only lost 1,000 of the 15,000 men of his South Luzon Force.

Already at their designated locations on Bataan eleven days earlier were the scattered units of the rump Far East Air Force. Then on December 29 a detachment of 19th Bomb Group men left Mariveles, on the southern tip of Bataan, for Cagayan, Mindanao, on the interisland steamer *Mayon*. They were ordered to build up defenses on Mindanao and assist Australia-based elements of the FEAF as they arrived back as reinforcements for MacArthur from Australia. For the other virtually plane-less personnel of the FEAF left on Bataan, a new role was assigned: to serve as infantry on beach defense. MacArthur's chief of staff gave the word to Col. Harold George, now chief of what remained of the FEAF in the Philippines, during a meeting on January 7.

On that same day, the defense of Bataan began officially with the assignment of commanding generals of two newly established forces: Wainwright for the I Philippine Corps, responsible for the western half of Bataan, and Parker for the II Philippine Corps, for the eastern half of the peninsula. Mac-Arthur now established a main battle position that extended eighteen miles in a line across northern Bataan from Mabatang on the east coast to Mauban on the west coast.

The supply situation of the defenders was grave right from the start. While WPO-3 had called for storage on Bataan of supplies for forty-three thousand men for six months, large-scale transfers to the peninsula began only with the orders to withdraw on December 24. It proved impossible to move the quantity needed for almost double the number of troops as well as fleeing civilians that ended up on Bataan, and that in only one week. Particularly serious was the shortage of rations, on January 3 estimated sufficient for only thirty days. On January 5, MacArthur was obliged to approve the recommendations of his quartermaster that troops and civilians on Bataan and Corregidor be placed on half-rations.

On the afternoon of January 9, the battle for Bataan opened with a Japanese artillery attack on II Corps. But they had misjudged the location of the II Corps line and were in turn subjected to a counterattack of artillery as they advanced down the east road of Bataan. During the next days, the elite 57th Philippine Scouts would bear the brunt of the Japanese infantry attack, but the II Corps would hold its ground on what was now known as the Abucay Line.

16. "I WISH THAT SOMEONE BESIDES SECOND LIEUTENANTS WOULD TURN UP TO FLY"

1 At Lubao Field on the morning of Friday, December 26, four of the P-40s hidden in their revetments were being readied by the men of the 21st Pursuit Squadron. They would lead off operations from the newly completed field. Capt. "Bud" Sprague, temporarily relieved of his desk job as operations officer of the 5th Interceptor Command, and Lt. Ed Dyess, CO of the 21st Pursuit, would fly a reconnaissance mission northwest over Lingayen Gulf to observe Japanese shipping activity there. Lt. Bill Hennon of the 17th Pursuit would also check out the Lingayen area, flying a different route. His squadron mate, Lt. George "Ed" Kiser, was ordered to fly southeast to obtain information about the status of the Japanese landing force in the Lamon Bay area.

In order not to give away the secret field to the Japanese, Dyess indicated that they would take off one by one, fly close to the ground for several miles, and only then climb for altitude over another area. The same procedure in reverse was to be followed in landing at Lubao.

After takeoff at 8:30, Dyess and Sprague flew north to Santa Maria and Asingan, where they were fired upon by 37-mm antiaircraft guns, but the bursts were too low. Continuing west to the town of Manaoag, just fifteen miles inland of Lingayen Gulf, they had a good view of Japanese operations offshore. Some fifty-five ships, all freighters, were identified.

On the way back to Lubao, five fixed-landing-gear Nakajima "Nates" jumped the P-40s, but the Americans eluded them. Then Dyess spotted a Mitsubishi "Ann" single-engine bomber, gave Sprague the high sign, and began to dive. Just before they reached firing range, the Japanese pilot saw the plunging pursuiters and dived too. Hurtling at much greater speed in their heavy ships, Dyess and Sprague soon caught up with the bomber. Just before Dyess shot past the Japanese, the adversaries exchanged fire: the "Ann" rear gunner put three rounds of 7.7-mm fire into Dyess's P-40, and Dyess riddled the Japanese with .50-caliber fire. Just over the treetops, the bomber straightened out, allowing Dyess to get in a long burst. The "Ann" burst into fire and went crashing into the woods.

On his mission, Bill Hennon, excited to be flying alone for the first time, approached Lingayen Gulf from the western Luzon coastline. He saw the same number of freighters in the gulf as had Sprague and Dyess. Turning inland, Hennon flew over Naguilian, whose airfield had recently been occupied by the Japanese, unknown to him. On the field, he could make out fifteen large single-engine planes. He then proceeded east to Baguio before heading back to Lubao.

Flying over the Alabat Island area on his reconnaissance, Kiser first spotted five destroyers northeast of the island, then some forty to fifty transports in the gulf between Alabat and the mainland.[1] He was so busy looking everywhere on his mission that he did not notice that a "Pete" had come up on his tail.[2] But when Kiser heard guns chattering, he looked back and saw the biplane with the big central float firing at him with its two 7.7-mm nose guns. Fortunately, the Japanese was way out of range and missed Kiser's P-40. Kiser went into a chandelle and headed for the maneuverable Japanese. As they approached each other, both fired head-on at each other. After the first pass, Kiser dove away and continued on his reconnaissance mission, mindful of the orders he had not to dogfight with anyone.

A little later, Kiser ran into a Type 96 pursuit flying in the same direction.[3] This time, the Somerset, Kentucky, native gave way to his instincts. He pulled up and fired at the Mitsubishi "Claude." The Japanese went into a shallow turn to the left and fired back at Kiser's P-40, then burst into flames. Kiser had his first victory.

Two days later, Dyess found himself in another scrape while on a reconnaissance mission, again over Lingayen Gulf. As he counted ships, barges, and truck trains, Dyess's wingman was weaving along his tail to keep Japanese away from him. But when Dyess had completed his mission and looked back for his wingman, he was nowhere to be found. Suddenly there was a loud boom, and his P-40 lurched. Banking, then looking down, Dyess spotted the cause of the incident: a "Nate" was just below and behind him, preparing to get in another burst of its 7.7-mm guns. Dyess now pulled over into a dive, building up distance between him and his adversary. Then he zoomed up, ending up behind and above the lighter fighter. The Japanese cut around and started up after Dyess, head on. Both planes fired. Tracers passed to the right, head-high, while others tore into the P-40's right wing, immobilizing one of its .50-caliber machine guns. By then, however, Dyess had got a bead on the Japanese and tore off the top of his motor with concentrated fire from his five remaining fifties. The flimsy "Nate" burst into flames and started its descent as Dyess passed over it. When Dyess turned his plane over to the mechanics upon landing back at Lubao, they counted twenty-seven holes in his right wing. The battery was also "all shot up."

Despite such heroics, the Japanese force that landed at Lingayen on December 22 continued its relentless movement down northern Luzon, meeting little opposition. General MacArthur's command stepped up aerial recon missions, now being flown in the morning and in the afternoon, to bring the vital information it needed on Japanese movements in order to plan holding operations.

On December 29, the focus of the recon missions from Lubao shifted to the south. With squadron mate "Dub" Balfanz on his wing following a daybreak takeoff, Bill Hennon flew over to the east coast of Luzon, then turned south down to Infanta and on to Paracale in Camarines Norte province, not spotting any ships or planes on his route. Losing Balfanz in the clouds before reaching Paracale, Hennon flew on alone, curving back to go over Alabat Island and Atimonan. There he observed twenty-seven boats near the shore, where the Japanese had landed five days earlier. Swinging over Lucena to the west, Hennon encountered antiaircraft fire but did not see any planes on the field. After passing over San Pablo on the home stretch, the Minnesotan landed back at Lubao at 10:00 A.M.

On December 30, Dyess and his wingman were again flying a reconnaissance in the Lingayen Gulf area. This time from 7,000 feet they spotted a truck convoy, inching along a hilly road in the direction of Baguio. Dropping down 2,000 feet, they got a good look at the seven-truck convoy and confirmed it was Japanese. When the Japanese saw the diving P-40s, they stopped the trucks and scattered for protection. As the P-40s ripped into the hapless convoy, "great chunks of truck bodies, motors, and cargo" flew in all directions. After two passes, three of the trucks were in flames, and the other four were torn to pieces. Dyess and his wingman had again exceeded their orders, albeit with definite consequences for the Japanese.

Some variety was introduced that afternoon in the Lubao operations. Japanese twin-engine navy bombers had been flying over the Lubao area every early afternoon from December 25, on their way down Bataan to bomb shipping in Mariveles Bay at the tip of the peninsula and (on December 29) Corregidor. Dyess now ordered six of the pilots to fly patrol over the approach path at 20,000 feet to catch the enemy planes on their daily run.

After takeoff, Bill Hennon, flying wing to Kiser, headed north and patrolled from noon to 2:30 in the afternoon with the others, but no Japanese showed up. Disappointed, the two pilots went into a Lufberry over San Fernando, ten miles northwest of Lubao, and then descended for the landing at their secret field. Later that afternoon, the pilots' irritation turned to frustration when they spotted fifteen Japanese bombers coming over again, heading south as usual.[4] The next day, six P-40s took off at 11:00 A.M. from Lubao on the same patrol over the same area in hopes of encountering the Japanese bombers on their daily run, but with the same negative results. Almost out of gas, the pilots landed in early afternoon.

When Dyess was not flying "reconnaissance" missions, he was busy supervising the final touches in camouflaging Lubao Field. The result was so good that the pilots were unable to locate it upon return from their missions except by reference to the adjacent road and a nearby sugar company plantation house. The Japanese could not spot the field either, although they were blasting targets on the highway continuously during the period.

Another weapon proved more effective against the so far untouched Japanese bombers. When Japanese Army Kawasaki "Lily" twin-engine bombers began attacking vehicles on the highway leading to Bataan later the afternoon of December 31, the 200th Coast Artillery Regiment, which had set up positions across the road from the airstrip, went into action for the first time. As one of the "Lilies" was heading in the direction of the field at 2,000 feet, bomb-bay doors still open, a 3-inch battery of the 200th opened up on it and scored a direct hit between the fuselage and port engine, partially obscuring the plane for a moment. Flames bursting through the open bomb doors and engines screaming, the doomed aircraft headed down, turning and twisting as it fell, in the direction of Dyess and others near him on the field. Only when it was within one hundred feet of the men did all scatter for safety.

With a terrific explosion, the "Lily" crashed into the cane field, spraying flaming gasoline in all directions and igniting the sugarcane. Filipino laborers and men of the 21st Pursuit and 200th Coast Artillery rushed to the scene. The bomber had dug a huge crater and scattered debris, bodies, and papers all over the area. It had just missed hitting five of the planes hidden in the cane revetment. Fortunately, no one on the ground was hurt in the crash. As some of the men began extinguishing the fire, others gathered up the maps, charts, and papers to give to Dyess according to his orders. Releasing their pent-up hatred of the Japanese, some of the Filipinos hacked the bodies of the Japanese crew. One handed Dyess the jawbones and teeth of one of the airmen.

2 Ten miles southwest of Lubao, another well-camouflaged field was also being used for reconnaissance missions in late December. This was Orani strip, at the northern head of Bataan, where the 34th Pursuit Squadron had arrived on December 26 from its old field at Del Carmen. Although the 2,800-foot strip was operational on the arrival of the 34th, the squadron had to take care of the camouflage, with the help of an engineer. This involved covering the field itself with rice straw. Mobile hay-

stacks were placed on crossbars and moved onto the strip. When a plane came in to land, the pilot would buzz the field. Filipino laborers would move the stacks off the field, then put them back in place after the plane had been hidden in the tree area. Later, half-circle revetments of sandbags were made for providing more protection of the aircraft.

Several pilots from the 20th Pursuit who had been flying from Lubao joined the 34th Pursuit at Orani on December 28, alternating flying missions with them and with a few pilots from the 3rd Pursuit. They would fly one reconnaissance at dawn and a second at sunset each day. Following an accident by Claude Paulger of the 34th, only five P-40s were available at the field for missions, with the other aircraft based at Lubao and Pilar fields.

From December 26, Don Steele of the 3rd Pursuit flew daily one or both missions from Orani, none of which were of much consequence, in his opinion.[5] He was not informed of the use of the information brought back and did not see "what we can do about it, anyhow." Steele was also chafing under the order to avoid all combat and keep as much under cover as possible during the flights. Another thing irritated the young flying officer. As he complained in his diary, "How I wish that someone besides second lieutenants would turn up to fly at some of the airdromes. Before the war a second lieutenant flew only routine and local missions and seldom got to take very many cross-country or pleasure trips. Now the first lieutenants and captains who enjoyed all the gravy before the war have affixed themselves to lovely desk jobs and we are, as usual, getting the undesirable end of the deal."

At Orani, Steele's gripe seemed valid. For instance, for the four morning reconnaissance missions of December 30, 2nd Lts. Tom Patrick, Erwin Crellin, and Dan Blass of the 20th Pursuit and Arthur Knackstedt of the 34th, all junior in rank in their squadrons, were the pilots who flew. At Lubao, however, the squadron CO, 1st Lt. Ed Dyess, took more missions than any other pilot in the 21st Pursuit.

On New Year's Day, 1942, Orani Field lost one of its few P-40s. Early in the morning, 34th Pursuit CO Ben Brown had called for two volunteers to fly a reconnaissance mission to Lingayen Gulf to check on the situation there. Second Lts. Stewart Robb and Frankie Bryant of his squadron volunteered for the job. Robb was to lead the way and Bryant to weave for him to protect his tail.

Shortly after takeoff at 7:15 A.M., machine gun fire from the 2nd Battalion, 31st Infantry, located at the "zigzag" overlooking Subic Bay, hit Bryant's P-40 over the combat lines, damaging his engine. When Bryant rendezvoused with Robb as planned over Subic Bay at 10,000 feet, Robb broke radio silence and informed Bryant that his plane was smoking. When Bryant leaned the fuel mixture, Robb radioed that the smoking had stopped, and both planes continued north. Shortly afterward, however, Bryant's plane burst into flames, unnoticed by Robb. The young Texan had no other option than to bail out. As he floated earthward, he was fired at from the ground. Were they Filipinos or Japanese?

After Bryant landed on the side of a mountain, the inhabitants of a small town above Subic Bay surrounded him and accused him first of being Japanese and then, on noticing his Caucasian features, of being a German spy. Brought before the mayor of the town, Bryant—helped by his red hair—protested until the community finally understood the error of its ways. Bryant was informed that the 31st Infantry was twenty miles to the south. Accompanied by five Filipinos, the relieved pilot started walking and finally reached the 31st's lines. There he was informed by the CO, Col. Charles Steel, that a Japanese spy had recently been killed at the front lines. Bryant made a deal with the colonel: provide transport for him to Orani, and the sergeant and corporal accompanying him could shoot him if he could not prove he was an American pilot with the 34th Pursuit.

3 On the afternoon of December 25, Major Grover had told Dave Obert to go to the dirt strip near the town of Pilar and get it ready for operations by his 17th Pursuit Squadron as soon as possible. This second airstrip on Bataan was just thirteen miles south of Orani, along the east-west Pilar–Bagac road, and had been hurriedly constructed mainly by hand labor over what had earlier been rice paddies. Within twenty-four hours of receipt of the orders, the field was completed, and camouflaged dispersals were built to accommodate the aircraft of the squadron. With the arrival of the 17th's ground crews the following day, maintenance services were now also set up.

Dust on the strip was a serious problem. Even though the squadron's sprinkling truck was used twenty-four hours a day, it was proving inadequate to keep the dust under control. Finally, on the morning of December 31, Obert, Steve Crosby, and two enlisted men took a truck and headed back to Manila in an effort to locate another sprinkling truck and a new pump so that water could be drawn from a stream near the airstrip.

After arriving in Manila, ablaze from burning oil stores all over the city, the 17th Pursuiters found what they were looking for, loaded up, and started back for Pilar. Obert, however, stayed behind in Manila for the evening, to spend New Year's Eve with his wife. Shortly after midnight, he was on the road again with the squadron truck, feeling "pretty blue" the whole way back on the crowded road to Bataan.

Squadron mate John Posten was also in Manila that evening, having left Pilar earlier in the day in his car with a few friends. After five days without a bath and wearing the same dirty clothes, he was "covered with crud" and "going crazy." He wanted a bath, and intended to celebrate New

Year's Eve in Manila. When they arrived in Manila, demolition crews were blowing up all the remaining oil and gas facilities of the city and what was left of Nichols Field, Fort McKinley, the port area, and Cavite naval base. The foolhardy young aviators were advised to get out of the doomed city at once, before the bridges to Bataan were blown up. Unfazed, Posten and his companions caught a New Year's Eve show before joining the tail end of a convoy back to Bataan. They had to leave in such a hurry they did not have time to look for Posten's car.

As Posten recorded in his diary, "We could hear them blowing the bridges behind us. On the way back we passed a dozen or more small villages laid flat by dive-bombers. We passed a railhead filled with am-munition cars burning; the ammunition was going off all around. I don't know how many cars we have seen wrecked and burning on the road." The convoy could proceed only at a snail's pace, since "the road was so choked with wrecks and retreating forces." Not until dawn did it reach Pilar.

On New Year's Day, Posten had alert duty and spent most of the day sleeping by his P-40. The first aircraft had now been flown into the field: three P-40Es. They apparently had been assembled at the Air Depot fa-cilities at Quezon City and flown out to Bataan, steps ahead of the Japa-nese entering the Manila area.[6] Pete Warden, assistant engineering offi-cer of the depot, flew the last one out himself.

4 Thirteen miles down the coastal road from Pilar, the men of C Com-pany of the 803rd Aviation Engineers were busy extending and widening the runway of Bataan Field, near the village of Lucanin, just three miles north of Cabcaben, and constructing aircraft revetments. Early in 1941, the strip had been built to a length of two thousand feet, too short for the operations now envisaged for it.

On Christmas Day, Colonel George had visited the field that was des-tined to become so famous as the base of his "Bastard Outfit of Bataan" in the three-month aerial defense of the peninsula. It was a completely bare area that day. Heavy equipment of the 803rd Engineers was being used to fill in two large bomb craters halfway down the strip; the day be-fore, twin-engine bombers made the first of the many visits the Japanese Army Air Force would pay to the field.

On December 26, a detachment of twenty-five enlisted men of the 24th Pursuit Group's Headquarters Squadron had arrived in a truck for detached service at the field, under the command of Capt. "Barney" Brodine, for-merly technical representative of Curtiss-Wright. The men were all skilled aircraft mechanics who would be responsible for those repairs to pursuit ships that could not be made readily on the flight line. One of the little group, Pfc Jesse White, was touched by the raw beauty of the location, a "barren strip carved out of the jungle, with no visible human life or

A detachment of mechanics of Headquarters Squadron, 24th Pursuit Group, with a P-40E in a revetment on Bataan Field, January, 1942. *Left to right, bottom row:* Charles Parman, Alan Waite, Brown Davidson, Henry McCracken, William Miller, Melvin Dixon, Lyall Dillon; *middle row:* Marcus Keithley, Jesse White, Ellis Holcomb, Chester Brown, Louis Tome, Michael Tardivo, Sid Wilkinson, John Dujenski; *back row:* Earl Akers, Richard Hunn, John O'Neal, Louis Myers, Clarence Hatzer, Henry Blair, William Alvis. *Photograph by Brig. Gen. Harold H. George; courtesy Jesse K. White*

facility," except for the 803rd Engineers, who welcomed them as they set up an area a few yards off the runway for their first bivouac.

Early the next day, the men had reconnoitered the field, familiarizing themselves with the hidden revetments the engineers had constructed and the jungle trails leading to them. They chose a big revetment nearest the runway, made of sandbags piled ten feet high on three sides and perfectly camouflaged, for the site of their general maintenance shop. Tools and spare parts were assembled in the revetment in readiness for the aircraft that would soon be flown to the field.

On December 29, the 16th Bombardment Squadron of the 27th Bombardment Group joined the aircraft mechanics and the 803rd Engineers at the field. Officers of the 16th had earlier been looking for an assignment for the planeless squadron, and Colonel George had assigned it to serve as the base squadron for the field. Bataan Field was now ready for operations. When would the pursuit pilots and their ships be coming in?

5 Headquarters, USAFFE, now based on Corregidor, was also wondering about the situation of its little air force, of which Colonel George had been put in charge. On December 28, it had radioed the War Department that as of that date, there were twenty-one pursuit planes on Luzon and two on Mindanao. Five days later, with the Bataan campaign beginning, MacArthur's chief of staff, General Sutherland, wanted to know from his air officer, Maj. Reginald Vance, the latest situation of aircraft availability. Vance believed about eighteen were serviceable but would check it out.

Valiant efforts were being made during the last week of December to save as many pursuit planes as possible from the relentless advance of the Japanese. Thus the last two P-40Es of the shipment of twenty-four that had arrived in the Philippines in late November had been assembled at the Philippine Air Depot's makeshift work area at Quezon City outside Manila by January 1 and flown out just ahead of the Japanese.

An even more daring attempt to save planes was accomplished by a few officers and men of the 20th Pursuit Squadron. In the hurried evacuation of Clark Field on December 24, several P-35As and P-40s were abandoned in dispersal areas in the adjoining woods because they were not flyable at the time. When it became clear that the Japanese invasion force that had landed at Lingayen on December 22 had still not reached the Clark Field area a week later, volunteers were sought from among the skilled mechanics of the squadron, now at Mariveles, to go back and attempt to salvage some of the aircraft.[7]

On the evening of December 29, at the request of M. Sgt. Bill Heller, S. Sgt. Ken Stanford agreed to lead a crew back to Clark. Selections were made from the volunteers on the basis of particular skills required to make a P-40 airworthy. In the case of Stanford, it was because of his specialty in engine changes.

At the crack of dawn on December 30, the men piled into a 1939 Buick touring car that had been commandeered earlier by the squadron and set out north for Clark. It had no top or windshield, but Stanford immensely enjoyed driving it on the uneventful trip, with no signs of war in the villages he passed. When the men arrived at Clark at about 8:00 A.M., they were struck by the eerie atmosphere. The base was completely deserted and devastated. Everywhere were blackened, twisted, burned, and shapeless masses of metal structures. Carcasses of what had been P-40s and B-17s were lined up on the apron; others lay in camouflaged positions around the edge of the field or in the skeletons of hangars.

All through the day, Stanford and his crew worked feverishly in the woods adjoining the field, selecting the least damaged P-40s and P-35As and robbing parts from the ones that were beyond repair. There was an occasional interruption when Japanese aircraft flew low over the field. The men were never spotted, however. When a plane was put in what was believed to be operating order, Stanford would taxi it out of its revetment in the woods and give it a "good run-up," checking all mechanical systems. By dusk, two P-40s and one P-35A were judged in flying condition by Stanford.[8]

Now the men could hear gunfire in the distance and were getting nervous. How close were the Japanese? Just after dark, 2nd Lts. Milton Woodside and Tom Patrick, under the command of 1st Lt. Charley Sneed, arrived at Clark in a car. Climbing into the cockpits of the renovated warbirds, they managed to taxi over the pitted field to the equally cratered strip and, without the benefit of lights, took off for Bataan. Two of the pilots had to make the flight with the landing gear of their aircraft in the down position, as they could not be retracted.[9]

Shortly after the pilots took off, the mechanics were ready to start back for their camp near Mariveles. By this time, the sounds of gunfire were very close, and the men were "scared as hell." Unknown to them, Wainwright's North Luzon Force was withdrawing that evening to D-5, the final delaying line on the central Luzon plain, about five miles north of Clark Field, with the Japanese right behind.

For Stanford and his men, the return trip was quite different. They inched along in pitch darkness with no headlights, their way impeded by natives fleeing south to Bataan. The Filipinos clogged the roads, walking or riding anything available to them, carrying all the possessions they could salvage. Finally, at about 8:00 A.M. on December 31, the dog-tired crew arrived safely back at Mariveles. They were appalled to find the town burning. They learned that the day before fourteen Japanese Army bombers had blasted the area for the first time in the campaign, though fortunately they had not hit the 20th's camp.

Stanford and his crew had left behind at Clark two P-35As and one P-40, as well as four Stearman biplanes of the Philippine Army Air Corps. That evening, a sergeant of the 75th Ordnance sent to Clark on another mission found them in the woods at the east end of the field and reported the matter to the FEAF. The following night, some men of the 698th Aviation Ordnance Company had found them, too, and reported the matter to the FEAF also but were told to "mind their own business." The P-40 was admittedly nonoperational, as were the Stearmans, all of which had had parts removed, but the ordnance men maintained that the two P-35As were in flying condition. In response to charges of abandoning the P-35As at Clark, Air Corps officers argued that the planes were obsolete. Even though they could have been flown on reconnaissance or observation missions, few pilots of the 24th Pursuit Group would have been willing to take such "sitting ducks" up in skies controlled by Japanese pursuit aircraft.

6 In late December Colonel George was still going ahead with his plans to send senior pilots of his command to Australia to fly back P-40 reinforcements. At noon on December 28, the ten pursuit pilots picked for this assignment reported in at Hank Thorne's newly established camp at Signal Hill on southern Bataan, along with all other flying officers who had no current assignments.

After they had arrived at Lamao early in the evening of December 25, Thorne's 3rd Pursuit had bivouacked near the town the first two days on Bataan. Then they moved west, high up on the peak of Mount Mariveles, at Signal Hill, two and a half miles from the main road. At the time it was occupied by the squadron, it was a completely primitive site, without a single building or even facilities for water other than a winding stream. But gradually Thorne and his men transformed the camp into a very comfortable one. They named the camp Shangri-La because it was such a very beautiful place. At two thousand feet above sea level, it provided welcome relief from the oppressive heat of the Bataan plain.

On December 29, from fifty to seventy-five Air Corps personnel were at Shangri-La, most unassigned. Don Steele, Thorne, and several others walked up one and a half miles to a cleared hillock on the west side of Mount Mariveles, where they watched the first Japanese bombing of Corregidor across the way in the early afternoon. They could see the bombs hit the water "and throw jets like a fountain to about 30 or 40 feet in the air," as well as score hits on the facilities at Fort Mills. It was frustrating for the pilots to watch the Japanese flying unopposed over the island, except for futile antiaircraft fire, and unloading their bombs.

Otherwise, life was proving very pleasant for the airmen at Shangri-La. Alcohol-inspired bull sessions lasted into the early morning. Other officers participated in wild pig hunts or just went hiking. One of the major diversions was singing obscene songs, facilitated by the combined knowledge of the lyrics by a large number of officers.

By now Carl Gies and the other pilots assigned to go to Australia were getting very restless. Had Colonel George forgotten them? Then Major Grover came to the camp on December 30 and informed them the operation would probably go through at about 3:00 P.M. that day. They waited around, and "sure enough it didn't come off."

Early the next morning, Walt Coss was roused by a phone call: the mission was on. Seven of the ten pilots were to report to Air Force Headquarters at noon. But three of the ten first had to be selected out, either on the basis of seniority or, as proposed by Jack Dale, flying time. This meant that Jim Rowland (41-D), Jim Alsobrook (41-D), and Randy Keator (41-C) lost out, much to their disappointment.

At their noon meeting with Colonel George, the seven fortunate ones —Walt Coss (40-A), Frank Neri (40-D), Joe Kruzel (40-H), Cy Blanton (40-H), Ed Gilmore (40-H), Jack Dale (40-H), and Carl Gies (41-B)—were instructed to report to Bataan Field, where a Beech 18 would be waiting to take them to Australia. George then briefed them on the objectives of their mission and on the airfields that would be available to them on their return to the Philippines in the new P-40s. On arrival in Australia, they were to report for duty to the commanding general, FEAF.

Following arrival at Bataan Field, happy and not realizing how danger-ous a trip it could be, the young airmen climbed aboard the red, twin-engined Beech, registration NPC-56 clearly displayed, which had been parked back in the woods off the strip. It had taken several hours of work to clear the camouflage off the plane and get the Philippine Air Lines veteran ready for the mission. The men filled five-gallon gas cans and brought them into the cabin so that the aircraft could be refueled from inside for the long trip.

At 3:00 P.M., Capt. Louis J. Connelly, a former Philippine Air Lines pilot who had flown the Beech in peacetime, lifted the overloaded trans-port off the strip and headed south. A page torn from an atlas was to serve as his route guide. At Connelly's side, Jack Dale was flying as copilot. All the way to Mindanao, the first stop, Connelly hedgehopped the Beech, never going higher than thirty feet off the water or ground. At 6:30 P.M., they arrived safely at Del Monte Field, where they were treated to a won-derful New Year's Eve supper and drinks at the Del Monte pineapple plan-tation club. Finally, at 1:00 in the morning, they all collapsed into bed, far from sober.

7 On the same afternoon that the seven pursuit pilots were getting ready to board the Beech for Australia, seven other officers of the 24th Pursuit Group were also preparing for their evacuation south, but by a different means of transport. All wounded in the Japanese attacks on Clark and Iba fields on the first day of the campaign, they were at Ma-nila's Sternberg Hospital. That morning, they had received the news that all the seriously wounded in the hospital were to be loaded on the old SS *Mactan* and taken to Australia that evening.

Of the seven airmen in that group, five were from the 3rd Pursuit. Of this group, 2nd Lt. Bartholomo "Bart" Passanante was the most seriously wounded; a leg had been amputated three weeks earlier at Sternberg fol-lowing his evacuation from Iba on December 8. First Lt. Jim Donegan and 2nd Lts. Robert "Jim" Hinson and John Hylton had also been wounded in the Iba attack, as had been 1st Lt. Reuben Hager, the 3rd's nonflying adjutant. Among the group injured in the Clark Field attack were 1st Lts. Ross Huguet, a nonflying officer of Headquarters Squadron, who like Passanante had lost a leg, and Fred Armstrong of the 20th Pursuit, who had been badly burned while attempting to take off in his P-40.

In late afternoon, all the officers and men in Sternberg selected for the ocean crossing were loaded into any form of available transportation — buses, taxis, army trucks, jeeps, and beer wagons — and driven down to Manila's Pier 7. Along with the seven 24th Group officers were 217 other seriously wounded American and Filipino troops who were being evacuated in the nick of time before the Japanese entered the city.

They must have wondered what their chances were to make it to Australia when they saw their ship for the first time. The *Mactan* was a tiny, forty-two-year-old interisland steamer, "not much bigger than a Staten Island ferry." Would it be able to survive the beating it would surely take on the high seas? By 7:00 P.M., all the passengers had boarded and claimed a spot to lie down somewhere in the incredibly cramped quarters, most on the open deck. At 8:30, the ship's old engines started pounding, and it began threading a path through the minefields of Manila Bay, the beginning of a long voyage that miraculously ended safely in Sydney, Australia, twenty-seven days later.

Not on board were 2nd Lts. Jim Pate and Jim Boone, two other 3rd Pursuit pilot patients at Sternberg who had also been wounded at Iba. Boone had not received the news of the *Mactan* evacuation and was "walking around" when the others were being taken from the hospital. By the time he found out about it, the *Mactan* had already sailed.

8 When news of the evacuation plans was being spread at Sternberg Hospital that morning, 1st Lt. Buzz Wagner was in the hospital too, recovering from the eye injuries he sustained on his December 22 mission to Lingayen. One eye was completely covered with a bandage, the other partially so. His close friend Jim Bruce, a pilot with the 28th Bomb Squadron who had received his wings at Kelly Field a year after Wagner, was visiting him.

Wagner sized up the situation. The Japanese were at the approaches of Manila, and the city would be surrendered without a fight; MacArthur had declared it an open city a week earlier to avoid its useless destruction, since his troops would all be safely on Bataan by the time the Japanese entered the city. Those in Sternberg Hospital not being evacuated would be taken prisoner by the Japanese. Wagner had no intention of accepting such a fate.

Assisted by Bruce, Wagner now got up and walked out of the hospital. The two then headed for the opposite end of the city from which the Japanese were approaching. En route, they picked up a machine gun. They were not going to be captured without at least a fight. Arriving at Manila harbor, Wagner and Bruce found someone loading two boats with TNT who told the airmen that he was headed for Bataan. If they were not afraid to ride on top of the explosives, they were welcome to join him. Accepting the offer, Wagner and Bruce climbed aboard the rear boat and set up their machine gun on top of the TNT.

A short while after setting out, a particularly serious problem developed. The two boats were attached to each other by metal bars, but the water was very rough, and each wave would buckle the second boat against the first. The captain was afraid they would buckle together too hard and set off the cargo of high explosives. Wagner and Bruce now tried to cross over to the first boat on the metal bars but could not manage it. Then they dove into the water in an effort to swim to the first boat. In diving, Wagner lost his eye bandage, and the salt water burned his eyes severely. After swimming a while but making no progress toward the first boat, he clambered back into the second one. But Bruce was still in the water, nearly fifty yards behind the second boat. Wagner persuaded the captain to swing around and pick Bruce up. Finally, both officers got into the first boat and cast adrift the second one.

Arriving at a harbor on Bataan where the captain intended to put in, the water proved so rough that he hesitated to attempt it because of his volatile cargo. Wagner and Bruce wanted to get off there, however, because an army camp was nearby. The captain gave them a rowboat that, as they discovered after pushing off, contained only one oar. After struggling with the boat in vain for a while, the two frustrated officers finally gave up and plunged into the water again. Reaching shore, they collapsed, exhausted, on the ground.

About noon, the hot sun beating down on them awakened them from their slumber. They then set out by foot for the army camp known to Wagner, about ten miles away. They would cover a short distance, then duck off the road into the ditches or the woods to avoid the attention of low-flying Japanese bombers and strafers. Finally arriving at the camp late at night, Wagner and Bruce dragged themselves into the first tent they saw and were soon in a deep sleep.[10]

The following morning, Wagner was awakened by Colonel George, slapping him on the back, and was taken to Hank Thorne's rest camp for Air Corps officers, up on Signal Hill. Colonel George informed him that he and a number of other pursuit pilots would be flown out to Australia that morning to bring back P-40s.

9 About eight o'clock that morning, an army staff car arrived at Lubao Field. The driver had been ordered to pick up 1st Lt. Red Sheppard and 2nd Lts. Bill Hennon and George Kiser, all pilots of the 17th Pursuit who had been flying out of the field the past week. Second Lt. Ben Irvin of the 21st Pursuit was also to join them. The Lubao pilots were to report

to Orani Field on northern Bataan for an evacuation flight to Australia. Hurriedly, with only about an hour's notice of their unexpected trip, the four collected a minimum of personal belongings and climbed into the staff car for the short trip down to Orani.

At Orani field, they were joined by Capts. Cecil S. McFarland, gasoline and oil officer of the FEAF, and Bud Sprague, operations officer of the 5th Interceptor Command, plus two other pursuit pilots: Wagner and Jim Rowland from their own 17th Pursuit. Except for Rowland (41-D), who had been originally selected for, but then cut off, the December 31 evacuation flight, the pilots were all senior level: Wagner the former CO of the 17th Pursuit and a 38-B flying school graduate, Sheppard from Class 40-A, Kiser 40-H, and Hennon 41-B. Irvin was also senior, a 40-G graduate of Kelly Field.

The aircraft that was to take them out was another Beech 18, number NPC-54, the sister ship of NPC-56 of the December 31 flight to Australia. But its condition was much worse than that of NPC-56. There were over 130 bullet holes in it, the consequences of being strafed and bombed at Nielson Field earlier in the campaign. The entire leading edge of the left wing had been replaced with a piece of sheet metal roofing material.

All the five-gallon cans of gasoline that could be obtained were loaded in the cabin. Then an improvised refueling line was made by taking a pipe and running it along the fuselage of the Beech. One end of the pipe was plugged, and the other end ran into the gas tank. The pipe was wrapped up as much as possible to prevent air from getting into the line. A hole was drilled in it near the cabin. A funnel was placed in the hole, into which gas from the five-gallon cans could be poured. After an atlas was produced, a page was torn from it to serve as a navigation aid. Better than nothing, they reasoned.

Finally, the men faced the question of who should pilot the plane. Though all of the eight officers had flown an old B-10 before, none had ever piloted a Beech 18. It was finally agreed among themselves that McFarland should take the controls, with Sheppard flying copilot. A little past 2:00 P.M., a heavily overloaded NPC-54 barely cleared the little strip on takeoff. Ahead of it lay 450 miles of water and islands before the first stop at Del Monte on Mindanao.

10 Back at Lubao late that afternoon, Ed Dyess received orders to abandon the field. Only by midmorning that day had the 21st Pursuit completed all work on the secret field. But Lubao was now almost on the front lines. The Japanese were reported to have occupied a barrio just two and a half miles down the road. Already there was a stream of traffic carrying men and matériel of the U.S. and Filipino forces out on Highway 7 that passed by the field, heading west toward Bataan. Dyess now gave the order for most of the nonflying personnel of his 21st Pursuit to join the exodus. By early evening, they were headed in a truck convoy for their new bivouac area at Kilometer Post 184.7, at the southern tip of Bataan near Mariveles. Bill Rowe and the other pilots at Lubao were also anxious to get out, but it was too late in the evening to fly the planes to the unlighted fields on Bataan.

Over at Pilar Field, twenty-three miles to the south, John Posten, Dave Obert, and several other pilots of the 17th Pursuit were awakened at 2:00 A.M. that night. They were ordered to get over to Lubao and help the remaining pilots there fly out their P-40s and P-35As. Reporting in at Lubao just before daybreak on January 2, they were informed that the P-40s were to be flown to Pilar and Orani fields and the P-35As, as well as the single A-27, further south to the new Bataan Field, near Limay.[11]

At 6:30, Bill Rowe joined the other 17th Pursuiters in taking off with the P-40s assigned to Pilar Field. While he and the others managed to land safely at Pilar, Bud Powell got too far over to the right of the strip and washed out his landing gear on landing and also damaged his propeller and a wing. Then Rowe's ship was damaged when the ground crew grazed a tree while pushing it into its camouflaged revetment, ruining the aileron.

Selected to fly the five P-35As[12] to Bataan Field were the most junior officers of the 17th Pursuit (41-D and 41-G flying school graduates): 2nd Lts. Oscar Wyatt, Bob Krantz, Earl Hulsey, Silas Wolf, and one other. After approaching Bataan Field on the short hop, Wyatt was circling to land when he suddenly ran into a hail of antiaircraft fire from USAFFE defenders at the field. With little or no training in the identification of aircraft types, and in the absence of any procedures to coordinate operations between aviation and defense units, these units had evidently mistaken the radial-engine P-35As for similar-looking Japanese aircraft. His aircraft smoking, the terrified Texan turned and headed back toward Pilar Field to the north. But his P-35A could not make it; it went into a dive and crashed at the edge of Manila Bay near the small barrio of Camachile, two miles southeast of Pilar Field. Wyatt and his plane were buried deep into the mud on impact, the young blond pilot killed instantly.

Also hit by the gunfire, but only in the windshield, was Krantz, Wyatt's flying school classmate.[13] Shaken by the sight of Wyatt's crash and with his view impeded by the broken windshield, the lantern-jawed officer from Yucaipa, California, decided to try to get down at Pilar instead. On touching down, he stood his P-35A on its nose when he overshot the field. Krantz was uninjured, but his ship was wiped out.

Hulsey and the other unidentified 17th Pursuiter also opted to abort the Bataan Field landing and came in behind Krantz, managing to set their P-35As down intact. Only Wolf held to his flight plan, continuing down the east coast of Bataan to Bataan Field, where he landed without incident.

17. "ONE OF THE MOST NERVE-WRACKING FLIGHTS THAT I HAVE EVER MADE"

1 At Pilar Field in the early evening of Saturday, January 3, 2nd Lts. Earl Stone and "Dub" Balfanz had just landed their P-40s. They had some exciting news for their 17th Pursuit squadron mates. On their reconnaissance mission to the north, they had spotted Japanese aircraft on the field at Cabanatuan. With Balfanz staying up to cover him, Stone peeled off and went into a strafing run across the newly occupied strip, burning one of the bombers. Then, pulling up, he encountered a Tachikawa Ki-36 "Ida," a single-engine army observation plane, approaching Cabanatuan Field to land. The Japanese pilot tried to elude the P-40 in the highly maneuverable two-seater, but Stone sent the machine down in flames.[1]

Resting after his mission, Stone was wondering if it was the last one he would fly from Bataan. That afternoon, before he had taken off on the mission, he had participated in a meeting of pursuit pilots called by Ed Dyess at Pilar. Dyess had driven from Orani to brief them on an important assignment that was being planned for the next day.

Evidently Colonel George had decided that with the rapid approach of Japanese forces to Layac Junction, where all the roads into Bataan joined, it was too risky to have his small, invaluable group of pursuit planes so near the front line. Consequently it was decided to fly them all down to Mindanao,[2] but only after one first, concerted attempt to intercept the daily "milk run" of Japanese bombers passing overhead each day on the way down to bomb targets at Mariveles and Corregidor. This interception would thus serve as a necessary morale booster for the pilots and the American and Filipino ground forces.

The eighteen pilots who were to participate in the mission had already been selected by Dyess. When they were all assembled, Dyess handed out a set of maps and laid out the plan for the next day. Dyess did all the talking. The eighteen P-40s on Bataan would be equally divided between Pilar and Orani fields. At 12:00 noon, forty-five minutes before the usual arrival of Japanese bombers over Bataan, Dyess would take off with the Orani group and 1st Lt. Fred Roberts with the Pilar nine. The two groups would rendezvous over Del Carmen, fifteen miles due north, then climb to 20,000 feet for the interception. After attacking the Japanese bombers, each group would return to its takeoff field, refuel, and head immediately for Del Monte on Mindanao.

Picked to fly under the 3rd Pursuit's Roberts (40-D) were Dave Obert of the 17th and Don Steele of the 3rd (both 40-H) as the other two element leaders plus John Vogel (41-B) and Walter Wilcox (41-C) from the 17th, Gordon Benson and Bob Newman (both 41-B) from the 3rd Pursuit, and Joe Cole (41-C) and Bob Ibold (41-D) from Dyess's 21st Pursuit. Taking off with Dyess (37-C) from Orani would be Marshall Anderson (40-D), Bob Duncan (40-H), Lloyd Stinson and Percy Ramsey (both 41-C) of the 20th Pursuit, Ed Woolery (39-C) and Dana "Chubby" Allen (41-B) of the 3rd Pursuit, and Bill Baker and Jack Hall (both 41-C) of the 34th Pursuit.[3]

To Don Steele, the Mindanao flight plans seemed ridiculous, if not impossible. As he wrote in his diary on January 3, 1942: "About two months ago, it would have taken an Act of Congress even to consider such a flight, and now they are sending 75 percent of the pilots in this field to an aerodrome that they have never seen, over territory they have never been to, without any hesitation whatsoever. I feel quite sure I could go around the peninsula and pick 50 pilots who are now on desk jobs that could make this flight, all of them quite experienced and quite familiar with all the terrain which we are to cover."

Steele was particularly apprehensive about the distance to be flown: some 520 miles as the crow flies. Equally concerned were Joe Cole and the others. "Getting to our destination was to be quite a feat," Cole wrote to his parents two weeks later. With no belly tanks available, the P-40's normal flying time was two and a half hours fully fueled, versus the four hours that Steele estimated they would need to reach Del Monte if they were able to stay directly on course. A direct route, however, would take them over "two strongly-held Japanese aerodromes," Steele determined. This meant they would probably have to circle the two fields "unless we were fortunate enough to get some weather where we could get above the overcast." As Steele wrapped his one blanket around himself and lay down on the cold ground off the field for a doubtful sleep, he rationalized that at least he would not be on Bataan another night.

2 At Pilar Field the next morning, all nine pilots were very excited and cheerful, their doubts of the day before about the mission cast aside. Already by 11:00 A.M. they were standing by their P-40s, one hour before the scheduled takeoff time. But at 11:10 a report came in to the field from headquarters that the Japanese would be taking off an hour earlier than usual. The P-40s were to get airborne immediately. Hurriedly, the pilots

climbed into their planes, started the engines, and roared down the dirt strip. By 11:15, all were in the air, heading out over Manila Bay before swinging around and proceeding northwest for the Del Carmen rendezvous with the Orani group. At 11:26, they were spotted maneuvering over Manila Bay by coast artillery units on Bataan.

Arriving over Del Carmen, the Pilar flight began circling at low altitude, searching for the Orani pilots. Soon the pilots began sweating heavily in their cockpits from the oppressive heat of midday in the tropics. Where were the others? Finally, after an hour's circling, Roberts and the others accepted that something had gone wrong and that the Orani flight would not be showing up. At any rate, they now did not have enough gas to climb to 20,000 feet and engage in combat. Dejected, they headed back to Pilar. But as they were descending to land, the pilots were angered to notice Japanese bombers overhead, heading south at the usual time.[4]

After landing at about 1:00 P.M., the nine P-40s were refueled for the flight to Del Monte, since no change in orders had been received at Pilar. Roberts took off first but did not circle overhead for the flight to form on him. Instead he just headed south. His wingmen, Joe Cole and Milt Wilcox, followed on their own. Then Dave Obert led off the second element, John Vogel and Bob Ibold on his wing, followed by Don Steele and his wingmen Bob Newman and Gordon Benson.

What had happened at Orani? Evidently the flight took off at the originally scheduled time of 12:00 noon; it had received no word of a time change. But the pilots had been given new instructions that canceled the Mindanao part of the mission. They were now to land at Bataan Field instead.

After Orani Field had been cleared of the stacks of rice straw, Marshall Anderson and his wingman, Lloyd Stinson, taxied out from under the trees and joined the others lined up on the strip. Taking off in two-ship element formation, they began their climb. At 15,000 feet, Stinson found that his liquid-cooled Allison engine was overheating and that he was unable to keep up with Anderson. To cool the engine, Stinson put his nose down and reduced power, then applied power and climbed again. When the engine started overheating again, he repeated the process.

Soon Stinson found himself alone. Looking up, he now saw a formation of Japanese bombers, but all he could do was watch them pass well overhead. Giving up in his efforts to gain altitude, Stinson headed south to Bataan Field. He found that he was the first of the Orani group to land. Then shortly afterward the others came in to land, too. None reported any success in trying to intercept the bombers. The enlisted men at Orani had seen the P-40s circling below the Japanese.

A check of Stinson's plane revealed why the engine was overheating.

On the takeoff roll, Anderson's P-40, slightly ahead of Stinson's, had blown loose rice straw around on the strip, and it had been sucked into Stinson's intake, blocking air to the cooler.

At Pilar, orders were received later that day countermanding the Mindanao mission. Apparently with Bataan Field, far to the south of the peninsula, now operational, the USAFFE and Colonel George felt the little force of P-40s was not in the grave danger they feared the day before.

3 After only twenty-five miles out of Pilar and approaching Cavite, southwest of Manila, the nine Mindanao-bound pursuiters ran into bad weather and went over to instruments. Having started out in very loose formation to conserve gasoline, they now lost sight of each other in the overcast.

Dave Obert had decided to alternate flying on instruments with flying by sight between layers of clouds, heading south on an approximate compass course. Finally, after some three hours, the cloud cover broke and Obert felt relief to find he was over the island of Cebu, over two-thirds of the way to his destination. All along, he had been thinking that the flight would probably run out of gas and end up somewhere over the Pacific.

Don Steele had also come out of the overcast somewhere over Cebu. Like Obert, he had lost sight of his wingmen somewhere during the flight. Occasionally he could make out Benson, but he had not seen Newman since he entered the clouds at the beginning of the flight. Cruising at about 7,000 feet, Steele had his carburetor leaned way back. His engine was overheating badly, and the temperature of the coolant was very high. But he had come out very nearly on course. Below, Steele could see large fires and smoke coming up from Cebu. Apparently the Japanese were raiding Cebu City. He expected to be intercepted, but no planes were seen rising from the area. And now his wingman, Benson, had spotted him and joined up with him.

With about a hundred-mile stretch of water ahead of them, "well-known to be shark infested," Steele figured it would take another forty-five minutes to reach Mindanao and another fifteen or twenty minutes to find the Del Monte strip. Grimly, now nearly out of gas, Steele and Benson hung directly on course, which would carry them over the island of Bohol next. Soon Mindanao came into view, but now all of Steele's tanks read "empty." Expecting the motor to cut out at any moment, Steele kicked off his shoes, in preparation for an unwanted swim. But their P-40s kept on flying as the minutes ticked by. And now the grass strip at Del Monte came into view.

Wasting no time, Steele now put himself into landing position and came right in, with Benson right behind him. Just as his wheels touched the ground, Steele's gas supply expired. He had enough to taxi off the field

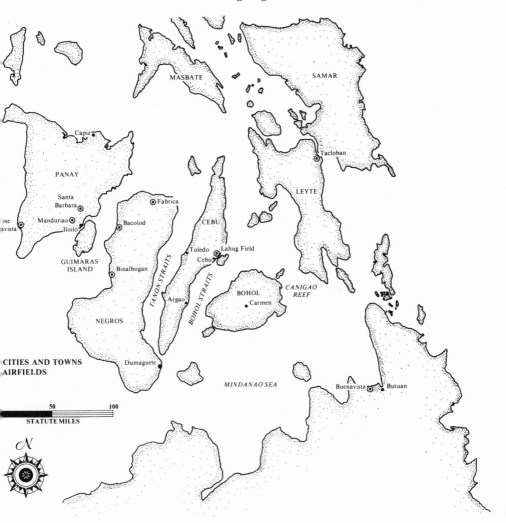

Map 6. Visayan Islands

only. "The gauge must have been inaccurate," Steele reflected as he climbed out of his cockpit, thankful to God for the imperfection. "This was probably one of the most nerve-wracking flights that I have ever made," Steele recorded in his diary that night. "A total of 532 air miles without auxiliary tanks—something that I did not believe could be done."

Already on the field were Roberts and Ibold. Roberts had run out of gas taxiing back up the field. Then shortly afterward, John Vogel, unable to locate the field and with only minutes of fuel left, opted to put down on a cart track in a pineapple field some ten miles from Del Monte, the most level-looking spot around. He made a perfect landing, with just enough room on each side for his wheels. His plane was undamaged. But Vogel's element leader, Dave Obert, had not arrived yet, nor had Bob Newman, Walt Wilcox, or Joe Cole.

Over Cebu, Obert had checked his gas gauges and come to the conclusion that he would not be able to reach Del Monte with the remaining fuel supply. He had been briefed that Cebu was probably in Japanese hands, but the alternative to landing there was a crash landing in the sea, a thought that did not appeal to him. He decided to investigate the possibilities on Cebu.

As Obert approached the field on Cebu, he saw that it was barricaded with gasoline drums. After he buzzed it a few times, Filipino soldiers came running out and started clearing the obstructions. Obert now began to wonder if perhaps the "Filipinos" were not actually Japanese in disguise. If they were, he would be ready to turn around and take off immediately after touching down. But when a white man, a Catholic missionary, rushed out to meet him on landing, followed by his "flock of Filipino airmen," Obert relaxed. The hosts were all excited; it was the first contact they had had with the outside world in days.

After his plane was refueled, Obert took off in the clear weather to resume his flight to Del Monte. But he knew that darkness would lay ahead of him on Mindanao. Crossing over Bohol and reaching the shore of Mindanao, Obert proceeded toward what he believed was the field at Del Monte. After circling for several minutes, he still could not make out any airstrip in the growing darkness. He now decided to fly back out to the coastline and look for a white beach on which to crash-land. But then he spotted a red flare in the distance. Heading in the direction of the marker, he could now make out car lights and a dim line of runway lights. Hitting the field roughly but safely, Obert taxied to the edge of the runway. "Lindbergh had nothing on this flight," the exhausted Oklahoman mused as he crawled out of the cockpit.

Flying a bit west of Obert's course and now approaching Negros Island, Joe Cole also came to the conclusion that he was not going to make it to Del Monte on his remaining gas supply. Dipping down, he decided to try to land at Fabrica Field, five miles inland of the northern shore. Noting that there were barrels on the strip, Cole signaled that he wanted to land. The local Filipinos, however, made no attempt to move them. Worried that he was too low on gas and desperate to get down, Cole decided to make a crash landing on a nearby sugarcane field. Coming in, he made a very rough landing, wrecking his plane and banging his head. Cole was dragged unconscious from the P-40 by employees of the Insular Lumber Company nearby. Two days later, he woke up in the local hospital.

Flying along with Cole, Walt Wilcox had elected to head to Cebu after they were unable to land at Fabrica. When he touched down safely, he found out that Obert had been there too. Not wishing to continue south, Wilcox spent the night on Cebu. Early the next morning, his P-40 refueled, Wilcox was off for Del Monte, flying at low altitude because of a heavy overcast. Over Bohol, he evidently developed engine trouble and crashed into a mountain at Carmen, in the middle of the island. He was killed instantly.

And what of Bob Newman? After flying for a while in the overcast, with no visibility, he decided that his chances for reaching Del Monte under the conditions he faced were too slim. Turning his P-40 around, he headed back to Bataan, landing in the late afternoon without incident.

The arrival of five P-40s at Del Monte that afternoon made quite an impact on the personnel at the base. The men thought that these were the first of the expected reinforcements and greeted the "tired and worn" pilots as "the saviours of the island." Capt. "Hoot" Horrigan arrived to pick them up and take them to a little barrio some miles away where they were given cold biscuits and beef stew for supper, the best meal they had had for weeks. Then Horrigan dropped them back at Del Monte Field, where they were directed to the nearby barracks and given two thin blankets for the evening.

After shivering and shaking for a few sleepless hours in the cold air of the plateau, two thousand feet above sea level, Obert decided to put his clothes on, wrapped himself in the small blankets, turned his canvas cot upside down and crawled under it, and finally succeeded in getting to sleep. Nearby, Steele and the others were trying to sleep with all their clothes on too but still were "freezing to death."

4 At about four o'clock the next morning, January 5, the Bataan Field pilots were "very rudely awakened" and hauled back to the little barrio, where they were given breakfast. Then they were told to go back to their P-40s on the main Del Monte field, where another pilot would meet them and lead them to a hidden field. The base commander did not want to leave his entire air force of five P-40s sitting out in the open as targets for the daily morning visits of Japanese dive-bombers.

Obert and the others got out to the field at daybreak and waited around for the pilot who was to show them the new field. When he did not show up right away, the Bataan group decided to go over to the barracks, where they loaded their belongings and cots in a car and sent them to where their new quarters were to be.

Obert had gotten all his things in the car and was just carrying his cot out when a car with some older officer in it was driven up to the location. As the officer charged up to Obert, the startled lieutenant jumped to attention and saluted. "Are you a room orderly or a pilot?" he roared at Obert. The Bataan pilot could see that the officer was very upset about something but did not know what had earned the wrath of the officer, who Obert now surmised was Col. Ray Elsmore, the base CO.

"I am a pilot," Obert weakly replied.

"Then why weren't those airplanes moved at daybreak?" Elsmore demanded to know.

Sensing that excuses were not in order, though asked for, Obert meekly replied, "No excuse, sir."

"Get those airplanes moved, and I want to see all of you at one o'clock!" Elsmore barked, then departed.

In the meantime the other pilot had arrived. It was squadron mate John Brownewell, General Sharp's reconnaissance pilot, who was now warming up the engine of Don Steele's P-40. A few minutes later, Brownewell took off in the lead, followed by Obert, Roberts, Benson, and Ibold in the other P-40s. After being airborne only a very short while, Brownewell led them down to about fifty feet, and only then could they make out a field, so well hidden it was. It was only about eight miles south of where they had taken off, a very narrow grass strip bounded on one side by big boulders and on the other side by a canyon about five hundred feet deep. Another end also dropped off into a five-hundred-foot canyon.

All five pilots landed safely, though Obert fully expected someone to plunge into the river below. No sooner had they gotten their P-40s pushed back under some trees than over came four Zeros. Obert figured they must have gotten word that planes had landed at Del Monte the night before. Hiding under a bush, Obert watched them search the area in vain then engage in a little strafing practice against a terrified officer driving in a command car nearby.

Leaving the 19th Bomb Group mechanics at the field, which was called the Del Monte No. 3, or Dalirig, strip, to work on the P-40s, about which the mechanics knew very little, Obert and the other three now headed back to the Del Monte base. The half-hour trip turned out to cover one of the most beautiful areas Obert had ever seen. The road wound down one side of a canyon, across a swift, clear mountain river, and then up the other side. Everything was so green and fresh-looking and the air so pure and crisp that it reminded Obert of a paradise on earth.

Arriving back at the Del Monte base area, the pilots drove on about ten miles to an outlying camp, known as Camp 29, where most of the base personnel were quartered. The old nipa shacks that the Filipino plantation workers had occupied before the war would be their new accommodations at the camp.

At the one o'clock conference with Colonel Elsmore, they were informed "in no uncertain terms" that he was the commander there and they would do as he said. To Obert, it seemed they were being treated "more as truant schoolboys than as combat pilots."

Brig. Gen. William F. Sharp, who was in command of all American and Filipino forces in the Visayas and Mindanao, proved even more antagonistic toward the cowed young men. Upon moving his command to Mindanao a few days later and meeting with them, he acted as if the pilots had flown from Bataan without orders, although he had received a radiogram from MacArthur on January 5 informing him of their arrival on Mindanao and putting them at Sharp's disposal.

Sharp already had two pursuit pilots under his command, both serving on his general staff as advisers. First Lt. Bill Feallock had arrived on December 31 after dropping off orders from MacArthur for Sharp to move his command and the bulk of his troops to Mindanao for the defense of that island and its Del Monte Field. Feallock joined John Brownewell on that day to fly special reconnaissance missions ordered by Sharp, including for the purpose of identifying suitable sites for new airfields in the region.

Brownewell had now completed two weeks of detached service at Del Monte for Sharp. His experiences had not been particularly eventful in this period, except for one mission that nearly cost him his life. On a reconnaissance flight on Christmas Eve to Davao, on the southern coast of Mindanao, Brownewell at 10,000 feet spotted three Kawanishi H6K "Mavis" flying boats on the water at Malalag Bay, in Davao Gulf. Under orders not to engage in combat but tempted by the target, Brownewell decided to go down after them in a strafing attack.

Only the left outboard of his six guns was working, but the eager native of Columbus, Ohio, still made three passes at them before the gun ran out of ammunition. One of the four-engine flying boats managed to take off, but one of the two remaining caught fire, ran aground, and blew up under Brownewell's relentless attack.[5]

After climbing to 1,000 feet after the third pass, Brownewell suddenly felt gunfire ripping into his P-40E, including the canopy. Startled, he turned to see that two Zeros were five hundred yards behind him. With no means to fight back and outnumbered, Brownewell quickly realized his only option was to get out of there as soon as possible. As the veteran 17th Pursuiter fire-walled his throttle to boost his speed, the two Zeros, at a higher speed and altitude, shot past him. They started climbing to lose speed, then went into a 360-degree turn to get back on Brownewell's tail. But by the time they caught up with the P-40, Brownewell had built up speed.

When the Zeros were about four hundred yards behind him, Brownewell glanced down at his instruments. His manifold pressure read only fifteen inches, yet he was registering 3,400 RPM. Perplexed, he cut back the throttle. To his amazement the needle dropped through the vacant space to the sixty-five inch mark. His Allison must have been putting out eighty inches.

With a reduced RPM, Brownewell worked his P-40 up to about 6,000 feet, weaving from left to right, to avoid a chance shot hitting him. But the Japanese were now gaining on him, so Brownewell, flying with his life on the line, decided to ignore the effects on his engine and once more shoved the throttle and propeller back to the maximum. Within a few minutes he began pulling away from his pursuers. Giving up the chase, the two Zeros broke off and headed back to base.[6]

Brownewell managed to get back safely to Del Monte. He was grateful to be alive. Who ever outran a Zero in a P-40 at an altitude disadvantage? But Colonel Elsmore was less than pleased with Brownewell's performance. General Sharp's reconnaissance pilot got a real bawling out that night for getting himself shot up. Elsmore wanted that P-40 kept intact. It was the only one available on Mindanao at the time.

The next morning, Brownewell inspected the damage to his plane. There were many bullet holes, and an aileron cable and the hydraulic system electric line had been shot out. With no pursuit maintenance men at Del Monte, the repair job was turned over to a crew chief of a destroyed B-18 bomber, Sgt. "Pappy" Nettles.

During the next few days of repairs, Brownewell stripped his plane to the bare minimum requirements to lighten it as much as possible. He wanted to improve his chances of survival in the event of another encounter with a Zero. First, since he had decided to fly at his optimum altitude of 10,000 feet most of the time, Brownewell had all his oxygen equipment removed. And since there were no communications facilities, out went his radio and associated equipment. Then he had all but his two inboard .50-caliber guns taken out, and he jury-rigged the ammo boxes to provide twice the normal amount of ammunition for the two remaining guns. On his next reconnaissance mission, Brownewell noticed a marked improvement in speed and maneuverability of his mount.

5 The six unwelcome pilots from Bataan were not very happy with the situation at Del Monte. Since Brownewell and Feallock flew only special missions for Sharp, the Bataan evacuees were expected to cover the other regular reconnaissance flights. One day, a reconnaissance was flown to the north, the next day to the south. The flights were scheduled to take off at the same time each day, covering the same route at the same time. With the Japanese now familiar with the rigid routine imposed by Elsmore, those flying the reconnaissance missions could not relax a moment while in the air. The pilots tried to convince Elsmore of the need to vary the routes and time schedules, but without success.

Living accommodations were also proving less than ideal. They were now quartered in a nipa shack village about ten miles from the field. The huts at Camp 29 were very dirty and infested with bedbugs, fleas, lice, cockroaches, and "everything you could possibly imagine," Don Steele complained in his diary. A slit trench was dug under each shack, and a hole was cut in the floor; in the event of a strafing attack, they should quickly get into the trench. During the day, they were required to remain inside their huts except when they were to go over to the field to fly.

After a few days at Del Monte flying the regular reconnaissance flights, John Vogel, Gordon Benson, and Don Steele were given an additional assignment on January 8. They were to transfer P-40s from one field to another in the Del Monte area and disperse them to new hideouts.

6 Back on Bataan, Colonel George's little remaining air force was preparing to evacuate another of its airfields. By the morning of January 7, the Japanese had entered northern Bataan and now controlled the north-south road as far south as Hermosa, only three miles north of Orani. With the transfer of the nine P-40s to Bataan Field on January 4, no aircraft now remained at Orani Field.

On January 3, 1st Lt. Robert Wray had engaged in the last aerial combat from the field. While flying a 5:00 P.M. reconnaissance mission that day north to Zambales, he was jumped by four Japanese aircraft. Wray radioed the field that he was being attacked and dove on the Japanese. Hit in Wray's attack, one smoked and disappeared over a hill. The others then took off after Wray, who was hedgehopping back to Orani Field. Trying to follow Wray back, one of the Japanese was seen to crash into the trees near Mount Pinatuba.

Wray, a 39-C graduate of Kelly Field, had been assigned to Orani on January 2 to take command of the 34th Pursuit from Ben Brown, who, as a 40-D flying school graduate, was evidently considered too junior by Colonel George to remain as the 34th's CO. Wray was ordered to move the squadron from Orani Field down Bataan to the Little Baguio area, where it was to be engaged as infantry on beach defense. On the morning of January 6, the squadron's personnel had completed packing and began moving south in their trucks.

Pilar strip, just ten miles down the road from Orani, was now the northernmost airfield of the American forces. Following the transfer of all its P-40s to Mindanao on January 4, five of the nine at Bataan Field were shifted to Pilar on the morning of January 5 to allow operations to continue.[7] At both fields, the pilots were on call to Maj. Gen. George M. Parker's II Philippine Corps, defending the eastern half of Bataan, to fly observation and reconnaissance patrols.

Operations at Pilar went into high gear on the morning of January 6, when three two-plane reconnaissance missions took off at just before seven o'clock. First off were Steve Crosby and LaMar Gillett, ordered to reconnoiter the western coast of Luzon and Lingayen Gulf. The second mission, being flown by Bud Powell and Bill Rowe, was to do a reconnaissance of northern Luzon and drop supplies to cut-off U.S. forces at Jones, in Isabella Province. Scheduled to reconnoiter Manila, Alabat, Batangas, and Bataan were Joe McClellan and Jim Ross.

Shortly after takeoff at 7:00, Crosby lost his wing man when Gillett's propeller went out and he had to turn back to Pilar. Now on his own Crosby followed the route up the west coast of Luzon and then to Lingayen Gulf. He spotted seven transports off San Fabian and fifteen vessels off Damortis, including a warship, and then turned out to sea for the return trip.

Arriving back at Pilar Field about 8:40, Crosby noticed that the "all clear" panel was not out. Very low on fuel, he decided to come in for a landing anyway, after a careful look around failed to disclose any Japanese planes in the air. But when he brought his P-40 down to about 1,000 feet and was ready to lower his wheels, tracers started flying from a Japanese single-engine plane sitting squarely on his tail. Reacting instantly, Crosby shoved the throttle and prop pitch full forward and started climbing and weaving as rapidly as possible. Then suddenly the Japanese pulled off; a P-40 had come right down on him in a whistling dive, all six .50s blazing.

Relieved of his adversary, Crosby dropped his wheels and started into his base leg, preparatory for landing. Suddenly, six bursts of antiaircraft fire exploded right in front of him. The 515th Coast Artillery boys near the field had become excited by the dogfight and were failing to distinguish between friend and foe. Shaken, his plane riddled from fire by friend and foe alike, Crosby somehow managed to get his aircraft down safely on the dirt strip.

On the ground, Crosby discovered that his savior in the air was Joe McClellan. His fellow 17th Pursuiter was coming in to land after an uneventful mission when he spotted the Japanese, a Mitsubishi "Ann" dive-bomber, firing his single wing-mounted 7.7-mm machine gun at Crosby. McClellan chased the Japanese to the north and was subsequently credited with a "probable" victory.

The mission of Bud Powell and Bill Rowe was no less eventful than Crosby's. Twenty minutes after the 6:45 takeoff, the two P-40s ran into two three-ship formations of Japanese twin-engine "Lily" bombers over the northern tip of Manila Bay, flying south. Against orders, Powell made a pass on the second three-ship element and was hit in the engine by fire from the rear gunners of the bombers. His P-40 smoking, Powell bailed out at 6,000 feet.

When Bill Rowe noticed that a few of the Japanese were heading back toward the parachutist, he began circling until Powell hit the water, wanting to frustrate any possible strafing intentions. Then, seeing that Powell was safe and was swimming toward shore near Orani, Rowe broke off his circling but decided not to continue the mission; he had used up too much gas to fly to northern Luzon and back. As he prepared to land back at Pilar Field, he saw that the "all clear" panel was not out; Japanese bombers had worked over the strip. He now decided to head north to Orani Field instead.

Coming in to Orani about 8:00 A.M., Rowe missed the field the first time around but was successful on the second try. But in trying to taxi his P-40 off the field into a narrow space under the trees, he banged his rudder and a wing tip against a tree. Jumping out and running over to the nearby road, he succeeded in eliciting the help of American soldiers to push the P-40 to safety under the trees and camouflage it. Then Rowe caught a ride back to Pilar with a colonel of the ground forces.

Later that day, a volunteer maintenance crew of the 17th Pursuit arrived from Pilar in an old Pontiac to replace the damaged rudder so that the P-40 could be flown out. As S. Sgt. Frank Chism, Pvt. Bill Duplisea, and the other men hurried to repair the plane, artillery fire boomed all around. This was the front lines now. In twenty minutes, however, they had finished the job. Second Lt. Bill Powell of the 3rd Pursuit had also arrived from Pilar and took off safely for Pilar Field in the repaired bird. Not a moment too soon: as Chism and his crew jury-rigged the decrepit Pontiac for the return trip, Japanese artillery fire began zeroing in on the strip.

When the 17th Pursuit mechanics arrived back at Pilar late that afternoon, a Japanese bombing attack was under way. Several holes were made in the runway, preventing takeoffs and landings, and telephone wires were knocked out. A reconnaissance ordered for that afternoon of the Hermosa–San Fernando–Tarlac area on Luzon had to be canceled.

Although the Japanese had discovered Pilar Field now, the P-40s were well hidden in the wooded area to the north and south of the east-west strip. Frustrated over their inability to locate any planes on the Bataan fields, the Japanese adopted the tactic of waiting for the P-40s to appear for takeoffs and landings. For the pilots, it was just getting too dangerous to fly recon missions under such circumstances. Beginning on January 7, such missions from Pilar were reduced to the very essential.

Another piece of bad news reached the 17th on the afternoon of January 6. Second Lts. Chuck Page and Truett Majors, 41-D flying school classmates, were dead. After the Wyatt tragedy of January 2, Page and Majors had been detached from the 17th to serve as assistant fire direction officers with Battery C of the 91st Coast Artillery, Philippine Scouts, located near Bataan Field. Bob Krantz and "Dub" Balfanz were also assigned to the battery as assistant executive officers. Majors and Page were to provide aircraft identification capabilities for the battery in its defense of

Bataan Field. When Japanese bombers raided the field on January 5, Battery C countered with its 3-inch antiaircraft guns. But a faulty fuse of World War I vintage caused one round to detonate over the battery's position. Majors, Page, and several Filipino Scouts were killed instantly by shell fragments from the muzzle burst. Both the commanding and executive officers of the battery were wounded, and the rangefinder was demolished. The battery would be out of action for several days.

The news of the deaths of Majors and Page did not improve the morale of the pilots at Pilar. They knew that the Japanese were pushing the defense line of the American and Filipino troops steadily back. There were reports that the Japanese were within a few kilometers of Pilar. Artillery fire was heard all night, and "the noise was terrible."

With Bud Powell's plane lost and Crosby's and Gillett's out of commission, the field was down to three operational P-40s plus three more at Bataan Field. And where were the reinforcements they were expecting? As John Posten recorded in his diary on the evening of January 7, "FDR made a speech and didn't even mention the Philippine Islands. All he talked about was the stuff we would all have by 1943—but we'll never hold out that long!"

7 At 10:35 on the morning of January 8, three P-40s took off from Pilar strip on what would turn out to be the last mission flown from the field. John Posten, Bill Rowe, and Wilson Grover were to reconnoiter the Cabanatuan-Tarlac area of central Luzon and Subic Bay to the west.

On the way north, the pilots spotted six bombers at high altitude approaching Mount Arayat near Clark Field. With orders to avoid combat, they did not attack. Then, on the way back, they noticed a large troop formation in the road near San Fernando, fifteen miles southeast of Clark Field. While Rowe and Glover covered him at about 5,000 feet, Posten went down to strafe the Japanese. Very low, he hit a tree with his left wing tip, but the P-40 continued to fly well as Posten poured .50-caliber fire into the troops. When one group of the Japanese did not recognize his plane as American and stood out in the road to wave at him, Posten refrained from firing at it.

Then it was Rowe's turn. Spotting troops concentrated in front of a large municipal building, Rowe dived. Approaching his target, he watched the tracers of his six fifties tearing into the Japanese as they hurried up the stairs of the building and through the three doors. He felt that hundreds must have been killed or injured in the two attacks.

Arriving back from Pilar, the pilots found that three single-engine "Ann" dive-bombers were attacking their field, With ammunition remaining from their strafing attack, Glover and Rowe went after them. Although their tracers hit the formation, the two 17th Pursuiters did not succeed in downing any of the Japanese. Another *shotai* (section) of three "Anns" coming up behind Rowe fled the scene without dropping their bombs. With Pilar Field not operational because of the condition of the runway, the three pilots headed south to Bataan Field and landed at 12:35.

The night before, the rest of the 17th Pursuit had evacuated Pilar Field for a new bivouac further south. Since the Main Line of Resistance of the American and Filipino forces was now only some eight miles north of Pilar, necessitating construction of defensive works on the field, it had been decided to abandon it.[8]

For Steve Crosby and the other pilots of the 17th at Pilar not assigned to reconnaissance missions or to the job of transferring the P-35As the next morning, it was the end of their flying days in the campaign. Crosby had been sent ahead to select a new campsite for the squadron and had decided upon Rodriguez Park, near Limay, eight miles down the road from Pilar. When the personnel of the 17th Pursuit arrived that evening at their new base site, they were informed they would be undergoing training as infantry, under a new CO, 1st Lt. "Spud" Sloan, a senior (40-A) pilot of the squadron.

Following the transfer to Bataan Field of the three flown by Rowe, Posten, and Glover, all of the P-40s remaining at Pilar were now at the new field. LaMar Gillett also flew the last of the two P-35As at Pilar over to Bataan Field. Hedgehopping at treetop level to avoid the attention of any marauding Japanese aircraft, Gillett suddenly found oil all over his windshield. He was being fired at from the ground by friendly forces and had caught a .30-caliber slug in the oil line. Gillett climbed to 1,000 feet, then came in at Bataan Field, landing with no further incident.

The night before, when pilots at Pilar were being solicited to fly the two P-35As to Bataan Field, no one besides Gillett could be talked into it. Stripped of their guns and with no armor plating, they were considered defenseless against Japanese aircraft. Since it proved impossible to find anyone willing to take the second P-35A, several enlisted men were assigned the distasteful task of destroying it prior to evacuation of Pilar.[9]

8 With the abandonment of Orani and Pilar fields, all flying operations of Col. George's mini air force would now be out of Bataan Field only. Available on the afternoon of January 8 were nine P-40s, two P-35As, and one A-27. The pursuit aircraft were to be used exclusively for reconnaissance ordered by USAFFE Headquarters on Corregidor.

Living conditions at Bataan Field were rough for the former Pilar and Orani pilots. They had no mess of their own; they went down the road to eat at an army ground forces mess. With no tents or cots, they slept on the ground under a big tree near their hidden aircraft, off the west end of the strip. Commuting back and forth from the army mess could also be a dangerous proposition for the pilots. On January 5, returning to Bataan Field in their big Packard convertible touring car after a meal,

Lloyd Stinson and several others were driving west along the runway when they looked up and saw trouble coming: a flight of dive-bombers was headed down after them. Slamming on the brakes, the pilots piled out and ran for the ravine at the side of the runway. From their haven they watched as the "Ann" dive-bombers, evidently out of bombs, resorted to a strafing attack on the old Packard, putting several holes in it.

Less lucky than Stinson during the attack was his best friend and squadron mate, 2nd Lt. Percy Ramsey. Immediately following takeoff in a P-40 on a reconnaissance mission with 2nd Lt. Dana Allen in another P-40, Ramsey ran into a Japanese force of over twenty aircraft approaching Bataan Field and was shot up by an Army Nakajima "Nate" fighter in a dogfight right over the field. Bailing out, he landed in a rice field, uninjured except for a slight head wound. Allen was unsuccessful in trying to drive off Ramsey's attacker but did manage to get back down on the field safely. But another of the precious few P-40s was lost.

After midnight on January 10/11, Bataan Field lost its A-27. MacArthur's air officer, Maj. Reginald Vance, had been ordered to fly Maj. Gerald Wilkinson, the British liaison officer with USAFFE, to Del Monte, Mindanao, on the first leg of his mission from the Philippines to meet with General Wavell in Singapore on possible help for the Philippines. But when the A-27's oil pressure dropped to zero following takeoff, Vance elected to abort the flight. Trying to land in the moonlight only, Vance misjudged and put the plane down abruptly from some fifty feet, "rolling it into a ball." Miraculously, Vance and Wilkinson sustained only slight injuries.

That morning after daybreak, and before another attack by Japanese dive-bombers on the field, the two remaining P-35As on Bataan were flown out. With Capt. Barney Brodine in the baggage compartment of one plane and 1st Lt. Joe McLaughlin, a senior pilot of the 20th Pursuit, in the other, Ed Woolery and Bob Duncan took off for Del Monte, claiming they had orders from Colonel George to go to Australia.

9 When the two P-35As landed at Del Monte on the afternoon of January 11, it was much to the surprise of the pursuit pilots and other officers at the base. No one believed their story that they had been ordered south, and they had no written orders to prove it. It appeared more likely that it was only Brodine, who was not a military pilot but rather a technical representative of Curtiss-Wright who had been given a wartime commission, who had been ordered to Australia.

The six former Bataan pilots who had flown down on January 4 were still flying daily reconnaissance missions around Mindanao. They now had three additional candidates for the flights with the arrival of Woolery, McLaughlin, and Duncan. John Brownewell and Bill Feallock continued to fly only special missions for Brigadier General Sharp. The two senior pilots were not very popular with the others. "They more or less tell us

A Nakajima Ki-27 "Nate," the principal Japanese Army fighter in the 1937–41 period. "Nates" were the main source of harassment of the Bataan Field Flying Detachment pilots in the January–March, 1942, period. *Courtesy Robert Mikesh*

what to do, much against our wishes," Steele complained in his diary.

The same day the two P-35As arrived, one of the reconnaissance missions came to grief on the beach at Cagayan, eighteen miles northwest of Del Monte. In Brownewell's stripped-down P-40E, Gordon "Squirrely" Benson had been down to Davao and now on his return flight had run into a flight of three Zeros. Twisting and turning at treetop level and unfamiliar with the characteristics of Brownewell's steed, the terrified Oregonian took machine gun fire in the P-40, then successfully evaded his pursuers by getting down into a canyon. But now his gas tanks had run dry. Too low to bail out, Benson rode the bullet-riddled Warhawk down. Crash-landing in the water just offshore, he planed it up on the beach like a surfboard. Shaken but uninjured, he extricated himself from the cockpit and ran for cover in the nearby bushes. The Zeros did not go after him but tore up the beached P-40 in strafing runs as Benson watched helplessly.[10] After relating the circumstances of the loss of his P-40 to an enraged Brownewell, who questioned his flying ability, Benson went back to Cagayan the day after his crash and spent the day stripping the P-40 for parts.

The next few days slipped by at the Del Monte base in their usual uneventful pattern. Steele and several others visited neighboring villages, raiding Japanese-owned grocery stores that had been vacated by their interned owners. The pilots now had a small supply of tinned goods stowed under their bunks to make up for any missed meals.

Orders had now also been received at Del Monte from Australia for Brodine to proceed south, but Duncan, McLaughlin, and Woolery were not included on the list. It was decided that a B-18 that Maj. Emmett "Rosy" O'Donnell, CO of the 14th Bomb Squadron, was repairing would be the means of transport. Sharp had asked O'Donnell if he could get the derelict B-18 in condition to fly to Australia with Sharp's G-3 operations officer, who was to establish communications between Sharp's command and American forces on Australia. After repairing the engines, O'Donnell's men rigged five gasoline drums in the fuselage to give the B-18 the fuel capacity to reach Australia. Four were put in the bombbay. A hole was then cut in the floor of the fuselage so that someone could have access to pump gas from the drums into the B-18's tanks with a wobble pump. Finally, the bomber's armament was removed to lighten it. At 3:00 A.M. on January 15, the jury-rigged B-18 lifted off Del Monte Field with its assorted passengers. Riding on top of the gas drums was Joe McLaughlin, the "fuel transferer" selected by O'Donnell.

On the morning of January 7, 1942, Colonel George was over on Corregidor for an important meeting with Major General Sutherland. George had briefed Sutherland on the current setup of his operations on Bataan and was listening as Sutherland explained to him and Major Vance the War Department plan for employment of the air force in the Far East. In the early afternoon, George made a further report to Sutherland on air fields and organization.

Still expecting aircraft reinforcements from Australia, MacArthur's strategy was to continue developing air fields on Mindanao for use of pursuit aircraft and bombers on arrival. Personnel of the 19th Bomb Group that had been sent to Mindanao from Mariveles on December 29 would be utilized to build up defenses on the island and defend the air installations. Except in support of operations at Bataan Field, remaining Air Corps units on Bataan would be assigned to infantry duties on beach defense, Sutherland informed Colonel George. However, Sutherland accepted George's argument that his men should be considered only on loan to infantry commands. The army units would have to relinquish the airmen for service in their original capacities when Colonel George could justify the reactivation of the Air Corps.

John Posten, 17th Pursuit, climbing into the cockpit of his P-35A at Iba, summer, 1941. *Courtesy William M. Rowe, Lt. Col. USAF (Ret.)*

Now assigned to Brig. Gen. C. A. Selleck's 71st Division, charged with defending the west sector of Bataan, were the Headquarters Squadron of the 24th Pursuit Group and the group's 3rd, 21st, and 34th pursuit squadrons. Being held in reserve were the 17th and 20th pursuit squadrons. The reaction of officers and men alike of the 24th Pursuit Group to their new duties was less than enthusiastic. As John Posten wrote in his diary

the evening of January 9 at Bataan Field: "It really must be getting serious when they have to take the mechanics and armament men and make
infantry men out of them. I sure wish we would get some help over here
soon. If we wreck any more planes here on Bataan Field I expect we will
be on beach patrol too!" Posten neglected to mention that all the pilots
of his 17th Pursuit and the other squadrons of the 24th Group, except
the few like Posten flying at Bataan Field, were also now assigned as infantry along with the enlisted men of the squadrons.

There was now much talk among the pilots at Bataan Field about the
likelihood of surrender of the USAFFE forces. Bill Rowe and others were
bitter. Why was MacArthur insisting on holding them there for reconnaissance against the wishes of Colonel George if the cause was hopeless?
With only nine planes available, they were a "suicide squad," Rowe felt.

Part Five
THE BASTARD OUTFIT OF BATAAN

In mid-January the Japanese were threatening to break through the Abucay Line in its center. Maj. Gen. George Parker called for reinforcements, which moved into position on the night of January 15/16. But the Japanese during the next days succeeded in driving in the II Corps' left flank and threatened to envelop the entire defensive line. MacArthur agreed to a tactical withdrawal to save the situation as from the evening of January 23. Under confused and demoralizing conditions, Parker's men during the next two days and nights fell back against heavy Japanese attack and by the morning of January 26 moved into positions along the new line of defense.

On the other side of Bataan, I Corps had also been ordered to withdraw and did so with little difficulty, so that the new line of resistance now extended continuously from Bagac on the west coast across central Bataan to Orion on the east coast, no longer broken in the middle by Mount Natib. Here MacArthur vowed to fight to the death.

In the meantime a threat to the defenders arose from a new direction. On the night of January 22/23, in an amphibious operation, Japanese troops had landed behind the lines on the west coast, in the Service Command Area of southern Bataan. One group had come ashore at Quinauan Point, and a second at Longoskawayan Point, some six miles south, near the southern tip of Bataan. At first estimated as only a small force, in the ensuing days the Japanese assault was taken more seriously as efforts to dislodge the enemy proved ineffective. Then on the evening of January 26/27 and again on the evenings of February 1/2 and 7/8, new landings were made in the

Anyasan Bay sector, just north of Quinauan. Only with the commitment of the 45th and 57th Philippine scouts to the operation, known as the Battle of the Points, did it prove eventually possible to wipe out the determined, tenacious Japanese groups — at Longoskawayan by January 31, Quinauan by February 8, and Anyasan by February 12.

Along the Main Line of Resistance, extending from Bagac to Orion across central Bataan, the American and Filipino forces were immediately subjected to strong Japanese attack from the day the defensive position was established on January 26. In what became known as the Battle of the Pockets, the Japanese suffered heavy losses during the three-week offensive and proved unable to break through the defenders' line of resistance.

With the failure of their offensives on the west coast and along the MLR, the Japanese command decided to break off its attack and withdraw the troops to more secure positions. The withdrawal commenced even before the conclusion of the west coast and MLR operations and resulted in the creation of a no-man's-land corridor between the opposing forces. The Japanese now intended to wait for reinforcements before launching a final offensive to seize Bataan. To weaken the defenders' capabilities, the blockade around Bataan was tightened, including the seizure of Mindoro Island, lying off the southwest coast of the peninsula.

Although the morale of the American and Filipino troops improved when the Japanese withdrawal and break-off of the offensive became known, practical matters of survival and shattered hopes during the next months soon sent it into a tailspin. The men were virtually starving to death on the rations allotted them. They scavenged for whatever form of supplementary sustenance they could find in the jungle, regardless of source. Clothing was also inadequate, and the men soon took on a ragged look. Malaria, dengue, scurvy, beriberi, and dysentery widely struck the men, already weakened by lack of food and required vitamins. By mid-March, the combat efficiency of the U.S. and Filipino forces was below 45 percent. When promised reinforcements also failed to materialize, the defenders became increasingly cynical and dispirited. MacArthur's evacuation for Australia on March 12 had the effect of convincing them that no reinforcements could be expected; they were doomed. They were indeed

the battling bastards of Bataan.
No mama, no papa, no uncle Sam
. . . And nobody gives a damn.

During the lull in the fighting that descended over Bataan beginning in mid-February, the Japanese prepared for the expected final offensive. Fresh troops poured in during the next six weeks while the veterans were being rested and trained. In mid-March sixty army heavy bombers arrived as aerial reinforcements, followed by a contingent of navy fighters and dive-bombers. This time, the Japanese made sure they would finish off the stubborn American and Filipino force, which had already ruined their original timetable for conquest of the Philippines.

18. "WE WANT A FEW 'EAGLES' TO CHASE THE 'HAWKS' OVERHEAD"

1 In response to USAFFE Field Order No. 2 of January 7, 1942, assigning them to the 71st Division, the 3rd, 21st, and 34th pursuit squadrons, plus Headquarters and Headquarters Squadron, began moving to their designated bivouac positions on the west coast of Bataan in the immediate vicinity of the beaches they were to defend. The 71st Division plus the attached 24th Pursuit Group squadrons were charged with preventing any enemy landings in the ten mile sector extending from Caibobo Point in the north to Mariveles in the south. Defense of the long and ragged coastline, heavily indented with tiny bays and inlets, with thick forest almost to the shoreline ending in abrupt cliffs, would be a formidable task.

After having laboriously moved its supplies down a steep hill to a new bivouac in a little valley along a stream above Mariveles on January 8, the 3rd Pursuit now received its orders transferring it to the 71st Division and assigning it to a position in the vicinity of the Biaan River, two miles northwest of Mariveles, at Kilometer Post 184.7 on the winding western road of Bataan. For Hank Thorne and his 17 officers and 112 enlisted men, to serve as infantrymen would be a new and strange experience.

With the help of the engineers at its new site, the squadron put up several strands of barbed wire along the sandy beach at the mouth of the river. Each man dug himself a foxhole, mounted whatever machine gun was available at the time, and settled into position.

During the next week, the 3rd collected an assortment of weapons, including Enfield rifles, .50-caliber aircraft machine guns, mortars, 37-mm cannon, and Marlin machine guns. The Marlin guns had been carefully greased and wrapped in newspapers dating from the early 1920s. With no mounts or tripods for any of these guns, the men had to improvise with tree stumps and logs until the ordnance shops at so-called Little Baguio helped them make swivel mounts.

Thorne faced difficulties in organizing a defensive position; his officers and men had little experience in ground operations. He finally suc-

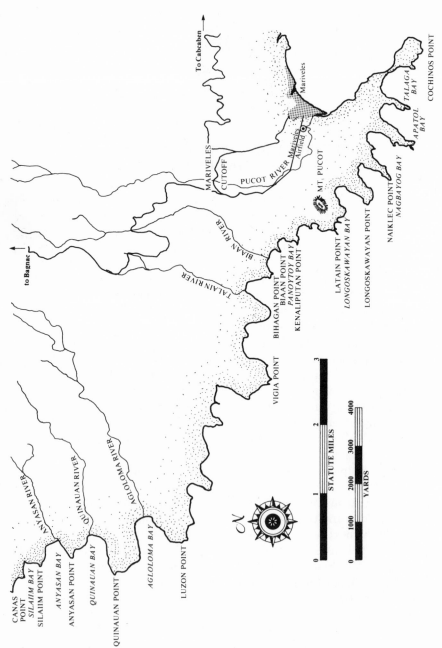

Map 7. Southwest Bataan and Mariveles Area

ceeded in working out a system of maintaining points of resistance around his main line, including along the shoreline, manned by mixed crews of officers and enlisted men. From defensive positions at the end of the promontories extending into the sea, the men could cover the approaches to Panoytoy Bay and its beach extending seven hundred yards between Bihagan Point to the north and Biaan Point to the south. The squadron was further reinforced by one-half a battery of Philippine Army field artillery, which now went into position on the slope of the hill on its left flank. Scanning the shoreline of the area, with its series of inlets and intervening promontories of volcanic rock, Thorne wondered whether the Japanese would really consider landing in such a forbidding place.

Not far from the 3rd Pursuit, the 21st Pursuit, with its 17 officers and 197 men, had been bivouacked near the Biaan River following its evacuation from Lubao on January 1. The bivouac was on a hill thick with jungle growth and had a creek that ran through the area. The men were sleeping on the ground. The area was quite mosquito infested, and many of the men were suffering from malaria. The twice-a-day rations were now quite meager, following the Bataan quartermaster's seizure during the second week of their bivouac of the canned goods that they had brought from Manila into Lubao.

Only a few men in the squadron had any previous infantry training. Under the supervision of Ed Dyess, who had joined the squadron after leaving Orani on January 4, a light schedule of training was introduced for the "willing but awkward" officers and men. The enlisted men were divided up into platoons of about fifty men each, with each platoon assigned a nonflying officer of the squadron. The three selected, all with previous infantry training, were 1st Lts. Herb Ball and Larry Parcher and 2nd Lt. Linus Schramski, in charge of the 1st, 2nd, and 3rd platoons, respectively.

For training, old Springfield and a few Enfield rifles were issued, plus a few automatic Garands, along with a clip of ammunition. The officers were instructed to take their men out and teach them to boresight and shoot their weapons. In addition, they were instructed on how to move through the jungle and how to take up defensive positions, but not much more.

The 21st had an unusual cache of weapons. It included some Marlin machine guns, .50-caliber machine guns from wrecked P-40s, two Browning water-cooled machine guns, six Lewis .30-caliber aircraft machine guns, hand grenades, and four Bren gun carriers (British-made tracked vehicles carrying light guns), plus the rifles used for training.

A little north of the 3rd and 21st's positions, the 34th Pursuit Squadron moved into its assigned beach defense position at Kilometer Post 188 on January 10. The men were coming from Little Baguio, where they had spent several days following their move from Orani on January 7. At Little Baguio, the men had been organized into groups to receive superficial training from a few of the old hands in the squadron who had served in World War I. One of them, T. Sgt. Michael Bruaw, seemed to the men a little too old and heavy to be racing through the jungle scrub, trying to teach them to set up a line of skirmish.

With the help of crude maps and compass directions, the 34th had located the bivouac site of its assigned beach defense position. Kitchens were set up, and a headquarters, supply area, and hospital were established. Each man cleared a place to sleep on the jungle floor. For the next ten days, the men lived "the life of Riley": "light duty, plenty to eat, ample supplies, and no enemy," as one of them described it. Some of the men made hammocks for themselves. At night, wild hogs would rummage through the sacks of flour, but attempts to shoot them to add fresh pork to their diets failed.

The squadron had been assigned to defend one mile of rugged coastline between Agloloma and Quinauan points. Four platoons, each of about three officers and fifty men, were set up to cover designated sections of the defense line. Officers were armed with .45-caliber pistols, and the men with Model 1903 Springfield rifles and a few Model 1917 Enfield rifles. The squadron also had four submachine guns and a fair supply of hand grenades. In addition, an attached group of Philippine Scouts was equipped with two mountain guns known as 2.95s.

2   Still in reserve on January 10 were the 17th and 20th pursuit squadrons. Two days later, however, Colonel Funk, G-3 of the Advance Echelon, USAFFE, recommended that the two squadrons be made available, along with Headquarters Squadron and the 93rd Squadron of the 19th Bomb Group, to Brigadier General Selleck, commanding officer of the 71st Division, for reinforcing the west sector's defenses.

On January 12, the 17th Pursuit had moved from Rodriguez Park on the east coast near Limay to the Saysain Point area, at Kilometer Post 205, high up the west coast, two miles south of Bagac. Then, three days later, the squadron shifted three miles south, to Caibobo Point, the northernmost point of Selleck's western beach defense sector, where they were to establish a coast defense position.

At Rodriguez Park, 1st Lt. Raymond "Spud" Sloan had taken over command of the 17th on January 9 from 2nd Lt. Maurice Hughett. One of the original group of 17th Pursuiters sent out in December, 1940, Sloan was now the most senior of the remaining officers of the squadron on Bataan. Under him were 16 officers and 164 men. The squadron defense was now organized into three platoons. Howard Connor and Jim Ross were put in charge of the first platoon, Dub Balfanz and Joe McClellan the second platoon, and John Gillespie and Maurice Hughett the third platoon.

By virtue of being the only officer in the squadron with infantry experience, Steve Crosby was made executive officer and given responsibility for training and tactics. He now introduced a rudimentary program of training of the squadron's personnel in marksmanship, bayonet and hand grenade techniques, and infantry combat principles. Each man was equipped with either a Springfield or a Garand, plus a .45-caliber pistol. The only other armaments the squadron had were four .50-caliber machine guns from wrecked aircraft, which the men had mounted on tripods, using homemade handles, ammunition racks, and sights. These guns were emplaced in pits to cover the bays just north of Caibobo Point. The beach was lined with barbed wire. The men were well dug into their positions, underbrush cleared away to discourage snipers from moving in on them.

All the way down the west coast from Caibobo Point and just northwest of Mariveles at Kilometer Point 181, known as the Mariveles cutoff, the 20th Pursuit Squadron was encamped. It had taken up this position from its earlier bivouac location near Pilar on December 27 on orders to prepare defenses for the airstrip being constructed at Mariveles by a civilian construction firm. Only a little more than three kilometers up the coast road was the 3rd Pursuit Squadron on beach defense.

The 20th Pursuit's camp was under giant jungle trees and growth so thick that the site was completely hidden from view from above. Mariveles River, clear and cold, ran along one side of the camp, and a gravel access road was in front of the bivouac area. There were no beds, barracks, tents, or showers, but the men prepared "a fairly cozy camp," with good foxholes, pit latrines, a canvas-covered field kitchen, and tree lookout stations.

On the morning of January 18, new orders went out for the squadron. Its 23 officers and 282 men were being assigned to one of the fourteen groups made up of USAFFE Bataan units previously in reserve, now to be on call as reinforcements for any attack on Bataan's east or west coasts. As part of Group No. 6, covering the Mariveles cutoff area, the squadron was to be put under the command of the Chemical Warfare Depot. Now the squadron faced an additional responsibility: to train itself in ground defense operations. Platoons of twenty-five men were formed, each under an officer. Like the other squadron pilots put in charge of a platoon, but with very limited or no previous experience in infantry tactics, 2nd Lt. Randy Keator felt very inadequate to the task.

3 At Little Baguio, behind-the-lines headquarters for the Bataan defense, on the slopes of nearby Mariveles Mountain, an important meeting was held on January 14 between Brig. Gen. Richard J. Marshall, Mac-

Arthur's deputy chief of staff, and Col. Hal George, commanding officer of the little Bataan air force. The II Corps had been complaining to MacArthur about the unhampered operations of Japanese observation and bombardment aircraft over its troops on the Main Line of Resistance on the eastern half of Bataan. Morale and fighting spirit had declined in recent days with the continued strafing and bombing attacks on the front lines and artillery positions of the defenders. The II Corps wanted help from Colonel George's air force.

Marshall had come over to Bataan from Corregidor to inform Colonel George of a change in the instructions that had limited his airmen to reconnaissance missions only. In the future, pilots flying such missions were also to watch for Japanese observation planes and shoot them down, if possible.

Actually, the day before, Colonel George's pilots had jumped the gun on the modified orders. Lts. Marshall Anderson, Bill Baker, and John Posten had taken off at 9:00 that morning to take out an observation plane that had been spotting artillery fire for the Japanese. Circling over the front line area, they could not find the plane, but Anderson, seeing a column of thirty or forty trucks on the Hermosa-Orani road, went down and shot it up in three passes, inflicting considerable damage. In apparent reprisal, nine Japanese dive-bombers, the ever-present Mitsubishi Type 97 "Anns," hit Bataan Field the next morning. "Shrapnel was flying all over," as Posten described the attack in his diary that evening, and two men of the 803rd Aviation Engineers were killed, though there was no material damage to the aircraft at the field.

That afternoon, four of the P-40s took off on a reconnaissance but three came back with engine oil troubles. Newly arrived 20th Pursuiter Varian Kiefer White continued on the mission but saw nothing to report. Later, rumor in the camp had it that the reconnaissance was to see if it was clear for a boat to leave for Mindanao with the pilots, but the plan fell through. Unknown to the Bataan pilots, their services were now of vital interest to the II Corps, as expressed to Colonel George that day by General Marshall. An evacuation of the pilots was out of the question.

The next day, January 15, the II Corps was in continuous communication with USAFFE Headquarters on Corregidor with requests for interceptions of the Japanese observation planes over the front lines, but with no positive response. Then, at 6:30 A.M. on January 16, the G-3 officer of the II Corps made his pitch. In a telephone call to his counterpart on the USAFFE staff, he said that "the 'birds' overhead, without interference and at all times, is [sic] having its effect—*increasing* effect. . . . We want a few 'eagles' to chase the 'hawks' overhead—or at least some 'coyotes' to bark at them and force them higher."

At Bataan Field, Marshall Anderson, John Posten, Lloyd Stinson, Jack

Hall, and Bill Rowe were already awake and ready to fly a mission when the call to Corregidor was made. Shortly before takeoff at 7:00 A.M., they got their orders: they were to head north up the coast of Bataan and provide protection to the defenders on the front lines from the Japanese aircraft overhead.

Patrolling over the Abucay area, Rowe spotted an observation plane near Orani and right under it made a firing pass but missed as the Japanese escaped into cloud cover. Acting as a lookout for the others, Posten became separated from them when they went into an overcast. Then he caught sight of a lone Japanese plane some 2,000 feet below him. Missing with his first burst in a diving attack, Posten worked himself into position again, but this time his guns failed.

Returning from their patrol, the disappointed pilots observed a convoy of six to eight trucks below them on the Hermosa-Orani road and went into a strafing attack, their .50-caliber tracers going through the trucks. Much to their surprise, Japanese antiaircraft guns opened up on them. It was the first time the Americans had ever seen flak put up by ground forces. In response, they now switched their attention to the antiaircraft positions in their strafing runs.

Below them, but unseen by the pilots, the II Corps troops cheered. The appearance of just a few American planes did wonders for their morale. The pilots had missed the dive-bombers over the front lines, having flown between them, and had not downed any of the observation planes, but no longer would the Japanese "hawks" be allowed to operate with impunity over the defenders' lines.

In reprisal, Japanese "Anns" dive-bombed and strafed Bataan Field at noon. "Plenty scared," Bill Rowe watched them in their dives on the field. An officer in the 803rd Engineers was killed, and another man was wounded. In a second attempt to knock out Bataan Field, the Japanese sent nine "Nate" fighters in a surprise strafing attack at dawn the next morning. Just as the pursuit pilots started to go up to the mess for breakfast, "all hell broke loose." Late-riser John Posten abandoned his bunk and jumped into his foxhole in his underwear.

Unintimidated by the attack, three of the flying detachment taxied their P-40s out from their hidden revetments at 10:25 for another interception of Japanese observation planes over the Main Line of Resistance. Marshall Anderson and Jack Hall got off all right into the solid overcast, but a tire on Lloyd Stinson's plane blew out, forcing the frustrated pilot to abort his participation.

Minutes after takeoff, Anderson and Hall spotted a Japanese observation plane eight kilometers east of Cabcaben on the east coast and went after it. Anderson shot it down into Manila Bay within view of the men on Bataan Field. Continuing up to the front lines, they went into a circling pattern looking for more enemy planes. Then they caught sight of a formation of nine light bombers and immediately took off in pursuit of it, but when the Japanese became aware of the approaching P-40s, they dropped their bomb loads in an empty field and headed back to their base, the P-40 pilots breaking off their attack.

Proceeding further north behind enemy lines, Anderson and Hall observed a convoy of from twelve to fifteen trucks on the Samat-Orani road and went down to strafe it. After having worked the trucks over for fifteen minutes, they sighted two more observation planes over Hermosa to the northwest. Hall went after them and shot one down; the other fled. Then, out of ammunition, the airmen headed back to Bataan Field and landed at 11:25, elated over their profitable hour of flying.

When General MacArthur was informed of the results of the mission, he directed that Anderson and Hall be awarded the Distinguished Service Cross. Not only were the Japanese being thwarted in their previously uninterrupted operations over the USAFFE lines, but the morale of his troops had been raised, jubilant as they were over the P-40 pilots' victories.

At 4:15 that afternoon, Bataan Field "really caught hell" for the morning's operations. Nine "Anns" arrived and proceeded to score hits on the runway as the pilots took cover in foxholes. The strip was too damaged for operations. A reconnaissance by Charley Sneed, Bill Rowe, and Kiefer White scheduled for 4:30 P.M. had to be canceled.

When it was informed that the afternoon mission had been aborted, USAFFE Headquarters via its air officer ordered a makeup mission to be flown the next morning of January 18. The rear echelon of the 31st Regiment was moving and required protection. At 6:45 A.M., Charley Sneed and Bill Rowe took off from Bataan Field (Kiefer White could not get his ship out of the revetment) and headed up to the designated area, the Pilar-Bagac road stretching east-west across Bataan. Over the front lines, they went into a layer of clouds at 6,000 feet and patrolled over and under it. Then Rowe noticed two "Anns" approaching from the east, above the clouds. Flying under the overcast to a point where he figured they were just above him, Rowe did a chandelle through the cloud cover and came out right behind them, pouring tracer fire from his six fifties into both ships until the Japanese rear-seat gunners stopped firing back and both planes fell, smoking, into the clouds.

Then Rowe went into the clouds too and pulled up and found a "Nate" that had apparently been flying cover for the dive-bombers. Opting for a quarter attack, Rowe closed in practically head-on and watched his tracers pepper the Japanese Army fighter. The "Nate" pulled up in a stall, then spun down through the clouds, engine smoking.

Sneed had missed the combat. He had not seen the two dive-bombers and had dropped down below the clouds to patrol. Rowe now joined Sneed for a while, then both headed back to Bataan Field. Just as they were about to land, they received a radio call that Japanese ships were nearby, so they climbed but did not see anything. The "all clear" now came in, and they landed safely.

Back at Bataan Field at 8:10, Rowe described his experiences. But since he was alone at the time and the Japanese aircraft would have crashed behind their own lines, there were no witnesses to the three apparent kills, and he thus could be given no confirmation for the victories. He had fired six hundred rounds of .50-caliber ammunition through the five functioning guns. Both he and Sneed received the congratulations of General Wainwright through Colonel George for having kept the Japanese planes from observing the movement of the 31st Regiment.

But that was not all the action that day for the Bataan Field pilots. At 3:45 that afternoon, Wilson Glover and John Posten took off on a mission to reconnoiter the Subic Bay area to the northwest for enemy activity. Just south of Silanguin Island, the pilots observed a large, three-stacked vessel, dark gray in color, headed east. It looked to them like a cruiser.[1] A catapult plane was circling the ship, but when it spotted the P-40s, it dropped two bombs into the sea and tried to flee. Both Americans poured .50-caliber fire into the hapless floatplane, leaving it dropping steeply and smoking heavily. Continuing on their recon mission, Glover and Posten swung east to the mouth of Subic Bay and spotted two smaller vessels, evidently a troopship and a destroyer. Now east of Binangan, they encountered a two-seat observation plane. Posten went after it, but the more maneuverable little plane "turned rings around me" and got away, as he confided to his diary that night. Both pilots made it back safely to Bataan Field by 4:45 P.M.

4 A significant development that would affect the operational effectiveness in the months ahead of the Bataan Field Flying Detachment, as it had now come to be known, took place on January 17. Col. Hal George had moved his command from Little Baguio near Mariveles to Bataan Field, where he would be able to supervise operations directly. This was no independent decision of Colonel George's but rather followed on the instructions left by Major General Brereton at the time of his transfer to Australia on December 24, 1941. According to Brereton's "plan of employment" for the rump Far East Air Force, an "advance interceptor command post" was to be established on Bataan peninsula in the vicinity of Bataan Field.

Actually, Colonel George's personal intervention in the operations at Bataan Field preceded his arrival by over a week. At that time he had decided to gather experts in all lines from his personnel, staff, pilots, and maintenance crews and assemble them at Bataan Field under his own command. He preferred this course of action to assigning one of his pursuit squadrons to cover flying functions at the field. The 16th Bombardment Squadron of the 27th Bombardment Group was to continue in its responsibilities for maintaining the field.

For flying personnel, Colonel George started with the former Pilar pilots who had flown into Bataan Field on January 8: Bill Rowe, John Posten, and Wilson Glover of the 17th Pursuit. in addition, he selected six of the nine former Orani pilots who had transferred their P-40s to Bataan Field on January 4: Marshall Anderson, Bob Duncan, and Lloyd Stinson of the 20th Pursuit; Ed Woolery of the 3rd Pursuit; and Jack Hall and Bill Baker of the 34th Pursuit. Percy Ramsey, who was shot down on January 5, and his wingman on that day, "Chubby" Allen, were evidently dropped from the detachment after the dogfight over Bataan Field that day. The ninth former Orani pilot, Ed Dyess, had gone with his 21st Pursuit Squadron on beach defense after the Orani-Bataan Field flight of January 4.

To replace Woolery and Duncan, who had departed for Del Monte on January 11, Colonel George on January 13 had selected 20th Pursuiters Charley Sneed and Kiefer White. By the time of George's shift to Bataan Field on January 17, the two new members of the detachment were already flying missions from Bataan Field. At the time George picked Sneed as a replacement, he also designated him as the flying commander of the detachment. Of the nine pilots, Sneed was the most senior.

On his arrival at Bataan Field, Colonel George immediately began establishing his bivouac, to the west of the field. The site had been selected a few days earlier by George himself and his engineering officer, Capt. Harold "Lefty" Eads. George now arranged for the construction of his headquarters and living quarters, a three-room bamboo shack with a lean-to, right out in the middle of the clearing. He figured that the Japanese would never expect a commanding office to be so foolish as to establish his command in a place where he could be observed. Colonel George, his intelligence officer Capt. Allison Ind, and Captain Eads slept in one room, and another was used as George's office. The lean-to in the back was for Captain Ind's radio.

Officers and enlisted men alike soon discovered that Colonel George was not typical of the higher-echelon officer corps with whom they had prior experience. He had grown a full beard, and the rest of his physical appearance (short stature, wearing glasses) did not suggest that he was a full colonel in the Air Corps. But more important, George immediately showed himself to be a very human person, concerned about the welfare of his pilots and men, displaying common sense, and disdainful of the privileges accorded his rank.

With Colonel George's arrival, living conditions for the Bataan pilots improved dramatically. That same day they moved into a camp where there were tents and cots to sleep on, instead of the ground under the trees. A mess hall had been set up, so they no longer had to eat at the ground forces' mess down the road. They also had the use of the big Packard convertible touring car for getting around the base. They were given the use of the makeshift outdoor shower that the 16th Bombardment Squadron had erected, with water provided from a nearby stream that the squadron had dammed. The pilots now could wash off the day's dirt.

Work was also proceeding on the upgrading of Bataan Field. Company C of the 803rd Aviation Engineers was extending and widening the strip beyond its original 3,750-foot length and 40-foot width to a length of 5,200 feet and a width of 100 feet. Revetments for twelve planes were completed, although the repair of damage to the field by the frequent Japanese bombing attacks had thrown the engineers somewhat behind their schedule.

To oppose the Japanese Army Air Force's squadrons on Luzon (composed at the time of thirty-six "Ann" dive-bombers, eleven "Nate" fighters, and twenty-one reconnaissance planes), Colonel George could muster only five P-40Es and two P-40Bs. But there were another six P-40s down at Del Monte, certainly excessive of the needs for recon flights there.[2] On January 14, George asked Brigadier General Marshall for four of them to be transferred back to his command on Bataan.

5 At Del Monte on the afternoon of January 17, the former Bataan pilots got news of a startling message received by Brigadier General Sharp from General MacArthur's Headquarters on Corregidor: "Four P-40s will return to Bataan as soon as possible." The pilots could not believe it; that would be a waste of pilots and planes. From what few reports they could pick up, Bataan was given up as lost and would be in Japanese hands in a few days. What possible use could anyone have for planes there?

Evidently of the same mind, and not wanting to give up the few planes he had, General Sharp now radioed back to Corregidor for confirmation of the message. That evening, "Squirrely" Benson was down at the radio shack when the radiogram from USAFFE Headquarters came in. When he came back to tell his fellow pursuiters that the earlier order was confirmed, everyone felt sick. Four of them would leave for Bataan the next day. "They would be staring death in the face," Obert felt. Speculation now ran wild as to who would be the unfortunates to have to fly the P-40s back. Don Steele expected there would be much rank-pulling to determine who would be selected to go. Already Ed Woolery and Bob Duncan were arguing that they were strictly P-35 pilots (having flown down to Del Monte in those ships); anyway, they were on special orders from Colonel George to proceed to Australia.

The next morning, Bill Feallock and John Brownewell, who were still on Brigadier General Sharp's staff as reconnaissance pilots and his aviation advisers, came to the operations shack and told the former Bataan pilots to decide among themselves which four of them were going to make the trip back to Bataan. After much debate, the six pilots—Fred Roberts, Don Steele, Dave Obert, "Squirrely" Benson, Bob Ibold, and John Vogel—agreed that the only way was to draw cards: the four getting the highest cards would have to fly. But several insisted that Woolery and Duncan, who were not present at the time, should also be included. Feallock and Brownewell said they would draw for them.

As the pilots commenced the draw, it seemed to Obert "that life it-self was at stake." Bob Ibold drew first, a ten of hearts. He did not know whether to feel good or bad, as the card was sort of halfway, and he fig-ured someone would draw an ace above him. Obert's heart almost quit beating as he reached down to pick up a card. He drew a seven of hearts, which made him feel better, as he figured it was a fairly low card. Don Steele was the seventh, and next to last, to draw. He got a two of clubs, "the best-looking two I had ever seen," he recorded in his diary that night. When the eight now laid their cards down, they breathlessly compared theirs with those of the others. There was a jack, Ibold's ten, an eight, Obert's seven, a six, and the rest were twos and threes, including Steele's. Woolery, Ibold, Benson and Obert had ended up with the high cards and would be going back to Bataan.

Since Woolery was not present for the draw, they figured he would pro-test, but when he was informed of his proxy selection, he took his bad fortune without complaint. As the most senior of the four by rank and the most experienced, too, Woolery was accepted as the leader for the return flight. Sizing up the situation and considering the condition of their aircraft, Obert felt that they would be lucky if three of the four even reached Bataan. And certainly none of them would ever leave it alive.

6 After deciding among themselves to fly to Cebu that afternoon and dash into Bataan from there "as best we could," Woolery, Obert, Benson, and Ibold took off from Del Monte at about 3:00 P.M. and pointed their ships north. By refueling at Cebu, 140 miles to the northwest, they would at least not be repeating the ordeal of the January 4 nonstop flight over the 520 miles between Del Monte and Bataan.

Soon after takeoff, the pilots encountered stormy weather and "had to fly practically on the ocean to see anything at all." The clouds finally got so low that they had to go up into the overcast and fly on instruments to get over the mountain on Bohol. Fortunately there was an opening over Cebu City, so they were able to descend and land without any trouble. The engines of both Obert's and Benson's ships had run very rough and with a loss of power toward the end of the flight, so both pilots decided after landing to work on the Allisons to try to get them performing better before resuming the flight to Bataan. The four were now taken to Lt. Col.

Howard J. Edmands, commanding officer of the Cebu Military Police Regiment, who put the young men up for the night.

The next day, January 19, Obert devoted almost exclusively to working on his P-40E. The others said they would fly their ships in their present condition. Plans for leaving for Bataan this day were shelved earlier by Woolery. The weather was closed in zero-zero. The pilots were now informed that San Jose, Mindoro, an airdrome between Cebu and Bataan, was still in friendly hands. Plans were accordingly made to fly from Cebu to San Jose the next morning, and then to leave San Jose just in time to reach Bataan as it began to get dark, when the risk of encountering Japanese pursuit was virtually nil. Woolery now sent a radiogram to USAFFE Headquarters on Corregidor, indicating they would arrive at Bataan Field at dusk on January 20 and asking USAFFE to have everything in readiness for them.

The next morning, the weather ahead had apparently cleared, and the much-delayed Bataan pilots were off. Their P-40s were much lighter now; they had removed most of their .50-caliber ammunition and given it to the troops on Cebu, who had practically no ammunition as all. But shortly after takeoff, the weather turned nasty again, forcing the pilots to go over to instruments the first half hour while trying to get above the overcast. Then, just as they began to break through, they received a call from Benson. Obert could not understand the message but looked back and saw Benson's P-40 begin to spin and dive seaward; his engine had evidently quit on him.

Obert followed the course of Benson's ship through the clouds as best he could, watching it plunge into the ocean. Moments later, Obert looked up and saw Benson floating down through the clouds in his parachute, then hitting the water about a half mile off the coast of Panay Island. Twice before since the outbreak of war, Benson had ridden P-40s safely into the water, but this time he had apparently opted to bail out because of the solid overcast below him.

Obert and the others circled for a few minutes to ensure that Benson had worked himself free of his chute. When they saw him in his Mae West swimming toward land, they figured he was OK and resumed their flight to San Jose, concerned about conserving enough gas to reach their destination.[3] The weather continued bad all the way to Mindoro. At times Woolery, Obert, and Ibold had to fly through blinding rainstorms right on the surface of the water in order to see at all.

As the three P-40 pilots now reached the southern extremity of Mindoro and moved up the southwest coast to San Jose, they dropped down to look over the airfield to see if it was in Japanese hands or not. After circling the field, they saw American troops come running out. The soldiers waved at the pilots, then began clearing the field of the fuel drums put there to block any Japanese landing attempt. On landing, they were met by a Lt. Warren C. Baggett, who informed them that his detachment of sixty-two men of the 48th Materiel Squadron had been there, out of contact with the rest of the world, since mid-December, when he and his men had arrived by boat on orders from some colonel in FEAF Headquarters to service the San Jose airfield. Baggett figured that the colonel had probably been subsequently evacuated to Australia and had forgotten to inform anyone of his sending the detachment to Mindoro.

After refueling at San Jose, the three pilots resumed their flight to Bataan late in the afternoon. At dusk, they had covered the 150 miles and landed safely at Bataan Field. The boundaries of the field were all lit up for their arrival, and the control tower was waiting for them with an "all clear" signal. Driven to the Bataan Field camp, Obert, Woolery, and Ibold found Colonel George and about ten of the Flying Detachment waiting for them. Evidently the situation was not as serious as they had been led to believe on Mindanao. After being given a cold meal of corned beef on bread, the three returnees turned in for the evening.

7 Before receiving the message on the delayed arrival sent from Cebu on January 19, USAFFE Headquarters evidently had expected the pilots to take off from Cebu in the small hours of the nineteenth to arrive before daybreak at Bataan Field, a flight of some 380 miles, and had notified Bataan Field and the batteries on Corregidor accordingly. The antiaircraft batteries on Corregidor were expecting four P-40s to show up "just before dawn" that morning; they had been cautioned not to fire on them.

At 7:00 on the morning of January 19, Marshall Anderson, Kiefer White, Lloyd Stinson, and Bill Baker had taken off from Bataan Field to cover the landing of the four P-40s expected in at that time from Del Monte. The pilots formed up, Stinson on Anderson's wing, and started climbing, heading west across Bataan peninsula. Reaching about 15,000 feet in good visibility, they crossed Bataan and continued west, circling the eastern shore of Subic Bay, then swung east, heading toward the front lines of Bataan.

Stinson now spotted eight Japanese planes below them and climbing in their direction. Stinson gave Anderson a signal and pointed to the Japanese. Then they did a wingover to get into a good firing position. As the Japanese came into better view, Stinson's heart sank. These were not the dive-bombers usually encountered over Bataan, but rather fighters.[4] As Stinson recalled thirty-six years later of the free-for-all dogfight:

One Zero had me in his sights. He was shooting and I thought he was going to come in the front windshield before pulling up. I did not see how I could be alive and the airplane still in one piece, with so many bullets coming straight at me. Anyway, about that time my aircraft stalled and I rolled off on a wing and dived down to get some air speed.

When I pulled up, I spotted one Zero and gave him a long blast. I now had speed and could better fight and protect myself. I rolled off that Zero and down and back up again. This time I spotted a Zero on a P-40. The Zero was firing away. I gave him a good long burst and rolled away again. I pulled back and looked around for a while, but could not find anyone. It was quite odd how the sky could be full of aircraft a few minutes before and then nothing.

During his last firing run, Stinson's guns were malfunctioning. He tried to recharge them, but the ones on the right would not work at all, and the left ones kept jamming. Then none of them would work. He decided to hit the deck and head back to Bataan Field.

On the ground after completing the half-hour mission, Stinson checked with White and Baker, who had also returned safely. Anderson was missing. Stinson figured that "Andy's" plane must have been the one he saw being attacked by the Japanese fighter.[5] White and Baker told Stinson they had not been in a position at any time where they could have fired on the Japanese, so any Japanese losses would have been due to Stinson or Anderson. Later, ground observers of the 17th Pursuit and the navy reported that two of the enemy had been seen to crash.[6] Stinson believed he had shot both down, but later Anderson was credited with one of the kills.

Hopes that Anderson, a good friend of Stinson's and one of the most popular pilots of the Bataan Field Flying Detachment, had survived his encounter were dashed when other ground observer reports came in. He had been seen bailing out near Bagac and then being strafed in his chute by two of the Japanese planes. His chute riddled, he had fallen the last 1,000 feet to his death. The story of this atrocity infuriated the American forces.[7]

Later, Stinson found out that on this his first encounter with Japanese fighters he had taken several hits in the right wing and some in the fuselage. One shell had gone through the fuselage fuel tank right behind him. The wing hits had severed the wiring to his three .50-caliber guns and made them inoperative.

After supper that evening, Colonel George called a meeting of all his pilots. With Allison Ind and Lefty Eads joining in, they started to "kill" a couple of bottles of whiskey, then proceeded in more mellow dispositions to thrash out a lot of troubles and try to get over the death of Anderson. It was decided that the detachment should operate as a squadron, with Charley Sneed remaining in command. In an expansive mood,

"Mort" Sneed allowed that all the pilots might be squadron commanders themselves soon.

8 On the morning of January 21, Woolery, Obert, and Ibold, after having passed a very uncomfortable night sleeping on the ground with just a blanket each, were called in by Colonel George to his operations shack. They were told that they had the choice of remaining at Bataan Field and flying the P-40s they had brought in the early evening before or joining their pursuit squadrons in beach defense positions. Colonel George warned them that the flying would be the hardest and most dangerous they would ever do. Without hesitation, all three pilots opted for the flying assignment. With the addition of Obert, Woolery, and Ibold, the number of pilots of the detachment increased to eleven: Sneed, Stinson, and White of the 20th Pursuit; Obert, Glover, Rowe, and Posten of the 17th; Woolery of the 3rd; Ibold of the 21st; and Baker and Hall of the 34th.[8]

On this date, the detachment included seven P-40Es and two P-40Bs, all in commission. In addition, there were several other aircraft on the field, including one Beechcraft Staggerwing, two basic trainers, two primary trainers, and an O-49 observation plane. They were being used for courier service to Corregidor and other noncombat operations.

Colonel George was still hoping for reinforcements from Australia. A week earlier he had impressed upon MacArthur's deputy chief of staff the importance of even minor additions of P-40s for his operations. Cabcaben Field, five miles to the south of Bataan Field, would be operational in a few days, following completion of construction of its 3,900-foot runway. Another field at Mariveles, on the southern tip of Bataan, was under construction, incorporating the present road as part of the runway. With Bataan Field, these strips could accommodate the reinforcements George was expecting.

Unknown to Colonel George, a meeting held two days earlier in Darwin, Australia, had ended any possibility of ferrying P-40s to Bataan. Major General Brereton, now the Australia-based commanding general of the Far East Air Force, had flown into Darwin on the afternoon of January 18 after returning to Australia from a nine-day series of meetings with AB-DACOM (American-British-Dutch-Australian Command) officials on Java.

At 8:20 the next morning, the pilots of the 17th Pursuit Squadron (Provisional) were assembled for a meeting with Brereton. The squadron had been organized only five days earlier on Brereton's orders and was composed of seventeen pilots under the command of Maj. Bud Sprague, formerly the operations officer of Colonel George's 5th Interceptor Command of Philippine days. Twelve of the pilots—Sprague, Gilmore, Kiser, Hennon, Gies, Neri, Rowland, Coss, Blanton, Dale, Irvin, and Kruzel— had been evacuated from the Philippines on December 31 and January 1. They had been at Darwin three days now, waiting to receive orders to fly their newly assembled P-40Es to the Philippines via Timor in the Dutch East Indies.

Brereton laid it on the line. Staging points in the Dutch East Indies for the P-40s along the ferry route were now either captured by the Japanese or about to be so. Their orders now were to proceed to Java instead. "You are a task force to delay the Japanese offensive," Brereton told them. The squadron's former Philippine pilots listened glumly to Brereton's speech. They had all looked forward to returning to help their beleaguered flying mates on Bataan, but now the matter was out of their hands.

19. "I KNOW MY MAMA IS FRANTIC ABOUT ME"

1 At the command post of the 3rd Pursuit Squadron, located in a banana grove near a cart-track dirt road that led down to Biaan Point on the west coast of Bataan, Herb Ellis was waiting for breakfast time. It was about 8:40 on the morning of January 23, 1942, and he and the rest of the squadron were hungry, as usual. For three weeks now, they had been on half rations, though it seemed more like one-fourth rations, with two skimpy meals, at 10:00 A.M. and 4:00 P.M. each day. The stillness of the morning was suddenly broken by the sound of a brief outburst of gunfire southeast of their position, then quiet once again returned to the area. A little while later the 3rd Pursuit received word that a Japanese patrol had surprised a small outpost of eight or nine men at Mount Pucot and killed all of them.

Now Ellis was being ordered by the CO of the 3rd Pursuit, Hank Thorne, to lead a patrol in the area of the gunfire to determine the strength of the Japanese force, in compliance with instructions Thorne had just received from headquarters. Ellis, the de facto executive officer of the squadron, selected Sgt. Lawrence Roach, who was Ellis's constant partner on patrols, to join him, as well as another enlisted man. Just as they were about to start out, four junior naval officers, who had arrived minutes earlier to confer with Thorne on the situation, asked to join the patrol too.

The men headed southeast in single file over a winding trail that took them over a few small open areas and then through a hillock of dense undergrowth before coming out into an open meadow stretching almost parallel to the ridge line on the far side of the meadow on which Pucot Hill was located. This ridge was shaped almost like a long loaf of bread; it was covered by thick tropical vegetation that looked impenetrable.

As they paused and rested against a mound near the bottom of the ridge, trying to figure out their next move, an enlisted man of the 3rd arrived with a can half full of hotcakes and syrup and a message from

Thorne for Ellis: What was the enemy's strength? Thorne was under pressure from higher-ups to provide an estimate.

After disposing of the more-than-welcome hotcakes with the help of Roach, Ellis told the courier that he had seen no indication of any Japanese activity in the area and that the shots that had been heard probably represented nothing more than the usual shooting incidents of trigger-happy friendly forces. Sergeant Roach then went back to the 3rd Pursuit's command post with the runner to make sure the message was not garbled.

About an hour later, Roach returned to Ellis's position with another communication from Thorne: he had been informed by higher headquarters that a large Japanese force had landed in the rear. Thorne had been irritated by Ellis's response to his runner's message and was expecting him to come up with an estimate of the Japanese strength this time.

No sooner had Roach finished giving the message to Ellis than a shot was heard way up on the hill to their left. Then another shot fired by someone about twenty-five yards up the hill directly in front of them, followed by a third shot. Now the whole hillside in front of them erupted. Rifle fire was extremely heavy, and several machine guns were firing at the same time. Ellis figured that there must be as many as five hundred men on Pucot Hill in front of them and wondered if that would be a good estimate to give Thorne.

But none of the fire was coming in the direction of little patrol; whoever was firing was not firing at them. But reasoning that if the firing force, assumed to be Japanese, came out of the jungle in front of them, they would be in a very bad position to receive it, Ellis decided to retire across the hundred-yard-wide clearing to the hillock, where a line was formed on the top. From this better position, they could withdraw along the trail back to the command post if the Japanese emerged from the jungle and started to cross the clearing in their direction.

As soon as the patrol took up the position on the hillock, Ellis sent Roach back to the 3rd's command post with a request that Thorne send the rest of the squadron to form a line on the patrol. He wanted to form a defensive line along the northwest side of the supposed enemy beachhead. This was in accordance with the squadron's assignment on the west coast of Bataan to contain any Japanese amphibious landing in its area until a regular infantry unit could take over.

Soon Sergeant Roach was back: reinforcements were on the way. As the day wore on, however, there was no sign of any help. Finally, as morning became afternoon, Ellis decided to check on the situation himself; the troops should have come up long ago. While crossing over the hillock on the east-west trail, he was surprised to run into the men; they had been deployed along the north-south trail running down the hillock and were advancing in line through the jungle. Not realizing that it was virtually impossible to move through jungle except on trails, they were now all tied up and making no progress.

After speaking to 2nd Lt. Lycurgus "Johnny" Johnson and the other second lieutenant in charge of the reinforcements, Ellis and the two officers finally extricated the men from the jungle and brought them up in single file along the east-west trail to the east side of the hillock. Here they were deployed in a north-south line along the edge of the hillock.

With the squadron's men in a good defensive position, they now waited for action. But as the afternoon wore on, the stillness of the area remained undisturbed by any sounds of warfare. Finally, in late afternoon, Thorne sent a message for the men to return to their assigned position in the 3rd Pursuit's beach defense area. A small force of Commander Frank Bridget's Naval Battalion of Marines and sailors, dispatched to the Mount Pucot area that morning to dislodge the Japanese, had succeeded in clearing the summit and slopes of the enemy. It was now evident that the rifle and machine gun fire that Ellis's men had heard earlier in the day was that being exchanged between Bridget's force and the Japanese.

Back at their command post and beach positions that evening, the officers and men of the squadron were all abuzz with the news of the Japanese landing one and a half miles to the south of their defensive position the previous evening. Evidently the Japanese had scaled the 130-foot cliff at Longoskawayan Point by driving long stakes into the face of the cliff and climbing up them, unseen by anyone; no troops had been assigned to cover Longoskawayan Point. A few days earlier, the infantry officer who served as the 3rd Pursuit's liaison and adviser had told Andy Krieger not to expect an attack from oceanside, since "the Japs will never be able to scale the face of that cliff." They were expected to land on the beaches between the promontories.

2 Late that same night, the officers and men of the 20th Pursuit Squadron, encamped a few kilometers from the 3rd Pursuit at the Mariveles cutoff area, were awakened and put on the alert. For the past five days the 20th had been on call as reinforcements in the case of any attack on Bataan's coasts. Now with the Japanese landing in the Longoskawayan area, the squadron was to get itself ready for a move to support the 3rd Pursuit in containing the landing force.

At 6:00 P.M. the next day, the order came through. Everyone piled into trucks and started out for the front. When the trucks had reached the point on the road nearest the area that the squadron was to defend, the men jumped out and lined up in two single files, several paces apart, for the hike down the jungle trail to the command post of the 3rd Pursuit near the coast.

As 1st Lt. Joe Moore led his men along the path on the moonlit night

Longoskawayan Point, Bataan. Though the photograph was taken in 1982, little has changed since January, 1942, when the Battle of the Points was fought. *Courtesy Franklin O. Anders, Lt. Col. AUS (Ret.)*

into a situation for which none had been trained and against an unseen foe, he felt awfully exposed. How he wished he could be in a P-40 instead, even if completely outnumbered! At 6:30 P.M., Moore and his men reached Thorne's command post. Here the 20th Pursuit was split up into three groups, with two to go to reinforce the defensive position of the 3rd Pursuit on two promontories of the coast and the third to beef up the defenses of the command post. Moore and Thorne would alternate the command of the combined force.

Assigned to reinforce the more southerly of the two strong points were 2nd Lts. Randall Keator and Jim Fulks, with ten men from Keator's platoon. They were given a guide and told to walk as silently as possible, in single file, and about ten feet apart. Snipers were scattered all through the jungle, and on this bright night the Americans would make excellent targets.

Upon arrival at the point, Keator and Fulks were met by 2nd Lts. Charles Sheeley and Burton Richard of the 3rd Pursuit, who with twenty men of the squadron were responsible for the defenses. Sheeley and Richard now took their two counterparts in the 20th Pursuit on a tour of the installation. The promontory that they were to defend was about five hundred feet long and two hundred feet wide and stood about fifty feet above the water, with almost vertical cliffs. Four machine guns were emplaced around the top rim of the point, with two having a field of fire covering the beaches on either side of the point. With the same layout on the point to the north of their position, any Japanese landing party on the beach between the two points would be caught in a cross fire from the two points. The men not manning the machine gun positions were positioned in foxholes around the rim, where they would be able to fire on any Japanese reaching the base of the cliff. And the entire beach was mined with cases of dynamite.

As the four officers stood and talked near the machine gun nest at the west end, they were suddenly startled when one of the guards down below on the beach shouted, "Halt!" There was no reply. The guard shouted again, but still got no response. When this was followed by several rifle shots fired in rapid succession, the officers, realizing they made perfect targets standing in the moonlight, ran over to the sleeping area at the center of the strongpoint for cover. Just as they reached this area, there was a blinding flash and a loud report, not more than ten feet in front of Keator. Jim Fulks fell at Keator's feet, hollering that he had been shot. Keator immediately hit the dirt and rolled behind a bush, fully expecting the next shot to be directed at him.

For the next ten minutes, no one moved, fearing that a sniper had slipped into their camp. Sheeley formed a line of men and swept the area in search of the sniper but found none. Then, suspicious, the officers asked if any of the men had fired the shot, but no admissions were forthcoming. When the officers threatened to smell each man's rifle barrel, one of the men confessed. He had been asleep, but the firing woke him up. When he saw the four officers running toward him, he fired, thinking they were Japanese.

After Fulks was given emergency first aid for multiple bullet wounds in the right leg, he was carried on a stretcher for a mile to the command post of the squadron, where he could be attended by the medics of the two squadrons.

The three officers then sought out the guard who had precipitated the evening's events. According to his explanation, seven Japanese had slipped around the base of the cliff directly below the Americans. When the guard had yelled for them to halt, they ran. He threw a grenade after them, but it was a dud and failed to explode. Three of the Japanese ran back around the cliff, two of them climbed a side of the cliff and ran through the rear of the camp, one of whom was wounded but managed to escape. A sixth Japanese, also wounded, dived into the bay and swam over to the northern strongpoint. Crawling onto the beach below the point, he called for an American doctor and was captured by Lt. "Johnny" Johnson, in charge of the defense on that point. It turned out he was an officer and willing to provide information to his captors.

No one did much sleeping the rest of that night. Sleeping time proved to be in short supply the next days too. The personnel of the two squadrons were put on duty eighteen hours a day at a stretch. Those on one shift went on duty at 6:00 A.M. and got off at midnight, while those on the second shift took over at midnight and were on duty until 6:00 P.M. It was a punishing schedule.

The night after Fulks's shooting incident, Herb Ellis had just finished his eighteen hour stint and was sound asleep on the ground at the command post when a tremendous explosion jolted him out of his slumber. Sitting bolt upright, he listened petrified as the sound of a falling shell became strong and stronger, like that of a freight train, until the projectile finally hit just a few hundred yards away. Then Ellis recalled that he had been told that Corregidor that evening would be bombarding the Japanese position on Longoskawayan Point with its 12-inch mortars of Battery Geary.

Ellis, a former artillery officer, now began following the flight of the 670-pound shells in his mind: they must be climbing to some fifteen miles before beginning to tumble end over end and crashing at the end of their seven-mile trip across Manila Bay to Bataan. The hair on the back of his neck really stood on end when on one of the rounds the rotating band of the shell apparently broke off and, continuing to rotate, made a sound like that of a woman in her death agony, lasting till the projectile detonated among the Japanese.

At the outset of the bombardment, Ellis's reaction was to get the hell out of there, but then he reasoned that he was probably in the safest spot he could be, in the little depression in the ground. And then, inexplicably, after enduring several rounds of mortar fire, he fell back asleep, exhausted from his day's schedule.

3 During the next few days, fighting between the Japanese force and the Naval Battalion raged on, but neither the 3rd nor the 20th pursuit were called in to participate. Their role continued to be defensive. When reinforcements were finally ordered to break the stalemate, it was the crack 57th Philippine Scouts, 2nd Battalion, that got the job. The five hundred men of the battalion arrived at dusk on January 27. This was not a surprising or unwelcome turn of events in the pursuiters' minds; they were not professional infantry and were just making the best of a bad situation.

While maintaining a vigilant watch on the water off the points on January 27, one of the men of the combined 3rd and 20th Pursuit force noted that a rock off Latain Point seemed whiter than normal. His report was checked out, and it was discovered that the rock in question had recently been painted white. This information was relayed to G-2 Intelligence on Corregidor, since it was suspected that the Japanese had painted the rock white to serve as a marker for possible sea reinforcements.[1]

Although the two squadrons were not engaged in any combat with the Japanese, there were incidents of sniper attacks on officers and men walking through the jungle between their defensive positions. Officers were known to be particularly targets of snipers and for this reason had removed their insignia and pinned it under their collars.

On two occasions, the 20th Pursuit nearly lost its commanding officer. Soon after having joined the 3rd Pursuit on beach defense, Joe Moore and his enlisted-man "runner" were walking down a path in the thick jungle with a group of Commander Bridget's Naval Defense Battalion. Coming to a small stream that crossed the path, they hesitated a moment to gauge the width of the stream, then leaped across. Just as they landed on the far side, they were startled to hear a shot ring out; a bullet splattered in the mud on the bank from where they had leaped. They saw no one but did not bother to search, instead scrambling down the path to get under heavier foliage. A sniper tied into a tree overlooking the spot had evidently taken a shot at them.

The second incident occurred late one night as Moore and three others were returning to the joint 3rd and 20th Pursuit command post after having strung a telephone wire from the post to a newly established observation position on one of the cliffs overlooking the sea. Moore was leading the group back, carrying his shotgun and the rifles of two of the men who between them were lugging the heavy spool of wire back to the post. Suddenly, a shot rang out off to their left. It was so close that it felt to Moore as if someone had slapped his hand across his left ear. All four fell flat on the ground, on which some foliage gave them a little cover. After laying there in the pitch darkness for a few minutes, "afraid to breathe," they crawled on their stomachs about fifty feet until they reached a small ditch near a banana grove, then made it back to the command post.

The next morning, they went back to retrieve the guns and wire, which they had left where they had fallen. They were still where they had dropped them. Exploring around the route they had taken back to the post, they found footprints near one of the banana palms about ten feet from where they had been walking. The footprints had the big toe separated from the rest of the toes, like the thumb of a glove, characteristic of the jungle footwear of Japanese soldiers.

4 Early on the morning of January 31, Herb Ellis and his squadron mate Bob Newman reported in at Mariveles naval base on a special assignment. They were to participate in a mopping-up exercise against the Japanese.

Although the 2nd Battalion of the 57th Philippine Scouts had completed the destruction of the Japanese on Longoskawayan Point by the afternoon of January 29, some of the enemy were believed to be still holed up in the caves along the face of the cliffs of the points around Longoskawayan. The day before, Comdr. Frank Bridget had ordered Lt. Comdr. Henry W. Goodall to take a forty-foot motor launch and a motorized whaleboat from the USS *Canopus*, modified the day before with a ⅜-inch-thick shield of boiler plate for protection and armed with a 37-mm and three .50-caliber machine guns, and capture or kill the remaining Japanese from seaside. This was the second day of the operation.

Ellis and Newman were assigned to the launch, along with the executive officer of the 2nd Battalion, Maj. Robert D. Scholes, all under the command of Goodall. Three Philippine Scouts and a chief petty officer (to handle the boat) were given the whaleboat. After about twenty minutes, the mixed party of eight reached Longoskawayan Point on a beautiful morning of calm sea. As the whaleboat and launch approached the point, someone pointed out bodies of Japanese hung up on the stone face of the cliff. They had either jumped, or been blown, off the point and fell down, to be caught by outcroppings of the cliff. After passing the face of the cliff, the launch and whaleboat turned northeast into a cove that reached back a hundred yards or so, between Longoskawayan Point and a small ridge to the north.

Ordered to fire into a cave on the end of the north promontory where some movement had been noticed, Ellis manned one of the .50-caliber guns with difficulty; the primitive mount allowed it to "jump all over the place," and it jammed after every few rounds. A Japanese fell into the water from a small shelf on the right side of the cave and floated facedown. After the whaleboat moved in and picked up the body, Goodall congratulated Ellis on his "good work," but the latter felt bad about the incident and did not want any praise for the shooting.

Then the launch and whaleboat moved up the cove. As soon as they reached a beach, the three scouts were put ashore from the whaleboat, one on the north shore of the inlet and two on the south shore. Scholes also got out on the north shore. Goodall instructed Ellis to sweep the underbrush on the right side of the cove to flush any Japanese that might be hiding there, but the recalcitrant machine gun kept jamming, then quit entirely.

In the meantime, the scouts were moving along both sides of the cove on narrow beaches of sand and pebbles. Then suddenly the scout on the north side of the inlet leveled his rifle and fired twice in the area of two rocks jutting out into the water. A Japanese pitched out on the narrow cliff between the two rocks and fell some fifteen feet into the water.

Now the launch and whaleboat party watched two other scouts, a fierce-looking sergeant with a full mustache and a private, as they reached a cave with a small opening, which looked like the entrance to a man-made tunnel and was completely unlike the other caves along the inlet. When the sergeant yelled into the cave for anyone inside to come out, he received no response, so he leveled his rifle and walked into the dark of the narrow opening. A few seconds later, the scout backed out, his rifle still leveled, followed by two unarmed Japanese.

For the trip back to Mariveles, Scholes brought the scout sergeant and his two prisoners, plus the body of the Japanese pulled out of the water, on board the launch. The legs of the body were all torn up from the .50-caliber slugs Ellis had fired.

5 Seven miles north of Longoskawayan on January 22, the men of the 34th Pursuit Squadron were covering a mile of the water's edge around the coastline promontory assigned them in the Quinauan Point area. To the north of them was Quinauan Bay; to the south, Agloloma Bay. The topography was similar to that at Longoskawayan Point: a heavily wooded area of tall trees and thick jungle undergrowth leading to steep cliffs of some fifty to sixty feet to the beach below. Across the face of the northern tip of Quinauan, the squadron had set up four machine gun positions, using .30-caliber guns, to guard against any possible Japanese sea landing. On the north side of Agloloma Point, about 1,800 yards to the south, a pair of twin-mounted .50-caliber machine guns covered the approach.

Sometime after midnight on January 22/23, Pvt. Larry Cohen, on guard in his machine gun site at Agloloma Point, spotted lights coming in from the sea around Quinauan Point to the north. Suspecting they were Japanese, he called in on the phone to the 34th's command post back of the defensive positions, but no one there expressed concern. Follow-up calls elicited no response either.[2]

A few hours later, the four-man crew of the squadron's northernmost gun position on Quinauan Point was surprised to see "Filipino" soldiers approaching them in the pitch darkness. But greetings yelled to them over the protecting rock barricade were answered by withering gunfire. Pfc John Morrell was killed outright. The other crew members fired their .30-caliber machine gun. The Japanese did not press forward but apparently went around the position instead. Two of the crew fled over the cliff, but the third, Pvt. Melville Jones, who had burned his hand trying to lift the hot machine gun on abandoning his position, ran down to the next gun position, manned by S. Sgt. Raymond High, Sgt. Ivan Foster, Pvt. Glen Flesher, and one other, who were firing sporadically into the dark at unseen targets.

Two of the squadron's machine gun positions were abandoned to the Japanese, who had scaled the cliffs undetected. In the confusion of the night, the invaders in short time succeeded in establishing themselves on about fifty yards of the coast line.

A small group, including Lt. Charles Gaskell, Cpl. Earl Ellsworth, and Pvts. Tom Blaylock and Ralph Keenan, had been driven down to the point where the Agloloma River runs into Agloloma Bay and ordered to spread out along the beach there on the north side of the little river until daylight, then fall back. They heard some machine gun fire and an occasional mortar burst from Quinauan to the north, as well as some rifle shots. But like most of the squadron's men, they neither saw nor participated in any combat this night.

Reacting to the news of the Japanese landing, which reached him at 2:30 A.M., Brigadier General Selleck ordered a battalion of his Philippine Constabulary at daylight to dislodge the enemy, whose strength was unknown to him. But by that time, the Japanese had dug in and erected defensive positions further down the point. The Filipinos were repulsed about six hundred yards from the coast tip of the thousand-yard-long peninsula.

At this point, Selleck decided to send in a detachment of Bren gun carriers and the 34th Pursuit as reinforcements, resulting in several combat engagements for the inexperienced and inadequately trained officers and men of the squadron. Lt. Jack Jennings was ordered to take a patrol of the 34th Pursuit into the Quinauan Point area where the Japanese had penetrated the night before. In the dense jungle, which impeded any movement, the patrol ran into a small force of the Japanese party, which it estimated at about fifty men. In trying to form a line, Jennings was hit in the knee by the unseen Japanese but continued in his efforts. Only when his mission was accomplished did he allow himself to be evacuated. For his action, he was cited for the Silver Star. Less fortunate was Cpl. Paul Duncan, from Ardmore, Oklahoma. Wounded in the thigh by a large-caliber weapon, he died in the squadron aid station that evening.

The next morning, the command post of the 34th Pursuit had a special visitor. Newly promoted Brig. Gen. Clinton H. Pierce, commanding officer of the famed 26th Cavalry Philippine Scouts, had come to talk to the 34th's CO, Robert Wray, just promoted to captain. Pierce had just replaced General Selleck that day, taking over command of his 71st Division, responsible for beach defense. Selleck was faulted for not being aggressive enough in pursuing the offensive against the Japanese landing party. The old cavalry officer, dressed in campaign hat, boots and spurs, and jodhpurs, was suggesting a "turkey shoot." Wray should lead a patrol down to sea level and around Quinauan Point and flush the enemy out.

Wray was lucky to escape with his life. Surrounded by the unseen Japanese and cut off from his own lines, he somehow managed to take his patrol over the cliffs down to the beach and then back to his own lines. But two men of his patrol, Cpls. Norman Johnson and Ralph Keenan, were wounded, Johnson in the leg and Keenan in the hand.

In another incident that morning, 2nd Lt. Claude Paulger was leading a patrol including Lts. "Shorty" Crosland and Jim Nicol, plus a few Filipinos, to relieve a night shift when a sniper began firing on them. As they hit the ground close together, they were raked by Japanese fire from the underbrush. Despite the efforts of Crosland and Nicol to stop them, the Filipinos broke and ran, leaving the .30-caliber machine gun behind.

Paulger did not get up; he had been hit, though the other officers did not know where. After throwing the machine gun ammunition into the trees, they carried Paulger back to the aid station, with the help of Tom Blaylock. There, the squadron medic, Dan Shapiro, removed the bullet, which had struck his left hand and right shoulder. Only a few days earlier, the young 2nd lieutenant from Lubbock, Texas, had been sharing his feelings about being assigned to Infantry duties with fellow pilot Ben Brown while the two finished off a can of pineapple. Only half in jest, he had told Brown, "I know my mama is frantic about me, but she ain't half as frantic as *I* am!"

Later that day, General Pierce himself became a casualty. While being given escort by Shorty Crosland and others to the front lines to inspect the progress of the fighting, he was shot straight through the foot by a sniper. The sniper was killed, and Pierce was carried back to the rear.

The 34th Pursuit now began to realize that the Japanese force was larger than originally believed. But large or small, it was proving impossible to really get at them. The squadron's men were reduced to firing in a general area only, as it was almost impossible to see beyond twenty yards in the dense foliage. Their ignorance of this type of warfare did not help matters either.

6 About midnight on the evening of January 23/24, the two hundred officers and men of the 21st Pursuit Squadron, on bivouac near the Biaan River, were rudely awakened by their first sergeant, Royal Huston. "All right, men, this is a battle call! Grab your gear. We aren't coming back," he yelled.

Huston, better known as Diz among the senior noncoms of the squadron, organized the loading of the men on waiting buses, most of whose tops had been sawed off. These buses had been taken to Bataan on the evacuation of Manila a month before and were now to provide the squadron transport for the seven-mile trip to the Quinauan area. The 21st had been ordered into combat to reinforce General Pierce's forces in an intensified effort to wipe out the stubborn Japanese party.

Arriving at their destination, the men were off-loaded in the jungle near the combat area. There they waited for orders the rest of the night, amid the crackling sound of rifle fire and blasts of mortar shell. Then, early the morning of January 24, the squadron moved on to the 34th Pursuit's bivouac area. A few of the 34th's wounded were being carried out and put in ambulances for the trip to the hospital. The 21st was ordered to comb the woods behind the coastline for snipers that might have slipped through. Slowly, the men worked themselves forward through the thick jungle in shadowy light to the point where the firing was going on. By nightfall, they had reached the 34th Pursuit's command post area.

On the morning of January 25, the 21st Pursuit was integrated with the Philippine Constabulary and Company A of the 803rd Aviation Engineers; the three units were to form a skirmish line to extend across the neck of the one-thousand-yard-wide peninsula protruding into the South China Sea between Quinauan and Agloloma bays. The 21st was on the right flank, the 803rd Engineers in the center, and the constabulary on the left flank. At ten o'clock, the mixed force began moving forward in an undulating fashion. First the flanks moved, then the center came up, and then the whole line moved in unison. Although the men were spread ten to fifteen feet apart, they could not keep a very straight line because of the density of the jungle and the thorny, sticky vines that tore their faces.

The men were very tense and became irritable in the heat, cursing and screaming at each other. At one point, the line became ragged and an officer on top of a hill shouted, "Maintain your interval!" One of the men then yelled back. "Let the son of a bitch who gave that order try to maintain it!" In a matter of seconds, one of the young pilots of the squadron came running down the hill, nearly falling down when he could not slow his momentum at the bottom. Following a consultation, the order was "somewhat modified."

The intermittent fire of rifles and the chattering of the engineers' machine guns added to the din. Every few minutes a sniper would be spotted in the trees, and the line would stop so that a man armed with an automatic rifle could wipe him out.

All that afternoon the line kept moving forward until the men had reached the edge of the ravine that ran in from the point. The 21st's men were stopped at the road that led down to the nearby cliff and began to dig in for the night. However, the 803rd Engineers kept on moving forward and at dusk went down into the ravine. When they got to the bottom of the ravine, all hell broke loose: there were Japanese in hidden foxholes waiting for the Americans to come down to their positions. They now fired into the surprised engineers, inflicting heavy casualties. Those who could, broke back to the 21st's position. Dyess then sent five of his squadron and thirty to forty constabulary to help fill the gap left by the 803rd. Those engineers who had not been hit were helping the wounded up the slope, but others remained pinned down in the ravine by the intensity of the Japanese fire. Some of the wounded were still at the bottom of the ravine but could not be reached by the medics. But the Japanese did not finish them off, leaving them to scream in the darkness all through the night.

Contact along the whole line had now been lost. Deciding to extricate his squadron from a bad situation where it it could easily be outflanked, Dyess ordered his men to move back at 2:00 A.M. It was so dark the withdrawal had to be done by touch. With rifles slung on their shoulders, each man behind took hold of the rifle of the man in front of him and groped through the jungle, stumbling into trees and tripping over vines for some two miles until they reached a spot where they could sleep for the rest of the night.

On the morning of January 26, the dispirited men set up a new line. This time, however, they remained in a holding position, combing the woods for Japanese who might have infiltrated through the lines. The men were tired and had eaten very little the past days, mainly salmon gravy on sourdough bread. Water was brought in a little tank truck, but it was warm and not enough.

Then on the morning of January 28, the 21st Pursuit was ordered back to its camp area. Along with the engineers and the Philippine Constabulary, it was being relieved by the 3rd Battalion of the crack 45th Infantry, Philippine Scouts. It was hoped that the five hundred professional soldiers of the scout regiment would be able to break the stalemated situation and wipe out the remaining Japanese bottled up on Quinauan Point.

7 Just after dawn on January 27, the 17th Pursuit Squadron, encamped near Kilometer Post 191 between the Quinauan and Anyasan rivers, listened to orders being called out by its first sergeant. The men were to join up with units of the Philippine Constabulary in the jungle south at "Quinine" to oppose a small force of Japanese. The squadron's cooks would keep the chow hot for the men, as the operation would take only until 5:00 P.M. The squadron had been shifted three days earlier from its former beach position at Caibobo Point to Kilometer Post 191, then into its present nearby bivouac the following day, where it was being held in reserve for defense of the sector.

The men soon found that instead of going south to "Quinine" they were heading north, to the promontory area between Anyasan Bay to the south and Silaiim Bay to the north. This was some two thousand yards north of the Quinauan area fighting. Evidently yet another landing of Japanese had taken place the night of January 26/27, this time in the Silaiim Point area. There was a risk this force would join up with the Quinauan Point Japanese. The 17th Pursuit was being called in to reinforce the Philippine Constabulary force defending the area and to oppose the Japanese movement toward the west road of Bataan.

Ignorant of the dangers of the situation, the 17th's men walked forward through the jungle "as if we were on a picnic," talking loudly and making "all kinds of noise." Then they reached an opening in the jungle, apparently the headquarters area of the 2nd Battalion, 2nd Philippine Constabulary.

Lts. Steve Crosby and Joe McClellan, at the head of the 17th's 2nd Platoon, were dumbfounded at the sight before them: a perfectly prepared camp, cleared of brush, with paths and various areas laid off with vines, the ground swept, bamboo living quarters erected, complete aid station with medicine and stretchers laid out, and even fires burning under full food pots. Only one thing was wrong: there was not a soul in the area. Crosby later recorded "[I] could feel the hair lifting right up the back of my neck."

After a meal on the food left cooking in the pots, Crosby at the head of the second platoon led the squadron's men down the trail that led into the jungle, then put them in a skirmish line when they reached the jungle. Slowly advancing, the men yelled back and forth at each other to keep the line straight and their courage up. Some of the men were asking the officers how to operate their rifles.

After the men had advanced some 150 yards into the jungle about 400 yards west of the main road, a heavy machine gun suddenly opened up on their center. It was joined by rifle fire from the trees. Instantly, Crosby's men fell on their stomachs and cut loose in the direction of the Japanese fire. Everyone was so relieved to have something to shoot at that they just fired away in the general direction of the Japanese, whether they saw anything or not.

The squadron's four air-cooled .30-caliber machine guns, mounted on little lightweight pipe tripods, were being fired in pairs because of their rapid rate of fire. When one got too hot, another was substituted. They were being fed from ammunition in metal-linked belts carried around each man's shoulders.

During a lull in the shooting, a bullet just grazed the helmet of Pfc Leo Arhutick, fired from the rear. He told a buddy in the squadron, and they went around to the opposite side of the tree that they had been behind and kept a sharp watch in the direction of the shot. About ten minutes later, they were rewarded; leaves and empty cartridge cases fell out of a tree, twenty yards to the rear. One less Japanese sniper.

Lt. "Spud" Sloan, the squadron's CO, phoned General Pierce's headquarters on the situation, but it refused to believe at first that the constabulary had fled their position and that there were so many Japanese around. But it managed to locate the constabulary unit, and later in the day the Filipinos were back, reinforcing the 17th Pursuit.

Around 8:00 that evening, when the firing had died down to spasmodic pops. Crosby tried unsuccessfully to advance a patrol. Leading a group of Filipinos, 2nd Lt. Jerry Brezina tried to flank the Japanese machine gun crew on the left but was killed when he walked into a vine attached to a hand grenade thirty or forty yards ahead of the squadron's men.[3] Then Pvt. Luchen Barnhart was hit in the right shoulder by a sniper. Crosby decided to suspend any further patrols and selected a spot for the night, where each man settled in behind "a sturdy log."

At 5:30 the next morning, the 17th Pursuit and Philippine Constabulary troops were joined by the 2nd Battalion, 45th Philippine Scouts, ordered by Brigadier General Pierce to support the stalemated U.S. and Filipino forces. Now equipped with sixteen Air Corps light machine guns, the three units under the command of Capt. Arthur Biedenstein, the battalion's executive officer, advanced against no Japanese opposition some two kilometers to the base of Anyasan Point, almost to the beach, before they ran into Japanese fire. For unknown reasons, the Japanese had withdrawn during the night from their line of the day before.

The Japanese were holding firm in their new position. That evening, the constabulary troops rushed the Japanese positions but then broke and fled when fired upon. The 17th Pursuit and the scouts were forced to withdraw two hundred yards that evening to their original position to reorganize the Filipinos and consolidate their forces.

At 1:16 P.M. on January 29, preceded by an artillery barrage, the units again attacked the Japanese, with the constabulary on the left, the scouts on the right, and the 17th Pursuit in the center. Encountering heavy machine gun fire, the units were again forced to withdraw about two hundred yards at sundown to reorganize and establish security for the night. The scenario was virtually repeated the following day. Additional help was needed to dislodge the stubborn foe.

On the morning of January 31, Crosby went north to try to contact Maj. John Primrose and his 12th Infantry, Philippine Army, which was being ordered in as reinforcements. After reporting in to the major and heading back down the line toward the north flank of the Philippine Scouts, Crosby was startled by 75-mm shells raining down on his position in the scouts' area. As the shell bursts in the trees showered fragments in all directions, Crosby hugged the ground "for all I was worth." Before the 88th Field Artillery's command post could be reached during the five-minute ordeal, four scouts from Company G had been killed and sixteen wounded.

Despite its losses, Company G in the afternoon made a spirited attack and advanced down to the beach at Silaiim Bay, followed by Company

E. The 17th Pursuit followed behind and covered the line of communications. But there was evident confusion about the location of the enemy and ignorance of its strength and capabilities. That evening the crack 57th Regiment, Philippine Scouts, less its 2nd Battalion and Company B, reported in as reinforcements. Brigadier General Pierce was determined to wrap up the drawn-out engagement, now the responsibility of Maj. Harold K. Johnson, the 57th's operations officer.

20. "THE BIGGEST, PRETTIEST, AND MOST THRILLING FIREWORKS SHOW WE'D EVER SEEN"

1 On January 23, 1942, three new pilots reported in at Bataan Field for duty with Colonel George's little air force: Ben Brown of the 34th Pursuit, Sam Grashio of the 21st, and Earl Stone of the 17th. All three were coming off beach defense with their squadrons, handpicked by George for their new assignments. The Bataan Field Flying Detachment was now up to fourteen pilots, an increase of six over the past four days. The 17th Pursuit was most heavily represented, with five (Obert, Rowe, Posten, Glover, and Stone), followed by the 20th (Sneed, White, and Stinson) and the 34th (Brown, Hall, and Baker) with three each. The 21st Pursuit had two (Ibold and Grashio), and the 3rd Pursuit one only (Woolery). Colonel George was still following his policy of selecting a few pilots with combat experience from each of the five pursuit squadrons under his command.

It was an easy enough matter for Colonel George to increase the number of pilots at Bataan Field from the large pool of flying officers available for such select duty, but another to expand the number of pursuit aircraft for them to fly. Arrival of the three P-40s from Del Monte on January 20 increased the total in commission only to nine: seven "E" models and two "Bs."

With fourteen pilots now available to fly missions, Colonel George decided to assign flight leaders. As the most senior officers in the detachment, Ed Woolery, Ben Brown, and Dave Obert were selected. Charley "Mort" Sneed continued as detachment commander; he would choose the flight leader for each mission scheduled by George.

Sneed had been assigning himself missions, but in recent days had aborted them under questionable circumstances. On January 22, he took off at 6:20 P.M. on a single-plane low-level reconnaissance over II Corps area on eastern Bataan, ordered by USAFFE Headquarters on Corregidor, but was "forced back" because of "engine trouble." Eight days earlier, he had taken off with Lloyd Stinson on his wing at 4:20 P.M., but forty-five minutes later was back at Bataan Field, also because of "engine trouble."

When Sneed reported the malfunction of one of the two aborted missions to the maintenance crew of the Headquarters Squadron detachment at Bataan Field, an engine check was run on the P-40, but nothing was found to be out of order. Then the engineering officer of Bataan Field brought a pilot of the detachment to the field to flight test the P-40. After really wringing the plane out, he landed and reported that nothing was wrong with it. Sneed was not told of the results of the test hop to avoid any embarrassment, but the pilots of the detachment were beginning to wonder if Sneed was suffering a case of the nerves.

On the morning of January 26, Sneed assigned himself and three other pilots for a reconnaissance mission over the front lines on Bataan and Subic Bay to the west. Sam Grashio was to fly the wing position on Sneed's P-40, and Earl Stone to fly as wingman for John Posten. Six 30-pound bombs were hooked under the wings of Posten's and Stone's P-40s.

After taking off at 9:20 and climbing into fine, clear weather, in places interrupted by huge, towering clouds, they passed over the lines without incident, then approached Subic Bay. There Posten and Stone spotted four boats one-half mile offshore, heading south, two being towed by the other two. The two 17th Pursuiters then went down in a bombing and strafing attack, inflicting casualties on all four boats.[1]

Heading back, down the west coast of Bataan, the two flights became separated. Then at 10:15 A.M. Posten caught sight of three Japanese dive-bombers about 4,000 to 5,000 feet below him at Luzon Point, just south of Agloloma Bay, coming up the coast. After signaling to his wingman, Posten led Stone down in a dive through a cloud on the unsuspecting Japanese, immediately sending one in flames into the ground—neither of the two crewmen got out. The other two "Anns" jettisoned their bombs then twisted and turned in a desperate attempt to escape, but the two P-40s got in several good shots on both before running out of ammunition. When Posten and Stone broke off combat, the two damaged dive-bombers were seen heading up toward the lines, losing altitude.

Grashio had spotted the dive-bombers below him too. Recognizing them as "easy meat," he got on the radio and sent a Morse code message to Sneed. When Grashio saw Sneed looking down, the 21st Pursuiter pointed down at the "Anns." But Sneed did not return any sign and continued flying along. Grashio assumed that he was choosing his time to peel off and go down after the Japanese. But when nothing happened as the dive-bombers were getting closer on their northward course, Grashio repeated his radio Morse code call to Sneed and again pointed out the planes to Sneed, who continued to fly along, much to the frustration of the junior pilot, since he could not leave his wing position without permission. When Grashio saw Posten and Stone go into their dives on the Japanese, Grashio was "ready to froth at the mouth."

Mitsubishi Type 97 "Ann" light bombers of the 16th *sentai* on their way for yet another raid on Bataan, March 3, 1942. *Courtesy* Mainichi Shimbun

Grashio followed Sneed back to Bataan Field and landed. After making his report, he remained at the field to await the arrival of Posten and Stone. Soon Posten came down over the trees and did a slow wingover over the field, followed by Stone in a repeat victory sign performance. Posten and Stone reported one dive-bomber kill, shared between the two. They were not sure about the other two "Anns." Both P-40s had been hit by Japanese rear gunner fire; Posten's hydraulic line had a hole in it, and Stone's oil line and crankcase were all shot up. The next day, good news was reported from I Corps: the second and third "Anns" had crashed up near the lines.[2]

The lopsided aerial victory for the Bataan pilots was a great shot in the arm for the morale of MacArthur's troops in the sector, the intended target of the dive-bombers that day. Sneed's performance, however, had cast a cloud on the esprit of the Flying Detachment. Grashio had reluctantly reported the failure of Sneed to attack the Japanese to George (pro-

moted on January 25 to brigadier general), and the incident quickly became known among the Bataan pilots. George listened closely to Grashio's
account but said little in reply. He knew he would soon need to make
a decision on what to do about the situation.

2 In the early evening of January 26, six P-40s were being readied for
a most unusual mission: a night raid on Nichols and Nielson fields in
Manila. Brigadier General George had been informed the day before that
a number of Japanese aircraft were on the two fields. He had obtained
permission from USAFFE Headquarters on Corregidor to stage a surprise
attack at an opportune time. On this evening, there was a full moon, offering good visibility for such a raid. In preparation for the raid, the antiaircraft operations officer on Corregidor had been informed that the P-40s
would be assembling over the island at 8:00 P.M. to gain altitude before
striking across Manila Bay for the attack.

Not a light showed on the blacked-out field on Bataan as the tugs pulled
the P-40s from their revetments to the clearing leading to the field. The
first three pursuit ships were now lined up and ready for takeoff, each
armed with six 30-pound fragmentation bombs under their wings. As Jack
Hall and Bill Baker roared down the strip and lifted off, Bob Ibold in third
position wheeled himself into position. But the 21st Pursuiter had become blinded by the swirling dust raised by Hall and Baker. Misjudging
the width of the strip on this his first mission from the field, he now
veered his ship too far to the right. His right wheel went into the rough
outside the runway, then his right wing dipped and hit a huge boulder.
The three fragmentation bombs on the wing exploded, setting off a tremendous blast. As men on the field rushed to the burning wreck to extricate Ibold, no one expected to find him alive. Miraculously, the young
native of Phoenix, Arizona, though badly burned and in a state of shock,
was not suffering from any fatal injury. The Bataan Field medical officer,
"Doc" Noell, rushed him to Bataan Hospital No. 1. Following Ibold's accident, General George canceled the second three-plane flight scheduled
for the mission.

After circling over Corregidor, Hall and Baker continued alone to Nielson Field when no other P-40s showed up for the mission. Shortly after
arriving over the field, they were surprised to find that the Japanese now
had turned on their landing and field lights for them, obviously thinking
that the two P-40s were their own planes. Aided by such a well-lit target,
Hall and Baker went down and dropped their bombs, then strafed the field,
encountering antiaircraft fire only toward the end of their attack. Back
over Bataan Field, the jubilant twosome came in on the blacked-out strip
for a perfect landing. As the irrepressible Hall climbed out of his cockpit,
he was "yelling like a cowboy."

When Hall and Baker reported the results of their attack, General

George decided to stage a follow-up attack for 11:00 P.M. This time the mission would be better organized and would use six P-40s, as originally planned. Ed Woolery was selected to lead Lloyd Stinson and Sam Grashio for a return strike against Nielson, while Dave Obert would take Bill Baker and Earl Stone for a makeup raid on Nichols.

Woolery was sure he could find Nielson even in the dark; he knew Manila well from flying in the area since late 1939. But on arrival over Manila and flying around the city for a considerable time, it was obvious to his two wingmen that their leader was having trouble locating Nielson, which was now blacked out by the Japanese.

Then Stinson spotted the field below and left the others to go in for the attack. Woolery now also went down, while Grashio remained up to fly top cover for the others. Diving across the field from west to east, Stinson fired his .50-caliber guns and then released his bombs over the aircraft parking area. Because of the pitch darkness, he could not be sure of the results of his attack.

To the south of Nielson, Obert and his wingmen also faced the problem of a blacked-out city, but he had no trouble in locating Nichols Field. As soon as the three P-40s came within range of the antiaircraft defenses of Nichols, the Japanese opened up on them with everything they had. "Big, firey red balls" came floating up toward the pilots from all directions. Looking down, they could see the flashes of the antiaircraft guns on the ground as they blazed away. It was "the biggest, prettiest, and most thrilling fireworks show" they had ever seen, even considering they were on the receiving end of it.

Obert picked out the spot on the field where the Japanese aircraft were reported to be located and started his dive. At some 2,000 feet the young Oklahoman released his six fragmentation bombs, then pulled out and looked back into the darkness. Just then, he caught a glimpse of a plane flashing by him, missing him by only a few feet. Obert had lost his two wingmen in the dive, and now they were all flying around blind in the pitch dark. "Things are getting too dangerous," he concluded. He decided to leave before there was a midair collision. The fireworks show was still going on, but the Japanese were evidently shooting at the sound of his plane only, Obert figured, since the tracers were always behind him. They seemed to be floating up so slowly that they could not harm anything, but Obert knew his eyes were deceiving him.

As he departed Manila, Obert headed his P-40 northwest across Manila Bay. He thought that he might pick up some target back of the front lines of Bataan and strafe it with his full load of .50-caliber ammunition. Just as he reached the north tip of the bay at ten minutes past midnight, Obert saw what appeared to be a grass fire off in the distance. After looking more closely, however, "I practically jumped up and down with joy at what

I saw." It was a large Japanese convoy of some fifty trucks, driving along the highway with all its lights on. Obert now circled around to get in front of the column, then dove in from about 1,500 feet, all six fifties blazing. Methodically working from front to rear, the excited pilot raked the entire column before the Japanese had time to turn their lights off. Absorbed in keeping his sights on the trucks, Obert nearly flew into the ground.

His strafing run completed, Obert now pulled his stick back with all his strength and started climbing in the night sky. The lights of the convoy had now gone out, so he headed for the front lines. Spotting some lights behind the lines, Obert went into another firing pass, but after only several bursts, his guns quit; he had exhausted his ammunition. Obert started back for Bataan Field, crossing over the lines and heading south. But antiaircraft fire from the American and Filipino positions began reaching up for him. Not wanting to share the fate of squadron mate Oscar Wyatt three weeks earlier, Obert headed out over Manila Bay, outside the radius of their guns.

As he approached Bataan Field, he picked up the green "all clear" light set out for him and put his wheels down. There were only a few lights on, just enough to demarcate the border of the narrow strip. Obert had to "feel" for the ground; he could not see it. And the runway looked "just about two feet wide" to him. Knowing that there was no margin for error, Obert concentrated to the fullest and made a perfect landing. After he had climbed out of his plane, he was told that everyone had been worrying about him. The other five P-40s had returned much earlier. Obert's strafing spree over northern Bataan had delayed his arrival home.

General George was as happy as a clam when he received the reports of his night fliers. Outside of Bob Ibold's near-fatal accident and the loss of his P-40, it had been a very successful night's work.[3] To celebrate, he dug out a quart of bourbon whiskey reserved for such an occasion and passed it around among the seven pilots.

In apparent reprisal for the Manila raid, the Japanese sent a flight of "Ann" dive-bombers over Bataan Field the next day. As in previous attacks on the field, no aircraft were damaged, although one P-40 was on the runway, and no one was injured or killed, despite Japanese claims to the contrary.

John Posten had missed the bombing this day. He had gone down to the hospital to see how Bob Ibold was doing and was happy to find that Ibold was not hurt as seriously as feared. But the sight of the other patients at the hospital nearly made him sick. Some had limbs missing, others were blind, and one had only half his face. The beds were right out in the open, with not even a tent over them. The hospital visit brought home to the young pilot the brutal reality of the ground campaign, of which he and the others of the Bataan Field Flying Detachment were not a part.

3 At 2:45 P.M. on January 29, Posten, Sam Grashio, and Kiefer White took off from Bataan Field on a combat mission, this time to shoot down another artillery spotter over the lines. After flying northwest to Subic Bay, they spotted eight small boats on the water below, then finally the observation plane over Subic they were looking for. The Japanese pilot headed for the clouds as soon as he saw the three P-40s after him. After ducking in and out of the clouds for fifteen minutes at 3,500 to 4,000 feet in a deadly game of hide-and-seek, the Americans finally caught the Japanese. On every pass the P-40s made, however, the nimble Oriental outmaneuvered his foe, with no hits scored on his machine. The tiny observation plane fled into another cloud and lost its adversaries for good. An hour after takeoff, the frustrated Americans were back at Bataan Field, with no results to show for their efforts.

Three hours before the failed mission, Bataan Field was subjected to its third bombing in three days. But again there was no real damage, and the 803rd Engineers filled the holes in the runway as usual. During the increasingly frequent attacks on Bataan Field, the 803rd and the enlisted men of the Headquarters Squadron detachment fought back at the raiders with whatever weapons they had at hand. Several gun pits along the field mounted .50-caliber guns that the men operated, while some of the engineers' carryalls, pulled by caterpillars, had guns mounted on them. Whenever Japanese planes appeared, the crews of the caterpillars would dive into the carryalls for protection and fire back at the Japanese. Other men on the field would shoot at the raiders with their antique Enfield rifles.

With the need to preserve themselves for flying duty, the pilots of the Bataan Field Flying Detachment were more concerned with finding a safe haven during the raids than with shooting down the enemy. During one attack, one-third of the detachment was nearly wiped out at one go. Kiefer White and four other pilots were huddled in a foxhole when a 30-pound bomb landed almost on the rim of the hole, only some three feet from White. All five officers were knocked unconscious. Dirt was caved in on all of them, one had his shirt ripped in two, and two suffered burst eardrums, but fortunately no more serious injuries were sustained. But White was left wondering what their fate would have been if that bomb had been twenty pounds heavier.

The frequent Japanese raids on the field were not always a cause for deadly serious concern, at least in retrospect. Thus, on one occasion, Pfc Jesse White of Headquarters Squadron was standing by near the strip, waiting to meet the P-40 for which he was the crew chief, standard practice for the field. White was becoming increasingly anxious, as the plane was overdue from a reconnaissance mission and obviously getting lower and lower on gas. Finally, the P-40 came into view and landed.

White ran out to the plane as the pilot jumped off the wing and began running. As he passed White, he shouted what sounded to the crew chief like "Take over!" Nonchalantly, White climbed into the cockpit and began taxiing the P-40 toward the end of the strip and the revetment area. Suddenly, from nowhere, machine gun fire began hitting the strip, just inches from the P-40's left wingtip. Looking up, White saw a single-engine Japanese fighter, a "Nate," firing at him. It had apparently been following the P-40 in.

As the Japanese passed just over White's head and began to circle, the terrified crew chief shoved the P-40's throttle forward and taxied quickly to the end of the runway, nearly colliding with the tug tractor used to tow the planes to the revetments. Barely had the Headquarters Squadron men gotten the tow bar of the tug connected and towed the P-40 into the camouflaged revetment area before the "Nate" returned to spray the field again with its 7.7-mm nose guns.

After the P-40 was safely in its revetment, White climbed out of the cockpit and jumped to the ground. Excited squadron mates eagerly wanted to shake his hand. Then everyone broke out with roars of laughter when White was told that the P-40 pilot had yelled "Take cover!" not "Take over!"

4 On January 29, General George called a meeting of his pilots. He had received a radiogram from San Jose, Mindoro, 160 miles south of Bataan Field. Twelve Japanese bombers had landed on Waterous Field, five miles from San Jose. This was bad news; Waterous Field was a good alternative to have for Bataan Field operations. It was decided to mount a bombing and strafing attack on the Japanese at Waterous at dawn the next day. Ed Woolery would lead the mission, with Jack Hall on his wing, and Dave Obert would head the second two-ship element, with Earl Stone as his wingman. That evening, the Bataan Field crews loaded each of the four P-40s designated for the mission with 30-pound fragmentation bombs and .50-caliber ammunition.

It was still dark in the small hours of January 30 when Woolery, Hall, and Obert lifted their P-40s off Bataan Field and headed south on their combat mission. They intended to strike Waterous before dawn's early light. Earl Stone was late getting off and could not find the other three to link up with them. Woolery, Hall, and Obert were obliged to continue to Mindoro without him.

Arriving over Waterous just about daybreak with Obert and Hall, Woolery started into a dive on the field. Obert had noticed some spots off one end of the field, apparently the Japanese bombers in question, and followed Woolery down. Woolery leveled out at about 100 feet, but did not drop his bombs. Right behind him, Obert released his load at that altitude. The explosion of the bombs tossed Obert around "like a kite" and nearly threw his P-40 into the ground, but he managed to right his plane and then circled to see what had happened. Was Obert feeling sheepish when he discovered that the "bombers" he had unloaded on were actually a few scattered bushes! He had looked so hard for planes that he had mistaken the bushes for them in the dim morning light. With Woolery and Hall still carrying their bombs under their wings, Obert now circled around to see if there was any enemy activity in the area. They could see none, so they came in to land on the field at nearby San Jose to check on the erroneous radiogram.

On the ground, the Bataan Field pilots were greeted by Lt. Warren Baggett, the 48th Materiel Squadron detachment CO, whom Woolery and Obert had met there ten days earlier. Baggett now drove them to the house of the sugar mill in San Jose for a big breakfast of eggs and venison, the best feast they had had in weeks.

The war still had not touched this island. In the beautiful country home of the sugar mill manager, full of his pretty daughters and nieces gathered around the Americans in worshiping wonderment, the pilots daydreamed of spending the rest of the war here, away from the hunger and agony of Bataan.

The whole countryside around San Jose was in an uproar about the bombing of Waterous Field. Rumors were multiplying about how the Japanese were bombing the whole area. The Bataan Field pilots had an difficult time explaining to the local people that the Waterous bombing was only a mistake on the part of Obert. As for the radiogram, it turned out that it had not been sent from San Jose after all. It was now believed that the Japanese had sent it with the purpose of luring the Bataan Field pilots out on a wild goose chase.

Since Bataan Field was short of sugar, the pilots now decided they would each carry back a hundred-pound sack in their planes. It proved quite a job loading the bags in the back of their P-40s. Obert worried that they might jam the controls, but all decided to take the chance anyway.

Since Woolery and Hall still had their bombs, it was decided that they would make an attack on the Japanese at the front lines before coming into Bataan Field. Obert, with no more bombs, would fly top cover for Woolery and Hall to protect them for any Japanese attack from above while they picked out a suitable target and dive-bombed it.

The three P-40s cleared San Jose Field at about 9:00 A.M. and arrived a half hour later over northern Bataan in a cloudless sky. Woolery and Hall were at about 7,000 feet, and Obert was weaving about 1,000 feet higher over and to the rear of them. Then, over the northwest corner of Manila Bay, about a half mile from Bataan's shore, Woolery and Hall apparently spotted a target and both went into a dive, Hall about 300 yards behind Woolery.

For a few seconds, Obert took his eyes off the two P-40s while looking around for Japanese aircraft. The sky seemed deserted, so he looked back at where the P-40s should be. But they were nowhere to be seen! Suddenly, he was surprised by a large midair explosion far below him and off to one side, then saw a parachute and fragments of a plane falling into the water. On starting down to investigate, Obert momentarily glimpsed another plane near the surface of the water just as it burst into flames and crashed.

Assuming that the two planes were low-flying Japanese dive-bombers that Woolery and Hall had spotted and shot down, Obert started looking for his two flying mates and any possible other Japanese dive-bombers to pick off before heading home. For about a half hour, Obert flew around the area but could find no flying activity of any kind. Thinking that Hall and Woolery must have already returned, Obert headed into Bataan Field to land himself.

But back on the field, Obert was told that he was the first to land. Now getting worried, he remained on the field for the next hour, anxiously waiting for Woolery and Hall to return. But when the point was reached when the two pilots would have exhausted their fuel supply, Obert was forced to give up hope. General George and the pilots at Bataan Field were broken up over the unaccountable disappearance of Woolery and Hall, two of the best pilots of the little detachment. Hall was always the life of the party; they loved his rendition of a ditty about Saturday night in a small town. He was a real ham.

Both Woolery and Hall were good friends of Obert. The thought of being the sole survivor of the mission gave Obert the jitters. Of the four who had flown back from Del Monte ten days earlier, Woolery, Obert, Ibold, and Benson, Obert was the only one who had not dropped by the wayside. "The odds are against me now," he thought. "How long will it be before something happens to me?"

Everyone at Bataan Field was wondering what had happened to Woolery and Hall. It must have been their planes that Obert had seen bursting below him, but how to explain the incident? Obert had not noticed any Japanese antiaircraft fire in the area. The only plausible explanation appeared to be that the bombs of Woolery's plane in the lead had gone off prematurely, wrecking the P-40 behind it too. The fragmentation bomb mechanism was not the best in dependability, as shown in Ibold's crash, when the bombs should not have exploded. Perhaps Woolery had armed the bombs during the dive, triggering an explosion before they were released.

To replace Woolery and Hall in the flying detachment, General George contacted the 3rd and 34th pursuit squadrons on beach defense and asked for an experienced combat pilot from each. Hank Thorne selected Andy Krieger from the 3rd, and Shorty Crosland was picked from the 34th.[4]

On the afternoon of the day that Woolery and Hall were lost, Obert was ordered to report to Brig. Gen. Spencer Akin, Signal Corps chief of the USAFFE staff, who had asked General George for a pilot to fly a courier mission to Del Monte. Since Obert was the only Bataan Field pilot left who knew flying conditions between Bataan and Del Monte, General George detailed him for the assignment.

On Corregidor, General Akin told the young officer that "it was a matter of life or death" to get a new secret code through to San Jose, Cebu City, and Del Monte. "If you get this code to its destination," General Akin emphasized, "you will have accomplished more than if you went up and shot down a dozen bombers." Obert reassured Akin that he was sure that he could deliver it safely.

Taking off from Bataan Field before daylight on January 31, Obert arrived at San Jose, Mindoro, at sunrise. There he was given another good breakfast at the sugar mill manager's home. His P-40 refueled, Obert started for Cebu, his next stop. Low clouds and rainstorms forced him to hedgehop along the shoreline of the islands on the way. On arrival at Cebu, he was warmly welcomed by Lt. Col. Howard J. Edmands and Col. John D. Cook. After sharing a bottle of scotch and downing a lunch offered by Edmands, Obert took off for Del Monte, his final stop.

For this easy leg of the trip into Del Monte, Obert was under less nervous strain than before. He felt "pretty frisky" as he arrived over the base and decided to have some fun. Diving in out of the sun at five hundred miles an hour, he scattered officers, troops, Filipinos, and horses alike in all four directions "like a covey of quail." Landing at Del Monte No. 2 field, Obert had just gotten his plane under cover when twelve Japanese pursuit ships suddenly appeared over the base. "If my arrival had been a few minutes later," he reflected, "my scalp would now be on a Nip's scoreboard."

Obert received a much better reception at Del Monte this time than he had on his January fourth arrival. Colonel Elsmore even insisted that the young lieutenant join him for dinner when he heard of the purpose of his mission. The colonel wanted to hear all about Bataan operations and his old prewar friend, General George.

General Sharp was not at Del Monte at the time to receive the code and would not be arriving for three days, so Obert spent the following days sleeping and feasting on the good food at Del Monte. Bombers had been flying in from Australia to bring in supplies and take out pilots, so he was also able to pick up some good rumors about likely aid to the

Philippines in troops and planes. Everyone believed that help was on the way, as promised by President Roosevelt.

Obert also learned that Bob Duncan, who was one of the winners of the card cut of January 18 to decide who would have to fly back to Bataan, had been flown to Australia on January 26 in one of the two B-24s that had arrived on the night of January 25/26. Don Steele was also selected for the evacuation flight that night. Both pilots were to report to Barney Brodine for engineering duties on arrival in Australia.

Fred Roberts had tried to get himself on the list of thirty-two Air Corps personnel to be evacuated in the two bombers but was unsuccessful. Also on board was Joe Cole, who had been injured in his crash landing at Fabrica, Negros, on January 4, on the flight to Del Monte from Bataan. He had since been taken to Del Monte by boat to await evacuation to Australia.[5]

On February 3, General Sharp came into Del Monte, and Colonel Elsmore took Obert to see him. Reporting in to the general in his underground tunnel office, Obert now faced his stare. Then, his 6'6" body rising up from his chair, the general boomed, "What are you doing here? Did someone send you, or did you get scared on Bataan and run off with one of the planes?" Then he added, "Do you have written orders with you, sending you down here?"

First dumbfounded, then just "so damn mad that I wanted to turn and walk out before I started throwing things," Obert recovered his control sufficiently to pull out the written order from his pocket that had sent him to Del Monte and handed it over to the "old fogie." General Sharp now studied it closely, perhaps trying to ascertain if it had been forged or not. "How could he have thought I had run away?" Obert wondered. The mail and code he had brought with him should have been ample proof of his assertions.

That night, Air Corps personnel at Del Monte were all gathered around the club house, waiting and hoping that they would be on the list to return to Australia with bombers expected in from Australia that evening. The planes never did show up, but someone had gotten a lot of beer, so they all had a good party instead.

On the morning of February 4, Obert prepared for the trip back to Bataan. Just before he was to leave, Colonel Elsmore called him in and gave him a packet containing the united allied code, with instructions not to let it out of his hands until he had given it to a responsible officer. As Obert took his leave of the now-amiable colonel, Elsmore grinned and asked, "Will you try not to scare my troops when you leave, because it took me nearly a day to get them rounded up after the scare you gave them the other day."

After flying through the worst weather he had ever encountered in the Philippines, skimming along a few feet above the water, Obert reached

Cebu at noon. There he was taken to Colonel Cook, who had assembled a stack of items to take to Bataan "that would have required a B-17 to haul." Obert now picked out the most essential items, dumped them in a car, and drove to the field to load his P-40. Included were four bottles of brandy, tobacco, pipes, and several large slabs of milk chocolate. He put them all over the cockpit and inside the fuselage.

On the takeoff, the war-weary P-40 "moaned and groaned" under the load but managed to get airborne. The weather was still bad, but Obert worked his ship above it. At San Jose on Mindoro, he spent the afternoon so as to time his arrival into Bataan just at dark. Obert did not want any combat with his plane loaded down like it was.

Taking off from San Jose for the last leg of his trip, Obert had begun a normal roll, but when he was about two-thirds of the way down the strip, he realized that the overload was keeping him from getting off the ground as he should. Shoving his throttle into the override position for emergency power and gritting his teeth, Obert reached the end of the runway still on the ground and shot off into the fifty-foot-deep canyon at the end of the field. The P-40 dropped almost to the bottom of the canyon before it picked up enough speed to climb. A close one.

Darkness was just falling over Bataan as Obert brought his ship into the field. When his flying mates saw what he had brought for them, they almost went wild with excitement. Unknown to Obert, he had unwittingly introduced the idea for the "Bamboo Fleet" that would haul medicine and supplies into Bataan from the south during February and March.

5 On the evening of February 1, shortly after the eleven pilots of the Bataan Field Flying Detachment had turned in and were shooting the breeze, a call came in to get up. General George then told them that a large ship had towed a group of barges to Agloloma Bay. The Japanese were preparing to make a landing in the Anyasan/Silaiim area after being repulsed by beach defense fire in their initial effort to land at Agloloma. The pilots were to get ready for takeoff at 11:15 P.M. in the four available P-40s to bomb and strafe the thirteen barges, carrying an estimated one thousand Japanese.

Eight of the eleven pilots available were now selected to fly the mission: John Posten, Earl Stone, Sam Grashio, Ben Brown, Wilson Glover, Bill Baker, Kiefer White, and Lloyd Stinson.[6] Of the other candidates, Bill Rowe was ill that night, and Andy Krieger had just arrived from beach defense.[7] Charley Sneed was apparently left out because of his recent psychological problems regarding combat flying.

Hurriedly, the men of the Headquarters Squadron detachment hooked up the 30-pound fragmentation bombs under the wings of the two P-40Es and two P-40Bs flying the mission and loaded the guns of the four ships with .30- and .50-caliber ammunition. Then, beginning at 11:20 P.M., their

Allison engines screaming at full throttle, the heavily loaded ships lumbered down the runway and took off at fifteen-second intervals. First off were the two P-40Es, followed by the two P-40Bs.

Lloyd Stinson was in the second P-40B taking off, the last ship to leave the field. After clearing Bataan Field, he turned south and went almost to the southern tip of Bataan, then swung up the west coast, looking for the barges. It was a moonlit night, so he anticipated no trouble in locating them. But somehow he missed the barges and got as far north as Subic Bay.

Looking around for some activity, Stinson thought he saw supplies and Japanese on some docks and went into a diving attack. Pouring .30- and .50-caliber fire into the target, he was surprised to find that the flash and tracers from his two nose-mounted .50s were blinding him; it was the first time he had fired the guns of a P-40B. Circling around Subic Bay once more, Stinson spotted what looked like a cruiser. Pointing his P-40 down again, he went into a firing run on the anchored ship, then pulled away. He was surprised that the big ship did not fire back at him.

By now, Stinson reflected that he was not carrying out the mission he had been ordered to fly. Turning south, he now went looking again for barges off the west coast of Bataan. This time he found them. By chance, he happened upon them in such a way that his plane's position formed a 90-degree angle with the barges and the moon. They were really clear, in the moon's reflection. "What a beautiful target," he thought.

In his first run over the barges, Stinson withheld his gun fire so as to see the target better for his bomb drop. Then, on the second run, his six bombs released, he poured machine gun fire into the hapless men on the barges until his ammunition was exhausted.

The pilots in the other three P-40s had found the barges on the first try, one mile off the coast. To Sam Grashio, "It was just like looking down at a theater show from the balcony." Searchlights from the shore silhouetted the barges against the dark water of the South China Sea. After releasing their wing bombs, the excited young men, guided by the flaming arrows of tracer fire from the shore, flew back and forth over their targets, no higher than 200 feet, "stitching" every barge again and again, from stem to stern, tearing the Japanese troops to pieces, until they had to break off to return to Bataan Field for reloading their guns.

But the Japanese fought back, firing machine guns and cannon mounted on the barges at the attackers. Several of the P-40s were hit. Pulling out of his bomb run, Ben Brown's ship was struck by a 20-mm shell in the bottom of the fuselage. Brown picked up fragments in his knee. He landed with two flat tires.

As the planes came back in ones and twos to Bataan Field, they were checked out by the ground crew men and rearmed for a second sortie over the Japanese landing force, with a fresh pilot to fly each P-40. On its return from the first attack, Jesse White's P-40E came in looking almost white with its crust of salt from the spray of the sea, and riddled with machine gun fire. Walking around the plane, the pilot remarked to White, "This ship will never fly again." Demurring, White replied, "You flew it back, didn't you? It will fly again." The young crew chief did a quick inspection of his P-40 and found no damage to the engine, fuel and oil systems, or controls. Within half an hour, it was being flown back again to the target area.

By 3:00 A.M., the Bataan Field Flying Detachment's work was done. Eight sorties in all had been flown by the four P-40s. According to the records kept of the mission, they had dropped thirty-six bombs and fired ten thousand rounds of ammunition. To the pilots, it seemed that every last Japanese must have died, either from gunfire or from drowning. General George was ecstatic. Chocolates and pie were laid out for the pilots on their return. Later that morning after sunrise, enemy barges were seen disabled along the beaches, dead Japanese lying all around them. Two barges were spotted going north early in the morning. Roperts indicated that nine of the thirteen barges had been destroyed and a few more badly damaged.[8]

That day the ground crews at Bataan Field were fully occupied in repair work of all kinds on the warbirds. A sheet metal man was called in to patch the badly damaged fuselages. One P-40 had a hole through the propeller from an armor-piercing bullet. The electronic gunsight control of Jesse White's P-40 had been shot away. But by 4:00 P.M. the next day, four of the field's ships, the two P-40Bs and two P-40Es, were in commission. Two other P-40Es still required work.

21. "A TEN-THOUSAND-DOLLAR PILOT SHOT TO HELL IN THE INFANTRY"

1 Over on the west coast of Bataan at the camp of the 21st Pursuit Squadron, Ed Dyess (promoted eight days earlier to captain) had just gotten new orders on the afternoon of February 3. He was to take his men back to the Quinauan Point area to reinforce the 45th Philippine Scouts. During the six days since the 21st Pursuit had been relieved of duties in the Quinauan fighting, the scouts had been unable to make much progress against the dug-in Japanese. They had managed to clear the cliffs on each flank, however, boxing the Japanese in on Quinauan Point on three sides, with only the cliffs overlooking the beach to their rear open to them now.[1] But even though the 3rd Battalion, 45th Philippine Scouts, had been reinforced with Company B of the 57th Philippine Scouts on the evening of January 28 and a platoon of three light Stuart tanks from Company C of the 192nd Tank Battalion on February 2, the scouts were not able to advance more than fifty yards against the bottled-up Japanese, and that at a loss of about 50 percent of their effectives. The area was too restricted for support by artillery, and their 81-mm mortars were virtually useless because 75 to 85 percent of the ammunition was duds. Even most of their hand grenades were defective. And the newly arrived tanks were proving ineffective under the jungle conditions and in the absence of radio control.

For the men of the 21st, being ordered back into the fighting was worse than being sent in the first time, for now they knew what to expect. They were scared to death inside but afraid to show it outside. During their six-day rest back at their camp, conditions had been rough, having to bunk on the soft jungle floor, without enough to eat, and with thousands of warfare-disturbed monkeys in the foliage around them making a tremendous racket, but anything was better than having to go back to Quinauan.

In the late afternoon of February 3, Dyess and his men reported in to Col. Donald B. Hilton, executive officer of the 45th Philippine Scouts, who had been brought in the day before to take charge of the operation. Standing in the steaming jungle, droning with insects, they listened solemnly as Colonel Hilton briefed them. Hilton did not mince any words on the severity of the situation. "You see those white sheets over there?" he asked, pointing to an open area. "There are 21 scouts under them, dead." Dyess later recalled that "the sight and stench of death was everywhere."

Many of the men now exchanged their old Springfield rifles for the Garands of the scouts made surplus by the heavy scout casualties. Although Colonel Hilton was not happy about the 21st's lack of familiarity with the Garand, he permitted the exchange in the interests of morale. Less effective were the grenades delivered in Coca-Cola boxes to the squadron; when picked up, powder poured right out of the bottom of many of them. Colonel Hilton was concerned about the lack of infantry training of Dyess's squadron, but he hoped with their "native intelligence" and their relatively fresh condition the men could swing the balance in favor of his efforts to crush the stubborn Japanese resistance.

Just after daylight on the morning of February 4, the scout battalion and its reinforcements made ready for the day's offensive. One of the 21st Pursuit's three platoons of fifty men each was assigned to the left platoon of the battalion's Company I, a second went into the line between the first and second platoons of Company L, and the third was held in reserve.

At about 8:30, five tanks and a radio car arrived for the attack and pulled into position along the battalion line. The plan today was to direct each tank in its movements through use of walkie-talkie radios among the troops and maintaining one tank's radio in communication with the radio control car. The tanks were to deploy across the front of the center units, with the foot soldiers following behind at close distance.

In a foxhole behind the tanks, waiting for the tank platoon leader's siren to be sounded to signal the charge, S. Sgt. Cecil Ammons was suddenly stricken with a case of buck fever for the first time in his life. "Oh, God, don't let that siren go off!" he murmured to himself. Then he lit up a cigarette, which immediately calmed him down. When the siren sounded, the two Filipino scouts in the hole with him asked, "You ready, Joe?" The three then climbed out of the foxhole and joined up with the others.

When the siren went off, the men in the other platoon of the 21st Pursuit remained petrified. No one moved. Then 1st Sgt. "Diz" Huston, the squadron's senior noncom, finally yelled, "Goddammit, men, I hate to tell you, but son of a bitch, we got to charge 'em!" Huston's men with those of the scout company now rose from their foxholes and joined the others following behind the tanks.

Despite the improved communications, the tanks were still passing up enemy machine gunners and riflemen, who engaged the American and Filipino troops as soon as the tanks passed. In one such incident,

2nd Lt. Jimmy May of the 21st Pursuit was killed when a Japanese in a bypassed foxhole rose up and shot him as May followed behind one of the tanks.

Although progress was being made all along the line, with the Japanese being pushed back about to the cliff line by the time the attack was halted, casualties were heavy among both the scouts and the airmen. In addition to May, the 21st Pursuit lost S. Sgts. Bill Fowler and Ben Kerr and Cpl. Merrill Riner, killed in action, as well as several others wounded, including Sgt. J. W. Bohner. Fowler, a popular guitar player from Tennessee, often used to entertain his squadron mates with his rendition of "The Yellow Rose of Texas."

Just before 9:00 on the morning of February 5, Hilton prepared to launch a new attack, using basically the same procedures as the day before. Hilton had established his command post thirty yards to the rear of the center company, where he would maintain telephone communications with the flank units and walkie-talkie contact with the others, as well as radio contact with the tanks from the tank command car next to him. He also had messenger facilities at his disposal. In this way, he would be able to control the movement of the tanks in reducing the Japanese machine gun positions passed by and assist the rifle platoons in situations apparent only to them.

As the tanks advanced, slowly and cautiously, they fired into all observed and suspected enemy positions with their 37-mm cannon and three .30-caliber machine guns. The scouts and 21st Pursuit men advanced steadily behind the tanks. But when they reached an area made bare of trees by the tanks' fire and milling around, Japanese return fire became very intense, halting the advance.

In an effort to push the 21st's left platoon ahead, Colonel Hilton then joined the men where they were held to the ground. As he was surveying the situation from immediately in the rear of a rifleman, one of the tanks, forty yards to the right front in the clearing, came to a stop. The turret of the Stuart opened sufficiently for one of the crew to yell back that an enemy soldier was under the tank and to point down toward his left track.

The rifleman in front of Colonel Hilton, Pvt. Rolland Chenoweth, had been watching and quickly sized up the situation. When he received a nod of approval from Hilton, Chenoweth jumped to his feet and ran across the exposed area to the tank. Reaching the Stuart, he brought his automatic rifle up to shoot into the foxhole, partly covered by the tank track. But just then the Japanese soldier in the hole fired, his shot striking and demolishing Chenoweth's left hand. In severe shock, Chenoweth dropped his rifle and staggered about in a dazed condition. Hilton helped him back to the cover of the woods before Chenoweth collapsed, applied a first aid bandage to his hand, then had him conducted to the aid station. For his gallantry, Hilton recommended Chenoweth for the award of the Silver Star.

By this time, riflemen were again advancing behind the tanks, and shortly before noon all platoons had reached the cliff above the beach at Quinauan Point. Then Hilton called in the third platoon of the 21st Pursuit from reserve to mop up.

The 21st had suffered only one fatality this time—Sgt. Jack McClintock. But the battle was not yet won. The surviving Japanese had taken refuge in caves in the cliff and among the trees, shrubbery, and large boulders of the beach below. And all approaches were covered by Japanese machine gun and rifle fire.

Near the cliff, "Diz" Huston and Cecil Ammons were sitting on a log, resting near one of the tanks, and having a smoke. Diz had a whole string of grenades and Ammons a Garand with bandoliers of ammunition around his chest. Then Ammons began wondering about a foxhole near them. "Gimme one of them grenades, I'm gonna throw it into that hole," Ammons told Huston. Standing up, pulling the pin, and counting to three, Ammons pitched it underhand. The grenade hit the bank and fell into the hole. Suddenly, a Japanese appeared from the hole, and Ammons unloaded his Garand on him. When Ammons then reached for his .45, it was gone. Diz had lifted it just before, ready to fire on any other Japanese coming out of the hole.

After this incident, the two senior noncoms worked together as a team and became well known for their effectiveness against the Japanese at Quinauan. Ammons picked up the nickname "Killer," given to him by his platoon CO, Lt. Jack Donalson.

One of the 21st's men whom Hilton had used as a runner between his command post and the front line the day before had a hair-raising experience. Sgt. John Cowgill had wandered way into the Japanese lines in his efforts to locate the constantly changing American/Filipino line. Realizing something was wrong, he reversed and ran a zigzag course as fast as he could as a hail of bullets whizzed past him. After resting ten minutes to recover his breath, he headed back out the right way to the lines. Reporting back to Hilton after his mission was completed, he told Hilton how rough it was to be a runner, without a compass, just going by feel. Laconically, the colonel replied, "I know, son, but that's war," and assigned Cowgill another message run.

At the end of the long day, Hilton's men dug in along the cliff line and put out patrols down along the beach to prevent any Japanese escaping through or around them during the night.

2 On the morning of February 6, Colonel Hilton tried various methods to get the remaining Japanese in the caves below the cliff line to surrender. Searching fire was delivered from every available position on the cliff

tops. The remaining hand grenades, including ones improvised with dynamite in bamboo stems, were thrown against the Japanese positions. Gasoline bombs were dropped off the cliffs. But all efforts proved futile. Any attempt to go below the cliff resulted in casualties.

Late that afternoon, Hilton attempted to get a gunboat to come up from Mariveles to shell the cliff from seaside, but one was not available for the next morning. Hilton decided to try dynamiting the cliffs instead to see if that would seal the Japanese in their caves.

Next morning, the dynamiting scheme was put into action. A detachment of engineers under Col. Harry Skelly lowered fifty-pound boxes of dynamite with time fuses over the cliff to each cave suspected to be harboring Japanese. When the boxes reached the cave mouths, they were detonated. This tactic collapsed only some of the caves but left considerable Japanese firepower.

That afternoon, Hilton called in Dyess. Hilton had received an order from General Pierce to send an officer and twelve men from the 21st Pursuit to Mariveles to embark on navy landing craft for transport during the night to Quinauan Point, where they were to assault the beach at daybreak on February 8. Hilton told Dyess to make up his landing party. Dyess put himself in charge of the operation and obtained twelve volunteers from his enlisted men. One, S. Sgt. Bob Miller, did not actually "volunteer"; Dyess wanted him along because of his demonstrated prowess with a rifle. Later, Jack Donalson asked to be included in the party too, and his offer was accepted. After Dyess departed with his group for Mariveles, a new survey of Japanese positions on the cliff was made, and each probable location was indicated by a white marker directly over the cliff top.

3 As the light of dawn broke over western Bataan on February 8, the American and Filipino troops on the cliffs were all in readiness for the arrival of the navy boats. But the boats did not materialize. Finally, at about eight o'clock, in broad daylight, the small force came into view. There were two motor launches, each towing a whaleboat.

Maneuvering in attack formation, the launches slowed down to avoid submerged rocks, then approached the cliffs within firing distance of the 37-mm guns mounted on the bow and their four .50-caliber machine guns, two mounted on each side. After the launches blasted the positions targeted the day before with the white markers, the two unarmed whaleboats carrying the landing party of the 21st Pursuit were cut loose and began to head in to shore under their own power. Just then, the men heard airplanes overhead and looked up. A formation of three Japanese dive-bombers was passing almost directly over them. Apprehensively, the men stared up at the planes; to their relief, the Japanese continued south along the coast.

One whaleboat carrying Dyess and his group now approached the south side of Quinauan Point, and the other whaleboat under Donalson's command was heading for the north side of the point. The plan was for the two groups to work themselves around toward each other, clearing out the Japanese as they combed the beach area.

As Dyess and his seven men prepared to jump out of their boat and wade in, the sound of firing from the beach transfixed them.[2] The men were just scared to death, sitting ducks as they were to the unseen Japanese. Then Dyess yelled loud and clear at his charges—"I thought you were men! Well, aren't you?" The spell broken, the men now all jumped out of the boat, landing in water up to their necks. Waves were rolling in and out. Sgt. John Cowgill found himself tiptoeing from large rock to large rock. Loaded down with a gas mask bag full of grenades, his rifle, and ammunition for S. Sgt. Jerry Karlik, he slipped and took some water, then gained his footing again.

Reaching the beach, Cecil Ammons, the senior noncom in Dyess's boat, assigned the six other men to clear out a brush area as he and Dyess sprayed positions on the beach ahead of the men with their heavy Lewis machine guns. Running across a Japanese lying down in the open, Ammons was suspicious and said to Dyess, "Captain, I don't believe that Nip's dead!" Wiggling his Lewis gun barrel up and down till he got it aimed on the head of the Japanese, Ammons fired a short burst. The Japanese bounced to a sitting position, then fell over. He had been alive, all right; he had his hand in his pocket on a grenade, playing possum.

Nearby, Sergeant Cowgill and the other enlisted men were making good progress. Cowgill and Karlik were working as a team. Cowgill would hurl grenades, then Karlik in front of him would spray the area with his Thompson submachine gun. He was using an asbestos glove to hold the gun barrel, which could become very hot.

Suddenly they heard the sound of a plane overhead and looked up. It was a Japanese dive-bomber low over the trees, and a stick of bombs was falling diagonally across the cliff and beach at them. Dyess had spotted the plane seconds before, and he and Ammons got down. But one of the fragmentation bombs landed near the six enlisted men, and the explosion sprayed shrapnel in their direction.

Karlik, who had just stood up to fire into a Japanese position, was hit in several places, leaving gaping wounds all over his body. Behind him, Cowgill, in a semicrouched position, was blown down. Since he was shielded by Karlik, he suffered only small shrapnel wounds in his neck and chest, and both eardrums broken.

Unable to find his rifle, and mad as hell as Karlik lay dying next to him, Cowgill yelled at some Philippine Scouts up on the cliff to come down and help him with Karlik. When they balked out of fear, Cowgill threatened them, and only then did they respond to the black-faced sergeant, who was overflowing with hatred for the Japanese as blood oozed from the many wounds of his buddy. But it was too late for Karlik. Also hit in Dyess's group in the bombing attack was Pvt. Perry Garrett, who had a finger blown off.

Just as they had reached shore, Lieutenant Donalson and his men from the other whaleboat hurriedly took cover as the dive-bombers passed overhead, but the Japanese did not drop bombs on their side of Quinauan Point. When the danger had passed, Donalson led his men in an equally action-packed operation. Firing his Lewis machine gun from the hip, he felt like he was reliving an adventure from an old movie of Victor McLaglen holding off a band of desert tribesmen. At one point, he was checking a group of "dead" Japanese when he noticed the belly moving of one who had a big leaf covering his head. Donalson fired, and the Japanese came straight up in a sitting position, his eyes rolling, then fell back, dead.

In addition to the bombs that fell on the beach and killed Karlik, others landed among the 21st Pursuit's men and the scouts on the top of the cliff. The three "Anns" had made a single pass over the area, with deadly results. S. Sgt. Frank Harangody lost a leg and Cpl. Maurice Freeland both legs to shrapnel, one above and the other below the knee. A Filipino that Lieutenant Parcher had sent for water was blown literally in half. Bombs also fell in a machine gun position in the rear manned by the 34th Pursuit, killing Pfc Orville Cox, blowing off the right arm of Pvt. Derrell Sharp, and wounding Pvt. Tom Chandler in the neck, back, and legs and Pvt. Jesse Marshall in the groin.

Then, as the two motor launches were proceeding back to Mariveles, the empty whaleboats left behind, they in turn were attacked by the persistent Japanese dive-bombers. A salvo of bombs crashed down on the leading boat, blowing a hole in its bottom, and the second launch was also hit. Two men were killed and fifteen wounded, including Lieutenant Commander Goodall, in charge of the operation, hit in the foot. The lead launch had to be beached, though the other damaged boat made it safely back to Mariveles.

At Quinauan Point, patrols of the scouts had now worked their way down to the beaches through the ravines, clearing out the few remaining Japanese from their entrenched positions. By 1:50 P.M., the sector was "completely cleared up," according to the operations officer of I Corps.

Colonel Hilton now tallied the losses on both sides of the bloody engagement. The Scout's 3rd Battalion had lost 74 men killed and 234 wounded out of a total strength of about 495, or over 60 percent casualties in the twelve days it was in action. Japanese losses were calculated at 408 killed and 6 taken prisoner. Of these, 385 had actually been buried by the scouts and the rest estimated by the number of graves as buried by the Japanese, with others contained in dynamited caves.

The 21st Pursuit had suffered relatively few casualties: six killed and an undetermined number wounded. The scouts just could not understand how the 21st Pursuit could have gotten off so lightly. A scout captain, an American infantry officer, expressed the feelings of the others when he told Dyess, "I don't know how in the world you have a man walking! You had no training in infantry and came down here like a bunch of wild Indians, and have 15 or 20 killed and wounded, and my company has got only 11 men left not killed or wounded!"

The next day, the 21st Pursuit participated in the search and cleaning up operations. It was a most unpleasant task, involving digging dead Japanese out of the caves and other positions. The stench of the dead and the swarms of flies in the battle-racked area were unbearable, making it difficult for the men to keep their meals down.

The following day, the 21st Pursuit was relieved of its duties and went into bivouac at Kilometer Post 184.7. The 34th Pursuit was being assigned to take over the Quinauan beach defense from the 21st. Colonel Hilton watched the 21st Pursuit's men as they marched out of the area along the jungle trail past his command post to their old bivouac area for a well-deserved rest. "I would have liked to thank each one personally for his splendid work," he reminisced five years later.

4 On the morning of February 2, the American and Filipino forces in the Anyasan/Silaiim area saw for the first time the extent of the destruction wrought before daylight on the Japanese force that had attempted to land on the beach below the cliffs. Disabled barges were drifting aimlessly about with dead Japanese lying all around them. One was near the beach. A couple of 17th Pursuit men swam out to look it over. They found only some stale bread, a rifle, and "plenty of blood."

But some of the Japanese force had managed to get ashore and now reinforced the other Japanese, who were bottled up at the edge of Anyasan and Silaiim points, concealed in canebrakes, thicket, and creek bottoms. The American and Filipino line extended four hundred to six hundred yards from the beach in a semicircle. The day before, north units had attempted to link up with south units, but had been turned back by heavy Japanese machine gun fire. During the next days, the 2nd Battalion, 45th Philippine Scouts, reinforced by the 3rd Battalion, 57th Philippine Scouts, made repeated attacks, gradually reducing the stubborn Japanese force.

Directly behind the assault battalions of the Philippine Scouts, the 17th Pursuit Squadron continued to patrol the trails. Then on February 4, the airmen moved up to the front line, occupying a position next to Company E of the 45th Scouts. Two days later they were shifted north to take over from the battalion of the 12th Regiment Philippine Army on the beach north of Silaiim Bay. They now covered the defenses from the Silaiim River north to Canas Point.

On the night of February 7/8, between 3:00 and 4:00 A.M., several new attempts were made by the Japanese to land reinforcements in Silaiim Bay. Some seventy-five Japanese managed to get ashore from two or three barges, despite being brought under machine gun fire by the 45th Scouts and the 17th Pursuit as well as strafing from P-40s that flew five sorties from Bataan and Cabcaben fields.

A renewed landing attempt on the evening of February 8/9 also was repulsed in the face of artillery and machine gun fire from the beaches. At dawn, seven barges were seen about five miles offshore and were immediately subjected to 155-mm fire from the beach. Several were sunk, and many Japanese were seen trying to swim to shore. One mile to the north, at Canas Point, Lt. Joe McClellan of the 17th Pursuit spotted some thirty to forty Japanese swimming to shore at 10:00 A.M. from a barge. Patrols were alerted to try to capture them.

With reinforcement efforts thwarted, the remnants of the Japanese force landed two weeks earlier were now desperate. Attempts to break through the line that encircled them on the afternoon of February 9 and morning of the tenth were repulsed. But at dawn on February 11, the north group of the Japanese attacked in force and broke through a gap in the line of the 45th Scouts. The Japanese first moved north to the Silaiim River, then east, following the river through the jungle. At the mouth of the Silaiim River, the Japanese reached the command post of the 17th Pursuit and immediately brought it under heavy attack. Relatively few men of the squadron were in the area of the command post; most were spread out along the beach between Silaiim and Canas Point.

Surprised by the unexpected intrusion of the enemy, 17th Pursuit CO, Spud Sloan, and 2nd Lt. Ted Bronk, the squadron's medical officer, hit the ground, pinned down by Japanese fire. Sloan soon realized that the Japanese outnumbered the small group in the immediate area of the command post. He now decided to try to reach his men to tell them to move back. During a lull in the shooting, Sloan got up and moved a short distance in the jungle, but when he reached the nearby footpath, where the Japanese force was concentrated, he was hit in the abdomen and thigh by 6.5-mm machine gun fire. A few feet away, Bronk could not see Sloan in the thick foliage but heard him cry out, "Doc, I'm shot!"

Just then, several of the squadron's men nearby ran back to the rear to escape the Japanese and had to jump over Bronk as he lay on the ground waiting for Sloan to return. Bronk's initial reaction was to run back with the men, but he now knew that Spud was shot and needed his help. Working his way forward, Bronk reached Sloan and proceeded to give him first aid. He had sustained a gaping wound in the thigh that caused him a great deal of pain and concern, but the first aid alleviated that. Bronk was much more worried about Sloan's abdominal wounds, though they did not disturb him more than his thigh injury. With the help of several men of the squadron that he was able to recruit, Bronk managed to get through the thick jungle with Sloan without being detected by the Japanese, even though there was shooting all around him. Finally reaching the main road, the group caught a ride to the main hospital at Little Baguio, arriving there late in the day.

On the way to the hospital, Bronk commented, but not to Sloan, that Sloan was developing peritonitis from his abdominal wound. Sloan was joking the whole way about his injuries and complaints of the pain, but Bronk felt very frustrated and sad; he knew the peritonitis would prove fatal. That night, on the operating table, Sloan died. His sense of humor now gone, his last words were, "A ten-thousand-dollar pilot shot to hell in the infantry."

5 On the morning of February 12, the group of Japanese that had overrun the Silaiim area was surrounded and wiped out by the scouts. By 3:00 P.M. the Scouts and the 17th Pursuit pushed through to the beaches. The Anyasan/Silaiim sector operation was now completed. Some four hundred Japanese were estimated to have been killed in the operation since February 1.

Finally relieved of its beach defense duties, the tired men of the 17th Pursuit now proceeded to rest camp at Kilometer Post 184 near the Biaan River. In the 2½-week operation, the squadron had lost two of its officers killed, but no enlisted men. A few days later, 1st Lt. Hugh "Tex" Marble of the 20th Pursuit was designated CO of the 17th Pursuit to replace Sloan.

22. "THAT'S HOW THE SLANT-EYED BASTARDS ARE WORKING NOW"

1 When Dave Obert arrived back at Bataan Field at dusk on February 4 after completing his mission south to deliver new secret codes, he found out that a similar mission had been flown from Bataan Field that morning. Capt. Bill Bradford, the forty-seven-year-old engineering officer of the field, had taken a former Philippine Air Corps O-1 biplane to Iloilo to deliver special codes and a letter of instruction to Brig. Gen. Bradford Chynoweth, commander of USAFFE forces on Panay. While there, he found his old NPC-9 Bellanca Skyrocket from PATCO (Philippine Aerial Taxi Company) days and arranged to swap his O-1 for it on his next trip to Iloilo. Other unusual missions were flown from Bataan that first week of February, including an attack on the Japanese landing party in the Anyasan/Silaiim area of the west coast on the night of February 1/2.

On the afternoon of February 1, five of the pilots—White, Stinson, Grashio, Baker, and Krieger—were selected to fly a mission to Manila and a few other places to drop propaganda leaflets. These were copies of President Quezon's speech denouncing the new Japanese-controlled Philippines government and urging Filipinos to keep fighting. Stinson for one was not happy with the idea of flying over Manila just to drop some papers. Arriving over the capital dutifully, he opened his canopy and threw bundles of leaflets out with his left hand while holding the stick with his right hand. His cockpit full of leaflets, he was glad not to have run into any Japanese interceptors that afternoon. Stinson and the others all returned safely to the field after the mission.

On the afternoon of February 4, MacArthur's chief of staff telephoned Capt. Ozzie Lunde, S-3 operations officer of the 5th Interceptor Command at Little Baguio, with an order for the Bataan Field pilots to fly a mission to northern Luzon to drop medical supplies to American and Filipino forces cut off at Jones, Isabella Province, two hundred miles behind Japanese lines. Charley Sneed and Bill Rowe were given the assignment but were unable to get off as scheduled the next morning, as their P-40s were not ready for the flight. At 6:00 A.M. the next day, February 6, they took off while it was still dark at Bataan Field in two P-40Es equipped with belly tanks for the long mission. A Japanese "Nate" that had been waiting overhead tried to intercept them over the field but was unable to catch them as they flew north without lights.

Arriving over Mount Arayat near Clark Field, Rowe found another Japanese aircraft with two red lights on its wings patrolling in the area. When Rowe approached him to attack, the Japanese put out his lights, obliging Rowe to abort his attempt. As he finally arrived in the area of Jones, Rowe spotted a schoolhouse with a white cross painted on it. Descending to 1,800 feet, he pulled back his canopy and then threw medical supplies, packed in containers that the Japanese had originally used for the same purpose, out the cockpit. Climbing to 19,000 feet, Rowe now headed home, alone. Looking down from his high vantage point, the veteran 17th Pursuiter was impressed with how small Bataan appeared to be. In a few minutes, Rowe was joined by Sneed at the high altitude, who passed him on the homeward flight.

As he neared Bataan Field, Rowe got an "all clear" signal on his radio and dropped his ship to 2,000 feet, preparatory to landing. Then suddenly his radio crackled with a voice warning of Japanese planes to the northeast of him. Spotting two enemy pursuit at about 8,000 feet, Rowe gave his P-40 the gun and climbed straight toward them, almost stalling out. As he got close under them, one peeled off and headed for him. Maintaining his position until he figured the Japanese would start firing, he now cut under the ship, but a bit too late; he had taken several hits in his wings. Then when the "Nate" half-rolled at him, Rowe went into a half-roll himself, then into a dive, doing 460 MPH with his belly tank still on. The Japanese did not follow. After getting the "all clear" signal from the Bataan Field operations post, Rowe now brought his ship in for a safe landing. Sneed came in moments later. The Japanese were still in the immediate vicinity, though.

This would be Charley Sneed's last mission for the Flying Detachment. He had lost the confidence of the other pilots at Bataan Field with his performance of the last three weeks, including aborting missions and declining to engage in combat on January 26. His nerves had deteriorated to the point where he could no longer function as a combat pilot, though no one questioned his courage or capabilities. On the recommendation of Lt. Col. Bill Kennard, the 5th Interceptor Command surgeon, General George decided to replace him on February 9 as the detachment flying commander. It was arranged to have him assigned to Little Baguio as assistant to Capt. Allison Ind, S-2 intelligence officer of the 5th Interceptor Command. As the most senior officer of the detachment, Ben Brown was now picked by General George to take over as the flying commander.

2 On the morning of February 6, Bataan Field was bombed by three "Anns," the third time in three days that the field had been hit by the troublesome single-engine dive-bombers. Although none of the field's planes had been hit on these raids, General George decided to shift half his force of eight P-40s that night to Cabcaben Field, two and one half miles south, for improved protection. The new field, built by contractor forces, was now operational, having been extended to 3,900 feet and turned over to Company C of the 803rd Aviation Engineers for maintenance. Kiefer White, Sam Grashio, Lloyd Stinson, and Bill Baker were selected to ferry the four P-40s to Cabcaben. The transfer was to take place at night, to avoid any unwelcome Japanese intentions and hide the movement from them.

The pilots were briefed on the new field's characteristics. Landings were to be made east to west, from Manila Bay toward the face of Mariveles Mountain, and uphill. With a high ridge on each side of the field and a mountain at the end, once committed to land, a go-around for a second landing attempt was considered impossible. Because of a postponement, it was not until 2:00 A.M. when the four pilots took off from Bataan Field. A few minutes later, as White approached Cabcaben Field and flashed his lights, the mobile night landing lights of the field were switched on, faintly outlining the strip. Making a straight-in approach, White brought his P-40 down safely. Before his plane had stopped rolling, Grashio signaled with his lights as he started to come in. He too landed without incident.

But when Stinson started to come in, the landing lights suddenly were switched off, signaling that something had gone wrong and constituting an order not to land. Unknown to Stinson, some water buffalo had been spotted crossing the field and had to be chased off. Reacting quickly, Stinson gunned the engine past the red line on the Allison's manifold pressure indicator, pulled up, then turned left over the left ridge, since it was lower than the one on the right, and barely cleared it. Right behind Stinson was Baker, who had also just barely pulled up his ship in time too.

As Stinson and Baker headed in for a second landing try, the lights were on again; the carabao had been chased off. Just as they approached the field, however, the lights were suddenly switched off again. The carabao had returned. Stinson cleared the left ridge again, and so did Baker, but then Baker's engine coughed, and the P-40 went into a stall just beyond the ridge. Crashing against a hill near Bataan Hospital No. 2 just south of Cabcaben, Baker's ship exploded in a fiery light.

Transfixed, the men at Cabcaben Field could see the red glow of the burning aircraft. The crackling sound of exploding .50-caliber ammunition of the P-40's guns added to the terror of the night scene. Then Grashio yelled, "Someone call General George and tell him Baker has crashed!"

Grashio figured that Baker, his classmate in 41-C at Kelly Field, was gone.

Getting into a command car, Grashio drove over to Hospital No. 2 to pick up help, but when the group minutes later tried to approach the scene of the accident, the P-40's ammunition was still exploding in all directions, and they were sure that there was no chance for Baker. Kiefer White, one of the more emotional members of the detachment, was practically crying.

But when the ferry pilots returned to Bataan Field later that evening, they were told by a sergeant that word had been received that Baker had survived, through some miracle. He had been found by men of the 200th Coast Artillery stationed near the field, staggering aroung in the woods. Evidently he had been thrown clear of the plane, which was demolished and strewn over five hundred feet of woods.

The next morning, Grashio and White visited Baker in the hospital. Although terribly burned and bandaged to the eyes, with a possible skull fracture, his situation was not critical. He had no recollection of what happened from the moment of impact until he regained consciousness and started walking in the woods. Although Baker returned to Bataan Field after his recovery, he would be flying no more missions for the detachment. The same was true for Bob Ibold, who eleven days earlier had also experienced a near-fatal crash and had returned to Bataan Field only on February 4.

The accidents to Baker and Ibold put the effective pilot strength of the Bataan Field Flying Detachment down to twelve. This figure included Shorty Crosland, who had reported in for flying duty on February 3 following his release from beach defense obligations with his 34th Pursuit Squadron. But with his P-40s reduced to seven following Baker's crash, General George felt no need to bring in more pilots. There were almost two pilots for each of his steadily dwindling number of pursuit planes.

3 That night, Grashio, White, and Stinson were back at Bataan Field after having visited Baker in the hospital. Then at 10:00 P.M., they were abruptly awakened from their slumber, along with the other pilots of the detachment. They were being put on alert for a possible bombing and strafing mission against Japanese barges observed northwest of Quinauan Point. An hour earlier, MacArthur's G-3 operations officer had telephoned General George with the order, and George had responded that he could have his pilots ready in an hour. George was to await a direct call from the chief of staff of I Corps on western Luzon for the mission to be flown.

But as the hours went by, no call from the I Corps came in. A rumor began circulating that the mission was off. But then, just after midnight MacArthur's G-3 phoned his counterpart in the 5th Interceptor Command at Little Baguio, Ozzie Lunde, that the pilots, by now restless to go back to sleep, were to stay on the alert until I Corps relieved them. Then at

3:30 A.M., the order came through. General George now instructed White, Grashio, and Stinson to go back to Cabcaben Field to fly the three P-40s there, while Obert, Posten, and Stone were to take the other three P-40s in commission at Bataan Field.

On his takeoff from Cabcaben, White ground-looped, wiping out the P-40E, but fortunately suffered no injury himself. Grashio and Stinson managed to get off all right.[1] Posten led off from Bataan Field and was rudely surprised to find his own antiaircraft firing at him, but it missed in the pitch darkness.

When the three Bataan Field pilots arrived over Silaiim Bay, they found several barges just pulling into shore. Experiencing difficulty picking out their targets in the shadows of the shoreline, Obert, Posten, and Stone released their 30-pound fragmentation bombs and poured machine gun fire into two barges. To his surprise, Obert found himself under attack by a Japanese night fighter and was shot at twice but was unable to follow the aircraft. Each of the five pilots flew only one mission, but it was 6:30 in the morning before they finished up. After eating breakfast at 6:45, they turned in, dead tired from having stayed up the whole night.

Unknown to General George and his Bataan Field pilots, General Wainwright, commanding I Corps, in the late afternoon that day had asked MacArthur's G-3 to request MacArthur's headquarters for an aerial reconnaissance of the west coast of Bataan each evening, to be flown just before dark. But two hours later, the G-3 officer called Wainwright's chief of staff to notify him that the request for that evening's air reconnaissance had arrived too late for execution. The G-3 also informed the chief of staff that I Corps was not to call General George directly for any reconnaissance missions, a procedure the chief of staff had evidently believed was approved. This time-saving arrangement applied only in the case of *combat* missions to repulse attempted Japanese landings, as agreed between USAFFE and I Corps on February 2 following the first aerial attack on Japanese landings of February 1/2.

That night, at 3:50 A.M., the Japanese made yet another landing attempt in the Siliaiim/Anyasan area, but this time General George's pilots were not called in to oppose it. Nor did USAFFE order them to fly any more reconnaissance missions over the west coast of Bataan, as requested by I Corps. Furthermore, when I Corps asked USAFFE on February 11 to request General George to mount a combat mission against dive-bombers attacking the area of the junction of the Cotas and Tuol rivers (in the Battle of the Pockets), it was flatly turned down: "We don't feel we can risk what we have on this mission." MacArthur was clearly concerned about maintaining what few P-40s he had for purposes vital to the campaign.

4 Beginning about 8:00 A.M. on February 6, USAFFE forces on Corregidor, Carabao, and El Fraile islands were subjected for the first time to artillery fire. The Japanese were now operating 105-mm batteries in the Ternate area just some ten miles across Manila Bay from Corregidor. Although efforts were made that day to get a fix on the location of the guns, they were unsuccessful, as the guns were in defiladed positions in valleys and were fired with the sun behind them, blocking observation of the gun flashes.

What was needed was photos of the Ternate area in order to pinpoint the Japanese artillery positions so that Corregidor could more accurately return the fire with its big guns. This would require an aerial photographic mission, but not by the P-40s of the Bataan Field Flying Detachment; aerial cameras could not be operated from such pursuit ships. An observation plane was needed, and the Philippine Army Air Corps still had a few two-seater Stearman 76D3 biplane trainers suitable for the job.

On the morning of February 6, MacArthur's chief of staff ordered the USAFFE's air officer on Corregidor to have the PAAC prepare to fly a photographic mission of the Ternate area. When the order was received by the PAAC on Bataan, Capt. Jesus Villamor, a flying hero of the early days of the campaign, volunteered for the job. He had had training in aerial photography before. Volunteering and selected to fly with Villamor as the photographer was M. Sgt. Juan Abanes of the 5th Photographic Squadron. Villamor would pilot the plane from the back seat, with Abanes up front with the big camera.

Since flying the old, unarmed, fabric-covered biplane, unable to make more than 100 MPH, would be suicide in the likely event of interception by Japanese fighters, General George arranged for five of his remaining six P-40s in commission to be flown as escort on the mission, which was now set for February 9. Assignments for the escort mission were now given out. Lloyd Stinson would take off from Cabcaben Field and fly top cover at 23,000 feet, serving as a lookout for the others. Dave Obert and his wingman, John Posten, were assigned at 19,000 feet, with Obert to take off from Cabcaben and Posten from Bataan Field, linking up after takeoff. Flight leader Ben Brown and his wingman, Earl Stone, would fly from Bataan Field and provide cover for Villamor from 17,000 feet. Villamor himself would fly at 15,000 feet after takeoff from Bataan Field.

At 1:00 P.M. on a balmy, clear day, with only a few broken clouds in the sky, Brown gunned his motor and raced down the 5,100-foot strip, followed within seconds by Stone. About fifteen minutes later, Villamor and Abanes in the old 76D3 were airborne, followed immediately by Posten. Over on Cabcaben Field, Stinson had taken off at 1:00 P.M., followed by Obert at 1:15 P.M. After gaining sufficient altitude, Villamor headed his biplane southeast, straight across the South Channel of Manila Bay for the Ternate region, only some sixteen miles distant from Bataan

A Stearman 76D3 armed trainer of the Philippine Army Air Corps. This was the type of plane flown by Lieutenant Villamor on February 9, 1942, on his photographic mission and also by pilots escaping from Corregidor in April, 1942. *Courtesy Boeing Company, via A. A. Anido*

Field. At staggered altitude above him were his five guardian angels. All the way, an anxious Villamor bobbed and turned, "scanning every corner of the sky." Shortly after Stinson, at 23,000 feet, reached the general area of the destination, he realized that he had lost sight of the others. He was not perturbed, however. He was looking more for Japanese aircraft at his altitude than down at his own, following his instructions.

Arriving safely over the Ternate region, Villamor wiggled his wings to indicate he was ready to begin his photo runs. Above him, Ben Brown acknowledged by wiggling back. Then Villamor begain weaving in a photographic pattern, making wide, slow turns so Abanes could get his shots. The sky was so peaceful. Where were the Japanese planes? Villamor wondered. Now more relaxed, he decided to stay over the area long enough to allow Abanes to finish the whole roll of 110 shots instead of the original plan to take 12 photos only. As the Stearman shuttled back and forth between Lake Taal to the southeast and the immediate Ternate region, four P-40s a few thousand feet higher were weaving for Villamor. No Japanese aircraft were in sight.

Unseen by the pilots, a Mitsubishi Ki-46 "Dinah" reconnaissance aircraft was flying north from the southern end of Manila Bay, spotted by the antiaircraft units on Corregidor.[2] High above the area, Stinson picked up calls on his radio of a twin-engine enemy observation plane in his vicinity, but though he searched the sky for the Japanese, he could not find him. Had the snooper seen the P-40s and the Stearman over the Ternate area?[3]

A few minutes later, Villamor's plane spiraled down, signaling that the photo work was finished. Now the four P-40s closed over him, and all headed toward Bataan Field. Over Corregidor, two-thirds of the way home, Villamor dropped to about 3,500 feet and made a few slow turns, then executed a "jaunty figure eight" over the heavily bombed and shelled island, to let the onlookers "share in the joy of my successful mission," as Villamor recorded years later.

Unknown to Villamor (his plane had no radio), the escorting P-40s had picked up a call just about the time they descended to link up with the Stearman trainer at the end of the photographic session. In quick, sharp words, Capt. Ozzie Lunde at Little Baguio had called, "9 M N to Leo, 9 M N to Leo, enemy pursuit taking off from hostile field . . . six enemy pursuit coming in your direction—Take care, Take care!"[4]

Now back over the Bataan Field area at 4,000 feet, the four P-40s circled as the Stearman started its descent to land. The pilots were keeping an eye out for the expected arrival of the Japanese. Over at neighboring Cabcaben Field, Stinson was now just landing and saw the biplane coming in at Bataan Field just north of him, the protecting P-40s above. Stinson himself had remained over the mission area until he figured the others had finished their work and then had headed back.

At Bataan Field, Obert now noticed a plane weaving down from behind the P-40s. He thought it was Stinson coming down from high altitude but then realized that it was Japanese. Ben Brown and the other two P-40 pilots also saw the Japanese, six of them, diving down from the left.

Below them, Villamor was about to swing into his landing pattern when he noticed the P-40s had broken from their protective net and had shot forward in a burst of speed. Then he saw the Japanese planes in their dive and realized that they were after him. To Villamor, it seemed the Japanese had figured it would be easier to get the photo ship on return over its field than in the open sky over Ternate, where it could escape.

Faced with the alternative of trying for a landing or bailing out, Villamor quickly opted for the former. Ignoring the warning he had been given not to dive with the rickety biplane, he now nosed the Stearman down in a steep descent, then pulled out at 1,000 feet. The wings held, and he found no Japanese on his tail.

There was no time for the four P-40s to gain altitude: the Japanese fighters, which looked to Posten like P-26s, but were later identified as

"Nates," were already upon them. Now Brown, Posten, Stone, and Obert turned up and into them, firing short bursts head-on from all six guns of their ships and then going into a sharp turn to the left as the Japanese planes passed over them.

Part of the way around in the turn, Obert spotted a "Nate" on the tail of one of the P-40s and fired a brief burst, then his guns jammed. Seconds later, Obert saw that the nimble fighters were coming around at him at the same time as their 7.7-mm tracers streaked past his P-40. In an effort to escape his adversaries, Obert went into a turning dive, then headed south for Corredigor.

Stone had picked out one of the "Nates" and gone after it, while his leader Brown went for one on his right, getting in flank bursts from his fifties, and then head-on fire at another Japanese as Brown passed him. Spotting another a little below and 90 degrees to his course, Brown got in a belly burst and some flank shots, but as he tried to turn with the highly maneuverable "Nate," he spun out. Now between Corregidor and the southern tip of Bataan, Brown put his ship into a dive.

During the wild dogfight, one of the Japanese went after the helpless 76D3 photo plane as it was about to land. As Villamor's wheels touched down, he saw spurts of dirt kick up as the 7.7-mm fire tore into the strip. While Villamor taxied hurriedly down the field and toward a revetment, bullets from the "Nate" and another that had joined him tore into both wings. Now abruptly braking the old biplane to a stop in a cloud of dust inside the revetment, Villamor jumped out, Abanes just ahead of him, clutching the film case of his camera.

Circling barely above the water near Corregidor, Obert had managed to clear his guns. Now he climbed for altitude. A few minutes later, he leveled off, then spotted one of the "Nates" below him at about 500 feet over the south beach of Corregidor. Obert caught up with him and opened fire, "getting in a fairly long burst before my guns quit again." He then headed back for Corregidor, cleared his guns again, and set out in a northerly direction.

In the meantime Brown had climbed back up in the Corregidor/Mariveles region and returned to the scene of the combat. But now the sky was clear of Japanese. He headed for Bataan Field and came in for an uneventful landing. It was 5:30 and he was the only one of the four back on the field.

Obert had landed at Cabcaben. Checking his P-40 for damage, he was surprised to find no holes in his ship. But where were Posten and Stone? At dusk, another P-40 appeared over Bataan Field and came in for a landing. It was Posten. He had been shot up in the swirling dogfight and had headed south to the field at San Jose, Mindoro, since he had no radio contact with the fields on Bataan and could not be sure if they were clear.

After refueling at San Jose, he timed his arrival at Bataan Field for dark to be on the safe side.

At Bataan Field, General George and the others of the Flying Detachment were becoming increasingly concerned about Stone as the evening wore on. One of the men of the 21st Pursuit, T. Sgt. "Jeep" Zieman, who had been near Mariveles on lookout duty during the dogfight, told the pilots that he had seen a Japanese fighter chasing a P-40 overhead, the Japanese gaining on the American. Then they went into and out of a cloud which enveloped the top of Mount Mariveles and he lost sight of them. After a few seconds, he heard an explosion. Stone, one of the outstanding pilots of the detachment, was now reported as missing.[5]

Although none of the P-40 pilots put in a claim for a victory, USAFFE Headquarters credited them with six victories and announced the score over the "Voice of Freedom" that night.[6] One of the Japanese fighters, trailing smoke, made an emergency landing on Pilar Field, now behind enemy lines, but was set on fire at 3:15 P.M. by a USAFFE battery of artillery that zeroed in on it.

The dogfight had provided quite a spectacle for those who watched it from the ground on southeastern Bataan. To Sam Grashio at Cabcaben Field, it was "like a Hollywood Special," as the American and Japanese fighters cut in and out over the sky, turned and dived, banked and climbed, rolled and looped. It had been the best show of the war so far.

The photo mission also yielded the results that were expected of it. Abanes's photos were rushed to Corregidor, where they were collated with the reports of the Japanese artillery at Ternate. Subsequently, counterbattery fire from Corregidor scored a number of direct hits on the concealed Japanese emplacements. The Japanese responded by moving their guns to new locations and resuming shelling, thus putting the situation back to square one.

5   At Bataan Field, a big organizational change took place on the evening of February 12. Capt. Ed Dyess and his 21st Pursuit Squadron arrived to take over flying operations at the field. A few days earlier, General George had visited Dyess in the bivouac area of the 21st on the west coast of Bataan to inform him of his decision to assign the squadron to Bataan and Cabcaben fields. General George had evidently felt that he needed the administrative capability of a formal squadron to run his Flying Detachment, and the 21st was to be given the opportunity to do the job. Lts. Leo Golden, Gus Williams, and Johnny McCown were immediately relieved of beach defense duties and were to report in to Bataan Field on February 10 for flying duties ahead of the other 21st Pursuit pilots.

With the takeover of Bataan and Cabcaben fields by the 21st Pursuit, personnel changes were made. Dyess now replaced Ben Brown as the Flying Detachment commander. Brown had served only three days in the position. The pilots who had been flying from the two fields remained but were now attached to the 21st Squadron, except for Lloyd Stinson and Kiefer White of the 20th Pursuit, who were to return to their squadron at Mariveles. Brown and Obert were to continue as flight leaders, as under the earlier arrangement under Charley Sneed. Leo Boelens of the 21st replaced Bill Bradford as the engineering officer and would be supervising the mechanics of the 21st in maintaining the aircraft of the Detachment.

For the small Headquarters Squadron group that had maintained the P-40s until now, the takeover by the 21st's men was a bitter disappointment. Henceforth, the Headquarters Squadron men would be responsible only for odd jobs in the maintenance revetment at Bataan Field.

Assigned to Cabcaben Field from the 21st were 1st Lt. Larry Parcher (a ground officer) and eighty of the enlisted men. With Cabcaben Field now operational, there was a need for pursuit aircraft mechanics to keep the few P-40s in flying condition. Headquarters and 93rd Bomb Squadron personnel of the 19th Bomb Group were to continue maintaining the field.

With the losses of three of the P-40s during the past week (those of Baker, White, and Stone), Dyess was left with only one P-40B and three P-40Es in flying condition as he took over operations. In addition, one P-40B and one P-40E were out of commission. In two days, however, his mechanics were able to get the P-40E operational, giving him a force of five P-40s to meet the reconnaissance and combat needs of the Bataan campaign.

On the afternoon of February 15, Bill Rowe and Andy Krieger were selected to fly the first missions under Dyess, set for the following morning. They were to drop ammunition to the cut-off USAFFE men at Jones. For Rowe, it was his second trip to that northern Luzon destination behind Japanese lines, and he had visions of it being his last one on earth. That night, premonitions of death kept him from sleep.

The next morning, Rowe was up at 5:00 A.M. and after a cup of coffee took off with only his running lights on at 6:30. Rowe's and Krieger's P-40Es each were loaded with 1,600 rounds of .50-caliber ammunition in bandoleers packed in boxes the Japanese had used to drop supplies to their men on the west coast. Rowe flew over Pilar, Plaridel, Cabanatuan, and San Jose to reach his destination, while Krieger followed a different route. After almost hitting a mountain, Rowe finally found the drop point, a white cross, and released the box of ammunition in its parachute at low altitude. Then Krieger appeared after descending through overcast from 5,000 to 2,000 feet and Rowe pointed out to him where to drop his box.

Their mission successfully completed, the two climbed to 16,000 feet and headed home via Rosales. Over Clark, Krieger noted several Japanese aircraft taking off as they passed by but did not try to intercept them.

At 9:00 A.M., they were back on Bataan Field, little gas left in their tanks, but safe and sound.

An hour and twenty minutes after Rowe and Krieger returned, Wilson Glover took off on another mission, this one to drop two thousand pamphlets at Lucena in central Luzon, east of Lake Taal. But his engine began to run rough as he approached his destination, cutting out at one point, so he decided to turn around and drop them at San Pablo, Batangas, Taal, and Bauan on his homeward leg instead. At 11:20, he arrived safely back at Bataan Field.

That afternoon, at 3:30, Dyess flew a mission himself, accompanied by one of the newly assigned pilots of his own squadron, Leo Golden. They also dropped leaflets, then continued south to spend the night at San Jose, Mindoro.

Before daybreak on February 20, Kiefer White took off from Bataan Field on a secret mission south, arousing the curiosity of his fellow pilots at the field. Unknown to them, he had been selected by Dyess to fly a letter to Brigadier General Chynoweth at Iloilo on Panay Island that MacArthur's chief of staff wanted delivered by a P-40. USAFFE Headquarters had cabled Chynoweth the day before that a P-40 would be arriving at Santa Barbara, Panay, at dawn on February 20 carrying "urgent dispatches" for him.

After delivering the message to Chynoweth and refueling, White took off in late afternoon the same day for the three-hundred-mile return journey to Bataan. Unknown to him, Dyess had decided that Dyess and Ben Brown should search Bataan for hostile aircraft to clear the way for White's landing, given the recent activity of Japanese aircraft over Bataan's fields.

After taking off at 5:00 P.M., Dyess and Brown carried out their mission without incident; no enemy aircraft were encountered. Then about 7:00 P.M. they spotted White returning to Bataan Field and headed toward him. With his wheels down just prior to landing, White caught sight of the two aircraft approaching the field. "Japs!" he thought, terrified. Reacting instinctively, he pulled his P-40 up so quickly and steeply that John Posten, watching from the strip, figured he would stall out. Recovering from his initial shock and recognizing the planes as P-40s, White came in for another landing try, with Dyess and Brown behind him. They all had a good laugh on the field. White distributed a lot of scotch and boxes of chocolates that he had brought back from Iloilo, which they consumed at General George's shack.

White was not the only one of the Bataan Field Flying Detachment pilots to be jumpy about Japanese aircraft lying in wait for them at the two fields. To John Posten, it seemed it was a new strategy of the Japanese to "hang around our fields waiting to catch us as we take off or land."

"That's how the slant-eyed bastards are working now," he wrote in his diary that evening.

On the morning of February 25, Bill Rowe had a close call. Getting ready to descend for a landing at Bataan Field after protecting Ed Dyess as he landed following another mission to Jones, this time to drop medical supplies, Rowe received a radio call from Ozzie Lunde at Little Baguio that a Japanese aircraft was flying to the northwest. When Rowe checked out the location, he found nothing, so returned to Bataan Field and began to head in.

Over the strip, the Bataan Field radio suddenly cut in and gave Rowe the danger signal: "enemy in vicinity." Rowe now pulled up in a big hurry, trying to get some altitude, and went into clouds over Manila Bay. Unfortunately, he picked just the spot where the Nakajima "Nate" was hiding. The next thing Rowe knew, the nimble fighter was firing its two 7.7-mm nose guns at him. Rowe tried to turn inside of the Japanese, but in seconds the "Nate" began firing again at Rowe's plane. Rowe now opted for escape in the heavy P-40, going into a dive. At that point, the Japanese succeeded in putting two holes in Rowe's wing before breaking off the combat and heading north.

After circling over Corregidor, Rowe climbed for altitude and positioned himself in the sun over Manila Bay. Lunde was now radioing him a report on a ship that Rowe realized was his own. Low on gas, the emotionally drained 17th Pursuiter came in to Bataan for an uneventful landing. Reflecting later on his experience, Rowe was peeved that Ben Brown and Shorty Crosland on the Bataan Field radio had not told him *where* that Nate was located. If he had known, he could have taken the Japanese out without being shot at himself.

With the stepped-up Japanese activity over Bataan's fields, the role of the field operations post in bringing the pilots down to a safe landing took on heightened importance. Physically, the post was a hole in the ground about six feet in diameter and four feet deep, ringed with sandbags about eighteen inches thick, located on the north side of the 5,100-foot runway at the east (Manila Bay) end. An experienced pilot of the Flying Detachment was always assigned to the post whenever missions were scheduled and the field's aircraft were airborne. The officer at the post operated a signal light gun (called a biscuit gun), like those used in control towers. As a P-40 would start to come in at low altitude and approach the east end of the field from the west, the operations post man would flash a green light if no enemy aircraft were in the immediate area. A red flashing signal indicated that the pilot should abort his landing: Japanese aircraft were approaching or in the vicinity. A steady red light meant that something was wrong with the landing, such as only one wheel down, and the pilot should not touch down. As a backup to the signal light gun, a Very pistol with green and red flares was available. There was also a field radio in the hole, which could be used for direct ground-to-air contact with P-40s overhead.

A field telephone at the command post at the other end of the field was used to provide the officer at the operations post with information about the presence of Japanese aircraft. Any visual sightings would be telephoned to the post; more important, it also received information on pickups by the radar sets on Bataan, telephoned in by the communications section of the 5th Interceptor Command's headquarters at Little Baguio, which was linked with the radar operations.

The communications operations at Little Baguio were under Capt. Ozzie Lunde, the operations officer of the 5th Interceptor Command. In addition to maintaining telephone lines to General George's communications center at Bataan Field, he was the telephone link of the command with USAFFE on Corregidor, via the air officer there, regarding missions to be flown. In addition, Lunde was also in telephone communication with the antiaircraft command post on Corregidor to provide it with information on takeoffs from Bataan's fields; otherwise the P-40s risked being shot at by Corregidor's guns as they approached the fortress.

In addition to the telephone communications to the various ground stations, Lunde had direct radio contact with P-40s in the air, utilizing the SCR-197 communications trailer in operation at Little Baguio. The facility was used sparingly, however, in view of the questionable security of radio communications. In an emergency, however, such as in the case of the February 9 Villamor photo mission, Lunde would not hesitate to break out in the open with a warning to the pilots of approaching Japanese aircraft. Lunde and his assistant S-3, 1st Lt. Ray Gehrig, also maintained an interceptor board, based on incoming reports of Japanese aerial activity from all sources.

Back of Cabcaben Field, the 200th Coast Artillery had set up a SCR-268 radar operation, meant for controlling antiaircraft fire, but here used for detecting Japanese aerial operations. In addition, a Marine air warning unit was established a few miles behind Bataan Field with a SCR-270B mobile radar unit. Both sets were linked to Lunde's operations. Sightings by these two radar units of Japanese aircraft, reported to the 5th Interceptor Command, which telephoned them to Bataan Field, provided the precious minutes' warning that the Flying Detachment needed for arranging takeoffs and facilitating landings, as well as for warning pilots in midmission if necessary. On occasion, however, Japanese aircraft were not detected by observers or radar, resulting in takeoffs or landings at Bataan Field made under strafing or bombing attacks. Fortunately, no planes or lives were lost as a result of such unexpected intrusions.

In addition to the air warning benefits of the Marine's set, Dyess had considered using it during bad weather to guide the P-40s into Bataan Field for instrument landings. Considering the primitive nature of radar at that time, Obert and the other pilots were not enamored of this plan; in the event, it was never put into practice.

Dyess and Ben Brown paid frequent visits to the Marine radar installation, reached by footpath about a mile distant from the west end of Bataan Field and screened from view by heavy jungle growth and huge trees. Dyess often consulted with the radar men and ate with them. He greatly impressed them with his self-assurance, deep sensitivity, and charming manners. The Marine radar men also enjoyed the company of Brown, a genuine wit in conversation who was also an "artist" in breaking wind. He always sat on one of the empty five-gallon square cans, which he favored for their amplifying properties!

It was not only the benefit of radar that protected Bataan Field operations from the unrelenting aerial attacks of the Japanese. Company C of the 803rd Aviation Engineers had constructed the field and its facilities in such a way as to minimize damage by enemy aircraft. The Flying Detachment's P-40s were kept in sunken earthen revetments off the far end of the strip, hidden from view by chicken wire and foliage cover. The large main revetment, on the south side of the field, was naturally camouflaged with overhanging branches and vines, completely obscuring it from view; it could hold up to five P-40s. Trails to the revetments were cut in the jungle just wide enough for a P-40 to pass through. Upon landing, a P-40 would be met by a tractor and towed off the field and through the downward-sloping trail to the safety of a three-foot deep revetment, all in thirty seconds flat. There was also a maintenance revetment, where mechanics worked to get nonoperational P-40s into commission. In all, the revetments at Bataan Field could shelter twelve planes.

Emplacements were also constructed for antiaircraft defense, the responsibility of the 515th and 200th Coast Artillery since mid-January, 1942. In addition to a 37-mm battery near the bivouac perimeter, General George had the use of thirty .50-caliber machine guns intended for use in B-24s. Company C of the 803rd Aviation Engineers also provided antiaircraft defense for the field with ten .30-caliber and four .50-caliber machine guns.

Facilities were constructed for gasoline, ammunition, and bomb storage, food, water supply, and communications. The mess hall was dug into the side of a hill, with steps leading down to it. Water was piped into the adjoining kitchen from a dam the men built. Later the mess and the kitchen were incorporated into a single building, over 80' × 30'. The dam also provided water via an iron pipe for the nearby showers the men improvised.

Brig. Gen. Harold H. George, commander of the Bataan Air Force, at Bataan Field in early March, 1942. *Courtesy Hugh J. Casey Papers, Historical Division, U.S. Corps of Engineers*

Out in the open, in the bivouac area, General George lived in a three-room bamboo shack, with an outside porch attached to it, which he shared with Capts. Allison Ind and Harold Eads of his staff. General George welcomed visits in the late afternoons by his pilots. He would sit in his cane chair on the porch, with his visitors at his feet on the porch floor. There was a strong feeling of empathy between this bearded, bespectacled little man, so unlike a general in appearance, and his youthful officers, most of whom regarded him as a father figure, so concerned was he for their welfare.

In the latter part of February, as the rainy season began to approach, General George encouraged his officers and men to construct suitable shelters to keep themselves dry. Bill Strathern, Andy Krieger, Pope Noell (the Bataan Field medic), Gus Williams, Ben Brown, and Sam Grashio, who had all been living together, spent a great deal of time constructing a pole-frame house spread with chicken wire that supported tar paper, with a floor of bamboo set one-half inch apart in the native fashion. Other officers also built themselves similar houses, but John Posten, Dave Obert, Wilson Glover, and Bill Rowe, who had decided to build one together, were less ambitious and elected to wait until the rains actually came before doing anything.

Jesse White and Sid Wilkinson, enlisted men of Headquarters Squadron engaged in maintenance of P-40s, teamed up to dig a small bunker, which they covered with bamboo poles to support two sheets of metal roofing and two layers of sandbags, under a huge tree near the center of the Bataan Field bivouac area. They used it as a storage area for their personal effects rather than as sleeping quarters and continued to sleep on a blanket spread out on the ground, with shelter halves for cover. White slept fully clothed, his rifle at his side and .45 automatic at his left shoulder. By now all he possessed was one change of coveralls, an extra pair of new shoes, his steel helmet, razor, and soap—but no underwear or socks.

6 On February 12, the 20th Pursuit Squadron was relieved of beach defense duties and returned to the 5th Interceptor Command, the same date that the 21st Pursuit Squadron was released from its beach defense responsibilities too. Not having been ordered into offensive action against the Japanese as had been the 21st, the 20th suffered much less during its west coast tenure, with only one wounded man (Lieutenant Fulks), and he by a fellow American in an accident.

General George decided to assign the 20th Pursuit to Mariveles Field, where it had been stationed prior to beach defense following its evacuation into Bataan. After Maj. Gen. Hugh Casey, MacArthur's engineer, had decided on January 7 to abandon the existing Mariveles airfield because of its poor location, it had been arranged that Contractors Pacific Naval Air Base should undertake for the USAFFE to build a new strip by widening and extending the road adjacent to the old airfield. By February 14, the field was 65 feet wide and 3,800 feet long. It was recommended to General George that Air Corps personnel be brought in to help construct revetments and maintain camouflage of existing revetments.

The 20th's CO, Joe Moore (promoted to captain on January 25), was happy to lead the squadron back to Mariveles after its unpopular infantry duties at Longoskawayan. On arrival, the squadron established a tent camp about two miles from the field, in heavy jungle near a fresh-water stream. Officers and enlisted men alike pitched in to help the contractors build revetments in the low-lying hills on the west side of the field.

Some of the revetments were made to accommodate awaited B-17s with their 105-foot wingspread. They also dug foxholes and constructed emplacements for three antiaircraft guns. After also having to walk from the camp to the field and back again every day, everyone was exhausted from the physical activity, too much on two small meals of rice and salmon per day.

With the new Mariveles Field now operational, General George decided to disperse his little stock of five P-40s wider. Two of the four P-40Es were to be transferred to Mariveles, with the remaining two P-40Es and the P-40B kept at Bataan and Cabcaben fields. Another P-40B was out of commission at Bataan Field. Selected to transfer the two planes to Mariveles were Dave Obert and Jack Donalson, the latter one of the pilots of the 21st Pursuit newly assigned to the Flying Detachment. After take-off from Bataan Field at 4 P.M. on February 23 for what turned out to be an uneventful patrol of the Subic Bay and Bataan area, they landed at Mariveles Field at 5:30 P.M. to the excited reception of the 20th Pursuit's officers and men. Now the squadron had aircraft again for the first time since evacuating Clark Field on December 24.

Earlier that day, Lloyd Stinson and Kiefer White, the only two 20th Pursuiters at Bataan Field, had been assigned back to their old squadron at Mariveles in anticipation of the reactivation of flying operations of the 20th. Stinson was made squadron operations officer on his return and was responsible for informing his squadron mates about the existence and conditions of airfields in the Philippines south of Bataan. Such information could be useful if air reinforcements were to come into Mariveles. But Stinson was not happy about the prospect of flying from the new field. He felt it would be worse than Cabcaben. When committed to a landing at Mariveles, there would be no going around for a second try.

Four days after receiving its P-40s, the 20th Pursuit was ordered on its first mission from Mariveles. Lts. Johnny McCown and John Burns of the 21st Pursuit had taken off at 5:05 P.M. from Bataan and Cabcaben fields, respectively, on a reconnaissance mission to Lingayen Gulf, but shortly after they left, Lunde's warning net at Little Baguio called in with a report of a flight of Japanese pursuit planes in the area. In response, Mariveles Field was ordered to send up its two P-40s to cover for the 21st's pilots. Joe Moore and Lloyd Stinson took off at 6:00 P.M. and linked up with McCown and Burns, but the mission proved unnecessary; the Japanese planes did not show up. Moore and Stinson brought their P-40s back to Mariveles Field at 7:10 P.M. without mishap.

By the end of the month, the squadron had moved from its tent camp into Mariveles town itself, much closer to the airfield, where all were hoping to see planes flown in from "down south" soon. Was that not the purpose of building the new strip and the many revetments?

Just as the squadron was unloading its equipment at its new home, a quarantine station that was nearly completed when war started, two Japanese "Ann" dive bombers came sailing down out of a low overcast and loosed a couple of "eggs," which made everyone hit the dirt immediately. The bombs burst about three hundred yards away and did no damage, except to everyone's already frayed nerves.

The squadron's officers moved into a three-story concrete structure "that would have been elaborate if it had been completed," in Randy Keator's view. They took up quarters only on the bottom floor so they could get out in a hurry if necessary. The enlisted men settled into the rear section of one-story barracks next to the officers' building.

To provide full security for Mariveles Field, General George had made plans for underground hangars and quarters. To translate the general's aspirations into reality, Contractors Pacific Naval Air Base personnel were now constructing two tunnels (M-1 and M-2) at the field.

7 On the afternoon of Sunday, March 1, at Bataan Field, Ed Dyess was getting ready for a second test of the new short-range air warning and interception system that Dyess and Lunde had been working on during February. This was an expansion of the network that Lunde had developed earlier at Little Baguio and was in effect a huge party line by which the antiaircraft batteries, radar units, listening posts, and airfields were all connected through Lunde's information center. Using reports from all the points, Japanese air activity over Bataan could be plotted and warnings sent out to the fields.

For this test, Dyess picked a new flyer at Bataan Field to fly with him. First Lt. Tom Gerrity, formerly a pilot with the 27th Bomb Group and more recently General Wainwright's air liaison officer, had accepted General George's offer to move to Bataan Field as a pursuit pilot, although he had never flown a pursuit plane before. He was anxious to fly anything after his prolonged assignment on the ground.

At 5:00 P.M., Dyess took off, followed by Gerrity, and then the two assembled two miles southwest of Mariveles at 1,500 feet. As they started to climb to 12,000 feet, the electrical propeller system on Gerrity's P-40 went out, the propeller going into a full low pitch. Gerrity indicated his problem to Dyess, who accompanied the disappointed novice pursuit pilot back to Bataan Field.

After Gerrity had landed, Dyess climbed to 18,000 feet off Luzon Point, where he maintained excellent radio contact with the interception center. Then on orders from the center he flew to the north of Bataan at 6:20, and then to the middle of Bataan at 6:30. No Japanese planes were in sight. At 6:35, Dyess headed north up to Subic Bay, where he spotted four small boats in the bay. Flying east to Orani, he crisscrossed back and forth over the Japanese lines but could not rouse any opposition. Finally, Dyess gave up and returned to Bataan Field for a 7:00 P.M. landing.

The first test of the air warning and interception net, on February 23, had also failed to lure any Japanese aircraft aloft. This was the mission in which Obert and Donalson subsequently landed at Mariveles to turn over the two P-40s to the 20th Pursuit.

Before the February 23 takeoff, Dyess had held a meeting of all the Flying Detachment pilots to discuss the new interceptor system, and they had practiced some codes. Then Obert, with Donalson on his wing, took off at 4:00 P.M. from Bataan Field and climbed to 22,000 feet, flying between Caibobo Point on the west coast of Bataan, Corregidor, and Mariveles Mountain. The two "made all the noise they could" over the radio to let the Japanese know they were up there, but no one came up after them. After circling for an hour, Obert and Donalson began the descent for Mariveles Field. Obert turned on the radio as if he were going to give landing instructions for a whole group of pursuit instead of just two P-40s. The objective was to entice the Japanese to investigate at the time that Ed Dyess and Gus Williams were taking off to relieve Obert and Donalson and continue the test. The Japanese did not accept the bait, and Dyess and Williams had an uneventful mission over Bataan too.

8 Shortly after Dyess landed at 7:00 P.M. following the March 1 second test of the new system, he approached Dave Obert with an unusual mission request. Would Obert be willing to take the old 76D3 Philippine Air Corps trainer, the one that Villamor had flown on February 9, and fly that night to San Jose, Mindoro, to pick up some alcohol and sugar? Bataan Field was out of both. Dyess explained that it was to be an experimental flight; if it worked out all right, there would be others to San Jose to pick up supplies. Obert was also to inquire about purchasing fresh vegetables and fruit.

Not having flown since transferring the P-40 to Mariveles six days earlier and knowing the conditions at San Jose rather well, Obert gladly took the mission. He also felt that he probably had the best chance of getting through because he had flown the route before and was familiar with all the landmarks. There would also be a full moon that night, which would help him identify the landmarks.

At 8:00 P.M., Obert crawled into "the old wreck," started it up, and took off. After flying pursuit so long, the trainer "didn't seem or feel like an airplane at all" to him. The exhaust section was throwing out a lot of flame, which made Obert nervous that he could easily be spotted from the ground or the air, so he started out across the water at only some 10 feet altitude while "silently praying that the Nips weren't looking in my direction that night." Obert would have been "cold turkey for any ambitious Japanese who happened to see me."

Crawling along at only 80 MPH, Obert headed south toward his destination. As he approached Mindoro, he started to climb, since he intended to cross over a mountain range some 1,000 feet high at the north end of the island to cut down the distance to reach San Jose at the south end. The old biplane, however, able to climb at only one hundred feet per minute, could not be coaxed to climb high enough to clear the mountains. Giving up, Obert turned to the west to follow the coastline instead.

Just as he rounded the northwestern tip of Mindoro, he spotted a ship out at sea flashing code. After going a little farther, he reached a small cove near Paluan Bay where he saw something that shocked him: a fiercely burning ship that had lit up the whole cove. It seemed to have run aground.

Continuing in a southerly direction down the coast of the island, Obert now developed engine trouble. The Stearman started losing power, and sparks began flying from the engine in showers. The problem persisted the rest of the way. Obert firmly expected to have to set down on the beach any minute during the last part of the flight. But finally he reached San Jose, circling the field until enough flares were lit for him to land by. His first landing in a Stearman was a good one. It had taken two hours to cover the 160 miles from Bataan Field.

After spending only about an hour at San Jose, making arrangements for the sugar and alcohol for his plane and for vegetables and fruit to be picked up in the future, Obert went back to the field to see about the return flight. There mechanics who had been checking the plane told him they had found a large hole burned in the exhaust manifold, which would explain the loss of power and sparks. The problem was not considered serious enough to prevent a return trip.

Loaded down with 150 pounds of sugar and twenty gallons of alcohol, Obert managed to take off all right, but he could not nudge the old biplane above 500 feet, and reaching even that altitude was difficult. And his visibility for the return was practically zero; some low clouds had blown over since he had arrived at San Jose.

After about one and one half hours in the dark night air, Obert made out some land that he thought was Bataan peninsula. Heading over to it, he quickly realized it was not Bataan at all but rather the Japanese base at Nasugbu, on the coast of southwestern Luzon below Bataan. Obert hightailed it back out to sea, evidently without waking the Japanese.

Finding Bataan fairly easily after his error, Obert started flying up the southeast coast of the peninsula toward Bataan Field. Locating the field, he passed over it at about 50 feet, then began to circle back for a landing. Then suddenly "every damn machine gun on the damn countryside opened up on me!" Tracers were flying all around the Stearman, uncomfortably close, "and there wasn't a thing I could do." Obert put the biplane into a dive to the treetops to come in for a landing. He landed without getting hit but was so mad when he got out of the plane "that I felt like taking a gun and starting a civil war right there!" It was 3:00 A.M.

After the enraged pilot had cooled down and the sugar and alcohol had been unloaded, Obert reported to Ed Dyess and General George that he had seen a burning ship in Paluan Bay. He was told that it was probably a blockade runner, trying to bring food and supplies to Bataan.

The next morning, General George's operations center at Bataan Field received a phone call from the air officer on Corregidor. MacArthur's chief of staff wanted an immediate reconnaissance to determine the location and condition of the steamship *Don Esteban*. A radio report had been received by USAFFE Headquarters that the ship, headed for Corregidor with anxiously awaited food and medicine, had been attacked by Japanese off Paluan Bay the evening of February 28/March 1.[7] "That must be the ship that Obert saw last night," General George exclaimed to his S-2, Capt. Allison Ind, who had given him the message from MacArthur's chief of staff.

On General George's order, Ind now telephoned Mariveles Field to instruct Joe Moore to fly the recon mission. At Palafox Red, the call sign for the field, Moore indicated he would be prepared to take off in a few minutes but was interrupted by Ozzie Lunde, who was visiting the field. General George's operations officer wanted to go on the mission too. He had not flown for ages and was afraid he would forget how to "strap on an airplane." Reluctantly, General George agreed. He did not like the idea of risking his valued S-3 but respected Lunde's ability and feelings.

At 10:50, Moore and Lunde took off in the field's only P-40s, Lunde on Moore's wing. When altitude had been reached, the two old friends and flying school classmates headed south, Lunde acting as weaver for Moore. After passing over the Lubang Islands, they flew southeast toward northern Mindoro. At the north end of Paluan Bay, near the shore, they could see a ship burning.

While Lunde remained at 4,000 feet as cover, Moore went down to investigate. He found what he suspected to be the *Don Esteban*, burned from stem to stern and still on fire near the stern. Moore could find no signs of the crew either on or around the ship, but there were people on the beach opposite the vessel. After continuing their mission over to the east of Mindoro to the coast towns of Calapan and Puerto Galera, Moore and Lunde headed back to Mariveles Field, landing at 12:15.

As soon as they climbed out of their cockpits, they were informed by Lloyd Stinson, the 20th Pursuit's operations officer, that General George had called twice in their absence. The two P-40s were to be loaded immediately with fragmentation bombs and two pilots put on standby for a combat mission to Subic Bay.

Ozzie Lunde of the 20th Pursuit Squadron in his newly received P-35A, spring, 1941. *Courtesy Oswald W. Lunde, Col. USAF (Ret.)*

A half hour after Moore and Lunde had taken off on their Mindoro mission, Captain Ind had received a call at Bataan Field for General George. Without asking for the identity of the caller, but assuming it to be from USAFFE on Corregidor, Ind called George to the telephone. "Two large tankers, three supply ships and an airplane in attendance are entering Subic Bay," the voice said. After hesitating for a moment, General George asked, "And what action does the Chief of Staff desire me to take?" After a short delay in responding, the reply came, "Why, he says you are to use your own judgment, sir."

General George reflected on the situation for a few moments. The past few days he had been receiving reports from lookouts on Bataan of Japanese ships entering Subic Bay, thirty-five miles northwest of Bataan Field as the crow flies. Already on February 28 AWARN (Air Warning) had reported two destroyers, a tanker, and a merchantman entering Subic Bay at 2:00 P.M. that day. But now, the buildup of supply ships in Subic Bay suggested a new Japanese operation against the west coast. And Corregidor itself seemed sufficiently concerned to call him about the situation.

It was 12:03 P.M. and General George had reached a decision on what to do. Ind was instructed to call Mariveles Field to order Moore to load his P-40s with bombs as soon as they were back from the *Don Esteban* mission. Then Ind was to call Dyess and ask him to report in at once.

On arrival at General George's shack, Dyess was briefed on the situation. Then General George asked if Dyess's homemade rig for releasing a 500-pound bomb from his P-40 was ready for a practical test. The general was referring to a double spring device, made up of valve springs, valve rods, and other salvaged parts from wrecked cars and aircraft that WO Jack Day and his ordnance team of five enlisted men of the 17th Pursuit had concocted that allowed a P-40 to carry a 500-pound bomb under its belly.[8] In a dive-bombing attack, the bomb would be swung away from the center belly bomb rack of the P-40 and be compressed against the two strong springs near the front of the bomb so that it would kick out and clear the cowl flaps of the plane when released.

"There was never a better day, General," Dyess replied. He was eager to lay some big eggs on the Japanese in Subic Bay with his P-40E, which he had nicknamed "Kibosh." Dyess was now instructed to load his P-40 with a 500-pound bomb and stand by for final orders.

As soon as Dyess had left, General George picked up the phone and got Capt. Bill Cummings, the USAFFE air officer on Corregidor, on the line. In double-talk, so as not to risk compromising the information on the Subic Bay buildup in case the Japanese were listening in, he asked Cummings to inform MacArthur's chief of staff that George was "very interested in the information" and "it would be soon." Cummings agreed to transmit the message to Sutherland.

At 12:50, on General George's instructions, Ind called Mariveles Field. Moore was now ordered to have his two P-40s take off for Subic Bay. The pilots were to stay high to avoid fire from warships and to take no unnecessary chances. Five minutes later, Ind was on the line to Dyess with the same orders for the two P-40Es and one P-40B at Bataan and Cabcaben fields. The raid was on.

23. "I'M GOING TO PUT A NEW PAIR OF SHOES ON THE BABY"

1 At one o'clock on the afternoon of Monday, March 2, 1942, John Posten lifted his P-40E off of Bataan Field, climbed for altitude two miles southwest of Mariveles, and then headed up the west coast of Bataan toward Subic Bay. Under each wing, he carried three 30-pound fragmentation bombs. He was leading off the attack on Japanese shipping in Subic Bay. Seven miles to the southwest, at Mariveles Field, Kiefer White, with Erwin Crellin on his wing, was also taking off. Each of the 20th Pursuit pilot's P-40Es also carried six 30-pound bombs. South of Mariveles, they climbed to 10,000 feet, then turned toward Subic Bay.

When Posten arrived over the target area, he spotted a tanker north of Grande Island at the entrance to Subic Bay and went down after it. Releasing his small bombs, he then pulled out of his dive. Posten could not see the results of his efforts but felt he must have overshot his target.

White and Crellin were now also over Subic Bay, where they first observed four large ships north of Grande Island. Continuing northeast inside the bay, they then saw what looked like a warship very near the docks at Olongapo, at the eastern end of the bay. Deciding on this ship as a suitable target, White peeled off to dive, followed by Crellin. When they got closer, they could tell that it was a cruiser, and it "was really throwing lead." After dropping his bombs, White pulled out. When he looked around for his wingman, he was nowhere to be seen. Posten landed back safely at Cabcaben Field at 2:15 P.M., and White about the same time at Mariveles, but alone. White reported in to Joe Moore. It was soon apparent that Crellin, a relatively inexperienced pilot, had been shot down by the cruiser's fire.

About twenty-five minutes before Posten and White returned to their fields, Ed Dyess was in his takeoff roll. Traffic on the north-south road of eastern Bataan was halted on each side where the east end of Bataan Field cut across the road. Spectators watched in awe as the P-40E, its 500-pound bomb slung under the belly, lumbered down the 6 percent grade of the field, heading toward the road, its wheels cutting into the sod because of the heavy load. As "Kibosh" crossed over the road, it took a bump, then continued to the edge of Manila Bay, its Allison engine racing at maximum RPM. Then the struggling warbird went over the edge and out of sight, and everyone held their breath. Suddenly, someone shouted, "There he is!" as he spotted Dyess just above the water and swinging west toward Corregidor.

At Cabcaben Field, "Shorty" Crosland in the P-40B had also taken off at 1:50 P.M., assigned to fly cover for Dyess. When the two linked up south of Cabcaben, they climbed for 12,000 feet altitude over the sea, then headed northwest for Subic Bay.

Over the target area, Dyess started across the bay to begin his descent with the sun at his back. At 10,000 feet, he saw that the big concentration of ships was not at Olongapo, as he had been informed, but rather back of him, near Grande Island. Here were many vessels, busily unloading their cargoes. Descending, Dyess saw two transports unloading on the north side of Grande Island. Then he observed two cruisers, two destroyers, and two other transports well inside the harbor, with other ships outside it. But no tanker was in sight, his primary goal on this mission.

Dyess decided on a medium-sized transport just entering Subic Bay, passing between Grande Island and the western shore. Three smaller vessels and a destroyer were near the transport. Dyess swung his P-40E over into a dive from 10,000 feet through the cloudless sky. At 2,000 feet, he released his 500-pound bomb and pulled away. Looking back, he saw it miss the transport by forty or fifty feet, sending a big geyser of water skyward.

Surprised to find so little antiaircraft fire from the island and the ships, Dyess pulled around and went into a shallow dive over the transport. In three passes, stern to bow, bow to stern, then stern to bow again, he poured machine gun fire from his six fifties into the ship, concentrating on its bridge.

Now Crosland was down too, and the two pursuiters began strafing in separate runs at targets of opportunity. Dyess first concentrated on four small warehouses on the shore near where the two transports were unloading, scattering Japanese on the docks. Then Dyess and Crosland shifted their attention to a wooden boat plying between Grande Island and the western shore of Bataan, evidently carrying supplies. Dyess focused his fire on its two forward guns at first, then started firing into the hull in strafing runs just above the water. The concentrated fire of Dyess's and Crosland's guns was tearing the sides out of the vessel. Their ammunition now exhausted, they left the hapless boat as it started sinking. Dyess called Crosland on the radio and told him they should head home.

When Crosland landed at Cabcaben at 2:50 P.M., his plane untouched by gunfire, he found that Sam Grashio had taken off thirty-five minutes earlier in the P-40E that Posten had brought to the field on his return from the first mission.

Grashio was now approaching Subic Bay, three 30-pound fragmentation bombs under each wing. North of Grande Island, the 21st Pursuiter observed three transports and one cruiser, then continued north over the bay. Spotting a lone transport, he now maneuvered his P-40 into position and put his ship into a dive. Lined up over the transport, he pulled the bomb-release handle, then pulled out. Glancing back, Grashio saw no splashes and assumed he had either missed the target or looked in the wrong direction. Disappointed, he started back for Cabcaben Field.

As Grashio began his descent and headed in to the field, he found to his surprise that he was getting the red light, "don't land" signal from the operations post. Then a few moments later, as he cleared the field and wondered what the problem was, a voice cut in on his radio—"9 M N to Leo—9 M N to Leo. . . . Your eggs are still on. . . . Your bombs are still on!" It was Lunde at Little Baguio, who had apparently been called by Cabcaben Field to radio Grashio on his dangerous situation.

Now Grashio realized why he had not seen the results of his bombing attack at Subic Bay. But what to do? Both his oil and Prestone temperatures were too high. "I've got to land—she's running hot!" Grashio anxiously called to Lunde. Grashio then thought of another alternative: bail out. If even one of those bombs he was still carrying around would drop while he was attempting to land, it would be all over for him. But the prospect of bailing out over the jungle or Manila Bay was not appealing either.

Grashio decided to head for Mariveles. There the runway is longer, he reasoned, which would make a "power on" landing, with its heavy braking requirement, more possible than at Cabcaben. Such a landing was less likely to jar the bombs loose than the standard "three point" landing would.

At 3:30 P.M., Grashio touched down at the near end of Mariveles strip, braked hard, and managed to stop the P-40 before it reached the other end. It was a perfect landing, and the bombs remained on the racks. The communications officer at the field telephoned Lunde, "Landed OK—Palafox." Examining the P-40 later, the ground crew at the field found the problem: the lock screw on the release handle had been set so as to make release of the bombs impossible.[1]

At Bataan Field, Ed Dyess had brought "Kibosh" back at 2:15 P.M. Despite the antiaircraft fire to which it had been subjected, only a single bullet hole was found, in the wing.

At 3:05 P.M., fifteen minutes after Crosland had landed at Cabcaben

Field, he received a phone call from Dyess; could he take another mission? When Crosland acceded to the request, Dyess told him, "I'm going to put a new pair of shoes on the baby—you be ready to pick her up by a certain time." Crosland knew exactly what Dyess meant by his doubletalk. Dyess was putting another 500-pound bomb in the makeshift rack of his P-40 and wanted Crosland to fly cover for him again. Indeed, as Dyess spoke to Crosland, "Kibosh" was being refueled and reloaded with another big egg and .50-caliber ammunition for a second mission to Subic Bay.

At 5:00 P.M. Dyess lifted off of Bataan Field and Crosland from Cabcaben Field, linking up again over southern Bataan before proceeding for another strike against Subic Bay. Over the target area, the situation looked the same to the two Flying Detachment pilots as it had during the first attack. Dyess now picked the two freighters still unloading at Grande Island as his targets and went into a dive from 10,000 feet, releasing his big bomb at 2,000 feet. This time the bomb overshot one of the two freighters by some forty to fifty feet and exploded among a nearby concentration of barges and lighters that were receiving cargo from the ships, damaging the barges and lighters extensively with flying fragments. Pulling up, Dyess saw many Japanese running from the two freighters to the docks. Swinging around, he poured machine gun fire into them, then sprayed the warehouses and two 100-ton motor vessels, exhausting his ammunition in the process. Crosland joined him in the strafing attacks.

At 5:40, Crosland was back at Cabcaben, and Dyess returned at 5:45 at Bataan Field. The 21st's mechanics found several antiaircraft holes in "Kibosh," including one large one next to the cockpit. After patching the holes, they serviced the veteran P-40E and hooked it up with another 500-pound bomb for a third sortie.

Daylight was fading on Bataan as Dyess and a new weaver, Lt. John Burns of his own 21st Pursuit, prepared to take off for a final mission against Japanese shipping in Subic Bay. At 6:40 P.M., Dyess roared down the Bataan Field strip in "Kibosh" again, while Burns in Crosland's P-40B lifted off of Cabcaben.

Five minutes later, at Mariveles Field, Lloyd Stinson and Jim Fossey of the 20th Pursuit, who had been on alert all afternoon expecting to be called into the action, took off in the two P-40Es. One of the P-40s was the one landed at Mariveles by Grashio three hours earlier and now back in service, its fragmentation bombs removed from the racks.

Over Subic Bay again, Dyess saw that his two freighters had now left the dock at Grande Island as he went into a dive at 10,000 feet, this time targeting big supply dumps at the northern end of the island. Then at 1,800 feet he released his bomb, scoring a direct hit that immediately started large fires. In deep twilight, Burns now joined Dyess in a dive for a strafing attack on the island dock area, resulting in more fires. This time, antiaircraft fire was coming at them from all directions, lighting up the sky.

On the return trip to Bataan, Dyess and Burns received a radio message from Lunde at 5th Interceptor Command headquarters: a heavily loaded ship was just leaving Subic Bay, with another large ship apparently getting ready to follow it out. Go after them! In response, the two 21st Pursuiters swung their P-40s back for Subic Bay again. The same message had been radioed to Stinson and Fossey, who were preparing at the time to join Dyess and Burns on the return to their fields. Now they also headed for Subic to join in the attack on the departing ships.

Flying north across Subic Bay, Dyess located the first ship, silhouetted against the sunset in the west, It looked about 8,000 tons, heavily laden, and was towing barges. Sweeping in for the attack, Dyess strafed it from amidships to the stern, then made a strafing pass over the bow and into the bridge. In separate attacks, Burns poured .50-caliber fire into the ship too. Fires broke out all along the deck. Then, suddenly, with Dyess only 1,800 feet overhead in another 45-degree dive, the ship blew up in a blinding flash, its sides seemingly dissolving in one big explosion. Debris shot high into the sky, far above the startled pilot, who pulled back on the stick to avoid flying through it. For several seconds, Dyess blacked out; when he came to, "Kibosh" was at 4,000 feet. Below him, there was only a mass of flame where the ship had been, and a few minutes later, it was gone. "It must have been loaded with explosives," Dyess thought.

Now Dyess turned south for the return, Burns weaving for him. But then the never-satisfied Bataan Field detachment leader spotted another ship, also silhouetted against the glow in the west, but even larger than the one that had blown up. It was too dark now for Dyess to tell what type it was, but it certainly sent up more antiaircraft fire than any ordinary transport or tanker. Without informing Burns, Dyess now began another strafing attack, this from the southwest. The ship was turning rapidly in an apparent effort to return to Subic Bay. After raking it from bow to stern, Dyess strafed the luckless vessel from the northeast in a stern-to-bow sweep, starting fires at both ends. In his third run, again bow to stern, Dyess poured all his remaining .50-caliber ammunition into the ship, hoping it would explode like the other one. Now completely in flames, the vessel veered ashore.

Since a huge fire was also raging on Grande Island, Dyess without thinking crossed over the Japanese-controlled western shoreline of Bataan instead of flying low over the water to reach American lines. Suddenly, "Kibosh" was bracketed with antiaircraft fire of an intensity Dyess had never experienced before. Cursing himself, the sobered pilot turned away in a climb.

In the meantime, Stinson and Fossey had arrived over Subic Bay but found no ships escaping from Subic Bay as expected. But at a point about one mile south of the west part of the bay, they noticed a large motor cruiser or launch of about 100 tons. With Stinson in the lead, they went down to strafe it from 4,000 feet and noticed they had started a fire. After repeated strafings, the small ship suddenly blew up. Evidently it had been loaded with ammunition.

As Dyess neared Bataan Field, he realized he was fighting a heavy tail wind. Heading into the field from Manila Bay, he landed roughly, but in one piece. Just as Dyess touched down, he was surprised to see a stream of tracer fire going up against Mount Mariveles from the direction of Cabcaben Field. Then he guessed the fire must be coming from a P-40 landing at Cabcaben—and that meant Burns. "He must have pressed the firing button on his guns accidentally," Dyess reckoned. He was correct in his surmise. The tail wind had tricked Burns and caused him to come in too fast. On each of his several bounces, his six .50-caliber wing guns sent fire spraying down the field. Then, continuing to roll past the far end of the field, Burns ran into stumps, swerved, and went over on one wing, tearing out the landing gear and damaging the wing and the propeller.

Moments after the P-40B came to a halt, Burns's armorer, Sgt. Al Sly, climbed up on the wing as Burns slid down from the cockpit. Shaken, Burns asked, "Has anyone got a cigarette?" Sly looked in the cockpit. Sure enough, the gun switches were set in the "on" position; Burns had forgotten to turn them off after his strafing attack. Trying to control the P-40B as he came in to land, his hand on the control stick, Burns had inadvertently pressed the trigger switch on the stick on each bounce.

When he found out about the accident, Joe Moore at Mariveles Field was particularly upset. It was his old No. 41, the last operational P-40B of the thirty-one that the 20th Pursuit had originally received in the Philippines. But before he got the news about his plane, Moore was witness to an even more disturbing pair of events at Mariveles Field that occurred shortly after Burns's accident.

Overhead, Stinson and Fossey were preparing to land. It was now dark, and the field was unlit. The strong 30 MPH tail wind that affected landings at Bataan and Cabcaben fields was also blowing in the Mariveles area. About to touch down, Stinson could not get his plane to sit down as it should; it just kept floating. Trying to get some drag, Stinson put the wheels on the strip, but it was not enough; the P-40E would not slow down. Now as it went off the end of the runway in a skid, the left wing hit the water truck, the right wing cutting the guard's bamboo shack in two. When the ship came to a halt, the left wing was hanging over a dry creekbed about ten feet deep, full of large rocks, and dust was flying everywhere. Fearful of fire, the shaken pilot stepped out onto the left wing, then in the darkness missed his footing and fell into the creekbed, landing on his back. The breath knocked out of him, Stinson lay immobile, unable to get up or call out.

When Joe Moore arrived at the scene, he assumed Stinson was half dead and helped carry him to a car for a trip to the hospital. About halfway down the side of Mariveles Field, Stinson got his breath back and told Moore that he was all right. Just then, they saw Fossey coming in to land and could tell he was in trouble too. History repeated itself; Fossey also could not manage the tail wind, overshot the field while riding the brakes, hit a tree with his wing tip, and washed out the landing gear. Both of the P-40Es were wrecked beyond repair.

2 That evening at General George's operations shack on Bataan Field, Captain Ind and General George were going over the reports of the Subic Bay pilots. Phone calls had also come in from ground observers verifying the heavy damage done by the P-40 attacks. An 8,000-ton heavily loaded ship had blown up, a very large 18,000-ton vessel was burning fiercely after being beached, and there were many fires and explosions all over Grande Island. But the price paid was heavy. Three of the five remaining P-40s of the detachment had been lost and another damaged. One of the pilots had been killed. They were now down to a single P-40, Dyess's "Kibosh."

General George took it philosophically. "Forget it," he told his pilots. "We couldn't have done better, and this was bound to happen sooner or later." In his view, the P-40 was not really fit for combat anyway, but it could be mass-produced when large number of pursuit were needed. The Air Corps had sacrificed quality for quantity. He then broke out a fifth of whiskey from his luggage.

At 7:43 P.M., a telephone message from General Wainwright was relayed to General George: "personal congratulations and thanks." A little while later, another phone call was received. MacArthur's chief of staff himself wanted to speak to General George. Sutherland was angry. He told George that he had not been informed of the intention to strike Subic Bay shipping.[2] And when he learned that three of the precious P-40s had been lost, his voice became even harder. After listening to a long lecture, General George finally was able to mention the damage his little air force had inflicted on the Japanese. Now somewhat mollified, Sutherland changed his tone. After the call, Ind prepared a detailed account for Sutherland of the Subic Bay operation.

The next day, a typical MacArthur communiqué was issued from USAFFE Headquarters on Corregidor. Reading it, one would have believed General MacArthur himself had planned the mission. In a radiogram to Washington the following day, MacArthur announced:

WE MADE A SURPRISE ATTACK ON OLONGAPO AND SUBIC BAY DESTROYING THE
FOLLOWING VESSELS COLON ONE OF TWELVE THOUSAND TONS ONE OF TEN THOU-
SAND TONS ONE OF EIGHT THOUSAND TONS AND TWO MOTOR LAUNCHES STOP
INFLICTED MUCH DAMAGE ON SMALLER CRAFT STOP LARGE FIRES WERE STARTED
AT SHORE INSTALLATIONS ON GRANDE ISLAND AND OLONGAPO[3]

The Bataan pilots were bitter about the communiqué. Not a word about
General George or their own role in the attack; "as if MacArthur had any
prior knowledge of this coup, or could have planned it anyhow," Andy
Krieger wrote later to his father.

3 Ever concerned about the welfare of his small group of pilots, General George now felt everyone needed a morale booster. The day after the
Subic Bay raid, he called Dyess in and suggested giving a party. He had
in mind to invite the nurses from Hospital No. 2 nearby and scare up
whatever ingredients were at hand for drinks and food. "If the war is going to be fought by our boys and girls," he told Dyess, "they might as well
have what little good times they can."

That evening, under a full tropical moon, the pilots and General
George's staff whooped it up at the thatched shack on stilts used as a
clubhouse with twelve nurses who had accepted General George's invitation. Outside the shack, Cpl. Robert L. Greenman of Dyess's squadron,
an accomplished concert pianist, was pounding out boogie-woogie on an
old salvaged piano they had set up to provide music for dancing.

Not having seen white women for so long, the pilots, in their best hand-
washed, unironed uniforms, without ties, were ill at ease with their lady
guests, who wore civilian dresses, as the party started. But as the shy young
men slugged down the punch concocted with water, lemon powder, and
the alcohol Obert had flown in two days earlier, their inhibitions faded.
Soon they were singing and dancing on the canvas spread over the shack's
bamboo floor. The music was hot, but there was no jitterbugging: the
men were too weak for that, and the shack too unstable. John Posten was
happy to be dancing with a girl who came from a town not far from that
of his girlfriend back home. Bill Rowe's date was a Chicago blonde, "a
little too big for me."

After the party broke up about 3:00 A.M., a sober Posten and a tipsy
Rowe had the pleasure of driving the lady guests back to the hospital in
Captain Eads's car and one of the trucks General George was using as
supplementary transportation. It was only a five-mile round trip, but driving with lights out, the pilots took until four o'clock to find their way
back to the field. Rowe had gotten lost and went the wrong way with
his laughing company.

Next morning, there was another treat for General George's charges.
He had cooked a batch of pancakes for them, an unheard-of delicacy for
perpetually hungry men on half rations. Somehow the general had lo-

The special breakfast for Bataan Field pilots on March 4, 1942, following their success in the raid on Subic Bay two days before. *Left to right, on left side of table:* Bill Bradford (obscured), Ed Dyess (flying commander of the Bataan Field Flying Detachment), and John Posten. All others are unidentified. *Courtesy John H. Posten, Jr., Col. USAF (Ret.)*

cated the ingredients and cooked the pancakes on a little Filipino stove. But few of the pilots could manage to get more than two down—their stomachs were too shrunken. Some even felt intoxicated after eating them.

As they sat eating at the long table on General George's verandah, the young men agreed that the party the night before was the best time they had had since the war started. They decided that they should put on two such parties a month. "Then maybe we can enjoy this damn war," Posten recorded in his diary that evening.

But now it was back to realities. They had exactly one P-40 with which to continue the campaign, and that one machine "looked like a patch-work quilt." "Kibosh" was painted olive drab, but the eighty-two patches of blue denim and khaki that the 21st Pursuit mechanics had glued over its battle-inflicted holes gave it a mosaic look.

Down at Cabcaben Field, other mechanics of the 21st were trying to repair the P-40B that Burns had ground-looped on his return from the Subic

Bay raid. With parts from the P-40E that White had wiped out on landing at Bataan Field on February 7/8 and the two Mariveles-wrecked P-40Es, plus a new (or overhauled) engine from the Air Depot, the men, supervised by Lt. Leo Boelens, managed to produce a hybrid P-40B/E by the afternoon of March 5. Although it was recorded in the daily S-3 operations reports as a P-40B, to the pilots it was known as the "P-40 Something."

Two days later, General George's two-plane air force was back in operation. A Japanese truck convoy had been reported moving north from Manila on the evening of March 7, believed to be heading for Bataan. At 12:30 A.M., Ben Brown took off in one of the P-40s to check out the situation in a rare night reconnaissance mission. Brown flew in bright moonlight all the way up Highway 3 to San Fernando, thirty-five miles north of Manila, then back down again. He saw nothing but two Japanese cars and came back in to land one hour later. Another false report.

On the afternoon of March 8, Dyess called a meeting of the pilots. There would be a rotation policy in effect now, with two pilots assigned to Cabcaben Field for one-week stretches, to fly the "P-40 Something" stationed there. For the first week, starting this day, Bill Rowe and John Burns were selected for the Cabcaben duty. While Dyess only had two P-40s for operation at Bataan and Cabcaben fields, Joe Moore down at Mariveles had none. His pilots were again unemployed as far as flying went. Lloyd Stinson had come back to Bataan Field to be with the rest of the pilots there.

Efforts were underway to give the squadron wings again, although not those of a P-40. S. Sgt. Howard A. Koppen and several other enlisted men of the 20th Pursuit were trying to salvage an old Grumman J2F Duck in Mariveles harbor. It was one of five single-engine amphibians of Patrol Wing Ten's utility squadron that had been dispersed in a semicircle near the beach, partially camouflaged, in early January, 1942. On the morning of January 5, four Zeros swept in at wavetop level and strafed them.[4] Their boat hulls punctured in the attack, they all sank in the harbor.

Wading out in chest-deep water, the 20th's men had checked the condition of the five seaplanes, two Curtiss SOC Seagulls, two Vought OS2U Kingfishers, and the J2F. They found that except for the Duck, their engines were all badly corroded by the salt water because of being fully submerged at high tide. But the J2F was high enough up on shore that its engine was above water at high tide and thus was salvageable. Using a block and tackle, the men, under the supervision of Lt. Harrison "Spec" Hughes, the 20th's engineering officer, managed to pull the Duck up onto higher ground. There they bailed out the water and plugged the holes in the hull with pieces of rubber from an inner tube.

During the next days, the men succeeded in refloating the amphibian and towing it across Mariveles Bay to the dock at the quarantine station.

Here one of the engineers of the Pacific Naval Air Base contractors used a drag line to lift the Duck out of the water and onto the Mariveles airstrip, where it was towed to a revetment for the squadron's mechanics to get it into flying shape.

4 Further south, at Mindanao, the situation of P-40 availability was also a serious problem. When Bill Feallock took off on a recon mission on February 9 from the unfamiliar Del Monte No. 3 field, a half mile from the barrio of Dalirig, eight miles south of Del Monte, he hit a rock with his left wheel. The accident left just a stub for the landing gear. Feallock was obliged to crash-land the P-40 at Del Monte No. 1 strip on return. That meant that all three of Colonel Elsmore's P-40s were now out of commission. His air strength was reduced to the two old P-35As.

Two days later, by transferring Feallock's undamaged propeller to one of the two out-of-commission P-40s, Elsmore got one P-40 back in flying condition. But he needed two more propellers, one belly cowling, and one complete left wing to bring the other two into commission. The air depot at Bataan Field had responded by loading its two remaining P-40 propellers on a submarine departing Corregidor that was scheduled to stop at Cebu, where they would be transshipped to Del Monte. By early March, the depot shipment evidently was received, for by mid-March, an additional P-40 was now in commission with a new propeller.[5]

Disaster struck on March 16, however, destroying one of the precious aircraft. A fire broke out in Dalirig barrio, soon engulfed the whole community, and spread to the adjacent Del Monte No. 3 field. The two P-40s were on this field at the time, and one was completely burned. The other was barely rescued. Elsmore was down to one P-40 again.

Two weeks later, however, Elsmore was about to reap a bonanza. Crates containing three brand-new P-40E-1s had been towed on a barge from Bohol to Butuan Bay, sixty-five miles to the northwest of Del Monte. The P-40s had been shipped on the blockade runner SS *Anhui*, which had left Brisbane, Australia, on February 22 with cargo destined for Cebu, but which had run aground on the Canigao Reef between Bohol and Leyte on March 9. The next day, the P-40 crates were offloaded and hidden in mangrove swamps along the Bohol coast, then reloaded on a barge for direct transfer to Mindanao. After arrival at the mouth of the Agusan River, just north of Butuan town, the crates were hidden in a covered area, then transferred ten miles up the western coast of Butuan Bay to covered positions near the Buena Vista airfield, two and a half miles south of Buena Vista village. Both movements were carried out at night, to avoid detection by Japanese observation planes constantly flying over northern Mindanao.

Awaiting the arrival of the crated P-40s were seventy-five mechanics specially selected from the 19th Bomb Group and the 440th Ordnance

Company, under the command of Lt. Col. Fred O. Tally, Elsmore's executive officer. This Provisional Mobile Depot Unit, as it was dubbed, was set up specifically for the purpose of assembling the just-arrived P-40s. First Lt. Henry "Pete" Warden, who had reported in from the air depot at Bataan Field, was in charge of assembly operations. By the evening of March 26, the men of the Provisional Depot had established camp in the barrio of Rizal, adjacent to the 4,800-foot-long airfield. They had also set up an assembly line in the nearby coconut grove selected for that purpose.

On March 29, the Provisional Depot completed the assembly of the first P-40E, and Warden took it up for a test hop. The next day, John Brownewell came up from the new Maramag Field in central Mindanao and flew the brand new bird back to Maramag. On March 31 the second P-40, and on April 2 the third one, were assembled and tested. Pete Warden and John Geer in separate flights flew them south to Maramag in late afternoon of April 2. On the way, Warden spotted a four-engine "Mavis" flying boat and chased it near the barrio of Esperanza, twenty-five miles south of Buena Vista, but lost it.[6] With four P-40s in commission on April 2, Elsmore's air force was now twice as big as that of General George on Bataan.

5 On Wednesday, March 11, General George received a peculiar order from MacArthur's chief of staff. Sutherland wanted a recon of the ocean south of Corregidor, down as far as the Cuyo Islands, one hundred miles south of Mindoro, to check on the presence of any Japanese warships in the area. No explanation of the purpose of the mission was given to George. At 3:00 P.M., Wilson Glover took off from Bataan Field, his P-40 equipped with a belly tank for the long flight.

As he watched Glover heading out over Manila Bay, Dave Obert, just recovering from a week's bout with malaria, worried for his squadron mate. To Obert, four hours over water in an old, worn-out airplane, with no hope of being rescued in case of engine failure, would be enough to make a "nervous wreck out of anyone." But all went well for Glover. On his return, he reported sighting a destroyer off the northwest coast of Mindoro, between Mamburao and Sigaras, and a destroyer or a cruiser heading north from a position southwest of Ambulong Island, off the southwest tip of Mindoro. South of Mindoro, in the waters between Panay Island and the Cuyo Islands, all was clear.

Shortly after Glover had returned from his long mission, Dyess and several other pilots were congregated near the command post off the strip when they were surprised to see General George approaching them, carrying luggage. Stopping at the command post, George announced in a few words that he was leaving Bataan. He was to go to Australia by boat on orders of the Far East Air Force command there. A PT boat would be picking him up at Mariveles at 7:15 P.M. for the trip over to Corregidor.

It was obvious to all that General George was leaving them only with the greatest reluctance. He promised to get some planes into Bataan "even if he had to go all the way to the States to get them." If he did not come back himself pretty soon, it would not be because he did not want to come back, he maintained. Then, with a silent handshake, the diminutive, bearded man climbed into his car and headed down the road to Mariveles. It was the last time any of them would ever see General George again. Dyess, unashamedly, sat down and cried.

That evening, the dispirited group at Bataan Field, "feeling like orphans," in Obert's words, got the word that their general had left with General MacArthur and his staff in four PT boats for Australia. Down at Mariveles Field, Randy Keator watched as PT 32 picked up General George, two other generals, and a colonel at 7:15 P.M. Keator felt that "we were really being deserted" and that the end of the Bataan/Corregidor campaign "must be drawing near."

At Cabcaben Field, Bill Rowe and the other officers assigned there were also feeling pessimistic. Japan controlled almost everything in the China Sea, and there was no help in sight for them. Anything that should come over would probably go to Australia instead. The Japanese could push them right off the peninsula if they got a strong enough force. The pilots at Cabcaben discussed what they would do in the event of a surrender. Some talked of making a break for it through the lines and hiding out with the natives; others suggested getting a boat and heading for an island in the southern Philippines to wait for help. All wondered what it would be like to be in a concentration camp.

Whatever the pilots' feelings, they were still on call for missions ordered by USAFFE Headquarters on Corregidor, now apparently under the command of Lt. Gen. Jonathan Wainwright, the senior officer in the Philippines. On the afternoon of March 14, MacArthur's deputy chief of staff, Col. Lewis C. Beebe, radioed Lunde at Little Baguio about a report of a large assembly of Japanese planes on Nichols, Nielson, Zablan, and Del Carmen fields, "which appear to indicate some large-scale operation in the making." Beebe wanted an aerial reconnaissance of these fields the same day. At 4:00 P.M., Lt. Col. Kirtley J. Gregg, General George's executive officer, radioed Beebe in reply that the reconnaissance would be flown that afternoon.

One hour later, Bill Rowe was on his way north from Cabcaben Field in the "P-40 Something" to check out the situation on the four airfields. It was Rowe's first time in a P-40B. Arriving first over Del Carmen, he buzzed the field and found nothing on it. Just north, at Clark Field, he sighted nine "Anns" parked in a semicircle at the north side of the field. Then, swinging south to Manila, Rowe found eight large bombers dispersed at the north of Nielson Field and on Nichols, ten large bombers parked in a circle at the northeast corner of the field, plus about four or five miscellaneous aircraft dispersed around the field. Since his orders were not to attack, Rowe took no offensive action against any of the Japanese planes, During the whole mission, the very nervous pilot constantly searched the sky for Japanese aircraft but saw none. At 6:00 P.M., Rowe was back at Bataan Field with a report that was transmitted to Beebe that evening.

When Rowe climbed into the "P-40 Something" for his reconnaissance mission, he found that it now sported an unusual logo on each side of the forward fuselage. Two days earlier, Sgt. Frank Mayhue and another of the men of the 21st Pursuit had painted a skull in a pilot's helmet and scarf with two playing cards alongside, the ace and jack of spades, on the "P-40 Something" and "Kibosh." Mayhue, a self-trained artist, had come up with the design in response to a request from Dyess, perhaps as a reaction to General George's departure the evening before.

The next day, a second recon was flown over the four fields, this time from Bataan Field by Lt. Leo B. Golden of Dyess's 21st Pursuit. During the one-hour flight in the "P-40 Something," Golden spotted four single-engine and five twin-engine ships on Nielson, five single-engine planes on Nichols, several dispersed ones on Clark, and none on Del Carmen.

6 To Dave Obert, "the bottom seemed to drop out of our entire organization" when General George left. Their commander had told his pilots at one time that he did not have a single competent high-ranking officer under him that he could leave in charge of the little air force, and now it seemed his words were prophetic. Each of the Air Corps brass hats was scrambling for a command position. In Obert's view, "We had an organization for our two planes large enough and loud enough to operate a complete Wing!"

The main struggle was between Lieutenant Colonel Gregg and Col. Lawrence Churchill, the latter the commanding officer of the Far East Air Service Command. As executive officer to General George, Gregg was trying to command the Bataan air force by direction of and as executive to General George, but his authority was not recognized by Churchill, who outranked him. In a letter to Beebe of March 26, Churchill complained that the Air Force organization "is so loose at the present time as to be practically no organization at all" and asked Beebe to make a decision on the matter. Three days later, Churchill was formally given command of the Bataan air force by virtue of his being the senior officer on duty with it.

In the event, Churchill elected to remain at Little Baguio and not involve himself in flying operations, unlike General George. Although he was in command of the 5th Interceptor Command, Gregg also opted to remain at Little Baguio and forgo such responsibilities. Tactical command of operations of the Bataan Field Flying Detachment thus fell to Orrin Grover (promoted on January 5 to lieutenant colonel), who on March 13 had been reassigned from his beach defense duties to the 5th Interceptor Command as S-3 operations officer, displacing Ozzie Lunde, who was now made assistant S-3 (and remained responsible for the interceptor net). Joining Grover at Little Baguio was Capt. Benny Putnam, his protégé from prewar 20th Pursuit Squadron days, who was also released from I Philippine Corps beach defense responsibility for service with the 5th Interceptor Command.

The dispute of the brass over who was to command the air force was of little concern to the Bataan Field Flying Detachment. Dave Obert, for one, felt "we could have gotten along very well without any of them." While most of the pilots were content to serve under the immediate command of Dyess, many of the original Bataan Field detachment pilots had never accepted the rationale for bringing in the relatively inexperienced pilots of the 21st Pursuit in mid-February when there were so few P-40s left to fly anyway. Bill Rowe and the other pilots originally assigned there had felt like outsiders after Dyess took over.

The detachment pilots' freedom from high-level brass was not to be. Soon after being appointed S-3, Grover decided to become more directly involved in tactical command of flying operations and moved up to Bataan Field from Little Baguio, taking up residence in General George's vacated shack. Although Obert and several other pilots had little confidence in Grover's capabilities, they tried to continue the same relationship with him that they had had with General George, taking the initiative in meeting with him informally on the porch of the shack. This was not Grover's style of operating, and he ordered the pilots to discontinue the visits.

Grover did not suppress another of General George's innovations, however: twice-a-month parties. On the evening of Saturday, March 21, the pilots arranged another one, following on the March 3 bash, and invited about twenty nurses from the hospitals. Returning at 10:00 P.M. from a visit to the front lines, John Posten almost missed it, but the last six hours, to 4:00 A.M., proved the best part anyway. "It was another drunken brawl, but everyone had a good time," Posten recorded in his diary the next day. But it looked like this might be the last one for the pilots. They were running out of alcohol.

More serious than the developing shortage of alcohol was the deteriorating food supply situation. Officers and men alike had been on a semi-starvation diet since January, and now its effects were becoming all the more evident. More than half of the pilots were so weakened by hunger that they were incapable of flying a mission, and those that did had difficulty even getting in and out of the cockpit. The enlisted men were just walking skeletons, and most were unable to do any work at all. By late March, daily rations were down to 14.5 ounces of food per man, reduced from 27 ounces set in mid-February. The two meals consisted of a small helping of nearly spoiled rice and one slice of bread, sometimes a piece of fish, supplemented occasionally by any monkeys, lizards, or horses they happened to find and shoot.

Debilitated by the effects of a near-starvation diet and lacking vitamins in their food, the men lacked the resistance to ward off or recover from disease. Nearly everybody had either malaria or dysentery, and many were down with both. There just was not enough quinine to go around to arrest the malaria, and there was nothing to be done for the dysentery.

Under such conditions, it was just as well that they only had two P-40s to fly and that mission requests from the Corregidor brass were now few and far between. Indeed, since the Subic Bay attack of March 2, only six missions, all for single planes, were flown during the rest of the month. Only two were flown from mid-March: Dyess on March 18 to Cebu (to pick up quinine), and Andy Krieger on March 25 to Vigan.

With so little demand on them for flying missions, the pilots of the Bataan Field Flying Detachment now found themselves with too much idle time on their hands, spent mainly in thinking about food and family and in exchanging the latest rumors of help on the way. Another major activity was searching the jungle for fruit, lizards, monkeys, snakes, and any other source of nourishment. To the limit of their strength, many who had not yet done so were building shacks in preparation for the rainy season. For the officers and men of the now-planeless 20th Pursuit and the squadrons left on beach defense, the situation was equally bad. The focus of activity was on ways to find local sources of edible items to supplement the rations.

At the 20th's camp at Mariveles, the most successful enterprise of food supplementation was run by Lt. Jim Fossey, an Oklahoma boy who had prewar experience cutting up steers and big game with his father. Just after every Japanese bombing raid on Mariveles, Fossey and his assistant hurried out in a small van-type truck to the site of the attack, looking for injured carabao. There was a quartermaster regulation against killing any of the locals' work animals, but what if the critter was already injured? Any such carabao they located, Fossey and his assistant skinned and dressed on the spot, using the knives kept in the truck, then brought the carcass back to the camp for all to share. Later when Fossey went out on evenings when there had been no bombing and still came back with carabao meat, Joe Moore began to have doubts about Fossey's allegations that the creature was injured but did not push matters further—the meat was too welcome.

Some two miles northwest of Mariveles, on the west coast sector between the Talain and Biaan rivers, Hank Thorne was trying to keep his 3rd Pursuit Squadron in a condition to carry out their duties in that sector, whose defense had been left exclusively to them on the transfer of the 20th Pursuit to Mariveles in mid-February. Dysentery had swept over the 3rd's camp at that time, probably caused by flies that had conveyed germs from the hundreds of unburied Japanese dead left at Longoskawayan Point. The squadron's medical officer had succeeded in locating some liquid quinine, which kept the incidence of malaria down, but now the supply was exhausted. And by late March, they were down to one meal a day, a small portion of rice, after going through their stock of canned salmon and a succession of 26th Cavalry horses and mules. With no further work required on building up defensive positions and no sign of any new Japanese beach landings, the officers and men spent any off-duty time in the search for additional things to eat. Some of the men turned to fishing with dynamite, with mixed results, while others took up hunting.

Further north, in the Agloloma-Quinauan Point areas, the 34th Pursuit had also been left on beach defense, now alone responsible for defense of the sector after the transfer of Dyess's 21st Pursuit to Bataan and Cabcaben fields in mid-February. In this area of such heavy fighting six weeks earlier, the squadron had built up a formidable network of gun positions and barbed wire to meet any new Japanese landing attempt.

As with the other squadrons, the officers and men of the 34th spent most of the time after their duty shifts hunting and cooking. Boar hunting with automatic rifles was very common with the constantly hungry men, but when these wild pigs proved hard to find, they went after monkeys and even the more elusive boa constrictor and python. Cpl. Robert Reynolds spent much of his off-duty time in the jungle looking for iguana, whose tail meat tasted to him like roast chicken. But the main supplement for their scanty rations of rice was fish dynamited from the sea. Cashew nuts were also collected from trees, but wisely the men roasted them first before eating them. Eating raw cashew nuts would result in blistered lips, swollen faces, and body rashes, as was the experience of several 20th Pursuit pilots.

More fortunate than the 3rd or 34th pursuit squadrons in adequacy of food was the 17th Pursuit. Under its new commanding officer, 1st Lt. "Tex" Marble, it had left its rest camp at Kilometer Post 184 on February 21 for a new location south of Mariveles, where it was assigned to defense of the extreme southern tip of Bataan from Naiklec Point to Cochinos Point, including Nagbayog, Apatal, and Talaga bays. Half of the squadron was sent to the Camp Levee area, and the other half went to the Talaga Bay area to the east. New defensive positions were established in both locations.

The personnel of the 17th were pleased to find that the navy had a good food supply at both sites and proceeded to figure out ways to avail themselves of the bounty before the navy should vacate the area. In the Camp Levee location, they opted for theft, but when some of the 17th's men were caught trying to make off with food, the navy moved their whole supply out when they were transferred.

But at Talaga Bay, the 17th's detachment there was luckier: they traded some of their Japanese souvenirs that they had collected during the Anyasan/Silaiim campaign for food. In the end, the navy men left their entire stock behind for them. By late March, however, the Talaga Bay stock was exhausted, and food had become very scarce. Fortunately, about that time some of the men discovered a barge out in Mariveles Bay loaded with fifty-pound sacks of flour. Several sacks were off-loaded and carried to the squadron's kitchen area, where the flour was made into pancakes. These supplemented the meager rations and the occasional sand shark caught out in the bay.

At this time, some of the 17th's officers were trading cartons of the squadron's cigarettes with several boat crews out in Mariveles Harbor for sugar, fruit juices, and jam. The officers, however, were not sharing the bartered goods with the squadron's men. One day a group of the men confronted the officers on the matter and asked why none of these items ever ended up on the squadron's tables. One of the officers finally admitted that they had been keeping them for themselves and still had some in their tents. However, they would sooner dump them back in the bay than let the men have them, he asserted. Looking the young officer in the eye, S. Sgt. "Patty" Clawson, the grizzled fifty-two-year-old World War I veteran of the squadron, then took out his .45-caliber automatic, laid it on the table, and said, "Lieutenant, I would think a little before I did that." The next day, the food was divided up for everyone, and the lieutenant left the area.

Sometime before this incident, in mid-March, another of the 17th Pursuit's officers had disappeared under mysterious circumstances. Lt. Maurice Hughett had been put in charge of moving food rations and other supplies in a motor launch at night from Mariveles Harbor around the tip of Bataan to the 17th Pursuit's camps. On this evening, Hughett, accompanied by Capt. Ralph S. Fralick of the Corps of Engineers and three Air Corps sergeants, had unloaded the cargo and was headed back out to sea for the return trip around Cochinos Point to Mariveles. They were never seen again by the Bataan defenders.[7]

7 At 4:00 A.M. on Tuesday, March 24, Joe Moore maneuvered down Mariveles strip and took off in an aircraft he had never flown before—a Grumman J2F Duck.[8] Several of the mechanics of his 20th Pursuit Squadron had succeeded in getting the previously submerged single-engine amphibian in flying condition, proving their numerous detractors wrong.

Occupying the observer's rear seat was Moore's old squadron mate, Capt. Bill Cummings, now reassigned from Corregidor to Bataan to work with Lunde's interception net at Little Baguio.

After clearing the field, Moore began to hand-crank the wheels up into the side of the massive pontoon of the biplane and set course for Mindanao, where he would pick up desperately needed medicine and other supplies for the men on Bataan. There was plenty of room for such items deep in the hull of the ship, which was where two additional men could be seated side by side to take photos and carry out other duties assigned to the general purpose amphibian.

Expecting to reach Del Monte before daylight, Moore found that he had misjudged the speed of the rebuilt veteran, which was not making over 100 MPH. That would have put him into Mindanao at 9:00 A.M., too late in terms of the risk of encountering Japanese warplanes marauding over northern Mindanao. Moore now decided to stop over in Cebu instead, 140 miles short of his original destination. One hour after daybreak, Moore brought the amphibian down at the airfield outside Cebu City after his slow 380-mile flight from Bataan.

Early the next morning, Moore and Cummings took off for Mindanao and landed less than two hours later on the Del Monte strip near the pineapple plantation. After loading the hull with huge five-gallon cans of powdered quinine and other items critically needed on Bataan, such as radio tubes and batteries, Moore took off for Cebu alone in early evening. Cummings was being left behind at Del Monte for rest and to pilot the Duck on its next flight north.

Back at Cebu, Moore talked to the quartermaster about the cargo situation. He had wanted to load the amphibian with food at Cebu, but General Sharp on Mindanao had insisted he fill the Duck to its capacity with medicine and other items. However, the quartermaster had a solution; he would take Moore's powdered quinine and process it into less bulky pill form with a pill-making machine he had. Moore could pick the reprocessed quinine up on his next trip north. Now the cans of quinine were off-loaded and several hundred pounds of desperately needed food substituted, alongside the nonmedicinal items Moore would continue taking north.

Just before daylight on March 26, Moore landed the overloaded amphibian on the Mariveles strip without incident. Then, less than twenty-four hours later, at about 3:00 A.M. on March 27, Moore took off again for his second mission in the old Duck. This time he was taking Lts. Kiefer White and Harold Cocanougher with him as passengers.[9] The two pursuit pilots (Cocanougher had originally been in Moore's 20th Pursuit before being transferred to the 27th Materiel Squadron) were to bring back two of the new P-40E-1s that were being assembled at Buena Vista on Mindanao.

After dropping the two pilots off at Del Monte that morning, Moore proceeded back to Cebu in the evening to pick up the load of quinine pills that the quartermaster had waiting for him. (Bill Cummings would be remaining at Del Monte to pilot the Duck back on the return leg of its third round trip during the early hours of April 1.) The amphibian was again overloaded for the return trip, with some nine hundred pounds of quinine pills jammed into the hull. Nevertheless, Moore managed to bring it safely in at Mariveles before daybreak on March 31.

The addition of the Duck gave what came to be known as the Bamboo Fleet a fourth aircraft to shuttle medicine, food, and other supplies from the southern Philippines to beleaguered Bataan. The vital little service had come into being in early March when Bill Bradford swapped a Philippine Air Corps Stearman 76D3 trainer for his old 1933 Bellanca Skyrocket, a discarded veteran of Bradford's Philippine Aerial Taxi Company of prewar days, at Iloilo on March 7 and proposed to fly it on a regular basis to pick up medicine and food. Joining the five-passenger Skyrocket, old NPC-9, on these dangerous missions were a Beechcraft Staggerwing, NPC-28, usually flown by Air Corps Capt. Hervey Whitfield, and a 1934 four-passenger Waco cabin plane. The Duck was based at Mariveles, with the other three operating out of Mindanao.

While the Bamboo Fleet carried vital medicine, food, and supplies into Bataan from the southern Philippines, its cargo going south from Bataan was of a quite different nature: human beings. Those flown south by the Duck were fellow pilots on particular missions, but the three civilian aircraft, especially "Jitter Bill" Bradford's Bellanca, were usually reserved for evacuating the brass to the south. To Dave Obert, it was amusing to watch the colonels and majors crowding around the aircraft at night, trying to catch a ride out of Bataan. There were terrible rows over who outranked whom that Dyess had to resolve in allocating the few seats, followed by unsuccessful efforts of the designees to load as much luggage as possible into the plane. When it was the Skyrocket providing the transportation south, Bradford, oblivious to their rank, would yell in his nervous, rapid-fire way, forcing them to strip down to the allowed thirty pounds each.

Despite the valiant efforts of the Bamboo Fleet to bring in food and medicine for the Bataan Flying Detachment, shortages persisted, and the conditions of the officers and men continued to deteriorate. By late March, it was a question as to whether any further flying could be done at all; pilots could not pass the physical exam to which they were subjected prior to being approved to fly a mission. John Posten had lost so much weight that his voice had changed to a very high pitch.

Finally, Lt. Col. William Kennard, the 5th Interceptor Command's flight surgeon, after consulting with Capt. William Brenner, the 21st Pursuit's medical officer, and Capt. Livingston "Pope" Noell, the Bataan Field medical officer, decided to report the situation to Maj. Gen. Edward King, Wainwright's successor as commanding general of the Luzon Force on Bataan. If the pilots did not get extra food, there would be no more flying. It was as simple as that.

On King's request, Wainwright now authorized a "training table" for twenty-five pilots, to start on March 27. Extra food and vitamins would be sent from Corregidor to provide three full meals for ten days to help build up the selected pilots to flying strength. It was essential to have a core of fit pilots at this time, because it was likely that a number of P-40s would be coming in as reinforcements.

Sensitive to the morale implications of this proposal, Dyess decided to call in several of the senior noncoms of his squadron to elicit their reaction. The first sergeant, "Diz" Huston, spoke for the men. "They think it's wonderful you're going to get extra grubb," he told Dyess. "If the new stuff isn't enough, they'll give you theirs!" Proud of and touched by the attitude of his squadron's men, Dyess now put the feeding program into effect. Nine of the 20th Pursuit's pilots at Mariveles were selected, and those on duty at Cabcaben were called back. Several experienced pilots still assigned to beach defense duties were also picked to bring the total on the training table up to twenty-five.[10]

For the first meal that evening, the fortunate few were served deviled ham, peaches, crackers, and coffee. Then the next morning they had pancakes, bacon, and all the tomato juice they wanted, followed by a lunch of soup and crackers. All agreed that the meals were wonderful, though for some it was hard to get the rich food all down, so shrunken and used to plain rice were their stomachs.

The pilots' consciences also bothered them. Here they were eating all this fine food while the nonflying officers and all the men were still on a once-a-day diet of molding rice. John Posten, for one, could "hardly look them in the face." He had seen three of the men keel over in chow line on March 28 and heard some were so weak that they had to have their rice carried to them.

If those excluded from the training table ever resented the privileged status of the pilots, they never showed it. However, when a frame covered with heavy chicken wire was installed at the entrance to the cave where the special rations were stored across from the pilots' mess and was secured with a padlock, Pfc Jesse White and other enlisted men who noted this sign of distrust felt a bitter indignation. "None of us would stoop to stealing food from fellow Americans," White later recalled of the incident.

During the next days, the physical condition of the pilots improved rapidly as a consequence of the new program. Their weight increased daily;

Bill Rowe was pleasantly surprised to find his up to 133 pounds in four days. Their basic resistance to disease, however, was still poor. For Dave Obert, down with malaria when the training table was introduced, it was still a great effort just to walk to the mess hall in his weakened condition.

Now the main concern of the pilots was shifting from their stomachs to overhead activities. Since March 24, they had been subjected to daily bombing attacks, some continuous during most of the day and even into the evening. And these Japanese were not the usual dive-bombers but the "big boys," the twin-engine high-flying bombers, coming in waves of from nine to twenty-seven planes. Targets were Bataan Field, Cabcaben, Mariveles, and, particularly, Corregidor.[11] As Dave Obert in his diary recorded:

> First, you would hear the droning of their engines in the distance, then you would see them flying high above. Just before they were directly overhead, you begin to hear a swishing sound, which starts out faintly, and then increases until it blankets out everything else, like a freight train bearing down on you. If you are near a hole, you flatten in the bottom of it. If not, you flop on the ground, face down. The few seconds the bombs are roaring down seem like hours, but at last there comes the terrific explosion and the whistling of shrapnel if you are near the explosion. You get up with a silent prayer of thanks while outwardly cussing the Japanese. The a/a guns have been cracking away in the meantime, but now you seem to see them for the first time. You hopefully watch the bursts of smoke high above and cheer madly when it gets near the planes. A few minutes and it is all over. The drone of the planes dies away and all that is left is the fire started by the bombs and the tiny puffs of A.A. smoke slowly disappearing high above.

It was a miracle no one was killed on the airfields during the first week of the bombing offensive. Some of the craters created at Bataan Field by the 550-pound bombs being dropped were forty feet in diameter and fifteen to twenty feet deep. Everyone wondered if the Japanese were making a final push against the beleaguered American and Filipino troops on Bataan.

On March 21, Japanese planes dropped leaflets all over Bataan, calling on General Wainwright to surrender to save further bloodshed. General MacArthur had deserted his men. Maybe the Japanese did mean business this time.

Part Six
THE FALL OF BATAAN

In mid-March the monthlong lull in hostilities on Bataan was broken with renewed Japanese aggressiveness. Skirmishes with Japanese patrols were on the rise, and aircraft in large numbers once again began to appear, attacking frontline troops and supply areas alike. Artillery fire was stepped up. Artillery and aerial bombardment against the sick and half-starved Americans and Filipinos of the recently established (March 21, 1942) U.S. Forces in the Philippines (USFIP) command was particularly effective in taking a psychological toll.

Then at 9:00 A.M. on Friday, April 3, Good Friday, the Japanese opened up with a massive artillery attack on the Main Line of Resistance that continued until 3:00 P.M. with only a half-hour pause. It was the most destructive barrage the defenders had yet experienced. And then the newly arrived heavy bombers added to the bombardment of the front lines in 150 sorties flown that day. Following the concerted aerial and artillery attack, Japanese units began to assault the part of the MLR that had borne the brunt of the attack and by the end of the day had penetrated deeply against little opposition from the terrified Filipino defenders, who were fleeing south.

The following day, the Japanese offensive was resumed with another artillery attack coordinated with aerial bombardment. Once again, the Filipino Army troops panicked and fled to the rear.

On Easter Sunday, April 5, the devastating artillery and aerial bombardment commenced again, but this time the defending Filipinos fiercely opposed the subsequent infantry attack, though being forced to give way. The next day, a desperate counterattack effort met a fresh Japanese offensive, ending in disaster for the defenders by nightfall.

Finally, on April 7, II Corps disintegrated in confusion in the face of relentless Japanese attacks preceded by yet another artillery and aerial bombardment. By the evening the Japanese had broken the entire MLR of II Corps and were poised to push forward all the way to Cabcaben on the southeast coast of Bataan.

On the morning of April 8, the decimated USFIP units took up new positions, but not according to any plan, because of the confusion and breakdown in communications during the withdrawal. The men were starving and exhausted after five days of unceasing bombardment, which once again commenced this day. By afternoon, the defenders had fallen back again, jamming the roads. Chaos reigned supreme.

That evening Corregidor ordered I Corps on the west coast to launch a counterattack, but Maj. Gen. Edward King, commanding all forces on Bataan, refused to transmit the order; he knew it could not be executed. The campaign was over. There was no possibility of halting the Japanese advance. King would not countenance any further loss of life. At midnight, General King called his staff together to inform them of his decision to surrender his forces. Then he notified all units and gave them instructions on carrying out the surrender, including destruction of all matériel of military value. Some two thousand of his force managed to escape to Corregidor by small boats and barges that evening. But the remaining seventy-eight thousand were left on Bataan to surrender to the Japanese.

At 9:00 on the morning of April 9, General King went forward to meet with representatives of the Japanese command at Lamao, on the southeast coast of Bataan. At 12:30, after protracted negotiations, King agreed to surrender his forces unconditionally. All troops along the road and on the adjoining trails were ordered to march to the east road, to stack arms, and to await further instructions.

24. "PLEASE DON'T BAIL OUT"

1 During the last days of March, no one was getting much sleep at Bataan and Cabcaben fields. Since March 28, the Japanese had kept their bombers overhead day and night, including during meal hours, when the select pilots at the special training table had to interrupt their meals and head for a foxhole. At night, searchlights in the area would try to pick up the high-flying Japanese, their thin fingers of light streaking the black sky, providing quite a spectacle for the defenders of Bataan. Then the antiaircraft would tune in, blasting away at the bombers.

For the pilots assigned to stand by the remaining P-40s at Bataan and Cabcaben fields each night, sleep was a particularly scarce commodity, grabbed during intervals in the daylight bombings of the area. A typical situation was that of John Posten. After having been on alert from 2:00 A.M. till morning with Wilson Glover next to "Kibosh" at Bataan Field on March 29, Posten was sent to Cabcaben Field the following evening with two other pilots to stand alert with "P-40 Something."

In response to a report on March 28 that the Japanese were planning a landing party on the east coast of Bataan, Ed Dyess was maintaining three pilots on alert at both fields, day and night. In the event of a landing, the two P-40s were to be moved down to Mariveles for safety.

To Bill Rowe and the other red-eyed pilots, it was beginning to look like the end of the Bataan campaign was at hand. They now began to hope for evacuation on one of the planes of the Bamboo Fleet, which were making frequent trips south with their human cargo. Rowe's opportunity had apparently come when Dyess ordered him to fly out with Bradford's Bellanca on the evening of March 28, along with two other pilots, but then Dyess unaccountably canceled the order, and the Skyrocket left without him two nights later after needed repairs.

The next night, March 31/April 1, it seemed like Grand Central Station at Bataan Field to Rowe. Lt. Willy Strathern flew in with the Beechcraft Staggerwing, bringing candy, radiograms, and news of old squadron mates now down in Australia and Java, picked up a few enlisted men, and headed back south the same evening. Then Capt. Jack Randolph flew an old Stearman 76D3 out with two passengers in the rear cockpit.

At 2:00 A.M., Capt. "Black Jack" Caldwell of the 5th Interceptor Command staff at Little Baguio took off in the Grumman Duck with three passengers: Ray Gehrig in the rear cockpit, and Benny Putnam and John Posten in the hull. On Dyess's orders, Posten and Gehrig were to fly the two P-35As on Mindanao back to Bataan, where they were more needed than down south.[1] Putnam was being sent to Mindanao to be put in charge of the four P-40s there, including the three newly assembled ones.

On the afternoon of April 2, Jack Donalson flew south in the "P-40 Something," but he was not being evacuated. Dyess was sending him to Cebu to pick up some morale boosters for the men at Bataan field. When Bill Rowe went over to Cabcaben to pick him up the next morning following his return, he found the rear of the P-40 loaded with candy, cigarettes, cigars, and a little liquor. Donalson had also brought back some radiograms sent from the United States, including one for Rowe that raised his spirits. Donalson's mission was uneventful, except for his being fired on while approaching Bataan by American and Filipino troops at Mariveles, who put two holes in the already crazy-quilt P-40B.

Back on Bataan that evening of April 2/3 was the hard-working Duck, flown in (evidently by Bill Cummings) from Del Monte after dropping off Caldwell, Putnam, Gehrig, and Posten. Its return trip was slightly delayed because of a flat tire suffered after arriving at Del Monte, but an old automobile tire was put on as a replacement.

Late that evening, the Duck was readied at Mariveles for yet another flight south after only a brief stopover on Bataan. This time it would carry one person over its capacity of four. Bill Cummings would fly it down, with Joe Moore on board as the return pilot and Lt. Tom Gerrity, CWO Jack Day, the armament whiz of the 17th Pursuit, and Air Corps Lt. John Wienert as passengers. Gerrity was particularly happy to be evacuated. He was tired of the lack of opportunity to fly. At 3:30 in the morning, the overloaded amphibian finally succeeded in becoming airborne after three tries and headed for Del Monte.

2 When John Posten and Ray Gehrig touched down at Bataan Field at 7:15 A.M. on April 4 with the two P-35As they had picked up at Del Monte, they had quite a story to tell about their flight south in the old Duck and their brief stay on Mindanao. Posten swore he would never forget that trip for as long as he lived.

Struggling alone at 95 MPH, the reconstructed amphibian had taken four and a half hours to reach Cebu. The Cebu–Del Monte leg of the trip was made in broad daylight, with Posten swapping positions with Gehrig and now sitting nervously in the rear seat behind the Duck's .30-caliber machine gun. Over the mountains of Cebu, the engine cut out twice, and it took two more hours before they reached Del Monte, all that time the aircraft constituting a "sitting duck" for any Japanese aircraft that might have been flying in the vicinity.

After having spent three grim months on Bataan, Gehrig and Posten now found themselves in another world. At Del Monte, they just sat around and ate all day, then at Cebu on the return trip in the P-35As, they were shown full hospitality by Col. Charles Cook, the quartermaster of the island. As Colonel Cook's guests, they were each given a room and bath to themselves in the big house Cook had commandeered. Walking around in Cebu City, where he had a shave and a shoeshine, Posten could not believe that just four hundred miles to the north, seventy thousand men were starving to death when there was so much of everything down on Cebu.

Before Gehrig and Posten had taken off for Bataan at 4:45 on the morning of April 4, their P-35As had been loaded with candy, cigarettes, cigars, quinine, brandy, and mail. The two veteran pilots had a difficult time navigating because of a partial overcast but managed to reach Bataan without incident after two and a half hours' flying.

As each man at Bataan Field now received his candy bar and pack of cigarettes, their haggard faces momentarily lit up with joy. To Obert and the other pilots watching the occasion, it was wonderful to see the men's reactions to such small gifts. Life was tough on Bataan for everyone, and little generosities were truly appreciated.

Posten mentioned during his debriefing that he had been told by Colonel Cook that fourteen boats had been lost in the past ten days trying to get food through from Cebu to Bataan. But Cook had also told him that Bataan could definitely expect help within a week. The Bataan pilots did not know what the colonel had in mind, but the news cheered them up, despite the deteriorating conditions under which they were serving on Bataan.

Later that morning, Dyess called Posten, Obert, and Krieger in for a hush-hush meeting. Without elaborating, Dyess asked them, "Do you want to stick your necks out a long way on a mission?" Since such a request did not seem out of the ordinary, the three highly experienced pilots agreed without hesitation. They were then told to be ready to leave for Del Monte that evening. It was a secret mission; they would get their instructions there.

At midnight, Capt. Hervey Whitfield flew his Beechcraft into Bataan Field from the south, with orders to pick up the pilots slated for the mission. Much to their surprise, Obert, Posten, and Krieger were now told by Lieutenant Colonel Grover that Grover himself would be going on the plane and that only one of the three scheduled pilots could join him. Grover explained that he had decided to direct fighter operations from that end. When Whitfield interjected that he could take one more passenger, Grover refused and said he did not want the plane overcrowded, as he would be wearing a parachute. The "bumped" two could come down on the Duck, due in at Bataan the following evening.

Grover's sudden and unexpected intervention and selfish attitude did nothing to improve his standing among the Bataan Field pilots. To Bill Rowe, he was "a bad apple," disliked by everyone. Unknown to the pilots, Grover had been ordered to Del Monte by Colonel Churchill at a suggestion on April 2 by Brigadier General Beebe, Wainwright's chief of staff on Corregidor. By a cut of the cards among the three candidates, Krieger was selected to fly with Grover in the Beechcraft. Shortly after midnight, Whitfield lifted the veteran Bamboo Fleet aircraft off Bataan Field for the trip south.

With only Obert and Posten now scheduled for the evening flight south on April 5, Easter Sunday, Bill Rowe felt he had a case for joining them. After all, he would be the most experienced pilot left on Bataan after the departure of Obert and Posten. He regarded Bataan as doomed, and he would be more valuable down south. But his arguments failed to convince Dyess, who turned his request down without explaining why. Something was up, and Rowe did not like it.

Fate now almost prevented Obert from going on the mission. The 21st Pursuit's medical officer, 1st Lt. William Brenner, was refusing to clear Obert for flying because of his malarial condition. However, 1st Lt. "Pope" Noell, the flight surgeon for the Bataan Field detachment, disagreed with Brenner's ruling, maintaining that Obert's malaria was not serious enough to impair his flying ability. When the matter was referred to Dyess for decision, a ruling was made in favor of Obert.

Late that evening, the mission of Obert and Posten was now confronted with another setback. On its flight in from Cebu, the old Duck had blown a cylinder about seventy-five miles out of Bataan. Joe Moore had barely been able to limp into Cabcaben Field at 4:00 on April 6 with the loss of power. It would not be going anywhere for several days.

But earlier that night, at 2:00 A.M., Jack Randolph had come in to Bataan with the Waco cabin plane, scheduled to fly out selected passengers. Now Colonel Gregg at Little Baguio ordered a switch, in view of the importance of getting Obert and Posten down to Mindanao for the secret mission; the intended passengers for the Waco were bumped. Capt. Dick Fellows, in charge of the air depot at Bataan Field, would also replace Randolph as the pilot, for some reason unknown to the others. Randolph insisted that he was the only one who knew how to fly the Waco but was overruled. At 3:00 the old cabin plane took off in total darkness with the two long-delayed passengers.

Following a stopover on Cebu for the day, where Obert and Posten were told by Colonel Cook that a "big show" was coming off but that he could not tell them what it was, Fellows took off for Del Monte about 4:00 in the afternoon. Obert was not happy about flying in daylight in the old, unarmed Waco; they would not have a chance against any Japanese plane that might find them. But his worries were over when the Waco touched down at Del Monte just before dark.

After a good dinner, Obert and Posten, with high hopes, were called to Lieutenant Colonel Grover's quarters for the expected revelations of what this secret mission was about. In the meeting room, they found Benny Putnam, Andy Krieger, and Grover already in conference. Now Grover locked all the doors and pulled down the blinds, adding to the suspense. "We have a very important mission scheduled," he intoned, "so listen closely while I explain it to you." Grover then began his briefing.

In Cebu, seven transports loaded with food were going to try to get through to Bataan. Between Cebu and Bataan, the Japanese had about seven destroyers and three cruisers, which were being used to blockade Bataan and other points, plus a number of fighter and bombardment aircraft. The pilots' job was to keep the Japanese Navy and Air Force from sinking the vessels. A formation of B-17s was expected in from Australia at any moment. They would attack Japanese aircraft on Luzon in the morning, return to Del Monte, then take off to bomb Japanese warships in Visayan waters and at Subic Bay in the afternoon.

Following the bombing attack on the first day, the four P-40s were to fly reconnaissance of the entire Visayan area. If any hostile surface craft remained in the area, the P-40s were to attack destroyers with strafing fire until they were neutralized and report any cruisers to Del Monte, which would dispatch the bombers to attack them. If the bombers did not arrive as planned, the P-40 pilots were also to strafe the cruisers and attack them with fragmentation bombs if Joe Moore could get some down from Bataan in the Duck.

As soon as Japanese warships in the Visayas were dispersed, the loaded relief ships would start their blockade-running voyage to Corregidor. The P-40 pilots would provide protection for the vessels en route against Japanese aircraft, operating out of Panay and Cebu when the ships were out of range of the Del Monte field. Two PT boats would also escort the ships. As the ships moved northward, the two P-40s on Bataan would join in flying cover too on the last day of the expected three-day voyage. If and when the convoy reached Corregidor, any survivors of the four Mindanao-based escorting P-40s would be landed at Bataan Field and join up with the two P-40s there in a resumption of normal operations from Bataan. Putnam, Obert, Posten, and Krieger would fly their first mission on the morning of April 8.

Concluding the briefing, Grover, in an apparent effort to bolster their morale, told the dumbfounded pilots, "I think you have a 75 to 25 chance of getting through this mission." To Obert, "that was the most optimistic statement of the war!" Grover knew "damn well" that we "didn't have any chance at all." With a lot of luck, they might be able to cripple one destroyer or two, but more likely the first warship they tried to strafe would "knock us ass over teakettle." Even if they survived being shot down, they would end up in shark-infested waters.

That evening, Obert and the others could not sleep, knowing it was probably their last night alive. Obert now began to see red. He had seen as much action as anyone, had gotten no thanks for it, and now was going out to sure death. Sure, he would go through with this suicide mission, but only because it would be in the cause of helping those he *personally* knew on Bataan, whose situation was desperate and who were dependent on the ships getting through to them with food and medicine.

3 On the evening of April 5 at Bataan Field, Bill Rowe was surprised to find a number of additional pilots reporting in for duty there, including his old squadron mates Bud Powell and Joe McClellan. Some of them, along with the pilots on temporary duty on Mindanao, were assigned to a new twenty-five-man training table; the ten days of the original training table were now up. Rowe found himself now on a six-man reserve training table, along with Wilson Glover, John Burns, Gus Williams, Jim Fossey, and another pilot. He speculated that perhaps they were the next ones to be sent south.

All morning of April 6, the men at Bataan Field were ducking Japanese bombers pounding the front lines. Rowe skinned his arm when he jumped for Charley Sneed's old foxhole. Later in the day, he took over John Posten's housekeeping possessions that Posten had left behind the previous night on his departure, including a very welcome mattress. But that evening he could not enjoy the mattress; he had been sent over to Cabcaben Field to operate the radio there, since a Japanese landing party was expected. The landing did not materialize, and he spent an uncomfortable night, with Ben Brown and Sam Grashio, in the tunnel, hot and bothered by mosquitoes.

When Rowe returned to Bataan Field early the morning of April 7, he found out at breakfast time that two more of the detachment had been flown south several hours before daybreak. "Jitter Bill" Bradford had taken John Burns and Wilson Glover out in the Beech Staggerwing that he had brought in the evening before from Del Monte. Rowe wondered when his turn would finally come, if at all.

Late that afternoon, flying classmates and good friends Gus Williams and Johnny McCown took off on separate recon missions ordered by Dyess earlier in the day.[2] Williams was flying the P-40E, Dyess's "Kibosh," up north to check out any Japanese bombers at Clark and Nichols fields, while McCown in the "P-40 Something" was going south to look for Japanese surface vessels. It was important to know of the disposition of any bombers or warships in connection with the imminent blockade-running effort from Cebu. Both P-40s were expected back just at dark, reducing the risk for surprise attacks by the marauding Zeros so in evidence the past days.[3]

After climbing together after takeoff to about 18,000 feet, Williams and McCown split, heading in their different directions. Flying over all the Luzon airfields, Williams observed many airplanes on them, but no bombers. After a totally uneventful mission, Williams headed south, came across Manila Bay, and swung into Bataan Field for the landing as darkness settled on the peninsula. Williams soon learned that McCown had come back unexpectedly early; he had aborted his mission south because of mechanical problems and had landed at Cabcaben. He thus was unable to report to Dyess on the situation of warships south of Luzon.

About 10:00 o'clock that evening, Williams walked over to the shack he shared with McCown and Bob Ibold and turned in. Three hours later they were awakened by the sound of approaching bombers, then moments later were knocked out of bed when a bomb exploded close by. By now, however, the Bataan Field pilots were inured to such nocturnal interruptions and moments later were sound asleep again. But Williams was hardly back to sleep when he was awakened again, this time by someone telling him that Dyess wanted to see him. Reporting in to Dyess's shack, the sleepy Arizonan was told he would be flying to Iloilo early that morning with Dick Fellows in the Waco. After collecting his musette bag containing all his possessions—a razor and a toothbrush—Williams walked in the darkness to the field. He also had with him a long list of requests from the nurses at the two hospitals: panties, brassieres, lipstick, bobby pins, and other female "necessities."

When Williams spotted the cabin Waco and headed for it, he found Bill Rowe there too, as well as "Black Jack" Caldwell, also scheduled for the flight south. Rowe had been awakened about 2:00 A.M. and informed by Dyess that he was to be flown south too. He had brought his musette bag and a blanket with him. After so many days of expectation, Rowe was relieved to be finally selected for evacuation but was still jittery from the bombing attack on the field that had jolted him out of bed earlier. The Japanese had unloaded just as Fellows was bringing the old cabin plane in for a landing, but fortunately it was not hit in the bombing.

Taking off from Bataan Field at 4:00 without lights, Fellows brought the veteran Bamboo Fleet ship safely into Iloilo at dawn. After disembarking, the four men went over to the club near the airfield, where they gorged themselves on breakfast unlike any they had had on Bataan: six fried eggs each, toast, and sausage.

Joining them at the table was Benny Putnam, who had also just flown in to Iloilo from Del Monte in one of the newly assembled P-40E-1s. Benny had flown a recon, searching the waters between Panay and Mindanao for enemy warships, as per the orders for the protection of the Cebu blockade-running mission. Later that day, Rowe met John Posten, who had completed a daybreak recon for the same purpose from Del Monte in another of the new P-40E-1s. Posten had spotted a minelayer on the way over, which fired at him "with all the antiaircraft guns it had" but missed.

Dave Obert had also flown a reconnaissance this morning in the third of the new P-40s but had found no ships in his search area and had come back to land at Del Monte, as ordered by Grover. For Obert, it was a relief to get back to flying; it kept his mind occupied and off the hopelessness of the mission.

The day before, Andy Krieger had flown the fourth P-40 up to Cebu a day ahead of the original schedule. There he reported in to Colonel Cook to make arrangements for the P-40 escort of the food ships. He had also been having discussions with the four PT boat officers involved in the blockade-running scheme: Lt. John D. Bulkeley and Ens. George E. Cox of PT-41, and Lt. Robert B. Kelly and Ens. Anthony B. Akers of PT-34. Later that day, Krieger received a wire from Grover at Del Monte: he should make arrangements at the airfield for the arrival of P-40s from Bataan that evening.

Apparently restless to start the mission, Grover had decided to send Putnam, Posten, and Obert on solo reconnaissances the morning of April 8, not waiting for the bombers from Australia to show up and deliver the opening blow against Visayan warships in advance of the P-40 reconnaissance of the Visayan waters. The three new P-40E-1s they would fly had been ferried into Del Monte that morning from their base at Maramag.[4]

Unknown to Grover, MacArthur that day had radioed Wainwright on Corregidor that the bombers, now identified as two B-17s and nine B-25s, would not be leaving Australia until the ninth of April—but more likely the tenth—to execute their role in the blockade-running mission. The exact time of departure depended on the completion of installation of extra gas tanks on the B-25s.

4 At 4:45 A.M. on April 8 at Bataan Field, Sam Grashio went down to the revetment where Dyess's "Kibosh" was hidden, climbed into the cockpit, and took off on a reconnaissance mission, the last that would be flown from Bataan. Dyess had asked him the day before to fly the recon mission aborted earlier that day by Johnny McCown.[5] He was to look for any Japanese naval forces in the sea between Corregidor and the Busuanga and Culion islands (in the Calamian Group), 170 miles to the south, located southwest of Mindoro. If he had not used up more than half his

gas supply in the fuselage tank and the belly tank by the time he reached the islands, he was to continue further south until he had reached the midpoint in his gas availability, when he should turn around and fly back to Bataan Field. Grashio was told that any information he collected was for the purpose of facilitating the evacuation of VIPs from Corregidor, but in actuality it was needed in connection with the still-secret Cebu blockade-running operation, about which the pilots on Bataan were still ignorant.

After climbing to 10,000 feet, Grashio proceeded south as instructed. Along the way, he noted the presence of some Japanese ships and duly plotted their number, type, location, direction, and the time in the navigation chart he had been given. But his thoughts were elsewhere. Would he be able to get back to Bataan at all? If so, would the dreaded Zeros be waiting there to jump him? Would he have enough gas left to have any chance against them?

The latest check on his fuel gauge now showed it was halfway down. Resisting the desire to keep going south and be free of surely doomed Bataan, the reluctant pilot swung his plane into a 180-degree turn and headed back to Bataan, planning to land at Cabcaben Field.

As Grashio approached the field at 7:00 A.M., the tower observer radioed him that the field was under attack and that he should circle around Corregidor, whose guns could provide him protection. Nervous about his dwindling gas supply, Grashio decided to try to land at Mariveles instead. But then an "all clear" call came in from Cabcaben.

Just as Grashio cut his engine after coming in to land at Cabcaben Field, a maintenance man rushed out to meet him, hooked up the P-40 to a tug, and began towing the P-40 to a revetment. He was hurrying because three twin-engine bombers were high overhead near the bomb release point. Realizing he was caught in another raid, Grashio sprinted for a foxhole, tripped over a tent stake, then fell into the shelter.

In addition to newly arrived "Kibosh," the "P-40 Something" was also on Cabcaben Field this morning, still undergoing repairs to get it back into commission after McCown's aborted mission. As soon as work on it was completed, it was to be taken up on another mission.

At about noon, Joe Moore at Mariveles was instructed by Lieutenant Colonel Gregg to be ready to go over to Cabcaben to pick up the hybrid P-40B, his old number 41, and fly down to Del Monte, where he was to report in to his former CO, Lieutenant Colonel Grover. Moore was slated to join the other pilots in the Cebu-Corregidor blockade-running operation.

On Bataan Field, several Japanese dive-bombers spent the entire morning, flying missions every fifteen to twenty minutes, hitting the bivouac area. Each time they attacked and went back for another load, Randy Keator and Jim Mullen would climb out of their foxholes and start digging a little deeper. Bill Powell of the 3rd Pursuit and Bud Powell of the 17th Pursuit were injured in the bombing, as were several others, including T. Sgt. Marcus Keithley of Headquarters Squadron, severely wounded by shrapnel. Keithley had made the mistake of remaining out of his foxhole during one of the raids.

As soon as the bombing let up, the area caught some incoming artillery shells. One missile struck the tree just above the bunker where Sgt. Sid Wilkinson and Pfc Jesse White of Headquarters Squadron were sheltering, terrifying the two maintenance men with its explosion and concussion. The upper third of the giant tree trunk was blown away, and the tree was denuded of foliage. Several pieces of shrapnel penetrated the sand bags and were protruding a few inches through the metal roofing above their heads.

In the afternoon, the dive-bombers resumed their activity. One bomb hit very close to General George's old shack, demolishing it in the blast. This time the "Anns" also dropped white phosphorous bombs, starting several brush fires that the men tried to put out between attacks.

All day, the screeching sound of the Japanese peeling off and diving down on them reverberated in the ears of the Bataan Field detachment. It was almost impossible for the pilots and field crews to get out of their foxholes long enough to grab something to eat. Without a doubt, it was the most terrific day of bombing the men had endured on Bataan. The bivouac area was in shambles by day's end.

When the bombing finally let up in late afternoon, Ben Brown, Sam Grashio, and Lloyd Stinson showed up at the field. They had just finished their alert duty at Cabcaben and were heading for the mess hall for the evening meal. Switching places with them for the Cabcaben alert duty were Shorty Crosland, Stewart Robb, and W. G. Coleman, all 34th Pursuiters. About five o'clock, Brown, in his role as operations officer of the detachment, informed Randy Keator, Jack Donalson, and Larry McDaniel that they were to go on the alert at the field that evening.

The day before, Dyess had received orders via 5th Interceptor Command Headquarters from Wainwright to hold his planes ready during hours of darkness for an attack on an expected Japanese landing party or artillery boats and barges. In recent evenings, artillery boats had been firing on the defenders' positions.

Keator was assigned to fly one of the P-35As and McDaniel the other, while Donalson was entrusted with "Kibosh," which had been transferred back to Bataan Field from Cabcaben.[6] Enlisted men of the 21st Pursuit were busy in the revetments hooking up three 30-pound fragmentation bombs under each wing of the three Bataan veterans and loading their machine guns with .30- and .50-caliber ammunition.

About six o'clock the three pilots experienced yet another noise: heavy artillery shells were whistling by over their heads. Were the Japanese shelling them again? Soon they found out that their own artillery had been forced to withdraw from their earlier positions and were now established and firing just behind Bataan Field. The airfield was now between the front lines and the enemy.

A few minutes later, the guard down on the runway phoned in to the command post and excitedly told the pilots that a captain had just stopped by and told him that the front lines had completely crumbled. Japanese tanks followed by infantry were advancing down the road and were now just four miles from the field. Then all the telephone communications went out. Not knowing what to do, Keator, Donalson, and McDaniel just sat tensely by their planes and waited for orders.

Soon afterward, the communication lines were repaired. A message now came in from Lieutenant Colonel Gregg at Little Baguio: the Bataan Field pilots should take off, bomb and strafe the Japanese piercing the front lines, and then head south for Cebu or Mindanao.

As darkness began to descend, maintenance men pulled the three warbirds out on the runway with the tugs. Just as Keator, Donalson, and McDaniel were now preparing to take off, Dyess arrived at the scene. He had heard the news directly from the captain and had rushed to the field. Going over to his squadron mate Donalson, whose fighting spirit he greatly admired, Dyess told him to take off immediately and bomb and strafe the approaching Japanese. But if the news was a false alarm and the Japanese had not broken through, he was to come in and land. Otherwise he was to pass over the field and rock his wings after attacking the Japanese as a sign the report was correct, then head south.

But Keator and McDaniel were to wait. Dyess wanted to call 5th Interceptor Command Headquarters to tell the brass of the situation and get fresh orders on how to handle the situation. He would be back as soon as possible, he told the two anxious young men. On the telephone to Gregg, Dyess was ordered to start evacuating the pilots in the remaining planes. Gregg specified the pilots to be evacuated: Moore (who was already scheduled to go out), Ozzie Lunde at 5th Interceptor Command Headquarters, Hank Thorne (who had been transferred to Bataan Field from the 3rd Pursuit's beach defense position on April 1), Ben Brown, and Dyess himself.

Gregg had picked the most senior and experienced pilots. He did not intend to go by rank, but rather on the basis of who could do the most for the war effort. But Dyess objected to being included on the list. "We haven't surrendered yet; I can't leave my men," he protested to Gregg.

Listening to the conversation at the command post, Sam Grashio was not surprised at Dyess's refusal to fly out. A few days earlier, when discussing the possibilities for evacuation, Dyess had indicated to Grashio and squadron mate Leo Golden that he intended to stay to the end with his men. Dyess had offered to have Sam and Leo, married men with a child each, evacuated, but when they learned of Dyess's position, they decided to stay with their commanding officer out of respect and admiration for him.

Before Dyess had gotten through to Lieutenant Colonel Gregg, Donalson had returned in "Kibosh" over the field. Dyess and the others watched as the pilot rocked the wings of the P-40E in confirmation of the Japanese breakthrough. Even before Donalson had gotten the wheels up following takeoff, he had seen the Japanese coming down the east road. Over the bridge on the road, Donalson dropped all six of his bombs, then went into several strafing runs on the Japanese troops before heading back over Bataan Field to give the signal. Now he headed for Iloilo.

Still waiting down at the strip in their P-35As, Keator and McDaniel watched as tracer bullets flew back and forth across the field, lighting the now-darkened sky like a neon sign. It was obvious to Keator that a pitched battle was now being fought not far from the north end of the runway where it crossed the north-south road. Then Keator noticed someone approaching him who had just arrived up the road in an old Chrysler car. It was Ozzie Lunde from 5th Interceptor Command Headquarters.

When Lunde told Keator that he had orders from Gregg to take the P-35A south, Keator's heart started pounding. In a state of shock, Keator climbed out of the P-35A's cockpit and handed Lunde his parachute and goggles. Then Keator thought about the big baggage compartment in the rear fuselage of the P-35A and asked Lunde if he could ride in it. Lunde agreed, and Keator opened the side panel door, climbed in, and shut the door. He sat down on the hard indentation in the floor where a seat-type parachute pack was meant to be fitted.

Lunde had his own problems. He suddenly realized that the map that he had prepared on which he had marked his route to Iloilo was not with him; he had left it in the Chrysler. "Jee-sus!" Lunde exclaimed as he watched his chauffeur drive the Chrysler down the runway for the return to Little Baguio. Lunde had never been to Iloilo before.

All Lunde had with him was his musette bag, his gun, and a toothbrush. And his pants were torn. Oh yes, he also had a copy of the Lord's Prayer given to him by T. Sgt. Louis Albin of his 5th Interceptor Command staff. When Albin told him just before he left headquarters that evening that his mother had given him the Lord's Prayer, Lunde was moved by the expression in Albin's eyes, that of a man who expected to meet his Maker soon.

Now Lunde was having problems getting the P-35A started. He had not been in one in months, and it was dark; he was tired, and there was shooting across the runway. Sweating out the situation in the baggage compartment, Keator had the worst thoughts. What if Lunde could not get the balky ship airborne and he piled up in the middle of the battle that was raging on the opposite end of the runway, with those six fragmentation bombs under the wings? Or what if machine gun bullets plowed into the baggage compartment as the plane passed over the battleground?

Lunde was still struggling to get the engine to start. Then Keator yelled from the back, "The choke! The choke!" Lunde had forgotten that in the P-35A, the choke must be pushed in. This time it started instantly. In his anxiety to get off, Lunde did not bother to wait to warm the engine up but headed down the runway with the engine sputtering. It suddenly caught, and he cleared the field.

Lunde now headed over the water and released his bombs into Manila Bay to lighten up the overloaded P-35A and build up speed. But neither he nor Keator were sure if all had actually dropped. Looking out the glass panel in the side door of the fuselage, Keator could see that it was now completely dark as they passed out of sight of Corregidor. He knew that they had a long, dark night ahead of them; the moon was not due to rise until two o'clock that night.

Back at Bataan Field, McDaniel was still in the cockpit of his P-35A, awaiting the return of Dyess. Then about eight o'clock, Hank Thorne and Ben Brown appeared out of the darkness. They explained to McDaniel that in a meeting near the field, Dyess had instructed Thorne to take the remaining P-35A south, with Brown as a passenger, in accordance with Gregg's orders.

Thorne believed he had been picked to fly the P-35A out because of his familiarity with the southern islands, gained during frequent cross-country trips flown during prewar days. But he was certainly not knowledgeable about Bataan Field. Although he had been assigned to the Bataan Field Flying Detachment since April 1, when he reported in to Dyess with squadron mate Howard Hardegree after being relieved of beach defense command of the 3rd Pursuit, he had not been asked by Dyess to fly any missions from the field until now.

Ben Brown pointed out to Thorne in the pitch darkness the direction of the runway, along which there were no boundary lights or illumination of any sort. The night sky, however, was lit up with the glow of burning ammunition dumps, set afire by the American and Filipino troops. Dyess's own men earlier had set charges to destroy the field's fuel stores, ammunition, and bombs, which they were now detonating.

Agreeing not to leave McDaniel behind, Thorne ordered him into the baggage compartment, which he would share with Brown. In Brown's pocket was a packet of razor blades and ten pesos, given to him the night before by Sgt. Jim Bass of his 34th Pursuit Squadron as payment for the telegram Brown promised to send on his behalf to Bass's wife on arrival south.

Thorne had no trouble starting the engine and at 8:15 roared blind down the unlit runway. As they reached the end of the strip and became airborne, Brown and McDaniel felt the impact of small arms fire in the wings; they were being shot at. With relief they realized that none of the hits were in the baggage compartment or in the six fragmentation bombs carried under the wings.

5 At Cabcaben Field, just south of Bataan Field, Lts. Stewart Robb, Shorty Crosland, and W. G. Coleman were on alert following their arrival from Bataan Field in late afternoon. Mechanics of the 21st Pursuit were working on the "P-40 Something" to get it back into commission as soon as possible. The three squadron mates had moved into the small tunnel at the end of Cabcaben strip, waiting for further orders. Then about seven o'clock in the evening, they picked up a walkie-talkie radio and listened to messages being excitedly exchanged between American and Filipino forces at the front line. It appeared to the 34th Pursuiters that the Japanese were making a strong push and had broken through the Main Line of Resistance in several places.

Now more anxious than ever for instructions on what do do, they continued to wait until finally they received a telephone call from Lieutenant Colonel Gregg at Little Baguio. The Bataan air force's executive officer told them that Joe Moore was coming to fly out the P-40B. They were also informed that Colonel Churchill, the commanding officer of the air force, accompanied by Lieutenant Colonel Kennard, the flight surgeon, would also be arriving. They were to fly out with Lt. Roland Barnick in the old J2F amphibian that Barnick had been repairing since Moore had landed it there on the early morning of April 5/6 with a broken cylinder. Barnick was to wait until the two colonels showed up before taking off. Gregg also authorized the three 34th Pursuit pilots to go out in the Duck, assuming that it was in flying condition.

Later that evening, Joe Moore showed up in a car from Mariveles to take out the "P-40 Something," having earlier been informed that the mission was now ready to be flown. Moore was still operating under orders to take the P-40 south to join the Cebu blockade-running operation; he had not been told at Mariveles that the Japanese had broken through the front lines just north of Bataan Field. At about 9:30 P.M., Moore was airborne and heading for Cebu.

Now relieved of their alert responsibility, Robb, Crosland, and Coleman headed over to the site where Barnick, the engineering officer of Cabcaben Field, was still struggling to get the amphibian in flying condition. Assisted by Lt. Leo Boelens, the engineering officer of the 21st Pursuit, and two enlisted men, Barnick had been working on the Duck night and day in shifts since Moore limped in with it on April 6. On that day, Barnick and his crew, with the help of the navy, had removed a barnacle-encrusted cylinder from another Duck, submerged in Mariveles Harbor since January 5, and subsequently found to their surprise that it was in good enough condition to be substituted for the blown cylinder of Moore's ship.[7] Now the three 34th Pursuit pilots volunteered their services to Barnick and the others, working feverishly by flashlight in a bamboo thicket to finalize the fitting and adjustment to the engine before the Japanese should break through.

Then at about ten o'clock, Ed Dyess showed up with a group of the pilots from Bataan Field. He was trying to get to Mariveles, where he hoped to find B-17s waiting to take the pilots south. Several of the enlisted men of the 21st based at Bataan Field were with him too. They had wrecked facilities at Bataan Field and were proceeding to their bivouac two and a half miles north of Mariveles, where they were going to be organized as mobile infantry.

Dyess had stopped by Cabcaben to check and see if Moore had taken the P-40B out all right and what was the situation of the remaining pilots at Cabcaben. He was also there to pick up the rest of his men assigned to Cabcaben Field for the Mariveles trip.

Talking with Barnick as he worked on the Duck, Dyess told him that he should include a Filipino colonel by the name of Carlos Romulo on the Duck's flight. Dyess had been informed earlier that Romulo, MacArthur's former press relations officer, would be coming from Corregidor for evacuation south on MacArthur's own orders. When the 34th Pursuiters asked Dyess to join them too, he again refused an evacuation offer; "he had his men to take care of." But Dyess wanted his engineering officer, Boelens, to go with the others. That would make six men for the flight, two over the Duck's capacity. And what if Colonels Churchill and Kennard showed up?

Shortly after Dyess left with his men, a car was noticed approaching, having been driven down to the far end of the runway from the intersection with the north-south road. It had dodged shellfire and exploding bombs before reaching the thicket where the men were working on the Duck. A Filipino officer jumped out of the car and called out for Barnick. It was Colonel Romulo. He had earlier been driven to Bataan Field from Mariveles after coming over from Corregidor but found it evacuated and under heavy shelling. Someone at Little Baguio had then told him to try for Cabcaben Field and a flight out in the Duck.

To Romulo, the amphibian was the funniest-looking plane he had ever seen. It looked like something reclaimed from a city dump. Watching the men in overalls working by flashlight on the engine, Romulo wondered whether they would really be able to get the thing to fly.

Just after midnight, Barnick and his crew finished the final adjustments, and none too soon; the men could hear small arms fire on the slope above them, just to the north of their position, and artillery firing over their heads. As Romulo sat in his car, the men spun the propeller. There was an immediate popping noise as the engine fired on the first try. After an initial "pup-pup-pup," the engine settled down for a fairly even hum, to the elation of all.

Barnick decided not to run any preflight tests on the ship; there was neither time nor facilities available for them. Instead, the men pulled the amphibian out of the thicket onto the strip. Shells were still falling, but the Japanese had shifted their main fire toward the Manila Bay coast away from the field. Barnick decided to wait for the moon to rise before venturing a takeoff. A fifteen-man detail of the ground personnel of the 21st Pursuit that had remained behind put out smudge pots along the runway to serve as a guide for the takeoff. Barnick and the others stretched out on the ground while waiting for the moon, listening to the gunfire now so close. Barnick was thinking of several reasons why he should be worried about the chance of success for the flight: the plane was greatly overloaded, he had never flown a Duck before, and there was no light in the cockpit by which to check the instruments.

Then Romulo noticed the moon finally edging above the lit-up jungle. It was 1:18 A.M., and Barnick now yelled for everyone to climb into the amphibian. Shorty Crosland climbed up into the back seat, where he had been designated to sit as copilot, and the others clambered into the hull, which did not have seats. There was no question of delaying the flight further for the arrival of Churchill and Kennard. It was now or never for the takeoff.[8]

When Barnick started the motor, the Duck began vibrating violently. Irritated, he yelled down at the passengers to stop shaking the plane, but was told no one was doing any shaking. Unknown to them at the time, an earthquake of a minute's duration had hit Bataan just at the moment of takeoff. As the old amphibian creaked and bounced down the strip, the passengers were not sure it would even hold together, let alone become airborne with its heavy load. No one was optimistic about making it out, but then anything was preferable to being taken prisoner by the Japanese. After clearing the end of the field, the Duck settled to within a few feet of Manila Bay. The load was just too great.

By running the engine at thirty-eight inches of manifold pressure, Barnick managed to pull the plane up to 70 feet of altitude. Then Japanese searchlights suddenly fixed on the ship. Soon both Japanese and American fire was being directed at the hapless aircraft, but no hits were noticed by the crew.

A few minutes later, Barnick passed a note to Crosland and dropped another one into the hull: "Throw out all extra weight! Hurry!" Romulo and the others began throwing out everything they had brought along:

baggage, parachutes, side arms, cushions, even shaving kits. Somewhat lightened, the Duck began to climb—but only to 125 feet.

After circling Corregidor, Barnick set a course for the south. Constantly checking his instruments in the dark cockpit with his flashlight, he was swearing constantly, so loud that even his passengers in the hull could hear him. He could not get the propeller to change into high pitch; it was stuck in low, preventing him from gaining altitude.

6 In the early evening of April 8, Jack Donalson was navigating "Kibosh" under difficult circumstances toward his destination of Iloilo, on the island of Panay, some three hundred miles south of Bataan. With his map as a guide, he now decided to go over one of the many straits of the Sibuyan Sea. Not only was it dark, but it was the time of year when the rice fields were burned off. The smoky haze obscured many of the important landmarks Donalson needed to see to make his way to Panay.

After several hours' flying, Donalson believed he had reached Panay and the Iloilo area. He could not be sure, however; the landscape below was dark and hazy, and there were no lights on what should have been the airfield. Deciding not to try to radio to the field in case there were Japanese planes in the area, Donalson now flew over what was apparently the Manduriao Field, two miles outside Iloilo town, and raced his engine. Immediately afterward, the field lights were put on; they had recognized the sound of his Allison engine.

After swinging into the landing pattern, Donalson tried to get his landing gear down, but with no success. Evidently the hydraulic system had been hit as he strafed and bombed the Japanese positions on Bataan. What to do? The anguished pilot knew how desperately each P-40 was needed, but he had no choice. He made a good wheels-up landing, causing only minimal damage to "Kibosh" and none to himself.[9] But the plane could not be flown again without some replacement parts.[10]

At Cebu that evening, Andy Krieger had alerted the airport defense troops upon receiving notification from Grover at Del Monte that P-40s were due in from Bataan for the food mission. Krieger instructed the Filipino commander to turn on the landing lights at the field if he heard aircraft engines. The officer, however, interpreted the request to mean that he should keep them *off*; that was so much safer for *him*.

About midnight, Krieger picked up the sounds of an aircraft overhead and rushed to get the lighting turned on, over the violent objections of the Filipino. It was a P-35A. On the first try it overshot the field but managed to land safely on the second try. Krieger went out to meet the pilot. It was his old CO, Hank Thorne. Much to Krieger's surprise, he found that two other pilots had flown in the baggage compartment, Ben Brown and Larry McDaniel.

Krieger now found out that Thorne was not sent down to participate in the Cebu blockade-running mission but instead evacuated a crumbling Bataan. Thorne described in graphic terms the situation on Bataan and his own flight. He had dropped six fragmentation bombs on some Japanese shipping south of Luzon then tried to fly under some weather en route before giving up and climbing on top of it. By changing course several times to avoid thunderstorms, he had made it to Cebu without difficulty.

At the time Thorne landed, Joe Moore was en route to Cebu himself but was in deep difficulty. Like the others, Moore this night was flying by dead reckoning and by sighting different islands along the route that he had come to recognize from having flown over them so many times before the war. But this evening he had run into a very large thunderstorm across the path he usually flew and had diverted to the west, to the right of his course, and tried flying around it. But he got completely disoriented. When he finally got around the storm, he could not identify anything below in the darkness.

After flying a long time and running low on fuel, he tentatively identified what he thought was the southern tip of Panay and Negros islands to the east. Now he set course east for Cebu. The weather began to improve as he neared Cebu. When he positively identified it, he came in and landed the P-40B safely at Lahug Field, just north of Cebu City. Moore was down to the last of his fuel. It was now about 1:30 A.M. It had taken four hours to cover the 360 miles as the crow flies. Exhausted from the nervous tension of the long flight, he talked to Krieger at the field, then headed for the officers quarters in Cebu City, where he collapsed into bed.

Like Moore, Ozzie Lunde in the P-35A had also gotten lost on his southward flight that evening. He was trying to find Iloilo, but if that proved impossible, he would try for Cebu. In pitch darkness, and unfamiliar with the area, Lunde began to descend over what he thought might be Iloilo, but no light was out. Then he headed over toward Cebu, but there were heavy clouds over the area, and he did not dare let down because of the risk of hitting mountains.

With the fuel gauge getting very low after three and a half hours of flight, Lunde now realized he was in deep trouble. He had to find a place to land, and soon. Thinking of Randy Keator in the baggage compartment, Lunde scribbled a note and passed it to his passenger. It stated that he was lost, low on gas, and would soon have to ditch the plane.

Keator was terrified at the thought of ditching in the water at midnight with him in the baggage compartment. Then another cold chill went up his spine; if Lunde opted to bail out instead, he would go down with the plane. With the aid of his penlight, Keator wrote on the back of Lunde's note, "Please don't bail out—you have my parachute up front." Keator had decided what to do if Lunde ignored his request. He had his

Joe Moore, CO of the 20th Pursuit Squadron, in front of his P-40B at Clark Field, summer, 1941. *Courtesy Joseph H. Moore, Lt. Gen. USAF (Ret.)*

.45 automatic at the ready. If Lunde had stood up in preparation to bail out, he would never have made it.

Lunde now began to descend, looking for a suitable place, but it was so dark he could barely make out the water below him. In the baggage compartment, Keator strapped on his steel helmet, then folded his blanket and a shelter half into a pad and held it on top of his head to cushion the shock of the crash.

Then the P-35A struck the water, bounced back into the air, and after several more bounces, finally came to rest on a sandbar in about three feet of water. Dazed after having hit his head on the instrument panel, Lunde climbed out of the cockpit and jumped into the shallow water to check on Keator, who had pushed the baggage compartment door open. He was unhurt, but Lunde had a bad cut on his eyebrow from banging his forehead.

Relieved to have survived the ordeal, Keator asked, "Captain, did you pray?" "I sure did," Lunde replied. "I put my arms around that stick and I prayed!"

Neither Lunde nor Keator had any idea where they were, nor did they know if the island was held by the Japanese or not. Then they heard voices on the beach and saw people approaching them in the darkness. They were surrounded. "We're Americanos, Americanos," they yelled. "We are Filipinos," came back the reply, the most welcome words they had heard in years.

To Keator, it seemed there must have been at least five hundred men, women, and children who waded out to them. They were armed with "everything from bows and arrows to muzzle-loading shotguns." He hated to contemplate their fate if they had been Japanese.

After the two Americans had given instructions on covering their P-35A with palm leaves, they were led by the natives to their small barrio located nearby, where they received the "warmest welcome" Keator had ever experienced. Keator figured they were the first white men that many of the villagers had ever seen.

While hundreds of inquisitive Filipinos crowded around the windows and doors to watch, the village doctor examined Lunde and Keator for broken bones. Finding none, he put a patch on Lunde's eyebrow cut. Then the two guests of the village were introduced to the mayor, a Mr. Flores, and taken to his home to spend the rest of the night after being given a meal. It was two o'clock in the morning.

Lunde and Keator had now learned that they were on the island of Leyte, some 150 miles from Cebu, their destination. Informed that the barrio had a telegraph line to Leyte's capital, Tacloban, they now telegraphed Tacloban to radio to American forces on Mindanao that they were safe on Leyte. The next day, the Bamboo Fleet Beechcraft would arrive to take them down to Mindanao.

And what of Barnick and his passengers in the overloaded Duck that night? As the amphibian's fuel load diminished, Barnick had managed to reach 300 to 400 feet altitude in the patchwork plane. After several hours' droning through the night sky, Barnick now began descending through broken clouds to 200 feet to get a bearing. Cebu should be near, the Duck's destination. But then long ribbons of white light began to cut the night sky in their direction; there were ships below. Assuming the ships were Japanese, Barnick lifted the Duck back up to 400 feet and set course for Iloilo instead, to the west.

But now Barnick had another problem: he was just about out of gas. Where could he land on Panay Island in a hurry? Fortunately, Romulo was able to produce a map of the secret airfields in the Philippines, which he now passed to Barnick. From the map, he could see that the closest airfield on the island was at Sara, some fifty miles northwest of Iloilo. As the Duck circled over the 3,600-foot strip, light flashed on two hundred feet below. It was 5:00 A.M. when Barnick touched ground with the old amphibian, its tanks almost dry. Much to his dismay, Barnick was informed that the field had no fuel. With little choice left him, Barnick took off again and headed south to the Iloilo area, hoping the little gas in his tanks would suffice. Dawn was breaking as the Duck put down at Manduriao Field, two miles northwest of Iloilo.

There was a little restaurant near the field. Barnick and his five passengers headed immediately for it. Starved after months on Bataan, they gorged themselves on fried eggs and coffee. It was a miracle, but they had made it, the last flight out of Bataan.

25. "YOU AMERICANS CAN'T BE TRUSTED"

1 After Ed Dyess had checked out the situation at Cabcaben Field shortly after 10:00 P.M. on April 8, he climbed back into his command car and proceeded to lead his miniconvoy of Bataan Field pilots in their two 2-ton trucks to Mariveles. He was following the instructions of Air Force Head-quarters at Little Baguio to take all the remaining pilots at Bataan Field to meet three B-17s at Mariveles Field, which would fly them south. The car and two trucks, however, did not have room enough for all the pilots. Some of them, including Fred Siler and Bill Akins of the 20th Pursuit, had been obliged to head out from Bataan Field on foot. Also walking were most of the men of the 21st Pursuit from Bataan and Cabcaben fields, who were heading for the squadron's assembly point two and a half miles north of Mariveles.

Following the zigzag road west into the interior instead of the coastal road south for security reasons was proving very slow going in the dark for the twenty some pilots benefiting from motorized transportation. Then, just after midnight, they ran into a traffic jam. Ahead of the snarl, ordnance officers were blowing up the main ammunition dump at Little Baguio, near the road. All traffic was ordered to a standstill.

Never had the pilots seen anything approaching the sight in pure hell-ishness. The enormous explosions and fires were coming faster and faster, feeding down the zigzag road and onto the Mariveles cutoff road, filling the air over the valley to 1,200 feet in an enormous pall of black smoke.

Dyess's little caravan had managed to work itself to the head of the line of traffic, where Col. George W. Hirsch, commanding officer of the Philippine Ordnance Department, had halted further movement. He con-sidered it too dangerous to let traffic proceed further. There they sat and waited as time ticked by. Finally, when it became a question of whether they would get to the field on time to meet the incoming B-17s, Dyess intervened with the colonel, informing him of his orders to get to Mari-veles and imploring him to let them through. Finally, Hirsch asked them to wait for about five minutes; they would have a chance to get through then during a break in the explosions.

Dyess now shifted an extra driver up front in the trucks, in case the first one got hit. The pilots riding in the trucks climbed into the back, put on their helmets, and lay down flat. Going like hell, the drivers then headed down the zigzag and got through to the bottom, at the foot of Mariveles Field. It was just past dawn.

Dyess's group was surprised to see men clearing the runway of trucks that had been parked on it. They were the last of a mass of vehicles, arranged in rows of ten each, that had completely covered the field the night before. How could B-17s ever have landed there?

It was a frustrated Ed Dyess who checked in at the Mariveles radio net and called Lieutenant Colonel Gregg, the second-ranking air force officer, who was still at Little Baguio. Gregg now told Dyess that the B-17s were not coming after all, but it had been arranged for a boat to take his pilots over to Corregidor, where a submarine would be waiting to evacuate them from the Philippines.[1] Dyess was to check with the captains of all the boats in Mariveles Harbor to determine which one was assigned to take his party the three miles across Manila Bay to Corregidor that morning.

The failure of the B-17s to come in affected more air force officers than just Dyess and his pilots. Unable to get to Barnick's Duck at Cabcaben because of the state of traffic, Colonel Churchill, the most senior air force officer on Bataan, and Colonel Kennard, the air force surgeon, had been waiting all night for the B-17s to come in to Mariveles to pick them up, along with other senior air force brass, including Lt. Col. William N. "Pinky" Amis and Maj. Maurice F. "Moe" Daly. When they received word that no B-17s would be coming after all that morning, the sixty-year-old Churchill, his spirit knocked out by dysentery, told the others they might as well give up. But Kennard decided to try to reach Corregidor by boat—and succeeded.

When Dyess's group finally located the boat intended to take them over to Corregidor, it was too late. A load of nurses was waiting to board the little vessel in their place, since Dyess and his men had not showed up in time. Gallantly, the disappointed pilots waved the nurses off.[2]

Unable to find any other means of transport to take them over to Corregidor, Dyess and the others now turned back and headed up Bataan to rejoin the enlisted men of the squadron north of Mariveles. Everywhere they saw white flags going up. Instructions were for each unit to pile its arms and ammunition in a heap and put a white flag over it. They were actually going to surrender. Despite clear signals that they were surrendering, Japanese dive-bombers were out in force again that morning, attacking the disarmed American and Filipino forces. Dyess was furious. He felt it was every man for himself how. He did not want to surrender to these barbarians. Suspending his plans to rejoin his men, Dyess now yelled to the group of pilots, "I know where there is a boat. A guy named Tex Marble has it and will let me have it!"

Dyess then told Sam Grashio and Joe McClellan to take his command car and collect all the food and gas they could after dropping him at Mariveles Hospital, near where Marble was believed to be. After collecting two drums of gas and some cans of tomatoes, Grashio and McClellan headed back to the hospital, near where they found Dyess walking on the dock with Bud Powell and Bill Powell. Dyess had found Marble, but he had refused to give up his boat to Dyess and his group. Since the death of Spud Sloan two months earlier, Marble had become the CO of the 17th Pursuit, which was still on beach defense. Marble had left his command when he had received word of the surrender. He had no intention of being deterred from reaching Corregidor. With his hopes for a boat for his pilots finally quashed, Dyess told them to find their squadrons so they could represent their men to the Japanese when the surrender formalities began.

Now, with only his own squadron's officers remaining, Grashio and Ibold, Dyess decided to check in on Air Force Headquarters for further instructions and headed back to Little Baguio in the command car, Ibold driving. On reaching Air Force Headquarters, Dyess, Grashio, and Ibold were approached by Lieutenant Colonel Amis, who had reported back from Mariveles strip after the B-17s failed to show. Amis told them that the surrender had gone through.

The three 21st Pursuiters could hear gunfire coming toward them from the road, about half a mile away. Running outside, they now took cover in the jungle beside the road. Then they saw two tanks clanking down the road, strafing on both sides. After the tanks passed by, Dyess decided to surrender his men, assembled at the designated meeting point two and a half miles north of Mariveles. The three pilots now came out of the jungle and tied white handkerchiefs to twigs, got back into the command car, and drove off after the tanks.

As they drove on down the road, Dyess, Grashio, and Ibold saw dazed Americans and Filipino soldiers coming out of the jungle and throwing up their hands in surrender. Then at a curve they were suddenly face to face with the tanks, which had turned around. One Japanese was standing out on the front of the lead tank, stroking the barrel of the gun.

The Americans got out of their car and held up the white handkerchiefs. In response, the Japanese motioned them to come closer, but when they started to, he shook his head and made a motion of driving, so they got back in the car and drove up to the tank. Then the Japanese suddenly yelled at them in English, "You Americans can't be trusted. You surrender, but you do not give up your arms!"

Dyess, Grashio, and Ibold now dropped their .45s, which they had forgotten they were wearing, and raised their hands. The Japanese then slapped Dyess's face. One of the other Japanese told Grashio to give him his ring, fountain pen, pencil, bracelet, and watch, and then motioned to them to get back in the car and continue back to their unit. Grashio looked back and saw the Japanese who had taken his things smiling at him, then with a sneer throwing them all into the road.

At Kilometer Post 181, where the 21st's men had congregated and stacked their weapons, Dyess told them that they had met the Japanese down the road and "they were not so bad." But the men were utterly dejected. Many were crying openly. How could such a thing happen? Later that afternoon, the Headquarters Squadron detachment from Bataan Field showed up too. Leaderless, they had been brought in by Lieutenant Brenner, the 21st's medical officer, who had assumed command of the little group.

2 Although Dyess and his group of Bataan Field pilots failed to get to Corregidor, some pilots and nonflying officers of the pursuit squadrons and the 5th Interceptor Command did, including Tex Marble. One of Dyess's administrative officers, 1st Lt. Larry Parcher, accompanied by a few men, reached Corregidor by skiff. Frankie Bryant, a 34th Pursuit pilot attached to the 60th Coast Artillery, evacuated with his battery to the Rock (a nickname for Corregidor).

Two of the senior pilots on Bataan, 1st Lts. George Armstrong of the 17th Pursuit, assigned since January, 1942, to the 71st Division, and Ray Gehrig, a former 3rd Pursuiter assigned to the 5th Interceptor Command net, had been ordered by Lieutenant Colonel Gregg to Corregidor the evening that Bataan went under. They were to go to Australia on a submarine, which was scheduled to pick up some twenty pilots and leave the next morning at 5:00 A.M.

At 11:00 that night, Armstrong and Gehrig were given Gregg's staff car and began working their way from Little Baguio to Mariveles. There they were to leave for Corregidor on the boat evacuating the army engineers who were to blow up all the ammo dumps in the area before embarking. After reaching Mariveles, Armstrong and Gehrig anxiously waited and waited while the dumps were being blown. Not until the first light of dawn was the work completed and they joined the engineers for the short water crossing to the Rock.

On Corregidor, they dashed to the navy pier but were told by a navy officer there that the submarine had already left before sunrise, earlier than planned because of the intensive Japanese activity on Bataan and the risks of departing Manila Bay during daylight.[3] The two dejected pilots were now assigned temporarily to the 4th Marine Regiment on beach defense.

3 When Lloyd Stinson and Jim Fossey split off from Dyess and his 21st Pursuit pilots at Mariveles and made their way to the 20th Pursuit's jungle bivouac area just north of the town early that morning, they found other officers of the squadron and the enlisted men preparing to surrender as a unit. Stinson and Fossey met 41-C flying school classmates Percy Ramsey, Jim Mullen, Jack Gates, and Fred Browne there too. Fred Siler and Bill Akins had now also reached the camp after an all-night walk from Bataan Field and the fruitless search for a boat to take them to Corregidor.

Following orders, officers and men of the squadron were stacking their weapons, but many refused to consider turning their arms over to the Japanese. Pfc Jim Brown dismantled his Colt .45 and 1903 Remington rifle, bashed the pieces with a rock, and threw them in a deep hole in the river.

With food supplies that had been given out and a variety of survival weapons, Fred Siler proposed to his 41-G flying school classmates Bill Akins and Max Halverson that they head for the hills, to avoid the Japanese on the coast and roads. But Halverson was experiencing a bad malaria attack, so he and Akins argued instead for staying with the squadron and surrendering. Siler went along with their decision.

A Japanese patrol then showed up, looked the assembled men over, took some pictures, and left. A short time later, another Japanese group arrived, accompanied by a civilian Filipino collaborator. The Americans were ordered to go down to Mariveles Field to surrender. As the most senior line officer of the squadron, 1st Lt. Robert F. Roberts, a nonflying officer, would formally surrender the 20th Pursuit.

4 When Tex Marble left the 17th Pursuit to take the boat to Corregidor, command of the squadron devolved to 1st Lt. Howard B. Connor, an administrative officer who was the most senior officer on hand. Connor, who had gained the respect of the enlisted men of the squadron during the Bataan campaign for his diligent response to his duties, was at Camp Levee, where one-half of the squadron was assigned on beach defense when he heard of the surrender order. He now immediately assembled the Camp Levee contingent and took it over to the Talaga Bay area to the east, where the rest of the squadron was located, and gave orders that the squadron should stay together here before departing for the surrender site.

Following orders, the men destroyed their weapons and defensive sites, as well as their gas masks and searchlight, though in some cases guns were kept, but minus key parts that were thrown into Mariveles Bay. Then at 3:30 P.M., the cooks prepared a big meal, using most of the remaining food items on hand.

At 6:00 P.M., the squadron set out for Kilometer Post 192, west of Mariveles Field, where the Japanese had ordered them to assemble. The men took whatever arms they had left with them, minus parts thrown away earlier, as well as any remaining food items that had been divided up among them. Each man also had a canteen, first aid kit, mess gear, blanket, shelter half, and toilet articles.

Strung out in single file, the men passed over the hills and reached Mariveles Field just as Japanese dive-bombers went into action again over the strip, bombing and strafing the men there, but with no casualties. They reached their destination just before dark and stacked their rifles before bedding down for the night. The next morning, there were Japanese "all over the place."

5   Late on the night of April 8/9 in the Agloloma–Quinauan Point area (Kilometer Post 191), word had reached the 34th Pursuit that Bataan was falling. The news came as no surprise to the men there, still on beach defense. They could hear the explosions of the ammo dumps being blown up to the east. Everyone then started gathering in the headquarters supply area. The men built a fire there and began throwing in their unloaded .45s and rifle bolts. S. Sgt. Tom Gage and Sgt. Arthur Sullivan drifted over to the supply trailer to see if they could get some new clothes. Gage put on everything new and picked out several pairs of socks and a new pair of brown army shoes, equipping himself for the inevitable ordeal ahead.

Eventually the squadron was told to move out. Most of the men were transported in three trucks to an assembly point, where they were to be put on trucks the next morning for the ride to the Mariveles cutoff, the designated site for the surrender of the squadron. Others who could not get transportation walked. As they were waiting to be transported, the men noticed that their commanding officer, Captain Wray, and the other officers of the squadron on beach defense had taken the squadron's cars and driven off, apparently in an effort to escape surrender by catching a boat to Corregidor.

The truck Tom Gage was loaded into would not start, so it was hooked up to another truck and towed down the hill. The men were standing and packed like sardines into the trucks. On the way down, they saw their first Japanese troops, stringing telephone wire along the road. Before the trucks reached the assembly point, they were directed to a burned-out area. The Japanese allowed no one off the trucks until morning light, when the guards let a few off at a time. Gage filled his canteen with ditch water and dosed it liberally with iodine.

They now faced a practical problem: the Japanese refused to accept their surrender, since it had to be offered by an officer, and the 34th was without one.[4] The matter was resolved, however, when 1st Lt. Warren

H. Markham, Coast Artillery, who had been assigned to the 34th at Aglo-loma Bay, in charge of the 3-inch rifle there, agreed to offer the 34th's surrender.

All the men were now unloaded from the trucks. Gage had with him his field bag and food, helmet, a book, and eyeglasses. Then the prisoners were marched back up the road they had come down in the trucks. At the Mariveles cutoff, they were pulled off the road and directed to a con-centration area. In the pen, the men of the 34th Pursuit searched for each other in the crowd of men from all units. Eventually all the men of the squadron were assembled in one area.

6 Two miles northwest of Mariveles, in its beach defense area between the Talain and Biaan rivers, the 3rd Pursuit by the early morning of April 9 knew that Bataan had fallen. After discussions with his men, 1st Lt. Herb Ellis, who had assumed command of the squadron on the departure of Hank Thorne on April 1 to Bataan Field, decided to make a last-ditch effort to get his men over to Corregidor. Ellis had heard earlier that Cor-regidor was sending barges over to the Mariveles area that day for the purpose of evacuating troops.

Ellis now began moving his men along rugged footpaths that zigzagged through the jungle near the southwest coast. Finally they reached a prom-ontory from which they could see Corregidor. They then tried signaling Corregidor by flashlight in Morse code to send a barge over to evacuate the squadron but received no response. Ellis was most disappointed at the nonreply. He had a number of litter cases, and only eighteen of his men were really fit for duty.

On the return to their beach defense position, several of the younger officers of the squadron approached Ellis with a burning question: would he report them as absent in desertion if they left the squadron to seek some means of transportation to Corregidor? Ellis replied in the nega-tive and wished them the best of luck. But when the 3rd Pursuit men reformed a few hours later at their camp, Ellis found that the officers had returned. They had not been able to find any kind of craft to take them to Corregidor.[5]

Following the surrender instructions radioed to Ellis, the men now dis-mantled their rifles, threw away the bolts, and stacked their rifles where they were. Then Ellis arranged for a last meal to be served the half-starved men from the remaining food before setting out for Mariveles Field to surrender.

Ellis now led the solemn procession by foot to their destination. The relatively fit carried the litter cases until a passing Japanese contingent made them get up and walk too. All that afternoon during the long, slow march, Ellis was repeatedly asked for permission to allow groups of strag-glers from other air force units to join his unit. Although not in favor of the requests in view of the very limited food supply available, Ellis reluctantly acquiesced. By the time they reached Mariveles Field, Ellis found he had almost double the number of men he had set out with.

When a Japanese officer approached to take the men prisoner, Ellis stood tall and saluted in a perfect military manner. Instead of returning the salute, the officer bellowed for the men to move out onto the airstrip and line up. He counted the men, then told them to strip down to be searched. Working in teams, many Japanese now went through every inch of the men's clothings and possessions.

7 By the morning of April 10, when the 17th Pursuit's men arrived, the personnel of all five pursuit squadrons were assembled on the Mariveles airstrip, along with men from other outfits. Dazed, dejected, half-starved, ill, unbelieving of what had happened to them, they would soon be starting out by foot on a long march north, the terror and brutishness of which few could have envisaged.

Part Seven
MINDANAO FINALE

With the fall of Bataan, the Japanese were now able to turn their attention to the conquest of Corregidor, where the USFIP command was located, and the southern islands of the Philippines. On the afternoon of April 9, a Japanese naval force was reported heading for Cebu from the south, and by early morning the next day had split into two groups—one proceeding along the west coast of the narrow island, and the other along the east. Just after dawn, the larger group began landing at Cebu City, the capital, and the other unit started coming ashore near the town of Toledo, on the western side of Cebu. Within one day, the Japanese had overcome light opposition and occupied the island. The surviving two hundred American and Filipino defenders retreated into the mountains.

Next, it was the turn of Panay, the larger island one hundred miles to the west of Cebu. Over four thousand Japanese troops came ashore at dawn on April 16, the larger force at Iloilo on the southeast corner of the island, and a smaller force at Capiz to the north. Two days later another landing was made at San Jose, on the southwest coast. By April 20, all the strategic points of Panay were occupied.

Now the large island of Mindanao remained as the last American-held territory in the area. Japanese plans envisaged a three-pronged attack toward the center. One of the forces to be utilized was already on Mindanao, on garrison duty at Davao and Digos, where it had landed four months earlier but had been unable to advance into the interior. The other two forces envisaged would be landed from the sea.

Early on the morning of April 29, one of the Japanese invasion forces landed at Cotabato and Parang, on the western coast of Mindanao, with some 4,900 men. By May 3, the Cotabato-Parang force had occupied southern and western Mindanao. Only in the north, in the Cagayan sector, was resistance continuing.

The third force envisaged for the seizure of Mindanao was now landing along the shore of Macajalar Bay, facing Cagayan and the American air base at Del Monte. In the face of Japanese advances, the American and Filipino command ordered a general withdrawal on May 4 to defensive positions about six miles south of the beach, to be executed that evening. But then the plan was overruled in favor of a withdrawal even deeper into Mindanao to benefit from natural barriers, to form the Mangima Line. The Japanese resumed their offensive on May 6, then on the evening of May 8 were able to infiltrate Filipino positions. The following night the Japanese force entered the town of Dalirig as the Filipinos retreated in a disorganized fashion. The Mangima Line had been breached, and the bulk of the defender's force defeated. The Mindanao campaign was over.

Three days earlier, on May 6, Corregidor was surrendered by General Wainwright following an amphibious assault on the bastion on the night of May 5/6. The defenders had poured fire from every weapon available into the landing force, inflicting heavy casualties, but it soon became clear that considerable numbers of the enemy were on the island, infiltrating the American line. When it became known that three tanks were also in action, against which the Americans on the tiny island had no defense. Wainwright decided not to risk unnecessary slaughter. He would surrender his forces.

26. "WE FELT THAT OUR LAST CHANCE HAD GONE"

1 At noon on April 9 Joe Moore woke up at the visiting officers' quarters in Cebu City following his exhausting flight down from Cabcaben late the night before. After dressing, he headed over to the Cebu headquarters of Col. Jack Cook. Entering the office, he found Dick Fellows and many of the other pilots who were just recently on Bataan in a bad emotional state. They had been listening to the 12:00 noon "Voice of Freedom" broadcast from Corregidor on Cook's radio and had just heard that Bataan had fallen. If he had arrived just as the announcement was being made, he would have found his fellow officers all bawling like children, overcome by the dreaded yet inevitable news. For Moore, this also meant his Cebu blockade-running mission was now off.

Looking around the room, Moore saw Hank Thorne, Ben Brown, and Larry McDaniel, who had reached Cebu on Thorne's P-35 an hour before Moore the night of April 8/9. Andy Krieger was there too, still temporarily based on Cebu. New arrivals on Cebu in the room were Jack Donalson and Bill Rowe, the latter two flown by Bamboo Fleet pilot Hervey Whitfield from Iloilo to Cebu in the Beech Staggerwing that morning. Jack Caldwell and Gus Williams were there too, also flown into Cebu from Iloilo that morning; Dick Fellows in the Waco had provided the transport.

Earlier that day, the Bataan evacuees (except slumbering Joe Moore) had been having a wonderful time on Cebu. Colonel Cook had put two big cars at their disposal for visiting Cebu City, which seemed virtually unaffected by the war. In high spirits after their Bataan ordeal, they went from store to store, buying items they had not seen for months. They also gorged their shrunken stomachs on hamburgers, ice cream, pie, and rum and cokes.

That morning, they were even treated to an exciting scene overhead, the "best fight" Williams had seen for a long time. Four Japanese float-planes were trying to sink a PT boat in Cebu City channel in repeated dive-bombing and strafing attacks while the boat fought back with .30- and .50-caliber machine gun fire from its twin turrets. But it was an uneven contest, the aircraft breaking off the attack after leaving the tiny craft dead in the water off Cebu Island.[1]

Several of the pilots who had escaped from Bataan that fateful night of April 8/9 were still stranded, short of their destination, by noon of April 9. Ozzie Lunde and Randy Keator were on Leyte Island, where Lunde had crash-landed his P-35, while Roland Barnick and his five passengers were on Panay Island with their immobilized Duck amphibian.

After dropping off Donalson and Rowe early on the morning of April 9, Whitfield with Bill Cummings had taken off from Cebu in the Beech on a mission to rescue Lunde and Keator, in response to the telegraph message sent from Leyte to Del Monte the evening before. Just about the time that Whitfield and Cummings touched down at Tacloban Field in late morning, Lunde and Keator arrived at the strip in a car driven by two officers of the Philippine Constabulary. The two Bataan veterans excitedly greeted their rescuers and climbed into the Beech. Two hours later, they arrived without incident on Mindanao, their interrupted flight to safety now completed.

On Panay, Barnick and his passengers on the morning of April 9 were busy trying to get the old Duck ready for the final leg of its originally planned flight to Mindanao from Cabcaben Field, so dramatically interrupted during the small hours of that day when it was forced to abort and land at isolated Sara Field. Waiting until evening for safety's sake, Barnick and the others now piled back into the amphibian for a renewed attempt to reach Del Monte. Still unable to climb higher than 800 feet, Barnick nevertheless was covering the two-hundred-mile distance to Mindanao when about one hour out of Panay, he ran into a cloud bank. Unable to climb above it and unwilling to risk losing his way in the solid overcast, Barnick decided to return to Iloilo. They would radio Del Monte for a replacement aircraft. It was no use trying with the old amphibian.

2 Back on Cebu on the afternoon of April 9, a brand-new P-40E-1 landed on Lahug Field, just north of Cebu City. Dave Obert had been ordered to fly the recently assembled Warhawk from Del Monte up to Cebu to exchange with Joe Moore's patchwork P-40B, so that the CO of the 20th Pursuit could more safely get down to Mindanao. Obert also carried orders for Moore to report immediately to his old CO, Lieutenant Colonel Grover, at Del Monte.

Early that morning, Obert had been waiting around in a fatalistic mood at Del Monte for the expected order to go on the delayed Cebu blockade-running mission when a call came in that a Japanese warship had come into Bugo Bay on the north coast of Mindanao and was making off with a supply ship. Grover then ordered Obert to take a P-40, load on a 100-pound bomb, and chase the Japanese away. Obert begged for a 500-pound bomb so that he might have a chance to sink the ship, but Grover refused the request. Irritated by Grover's further warning not to lose his plane ("as if I'd lose the damn thing on purpose"), Obert took off from Del Monte on his mission. After having climbed to 10,000 feet, Obert spotted the warship in question and identified it as a light cruiser. Not being able to tell if it was Japanese or American, he began to circle down and over it to determine its nationality. Then, at about 5,000 feet, he received an abrupt answer to his query when an antiaircraft shell exploded right behind him, "much too close for comfort!"

Immediately, Obert whipped over into a dive on the Japanese, which had now cut loose from the vessel it was towing and was headed out to sea. At a little under 3,000 feet, Obert released his bomb, pulled up, and rolled out into a turn to observe its effect. The whole ship seemed aflame, with the sky behind him full of antiaircraft fire. Having chased the Japanese away and thus fulfilled his orders, Obert headed back to Del Monte.[2]

On reporting back to Lieutenant Colonel Grover, Obert was informed that a message had been received from Joe Moore on Cebu that the Japanese had broken through the lines on Bataan. Deciding to suspend the blockade-running mission until he had further news of developments on Bataan, Grover now ordered Obert to fly to Cebu for the P-40 exchange. Then, as an afterthought, he told Obert to take along another 100-pound bomb and dive-bomb the cruiser again.

After having another bomb put on his plane, Obert took off for Cebu. With the dreaded blockade-running mission called off, he felt he had "a new lease on life," despite recognizing symptoms of another attack of malaria coming on and feeling "rotten physically." Spotting the cruiser again, still heading out to sea, Obert got between the warship and the sun and started to dive. Releasing at about 4,000 feet, he saw the bomb explode "very close" to the Japanese. The cruiser scarcely got a shot off at Obert this time, its gunners blinded by the sun.

On Obert's arrival at Lahug Field, he was met by Andy Krieger, who gave him the sad news of the fall of Bataan. In Cebu City, he met the other Bataan evacuees and was brought up-to-date on the various hair-raising flights out of Bataan. Joe Moore went out to the field to fly out the P-40E-1 Obert had brought in for him and took off for Mindanao. Just after dusk, he reached his destination.

At six o'clock that evening, Obert and the others on Cebu listened to the "Voice of Freedom" broadcast. The fall of Bataan was again announced. None of the pilots wanted to hear any more about it. Obert pictured the soldiers on Bataan, "starved, tired, and most of them sick," captives of the Japanese. "They had waited and waited month after month for help they knew must come and had never given up hope even until the last day, but now it was all over; help had not come," Obert recorded in his diary that evening.

After the broadcast, Andy Krieger went out on a reconnaissance in his P-40E and spotted a convoy of Japanese ships just off the southern end of Cebu island as daylight was fading: three cruisers and eleven transports. He reported back to his fellow officers that they were just lying there, but they knew the Japanese were just waiting for nightfall to move north for a landing on the island. Anticipating the invasion of Cebu, Lieutenant Colonel Grover radioed orders to the pilots: they were to return all flyable aircraft to Del Monte. The Cebu pilots now made plans to proceed at first light. Thorne would take off in the P-35, with Williams and Donalson in the baggage compartment; Fellows would take the Waco, with Jack Caldwell, Ben Brown, Bill Rowe, and Larry McDaniel as passengers; and Krieger would fly out alone in his P-40E and Obert in Moore's old P-40B. They figured their timetable should put them one step ahead of the Japanese landing party expected at daybreak. Then they all, except for Obert, headed out for Lahug Field, to camp down in a nipa shack near their aircraft. If the Japanese should land at night instead, the pilots were resolved to take off in the darkness. Under no circumstance were they going to risk being captured.

Feeling that the others needed sleep more than he, Obert volunteered to stay at the radio station in Cebu City to send and receive messages all night. At a little after midnight, Obert received a call that the Japanese were approaching southern Cebu. When at about 4:00 A.M. Obert got word that the Japanese had landed and were now on their way to Cebu City, Colonel Cook gave orders to start the destruction of all ships and supplies. After sending a radio message to Del Monte that the pilots would be arriving shortly, Obert dashed out to Lahug Field, where he alerted all the other pilots.

As the others prepared to take off, Obert approached his P-40B, carrying many cartons of cigarettes, which he knew would be in great demand on Mindanao. Crawling into the cockpit, Obert was apprehensive about flying a P-40B for the first time. Suddenly, there was a terrific explosion that rocked the whole Cebu City area. Obert was so startled he practically jumped out of his plane.

Now the other planes began taking off, evidently without even warming up their engines. First off was Fellows in the Waco. Sure that the Japanese were almost on them. Obert started his engine in a hurry and raced toward the end of the runway. In his blind haste, he nearly got run over by Andy Krieger, who was just taking off in his P-40E. Now Obert realized what had caused the terrifying explosion. It was a huge gasoline storage tank that had been blown up by Colonel Cook's demolition men. Burning fiercely, it threw a ghastly light over everything.

Obert noted that only his P-40B and Thorne's P-35A were still on the

field now. Thorne was having trouble starting his plane and was still trying as Obert gave his the gun and started his takeoff roll. Starting to turn
to the right after his wheels left the ground, Obert was looking out the
left side of his plane, keeping himself oriented by the field lights on that
side. Then, something made him glance to the right and ahead. Right
in front of him, only a few feet away, was the field's hangar, which he
had completely forgotten about in all the excitement. Instinctively, Obert
kicked and yanked to the left and upward at the same time. Barely clearing the hangar, he thanked "the old wreck," more responsive on the controls than the P-40E to which he was used, for saving him from certain
death.

Still on the field, Hank Thorne was having real trouble starting his
P-35. After exhausting the battery in a fruitless effort, Thorne enlisted
the help of Williams and Donalson in hand-cranking the balky veteran.
Try as they might, the engine still would not turn over. Then Thorne
solicited the aid of some Filipino Army Air Corps troops. Donalson and
Williams climbed into the baggage compartment and closed the door.
The Filipinos cranked away, but with similar results.

Suddenly, there was the terrific explosion that had shaken Obert, and
Donalson and Williams scrambled out of the compartment. The Filipinos
scattered in terror, leaving Donalson and Williams to return to their cranking work. By now, it was beginning to get light, and everyone was getting
nervous.

Then the pilots noticed an aircraft coming in to land at the far side
of the field—it was the Beech Staggerwing! Donalson and Williams kept
cranking the P-35, but after a few minutes Thorne made a welcome suggestion: head over to the new arrival and try to catch a lift with it instead.

When Donalson and Williams reached the Staggerwing, they realized
that Thorne had not accompanied them; he had stayed on to continue
trying to start the P-35. Then they heard the P-35's engine turn over. Opting to remain with the Beech, Donalson and Williams climbed into the
cabin plane and recognized Hervey Whitfield as the pilot. As they took
off, they looked back and saw that Thorne was airborne behind them.
It was now daylight.

Shortly after the hard-working Beech landed on Mindanao, it was scheduled for yet another rescue mission—this time to Iloilo to pick up Barnick and his passengers. When Bill Bradford landed the Staggerwing at
Iloilo field that afternoon,[3] he found that Barnick was reluctant to abandon the old Duck and had decided to give it another try to Del Monte.
Leo Boelens and Bill Coleman opted to stay with Barnick, leaving Romulo,
Stewart Robb, and Shortly Crosland as passengers for the Beech. Early
that evening, having landed at Del Monte following the uneventful two-

hundred-mile flight, Bradford and his passengers were surprised to find Barnick, Boelens, and Coleman already there; the old amphibian had arrived ahead of them.

3 The April 10 Japanese invasion of Cebu was unopposed from the air—with the exception of the efforts of a single pilot who was disobeying orders. On the afternoon of April 9, on returning to Panay after a long recon mission to Palawan to the west, Benny Putnam heard of the Japanese naval force moving in to Cebu. Excited about the prospect for some action, he called Lieutenant Colonel Grover at Del Monte for help in attacking the Japanese. Instead, he was told to stick to his orders—flying recon—and to leave the Japanese alone.

The next morning, Putnam decided to go over to Cebu to take a look at what was happening. As he approached the Tanon Straits, separating Negros from Cebu, he spotted the main part of the Japanese convoy, moving slowly north up the Bohol Straits on the other side of the narrow island. Then, on his left, Putnam noticed a large ship docked at Argao, some thirty-five miles down from Cebu City on the east coast of the island. Black smoke was rising straight up from the vessel, smudging the beautiful blue sky that morning.

Descending to get a better look at the vessel, he saw it was a troop transport, with a dozen landing barges clustered around it. Putnam then circled the transport a few times in order to make an identification. When he saw the rising sun flag, his suspicions were confirmed. Coming over the ship again, Putnam gave it a long burst with the six .50-caliber guns of his P-40E. Preparing for a second run, he spotted a motor launch leaving the shore and headed for it, giving it a two-second burst that tore pieces out of it. Now turning his attentions to the landing barges, he lined them up with the transport and came in on a flat approach and proceeded to pour fire into them and the engine room of the ship.

After the fourth run on the target, Putnam found himself the subject of attention of one of the escorting cruisers, which was steaming down the strait to Argao. Black bursts of antiaircraft fire were bracketing his P-40, some so near that they rocked the little fighter. At this point, his ammunition exhausted and fuel running low, Putnam elected to return to Santa Barbara field on Panay. While the P-40 was refueled and guns reloaded, Putnam counted seventy-three holes in the plane.

Just after noon the worked-up pilot was off again for a return engagement in his "one-man war" with the Japanese landing force. This time Putnam picked out the last troopship in the line of four, a large one. Diving out of the sun, he unleashed a stream of fire into the hapless Japanese troops packed on the deck, literally cutting the green-clad bodies in two. Fragments from the deck flew up in the air, mixed with pieces of equipment and flesh.

But now Putnam could feel small-arms fire from the four transports tearing into his ship. And the two cruisers had approached close enough to begin sending up ack-ack against him too. Putnam had just finished his fourth pass and was climbing when he ran into two floatplanes. Surprised, the Japanese climbed for altitude. Putnam went up after them, but his damaged engine was laboring. Then the two Japanese turned head-on into the P-40, but Putnam, concentrating on one, gave it a short burst with his two guns that still functioned. Pieces of the floatplane came off in all directions; Putnam turned sharply to the right to avoid the fire of the second Japanese, then watched his victim heading into the sea in flames. The other floatplane, breaking off combat, was heading down for the transport and the protection afforded by the cruisers' guns. Putnam dove and caught the unfortunate Japanese from the rear only 50 feet over the water, sending it flaming into the sea.[4]

Escaping harm from the two cruisers firing madly at him, Putnam pulled up and then headed back to the transport he had shot up on his first run. But this time, neither of his two remaining functional guns would fire. Reluctantly, he headed back to Santa Barbara.

On the field, Putnam and his crew checked the Warhawk over for damage. The plane was a sieve, but fortunately for the pilot, all the hits had been made by small arms: not one of the larger antiaircraft shells fired by the cruisers had touched him, even though some had been so close that the explosions had hurt his ears.

That afternoon, the crew managed to get Putnam's steed in flying order again, using parts cannibalized from Dyess's "Kibosh," still lying wrecked on the Manduriao Field, just outside Iloilo, where it had come to grief on the evening of April 8/9. But his guns could not be repaired; the electrical system still was not functioning. That night, Putnam received word from Grover that he had sunk two transports, a motor launch, and a number of landing barges, plus shot down two floatplanes.[5] At the end of the message, he was ordered to abstain from any other missions not assigned by Grover; all ships were to be used for recon only.[6]

4 At Del Monte, a little before noon on April 10, Dave Obert was awakened on the clubhouse cot where he had collapsed dead-tired after arriving in the P-40B only hours earlier from Cebu. Lieutenant Colonel Grover wanted him to fly another recon. "Why in hell doesn't someone else do some flying around here besides just a few of us!" Obert moaned as he got up and staggered to lunch. After the big meal, however, he felt better and agreed to take the mission for one reason only: he was going to break all regulations and "buzz the hell out of headquarters." Maybe that would make Grover sore enough to ground him for a while.

Obert's recon was a big circle over the ocean to the north of Del Monte to look for Japanese ships. He saw none but did observe a huge cloud of smoke over Cebu. On his return, he did give headquarters a good buzzing, but on landing heard not a word about it.

Early that morning, when Dick Fellows in the Waco, Hank Thorne in the P-35, and Andy Krieger in the P-40E had landed at Del Monte No. 1 field, they were met by an officer of the field, who told them to proceed immediately to Maramag. Since this was a new field that would be unknown to the pilots, it was arranged for a P-40 pilot familiar with the field to lead the three aircraft to Maramag. After Fellows, Thorne, and Krieger had taken off, they linked up with the P-40, piloted by John Geer, a former 20th Pursuiter now flying recon missions on Mindanao under John Brownewell, and followed it south to the Maramag field. The field was so well camouflaged that a pilot who had not previously been there would have had a very difficult time locating it.

On landing on the straight, grassy plain used as the airstrip, the pilots taxied their aircraft under trees that bordered one end of the four-thousand-foot-long field and completely obscured aircraft from aerial view. About twenty-five officers and enlisted men operated the base, mainly from the 19th Bombardment Group. The new arrivals headed for the mess for an early morning breakfast.

After the hearty meal, they looked around the new field. A regular city was being developed in the jungle. Revetments were being built under the trees large enough to accommodate B-17s, in addition to those already constructed for P-40s. Native workmen were constructing a hospital, barracks, roads, and bridges. Bombs and gasoline were stored in the woods. Clearly, a major role was planned for this air base.

That evening, Bill Rowe was looking forward to a good night's rest after the nervous exhaustion of the evacuation from Cebu in the Waco. But it was not to be. "For some damned reason or the other," he was ordered to go back to Del Monte from where he had arrived only that morning, along with recon pilots John Brownewell and John Geer. At 1:00 A.M. on April 11, he climbed into a staff car with the others for the rough fifty-mile ride north over mountainous territory, finally reaching Del Monte at 4:00 a.m., when he turned in for one hour's sleep.

A few hours after the arrival of Brownewell, Geer, and Rowe at the Del Monte base, orders went out for Obert, John Posten, and Kiefer White to get down to Maramag. The three veteran Bataan Field pilots assumed they would be operating for a while from the new field, where the three new P-40E-1s were based. On arriving at Maramag after the bumpy ride in the staff car, they were impressed by the layout. To Obert it was the "best field for pursuit operations" that he had ever seen.

5 On the island of Panay, about 6:30 in the morning of April 11, Benny Putnam was off again from Santa Barbara, this time ordered on a recon mission all the way north to Nichols Field. Grover had received word

that a heavy force of Japanese aircraft was assembled there and wanted confirmation.[7]

This mission would involve a round-trip flight of 560 miles without refueling. It was a longer distance than even the 532 miles the Bataan Field pilots had flown on the terrifying January 4 mission to Del Monte. But Putnam, an experienced pilot, planned to get maximum range from his battle-scarred Warhawk by manually maintaining his prop in a fixed position and keeping the fuel mixture as lean as possible without losing power.

A few hours later, Putnam arrived over Nichols Field at 10,000 feet. Surprised to find no antiaircraft fire to greet him, he took his fighter down to 5,000 feet for a better view of the situation. Putnam was astonished at the sight below. More than one hundred aircraft of all sizes were parked, wing tip to wing tip, in neat rows! Transfixed by the scene, he continued to circle at lower and lower altitude, coming all the way down now to 500 feet. Yet there was still not a sign of opposition to his brazen snooping. "Perhaps they take my plane as one of theirs," Putnam thought.

Now Putnam switched on his six fifties and began a dive to carry him along the entire length of one line of the sitting ducks. "To hell with orders," he decided; he was not going to pass up this golden opportunity. But when he pressed the trigger switch, Putnam got no response. None of his guns would fire. Nor would the hydraulic gun charger clear the jam.

Powerless to carry out his intentions, the disgruntled aviator broke off his strafing attempt and turned his P-40 in the direction of Corregidor. He had been ordered to radio his recon results at 10,000 feet to USFIP Headquarters there but soon found out that his radio was not working, a victim of the Cebu strafing mission of the day before. To add insult to injury, Corregidor opened up on him with very heavy ack-ack as he passed over at the assigned altitude.

Safely back at Santa Barbara in late morning, Putnam radioed his report to Lieutenant Colonel Grover at Del Monte. Wisely, he did not mention his frustrated attempt to shoot up Nichols Field.

6 Grover had a good reason for ordering the reconnaissance of Nichols. A force of B-17s and B-25s, under the command of Maj. Gen. Ralph Royce, was due in that afternoon from Australia for bombing attacks on Cebu, Mindanao, and Luzon. The long-range B-17s would be assigned suitable targets in the Manila area, and Nichols Field was a prime candidate for attention. The force would be arriving too late to play its earlier-envisaged critical role in the Cebu blockade-running mission, but it would still be a morale-damaging blow against the Japanese.

On the afternoon of April 11, in one of the rooms of the Del Monte Officers Club that had been made into a war room, Joe Moore was working with Lieutenant Colonel Grover on plans for the missions of the bombing force and P-40 support for it. Grover also had issued orders to Benny Putnam to report back from Iloilo in his P-40E and take over operations at the Maramag base, which would be heavily involved in support of the Royce mission. Moore and Putnam were closer to Grover than any other flying officers on Mindanao, ever since their prewar service under him when Grover commanded the 20th Pursuit.

At about five o'clock in the afternoon the Del Monte base was startled by three rifle shots fired from a nearby hill, the signal for an air raid. Bill Rowe joined the others and dove into the nearest foxhole in anticipation of another Japanese raid on the field. As the unidentified planes circled overhead, Rowe raised his head slightly for a look. There were stars on the wings of the strange twin-engine aircraft. They must be American, but what were they? At once joyous and curious over the unexpected visitors, the personnel of the Del Monte base climbed out of their holes and watched the aircraft as they put down on the Del Monte No. 1 strip. There were three B-17s and ten twin-engine bombers that no one had ever seen before but were now identified as B-25s.

At the field to greet Maj. Gen. Royce was Brigadier General Sharp, commander of all American and Filipino forces in the Visayas and Mindanao, Colonel Elsmore and other members of his 5th Air Base Group staff, and Lieutenant Colonel Grover. They all immediately headed for the war room of the officers club, its walls covered with situation maps, to confer on planned operations for the bomber force in a meeting that would last into the small hours of next morning.

Shortly after the aircraft had landed, John Geer took off in a P-40 and climbed over the Del Monte area to keep a lookout for any Japanese dive-bombers that might try an attack on the open, uncamouflaged field and its tempting targets. He continued to fly until after dark, then came in to land. The Japanese obviously had no intelligence on the arrival of the Royce force.

For the Royce mission planners, the first order of business was to disperse the bombers to fields lesser known and better camouflaged than Del Monte No. 1. Del Monte Headquarters had assumed that the B-17s and B-25s would be dispersed immediately to Maramag and Valencia and had ordered the two well-camouflaged fields to be ready to receive and service the aircraft that evening. At Maramag, Obert and the others had lit flares and were waiting at the field for the arrival of the B-17s and B-25s, for which suitable, well-hidden revetments were now ready.

For some reason, General Royce refused to accept the recommendations of the Del Monte base to disperse his total force, despite warnings of the likelihood of Japanese reconnaissance planes over the open field in the morning. He did agree to have one flight of five B-25s move forty miles south to the Valencia Field for the evening and somewhat implausibly to shift the other flight of five B-25s over eight miles to the Del Monte No. 3 field (known as the "Dalirig fighter strip"), which afforded some cover and had field lights that were now ordered turned on. The three B-17s, however, would remain at Del Monte No. 1.[8]

Down at Maramag at midnight, Obert and the others watched a heavy fog settling over the field. No aircraft would be able to land here now for sure, they figured. Wondering what had gone wrong with the plans, they headed back to their quarters to turn in for the rest of the night. No sooner had they gotten to bed when another message came over the radio. At sunrise, Lieutenants Obert, Posten, and Brown were to strafe the Japanese airdrome at Davao, sixty-five miles to the southeast, and destroy all enemy aircraft on it. They were also informed that the Royce bombers had landed at Del Monte but would be coming into Maramag in the morning.

At sunrise on the morning of April 12, the Maramag field was still fogged in, so the three fighter pilots could not take off for their Davao strafing mission. Finally, at about eight o'clock, the fog cleared and they were off. Just after takeoff, Obert looked up and was startled to see five twin-engine bombers flying right at them. So surprised that he almost started shooting at them, thinking they were Japanese, Obert then recognized the white stars on their wings and fuselages and realized they were *American* bombers, the first he had seen in the air since the first days of the war.[9]

After looking at the bombers for a while, the three fighter pilots started across the mountain range toward Davao. In about thirty minutes they came in over the city at about 10,000 feet. They looked around for quite a while but could see only two aircraft on the field.

Ben Brown started his dive first, followed by Posten and then Obert. They showered the entire airdrome with .50-caliber fire from their P-40Es, concentrating mainly on the two aircraft and the big hangar. A large, twin-engine bomber was set on fire, but the second plane, a small noncombatant type, stubbornly refused to burn. Then they all split up. Posten turned back to make another pass at the field, while Brown and Obert went their separate ways. Brown's guns had quit firing at the beginning of the attack, causing him considerable disappointment.

Obert noticed some trucks driving along a road, nosed down, and gave them a good, long burst. Then he ran across a Philippine Army barracks, into which he fired steadily. Japanese came tearing out of every opening. On a second pass, he nearly flew into the structure, so intent was he on the "show and confusion" he was causing below. Obert found he was enjoying himself greatly, seeing the Japanese do what he had been doing for so long on Bataan. Passing over a small village, where he saw Japanese soldiers in the streets, he held his fire, however, because there were Filipinos everywhere too. But when he spotted a big house, sure that it was occupied by Japanese officers, since it was the best house in the village, he strafed it, too, with unknown results.

Realizing that his ammunition must now be getting low, Obert headed back to Maramag, saving a few rounds in case he should be jumped by Japanese before getting back. On the uneventful return flight, Obert came to an unsettling conclusion about his character. He had become a killer, "not in the heat of battle, but cooly and deliberately because the laws of warfare said it was no crime." His conscience was not bothering him a whit that he had killed a number of defenseless Japanese soldiers that morning. Six months earlier, however, he even felt bad when he shot a rabbit or bird while hunting with his squadron mates at Iba.

Just after Brown and Obert landed, John Posten came in. Brown and Obert "gasped in astonishment" at the sight of his P-40E. His right wing-tip and just about all of the aileron were missing! On his final dive at Davao Field after Obert and Brown had departed, Posten had hit the wind-sock on top of the big hangar—with predictable results. All the way back to Maramag, it took all his strength to hold the left wing down and main-tain level flight with half his right wing gone. Fearful of stalling out on landing, Posten brought his crippled warbird in at way above safe landing speed, about 150 MPH.

7 At Del Monte No. 1 field, two of the three B-17s had taken off at about 7:30 on the morning of April 12 to bomb assigned targets on Luzon. The B-17 flown by Capt. Frank Bostrom was to attack any ships that might be blockading Corregidor, otherwise to hit Nichols Field. The second B-17, piloted by Capt. Edward Teats, headed for Batangas to hit any shipping there. But the third B-17, which had limped into Del Monte from Austra-lia on three engines, was left behind for repairs.

Shortly after the two B-17s had left on their mission north, single-engine Japanese floatplanes began appearing over Del Monte, as expected by base officers. They arrived in pairs, each carrying two light bombs, and would look over their targets after cutting their engines and gliding over the field as low as 2,000 feet. Then they would swing back and go into dives, release their bombs, and head back to base. A discomfited General Royce watched this shuttle exercise all morning, but fortunately the B-17 under repair was not hit.[10]

Between 1:00 and 2:00 P.M., the two other B-17s returned to Del Monte after accomplishing their missions. While they were being gassed and rearmed for another mission, two more floatplanes appeared over the field. They immediately picked out the three B-17s as targets and released their bombs in diving attacks. The B-17 undergoing engine repairs was hit squarely in the fuselage, practically destroying it. Other bombs fell near the other two B-17s parked nearby, riddling the tails of both. Then in a return trip, two more floatplanes dropped bombs thirty and seventy-five feet from the damaged B-17s, the shrapnel tearing up the wings and damaging the sides of Teats's B-17. There would be no late afternoon mission for the B-17s.

Following one of these shuttle attacks, Kiefer White had taken off from Maramag to intercept two floatplanes as they headed back to their Davao base. At 11:50 White ran into the "Petes" over Malaybalay, but in the dogfight they managed to escape and return to Davao, with no damage to either side.

The fighter pilots witness to the sad state of affairs at Del Monte were furious. John Geer recorded in his diary that evening that "after all our work to build revetments for these planes, the high command screws up and lets them sit out in the open to be destroyed!" To Bill Feallock, who with the others on Mindanao was "pretty well pissed off" at Royce's refusal to disperse the B-17s, it meant that "18 fewer fighter pilots would be able to evacuate Mindanao."

Fortunately all the B-25s were undamaged after their first missions and were now being readied at Maramag and Valencia for afternoon attacks on Cebu and Davao. After their successful attacks, all returned safely to their camouflaged fields as evening approached.

All that evening, ground crews at Del Monte worked feverishly to repair the two damaged B-17s. By dawn they were ready to fly back to Australia. The crew of the destroyed B-17 was loaded on the other two aircraft, along with four select passengers, including Comdr. John Bulkeley of PT Squadron 3 fame, and Jack Donalson, the only pursuit pilot to manage a ride out, who was lying in the crawlway that extended from the nose aft (in his diary, Bill Rowe referred to him as a stowaway).[11] General Royce himself elected to remain behind and fly out with a B-25 instead.

Just before dawn on April 13, the two bombers lifted safely off of Del Monte with their heavy loads and set course for Australia. Bostrom's hydraulic system was still out from bomb damage, so his B-17 had no supercharger or brakes, but it managed to hold together.

Shortly after the B-17s took off from Del Monte, 1st Lt. Harold F. Cocanougher was airborne in the P-35A—the last surviving one of the Philippines campaign that Thorne had brought in from Bataan. He had been ordered the day before by Capt. Ozzie Lunde, now serving as Lieutenant Colonel Grover's executive officer, to go up in the P-35A from the Del Monte No. 3 (Dalirig) strip and fly cover over the two surviving B-17s being repaired at Del Monte No. 1, eight miles to the north. Grover's headquarters was upset over the failure of its fighters to ward off the pesky Japanese floatplanes and did not want to see a repetition of the performance of the day before. It had failed to inform Cocanougher, however, that the B-17s had already departed at daybreak.

Over Del Monte, "Coke" ran immediately into two floatplanes, which had arrived at 5:20 A.M. with hopes for further damage to the base. Cocanougher was above them and went into a dive, emptying his .50-caliber wing guns at them until the guns jammed. Then the P-35 and its adversaries went back and forth after each other, making pass after pass, exchanging .30-caliber fire, with neither side able to score any hits.

Shortly after Cocanougher had become airborne, Gus Williams taxied out on the same Dalirig strip in the P-40B behind John Brownewell in a P-40E for a reconnaissance and strafing raid of Davao. As they reached the far end of the narrow, six-thousand-foot-long strip to turn around, Williams noticed two floatplanes overhead and was anxious to take off before the Japanese spotted them. (These evidently were another pair of floatplanes that had arrived with the two that Cocanougher had mixed it up with.)[12]

Shortly after takeoff, Brownewell also saw the Japanese, and both P-40s started a steep climb to get above them. But Williams's P-40B kept falling further and further behind Brownewell's P-40E. The floatplanes now separated, and at about 11,000 feet, one of them turned and made a head-on attack on Brownewell. Just before passing each other, the two antagonists fired at each other. His .50-caliber guns working well, Brownewell scored hits on the "Pete's" engine or pilot. The floatplane immediately went into a spiral dive and crashed a few miles south of Del Monte.[13]

As the mortally stricken Japanese aircraft went spiraling past Williams about two thousand feet below Brownewell, Williams started circling to watch for a bailout. But in the fairly tight turn, Williams's P-40B suddenly snapped to the outside, throwing off the canopy cover and leaving Williams halfway out of the cockpit, minus his goggles and helmet. At full throttle, the aircraft went into wild gyrations, preventing Williams from getting back into the cockpit and reaching for the throttle. Finally the engine quit and the terrified pilot was able to get back into the cockpit and recover from the spin at about 1,500 feet over the Dalirig strip. Preparing for a landing with a dead engine, Williams dropped his landing gear and was only about six feet off the field when the engine started wide-open. With too high RPM, Williams aborted the landing attempt and went around for another landing at reduced airspeed and came in without further incident. In the meantime, Brownewell had continued his flight down to Davao, where he was credited with strafing four aircraft.

During the inconclusive dogfight between Cocanougher and the other two floatplanes, the Japanese had managed to drop their bombs on their target—the wrecked B-17 of the day before that had been fixed up to serve as a decoy for the Japanese. Just before six o'clock, they succeeded in blowing up this useless B-17. At 10:40 A.M., two more "Petes" were back over Del Monte, looking for remaining targets.

About noon, Lt. John Burns was assigned to fly a patrol from the Dalirig strip. Not familiar with the characteristics of the narrow, long field, which still had rocks left alongside it, feeling unwell from a malarial condition carrying over from Bataan days, and not having flown for a long time, he reluctantly accepted his orders and climbed into the P-40E. On take-off, Burns failed to line himself up in the center of the two-hundred-foot-wide strip and before becoming airborne ran off the edge of the field, hit a boulder, and fell into the canyon bordering the field, where his plane caught fire. No one could get to him; the field had no fire-fighting equipment, and he burned to death in the cockpit. That evening, John Geer and the base medic recovered his body from the still-smouldering airplane.

8 At Maramag on the afternoon of April 13, Dave Obert and most of the other pilots at the base were ordered back to Del Monte. "We whooped with joy because we thought we were going to get our ride out of the Philippines," Obert recorded in his diary. They had finally realized that no help was on the way and that all the Philippines would soon be in Japanese hands. The elated pilots loaded into a truck and started out for Del Monte, not even complaining a bit of the long, rough, four hours' ride. Late in the afternoon they reached Del Monte.

But disappointment waited for them at the base. They were informed that most of them would not be catching a lift out with the B-25s when they departed that evening after all. However, Obert was told to get his things packed. He would be one of the few to go out.

With nothing really to pack, Obert opted to spend the waiting time in bed, since he was not feeling well. No sooner than he had gotten to sleep than Joe Moore woke him and told him that Lieutenant Colonel Grover wanted him to get another pilot and fly patrol over Del Monte while the B-25s came in to land after their final mission, this one over Davao. He was informed that his name had been taken off the list of evacuees because there were some civilians and other officers to go instead of pilots.[14] Obert was bitterly disappointed at this turn of events.

Obert now asked among the pilots for someone to go with him on the patrol flight, but everyone said they did not feel like flying. Nearly everyone was sick, including Obert, but he was "too proud and stubborn" to ask Grover to get someone in his place. Why had Grover not asked some of the other pursuit pilots who were healthy and strong and hanging around headquarters but who had done very little flying?

Finally, Kiefer White volunteered to fly with Obert, indicating he felt well enough for yet another mission. After taking off, they gave headquarters a good buzzing to express their feelings about the situation and then went on patrol over the Del Monte area. They remained up until after nightfall and then came in for a very dark, tricky landing.

The B-25s had come in at dusk. Now the Del Monte crews were busy reinstalling the long-range fuel tanks and servicing the aircraft to ready them for their long return trip to Australia. Each B-25 was so heavily loaded with gas that it could carry only three passengers. Only Hank Thorne and Joe Moore had gained final selection among the pursuit pilots to be evacuated. General George in Australia had requested General Royce to bring out any of the pursuit squadron commanders that he could locate on Mindanao, as they were sorely needed in Australia. Thorne of the 3rd and Moore of the 20th were the only candidates.[15]

At about midnight, nine of the B-25s took off from Del Monte for Australia. The tenth one, piloted by "Pappy" Gunn, had lost its extra fuel tank to one of the Japanese attacks on Del Monte. It would take two anxious days for its crew to adapt two B-18 tanks for it before they all could leave, with Hank Thorne as one of its five passengers.

Earlier that evening, Obert and the other pursuit pilots left behind sent a message to General George, informing him that most of his old Bataan Field pilots were at Del Monte and wanted very much to join him in Australia. They felt sure that if it were possible, he would send a plane back for them. Nevertheless, when the B-25s took off that night, "we felt that our last chance had gone," a dejected Obert recorded in his diary that evening.

27. "GET ABOARD. THERE'LL BE NO TOMORROW"

1 During the last mission of the B-25s, on April 13, one had been detached from the mission and ordered to Santa Barbara on Panay on a special assignment: to pick up four persons scheduled for evacuation to Australia on the B-25s and the USAFFE G-2 and G-3 journals flown out of Corregidor by Lts. Ray Gehrig and Jack Randolph before dawn that day. The two Bataan veterans had experienced several nerve-racking days and nights since arriving separately on Corregidor the morning of April 9 and missing their submarine trip out to Australia.

After giving up on the possibility of the submarine evacuation in late morning April 9, Randolph had run into Colonel Kennard, who had also reached Corregidor after failing to get out of Bataan by air earlier that morning. They had found out that there were four old Stearman 76D3 armed trainers of the Philippine Army Air Corps on Corregidor's Kindley Field. The biplanes were being guarded by Sergeant Ojeda of the PAAC. Since Kennard was still authorized for evacuation south, they decided to approach Col. Charles Savage, air officer of the USFIP command on Corregidor, for permission for Randolph to fly Kennard south in one of the two-seaters.

Colonel Savage was half-asleep in Malinta Tunnel when Kennard and Randolph approached him. At first, he refused to authorize the flight but eventually acquiesced. Then Col. Harry Porter, the air force's engineering officer, found out about the arrangement. He now wanted to go out in one of the 76D3s too. After all, he was originally authorized to fly out with Randolph.

But who would fly the second Stearman south? Randolph proposed Gehrig, and the three of them went looking for him. Upon learning of this proposal, Gehrig discussed the matter with George Armstrong, who with Gehrig had missed his scheduled evacuation from Corregidor on the morning of April 9. They agreed that Gehrig would take the Stearman on this mission and Armstrong would fly one of the two remaining biplanes out the following night. Gehrig, Kennard, Randolph, and Porter went back to Colonel Savage for authorization for the second Stearman. Savage wrote out a release for a second ship to give to Sergeant Ojeda.

At 4:15 that night, Gehrig and Randolph took off from tiny Kindley Field with their two passengers. After refueling and laying over during the afternoon at Santa Barbara on the island of Panay, they landed safely at Del Monte the evening of April 10. The next day, all four were ordered to report to General Sharp. Standing in disbelief before Sharp, they were read an order from General Wainwright instructing Sharp to arrest the four of them, plus a Lieutenant O'Brien and a Sergeant Madden, who had taken a third Stearman out the night after Randolph and Gehrig had left Corregidor, and have them returned to Corregidor under suitable guard.

Sharp declined to arrest Kennard and Porter and later agreed to a suggestion by the four to radio a message directly to Wainwright, asking him to send for Sergeant Ojeda and have him produce the release slips for the two Stearman trainers that Randolph and Gehrig had flown out. That afternoon, a reply was received from Wainwright. Kennard, Porter, Randolph, and Gehrig were "exonerated without prejudice."[1] The message also ordered Gehrig and Randolph to fly back into Corregidor on a special mission: to pick up the confidential USAFFE G-2 and G-3 journals and to evacuate four important passengers: UPI correspondent Frank Hewlett, China liaison officer Col. Chih Wang, and two nisei interpreters in U.S. Army intelligence, Col. Clarence Yamagata and S. Sgt. Arthur Kumori. The last three risked execution if captured by the Japanese.

At about 4:00 in the afternoon of April 11, Randolph climbed into the pilot's seat of the four-passenger Waco cabin plane of the Bamboo Fleet, loaded down with medicine, vitamin pills, and chocolate for the troops on Corregidor, and took off from Del Monte. With him was Gehrig in the Stearman he had flown south from Corregidor. After refueling at Santa Barbara and laying over until about 1:30 A.M., Gehrig and Randolph took off again for Corregidor. To facilitate their locating Corregidor and Kindley Field in the middle of the night, Randolph and Gehrig had asked Wainwright for searchlights to be turned on, straight into the sky for a few minutes every half hour.

At 4:30 on a moonless night the two vintage aircraft arrived over Corregidor, but without the benefit of searchlights. None had been turned on. After making three passes, Randolph brought the Waco down in total darkness, without any landing lights, but not before banging his right landing gear against a huge rock sitting right out in the middle of Kindley Field. The accident spun the Waco around 180 degrees.

After climbing out of the Waco, Randolph anxiously watched as Gehrig now tried to bring the Stearman down. On the fourth pass, Gehrig brushed a treetop with his wing at the end of the strip, then on the fifth try, he finally touched down. Gehrig was afraid he was going to run into the Waco sitting on the strip; with the benefit of his landing lights, Gehrig spotted the cabin plane but then ran off the strip and nosed up, bending his propeller.

Among those at Kindley Field to meet the two aircraft were George Armstrong, the UPI correspondent, the Chinese liaison officer, and the two nisei. Cheated out of flying the third Stearman out the night before, Armstrong had been assigned by Corregidor to fly the Waco back to Del Monte. After heated discussions in the pitch darkness, however, Randolph refused to give it up, and Armstrong and Colonel Savage backed down.

At any rate, the Stearman and the Waco would not be going anywhere the next hours. That day, April 12, was devoted to repairs of the two damaged aircraft. The ordnance shop on Corregidor managed to straighten Gehrig's propeller, and the Waco had its right tire changed and its landing gear strut repaired.

As darkness fell over Corregidor that evening, Randolph went down to Kindley Field, pulled cushions out of the Waco, put them under the aircraft, and settled in for the evening, his .45 next to him. He had heard about O'Brien stealing the third Stearman on Corregidor two nights before and was not going to take any chances with the Waco of another theft.

In the early hours of Monday, April 13, Gehrig showed up at Kindley Field. Shortly afterward, at 3:00, the UPI correspondent, the Chinese liaison officer, and the two nisei interpreters arrived, hoping that this evening they would be able to leave after the aborted effort the previous evening. Carrying the heavy files of the G-2 and G-3 journals, Hewlett climbed into the front seat of the 76D3 as Gehrig took over the pilot's controls in the back seat. The other three passengers boarded the Waco with Randolph.

Then at 3:50, Gehrig in the Stearman and Randolph following behind in the Waco worked their way down the dark strip as the harbor defense lights gave some light on the field at intervals of thirty seconds. Taking off without incident, they headed skyward for Iloilo, the layover destination.

It was 7:00 A.M. when the Waco and the Stearman touched down at Santa Barbara field and began taxiing up the strip. Then Sergeant Kumori, sitting up front in the right seat, called to Randolph to look at the right landing gear. Something was wrong! Randolph looked over and saw that it was moving backwards and forwards about six inches. Gehrig also had his problems. His repaired prop had vibrated badly all the way down from Corregidor.

Neither pilot intended continuing south with their passengers and cargo with their aircraft in disrepair. Instead, they radioed Del Monte for transportation for the others and the journals and a new prop for the Stearman and parts for the Waco. In the meantime, Randolph put some airline mechanics at Santa Barbara at work on the Waco, now parked under an oak tree off the strip in the jungle. That afternoon at 3:00 P.M., when the B-25 came in from Mindanao in response to their message, there was no prop or parts for the two pilots. After the passengers and journals were loaded on the B-25 and flown out, Gehrig and Randolph settled back to wait for the materiel they needed to get airborne.

Also at Santa Barbara that afternoon but under less honorable circumstances were Lt. Forrest O'Brien and Sgt. James E. Madden of Headquarters Squadron, 24th Pursuit Group. However, they avoided any contact with Gehrig and Randolph. Anxious about getting off Corregidor after the fall of Bataan, O'Brien had gone down to Kindley Field with Madden and secretly climbed aboard one of the two remaining Stearmans on the field that was scheduled to be taken out to Del Monte by Armstrong at 2:30 A.M. on April 11. At 2:00, O'Brien had taken off with his passenger without any lights on the field and landed before daylight at Santa Barbara. Evidently O'Brien had decided after landing at Santa Barbara not to continue on to Del Monte, where he figured (correctly) he would be placed under arrest. Indeed, orders calling for his arrest, along with that of Sergeant Madden, had been received two days earlier at Del Monte, as well as for Randolph, Gehrig, Kennard, and Porter.

And what of the fourth Stearman on Corregidor? This last 76D3 biplane had been assigned by Colonel Savage to Capt. Charley Sneed, former flying commander of the Bataan Field Flying Detachment and subsequently assigned to the 5th Interceptor Command staff, and 1st Lt. Perry Franks, at the time assigned to Headquarters Squadron, 24th Pursuit Group. They were under instructions of General Wainwright to evacuate Dean Schedler, a twenty-eight-year-old Associated Press correspondent, the last news reporter remaining in the islands, down to Mindanao.

In pitch darkness at Kindley Field in the small hours of April 12, Sneed and Schedler climbed into the rear seat of the old biplane, somehow managing to squeeze into a place intended for a single person, as Franks, a bulky man, took the front seat. A few minutes later, the overloaded Stearman was airborne, heading south at low altitude.

North of Mindoro, they sighted a concentration of Japanese warships running blacked out. The ships opened fire and tracers climbed under the Stearman's wings. Struggling to gain altitude to escape the fire, they frantically threw out their sidearms, seat cushions, some instruments, and everything else they could pry loose. When they reached 10,000 feet, they succeeded in evading the antiaircraft fire. But now they were shivering with cold in the open cockpits.

At first light, several hours into their odyssey, they found themselves over open sea. They were obviously far off course, their aircraft having been buffeted by strong winds all night. Franks was worried. His gasoline was running low, and he would need to put down somewhere soon. Then he spotted a small island through heavy ground fog. He did not know whether it was occupied by the Japanese or not, but had no choice but to try to land.

Banking over the trees, Franks lined himself up with a curving beach. Touching down safely, the Stearman rolled several hundred feet on the soft sand, then nosed over. Schedler, Sneed, and Franks were all thrown out onto the beach but were only scratched. They saw no signs of life but were too exhausted to investigate and crawled into a palm grove to sleep, oblivious as to whether the island was in Japanese hands or not.

About noon, small Filipino children timidly approached the plane and awakened them. When they saw the white stars on the wings, they ran away, shouting "Americano aviators," then soon returned with adults from a nearby village, who were friendly and spoke some English. They informed the Americans that they were on the northern end of Palawan Island, over four hundred miles west of Iloilo, their intended touchdown point.

After giving their visitors some coconuts, the Filipinos managed to right the plane. A cursory examination indicated that the fabric on one wing end was torn, the propeller and tail rudder were bent, and there were a few sand tears elsewhere in the fabric. Sneed started taking sand and water out of the engine, then began to make rudimentary repairs, using only a bolo and a small screwdriver.

In the meantime, natives within a radius of twenty miles offered to bring gasoline. The Americans were skeptical, however; there were not any automobiles on the island. Nevertheless, Schedler and Franks began building a makeshift runway of palm leaves across the sand with the help of a few natives and one shovel. As the sun descended on Palawan on April 13, the Stearman had been sufficiently repaired to attempt a flight to Iloilo. But would the Filipinos be able to find them any gas?

2 In the Del Monte area on the morning of April 14, it was raining heavily. Lieutenant Colonel Grover had ordered most of the pursuit pilots back to the Maramag base following the completion of the Royce mission, but Dave Obert was feeling so bad he did not want to make the long, bumpy ride. Then about noon he developed an awful chill. He tried to warm up on a bottle of brandy, but that only made matters worse. The malaria had hit him full force again. He was now loaded into a car and driven to the Del Monte hospital, where he was put to bed and started on a heavy course of quinine.

After Obert had been in the hospital several hours, someone came in with a report that Lt. Larry McDaniel had cracked up and been killed. Evidently he was transferring the "P-40 Something" from Del Monte No. 1

to Del Monte No. 3 Dalirig strip in the rain that afternoon when the rebuilt aircraft stalled and crashed on the final approach for the landing.
He was found badly mangled near the scattered pieces of the aircraft, and
he died later of a fractured skull without regaining consciousness.

This latest tragedy was too much for Obert, so sick with malaria now
he was nearly out of his mind and awaiting the expected fall of Mindanao.
He broke down and cried like a baby. Later, regaining his composure, his
feelings turned to anger. McDaniel should never have flown that day. Another more senior pilot had originally been ordered to move the P-40B,
but it was raining, so he got McDaniel to do it. The 34th Pursuiter had
not flown for months, he knew nothing of the tricky characteristics of
the Dalirig strip, and he was in poor physical condition.

Gus Williams could add another factor to account for McDaniel's death:
the aircraft was not safe to fly. It had nearly killed Williams the day before when it snapped on him and stalled. He had recommended that it
not be flown again until they found out what was wrong with it. His warning went unheeded.

The next day was hot and sultry following the heavy rains of April 14,
good weather for a visit of the Japanese floatplanes expected back in re-
venge for the Royce raids. Sure enough, at noon two of the dive-bombing
aircraft showed up and started wreaking destruction on the Del Monte
area.

One bomb fell right in the center of the Del Monte Club; the resultant
fire burned the popular clubhouse to the ground. Then the Japanese started
strafing and bombing cars and other targets on Del Monte No. 1 field as
the base's personnel cowered in foxholes. Bedridden in the hospital, Dave
Obert and two of the other pursuit pilots also down with malaria, John
Posten and Bill Coleman, were "nervous wrecks" by the end of the day.
All of the big buildings at the base had been hit by the Japanese except
for the hospital. They fully expected to be bombed next.

About 8:00 on the morning of April 16, base personnel at Del Monte
heard a plane approaching the number 1 field, but it was not Japanese.
They recognized Bill Bradford's old camouflaged Bellanca Skyrocket coming in for a landing. But just as Bradford put the wheels down, two more
Japanese floatplane dive-bombers arrived high over the field. Hurriedly,
Bradford taxied the twin-engine veteran to a hiding spot, then with his
passengers jumped out and headed for a barrio near the field. As the Japanese came down and started bombing the field, they all took to a ditch
for safety.

But now another Bamboo Fleet veteran appeared over the field, circling and descending to make a landing. It was the Waco cabin plane.
About 2,000 feet above the defenseless aircraft, one of the floatplanes
spotted the enticing target, jettisoned its bombs, and screamed down, fir-

ing its 7.7-mm guns at the Waco. Touching down, the Waco pilot took off again, tried another landing, then crashed.

When Del Monte base personnel reached the wrecked Waco, they pulled Lt. Forrest O'Brien and his two passengers, Sergeant Madden and a navy man later identified as John L. Howard, out of the plane and took them to Del Monte hospital, but all died as a result of their injuries. O'Brien had evidently learned that the Japanese were beginning to land on Iloilo in the early morning darkness of April 16. He now decided that arrest on Mindanao was preferable to POW status on Iloilo. Having linked up with the navy man on Iloilo, O'Brien and Madden needed the larger Waco to get off the island. Despite its damaged landing gear, they decided to steal it from Randolph, who was not on the field at the time.

Later that morning, Bradford's passengers—Dean Schedler, Charley Sneed, and Perry Franks—described to Del Monte base personnel their hair-raising experiences of the past four days in the old Stearman 76D3. After recounting the events of April 12 and 13, they related that on the afternoon of April 14, Filipinos had appeared at the site on northern Palawan where the three were marooned. The natives were rolling a big fifty-five-gallon drum of aviation gasoline plainly marked "Cavite Navy Yard." The Filipinos told them that it had washed ashore some time ago. Sneed and Schedler strained the gasoline through a handkerchief and poured it into the Stearman's tank. They figured that the fifty-five gallons would be sufficient to reach friendly Iloilo.

Then Franks, who had been exploring in a native double outrigger canoe, returned with word that Japanese on a nearby island had picked up the news of the Americans' plight. They had to clear out as soon as possible. After a last inspection of the crudely fashioned "runway"—six hundred feet long and only two feet wider than the biplane's landing gear—they shook hands with the Filipinos and thanked them for their help. It was 5:03 P.M.

In a switch, Franks got in the rear seat with Schedler and Sneed climbed into the pilot's seat. At full throttle, Sneed gunned the old Stearman down the improvised runway of palm leaves, zigzagging all the way. Finally, it lifted off and cleared coral rocks at the end of the beach by a few feet.

Sneed soon found that the still-bent propeller, "rattling like an old car," was unable to pull the plane above 2,000 feet. After thirty minutes, the head wind grew stronger, while threatening black clouds came closer and closer. Near sunset, the 76D3 was completely enveloped by the rain-bearing clouds, which now drenched the Americans in the open cockpits.

Sneed then rolled and banked, anxiously searching for an opening in the clouds while trying to maintain his eastward course. He wanted to reach a shoreline before dark. After continuing through the clouds for an hour, it had become pitch dark. Finally he spotted the shoreline of an island. As the pilot circled low, his passengers saw tall, waving palms without an open space in sight. It was raining harder and harder.

Sneed now announced that they only had ten more minutes' flying time left to find a cove where they could set the plane down in the water before their gas was finished. Schedler and Franks tightened their Mae Wests. Franks tied a safety belt around his right leg and Schedler's left, since it was not long enough to encircle both men. Sneed reached back, shook his passenger's hands, and said, "Well, this is it." He was going to try a water landing.

As he brought the old biplane lower and lower, the engine barked and spit fire. The Stearman skimmed along perfectly, then the prop touched the water. Immediately, Sneed cut the engine, so hot after four hours' flying that they feared an explosion.

The 76D3 hit the water easily, but as it sank, it flipped over on its nose. Sneed was thrown clear, but Schedler and Franks were left hanging in the air. After loosening their safety belt, they tumbled into the water, went under, then came to the surface, where they clung to the wings.

After regaining their composure, Franks and Schedler started paddling to the shore some three hundred to five hundred yards away. But the life preservers were choking them. A nonswimmer, Franks twice swallowed water and sank, despite his Mae West, but each time Sneed answered his calls for help, pulled him up, and supported him. Schedler struggled for an hour with the high waves and outgoing tide, then finally reached shore, totally exhausted. He climbed the rocks on the coastline and with the flashlight he had retained shone a beach light for Sneed and Franks.

After they were all safely ashore, they made an inventory of their possessions: wristwatches stopped by salt water, one compass, one .45 automatic, a package of soaked cigarettes, and wallets. Franks had lost his shoes in the crash, so they used underwear and handkerchiefs to protect his feet. Utterly exhausted, the three lost Americans wanted to drift to sleep, but rapacious sand flies kept them awake. All night they lay awake, wondering where they had landed and if the island was Cebu, which they knew to be in Japanese hands since April 10.

At dawn on the next day, April 15, friendly natives came to the beach and gave them food, including overripe eggs and items salvaged from the submerged Stearman. The Americans were told that they were on the island of Guimaras, south of their destination of Panay.

After obtaining the services of a fishing boat, they set out on a slow daylong trip north to Panay Island. On arrival, they were informed that eight Japanese ships were heading in to make a landing, expected for the next morning. Much later in the day, they were treated to a hearty dinner with U.S. Army officers at Iloilo City, then they turned in for the evening.

Before dawn on April 16, the three were awakened and told that the

Japanese were landing only four miles away from Iloilo. They were driven down to Santa Barbara field outside Iloilo to meet Bill Bradford, the veteran Bamboo Fleet pilot. Bradford had spent several days at Iloilo after experiencing engine trouble with his old Bellanca and fortuitously had finished repairs and was preparing to leave just at the time Sneed and the others reached the area.

Taking aboard the three Stearman survivors, Bradford now took off for Del Monte twenty minutes before daylight. Bradford and his passengers could hear the Japanese shooting up Iloilo City as the old Bellanca cleared the field. For Sneed, Franks, and Schedler, their four-day odyssey—the longest and most obstacle-beset escape of any from Bataan and Corregidor—was over. Both Sneed and Franks were subsequently awarded the Distinguished Flying Cross for their feat.[2]

Another escapee from Iloilo that morning was Capt. Bill Cummings. He had flown out of the doomed town in the last remaining P-35A in the Philippines.

3 On the early evening of Thursday, April 16, Dave Obert was feeling much better and asked the Del Monte hospital doctor if he could be released. The doctor told him no. Fellow patient Bill Coleman was getting ready to leave at the time, so Obert got out of bed and left with him anyway.

That night, they slept at Camp 29, the vast pineapple field near Del Monte where the 19th Bomb Group's personnel were ensconced in nipa shacks. The following night the two airmen caught a ride to Maramag on a truck loaded with bombs and fuses. What a ride! No lights, over a mountainous road, and "loaded with enough explosives to level a small-sized city." Obert crawled on top of the cases of fuses and slept most of the way.

On arrival at the Maramag base, Obert and Coleman found that most of the other pilots were already there. The remaining pilots were scheduled to move there in the near future. By now, the pursuit pilots had just about given up hope of being evacuated from Mindanao. But they had all agreed not to be taken prisoner by the Japanese. The fifteen or so of them planned to stay together in a group and work their way to the coast in order to escape by boat when the opportunity arose. With this objective in mind, they began collecting food, weapons, ammunition, and other supplies at Maramag for a protracted stay in the jungle. The jungle kit that Obert put together contained more quinine than anything else. He was taking thirty grains a day against the malaria attack that still held him in its grips.

For the time being, Obert and the others were living pretty comfortably at Maramag. Food was plentiful. They were getting all the beef and potatoes they could eat and were supplementing it with canned goods, fruit, and candy they bought from the native stores. In addition to walks in the beautiful countryside, they loafed, read, and played cards at the Alligator Club, a large, wall-less building with a grass roof and a rough floor back in the forest where all the pilots stayed. The club also had a bar constructed at one end, but the only drink they could get was a native concoction appropriately called "very special brandy."

After breakfast on April 19, the pilots heard that orders were out for someone to fly the old Bellanca to Corregidor to bring in sorely needed medicine to the beleaguered fortress.[3] Evidently General Wainwright had radioed the day before with the request, but Lieutenant Colonel Grover had resisted. He had talked to Bill Bradford about the chances of getting through, given that the Japanese were believed to be in control of all territory north of Mindanao.. Bradford replied that he thought the chances were exactly zero.

When Benny Putnam, now at Maramag in charge of flying operations, heard of the request, he tried to get permission for one of the pilots to take the P-35A and drop the medicine by parachute instead, but Wainwright's command on Corregidor refused this alternative and insisted the Bellanca be flown in. If no one would volunteer for the flight, someone would have to be ordered to go.

When the ultimatum was presented to the Maramag pilots, no one offered to go. They all felt they had been kicked around so much that if they did not begin to look out for themselves, no one else would. They had gotten no thanks or credit for what they had done so far, so why should they stick their necks out again now? This mission, they felt, was certainly a hopeless one. Even if the defenseless Bellanca could refuel at Negros Island, which might be in Japanese hands, and at 110 MPH make it through Japanese-controlled skies to Corregidor, it would still have to run the gauntlet of Japanese artillery fire zeroed in on Kindley Field and probably have to crash-land on the shell-pocked strip, and the pilot would have to remain on the doomed island.

As the air force officer in charge of operations at Maramag, Putnam decided that the pilots would draw cards and the low man would make the flight, although many did not even know what the Bellanca looked like or how to fly up to Corregidor. Bill Rowe and some of the others argued that it would be fairer if all the pilots on Mindanao participated in the drawing, but Putnam wanted it restricted to the Maramag group only. Obert, Posten, and another of the pursuit pilots who were still down with malaria and thus unable to fly were excused from participating.

At one o'clock that afternoon in the lounge of the Alligator Club, about fifteen pilots gathered for the draw. Just before starting, Bill Bradford asked to shuffle the cards. He took the deck, played with the cards a bit, and then handed them back to Putnam. One by one, the nervous group of pilots picked cards. "Life and death are high stakes to play for with cards,"

Obert thought as he watched the drawing, relieved but feeling guilty for not participating.

The ones who drew high cards gave out a sigh of relief, while the low-card drawers became more and more tense as they compared their cards with the others. Bill Rowe had drawn a five but found there were lower cards than his.

Then Bill Bradford produced a deuce of diamonds. It was the low card. The veteran Bamboo Fleet pilot now told the relieved pilots that it was probably a good thing that he would be making the flight because only he knew the Bellanca and the route to be followed and thus was more likely to get through than any of the others, what with his long years of experience as a civilian pilot in the Philippines. "Who knows, I might even have a slight chance of getting back," he declared.

Bradford now packed his few things, collected the quinine and other medicine for the trip, and headed out for Valencia Field, some ten miles away where the Bellanca was parked. Putnam would be scouting for him in the Maramag P-40 up as far as the coast of Negros, where Bradford would refuel; it was assumed that Bacolod Field on Negros was still in friendly hands.

Shortly after Bradford had left the clubhouse, the pilots were talking about the nerve-racking experience of the card draw when a thought occurred to one of them. "Jitter Bill had that deuce all the time!" he blurted out. "Remember him playing with the cards before the draw? He slipped it out then because he thought he should go."

The whole thing was clear to the pilots now. Rather than see any of them go, Bradford had palmed the deuce before the draw so that he would be sure to go.[4] To Obert, Bradford's act was "the biggest, the most unselfish and the bravest thing I had ever seen a man do." Yet when that same officer, who had been informed the day before by Corregidor that he had been promoted to major and was now wearing his oak leaves around the base, had radioed Corregidor for confirmation of his promotion, the reply was that he had *not* been promoted.

At this point, the Maramag pilots were so mad at the command that "anything is liable to happen," Bill Rowe wrote in his diary that evening. He believed that if any of the Maramag group had been picked instead of Bradford, "he would have flown south instead of to Corregidor and found himself a deserted island."

A few days later word reached the pilots from Corregidor that Bradford had landed safely, but while trying to take off the following night, he had come too close to the edge of the runway and had nosed over and crashed, though neither Bradford nor his passengers were injured. "We felt like murdering the people who had ordered the mission," Obert recorded in his diary that night.

4 On Wednesday evening, April 22, Benny Putnam received a message from Lieutenant Colonel Grover at Del Monte. All pilots were to report to Del Monte field the next day at 6:00 in the afternoon. A plane would be coming in from Australia to evacuate a load of pilots. The news immediately lifted the spirits of the Maramag group. The young men "whooped, jumped, and shouted with joy!" Another chance for them to get away before the Japanese arrived. The next morning, the pilots piled into a 2½-ton truck for the bumpy, tiresome road north to Del Monte, arriving in the afternoon.

After gorging themselves on pineapple and putting away a heavy meal at dinnertime, they sat back to wait for the arrival of the rescue aircraft. They were joined by the senior pilots in staff jobs at Del Monte plus others still flying recons from the Del Monte No. 1 and No. 2 and Dalirig strips, including John Brownewell and John Geer. No one knew if his name was on the list for evacuation or not. They would have to sweat it out until the plane arrived.

Two surprise candidates for the flight out were there too, Ray Gehrig and Jack Randolph. Most of the pilots thought that they had been captured on Panay when the island fell to the Japanese on April 16. However, they had hidden out under some concrete steps of a house that day, literally under the nose of searching Japanese troops, then had started off at dark for a three-day hike through Japanese lines and caught a lift over to Negros Island by canoe. On Negros, they were given a ride to Binalbogan, where they radioed Del Monte on April 21 for a rescue flight.

As the Del Monte pilot most experienced with conditions in the southern islands, John Brownewell answered Grover's call for a volunteer. He decided to take the old P-35A, figuring correctly that the baggage compartment could hold both the grossly underweight men. Taking off in the early morning of April 23, Brownewell accomplished the rescue mission without incident, much to the gratitude of the two stranded pilots. For that flight Brownewell was subsequently awarded the Distinguished Flying Cross.

At 11:00 o'clock on the evening of April 23, an LB-30 four-engine Liberator bomber approached Del Monte No. 1 field, circled, then came in to land. The pilot produced a list of evacuees and gave it to Grover. The names were arranged according to seniority. With only one exception, Col. Carlos Romulo of MacArthur's staff, they were all aviators, not army brass. Evidently Brigadier General George had drawn up the list and had it approved by Lt. Gen. George H. Brett, the highest ranking air force officer in Australia, and MacArthur.

All the pursuit pilots of General George's old command were evidently on the list, as well as their current CO, Grover. However, five of the Bataan veterans were removed from the list to make place for more senior air force staff members. Charley Sneed's name was also removed at the request of General Sharp, who wanted his recently appointed air officer to remain with him to arrange for further aerial missions.[5] When he found that his name had been taken off the list, a dejected Randy Keator was obliged to go around through the assembled crowd and reclaim all the things he had given away minutes before.

Gus Williams was wondering if his name was going to be cut from the list too, but at 1:00 in the morning as the LB-30's engines started up, he was still on the list and began running to board. The last of the twenty-four finally designated evacuees to reach the bomber, Williams grabbed hold of the bomb racks and pulled himself up through the bomb bay just as its doors began closing. Minutes later, the LB-30 thundered down the runway and lifted off, then circled and headed south to freedom.

Back on the field, a crestfallen Bill Rowe now joined Randy Keator and Bill Coleman in collecting their belongings for the ride back to Maramag. They were afraid if they stuck around Del Monte headquarters, they would get "some lousy job." Also cut from the list, Wilson Glover and Shorty Crosland would be returning to the Maramag field, too.

5 April 24 was a lazy day for Rowe and the few other remaining pursuit pilots at Maramag. After a late breakfast, they dozed most of the day, sleepy from not having arrived back at Maramag until 4:30 that morning. During their waking hours, the main subject of conversation was the likelihood of their being evacuated before the Japanese invaded Mindanao, expected very soon. Rowe figured that an effort would be mounted to get Colonel Elsmore out, and in that case the pilots might be evacuated too, if they were high enough on the list.

The next day, an ordnance major picked up Rowe and Keator and drove them up to the Dalirig fighter strip, while Coleman and Cocanougher were taken there by Colonel Elsmore. They had been assigned to help fly the reconnaissance missions that had fallen exclusively to John Geer and former 19th Bomb Group pilot Marne Noelke following Brownewell's evacuation two days before.

On arrival, the four were driven over to Brownewell's old house near the strip, which they would be sharing with Geer and Noelke. They were given mattresses on the floor to sleep on and were informed that they were to use the shower and latrine located in the schoolyard near the barrio. Meals would be with the 701st Ordnance down the road. Rowe noted all the goats wandering around the house.

On April 26, after a shower and a shave, Rowe paid a visit on General Sharp's command post at Del Monte. He found that the headquarters of the commanding general of U.S. and Filipino forces in the Visayas and Mindanao was a large tunnel dug deep into the ground, with regular rooms occupied by the staff. Rowe spotted his old Bataan Field Flying Detach-

ment chief Charley Sneed there behind a desk and went over to discuss
the situation with him. Sneed mentioned to Rowe that he was serving
as Sharp's air officer; he was now the most senior pilot left on the island
after the April 23 evacuation. Sneed also told Rowe that he would try
to arrange for Rowe's promotion to first lieutenant and see that he got
on the next evacuation flight. At the moment, Sneed was making arrangements for Filipino pilots at Del Monte to check out in the remaining P-40s
and the P-35A so that the American pilots left behind so far could leave
for Australia if another plane did come in.

That afternoon, Randy Keator brought back distressing news from his
reconnaissance flight up north to southern Cebu and Bohol islands. He
had spotted six Japanese transports and two destroyers just leaving Cebu
and heading in a southeasterly direction. Thoughts of Japanese invasion
now filled the pilots' minds. Keator despaired of the possibilities of the
U.S. and Filipino force defending itself. He knew that it had no artillery,
just a few mortars, .30- and .50-caliber machine guns, and 1903 Springfield rifles. There were not enough rifles to go around, and they were short
of ammunition.

Geer figured the defensive strategy was to move south, into the mountains, since he noticed that most of the fuel, heavy equipment, and radio
equipment was being moved to the air bases at Valencia and Maramag.
He and the other pilots intended to make for Australia by boat if it ever
came to the worst. But early the next morning, on a reconnaissance flight
north ordered by Sneed, Bill Coleman did not see a trace of the Japanese
force sighted the day before. And Noelke, flying in a P-40 for the first time,
reported back after his afternoon reconnaissance flight that he had not
found anything either. Where *were* the Japanese?

On April 28, Capt. Ramon Zosa, a Philippine Army Air Corps pilot,
came down to Dalirig field for a checkout in the P-35A. Geer spent most
of the afternoon with him, instructing him on flying procedures, then
Zosa took the ship out on a reconnaissance in place of Rowe. He spotted
the transports of two days before at Zamboanga and then headed east
toward Davao. Then he flew the ship up to Valencia, where he was to
use it on recon to the south. That left only one P-40 at Dalirig and one
flyable one plus the inoperative P-40E minus its wing tip at Maramag.

The next morning the pilots got the inevitable news: the Japanese invasion force had landed at Cotabato and Parang on the west coast, only
ninety-five miles west of them. With the state of defenses on Mindanao,
Rowe and the others knew that "they could easily walk up here."

Then at noon, after lunch, Rowe took the P-40E on a recon to the north
over the Mindanao Sea to look for any other possible Japanese invasion
forces. North of Bohol, he spotted a large group of about 150 powered
bancas, dispersed around a large transport and heading south toward Min-

danao. As Rowe approached them, the native boats scattered and began to maneuver defensively. But Rowe did not attack them; his orders restricted him to reconnaissance only.

On the return trip to Dalirig, Rowe got lost and landed almost out of gas. He overshot the field, with no flaps, but did not damage the warbird. Rowe believed something was wrong with the plane. He had to hold the stick over to one side in order to adjust for a "heavy wing." He was later told he had a P-40E wing on one side and a P-40B wing on the other.

Just before dark, the pilots noticed the gas trucks heading for the Del Monte No. 1 field and realized something was up. At the time, they were discussing arrangements for flying a mission to Davao ordered by Sharp for the following morning at dawn to strafe Japanese troops there while American forces pushed the lines. Since it was up to the pilots themselves to decide who should fly the mission, they had decided to cut cards for it that evening. But now with the evidence that another evacuation plane was coming in, they decided to postpone the drawing and hang around to see what was happening.

About 8:30 P.M., the pilots at Dalirig got a call from Colonel Elsmore at the same time they heard an airplane coming in. They were told an LB-30 was landing and that they should report over to the number 1 field right away. Elsmore indicated he did not know who would be going out, but they had better be there in case their names were called. Unknown to the Dalirig pilots, he had also called down to the bases at Maramag and Valencia in the late afternoon to inform the officers there to get up to Del Monte as soon as possible too. Excitedly, the Dalirig pilots collected their meager possessions and headed over to the field. Practically everyone at the base was there, anxiously wondering if they were going to be flown out or not.

Colonel Elsmore opened the letter delivered him by the pilot, Capt. Alvin Mueller, and found that it was from Brig. Gen. Ralph Royce. Elsmore and three majors on his staff were ordered to return to Australia on the aircraft. Selection of the balance of the thirty evacuees was left to Elsmore's discretion by Royce.

Elsmore then produced the list he had prepared earlier that day following receipt of a radiogram from Australia announcing the arrival of the LB-30. He had listed the remaining air force officers by rank, then seniority within rank, and finally, alphabetically. Those whose dates of commission were unknown were lumped together at the end of the list for each rank.

Randy Keator was happy to find himself high up on the list of second lieutenants to be evacuated. But with a date of commission unknown to Elsmore and a family name at the low end of the alphabet, Rowe was angry at his position on the list: next to last. Here he was, a veteran pilot of the Bataan period, and pilots with no combat experience were placed ahead of him! What sort of a selection process was that?

In making up his list, Elsmore had included officers of his 5th Air Base Group staff not cited in Royce's letter plus all other air force flying and nonflying officers on Mindanao. But now below the rank of major he reduced his list to include only pilots. Elsmore still had more names on his list than remaining places available on the LB-30. Thirty-nine were 19th Bomb Group pilots alone.

But then the word was spread that General Sharp had asked to keep four of the pursuit pilots back to fly the Davao strafing mission the next morning and any other missions that might be required after the departure of the LB-30. The pursuit pilots knew that the candidates were Rowe, Coleman, Keator, Geer, Crosland, and Glover.

Elsmore had set a deadline of 11:30 P.M. for the LB-30 to take off in order that the bomber could reach Darwin, Australia, at dawn. Any later arrival in the morning would risk running into the usual Japanese early-morning attack. Anyone on Elsmore's list of the top thirty candidates who did not make it to the field by then would have his place taken by the next lower person on the list.

About 10:45 P.M. Elsmore's aide began calling names to board the aircraft. Some of Elsmore's staff were still not there, but their places were being held for them till the last minute, as well as the places for the other higher-rank officers listed among the top thirty. When Bill Coleman's name was called, he was called back, as were Geer and Keator. Along with Rowe, who was not listed among the top thirty, they would have to stay behind to fly the P-40 missions Sharp wanted.

It was now just before 11:30, and several of the thirty top-listed officers had still not shown up, including Maj. Wilfred Rotherham of Elsmore's staff down at Valencia and Capt. Charley Sneed, over at Lake Lanao on other duty. Nor had Wilson Glover at Valencia and Shorty Crosland at Maramag, the other candidates for the P-40 missions.

With several places left on the LB-30, Coleman, Geer, and Keator were called to board, in contravention of Sharp's order that they remain. Coleman climbed aboard, but when Geer approached, an aide to Sharp called him and told him he was needed for the recon in the morning. Colonel Elsmore then interceded, yelling, "Get aboard, Geer, there'll be no tomorrow!" Elsmore had apparently decided that low-listed Bill Rowe and the two nonshows, Glover and Crosland, would suffice for the reconnaissance missions Sharp wanted.

There was one last place remaining on the LB-30. Then Bill Rowe's name was called, and he replied "Here!" so loudly that everyone at the field could hear him. But as he ran out to the bomber, he was called back and asked by Colonel Elsmore if he was not scheduled to fly the Davao mission in the morning. Rowe acknowledged that he was and was told he would have to stay.

But then his old 17th Pursuit Squadron mate, 1st Lt. "Hi" Messmore, assigned since December 9, 1941, to the 19th Bomb Group and already selected as one of the thirty to go, did something against normal army protocol. He approached Colonel Elsmore and said, "Sir, there are two pursuit pilots who haven't shown up yet. Why don't you let Rowe go; they can fly that mission."

Reflecting a moment, Elsmore accepted the rationale of Messmore's argument. Two pilots should be sufficient to handle the reconnaissance missions Sharp wanted. Then he responded, "Rowe, if you can find a place on that airplane, you can go." Rowe ran over to join the other twenty-nine officers assembled near the bomber. Since the passengers were boarding in reverse order, he was the first into the aircraft and was assigned the nose, where he was immediately joined by two other evacuees, making for very cramped conditions.

At 11:30 P.M. sharp, the heavily loaded LB-30 roared down the runway for takeoff, then circled to head south. Unknown to all, it would prove to be the last plane to come in to Mindanao to evacuate the trapped remnants of the disastrous Philippine campaign.[6]

28. "THIS IS THE FIRST TIME P-40Es HAVE BEEN CAPTURED?"

1 Charley Sneed had missed his ride on the April 29 Del Monte evacuation plane because he was elsewhere, still occupied in carrying out an assignment given him by Colonel Elsmore days before. On April 25, Elsmore had told General Sharp that he was going over to the seaplane base at Lake Lanao to supervise personally the handling of the two PBY Catalinas expected in from Australia on an evacuation mission to Corregidor, but Sharp had told him to send someone else instead; he wanted Elsmore at Del Monte in case other land planes came in at Del Monte to evacuate personnel. Elsmore then got Sharp's permission to send Sharp's air officer, Sneed, to take charge of both the incoming and outgoing staging stops of the PBYs at the Mindanao lake, some forty miles southwest of Del Monte.

At about 5:45 in the morning of April 30, just at daylight, one of the flying boats circled Lake Lanao and came in for a landing on its return flight from Corregidor. About an hour later, the second PBY also now arrived; it had been delayed because of having to make an ocean landing earlier because of haze. The two Catalinas were guided by small boats to hiding places on the shore of the lake. After disembarking, the passengers were taken to a hotel at Dansalan, on the northeastern shore of Lake Lanao.

Waiting at the Dansalan Hotel to greet the new arrivals was Charley Sneed. He recognized several of the air officers. "Jitter Bill" Bradford and Capt. Tex Marble, his 20th Pursuit squadron mate during pre-Bataan days, were on one of the PBYs, and 2nd Lt. Ed Erickson of the 17th Pursuit was on the other. Bradford had been authorized by General Wainwright to go out on the PBY evacuation mission days after his crack-up in the Ballanca on Kindley Field. Both Marble and Erickson had gotten to Corregidor just before the fall of Bataan and were also assigned seats on the Catalinas, the last pursuit pilots left on Corregidor to escape.[1]

About 6:00 P.M. the passengers all reboarded the two flying boats for the final leg of the evacuation trip to Australia. The PBYs had been provided good hideaways on the lake during the day; it was considered too risky to fly the slow navy flying boats during daylight hours, since the skies over the Philippines were controlled by the Japanese.

The lead PBY was being towed tail first toward its takeoff position on the lake when it hit submerged rocks and began taking on water. Aborting the takeoff, the pilot headed the damaged flying boat back to shore. Overhead, the second PBY was circling, waiting for its sister ship to join up. But after darkness began to descend, it headed south alone.

Dejected, Ed Erickson and the other passengers on the damaged PBY were taken back to the hotel in Dansalan by Charley Sneed. They would spend the evening there while the PBY crew worked feverishly to try to repair the flying boat. But after several hours, the situation looked hopeless. The PBY captain early the next day radioed Australia to send a four-engine bomber to Del Monte to evacuate his stranded passengers.

Late the next afternoon the Corregidor evacuees returned to the site of the PBY on the lake to check out the situation and see if there was any slight chance the flying boat would be able to leave that evening. To their amazement, they found that it had left just before their arrival! Someone told them that the crew had evidently made repairs adequate for the PBY to take off, and it had left about 5:00 P.M. Ten other passengers had been taken aboard—the pilot had reasoned that there would not have been time to locate and assemble the original passengers for the hurried takeoff, and they would be picked up by the alternative rescue plane from Australia. But he had not informed them of his request for another aircraft to evacuate them.

2 Just after daybreak on Thursday, April 30, a P-40 approached the Del Monte No. 1 field and landed. The pilot was Shorty Crosland, reporting in to General Sharp from Maramag Field. Crosland had been expected to join the other candidates for the LB-30 evacuation flight the evening before but had been ordered by Sharp to come in with the P-40 at Maramag. Since unknown to Sharp the Maramag field had no lighting, Crosland had to wait until it was light enough to see the runway and thus arrived hours after the LB-30 had departed.

Later in the morning, Wilson Glover arrived at Del Monte from Valencia Field by ground transportation. He also had missed the evacuation call. Glover had been very busy at Valencia (as had Geer two days earlier at Dalirig) familiarizing Philippine Army Air Corps Capt. Ramon Zosa with the characteristics of the P-35A. The evening before, Zosa had taken the veteran warbird, loaded with two 100-pound bombs, and flown west to Parang, where he bombed Japanese invasion ships in the harbor, but with unobserved results.

When Crosland and Glover met with General Sharp and his air offi-

cer, Charley Sneed, they were informed that they should take the two
P-40s on a recon/combat mission the next morning.[2] They were to support an attack by the 81st Infantry on the Moncayo Front, in the hopes
of putting pressure on the Japanese to shift troops from the Digos Front
to the south. But when Crosland and Glover reported back the next day
after flying the mission, they told Sneed and Sharp that it was a failure.
They could not find any Japanese on the road in the area.

On the following evening, General Sharp called Crosland, Glover, and
Zosa into his command post at Del Monte for new orders. A Japanese
invasion force of four transports and two destroyers was heading into Macajalar Bay, just fifteen miles from the Del Monte base. Sharp wanted the
pilots to take the remaining operational aircraft of his command, the P-35A
and two P-40Es, and dive-bomb the ships that night.

"Well, this is it!" the last veterans of the Far East Air Force thought
as they headed over to the Del Monte No. 2 strip, a short emergency runway parallel to Del Monte No. 1. There the aircraft were loaded with bombs
for the mission. Zosa's P-35A would carry two 100-pound bombs, while
the shop-built racks of Crosland's and Glover's P-40Es had been fitted to
carry a 500-pound egg each.

The ground crew had strung lights down the 3,300-foot length of the
strip. Since the runway was too short to allow landings, it would be used
only for the takeoff; they would land on Del Monte No. 1 and taxi back
to No. 2 strip after the mission. Del Monte No. 1 was too exposed to keep
aircraft there during the day.

Scheduled to lead off, Glover raced his heavily loaded P-40 down the
rough, unfamiliar strip. But his ship was not getting up sufficient speed
and veered to the left and crashed off the runway. Glover was not seriously injured—just a broken collarbone. Fortunately the 500-pound bomb
had not detonated. Shaken by the accident, Crosland nevertheless kept
his composure and applied full takeoff power. Seconds later he cleared
the strip and headed for his destination, Zosa following behind.

About midnight, Crosland arrived over the invasion force as it was
entering Macajalar Bay. The veteran 34th Pursuiter could make out a large
transport in the middle of the bay and selected it as his target. Diving
down, he released his heavy bomb but saw that he had missed the transport. Undaunted, Crosland gave the transport several bursts from his six
fifties in a strafing pass and noted that it had caught fire. Zosa had been
unsuccessful in his bombing attack too. It was clear to both pilots that
bombing attempts at night were useless. The targets could not been seen
adequately for an effective attack.

After landing on Del Monte No. 1 and reporting in to General Sharp,
the pilots were ordered on another mission against the Japanese force,

to be flown at daybreak. Because of the heavy overcast impeding bombing possibilities, it would be a strafing attack.

At dawn on the morning of May 3, Crosland and Zosa were off again with only a few hours' sleep. They hit the Japanese transports as they were beginning to disembark the invasion troops but were unable to disrupt the landings. As they broke off their strafing attack, three "Nate" fighters arrived over the force on a patrol mission, but neither side noticed the other.[3]

Sharp then ordered Crosland to fly the P-40E down to Maramag. It was overdue for an engine overhaul. At the hidden jungle base, ground crews had earlier repaired the other P-40E that had been out of commission since Posten clipped off part of its right wing on the April 12 strafing mission to Davao. The LB-30 that flew in on the evening of April 29th had brought with it a right wing tip and aileron required to get the P-40E into flying condition again, though its Allison engine was not in good order. The maintenance men also had painted a shark's head on the engine area of each of the two P-40s, perhaps inspired by photos they may have seen of the "Flying Tigers."

With the Japanese troops advancing steadily from the Cagayan area during the next days, forcing the U.S. and Filipino forces south toward Malaybalay, it was clear that it was only a matter of time before Mindanao would fall. Sharp ordered no more missions for the two P-40s and the P-35A after the Cagayan strafing attack. Captain Zosa flew his P-35A to a small airstrip near the northern tip of Mindanao and hid it on a nearby plantation.

At Maramag, Crosland and Glover were making plans to escape. They had 100-gallon belly tanks that had been brought in by the LB-30 installed on the two Warhawks and stripped them down to mimimize weight, to gain the maximum possible range for the aircraft. But then word was received that Sharp had surrendered and that the two pilots were not to try to escape—it would only make it harder on the others who had surrendered. A quartermaster major ordered a maintenance sergeant to take the distributor caps off the two P-40s and throw them in a toilet.

On May 10, Crosland, Glover, and other personnel at the Maramag base loaded cots, bedding, and food on vehicles at the base and started driving north toward Del Monte. Then, along the way, horse-mounted Japanese troops intercepted them and took them prisoner. After being searched, the Maramag group moved on under escort to the main camp at Malaybalay, where the rest of the U.S. and Filipino prisoners had been assembled.

In the Malaybalay camp, the Maramag garrison was reunited with the rest of Sharp's forces. The deserted passengers of the second PBY were also there, including Ed Erickson and the nurses. With them was Charley Sneed, who had left Sharp's post following the cessation of aerial missions and stayed with the PBY group until their capture.

So close to having escaped from the Philippines, the PBY passengers had been consumed with impractical schemes to get down to Australia. Then, late one night, they had heard the motors of a plane droning far above them, the aircraft flying around and around, as if searching for a landing. Had a plane come for them? But after a few minutes the sound became weaker and weaker as the plane moved away from the area.[4]

3 On the morning of Tuesday, May 19, after over a week in the POW compound, Charley Sneed had visitors. Lt. Yasushi Ushijima, a pilot of the 84th *dokoritsu chutai* of "Nate" fighters assigned to support the final phase of the southern Philippines campaign, accompanied by a Japanese officer serving as an interpreter-guide, had come to meet the commander of the remnant American air force.

The day before, Ushijima had been taken by an officer of the Japanese ground forces at Malaybalay to Maramag to inspect two P-40s discovered by the Japanese in hiding places. After a half hour's drive, they had entered a forest packed with gasoline drums. Returning to the main road, they drove on a little while until they reached another forest on top of a small hill. The guide continued through an opening about forty-five feet wide between the trees. Continuing along the path, tire marks evident on the ground, the Japanese drove up to a nipa hut holding spare aircraft parts, then on to a building made of rough wood, with a floor raised high off the ground. Climbing up the ladder, they reached a porch with a railing all around. The building was divided into small rooms. They opened the door of one of them and went inside, where they found some pinup photos on the wall and an open trunk on the floor, with some uniforms and other clothes spilling out. The room appeared to the Japanese to be a pilots' or officers' quarters.[5]

Returning to the car, the Japanese officers drove deeper into the forest, turned right, then left, and suddenly found themselves face-to-face with a strange-looking aircraft with a sharklike design painted on the engine area. Ushijima realized that this must be one of the P-40s. A rudimentary inspection suggested the old warbird must be in flying condition. Nearby, they located the other P-40, also wedged into the woods and sporting a shark mouth too. To Ushijima, it seemed rather worn, but flyable nevertheless. The guide then led Ushijima to a biplane, which struck him as quite old but probably in flying condition too.

That evening Ushijima dined with the battalion commander of the Japanese forces at Malaybalay. Ushijima described his visit and indicated that all three aircraft looked flyable, if their engines were in good shape. "This is the first time P-40Es have been captured, is it?" Ushijima's host asked. Ushijima replied in the affirmative and urged that they be sent to Japan to obtain firsthand knowledge of the aircraft's relative performance. It was agreed that Ushijima should visit the POW compound the next morning to solicit the help of any pursuit pilots in custody in having the aircraft transferred to the Malaybalay field.

Now, at the invitation of his Japanese visitors, Charley Sneed climbed into their car, while two other American pilots and maintenance men followed behind in their own truck. Through the guide, Ushijima asked Sneed a number of questions about the performance and handling of the P-40 as they proceeded to the Maramag base. But the guide's vocabulary proved too limited, so Ushijima began conversing directly in his faltering English, being more familiar with aircraft terminology even in English than the guide.

When they reached the site of the first P-40 Ushijima had seen the day before, the maintenance men jumped out of their truck and began checking out the old warbird. It was indeed in good condition. But the engine of the second, older, P-40E was not in the best of condition, they found.[6] It was the P-40E whose right wing tip and aileron had been repaired before the surrender. Sneed mentioned to the Japanese that he and another pilot had planned to fly out of Mindanao in the two P-40s but that the other pilot's aircraft had developed trouble, so Sneed had decided to stay behind too.

The old Stearman 76D3 was flyable. The Americans recognized the Philippine Army Air Corps biplane as the one that Jack Randolph had brought down from Corregidor on the evening of April 10.

Ushijima now spoke to Sneed about transferring the three aircraft to Malaybalay Field. It was agreed that Sneed would fly the newer P-40, while the two pilots with him would fly the Stearman and the older P-40.[7] Led by the pilot of the Stearman, Sneed and then the pilot of the other P-40 (Wilson Glover?) taxied their way along the forest road, just wide enough for the P-40's wing tips to clear the bordering trees. Following the hand directions of the maintenance men, they threaded their way out to the entrance to the forest, then down the grass flying field to the edge of the road, which they would use for the takeoff.

The Stearman rolled down the road and lifted off, floating up to about 600 feet, passing low over the heads of the Japanese, then heading for Malaybalay. After a long ground run on the narrow road, his Allison engine roaring, Sneed took off. After climbing to a high altitude, he decided to perform some aerial maneuvers before proceeding in the direction of Malaybalay. Finally, the other pilot headed off in the old P-40, giving out noticeably less power than Sneed's Warhawk, and linked up with the Stearman for the flight to Malaybalay.

Shortly after landing at Malaybalay Field minutes later, Sneed and the other two pilots waited to rejoin their Japanese "colleagues," who were driving over in their car. In preparation for flying in the P-40, Ushijima asked Sneed to go up with him in the Stearman so that he could familiarize the Japanese with the instruments and characteristics of an American aircraft. Airborne, with Ushijima in the front seat as the trainee, Sneed frequently took hold of the controls to correct the mistakes of the Japanese as they practiced takeoffs and landings.

Back on the ground, his orientation in the 76D3 biplane completed, Ushijima wanted to fly the P-40. Sneed advised against it, because Malaybalay Field was short, only 2,800 feet long, and would give him trouble. He told Ushijima it would be better to wait until he could fly from a larger field.

Arrangements were now made for Sneed and the other P-40 pilot to fly their aircraft to Davao, while Ushijima would take the Stearman. The Japanese carefully briefed the two Americans on the layout of Davao Field and the correct flight patterns to be followed to avoid their being shot at by base personnel. Then with a P-40 mechanic in the front seat, Ushijima took off in the old biplane ahead of the others.

After landing at Davao, Ushijima waited for the two P-40s. The eyes of all the Japanese personnel at the base were on the two American fighters as they followed the correct approach pattern, skimmed just over the palm tree grove at the edge of the field, and came down for a perfect landing.

On the field, the two Americans were offered cool drinks by the commanding officer of the Japanese air unit, Colonel Hoshi. But the Japanese had a request to make. Could Sneed put on a demonstration for them of mock combat maneuvers with some of the aircraft of the Davao base? Responding in the affirmative, Sneed now took the P-40E up to a high altitude and proceeded to put on an impressive show, diving, turning, and "really wringing the aircraft out," in the estimation of Ushijima.

4   Among the spectators on the ground watching Sneed's performance were Shorty Crosland, Ed Erickson, John Valkenaar, and two air force sergeant mechanics, all of whom had been trucked down to Davao that day from the POW compound. The three pilots had been selected to fly the two P-40s and the 76D3 to Nichols Field that day, taking along one of the mechanics in the Stearman. Sneed and a few other officers of Sharp's staff had told them at the camp that Sharp wanted them to carry out this request of the Japanese, but they were not informed of the circumstances under which Sharp had acquiesced.[8]

That afternoon, Crosland and Erickson climbed into the P-40s and Valkenaar and one of the mechanics into the biplane.[9] They were not allowed to take parachutes with them. For Crosland this was a real prob-

One of the two captured P-40Es flown by either Sneed or another pilot from Malaybalay to Davao, May 10, 1942. *Courtesy Hal Hitchcock*

lem, as suggested by his nickname; without the usual parachute pack on the seat, he could not see out of the windshield. A substitute pad was given him to overcome his problem.

If the American POW pilots harbored any thoughts of escape, they were quashed with the news that three twin-engine Mitsubishi Ki-46 "Dinahs," sleek, modern army command reconnaissance planes capable of speeds up to 360 MPH and armed with a 7.7-mm machine gun in the rear seat, would be escorting them to Nichols.[10]

The two P-40s and the Stearman now headed north at about 120 MPH, all three under the watchful eye of their escort. Erickson and Crosland had the Allison engines leaned out to the maximum, their ships, stripped of their guns, radios, and other heavy and unnecessary equipment, held down to 1,500 to 2,000 feet, to be able to cover the 630 miles to Nichols nonstop. Flying under such conditions was very hard on the old engines.

About fifty miles out of Nichols, Crosland's plane (evidently the older P-40, with engine trouble) began to cut out on him. Low on gas, Crosland then ran into a rainstorm. Descending below the black clouds, he spotted a small strip and decided to come in and land. He had lost his escort.

On the field, Crosland could make out a barracks, but that was all; there were no people and no gas. His fuel gauge read empty. For a moment, he thought of taking off into the bush but then realized that he had nothing with which to survive. Climbing back into the P-40 after the weather had improved, Crosland flew on to Nichols Field, hoping there was still enough fuel in the tanks to cover the short hop.

On his arrival at Nichols, Crosland was met by Valkenaar and Erickson and the sergeant mechanic. They had been getting anxious with the no-show of Crosland. They had been told before takeoff from Davao that if any of the three pilots tried to escape, the others would be shot. Crosland, Erickson, and Valkenaar had flown the last mission of the Far East Air Force in the Philippines campaign.[11]

Epilogue

The fall of the Philippines to Japan in April–May, 1942, was the most humiliating military defeat the United States had ever suffered in its history. The failure of the Far East Air Force to live up to the high expectations for it was one of the major factors in that defeat. In particular, its 5th Interceptor Command had not succeeded in carrying out its critical mission: meeting and destroying enemy aircraft violating Philippine airspace. Indeed, not a single successful interception of Japanese bombers or fighters was ever mounted by the command during the five-month campaign.

It took the Japanese only three days to wipe out two-thirds of the pursuit force of the command. By the afternoon of December 10, 1941, sixty-four of its ninety-two P-40s, the only aircraft capable of stopping the enemy's air thrust, lay in wreckage all over Luzon. The Japanese had succeeded only too well in meeting their initial objective in the Philippines campaign: destroying MacArthur's air capability.

With the parallel destruction of his observation squadron, MacArthur turned to the remnants of his interceptor force to provide him the reconnaissance capacity he desperately needed to monitor the movements of the Japanese invasion forces on Luzon. In the ensuing months, the pursuit pilots proved effective in this unwanted role, but their P-40s dwindled day by day as they also took on other assignments of a combat nature, most of which were unsanctioned by MacArthur: strafing and bombing Japanese landing forces, airdromes, shipping, and truck convoys, and taking out Japanese light bombers and observation ships over the front lines of Bataan. Many instant heroes were created in often spectacular attacks, but such heroics had little bearing on the course of the campaign. By March 3, 1942, MacArthur's mini air force was down to a single operational P-40.

In his attempts to color his losing effort with the glory that his ego required, MacArthur grossly exaggerated the modest accomplishments of his pilots in the frequent, grandiose communiqués he issued from his Corregidor headquarters. Months after the end of the campaign, his pursuit commander credited 103 aerial victories to his pilots, but in actuality it would appear, based on my own analysis of each engagement, that they had destroyed no more than 30 Japanese aircraft in the air. Although this number of victories was gained at a price of only 25 P-40s and P-35s shot down in aerial combat, losses of aircraft caught on the ground, damaged beyond repair in air action, or through accidents and antiaircraft fire of U.S. and Filipino forces accounted for the rest of the strength of 114 operational P-40s and P-35s of the 24th Pursuit Group at the outset of the campaign.

The human loss was even more depressing. Following the fall of the Philippines in April–May, 1942, half of the 165 pilots of the group entered Japanese POW camps in the Philippines. Another fifth (33) had been killed earlier in the campaign, either in combat or in accidents. The balance, a fortunate 30 percent (49), had been evacuated to Australia before the defeat.

For the 27 non flying officers and the 1,144 enlisted men of the group, the outcome of the campaign was dismal. Only one of the officers had been evacuated, and one was killed in action, with the remaining 93 percent going into POW camp. Of the enlisted men, only 1.4 percent had been evacuated (all wounded men going out on the hospital ship *Mactan*), 3.3 percent were killed in action, and the balance of 95.3 percent ended up as prisoners of war.

How can we explain the disastrous outcome for the 24th Pursuit Group, to the extent it was not a result of factors affecting the USAFFE as a whole? Were the pilots grossly outnumbered as Colonel George so dramatically had informed them two days before the Japanese onslaught? An analysis of Japanese wartime records covering the campaign indicates that the Japanese Naval Air Force had committed 117 twin-engine "Betty" and "Nell" bombers from three *kokutai* to the initial attacks, while the Japanese Army Air Force had 54 medium and heavy bombers, for a total bombing force of 171 aircraft. To escort the navy bombers and to engage in strafing attacks on the American airfields, two *kokutai* of 89 Zeros were utilized. (The IJAAF had also provided 36 pursuit from one *sentai*, but these could be put into play only after December 10, when Philippine bases had been secured, as they were too short-ranged to attack from Formosa.) Against this force of 260 aircraft, Colonel George controlled 114 interceptors.[1] Outnumbered? Yes, but not as heavily as Colonel George had expected. Certainly the Japanese *fighter* force was not greater than that of Colonel George.

For Max Louk and many of the other pursuit pilots, the anxiety of engaging the Japanese was based more on apprehensions about the *quality* of the equipment the Americans would be using. Louk was correct in his lament that the best pursuit they had to operate, the P-40, was not adequate to do the job in the event of a Japanese aerial attack. As an interceptor, it could not perform adequately at the altitude the Japanese would choose in their bombardment of Luzon's airfields, above 18,000 feet; in any case, its rate of climb was too slow to reach that altitude in time to be able to intercept. In combat with the Zero, its principal nemesis, the P-40 had no chance if the pilot should try to dogfight. It simply could not maneuver with the Japanese.[2]

Yet in trying to account for the reasons why the Philippines pilots fared so badly against the Japanese, one inevitably brings into comparison the performance of another group of American pilots flying the same machine in the same time period against similarly greater numbers of the same types of aircraft of the same enemy, and also in a losing campaign: the American Volunteer Group in China. Why was the AVG able to chalk up such a remarkable record against the Japanese in the face of similar odds? Was the 24th Pursuit Group "doomed at the start" because of factors other than aircraft quantity and quality considerations that the AVG did not face?

To intercept successfully a high-flying Japanese force in P-40s, as shown by the outstanding successes of the AVG, the pilots needed adequate warning time to pull their slow-climbing ships up to altitude, accurate information on the location and altitude of the force, and a machine that could deliver the necessary firepower to down the intruders. In China, Chennault, based on his preoccupation with the question and his long experience in the Army Air Corps, had given high priority to development of an air warning system. Although it was relatively primitive, it proved effective in giving his pilots the time needed to get airborne and in position to attack high-flying Japanese bombers. In contrast, the 24th Pursuit Group was invariably caught on the ground with only minutes' notice of an approaching Japanese force, at least in the early disastrous days of the campaign, because of lack of air warning relayed by the FEAF's air warning system. The exception was the first day, when Iba radar had provided warning to Iba and Clark fields way in advance, but in a confused situation of conflicting reports coming from other sources in the Philippines net, the 24th Group's commander made erroneous judgments that would cost the destruction of virtually a whole squadron of pursuit and most of the B-17s at Clark. And the invaluable Iba radar station was knocked out on the first day, leaving warning to the local Filipino watchers, a system that proved ineffective.

But even if the pilots of the 24th Group had received advance warning adequate to allow them to climb to altitude and locate the enemy force, their lack of practice in bomber interception before the outbreak of war would have handicapped them against the Japanese.[3] Colonel George had been preoccupied with logistics and supply problems at a time of rapid expansion of his command, while the 24th Group Commander, Major Grover, had not given the development of suitable combat tactics the attention it required, a result in part of reasons beyond his control. The major factor here was that the P-40Es earmarked to two of his squadrons were not turned over until just six weeks before the outbreak of war.[4] The pilots were preoccupied in trying to learn how to handle the new pursuit, whereas the AVG had months to familiarize themselves with their ships.

The long period the AVG pilots had to learn how to handle their P-40Bs also provided the time necessary to work the bugs out of the gunnery operations of their ships. As was the case in the 24th Group, jamming of the guns of the AVG's P-40s was a common problem in the early period, but by the time war broke out, they invariably operated well, thanks to the efforts of the AVG armorers to overcome reasons for gun stoppages. For two squadrons of the 24th Group (the 3rd and 17th), the guns in the P-40Es were installed just weeks before December 8 and were never test-fired to determine whether they would even work. Similarly, the 21st Pursuit had received its P-40s and had guns installed just days before December 8 and had never test-fired them. Although the 20th Pursuit with its P-40Bs had .30- and .50-caliber machine guns mounted considerably earlier, a shortage of belted ammunition prevented it from ever test-firing its guns too.

As a result of inadequate time or ammunition for test-firing, the 24th Group entered combat with guns that invariably did not work, unlike the case of the AVG. It was a miracle that more 24th Group pilots were not killed in combat with Zeros in those initial days of the campaign.

Chennault had drilled into his pilots never to dogfight with a Zero and had developed tactics of hit-and-run instead, which was the key for the AVG's success against Zeros and the equally maneuverable army "Nate" fighters. While the 24th Group had some limited information on the Zero, it was never translated into effective use by the pilots. Only through sheer trial and error did individual pilots during the first three days of combat learn on their own to use the tactics practiced by the AVG in order to stay alive.

Another final factor should be introduced here: *luck*. The devastating success of the Japanese on the first day of hostilities was largely a result of the IJNAF's arrival over Clark and Iba much later than it had planned. An unseasonal fog had kept its aircraft on the ground at Formosan bases until late morning, when it finally lifted. The arrival of the Japanese bombers and fighters over Clark Field followed by less than two hours the

The emotional reunion of John Brownewell with other pilots of his 17th Pursuit Squadron shortly after their release from POW camp in September, 1945. *Left to right:* Steve Crosby, George Armstrong, James Ross, Brownewell, La Mar Gillett, and Willis Culp. *Courtesy John L. Brownewell, Lt. Col. USAF (Ret.)*

end of the 24th Group's patrol to the north of Clark, which the Japanese would have met had they taken off earlier that morning as scheduled.

The AVG pilots were better trained in the realities of combat than were those of the 24th Pursuit Group, thanks to the superb leadership of Chennault (a quality of leadership that was lacking in the Philippines). In addition, the AVG pilots had flying experience in the United States, whereas most of the 24th Group was sent to the Philippine Islands fresh from flying school. However, there was no intrinsic superiority of the AVG pilots over those of the 24th Group. The unimpressive results of the Philippines aerial campaign were not the fault of the individual pilots. They did the best they could with what they had and under the conditions extant. Carefree and fun-loving youth in the months prior to December 8, they quickly shaped up once the curtain rose.

For the POWs of the 24th Pursuit Group, it would prove to be a long incarceration—for those who survived their experience. Of the 83 POW pilots, only 34 made it back home. Seventeen died in POW camps in the Philippines and Japan, and 32 perished on the infamous "hell ships" trans-

porting prisoners to Japan in 1944–45 and attacked by American sub-
marines and aircraft. Of the 25 nonflying officer POWs, 15 died in camp
or on hell ships.

The death rate for the 1,090 imprisoned enlisted men of the group was
similarly high. As compared with the rate of mortality of 59 percent for
the pilots and 60 percent for the nonflying officers, 61 percent of the enlisted men POWs perished. Nine of ten died in POW camps; relatively
few had been put on hell ships in 1944–45 for transfer to Japan.

The war was not over for the 49 pilots who had been evacuated to
Australia before the fall of the Philippines. Eleven were killed later in
wartime combat or accidents. One of the former POW pilots was also
killed in a wartime mishap: Ed Dyess, who with Sam Grashio and other
officers had escaped as a POW and returned to the United States, lost his
life there in a P-38 accident on December 22, 1943.

Following the end of the war, 71 of the 165 pilots were alive and well
in the States again, comprising 38 evacuees and 33 former POWs. Postwar aircraft accidents claimed the lives of 8 of them, and by natural causes
a further 18 passed from the scene by mid-1991, including in the past few
years Dave Obert, Frank Neri, Andy Krieger, Fred Roberts, Randy Keator,
and Ed Gilmore, whose experiences are prominently featured in this history. Of the 45 survivors in mid-1991, all are retired, men now in their
seventies, almost all of whom shared their experiences with me to make
this story possible.

Appendix A

AIRCRAFT ASSIGNED: PURSUIT SQUADRONS OF THE 4th COMPOSITE GROUP AND (from September, 1941) 24th PURSUIT GROUP

Type	No. received[a]	Date received	Serial nos.
Boeing P-26A	34	Mar., 1937– Nov., 1940	33-31 33-36 33-38 33-40 33-47 33-50 33-54 33-58 33-59 33-61 33-62 33-67 33-73 33-81 33-83 33-90 33-96 33-99 33-102 to 33-106 33-108 33-109 33-111 33-114 33-116 to 33-118 33-120 33-121 33-131 33-138
Seversky P-35A	57	Dec., 1940– Mar., 1941	41-17434 to 41-17473 41-17477 to 41-17493
Curtiss P-40B	31	May 17, 1941	41-5258 to 41-5282 41-5284 41-5285 41-5287 to 41-5290
Curtiss P-40E	50	Sept. 29, 1941	40-462 to 40-483 40-488 to 40-491 40-496 40-503 to 40-509 40-514 to 40-517 40-522 to 40-524 40-529 to 40-531 40-536 to 40-538 40-543 to 40-545
Curtiss P-40E	24	Nov. 25, 1941	40-615 to 40-626 40-634 40-635 40-638 40-639 40-642 40-643 40-646 40-647 40-650 or 40-651 40-654 40-655 40-659
Curtiss P-40E	3[b]	Mar. 9, 1942	[serial nos. unidentified]
North American A-27	10[c]	Mar. 8, 1941	41-18890 to 41-18899

[a]Except as indicated in note b, all aircraft were received at the Philippine Air Deport, Nichols Field, Manila.

[b]These aircraft were part of a shipment of 111 that arrived in Australia on Feb. 4, 1942. On Feb. 22, the 3 were transshipped to the Philippines on the SS *Anhui* and ultimately were received at Bohol.

[c]Five of these ten aircraft were assigned to pursuit squadrons of the 4th Composite Group.

Appendix B

ROSTER OF FLYING OFFICERS OF THE 24th PURSUIT GROUP

(as of December 8, 1941)

HEADQUARTERS AND HEADQUARTERS SQUADRON

Rank	Flying school class	Service no.	Hometown	Date of Death
Maj. Orrin L. Grover	[unk.]	0-16831	New York, N.Y.	Jan. 13, 1969
1st Lt. W. Ben Putnam	38-B	0-22508	Oklahoma City, Okla.	—
1st Lt. William Cummings	38-B	0-369651	Lawrence, Kans.	—
2nd Lt. William A. Parsons	40-H	0-401039	Wichita, Kans.	July 29, 1946
2nd Lt. John G. Griffith	40-H	0-401221	Cincinnati, Ohio	MIA Jan. 9, 1945
2nd Lt. Forrest S. O'Brien	41-B	0-406580	San Jose, Calif.	KIA Apr. 16, 1942
2nd Lt. Joe DeGraftenreid	41-C	0-411945	Sacramento, Calif.	July 12, 1942

THIRD PURSUIT SQUADRON

Rank	Flying school class	Service no.	Hometown	Date of Death
1st Lt. Henry G. Thorne	37-A	0-21527	Fort McPherson, Ga.	—
1st Lt. Edward R. Woolery	39-C	0-24120	Dayton, Ohio	KIA Jan. 30, 1942
1st Lt. Herbert S. Ellis	39-C	0-383712	Elizabeth, N.J.	—
1st Lt. Gerald M. Keenan	40-A	0-388608	Chicago, Ill.	KIA Feb. 27, 1942
1st Lt. Raymond M. Gehrig	40-A	0-388660	Cohocton, N.Y.	—
1st Lt. Robert T. Hanson	40-A	0-388665	Oakland, Calif.	KIA Dec. 13, 1941
1st Lt. Fred D. Roberts, Jr.	40-D	0-396314	[unknown]	Apr. 9, 1980

Name	Serial	Class	Home	Date
1st Lt. James D. Donegan, Jr.	0-396396	40-D	Paterson, N.J.	Jan. 13, 1980
1st Lt. Frank V. Neri	0-396658	40-D	Rochester, N.Y.	Apr. 17, 1988
2nd Lt. George O. Ellstrom	0-401152	40-H	Sellersville, Pa.	KIA Dec. 8, 1941
2nd Lt. Andrew E. Krieger	0-401182	40-H	Salamanca, N.Y.	Oct. 29, 1988
2nd Lt. Donald D. Steele	0-401256	40-H	Akron, Ohio	—
2nd Lt. Howard Hardegree	0-406541	41-B	Ben Wheeler, Tex.	MIA Jan. 9, 1945
2nd Lt. Robert W. Newman	0-406579	41-B	Santa Barbara, Calif.	Aug. 13, 1942
2nd Lt. Vernon R. Ireland	0-406684	41-B	Long Beach, Calif.	KIA Dec. 8, 1941
2nd Lt. Gordon S. Benson	0-406706	41-B	Klamath Falls, Oreg.	MIA Jan. 7, 1945
2nd Lt. James R. Field	0-406728	41-B	Palo Alto, Calif.	Nov. 11, 1942
2nd Lt. Dana H. Allen	0-407049	41-B	[unknown]	July 31, 1942
2nd Lt. William H. Powell	0-407091	41-B	Weston, Oreg.	—
2nd Lt. Richard L. Root	0-407094	41-B	Buena Vista, Colo.	KIA Dec. 8, 1941
2nd Lt. William L. Longmire	0-392548	41-C	Palo Alto, Calif.	Feb. 13, 1943
2nd Lt. Edgar B. Smith, Jr.	0-408862	41-C	Mayfield, Ky.	MIA Jan. 8, 1945
2nd Lt. Andrew F. Webb	0-408872	41-C	Forest, Miss.	KIA Dec. 8, 1941
2nd Lt. Joseph L. Burke	0-411686	41-C	Troy, N.Y.	MIA Jan. 9, 1945
2nd Lt. John T. Hylton, Jr.	0-411702	41-C	Danville, Va.	—
2nd Lt. John F. O'Connell, Jr.	0-411725	41-C	Chicago, Ill.	KIA Dec. 8, 1941
2nd Lt. Burton R. Richard	0-411733	41-C	Hagerstown, Md.	Jan. 25, 1945
2nd Lt. Cleitus R. Garrett	0-411825	41-C	Chestnut, La.	MIA Oct. 24, 1944
2nd Lt. James E. Boone	0-411923	41-C	Delta, Colo.	—
2nd Lt. Glenn E. Cave	0-411937	41-C	Santa Ana, Calif.	—
2nd Lt. John Ship Daniel	0-411939	41-C	Mullins, S.C.	Oct. 27, 1942
2nd Lt. Harold E. Finley	0-411951	41-C	Iola, Kans.	—
2nd Lt. James H. Pate	0-412149	41-C	Tyler, Tex.	Aug. 2, 1942
2nd Lt. Bart A. Passanante	0-412318	41-C	Philadelphia, Pa.	—
2nd Lt. C. Philip Christie	0-412681	41-C	Williamstown, Mass.	Aug. 19, 1973

Rank	Flying school class	Service no.	Hometown	Date of Death
2nd Lt. Lycurgus W. Johnson	41-C	0-412691	Denver, Colo.	Aug. 1991
2nd Lt. Donald H. Miller	41-C	0-413476	South Gate, Calif.	Oct. 1947
2nd Lt. James E. Mackey	41-C	0-413532	Portland, Oreg.	MIA Sept. 7, 1944
2nd Lt. James E. Alsobrook	41-D	0-417922	Magnolia, Ark.	Apr. 9, 1949
2nd Lt. Charles A. Sheeley	41-D	0-418177	Pueblo, Calif.	—
2nd Lt. Paul O. Mock	41-D	0-418433	Goose Creek, Tex.	Aug. 18, 1942
2nd Lt. William H. Brewster	41-G	0-426551	Spokane, Wash.	KIA Dec. 15, 1944
2nd Lt. Robert James Hinson	41-G	0-426565	Lufkin, Tex.	—
2nd Lt. Paul Racicot	41-G	0-426576	Mare Island, Calif.	MIA Oct. 24, 1944

SEVENTEENTH PURSUIT SQUADRON

Rank	Flying school class	Service no.	Hometown	Date of Death
1st Lt. Boyd D. Wagner	38-B	0-21623	Johnstown, Pa.	Nov. 30, 1942
1st Lt. William D. Feallock	38-A	0-23358	Cleveland, Ohio	—
1st Lt. John L. Brownewell	39-A	0-373805	Columbus, Ohio	—
1st Lt. George H. Armstrong	39-A	0-373852	Billings, Mont.	—
1st Lt. William A. Sheppard	40-A	0-364059	Pittsburgh, Pa.	—
1st Lt. Russel M. Church	40-A	0-374264	Dumont, N.J.	KIA Dec. 16, 1941
1st Lt. Raymond A. Sloan	40-A	0-377421	Marion, S.C.	KIA Feb. 11, 1942
1st Lt. Walter L. Coss	40-A	0-388651	Brighton, Pa.	—
1st Lt. Allison W. Strauss	40-A	0-388826	Wadesville, Ind.	KIA Apr. 27, 1942
2nd Lt. Jack D. Dale	40-H	0-401140	Willoughby, Ohio	Dec. 10, 1990
2nd Lt. George E. Kiser	40-H	0-401180	Somerset, Ky.	—
2nd Lt. Joseph J. Kruzel	40-H	0-401183	Wilkes-Barre, Pa.	—
2nd Lt. David L. Obert	40-H	0-401305	Apache, Okla.	Feb., 1991
2nd Lt. Nathaniel H. Blanton	40-H	0-401361	Shawnee, Okla.	—

Name	Class	Serial No.	Hometown	Status
2nd Lt. John E. Vogel	41-B	0-406069	Columbus, Ohio	KIA Sept. 29, 1945
2nd Lt. John H. Posten, Jr.	41-B	0-406333	Atlantic Highlands, N.J.	—
2nd Lt. William M. Rowe	41-B	0-406336	Lynn, Mass.	—
2nd Lt. Hiram A. Messmore	41-B	0-406422	Lincoln, Nebr.	KIA Mar. 31, 1943
2nd Lt. William J. Hennon	41-B	0-406549	Mound, Minn.	July 25, 1989
2nd Lt. Maurice G. Hughett	41-B	0-406561	Waco, Tex.	KIA Dec. 9, 1941
2nd Lt. Lawrence K. Lodin	41-B	0-406574	Minneapolis, Minn.	1985
2nd Lt. Elmer B. Powell, Jr.	41-B	0-407090	University City, Mo.	
2nd Lt. Stephen H. Crosby	41-C	0-390710	Greenwood, Miss.	KIA Feb. 9, 1942
2nd Lt. Earl R. Stone, Jr.	41-C	0-390872	Los Angeles, Calif.	—
2nd Lt. Robert J. Leyrer	41-C	0-392233	Clintonville, Wis.	MIA Jan. 27, 1945
2nd Lt. Wilson Glover	41-C	0-397575	Greenville, S.C.	
2nd Lt. James M. Ross	41-C	0-408850	Aberdeen, Idaho	KIA Jan. 5, 1942
2nd Lt. Walter V. Wilcox	41-C	0-408878	Long Beach, Calif.	KIA Jan. 27, 1942
2nd Lt. Jerry O. Brezina	41-C	0-411927	Fort Collins, Colo.	
2nd Lt. Charles W. Burris	41-C	0-411933	Tulsa, Okla.	MIA Jan. 9, 1945
2nd Lt. James A. Phillips	41-C	0-412159	Lewiston, Idaho	July 13, 1942
2nd Lt. Joseph L. McClellan	41-C	0-413466	Butte, Mont.	July 29, 1946
2nd Lt. A. W. Balfanz, Jr.	41-C	0-413561	Abilene, Tex.	KIA Dec. 10, 1941
2nd Lt. Forrest M. Hobrecht	41-C	0-413595	Dallas, Tex.	
2nd Lt. Edward A. Erickson	41-D	0-417948	Mankato, Minn.	—
2nd Lt. R. LaMar Gillett	41-D	0-418038	El Centro, Calif.	KIA Apr. 13, 1942
2nd Lt. Robert A. Krantz	41-D	0-418040	Yucaipa, Calif.	KIA Jan. 5, 1942
2nd Lt. Truett J. Majors	41-D	0-418046	Greenville, Tex.	KIA Jan. 5, 1942
2nd Lt. Charles W. Page	41-D	0-418162	Spokane, Wash.	KIA Jan. 2, 1942
2nd Lt. Oscar D. Wyatt	41-D	0-418186	Fort Worth, Tex.	KIA Feb. 1, 1942
2nd Lt. James M. Rowland	41-D	0-418435	Fort Worth, Tex.	
2nd Lt. Willis P. Culp III	41-G	0-426558	Elgin, Tex.	Aug. 24, 1942

Rank	Flying school class	Service no.	Hometown	Date of Death
2nd Lt. Silas C. Wolf	41-G	0-426583	McAlester, Okla.	—
2nd Lt. Earl H. Hulsey	41-G	0-426670	Dallas, Tex.	MIA Jan. 26, 1945

Twentieth Pursuit Squadron

Rank	Flying school class	Service no.	Hometown	Date of Death
1st Lt. Joseph H. Moore	38-B	0-22527	Spartanburg, S.C.	—
1st Lt. Charles R. Sneed	39-A	0-373918	Hamilton, Tex.	MIA Jan. 9, 1945
1st Lt. Glen M. Alder	39-B	0-22860	Los Angeles, Calif.	KIA Dec. 10, 1941
1st Lt. Joseph P. McLaughlin	40-D	0-396289	——, Mont.	MIA Mar. 19, 1943
1st Lt. Hugh H. Marble, Jr.	40-D	0-396291	Houston, Tex.	Nov. 29, 1949
1st Lt. Fred M. Armstrong, Jr.	40-D	0-396353	Indianapolis, Ind.	—
1st Lt. Marshall J. Anderson	40-D	0-396368	Oklahoma City, Okla.	KIA Jan. 19, 1942
2nd Lt. Robert P. Duncan	40-H	0-401149	Dallas, Tex.	KIA Sept. 23, 1943
2nd Lt. Edwin B. Gilmore	40-H	0-401165	Highland Pk., Mich.	Oct. 14, 1988
2nd Lt. Morgan S. McCowan	40-H	0-401199	Leoti, Kans.	KIA Dec. 10, 1941
2nd Lt. Frank A. Ansley	40-H	0-401351	Niagara Falls, N.Y.	MIA Sept. 7, 1944
2nd Lt. Erwin B. Crellin	41-B	0-407037	Anthony, Kans.	KIA Mar. 2, 1942
2nd Lt. Harrison S. Hughes	41-B	0-407057	Pullman, Wash.	MIA Oct. 24, 1944
2nd Lt. Carl Parker Gies	41-B	0-407083	Salem, Oreg.	July 3, 1964
2nd Lt. Max Louk	41-B	0-407114	Lawrence, Kans.	KIA Dec. 8, 1941
2nd Lt. Eugene B. Shevlin	41-B	0-407128	Courtland, N.Y.	MIA Sept. 7, 1944
2nd Lt. Varian Kiefer White	41-B	0-407132	Blackfoot, Idaho	May 18, 1943
2nd Lt. Milton H. Woodside	41-C	0-396134	Charlotte, N.C.	July 1973
2nd Lt. Percy E. Ramsey	41-C	0-408845	Hope, Ark.	MIA Oct. 24, 1944
2nd Lt. Henry C. Rancke	41-C	0-408846	Rockingham, N.C.	Sept. 19, 1942
2nd Lt. Lloyd H. Stinson	41-C	0-408869	Greenwood, Miss.	—

Name		Serial	Class	Hometown	Date
2nd Lt. Custer E. Wake	0-409071	41-C	[unknown]	Sept. 17, 1947
2nd Lt. William B. Carter	0-411690	41-C	Downsville, La.	Dec. 13, 1942
2nd Lt. Edward J. Tremblay	0-411740	41-C	Springfield, Mass.	June 24, 1942
2nd Lt. Edward Houseman	0-411836	41-C	Philadelphia, Pa.	MIA Oct. 24, 1944
2nd Lt. Harlan F. Rousseau	0-411848	41-C	Oconto, Wis.	MIA Jan. 12, 1945
2nd Lt. Fred B. Browne	0-411930	41-C	Memphis, Tenn.	MIA Dec. 27, 1944
2nd Lt. W. James Fossey	0-411956	41-C	Buffalo, Okla.	—
2nd Lt. James W. Fulks	0-411958	41-C	Mena, Ark.	MIA Jan. 23, 1945
2nd Lt. Daniel L. Blass	0-411981	41-C	Le Compte, La.	ca. 1947
2nd Lt. J. Jack Gates	0-412099	41-C	Lonoke, Ark.	—
2nd Lt. Thomas W. Patrick	0-412150	41-C	Chester, S.C.	MIA Jan. 9, 1945
2nd Lt. James E. Mullen	0-412186	41-C	Trinidad, Colo.	Jan. 30, 1945
2nd Lt. Randall D. Keator	0-412276	41-C	Compti, La.	Feb. 4, 1981
2nd Lt. Jesse A. Luker	0-412524	41-C	Porterville, Calif.	KIA Dec. 8, 1941
2nd Lt. Melvin E. McKnight	0-412694	41-C	Sioux City, Iowa	Aug. 21, 1942
2nd Lt. Guy W. Iversen	0-417694	41-D	Cedar Falls, Iowa	MIA Oct. 24, 1944
2nd Lt. James T. Drake	0-418430	41-D	Dallas, Tex.	KIA Dec. 8, 1941
2nd Lt. William Tom Akins	0-426546	41-G	Hillsboro, Tex.	between 1947 and 1949
2nd Lt. Max B. Halverson	0-426563	41-G	Salt Lake City, Utah	MIA Oct. 24, 1944
2nd Lt. Lowell J. Mulcahy	0-426571	41-G	Tulare, Calif.	KIA Dec. 8, 1941
2nd Lt. Fred L. Siler	0-426578	41-G	Pocatello, Idaho	—

Twenty-First Pursuit Squadron

Name	Serial	Class	Hometown	Date
1st Lt. Wm Edwin Dyess	0-22526	37-C	Albany, Tex.	Dec. 22, 1943
2nd Lt. Ben S. Irvin	0-399532	40-G	Washington, Ga.	Nov. 2, 1968
2nd Lt. John P. Burns	0-390803	41-A	Akron, Ohio	KIA Apr. 13, 1942
2nd Lt. Joseph P. Cole	0-396106	41-C	Kingstree, S.C.	KIA July 15, 1942

Rank	Flying school class	Service no.	Hometown	Date of Death
2nd Lt. Lloyd A. Coleman	41-C	0-411963	Doddsville, Miss.	Jan. 25, 1968
2nd Lt. Leo B. Golden, Jr.	41-C	0-412104	Mobile, Ala.	MIA Jan. 9, 1945
2nd Lt. Robert D. Clark	41-C	0-412166	Cleveland, Ohio	KIA Dec. 9, 1941
2nd Lt. Samuel C. Grashio	41-C	0-412503	Spokane, Wash.	—
2nd Lt. Robert S. Ibold	41-D	0-417962	Phoenix, Ariz.	Dec. 10, 1942
2nd Lt. James E. May	41-D	0-418157	Quartzsite, Ariz.	KIA Feb. 4, 1942
2nd Lt. John L. McCown	41-E	0-421120	Grandview, Tex.	MIA Sept. 7, 1944
2nd Lt. Augustus F. Williams	41-E	0-421150	Globe, Ariz.	—
2nd Lt. I.B. Jack Donalson	41-F	0-424927	Tulsa, Okla.	—

Thirty-Fourth Pursuit Squadron

1st Lt. Samuel H. Marett	38-B	0-22854	New Braunfels, Tex.	KIA Dec. 10, 1941
1st Lt. Ben S. Brown	40-D	0-396370	Hawkinsville, Ga.	July 3, 1942
2nd Lt. Donald E. Pagel	41-A	0-404060	Aurora, Ill.	Feb. 18, 1943
2nd Lt. William L. Baker, Jr.	41-C	0-411915	University City, Mo.	KIA Aug. 15, 1944
2nd Lt. William G. Coleman	41-C	0-411964	——, Miss.	KIA Jan. 30, 1942
2nd Lt. Jack W. Hall	41-C	0-412108	Liberty, Mo.	KIA Apr. 14, 1942
2nd Lt. Lawrence E. McDaniel	41-C	0-412170	Jackson, N.C.	MIA Sept. 7, 1944
2nd Lt. Arthur B. Knackstedt	41-C	0-412506	Saint Louis, Mo.	—
2nd Lt. Stewart W. Robb	41-C	0-412881	Bakersfield, Calif.	—
2nd Lt. Donald M. Crosland	41-D	0-417944	Mineral Springs, Tex.	MIA Jan. 9, 1945
2nd Lt. Claude W. Paulger	41-D	0-418164	Lubbock, Tex.	MIA Sept. 7, 1944
2nd Lt. James C. Nicol	41-D	0-418305	Fort Worth, Tex.	—
2nd Lt. Frankie M. Bryant	41-D	0-418516	Graham, Tex.	MIA Oct. 24, 1944
2nd Lt. Charles E. Gaskell	41-E	0-421072	Dallas, Tex.	MIA Oct. 24, 1944
2nd Lt. James M. Henry	41-E	0-421089	Kingsville, Tex.	

Notes

CHAPTER 1

1. Days before, five of the 17th's P-26As had been flown to Clark for transfer to the Philippine Army Air Corps. Five others from the 3rd and 20th pursuit squadrons were also transferred at that time, leaving only twelve in the three squadrons as hacks. With the completion of transition training to the P-35A by the squadron's newies, the P-26As were no longer needed for regular duty (Messmore interview, Jan. 11, 1981; *Aircraft Status Report,* June 30 and July 31, 1941; Memo, August 14, 1941, Col. George to Gen. MacArthur).

CHAPTER 2

1. Krieger had obviously studied War Department Field Manual 30–38, *Identification of Japanese Aircraft,* issued in March, 1941, and sent to the Philippines in May, 1941, which included among the list of Japanese Army aircraft the Messerschmitt 109. Evidently the War Department believed the Germans had exported numbers of their high-performance pursuit aircraft to Japan.

CHAPTER 3

1. The remaining pilots of the 21st and 34th pursuit squadrons left San Francisco for the Philippines on the *Republic* on November 21, while Headquarters and the 70th Pursuit squadrons were set to sail for the Philippines on December 1 (Memo for Asst. Secretary of War from Brig. Gen Gerow, Nov. 10, 1941; Memo, W. W. I. to Gerow, Nov. 26, 1941).

2. These P-40Es were serial numbers 40-615 to 40-659, with breaks, and were the first part of the fifty P-40Es taken from the production line to equip the two squadrons, with estimated delivery to the Air Corps on November 1 and December 1 in groups of twenty-five aircraft each (Memo, Army Air Corps to Commanding General, Air Force Combat Command, Sept. 25, 1941; Memo, Wright Field to Materiel, OCAC, Oct. 14, 1941).

3. The equipment was a SCR-270B mobile radar unit, operated by a detachment of the Air Warning Company of the Far East Air Force.

4. Effective November 16, the Air Force USAFFE was redesignated the Far East Air Force (USAFFE General Orders No. 28, 14 Nov. 1941).

5. Since pilots of the 21st Pursuit did not go with Mahony to pick up the P-35As (Williams, Feb. 6, 1988; phone call from Grashio, Jan. 27, 1988), it is assumed that pilots of the 17th Pursuit made the ferry trip. Mahony did not identify the squadron affiliation of his passengers in the reference letter to his mother. The 17th was highly experienced in flying the P-35A. None of the surviving members of the squadron, however, recalls going to Iba for the purpose.

6. Memo, Crawford to Gerow, Dec. 1, 1941; Letter, Adm. Stark to Gen. Marshall, Dec. 3, 1941. In convoy with the *Blomfontein* was the USAT *Republic* carrying the balance of the pilots of the 21st and 34th pursuit squadrons to the Philippines (Memo for Asst. Sec. of War and Depot C/S from Gerow, Nov. 10, 1941).

CHAPTER 4

1. This was the Malaya invasion force of the Japanese 25th Army, which had left Hanoi in two convoys on December 4. On December 6 it was nearing southern Thailand and Kota Bharu, Malaya (Morton, *Strategy and Command,* p. 123).

2. According to an officer of the 19th Bombardment Group based at Clark, the B-17s "could fly circles around the P-40s at 20,000 feet—when we could get them up that high" (Cappelletti overseas log, p. 1).

3. On December 1, 1941, as against .50-caliber requirements of 6 million rounds for air and 13.3 million rounds for ground, only 3.8 million rounds were available, or less than one-fifth of the needs (Memo, Crawford to Gerow, Dec. 1, 1941). The *effective* supply of .50-caliber ammunition for aircraft was even less, for it had to be belted before being loaded. By mobilizing all ordnance troops that could be spared, the recently arrived 680th Ordnance Company (Aviation Pursuit)—responsible for supplying the 24th Pursuit Group with belted ammunition—organized a twenty-four-hour belting party at Nichols during the first week of December to hand-belt ammunition; by the end of the week several missions' supply was ready for the pursuit ships (Whittenburg, "Brief History of the 680th Ordnance," pp. 3–4, and letter to author, Oct. 5, 1981).

4. An additional three pilots had been temporarily assigned to the understrength 21st Pursuit.

5. The Wright Field Maintenance Command had issued a new technical radiogram on October 14, 1941, calling for removal of the plugs on the gun charger valves and certain alterations to be introduced, but the order evidently had never been received by the Philippine depot.

6. There is disagreement on the numbers of P-40Es delivered to the 21st by December 8. In a 1943 POW interview, Dyess indicated twenty-two, the

figure used here (Priestley 1943 interview of Dyess). They were from the serial numbers 40-615 through 40-659 (Aircraft history cards for the P-40E).

7. The last two of the twenty-four P-40Es received and delivered to the 21st on December 8 were equipped with an improved gun charger hose and were not subject to the order of September 19, 1941, to deactivate the hydraulic gun charging system (Wright Field Technical Radiogram, Oct. 14, 1941; Hoffman to author, Oct. 21, 1986).

8. There is disagreement about the time of the radar sighting. Radar operator Brodginski gives it at "just after midnight," which is the time used here, but Thorne indicates that it was about 1:00 A.M.; the 16th Naval District, 1:30 A.M.; and Wimer, "before midnight." The official Japanese war history, *Senshi Sosho,* indicates the Japanese planes were over Corregidor at 12:30 A.M.

9. In his wartime diary, Don Steele, who was flying as a wingman in Thorne's flight this night, recorded that the flight *was* in radio contact with Donegan the whole time, but Thorne and other sources indicate it was not. Steele's account seems unlikely; only Keenan's radio was set to receive the Morse code calls from Donegan, so Steele would not have known of any radioed instructions unless Keenan had informed him of them after they had landed.

10. The Japanese intruders were four navy twin-engine attack bombers on a weather reconnaissance. The did a U-turn twenty-five miles off Corregidor to return to Formosa (*Senshi Sosho* 24:175; Mori, *Kaigun Sentokitai,* p. 163).

CHAPTER 5

1. In his wartime flying log, Grant Mahony, Nichols Field operations officer, records that he flew two patrols for a total of five hours on December 8. It is assumed he flew with the 17th Pursuit, to which he was assigned for tactical operations in the event of war (Mahony Individual Flight Record, entry for Dec. 8, 1941; Hoffman to author, Sept. 7, 1986). However, squadron mates Dave Obert and Red Sheppard do not recall Mahony flying with the 17th this day (Obert to author, Feb. 5, 1988; Sheppard to author, Mar. 3, 1988). Sheppard indicated in a 1944–45 narrative that Manony led a six-plane patrol over Manila Bay from Nichols Field from about 12:15, when the 17th Pursuit at Clark was ordered on such a mission (see chapter 6), but he does not mention an earlier first patrol by Mahony (Sheppard/Gilmore statement, p. 4).

2. At 9:31 FEAF Headquarters informed the 16th Naval District in Manila that the patrol had made "contact with hostile forces over Clark Field," but this was typical of the incorrect reports of this day (16th Naval District War Diary, Dec. 8, 1941). The report is not mentioned in the FEAF Summary of Activities. The 34th Pursuit over Clark had not encountered enemy planes either.

3. The two groups of Japanese bombers that attacked Baguio and Tuguegarao were short-range army planes, whose Philippines targets were limited by army-navy agreement to those north of 16 degrees latitude. Eighteen twin-

engine "Sally" bombers hit Baguio's Camp John Hay barracks from 12,000 feet, and twenty-five "Lily" twin-engine light bombers struck Tuguegarao, 110 miles northeast of Baguio, each shortly after 9:00 ("Brief Summary of Action in the Office of the Chief of Staff," Dec. 8, 1941, entry for 9:05; Japanese Monograph No. 11, p. 9; *Senshi Sosho* 34:203–204; FEAF Summary of Activities, Dec. 8, 1941, entry for 9:23.

CHAPTER 6

1. The SCR-270B scope man on duty at Iba between 10:00 and 12:00 noon recalled in 1943 that he had picked up two flights: one toward Iba at 129 miles to the northwest, and the second in the direction of Clark Field (Interview of Pvt. Thomas Lloyd, Air Warning Service, in Priestley interviews, book 8, pp. 144–45). These reports, like all at Iba, were radioed to AWS at Nielson (Wimer report).

2. In his 1942 narrative (p. 4), Grover refers to the 34th Pursuit as the 21st Pursuit, and vice versa. He recalled ordering only the 34th Pursuit ("the 21st") to cover Clark, but evidently he did order the 21st at Nichols to fly to Clark to provide cover too. The 34th, which had landed back at Del Carmen after its uneventful patrol over Clark in the morning, never received the second order of Grover to cover Clark again (Priestley 1943 interview of Baker).

3. It is believed that the wingmen of A Flight were Gordon Benson, Vern Ireland, and Howard Hardegree, but it has not been possible to determine to whose elements they were assigned this day.

4. Ellstrom is not confirmed as Roberts's wingman, but Ellis recalls that Ellstrom usually flew in his C Flight before December 8.

5. Thorne's A Flight did not pick up this radio call and continued to climb to 15,000 feet over Iba. No mention of any new orders radioed to the 3rd Pursuit is made in Grover's 1942 narrative.

6. Grashio believes Clark, a 41-C classmate, was the flight leader, but it would seem more likely that Dyess would have assigned a more senior pilot to the position, perhaps John Burns (41-A). The second-ranking pilot in the squadron, Ben Irvin (40-G), was flying in Dyess's formation, probably as B Flight leader (Grashio to author, Mar. 28, 1983; phone call from Grashio, Jan. 16, 1987; interview of Ben Irvin in *Atlanta Journal*, Nov. 20, 1942).

7. In his 1942 narrative, Grover does not mention radioing the 21st Pursuit with the new orders, one of many omissions and erroneous statements in his recollection of events.

8. Unlike Dyess and Williams, Grashio does not recall original orders to go to Clark and indicates that in the absence of any mission destination, he decided to take the four ships to Clark (Grashio, *Return to Freedom*, pp. 4–5; Grashio/Donahoe interview with Edmonds, Apr. 2, 1945; phone call from Grashio, Jan. 16, 1987).

9. This time allows for five minutes' delay in getting the report to the district, which recorded it at 12:15. It is assumed that it was Woolery's group

that Carided spotted, for it was the only group heading for Manila at this time. It is also assumed that all four of the splintered C Flight went with B Flight to Manila, although Powell recalled that he and Roberts did not join up with the others until *after* they had reached Manila (Powell diary, p. 3).

10. Allowing about thirteen minutes to cover the fifty miles to Clark Field, where they apparently arrived at 12:30, it must have been about 12:17 when Krieger picked up this call. Neither Powell in C Flight nor Gehrig in B Flight remembers receiving such a call over their radios. The origin of the call is still unknown.

11. It is assumed that this message reached Major Grover, though neither he nor his staff have acknowledged receiving it. The teletype had functioned perfectly that day. One wonders if the message was received and served as the basis for the frantic "Tally Ho, Clark Field!" calls that Krieger and (about ten minutes later) Steele picked up on their radios. Some radiomen in the 24th Group Headquarters Squadron recall "Tally Ho" calls sent out to airborne pilots over their SCR-197 communications trailer at this time. Colonel Campbell, head of the AWS, became increasingly restive following the reports coming in of Japanese planes flying south in the direction of Clark and relayed this information to group operations at Clark (Col. Campbell notebook).

12. The 34th Pursuit was also still on the ground at Del Carmen, but it is not known if Grover was aware of this. According to its officers, no order had been received from the 24th Group since its return from morning patrol over Clark.

13. The identity of the two pilots remains unknown. They may have been from Hank Thorne's A Flight, which had splintered while on high-altitude patrol of Iba from about 12:15.

CHAPTER 7

1. There were actually only fifty-three. One plane in the first wave of twenty-seven suffered a blowout on takeoff from Formosa and crashed.

2. Joe Cole and Gus Williams in Grashio's flight recall receiving radio instructions before the call from Clark Field to intercept Japanese bombers off the west coast of Luzon (i.e., Iba) after joining up with Woolery's group and heading for Iba together, but Grashio does not recall such instructions, nor do any of the surviving pilots of Woolery's group recollect joining up with Grashio's flight and continuing together in the direction of Iba.

3. It is assumed that Vern Ireland and Gordon Benson did proceed to Clark with Thorne, Hanson, and Hardegree, since they apparently were subsequently engaged in combat there.

4. Since Steele and Daniel arrived over Clark about 12:39 P.M. (shortly after the Zeros had started strafing) and assuming the call was heard at 12:35, when the bombers began their attack on Clark, and that the ground speed of their P-40s was 240 MPH for the high-speed run into Clark, then the pilots would have been sixteen miles out of Clark.

5. Author's estimate, based on the fact that on their arrival at Iba an

estimated nine minutes later, no Japanese aircraft were still operating over Iba, having left minutes before for Clark.

6. Assuming Woolery's group left Clark at about 12:32 and Roberts and Powell were two minutes behind them (at 12:34, one minute before the bombing of Clark). Two-thirds of the way to Iba would take about six minutes from Clark.

7. The identity of the P-40s' pilots is unknown. They were probably either Steele and Daniel or Grashio and Williams. Cole would have left for Nichols before Roberts and Powell arrived at Clark. In his diary, Powell indicated the P-40s were from the 17th Pursuit, but that squadron was flying over Manila Bay at the time.

8. In his retrospective diary Powell maintained that he was being hit by the rear gunner of the two-place ship in front of him, but no such Japanese aircraft were in combat over Clark that day. Roberts, his element leader, recalled that he was fired on by a plane behind him, flying in a Lufberry (Powell diary, p. 3; Powell to author, July 26, 1979; author's interview of Roberts, Mar. 23, 1980).

9. Author's estimate; it would take about ten minutes to fly the thirty-seven miles back to Iba, and the Japanese were still operating there on arrival, not departing until about 1:00 or 1:05 (see chapter 8).

10. This assumes that Thorne headed for Clark at 12:36 after picking up the call from Clark a minute earlier and allows ten minutes to cover the distance to Clark from Iba.

11. This must have been a call from Andy Krieger, who had radioed from Iba about 12:50, after the bombing of Iba Field (Krieger narrative, pp. 6–7; see chapter 8).

12. Thorne acknowledges that his flight had become splintered but does not recall who left it. The 3rd Pursuit pilots learned at the end of the day that Ireland had spun out of control and crashed into Mount Arayat, ten miles east of Clark Field, evidently a victim of Zeros over the field (Krieger narrative, p. 10).

13. The 34th Pursuit had evidently never received the 11:30 order from group operations to take off and patrol over Manila Bay.

14. The number of P-35As taking off from Del Carmen on this initial war mission of the squadron is subject to disagreement. Stewart Robb in 1944 recalled sixteen, as did Ben Brown in 1979, but Frankie Bryant in 1979 thought there were sixteen to eighteen. Robert Reynolds, a 34th enlisted man, mentioned fourteen in a 1951 book. In a 1942 interview, Claude Paulger put the total as only between nine and twelve.

15. The SCR-197 communications van of QA-1 had been knocked out of service at about 12:42 during the Japanese strafing attack. None of the 17th's pilots had picked up the distress call of the SCR-197 at the time of the bombing attack on Clark, calling all pursuit to the base, though Willie Feallock heard "a lot of chatter and yelling" on the frequency but was not able to make it out (Feallock to author, Feb. 27, 1978). Considerably behind his squadron mates because of his late takeoff from Clark, Feallock was much closer to

Clark and thus in a better position to pick up the call when QA-1 radioed its distress message.

CHAPTER 8

1. Gehrig, Krieger, and John Lester believed that Root was shot down by Zeros while attempting to land, but none was an eyewitness, as was the source for this version of the incident (author interview of Bland, Jan. 30, 1983). The strafing of Iba by Zeros did not occur until *after* the attempted landing by B Flight.

2. Perhaps from the radios of P-40s in combat over Clark at the time (ca. 12:55), as the SCR-197 communications van at Clark had been knocked out of service by this time.

3. Ellis's count was correct. The Takao and Kanoya *kokutai* had each left Formosa with twenty-seven Mitsubishi G4M1 "Betty" bombers for the attack on Iba, but one from the Kanoya unit had returned to base because of mechanical trouble (*Senshi Sosho* 24:180).

4. Apparently Ellis entered into combat with the Zeros after Krieger had broken off his own combat with them, as neither pilot ever saw the other. Krieger had flown directly into their right-hand pattern, a more dangerous tactic than Ellis was following.

5. Japanese official records acknowledge the loss of only two of the attacking force of fifty-three Zeros of the 3rd *kokutai* that strafed Iba after the Japanese bombing and subsequently shot up Clark Field (see chapter 9); both were evidently lost over Iba.

6. The three Zeros that attacked Neri and Keenan were probably a *shotai* of the 3rd *kokutai* that had finished strafing Iba and was on its way to Clark between 1:05 and 1:10 P.M.

7. Roberts and Powell both claim that Roberts was shot down by the rear gunner of a two-seat plane, but only single-seat Zeros were operating over Iba. A two-seat reconnaissance plane (Mitsubishi C5M2) did come over Iba at 1:00 P.M. to survey the effects of the attack, but it was unarmed (*Senshi Sosho* 24:180; Masami Miza, *Maru*, Feb. 1962).

8. These were most likely the fifty-three "Betty" and "Nell" bombers that had bombed Clark twenty-three minutes earlier. They had slowly swung north from a point south of Clark for the homeward flight and were now passing over Iba. The Iba attack force bombed Iba only once, from north to south (Ozaki to author, Mar. 16, 1981).

9. This estimate is based on rate-of-climb data from 15,000 feet for a combat-loaded P-40E, as derived from P-40 operations manual and correspondence with Herb Ellis (Ellis to author, Sept. 17, 1979, and Jan. 13, 1980).

10. Allen eventually landed at O'Donnell, an auxiliary field twelve miles north of Clark (Gies diary, Dec. 8, 1941).

11. McBride and many of the enlisted men of the squadron maintain that they were bombed by this second group of Japanese bombers passing over Iba, but Japanese records do not indicate two separate bombings of the base. These

were evidently bombers from the Clark attack passing over Iba on their return trip to Formosa. McBride recalls a bomb fragment striking him, but it may have been a bullet from one of the Zeros.

12. Cave noted that the attack began at 12:44 and ended at 1:05. This coincides exactly with Japanese records. These records, however, indicate that only a single bombing run of fifty-three planes from 12:44 followed by a single strafing by forty-two Zeros until 13:05 were mounted against Iba. Like other 3rd Pursuiters, Cave recalls that the second group of bombers passing over Iba also dropped bombs on the base. The Zeros that Cave recalls strafing Iba after the second group of bombers passed over may have been just interrupting their attack so as not to be on the deck when bombs fell from this group, not realizing that this group was not on a bombing mission but was just returning to Formosa. Several 3rd Pursuiters as well as Iba radarmen recall bombers returning from the south in a second attack, followed again by strafers (see, e.g., Priestley's 1943 interviews with radarman Brodginski).

CHAPTER 9

1. The Zero was piloted by Flight PO 3rd Class Yoshio Hirose, wingman to the *buntai* leader Lt. Sachio Maki. Maki's nine Zeros were on their way to Clark Field after having strafed Iba (correspondence with Hideki Shingo, former flying CO of the Tainan *kokutai*, Feb.–Apr., 1979).

2. Later, Ellis found out that it was Johnny McCown of Grashio's flight, flying alone near Mount Arayat twelve miles to the east of Clark, who had spotted his predicament and had come to his rescue (Ellis, June 2, 1978; Grashio/Donahoe interview).

3. The 3rd *kokutai* Zeros had now finished their strafing attacks on Iba and had left for Clark Field.

Persistent allegations by P-40 pilots in the Philippines campaign that Ellstrom had been strafed and killed in his chute are proved to be without foundation with the discovery of the item in Mallonee's unpublished diary. Indeed, Lt. Hideki Shingo, flying commander of the Tainan *kokutai*, insists that none of his pilots ever strafed American pilots who had bailed out (Shingo, May 16, 1981). The absurd stories that American pilots spread from secondhand information under the crisis of war conditions are illustrated in this case by the one that Andy Krieger, a close friend of Ellstrom, had heard on the circumstances of his death; namely, that Ellstrom had engaged several Zeros over Clark and had shot down three in twenty minutes before running out of gas. He jumped and was shot in his parachute (Krieger narrative, p. 10).

4. It is assumed that Daniel managed to land his original P-40 and that it was too shot up to fly again, though no documentation is available to confirm this.

5. At 300 MPH indicated airspeed—the "fastest level flight" that Steele had ever heard of (Steele diary, p. 8)—ground speed would have been 330 MPH at 5,000 feet, requiring eleven minutes for the fifty-eight-mile trip. P-40 pilots were not supposed to use full military power (3,000 RPM, 44.6 inches of mani-

fold pressure) for more than five minutes ("Pilots Manual for the Curtiss P-40 Warhawk," p. 15B).

6. The only other 3rd Pursuit pilot who was unaccounted for who could have landed at Rosales was Gerry Keenan.

7. It is assumed that Neri covered the twenty miles from Mount Pinatuba to Clark in five minutes, and the fifty miles from Clark to Rosales in twelve minutes. If he left Mount Pinatuba at about 1:08 P.M. and circled Clark for about three minutes, he would have reached Rosales at 1:28 P.M.

8. The *Senshi Sosho* indicates that three *buntai* of the Tainan *kokutai* strafed Del Carmen after combat with American fighters over the base, but it would appear that only two Zeros actually attacked the field. The CO of the Tainan *kokutai* maintains that his pilots had no orders to attack Del Carmen (correspondence with Hideki Shingo).

9. Some of the 17th Pursuit pilots who maintain they saw dust and smoke around Clark while they patrolled over Manila Bay are John Brownewell (Brownewell interview, June 2, 1945), George Kiser (Kiser statement), Cy Blanton (Blanton tape, Nov., 1980), and Walt Coss (correspondence, May 6, 1978), but evidently they did not radio the sight to the others of the squadron. Obert had his eyes glued on the plane ahead of him in the formation all the time not to lose his position (Obert correspondence, June 2, 1979). In his wartime diary, Col. James V. Collier, a G-3 officer in USAFFE Headquarters, faults the CO of the 17th Pursuit for making no effort to investigate the situation at Clark, which Collier maintains he must have seen from Manila Bay (Collier Notebooks, book 1, p. 58).

CHAPTER 10

1. The B-18 had been flown into Rosales from Clark Field during the bombing attack on Clark.

2. Killed in action were S. Sgts. Bill Hainer and Andy Kapalko and Pvts. Cornelius Bumbar, Edwin Wissing, and Vernon Wyatt.

3. The fifty-three "Nell" and "Betty" bombers had dropped a total of 636 bombs of 132 pounds each (*Senshi Sosho* 21:180).

4. They were S. Sgts. Cecil Commander and Walter Foster, Cpls. Gerald Dumais and John Jurcsak, Pfcs Orin Gillett and Leo Mack, and Pvts Henry Colvin, Joe Deschambeau, Kenneth Messenger, Karl Santschi, and Arthur Space. Foster, Santschi, and Space are listed in army records as KIA at Iba on December 12, and Commander as KIA on December 29, but these dates are clearly erroneous.

5. There are no known records that indicate how many of the enlisted men were wounded. One source estimates about twenty-five (Toland interview of Grow). Eight of the 3rd Pursuit's wounded enlisted men (Benedict, Corbett, Douglas, Fritz, Jones, Mollohan, Nelson, and Preston) were evacuated to Australia on the hospital ship *Mactan* on December 31, 1941.

6. By dusk Headquarters Company of the 803rd Aviation Engineers at Clark had filled in the craters on this strip enough so that planes could land

on it (Goldblith, "The 803rd Engineers in the Philippine Defense," p. 323).

7. Their identity is unknown, but the only candidates would be Gerry Keenan and Ship Daniel.

8. Shot down were the aircraft of Ireland, Ellstrom, Ellis, and Roberts; Woolery's original P-40 and Root's were destroyed on landing at Iba; Neri's and Daniel's original P-40s were severely damaged and written off at Rosales and Iba, respectively. Powell's P-40 was a wreck at Lingayen (see chapter 11), and four of the six spare P-40s at Iba were evidently destroyed on the ground in the Japanese attack on the field.

CHAPTER 11

1. On his return to Nichols, the 17th Pursuit mechanics checked his P-40E out and found it in good working order. Lodin subsequently regained his composure and rejoined his squadron over Clark as it waited for the 21st Pursuit to land (Wright narrative, pp. 3–4; Wright to author, July 8, 1978).

2. There is disagreement on the number who flew this mission. Posten in 1945 recalled that twelve were assigned, while Burris in 1978 cited eighteen (Edmonds 1945 interview of Posten; Burris to author, Dec. 11, 1978).

3. In a 1942 interview, the squadron's administrative officer, Lawrence Parcher, confirmed that the 21st lost four P-40s in takeoff accidents this morning (Chunn 1942 interview of Parcher).

4. FEAF Headquarters was also wondering where the B-17s were. At 10:20 A.M., the CO of the 19th Bombardment Group responded that he had no information on the Del Monte flight. Not until 2:30 P.M. did the six awaited B-17s show up at Clark—their takeoff from Del Monte had been delayed (FEAF, "Summary of Activities," p. 5; 19th Bomb Group Diary, p. 2).

5. Wagner may have left a few additional of his P-40s at Nichols and taken only twelve to Clark, though there is no documentary evidence to this effect. In addition to Obert and Rowe, at least six other 17th Pursuiters were at Nichols next morning: Feallock, Earl Stone, Forrest Hobrecht, Wilson Glover, Jim Phillips, and "Dub" Balfanz.

6. The 11th Air Fleet on Formosa had planned to attack Nichols Field and the ships in Manila Bay in separate strikes to take off at 9:30 A.M. It was forced to abandon its plans, however, when heavy fog over the island persisted past the revised departure time of 10:00 A.M. (Senshi Sosho 24:184).

CHAPTER 12

1. Dale at first refused the award, arguing that he had done no more than anyone else on the mission. He was then reprimanded by Col. Brady and ordered to accept it (Edmonds interview of Dale, Nov. 24, 1944).

2. Marett's machine gun fire had detonated depth charges stacked on the rear deck of Minesweeper No. 10 at 9:33 A.M., according to Japanese records. The vessel sank immediately with a loss of seventy-nine killed and seventeen injured (Senshi Sosho 24:211; SRN 129,733, Dec. 11, 1941, 16:00; SRN 129,912, Dec. 18, 1941, 16:00).

3. According to Japanese records, only one transport, the *Oigawa Maru,* was set afire in the attack. Sixteen of its complement, including its captain, were injured, though no one was killed *(Senshi Sosho* 24:214).

4. Most likely, the pilot was from the 20th Pursuit Squadron, flying the second attack mission from Clark in the P-40Es flown by the 17th Pursuit in the first mission. See below.

5. The Japanese aircraft were Army Kawasaki Ki-48 "Lily" bombers of the 8th *sentai* (Flying Regiment), supporting the Vigan landings.

6. Japanese records acknowledge loss of a "Lily" bomber of this unit.

7. A combat-loaded P-40E weighed 9,200 pounds vs. 7,600 for a similarly loaded P-40B, a good 20 percent more, with the same supporting wing area.

8. They were Army Nakajima Ki-27 "Nates" from the 24th *sentai,* guarding the landing force *(Senshi Sosho* 34:299).

9. He was S. Sgt. Wilmer Inlow of the 20th Pursuit (Gies diary, Dec. 10, 1941).

10. Japanese records indicate that eighteen Zeros of the Tainan *kokutai* attacked Del Carmen, but Claude Paulger in 1942 recalled only "six or eleven," and a report of the resident 803rd Aviation Engineers noted that the field was strafed by seven planes only *(Senshi Sosho* 24:187; Chunn 1942 interview with Paulger; report of 1st Lt. James D. Richardson, 803rd Aviation Engineers, to Engineer, USAFFE, Dec. 26, 1941).

11. The Japanese were actually heading for the Manila area—including Nichols Field—and Del Carmen rather than Clark Field. The bomber force consisted of twenty-six G3M "Nells" of the 1st *kokutai* (Cavite naval yard), twenty-seven G4M "Betties" of Takao *kokutai* (Nichols), and another twenty-seven G4Ms of Takao *kokutai* (Del Carmen, switched to Manila Bay) *(Senshi Sosho* 24:188).

12. Gies's Distinguished Service Cross citation gives him credit for two Zeros, while Gilmore and Strauss are credited with one each. Japanese records, however, indicate that only one Zero, piloted by NAP 1/C Masaharu Higa, was shot down, although another was badly damaged and crash-landed off the coast of Formosa on the return trip. There is no way to determine which P-40 pilot downed Higa or damaged the other plane *(Senshi Sosho* 24:188; Shingo to author, Apr. 4, 1979; Gies DSC citation; Sheppard/Gilmore statement, pp. 10–11).

13. Figures here on the extent of damage derive from 1942–43 statements by officers of the squadron (Chunn 1942 interview of Paulger; Priestley 1943 interview of Baker). Since they are the closest to the date of the attack, they are accepted here. In a 1944 statement, Ben Brown recalled twelve destroyed and six damaged, but another wartime report by a nonsquadron officer mentioned only five destroyed (Lester report, p. 3). Postwar recollections by the pilots give all destroyed except one (Crosland to author, Mar. 6, 1979) and all destroyed except three damaged (Bryant to author, Jan. 10, 1979). The Japanese claimed they strafed and burned twenty P-35As, but this figure can be discounted *(Senshi Sosho* 24:188).

14. Krieger's estimate was accurate. There were thirty-four Zeros of the

3rd *kokutai* mixing it up with ten P-40s of Feallock's flight (*Senshi Sosho* 24:188; Rowe Combat Report, Dec. 10, 1941).

15. The bombers were twenty-seven G4M1 Betties of the Takao *kokutai,* which began unloading on Nichols at 1:00 P.M., following the five-minute strafing of the base by the thirty-four Zeros of the 3rd *kokutai* (*Senshi Sosho* 24:188).

16. By the author's calculations, nineteen P-40Es from the 21st Pursuit, eighteen P-40Es in the 17th, eleven P-40Es in the 3rd, and three P-40Bs of the 20th. These figures take into account losses on December 9 of two for the 17th (Lodin's and Hughett's ships) and four for the 21st.

17. Only thirteen of these losses have been documented in this chapter (the aircraft of McCowan, Newman, White, Woodside, Krieger, Gehrig, Benson, Sheppard, Hobrecht, Glover, Phillips, Feallock, and Burns). A number of the other losses were apparently from the 21st Pursuit, but information is not available. One account has six of the 21st's P-40E pilots landing through the obstacles at Maniquis Field (Edmonds interview of McMicking, June 5, 1945), rather than just the one reported here (Burns).

18. In the dogfight and strafing attacks over Del Carmen and Manila, the Japanese lost three planes and pilots of their forces of fifty-two Zeros, plus one Zero crash-landed off Formosa on return. Sixteen other Zeros had suffered hits (*Senshi Sosho* 24:188).

19. A week later, one of the 24th Pursuit Group's pilots confided to a Signal Corps officer that he had deliberately run out of gas and bailed out while on patrol over Manila Bay on December 10—"and he would be damned if he would fight a Zero in a P-40." He also told the Signal Corps officer that he knew of several other 24th Group pilots who had done the same (Reminiscences of Lt. Col. Howard W. Brown, SRH-045, Aug. 1945, p. 26).

20. In mid-December, without waiting for authorization from the United States, the Depot ordered that the hydraulic gun-charging systems be reconnected in the P-40Es, thus permitting the pilots to charge their guns while airborne (Fellows report, pp. 2–3). Hydraulic system charging could clear some types of gun stoppages of a technical nature (Obert to author, Apr. 9, 1989; Sly to author, May 30, 1989), but it could not overcome the more common jams due to tight headspace, congealed dust or dirt, or ammunition belts hanging up in the chutes.

CHAPTER 13

1. At the time of Wagner's attack on Aparri, there were thirty-four Nakajima Ki-27 "Nates," fixed-landing-gear pursuits, of the Japanese Army Air Force's 50th *sentai* based there. They had flown in the day before from their Formosa base, staging through Basco Island, to support the Aparri landing force's advance south. According to the memory of the CO of the 50th *sentai,* the only loss suffered by his unit to Wagner's attack was a single Ki-27 burned on the ground. Japanese contemporary records, however, indicate a loss of eighteen Ki-27s of the 24th and 50th *sentai* during the week December 8–15, but only eight airmen from a total loss of twenty army planes of all types during this

period. Since Wagner's attack was the only offensive against the bases of the Japanese Army pursuit aircraft in this period, his claim of two in the air and five on the ground seems very plausible (*Senshi Sosho* 34:372; Tagaya to author, Dec. 6, 1977).

2. It was actually 1:45 A.M. (2:45 Japan time) when the Japanese came ashore at Legaspi (SRN 129,751, Dec. 12, 1941, 0700).

3. More likely it had taken off during the chaotic December 10 evacuation of Clark, when many of the P-40s had not yet been refueled.

4. These decoys and boneyard planes were evidently those claimed as destroyed by Japanese Army Air Force fighters and bombers in their frequent raids (several a day) during this period (*Senshi Sosho* 34:372–77).

5. At a FEAF staff conference at 8:00 A.M. on December 13, Major General Brereton ordered that all damaged aircraft be used as decoys, but it appears that the local FEAF commanders initiated the idea before Brereton's order (FEAF, "Summary of Activities," entry for Dec. 13, 1941).

6. Two days after the incident, Coss had phoned the CO of the 24th Pursuit Group that he had counted seventeen pursuit on his tail (USAFFE G-2 Journal, Dec. 16, 1941, entry for 01:13).

7. Although Coss recalls the plane that strafed him as having a very large engine and a retracted landing gear, no Zeros were based at Aparri or operating near there on December 13. The two planes must have been Nakajima "Nates" of the 50th *sentai*, the type Wagner encountered the day before and that were based at Aparri.

8. This was the support force for the Legaspi landing, which included the carrier *Ryujo* (*Operational Situation of the Japanese Navy in the Philippines Invasion Operations*, Japanese Monograph No. 80, p. 12; Dull, *The Imperial Japanese Navy*, p. 31).

9. At 12:40, twenty-seven Mitsubishi G4M1 "Betty" bombers of the Kanoya *kokutai* arrived over the Nichols area and dropped 216 bombs of 132 pounds and sixteen 550 pounders, followed ten minutes later by twenty-six G3M2 Nells of the 1st *kokutai*, which unloaded 316 bombs of 132 pounds each. The three waves referred to by Krieger would be nine-place *buntai*s of one of the two *kokutai*s. Each *kokutai* reported that it had hit Nichols Field, but one of them in actuality missed Nichols "almost entirely" and dropped its load west of the field in the native villages and shacks near where Hanson and Krieger were sheltering (*Senshi Sosho* 24:192; Thorne narrative, p. 21).

10. The FEAF "Summary of Activities," contrary to Krieger's wartime narrative, records at 14:35 and 15:22 that the Legaspi recon mission did not get off because of lack of communications and the air raid.

11. Manony told war correspondent George Weller in February, 1942, while operating from Java, that he had seen "12 big bombers of the type hitting Cavite," "about 28 Zeros," and "a Lockheed transport" (Weller, "Luck to the Fighters," part 2, p. 45; Will Stevens, "Capt. Grattan Mahony, Most Chased Pilot in Far East," *Vallejo Times Herald*, Mar. 1, 1942). This was an exaggeration. Three hours before Mahony's attack, nine Zeros and six "Betty" bombers had landed at Legaspi, the first Japanese aircraft to occupy the field there (SRN 129,842, Dec. 14, 1941, 23:50).

12. In his flight log, Mahony indicated that he destroyed on the ground the transport plane, two "Betty" bombers, and two or three Zeros. Immediately following the attack by Mahony, the Japanese at the base reported that two Zeros and five "Betty" bombers had been hit and were damaged. Two days later they indicated that four of the nine Zeros had been damaged and were inoperative. Their earlier report did not acknowledge the combat between four of the Zeros and Mahony. Rather it mentioned that two Zeros were stationed directly above the base for protection, but they were very high up and "didn't discover the P-40" (Mahony flight log, December 13 [sic] 1941; SRN 129,842, Dec. 14, 1941, 23:50; SRN 129,868, Dec. 16, 1941). Evidently the Legaspi base, in order to save face, did not want to acknowledge the unequal yet unsuccessful combat with a single American plane.

13. To the eighteen Nakajima "Nates" of the 24th *sentai* based at Vigan from December 11 were added the next day several more "Nates" from the 50th *sentai* based at Aparri and some of the observation aircraft of the 10th *dokoritsu hikotai* on December 13. These were the planes spotted by Church during his recon mission (*Senshi Sosho* 34:372-74).

14. Strangely enough, there is absolutely no mention in the official Japanese war history or other sources of this devastating attack. A considerable number of "Nates," however, were lost in the period December 8, 1941-January 7, 1942, according to Japanese records, most on the ground, so some are probably accounted for by this attack.

15. The Japanese were apparently impressed with Church's bravery. Posten notes in his diary for January 7, 1942, that the Japanese "announced over the radio that they had buried a Lt. R. M. Church with full military honors."

CHAPTER 14

1. Coss's observation is quite curious. Three days earlier, about two thousand troops had disembarked from six transports, and after seizing the airfield, part of the landing force made rapid progress south. No troops were landing on December 13 (Dull, *Imperial Japanese Navy*, p. 30; Morton, *Fall of Philippines*, pp. 103-106).

2. At 1:00 P.M. on December 18, Mitsubishi Ki-30 "Ann" single-engine bombers hit Nichols Field (Japanese Monograph 11, p. 19).

3. Although McAfee recorded that he took over Nielson "yesterday" (i.e., December 11), and Brereton in his published diaries (p. 52) indicated that the move to McKinley occurred on December 12, more authoritative is the entry of December 14, 08:07 A.M., in the FEAF "Summary of Activities," where it is recorded that the movement of FEAF Headquarters to McKinley was made "this morning."

4. No aircraft were lost to Japanese attacks at Nielson during McAfee's tenure there (Dec. 14-24).

5. Four days earlier, Sutherland had instructed Sharp to arrange for reconnaissance missions in his command area "to determine all possible potential landing fields . . . capable of ready construction." The expected early arrival of large additional air reinforcements required the earliest possible provision

of such fields (Sutherland to Commanding General, Visayas-Mindanao Force, Dec. 16, 1941). With no capability for flying such recon missions, Sharp must have asked Sutherland for a suitable pilot.

6. The Japanese had learned of the existence of the Del Monte base from their interception of repeated USAFFE radio calls to Del Monte on December 11, requesting weather information. Bad weather had caused the postponement of earlier planned attacks by the Japanese. The four Zeros that shot up the base were from a detachment of the Tainan *kokutai*, based at Legaspi, 325 miles to the north (*Senshi Sosho* 24:247; SRN 129,961, Dec. 20, 1941, 23:50).

7. The timing of Brereton's request for dispersal of pursuit aircraft at Clark because of Japanese bombing attacks is difficult to understand. During the three days prior to his order, Clark Field was left unmolested by the Japanese Army and Navy Air Forces (Posten diary, Dec. 16–18; *Senshi Sosho*).

8. The FEAF had evidently based its assertion to Dyess on a message to USAFFE Headquarters from Lieutenant Colonel Manzano of the Engineers, Philippine Department, who had been informed by the chief civilian engineer for the Bataan area on the afternoon of December 13 that the field would be operational at noon on December 14 (Memo, Lt. Col. Narciso Manzano, Dec. 13, 1941; Engineer, USAFFE to Commanding General, FEAF, Dec. 16, 1941).

9. In his 1947 narrative Thorne recalled that a total of twenty-four revetments were being built, all for pursuit ships only, but Steele in his wartime diary indicated the number and kind of revetments as cited here (Thorne narrative, pp. 22–23; Steele diary, Dec. 19, 1941).

10. Crosby had apparently been attacked by a group of "Nates" that had strafed Nichols, Del Carmen, Cabanatuan, and Iba fields in the early afternoon of December 20 (*Senshi Sosho* 34:382).

11. The Japanese force actually landed at Lingayen at 4:45 A.M. (5:45 Japan time) to "almost no resistance" (SRN 130,013, Dec. 22, 1941, 05:50).

12. The Japanese planes were fourteen Kawasaki Ki-48 "Lily" twin-engine bombers, which hit Nichols at 7:30 A.M. from 15,000 feet (Japanese Monograph 11, p. 25).

13. It is likely that the B-17s expected were those that flew from Del Monte at 3:15 A.M. on December 23 on a mission to attack shipping in Lingayen Gulf. They had orders to land at San Marcelino, eighty miles south of Lingayen, after the attack, but apparently their original destination was to be Tanauan. At any rate, the pilots refused to land at San Marcelino "due to the prevalence of enemy pursuit in the vicinity." One ended up landing at San Jose, Mindoro, and the rest put down at Ambon Island, all the way south in the Dutch East Indies (19th Bomb Group Diary, p. 10).

CHAPTER 15

1. Gillett recalls that only he and one of the other pilots got off, but Stinson in 1943 and Japanese records indicate that all four were in the attack (Stinson/Priestley 1943 interview; *Senshi Sosho* 24:277).

2. These were from the Tainan *kokutai* attachment based at Legaspi to the south, who were patrolling over Lamon Bay. (SRN 130,314, Dec. 27, 1941).

3. Stinson and Gies both recorded that Anderson and Gillett each shot down a Zero, while Gillett recalls that he definitely got one. Japanese records, however, indicate that only one Zero was lost in the dogfight (Gies diary, Dec. 25, 1941; Stinson/Priestley 1943 interview; SRN 130,314, Dec. 27, 1941).

4. It is not known how many P-40s were in commission at Nichols, but there could not have been more than two or three, considering the number at Clark that day (ten?) and the total number (twelve) reported at Lubao and on Bataan on December 31. (Memo, Captain Mamerow, Headquarters, 5th Interceptor Command, to Commanding General, USAFFE, Dec. 31, 1941).

5. The USAFFE Engineer, Brig. Gen. Hugh Casey, had assigned 1st Lt. Thomas H. Delamore of his command the responsibility for wrecking Nichols and Nielson fields, including the hangars and any out-of-commission aircraft (USAFFE Engineer, "Summary of Directions with Respect to Demolition," Dec. 31, 1941).

6. The Lamon Bay force did not reach Tanauan until December 28 or 29. See Morton, *The Fall of the Philippines*, p. 195. The evacuation train did not show up until the next day (Chunn 1942 interview of Ellis).

7. Rowland was at Nichols, where he reported in after his crash into Laguna de Bay early in the afternoon.

8. At midnight on December 24, veteran pilot Pappy Gunn flew out Lt. Col. Charles Caldwell, Lt. Col. Les Maitland, Maj. Bill Hipps, Capt. Louis Hobbs, and Lt. Wade Hampton in a Beech 18, and Capt. Harold Slingsby flew out five others in the other Beech 18. These planes were apparently the ones intended for the pursuit pilots (Kenney, *Saga of Pappy Gunn*, pp. 34–35; "The 27th Reports").

9. In a 1943 interview, Milt Woodside of the 20th Pursuit indicated that eighteen P-40s and three P-35As were flown out, and Dyess in the same year recalled twenty-five in all, but these numbers seem excessive. Sheppard/Gilmore recalled "about 15 P-40Bs, P-40Es, P-35As, and an A-27," which seems a likely number, since on the morning of December 22 there were only twelve flyable P-40s at Clark and Sheppard and Rowland each lost one on December 22 and 24, respectively (Priestley 1943 interviews of Woodside and of Dyess; Sheppard/Gilmore statement).

10. It is likely the P-40 is the one that Pete Warden flew to Nichols Field on December 24 from the Air Depot at Quezon City, outside Manila, the first of four the depot saved after the Bataan evacuation order (Fellows to Edmonds, Jan. 14, 1947).

11. Brereton had informed MacArthur just before his evacuation to Australia on December 24 that pursuit aircraft could be transferred to the Philippines from Australia by hopping from Darwin to Koepang (Timor), thence to Makassar, Balikpapan, and Tarakan, and finally into Del Monte (Memo, Brereton to Commanding General, USAFFE, "Plan of Employment, FEAF," Dec. 24, 1941).

CHAPTER 16

1. Kiser's count was way off—only twenty-four transports brought the Lamon Bay landing force (Morton, *Fall of the Philippines,* p. 140).

2. This Mitsubishi F1M floatplane was from the seaplane carrier *Mizuho,* which was maintaining an aerial cover for the Lamon Bay force (Japanese Monograph 80, p. 15).

3. The only Type 96 "Claudes" operating in the Philippines at the time were off the carrier *Ryujo,* but on this day it was supporting the Jolo landings far to the south, off the western extremity of Mindanao (Dull, *Imperial Japanese Navy,* p. 33).

4. Unknown to them, these Japanese planes were not navy but rather army bombers—twin-engine "Sally" aircraft—which were not flying the same schedule as their navy counterparts. They bombed Mariveles on this day when the navy bombers were taking a few days off (Japanese Monograph No. 11, p. 30).

5. In his diary, Steele does not identify the field on Bataan from which he flew as Orani, but it appears to be the only candidate.

6. In his report on depot activities, Dick Fellows records that two of the P-40Es the depot was getting into commission at Quezon City were flown to Bataan on December 27, and the last one on January 1. An aircraft status report for December 31 indicates that two P-40s were being overhauled in the Manila area, most likely the same aircraft. In his report, John Lester notes that Pete Warden of the depot flew one of the P-40s to Pilar. It is assumed that the other two were flown to Pilar also, but at a later date than December 27. There were no planes at Pilar on December 28, according to Posten and Cowboy Wright.

7. This request may have been in response to information received by Major Vance, air officer on Corregidor, when he was apprised by 1st Lt. Tom Gerrity of the abandonment of aircraft at Clark following the evacuation into Bataan (The 27th Reports, p. 39).

8. In 1978 Stanford recalled that five P-40s were put in operational condition, but a 1943 interview of one of the pilots involved indicated two P-40s and one P-35A were salvaged (Stanford 1978 narrative; Priestley 1943 interview of Woodside).

9. It is not known to which airstrip the planes were flown. Most likely they were taken to Lubao, where Sneed had led the aircraft evacuated from Clark on December 24.

10. Assuming that the "two wounded airmen" were Wagner and Bruce, a PATWING 10 pilot recalls the evacuation story in slightly different version. See Messimer, *In the Hands of Fate,* pp. 181–84.

11. Dyess in his wartime memoir (*The Dyess Story*) indicated that there were eighteen P-40s and that half were to go to Pilar and half to Orani. The number of P-40s seems too high—Orani Field already had a few P-40s at the time. In his wartime diary Rowe wrote that *all* the P-40s were to go to Pilar, but a few definitely went to Orani to supplement those already operating from that field.

12. One of the original six P-35As would not start and was destroyed by

several enlisted men of the 21st Pursuit still at the field (Rowe diary, Jan. 2, 1942; Ammons interview, Apr. 1, 1980).

13. Evidence suggests that it was Company C of the 803rd Aviation Engineers that fired on Wyatt and Krantz (J. White narrative, p. 2).

CHAPTER 17

1. Later, as a POW of the Japanese, Ed Dyess was informed by a Japanese pilot that Stone had killed "his squadron leader" in the attack (*Dyess Story*, p. 146). This fact is corroborated by the official Japanese history of the Pacific War, which indicates the Japanese was CO of the 74th *dokoritsu chutai* (Independent Flying Squadron), which had recently been transferred to Cabanatuan (*Senshi Sosho* 34:397).

2. According to Obert, Steele, and Posten, but Ind and Lester indicate that only half were scheduled to go to Mindanao (Ind, *Bataan: Judgment Seat*, pp. 216–17; Lester report, p. 5).

3. This composition has been compiled from information on pilots at Bataan Field in early January. Inclusion of Ben Brown of the 34th Pursuit and four 17th Pursuit pilots (Posten, Rowe, Stone, and Glover) cited in the Obert statement (p. 6) would appear erroneous.

4. One group of nine G3M "Nells" hit Mariveles at 1:03 P.M., the other of forty-four G4M "Betties" bombed Corregidor at 1:30 P.M. (Sutherland, "Brief Summary," Jan. 4, 1942; Braly log, Jan. 4, 1942).

5. The flying boats were a detachment from the *Toko kokutai*, based at Palau to the east of the Philippines.

6. The Zeros were from the 3rd *kokutai*, based at Davao. In their operations report, the Japanese recorded for December 24 that the unit had "chased and repelled one fighter" (SRN 130,314, Dec. 27, 1941).

7. Bob Newman had returned to Pilar in his P-40 after his aborted attempt to reach Mindanao.

8. Curiously enough, another field—Pilar No. 2—was still under construction by the 803rd Engineers. By January 17, the runway had been built to a length of 7,500 feet, and by January 24 it was declared operational. Two days later, however, it had to be abandoned, at the conclusion of the "Abucay withdrawal" operation on that date (Engineer Operations, Week Ending Jan. 17, Jan. 24, and Jan. 31, 1942; Morton, *The Fall of the Philippines*, p. 291).

9. To cover up the fact that a flyable aircraft was wantonly destroyed, the S-3 report for the day recorded that it was destroyed because it was "not flyable" (S-3 Report No. 8, 5th Interceptor Command, Jan. 8, 1942).

10. The Zeros were from the 3rd *kokutai*, based at Davao. Three had attacked Cagayan on January 11, curiously, with "no results" reported (*Senshi Sosho* 24:312; SRN 131,025, Jan. 16, 1942).

CHAPTER 18

1. The three-stacker was the Japanese light cruiser *Kuma*, engaged in operations protecting the departure of minesweepers from Subic Bay. An in-

tercepted Japanese communication mentions the planes of the *Kuma* engaging "three enemy planes," without acknowledging the loss of one of their aircraft (SRN 131,202, Jan. 19, 1942).

2. Added to the two original P-40s (Brownewell's and Feallock's) were the six that made it down from Bataan Field on January 4. Benson, however, had wiped one out, and Feallock had damaged his (Rowe diary, Jan. 20, 1942).

3. Benson was subsequently hospitalized at Iloilo, Panay, until February, when he left to become a member of the staff of Brig. Gen. Bradford Chynoweth, commanding general of the Visayan Force (Chynoweth statement).

4. Stinson refers to them as Zeros in his postwar narrative, as does the S-3 report and the Lester report, but no Zeros were operational in the Philippines at this time. They must have been Nakajima Ki-27 "Nates" of the 50th *sentai*, a *chutai* (nine planes) of which was based at Clark Field at this time. Stinson recalls, however, that they did not have a fixed landing gear, but the "Nate" did. Curiously enough, there is no mention of this dogfight in the volume of the official Japanese history of the Pacific War that covers IJAAF operations in the Bataan campaign (Stinson, July 19, 1978; *Senshi Sosho* 34:400).

5. A pilot of the 50th *sentai*, 2nd Lt. Noboru Mune, is credited with a P-40 over Bataan in January 1942—he may have been the one who shot down Anderson (Izawa and Hata, *Japanese Army Fighter Units*, p. 307). No other P-40s were lost to "Nates" in the Bataan campaign in January 1942, except for that of Percy Ramsey on January 5.

6. According to Japanese records, no 50th *sentai* pilots were killed on this date (Izawa and Hata, ibid.). It is possible the planes crashed and the pilots were rescued by the Japanese behind their lines.

7. Anderson's body fell behind enemy lines and was never recovered.

8. Obert recalls Ben Brown of the 34th and Earl Stone of the 17th as members of the detachment at this time too, but Rowe's diary indicates they arrived only on January 23.

CHAPTER 19

1. The Japanese force had landed further south than intended, and their position was apparently unknown to their headquarters at Moron, up the coast of western Bataan.

2. A navy PT boat had intercepted some Japanese landing boats just off Agloloma Bay, resulting in a "small scale naval engagement." It was reported that "machine guns and rifles from the beach" joined in shooting at the Japanese boats (J. V. Collier, Asst. G-3, G-3 Information Bulletin, 4:45 P.M., Jan. 23, 1942). The men of the 34th Pursuit Squadron on beach defense, however, do not recall this incident today.

3. Another version, related in 1946 by one of the squadron's men, has Brezina cut down by fire from the Japanese machine gun as he moved forward with hand grenades (letter of Edsall to Mrs. Brezina, Oct. 2, 1946). When Brezina

was killed, the Filipinos in his patrol abandoned him and would not tell the Americans what had happened (Chunn 1942 interview of Crosby).

CHAPTER 20

1. These boats were evidently heading for Anyasan/Silaiim, where landings were later made that evening.

2. The Japanese official war history claims that the three Ki-30 "Anns" of the 16th *sentai* shot down one of the attacking two P-40s for the loss of only one of their planes (*Senshi Sosho* 34:401).

3. Reports received later from Filipino sources in Manila indicated that fourteen Japanese aircraft at Nielson and Nichols had been destroyed and seventy Japanese killed. The official internal Japanese report of the attack, however, mentioned only that in two attacks by four U.S. fighters on the city of Manila, no damage had been sustained. To the Filipino population, the Japanese announced that innocent women and children had been killed, not indicating that the raid was limited to the two airfields only, and threatened that if the "brutal" pilots were caught, they would be executed (Obert diary, p. 10; Grashio, *Return to Freedom*, p. 20; SRN 132,001, Feb. 3, 1942; Rowe diary, Feb. 1, 1942).

4. Krieger narrative, p. 27; Rowe diary, February 3, 1942. Krieger evidently reported in at Bataan Field on February 1, though the date of his arrival is not recorded anywhere.

5. Evidently John Vogel was also evacuated on this flight. He had been on Mindanao since arriving at Del Monte on January 4 with Cole and the other Pilar pilots from Bataan. Of the four pilots then on Mindanao who had flown there from Pilar on January 4 (Roberts, Vogel, Cole and Steele), only Roberts was not selected for the January 26 evacuation.

6. Wilson Glover's diary excludes Posten and Stone but includes Shorty Crosland of the 34th Pursuit, but he did not arrive at Bataan Field until February 3 (Rowe diary, Feb. 3, 1942). In a wartime interview, Grashio indicated that Posten and Stone flew with him (Edmonds interview of Grashio and Donahoe, Apr. 2, 1945).

7. Glover's diary and Grashio's wartime interview also cite Andy Krieger as flying the mission, but he is not listed in the Silver Star citation for the eight who did fly.

8. Japanese records confirm the devastation caused by the P-40s. About 350 of the 700 Japanese of the Kimura detachment being carried in the thirteen barges were estimated to have been killed as a result of the air attack (Provan to Stinson correspondence, in Stinson to author, Aug. 18, 1978).

CHAPTER 21

1. They had also beaten off another Japanese seaborne landing attempt in the Quinauan area in the early evening of February 1, forcing the Japanese barges north to the Anyasan area (History, 3rd Battalion, 45th Philippine Scouts, pp. 11–12; Hilton to Edmonds, Mar. 10, 1947, p. 2).

2. There is disagreement over the number of men in each boat. In a 1947

letter Hilton implied there were seven, Parcher in 1942 recalled eight, Joe Ward in 1986 recalled nine, and Dyess in his 1944 book indicated ten.

CHAPTER 22

1. Neither Grashio nor Stinson recollect this mission today, but it appears from the S-3 report on the mission that they did participate, as the report mentions five combat sorties flown (5th Interceptor Command, S-3 Report No. 38, Feb. 7/8, 1942).

2. This must have been one assigned to the 76th *dokoritsu chutai*, which operated "Dinahs" during the Philippines campaign.

3. It had indeed spotted the Americans. The USAFFE radio intelligence unit on Bataan intercepted radio communications between the Ki-46 and a Japanese ground base in which the "Dinah" reported four enemy fighters over Limay (Howard Brown, SRH-045, p. 38).

4. The USAFFE unit had just radioed Lunde that Clark Field had sent six fighters to intercept the P-40s and the Stearman sixteen minutes after the unit had intercepted the P-40 report from the "Dinah" (Howard Brown, SRH-145, p. 38).

5. Stone's plane and body were never found. He is believed to have crashed into Mount Mariveles (Brown 1944 statement). A few days later, a search party found the wreckage of a Japanese fighter in a deep gulch next to Mount Mariveles, bits scattered over hundreds of feet of jungle. The pilot's body lay nearby. This was evidently the plane pursuing Stone, which had met a similar fate (Ind, *Bataan*, pp. 292, 295; Posten diary, Feb. 14, 1942; Rowe diary, Feb. 13, 1942).

6. Japanese records indicate that six Nakajima "Nates" of the 50th *sentai* (not Zeros, as reported by most American accounts) engaged the P-40s this day. They were responding to a report of the reconnaissance plane that had spotted the P-40s (and evidently the 76D3). One "Nate" piloted by the *shotai* leader, Second Lieutenant Kanamaru, force-landed his ship at Pilar strip after suffering hits by the P-40s and was subsequently destroyed by artillery fire. Another, piloted by Sergeant Kurosawa, never returned. (This would be the "Nate" that crashed at Mariveles.) There were no other losses, although the aircraft of Sergeant Major Nakaue was slightly damaged The Japanese claimed three P-40s shot down (not including Stone; Diary of Anabuki, Feb. 9, 1942, via Yasuho Izawa, Dec. 10, 1984; Izawa and Hata, *Japanese Army Fighter Units*, p. 132).

7. The 1,500-ton U.S. Army-chartered *Don Esteban* had been attacked by three Japanese aircraft off of Mamburao, just south of Paluan Bay. Machine gun fire ignited gasoline in its cargo, forcing the crew to abandon ship. By the time the crew reached shore, the ship had become engulfed in flames. It was carrying a cargo of foodstuffs loaded at Iloilo and Cebu City (Underbrink, *Destination Corregidor*, p. 150).

8. The other men were S. Sgt. Robert D. Pannier, Sgts. Charles E. Stafford and Hyman Bernstein, Cpl. Carroll Ferguson, and Pfc Ernest Essen (USAFFE General Order No. 40, Mar. 13, 1942).

CHAPTER 23

1. Grashio's armorer, Sgt. Al Sly, recalls the problem as other than cited here in the 5th Interceptor Command report—Grashio had not pushed the bomb release handle forward all the way to the bomb release point (author's interview of Sly, May 9, 1986, and Sly correspondence, July 1986; *Pilots Manual for Curtiss P-40 Warhawk*, pp. 7, 19).

2. Evidently the telephone call that General George had received that morning suggesting he take whatever action he wished against the Subic Bay buildup was not from Sutherland's office, as George had thought, but from George's own S-2 office, relaying a message from his executive officer to George. (Ind, *Bataan*, pp. 320–21).

3. A navy observer at Signal Hill reported on March 3 as sunk or damaged: one 10,000-ton vessel, blown up; one 18,000-ton vessel, set afire and still burning; one 8,000-ton vessel, caught on fire from vessel or dock adjacent to it; and two motor cruisers, about 100 tons each, sunk (USAFFE G-2 Journal, Mar. 3, 1942, 8:15 P.M.). Japanese records, however, indicate only a 385-ton converted subchaser as sunk or damaged (*Imperial Japanese Navy in World War II*, Japanese Monograph No. 116). Just before the attack, four supply ships and a 300-foot tanker were reported entering Subic Bay—the ships hit were evidently these (USAFFE G-2 Journal, Mar. 2, 1942, Message No. 860).

4. The Zeros were part of the nine plane *buntai* of the Tainan *kokutai*, based at Legaspi.

5. In his 1943 report on Philippine Air Depot operations, then Major Dick Fellows indicated that the shipment of the two propellers "never reached their destination" (p. 30). Since this statement was obviously not based on personal knowledge—in fact two P-40s were in commission in mid-March—the propellers must have been received.

6. A member of the Provisional Mobile Unit (S. Sgt. Richard D. Hough) recorded in his diary that Warden shot the "Mavis" down, and a fellow officer at the depot during the Manila period had been informed he did (Hoffman, Sept. 7, 1986, to author), but the diary of John Geer indicates Warden did not. Warden is not credited with such a victory in 5th Air Force records.

7. After the war, it was found that Hughett, Fralick, and the sergeants were POWs of the Japanese in French Indochina, where they had come ashore in the boat. Hughett indicated that the engine of the launch quit in the sea and they were blown out of sight of land by the next morning. Deciding not to return to Bataan, as the wind was blowing in the wrong direction, and fearful of the coast defense guns, they made a crude sail and set out for China, then shifted course for Indochina instead, arriving about three weeks later. They were turned over to the Japanese by the French officers who met them on landing (Posten diary, Mar. 20, 1942; Hughett round-robin letter, 1982; Hughett to author, Apr. 17, 1981).

8. There is no documentation that the first flight of the Duck took place on this date, but in reconstructing the subsequent flights of the amphibian and its pilots, it can be deduced that it took place at this time if we accept

Moore's assertion that he made three round-trips in the Duck. (Toland interview of Moore).

9. Squadron mates Stinson and Woodside in 1943 interviews stated that White and Cocanougher were taken south in the Duck's *first* flight, but the evidence suggests it was rather during the Duck's second mission (Priestley 1943 interviews of Stinson and Woodside).

10. Selected from the 20th Pursuit were Lloyd Stinson, Randy Keator, Percy Ramsey, Jack Gates, Jim Fossey, Jim Mullen, Bill Akins, Fred Siler, and Max Halverson (Keator diary, Mar. 24, 1942; Moore to author, May 18, 1979). Kiefer White was down on Mindanao at the time, where he was eating well to get in shape. Called back from Cabcaben were John Posten and Andy Krieger (Posten diary, Mar. 27, 1942). From the 34th Pursuit were Stewart Robb, W. G. Coleman, Shorty Crosland, and one other (Robb statement, p. 34; W. G. Coleman to Glover, Jan. 28, 1943). Pilots already at Bataan Field included Ed Dyess, Dave Obert, Bill Rowe, Wilson Glover, Gus Williams, John McCown, Sam Grashio, John Burns, Ben Brown, and Tom Gerrity (Rowe diary, Mar. 27, 1942; Gerrity diary, Mar. 26, 1942; Obert diary, p. 29; Williams 1978 taped narrative).

11. Unknown to the pilots, the Japanese had begun their second Bataan offensive on March 16. From March 24, the newly arrived 60th and 62nd *sentai* of the Japanese Army Air Force, flying Ki-21 "Sally" bombers, reinforced by G3M twin-engine "Nell" bombers of the Japanese Navy, went into action against Bataan and Corregidor (Japanese Monograph No. 11, pp. 43–45; Okumiya to author, Apr. 27, 1977).

CHAPTER 24

1. Five nights earlier, Kiefer White and Harold Cocanougher had been sent south on the Duck to bring back two new P-40s, but the first one was not even assembled until March 30. In the event, White and Cocanougher never returned to Bataan.

2. In his wartime diary, Bill Rowe recorded that it was Donalson rather than Williams who flew the recon with McCown this day, but Williams clearly recalls he was the pilot (Williams taped 1978 narrative).

3. On March 22, nine A6M2s were detached from the Tainan *kokutai* based at Den Pasar in the Dutch East Indies and transferred to Clark Field for escorting bombers attacking Bataan and Corregidor (Izawa and Hata, *Japanese Navy Fighter Units*, p. 104).

4. John Brownewell, Bill Feallock, and John Geer were the pilots who transferred the P-40s that morning (Geer diary, Apr. 8, 1942).

5. Grashio recalls that Dyess had told him that it was Williams rather than McCown who had aborted the mission that day (phone call from Grashio, Oct. 27, 1986), but Williams maintains it was McCown. No S-3 report is available that could resolve the disagreement.

6. Although there is no information indicating so, it is assumed that after "Kibosh" was landed at Cabcaben in the morning, it was subsequently flown back to Bataan Field, since it was there in the early evening of April 8.

7. There was reportedly only *one* Duck at Mariveles on January 5 (see

chapter 23), but a second one had apparently been shot up by the Japanese on that date too.

8. Kennard had started out late for Cabcaben from Little Baguio and found the road blocked with retreating troops and civilians. He saw it would be impossible to reach the field with Churchill at the agreed takeoff time for the Duck and tried to call Barnick at Cabcaben to tell him to take off without them but was put through to Bataan Field instead and was told that both fields were being evacuated (Kennard 1945 interview for Edmonds).

9. Donalson's account of the crash landing given here is at odds with that of Dick Fellows, who was at Iloilo at the time. According to Fellows, who heard the unmistakable sound of the P-40's Allison engine overhead between 9:00 and 10:00 P.M., Donalson opted to land through barricades at Manduriao Field instead of going to Santa Barbara Field, some seven miles west of Iloilo, and thus wiped out the P-40 (Fellows to author, Sept. 14, 1986).

10. A few days later, Bill Cummings flew in to Iloilo with the necessary parts so the P-40 could be flown out of Iloilo, but when he arrived, "Kibosh" was burning. Someone had set it on fire (author's interview of Cummings, Mar. 30, 1980).

CHAPTER 25

1. Stinson, Gates, and Fossey in Dyess's group do not recall a plan to fly the pilots south but do remember one to take them out by submarine (Stinson to author, Nov. 23, 1986; Gates to author, Aug. 4, 1986; Fossey to author, Oct. 2, 1986). Grashio maintains, however, that B-17s were due in for them (Grashio to author, Aug. 20, 1986).

2. The nurses were from Hospital No. 2 and had missed their originally assigned boat when they reached Mariveles only at daybreak. They were later assigned another boat, evidently that originally intended for Dyess's group (Schultz, *Hero of Bataan*, pp. 240, 246).

3. The submarine *Seadragon* arrived off Corregidor at 8:53 P.M. on April 8, boarded twenty-one passengers, then cleared the area at 9:29, evidently because of the situation on Bataan (USS *Seadragon*, Report of War Patrol No. 2, Apr. 26, 1942, p. 5). This was apparently the submarine intended to pick up the twenty pilots. Another submarine, the USS *Snapper*, arrived off Corregidor on April 9 at 10:32 P.M. and left later that night at 12:55 A.M. with twenty-five passengers (USS *Snapper*, Report of War Patrol No. 2, Apr. 25, 1942, p. A-11). Evidently since Gehrig and Armstrong had made arrangements for flying out of Corregidor that and the following evenings (see chapter 27), they were not considered for the *Snapper* evacuation (Armstrong to author, Aug. 8, 1986).

4. During the three-day period the men of the 34th were in the concentration area, Captain Wray and the other officers with him came straggling in. They evidently did not get very far down the road before the Japanese pulled them out of their cars.

5. Two of the enlisted men from another group found a banca, however, and made it to Mindoro, where they were subsequently captured (Chunn 1942 interview of Ellis; diary of Stewart).

CHAPTER 26

1. The floatplanes were from the seaplane tender *Sanuki Maru*, which had been ordered south from Manila Bay to support Japanese landings on Cebu. After the initial attack on PT 34 at 7:30 A.M., the aircraft returned at 11:40 to find the hapless boat stranded off Cauit Island, whence it had taken refuge, and destroyed it (War Diary of the Sanuki Maru, Apr. 9, 1942; Bulkley, *At Close Quarters*, pp. 24–25)

2. Obert's action was observed from the ground. A subsequent report indicated that the P-40's bomb fell about a mile inland from the cruiser, whose tow lines had parted. Earlier the cruiser had put a prize crew aboard the vessel, the M/S *Katapunan*, anchored in a cove off Tagaloan, and was attempting to tow it away after its Filipino crew had put it out of commission (Col. Melville S. Creusere, "QMC Report," p. 38, n.d.).

3. Bradford's flight log indicates that he flew the Beech into Iloilo on April 9, leaving the following day for Del Monte, but on April 9 the Beech was fully occupied evacuating Lunde and Keator and before daylight the following morning had been flown into Cebu. It is thus assumed Bradford flew the Beech into Iloilo on April 10.

4. The version of the dogfight incident as reported in the war diary of the seaplane tender *Sanuki Maru* is quite different from that of Putnam. According to the former, at 12:30 P.M. the P-40 made its first attack and dropped bombs (evidently on the troopship) at an altitude of 2,400 feet after diving from 4,500 feet, about seventeen miles southwest of Cebu City. Putnam was sighted by two "Pete" floatplanes patrolling nearby from the *Sanuki Maru*. The "Petes" chased the P-40, which went into a cloud at 3,600 feet after it had reversed its course after the attack. Putnam then came out of the cloud for a second attack, but on the third pass he was met head-on at 12:44 P.M. by a "Pete" piloted by Kyooi Takayasa at 4,000 feet as Putnam was beginning a dive. Machine gun fire was exchanged, and the P-40 went into a dive and crashed. The "Pete" took three hits but returned safely at 1:15 P.M. to the *Sanuki Maru*. Its fuel tank was destroyed, but the plane was repaired (War Diary of the *Sanuki Maru*, map and entry of Apr. 10, 1942, 13:44 and 14:15 hours, Tokyo time).

Clearly, Putnam did not down two "Petes," only damaging one of them, nor did the "Pete" shoot down the P-40. There was no American witness to Putnam's combat with the floatplanes who could verify one version or the other of the incident. In 1979, Putnam maintained to the writer that the description of his combat that day as reported by Roosevelt der Tatevision, ghostwriter of the Scott book in which Putnam's story was published, was correct.

5. Japanese records compiled after the war do not indicate any combatant or noncombatant ships damaged or sunk in the Cebu area in April, 1942.

6. On "April 10 or thereafter," John Brownewell was ordered to Iloilo to take over command from Putnam. Brownewell apparently arrived on the morning of April 11 and remained only two days before being ordered back to Mindanao (Brownewell, Journal).

7. Putnam gives the date as Sunday, April 12, but also notes that it was

the day after his Cebu "one-man war" mission, which would put it at April 11 (Putnam, *Damned to Glory,* p. 113).

8. In a 1945 interview, Royce indicated that arrangements were made to disperse the B-25s at "three different airfields" [*sic*] but did not explain why he refused to move his more valuable B-17s, including his own aircraft, to a more secure field (Royce interview, Mar. 10, 1945).

9. The B-25s were Col. Robert Strickland's flight that had spent the evening at Del Monte No. 3 and was now returning to the Maramag base as per orders after having attacked shipping and dockside targets at Cebu City with the other five B-25s at 6:10 A.M. (Alcorn, "The Grim Reapers," p. 8; War Diary of the *Sanuki Maru,* Apr. 12, 1942).

10. Geer's diary, however, records that it was seriously damaged by a single floatplane (Geer diary, Apr. 12, 1942).

11. The others were Lt. Col. Arthur Fischer, carrying vital quinine seeds; Col. Charles Backes, CO of the Philippine AAC; and 1st Lt. Howard W. Brown, of the Signal Corps (Brown, SRH-045, p. 47).

12. Four "Pete" floatplanes from the seaplane tender *Sanuki Maru* had left the Cebu area at 3:45 A.M. to attack the Del Monte base (War Diary of the *Sanuki Maru,* Apr. 13, 1942, entry for 04:45, Tokyo time).

13. Brownewell's victim was a Mitsubishi F1M "Pete" from the seaplane tender *Sanuki Maru,* piloted by Susumu Hiromara, that the seaplane tender reported as lost on the 5:20 attack of Del Monte (War Diary of the *Sanuki Maru,* Apr. 13, 1942, entry for 09:30, Tokyo time).

14. Cocanougher's name was also dropped from the list. He was twenty-ninth on the list of thirty scheduled for evacuation and had given all his goods away when he got word he was being bumped.

15. Tex Marble of the 17th was on Corregidor, and Ed Dyess of the 21st and Robert Wray of the 34th were in Japanese hands on Luzon.

CHAPTER 27

1. Gehrig recalls being ordered back to Corregidor with Randolph to face the accusation of having taken the two 76D3s without authorization, but Randolph and Kennard maintain that they were cleared of the charges on Mindanao and were ordered back for the special mission only.

2. The citations for the medals for this flight indicate takeoff on April 9, but the date is clearly incorrect.

3. The more modern Beechcraft Staggerwing had been destroyed four days earlier at Malaybalay by Japanese floatplanes, so the Bellanca was now the last survivor of the Bamboo Fleet (Rowe diary, Apr. 15, 1942; author's interview of Lunde, Apr. 2, 1980).

4. In a 1944 Army Air Force interview, however, and again in a 1980 interview with the author, three years before his death at eighty-eight years of age, Bradford maintained that he had not done so; he had drawn equally with the others (Bradford interview for Edmonds, Mar. 27, 1944; author's interview of Bradford, Mar. 30, 1980).

5. At least three of the Bataan pilots indicate that the list was revised

at the last moment to accommodate more senior officers (Keator diary, p. 72; William 1978 taped narrative; Krieger interview for Edmonds, Feb. 21, 1945). It is not clear by what authority the Del Monte brass felt it could countermand orders issued by higher-level officers in Australia.

6. On arrival at Batchelor Field, Darwin, at 7:30 the next morning, the evacuees noticed a wrecked C-40 transport on the runway. They were shocked to learn that General George had been fatally injured the night before when a P-40 in taking off had crashed into the transport. Fragments had hit him while he was standing near it before takeoff (Geer diary, Apr. 30, 1942; Obert diary, p. 42; Elsmore retrospective diary, Apr. 30, 1942).

CHAPTER 28

1. Still remaining on Corregidor were 1st Lt. George Armstrong, who had missed all his chances to leave, and 2nd Lt. Frankie Bryant, assigned to a Coast Artillery battery on the Rock. Another pursuit pilot who had made it to Corregidor earlier, 2nd Lt. Bob Krantz of the 17th Pursuit, had been fatally wounded on April 13 by Japanese artillery fire while assigned to the 91st Coast Artillery.

2. Apparently the mission originally scheduled for that morning had been called off by Sharp.

3. The "Nates" were from the six-plane 84th *dokoritsu chutai* of the army air force, detached to the Philippines for the period April–May, 1942, to defend the Japanese-held islands in the Philippines (Yasushi Ushijima, "Japanese Warhawk").

4. This aircraft may have been the LB-30 piloted by Captain Mueller on the last planned rescue flight to Mindanao, this time to take out the stranded nurses and other passengers of the PBY flight from Lake Lanao. On the evening of May 6, he had circled Del Monte as usual, but when no field lights came on, he proceeded to Maramag and Valencia fields. No lights were turned on there either—or at least none were seen by Mueller. (Crosland recalls that lights were put out on the highway next to Maramag field [Crosland to author, Oct. 28, 1987].) After flying over the other subbases at Malaybalay and Anakan with no signals, Mueller started back to Australia, although he was too low on gas after the three-hour search over Mindanao to make it all the way back. He crash-landed at Yu Island in the Dutch East Indies, a preselected site for such an eventuality (Capt. Paul Cool, "Adventure over—and on—the Pacific," *Detroit Free Press*, Oct. 25, 1942).

5. The Japanese had inspected the Alligator Club pilots' quarters of the Maramag base.

6. Evidently the distributor caps of the two P-40s, thrown into a toilet before the surrender, had since been retrieved and put back on the aircraft. An enlisted man recalls P-40 parts being fished out of a toilet at Valencia Field just before the surrender (Young to author, July 31, 1979).

7. It has not been possible to identify the two pilots with Sneed. One was probably Wilson Glover, to fly the older P-40, which, according to Ushijima, was "his" aircraft. The other may have been John Valkenaar, who before the war served with the 20th Pursuit in the Philippines but was subsequently

transferred to the 19th Bombardment Group. Both Shorty Crosland and Ed Erickson, the other candidates, indicate they did not fly the aircraft to Malaybalay. Ushijima referred to one of the pilots as "2nd Lt. A" (flying the Stearman) and the other as "2nd Lt. B" (flying the old P-40E). Ushijima does not indicate any problem in securing the agreement of the three pilots to fly the aircraft for the Japanese. In his account he emphasized rather the excellent personal relations between the former adversaries. Nevertheless, one wonders if the Japanese threatened dire consequences if the Americans did not acquiesce to the request.

8. Erickson maintains that pressure was put on Sharp, but the circumstances appear lost to history.

9. Ushijima indicates in his narrative that *he* flew the biplane to Nichols, but both Crosland and Erickson maintain that it was Valkenaar who did, not the Japanese. Ushijima also incorrectly reported that Sneed and "Lt. B" took the P-40s to Nichols from Davao, after flying them to Davao from Malaybalay.

10. In his narrative Ushijima refers to only one Ki-46 as an escort, but Erickson and Crosland each recall that three aircraft escorted them, though they could not identify the type. They were apparently "Dinahs" of either the 74th or 76th *dokoritsu chutai*, each unit operating in the Philippines at the time. Crosland recalls them, however, as single-engine two-place ships, with a machine gunner in the rear seat (Crosland to author, Oct. 28, 1987).

11. The two P-40s were subsequently flown by Japanese pilots from Nichols to Clark Field and then on to Japan.

Epilogue

1. The Japanese had also committed the light carrier *Ryujo* to the initial offensive against the Philippines, but it was assigned to attack the Davao area of Mindanao to the south, not Luzon. The *Ryujo* carried a force of twenty-two outmoded Mitsubishi A5M4 "Claude" fighters and sixteen Nakajima "Kate" level bombers (Brown, *Carrier Operations in World War II* 2:25).

2. In a May, 1942, evaluation of the P-40's capabilities, Buzz Wagner informed the air force that the P-40 "at medium altitude, 10,000 to 18,000 feet, is considered an excellent anti-bombardment fighter," but "above 18,000 feet, its performance is sluggish. Rate of climb is considered too low at all altitudes and wing loading is too high to maneuver with Japanese fighters" (Memo to Headquarters, Pursuit Section, Northeastern Area, Townsville, Queensland, May 11, 1942).

3. As maintained by a senior pilot of the 17th Pursuit, "None of us spent significant time in devising us-vs.-them tactics or in realistic practice other than occasional dogfights, which, of course, were the wrong thing to practice" (Sheppard to author, Oct. 30, 1988).

4. Another of the squadrons received its P-40Es only days before hostilities began, but it had already gained experience in flying the aircraft before it was transferred to the Philippines.

Sources

This account of the experiences of American pursuit pilots in the Philippines campaign has been constructed from a myriad of sources. Indeed, a book could almost be written on the experiences of the writer in identifying, tracking down, and collecting any item that touched on the wartime or immediate prewar activities of the pursuit squadrons.

As a starting point, I worked with the materials that Walter D. Edmonds had assembled for his 1951 classic *They Fought with What They Had*, held at the Albert F. Simpson Historical Research Center of the U.S. Air Force at Maxwell Air Force Base, Alabama. Particularly valuable in this collection were the transcripts of the 1944–45 interviews by the USAF of many of the pursuit pilots and written statements and narratives several of them had prepared in 1944–47 of their experiences. Unavailable to Edmonds at the time he prepared his account were the records of General MacArthur's USAFFE command that had been flown out of Corregidor to Mindanao and on to Australia on April 13, 1942. These primary source materials were believed lost until they turned up in the collection of General MacArthur's papers donated by the general in 1960 on the occasion of the establishment of the MacArthur Memorial in Norfolk, Virginia. Particularly useful from the MacArthur Memorial archives in the preparation of this volume were the entries in the G-2 and G-3 journals on the reconnaissance missions flown by the pursuit pilots in December, 1941, and the S-3 reports of the 5th Interceptor Command covering missions flown during the Bataan period, January–April, 1942.

Other than these items, however, and the Far East Air Force's valuable war diary "Summary of Activities, 8 December 1941–24 February 1942," there are virtually no official contemporary accounts covering the operations of the pursuit pilots in the Philippines campaign. This absence of information is particularly severe for the period of the first two weeks of the campaign, when the only large-scale combat missions of the campaign were flown against the Japanese attackers. This is not surprising, given the suddenness of the Japanese onslaught and the chaotic conditions created among the defenders in the wake of the relentless assault.

To obtain a more complete picture of what happened, as well as to give a human dimension to the story, I endeavored from the start to learn of the individual experiences of as many of the surviving officers and enlisted men as I could via interviews and correspondence. Over the thirteen years from 1976 to 1989, interviews were held with 25 persons, correspondence exchanged with some 120 individuals (including surviving relatives of the deceased), and written and taped narratives for my use received from 23 survivors. Supplementing these personal accounts that relied on the memories of the participants were transcripts of interviews in 1942–43 in POW camps of fourteen pilots and two enlisted men by two POW infantry officers (Chunn and Priestley Papers, National Archives Record Group 407, Philippine Records). Most important, I was entrusted with the personal wartime diaries of nine of the pilots (Geer, Gies, Hennon, Keator, Obert, Posten, Powell, Rowe, and Steele) that had never before been made available to anyone attempting to write on this aspect of the Philippines campaign and that have served as the foundation of this story.

Japanese sources were indispensable for cross-checking the accuracy of American official and personal accounts. The volumes covering the Philippines campaign in the official Japanese war history, *Senshi Sosho* (in Japanese), were particularly useful in providing a detailed account of the intensive Japanese aerial attacks of December, 1941, and Japanese air operations during the Bataan period. Translations of intercepted Japanese naval messages (SRNs; National Archives Record Group 457) were also valuable in pinpointing particular aerial operations in the period between December, 1941, and January, 1942, as was the war diary of the *Sanuki Maru* (in Japanese) for Mindanao operations in April, 1942. Tapped also were accounts published in Japanese of several Japanese Naval and Army Air Force pilots who participated in the aerial attacks against the Philippines (Sakai, Yokoyama, Miza, Ushijima). Several of the IJNAF bomber and Zero pilots who flew in the Philippines campaign, including the late flying commander of the Tainan *kokutai*, Hideki Shingo, also kindly cooperated with me in this project by responding to my detailed questions on their experiences.

Material for the prewar section of the book was derived heavily from the letters sent from the Philippines by twenty-one of the pilots to family members and friends in the United States between November, 1940, and November, 1941. This period immediately before the attack of the Japanese on the Philippines is practically unknown to history, despite its importance for understanding the conditions under which the pursuit pilots entered the war.

ORAL HISTORY

INTERVIEWS WITH AUTHOR

Ammons, Cecil. April 1, 1980. Dallas, Texas.
Bernstein, Hyman. August 17, 1979. Orlando, Florida.
Bland, Albert. January 30, 1983. Joppatowne, Maryland.
Bradford, William. March 30, 1980. San Antonio, Texas.
Chiles, Lucy Hall. May 19, 1986. Reston, Virginia.
Coss, Walter. February 2, 1981. Fairfax, Virginia.
Cummings, William. March 30, 1980. San Antonio, Texas.
Dimson, Jaime and Juan. November 11, 1979. Lubao, Philippines.
Ellis, Herbert. August 16, 1979, and November 22, 1986. Orlando, Florida.
Hinson, Robert James. January 12, 1981. Austin, Texas.
Lunde, Oswald. April 2, 1980. McLean, Virginia.
Messmore, Hiram. January 11, 1981. Houston, Texas.
Millett, Sally Blaine. April 17, 1983. Falls Church, Virginia.
Moore, Joseph. June 11, 1981. Geneva, Switzerland.
Neri, Frank. March 29, 1980. Philadelphia, Pennsylvania.
Passanante, Bartholomo. January 29, 1983. Reston, Virginia.
Randolph, Jack. March 31, 1980. San Antonio, Texas.
Richardson, James. September 4, 1982. Arlington, Virginia.
Rizzolo, John. February 18, 1986. Washington, D.C.
Roberts, Frederick. March 23, 1980. Indialantic, Florida.
Robinett, Blair. March 21, 1983. Sterling, Virginia.
Rowe, William. May 9, 1986. Orlando, Florida.
Sly, Allen, and Omar McGuire. May 9, 1986. Orlando, Florida.
Ward, W. Joe. May 9, 1986. Orlando, Florida.

INTERVIEWS WITH OTHERS

With Calvin Chunn, 1942, Cabanatuan POW Camp
(in National Archives, Record Group 407, Box 1443)

Crosby, Stephen
Ellis, Herbert
Fulks, James
Parcher, Lawrence
Paulger, Claude
Anonymous officer of 5th Interceptor Command

With Walter D. Edmonds, G. A. McCulloch, or E. R. Emmett
(in Walter D. Edmonds Collection, Albert F. Simpson Historical
Research Center, Maxwell Air Force Base, Alabama)

Bolitho, S. Sgt. Hayes, and Sgt. Walter Alexander. April 8, 1945. Spokane,
    Washington.
Bostrom, Lt. Col. Frank. March 25, 1944. El Paso, Texas.
Bradford, Lt. Col. William. March 27, 1944. San Antonio, Texas.

Brownewell, Lt. Col. John. June 2, 1945. Manila, Philippines.
Carlisle, Col. Richard. February 27, 1945. Orlando, Florida.
Connally, Col. James. May 20, 1945. Tinian, Marianas.
Dale, Lt. Jack. November 24, 1944. Orlando, Florida.
Eads, Col. Harold. August 7, 1945. Tampa, Florida.
Elsmore, Col. Raymond. June 12, 1945. Hollandia, New Guinea.
Eubank, Brig. Gen. Eugene. November 29, 1945. Washington, D.C.
Feallock, Lt. Col. William. May 30, 1945. Fort Stotsenburg, Philippines.
Grashio, Maj. Samuel, and Sgt. Jack Donahoe. April 2, 3–4, and 7, 1945.
    Spokane, Washington.
Gunn, Col. Paul. April 2, 1945. Auburn, California.
Hunt, Capt. Ray. June 3, 1945. Manila, Philippines.
Kennard, Col. William. April 3, 1945. Spokane, Washington.
Krieger, Lt. Col. Andrew. January 22, 1945, and February 21, 1945. Orlando,
    Florida.
McMicking, Lt. Col. Joseph. June 5, 1945. Manila, Philippines.
O'Donnell, Brig. Gen. Emmett. July 2, 1945. Saipan, Marianas.
Posten, Maj. John. February 23, 1945. Orlando, Florida.
Putnam, Col. Walter. February 23, 1945. Orlando, Florida
Royce, Maj. Gen. Ralph. March 10, 1945. Atlantic City, N.J.
Sutherland, Lt. Gen. Richard. June 4, 1945. Manila, Philippines.
Whitcomb, Capt. Edgar. March 20, 1945. Wilmington, Delaware.

With George von Peterffy

Heinzel, Jack. May 9, 1985. Albuquerque, New Mexico.

With William Priestley, 1943, Cabanatuan POW Camp
(RG 407, "Philippines Records")

Baker, William   Lloyd, Thomas
Brodginski, Henry   Maverick, William
Crosland, Donald   Smith, Edward
Dyess, Edwin   Stinson, Lloyd
Ellis, Herbert   Woodside, Milton

With Reno, Nevada, radio station, ca. 1943

White, Varian K.

With John Toland, ca. 1958 (in materials of John Toland
for But Not in Shame, *Library of Congress, Washington, D.C.)*

Cave, Glenn   Moore, Joseph
Grow, Floyd   Roberts, Fred

TAPED NARRATIVES TO AUTHOR

Armstrong, George. May and October, 1977, January 4 and April 4, 1978.
Blanton, Nathaniel. November, 1980.

Brown, Ben, with Lloyd Stinson. March 3, 1979.
Cave, Glenn. April 4, 1981.
Jones, William. January 23 and February 28, 1981.
Madden, James. February 20, 1982.
Pitts, Enoch "Red." November 11–14, 1978.
Rogers, Jack, with James Bitner. June 15, 1986.
Thorne, Henry. May 4 and June 12, 1979.
Williams, Gus. May 7 and September 26, 1978.

TAPED NARRATIVES TO OTHERS

Brownewell, John, to Col. John Bradley. February, 1971.
Erickson, Edward, to John Brownewell. November, 1978.
Sheppard, William, to Charles Provan. October, 1974.

CORRESPONDENCE

PHILIPPINE DEPARTMENT/USAFFE WITH AGWAR AND USAAC

Brady, Col. Francis M., to Brig. Gen. Carl Spaatz. November 13, 1941.
MacArthur, Gen. Douglas, to Gen. George C. Marshall. November 29 and
    December 1, 1941.
Marshall, Gen. George C., to Maj. Gen. George Grunert. September 20, 1940,
    and February 8, 1941.

PILOTS AND OTHERS TO FAMILY MEMBERS AND FRIENDS

Armstrong, George, to wife. July–November, 1941.
Balfanz, A. W., to parents. July–November, 1941.
Brezina, Jerry, to parents. July, 1941.
Cole, Joe, to parents. January 22, 1942. (Published in *Greenville* [S.C.] *Pied-
    mont*, March 26, 1942.)
De Filippo, Lawrence, to parents. May, 1941.
Fisch, Ted, to wife. July, 1941.
Gies, Carl, to parents. May–November, 1941.
Glover, Wilson, to parents. July–November, 1941.
Hennon, William, to parents. May–October, 1941.
Hobrecht, Forrest, to parents. June–November, 1941.
Hummel, Frank, to Emmett Mahony. March, 1941.
Irvin, Ben, to mother. January, 1942.
Knackstedt, Arthur, to parents. November, 1941.
Krieger, Andrew, to father. March–November, 1941.
Lodin, Lawrence, to parents. May–November, 1941.
Louk, Max, to parents and sister. May–November, 1941.
McCowan, Morgan, to Bryant Holmes. June, 1941.
McCowan, Morgan, to parents. September–November, 1941.
Mahony, Grant, to "Marian." November, 1942.
Mahony, Grant, to mother. November, 1940–November, 1941.

Miller, Don, to parents. June–November, 1941.
Myers, Bertram, to parents. November, 1941.
Neri, Frank, to wife. May–November, 1941.
Ramsey, Percy, to parents. July, 1941.
Sheppard, William, to parents. November, 1940–February, 1942.
Sneed, Charles, to sister. December, 1940–November, 1941.
White, Varian Kiefer, to sister. May, 1942.

PILOTS AND OTHERS TO AUTHOR

Headquarters Squadron, 24th Pursuit Group

Cummings, Bill. 1978–79.
Franklin, Gene. 1982.
Hatzer, Clarence. 1978.
Madden, James. 1981–82.
Putnam, Benny. 1979.
White, Jesse. 1977–86.

3rd Pursuit Squadron

Boone, James. 1979.
Bradley, Hardy. 1982–83.
Cave, Glenn. 1981.
Ellis, Herb. 1978–89.
Gehrig, Ray. 1978–87.
Hinson, Jim. 1980.
Krieger, Andrew. 1979–83.
McBride, Woody. 1981.
Pitts, Red. 1978.
Powell, Bill. 1978–84.
Roland, Orville. 1980–82.
Schramm, Eric. 1981.
Sheeley, Charles. 1981–83.
Thorne, Hank. 1978–87.
Tyson, Herb. 1979–80.

17th Pursuit Squadron

Armstrong, George. 1976–88.
Bronk, Ted. 1982–83.
Brownewell, John. 1977–89.
Burris, Charles. 1978–79.
Coss, Walter. 1978–80.
Crosby, Steve. 1977.
Edsall, Carlton. 1978–81.
Feallock, Bill. 1978.
Gillespie, John. 1979–86.
Gillett, LaMar. 1982–84.
Hobrecht, Alfred. 1982.
Hughett, Maurice. 1981.
Kiser, George. 1979–84.
Lower, Joe. 1989.
Messmore, Hi. 1981.
Obert, Dave. 1978–89.
Rowe, Bill. 1978–89.
Sheppard, William "Red." 1978–89.
Wolf, Silas. 1980.
Wright, William "Cowboy." 1978–83.

20th Pursuit Squadron

Bowers, Glenn. 1978–80.
Brown, Jim. 1978–86.
De Jonge, Marian. 1983.
Fackender, Ken. 1986–89.
Fossey, Jim. 1978–86.
Gates, Jack. 1978–86.
Gilmore, Edwin. 1977–82.
Idlett, Doug. 1985.
Jones, Bill. 1981.
Keator, Randy. 1978–80.
King, Bill. 1979.
McClellan, Bob. 1985.
Moore, Joe. 1978–89.
Ramsey, Frank. 1983.

Rizzolo, John. 1985–86.
Siler, Fred. 1983.

Sperr, Roy. 1978–79.
Stinson, Lloyd. 1978–87.

21st Pursuit Squadron

Ammons, Cecil. 1980.
Bailey, Laura Irvin. 1987.
Baits, Bill. 1978.
Cowgill, John. 1981–88.
Ernst, Norm. 1980.
Gifford, Fred. 1978.
Grashio, Sam. 1977–86.

Hunt, Ray. 1978–79.
McGuire, Omar. 1982.
Mayhue, Frank. 1985.
Miller, Bob. 1985–86.
Sedlar, Joseph "Whitey." 1981.
Sly, Allen. 1986–89.
Williams, Gus. 1978–88.

34th Pursuit Squadron

Aguilar, Lorenzo. 1980.
Bass, Jim. 1979.
Brown, Ben. 1988.
Bryant, Frankie. 1979–85.
Chandler, Tom. 1978.
Coleman, Elbert. 1979.
Crosland, Don. 1979–89.

Gage, Tom. 1978–89.
Ostreich, Dave. 1982–83.
Pagel, Mrs. Henry. 1982.
Reynolds, Bob. 1980–81.
Robb, Stewart. 1978–88.
Smetts, Bob. 1980.

Others

Anders, Frank. 1986.
Anloff, Garry. 1979–86.
Bardowski, Zenon "Bud." 1983.
Bostrom, Frank. 1987.
Carpenter, John. 1979.
Chestnut, Albert. 1988.
Cocanougher, Harold. 1987.
Dickson, Ronald. 1981.
Fellows, Dick. 1986–87.
Goldblith, Samuel. 1982–83.
Hileman, Millard. 1982.
Hoffman, Fred. 1986.
House, Walter. 1979–80.

Lape, Ralph. 1986–87.
Michie, Robert. 1982.
Okumiya, Masatake. 1977.
Olson, John. 1985.
Ozaki, Saiji. 1980–81.
Pray, John. 1984.
Rogers, Jack. 1986.
Roseen, Everett. 1984.
Shingo, Hideki. 1979–82.
Shoss, Morris. 1981.
Tagaya, Sam. 1977.
Wang, Chih. 1988.
Young, Jim. 1979.

OTHER CORRESPONDENCE

Begley, Wild Bill, to Tom Gage. December, 1981.
Bell, Gilmer, to Walter D. Edmonds. March, 1947.
Boghosian, Sam, to John Brownewell. November, 1973.
Churchill, Lawrence, to Lewis Beebe. March, 1942.
Coleman, William, to Wilson Glover. January 28, 1943.
Davis, Kelly, to Mike Drake. December, 1981.
Edsall, Carlton, to Mrs. Ada Brezina. October, 1946.
Ellis, Herb, to William Leary. June, 1985.

Fellows, Dick, to Walter D. Edmonds. January, 1947.
Fry, Ralph, to John Brownewell. July, 1983.
Gehrig, Ray, to Frank Schirmer. August, 1979.
Hilton, Donald, to Walter D. Edmonds. March, 1947.
Krieger, Andy, to Walter D. Edmonds. October–November, 1945, and April, 1946.
Lape, Ralph, to John Brownewell. August, 1983.
Maitland, Lester, to Walter D. Edmonds. November, 1950.
Miller, Robert, to John Whitman. Ca. 1980.
Moore, Joseph, to Jim Brown. March, 1978.
Moore, Joseph, to William Leary. June, 1985.
Moore, Joseph to Robert Underbrink. July, 1967.
Obert, David, circular letter. 1980.
Pierce, Clinton, to Walter D. Edmonds. March, 1947.
Sheppard, William, to Charles Provan. October, 1974.
Sheppard, William, to Frank Schirmer. N.d.

Unpublished Written Materials

REPORTS AND STATEMENTS

Blanton, Maj. N. A. "Statement of Activities during the Early Days of the War." February 20, 1945.
Bradford, William R. "Intelligence Report, 7 February 1942."
Bridget, F. J. "Action of Longoskawayan Point against Japanese Forces." February 9, 1942.
Brown, Maj. Ben. "Statement." October 25, 1944.
"Cebu—Southern Islands Report." In William Priestley notebooks, Books 1 and 2.
Creusere, Lt. Col. Melvin S. "Quartermaster Report." N.d.
Darvall, Group Capt. Robert Charles. "Notes on the Defense Problem of Luzon." Manila, November, 1941.
Elsmore, Col. Ray T. "Statement. [Ca. 1945].
Hilton, Col. Donald B. "Statement." March 10, 1947.
"Historical Report, Visayas-Mindanao Report—Battle of Mindanao." N.d.
"A History of the Cebu Military Police Regiment and Cebu during the War Period." N.d.
Ind, Allison. "Composite Operations, Pilots' Report." March 2, 1942.
Keator, Col. Randall. "Supplementary Statement." April 5, 1974.
Kiser, Lt. Col. George E. "Statement." [Ca. 1944].
Obert, Maj. David L. "Activities of Fighter Units in the Philippines." April 25, 1945.
Obert, David, and I. B. J. Donalson. "Pilots' Report—February 23, 1942."
"Pilots' Report, Lt. Gehrig and Lt. Posten." April 4, 1942.
Quinn, Col. Michael A., QMC. "Operations of the Philippine Motor Transport Depot and the Motor Transport Service, Luzon Forces, P.I., during 1941–42." 1946.

"Report of Airdromes under Jurisdiction of Visayan-Mindanao Force, USAFFE."
February 2, 1942.
"Report of Operations in the Samar-Leyte Sector and in the Agusan Sector."
N.d.
"Report of the 17th Pursuit Squadron (Provisional) Activity in Java." N.d.
Robb, Maj. Stewart W. "Statement." November 30, 1944.
Rowe, Capt. William M. "Combat Reports, 10 December 1941–29 April 1942."
N.d.
Sackett, Comdr. E. L. "Bluejackets on Bataan." N.d.
———. "Operations of U.S.S. Canopus during War Period." June 17, 1942.
Sage, Brig. Gen. Charles G. "Report of Operations of the Philippine Provi-
sional Coast Artillery Brigade (AA) in the Philippines Campaign." N.d.
USS *Seadragon.* "Report of War Patrol #2." April 26, 1942.
Small, WO Ballard B. "Statement." October 15, 1942.
USS *Snapper.* "Report of War Patrol #2." April 25, 1942.
"27th Bomb Group Reports." N.d.
Whittenburg, Floyd E. "Brief History 680 Ord. Co. (Avn Pur) and the 2nd and
3rd Platoons of the 693 Ord. Co. (Avn Pur)." N.d.
"William Gay/Thomas Delamore Inspection Trip, January 19–20, 1942." N.d.
Wimer, Capt. C. J. "History of Signal Corps Radar Units in the Philippine
Islands, 1 August 1941–6 May 1942." 1946.
———. "Report on Enemy Air Activities over the Philippines up to and In-
cluding the First Day of War, as Observed by S.C. Radar." 1946.

UNIT DIARIES, HISTORIES, AND NARRATIVES

Amato, Capt. Ralph, Jr., and Louis F. Murphy. "History, Second Battalion 45th
Infantry P.S., December 8, 1941–April 9, 1942." In Chunn notebooks, RG
407, Box 1443.
Army Air Action in the Philippines and Netherlands East Indies, 1941–42.
USAF Historical Study No. 111. Washington, D.C.: Assistant Chief of Air
Staff, Intelligence, Historical Division, March, 1945.
Army Air Force in Australia to the Summer of 1942. USAF Historical Study
No. 9. Washington, D.C.: Assistant Chief of Air Staff, Intelligence, Histori-
cal Division, 1944.
Braly, Col. William C. "Operations Log, Corregidor, 7 December 1941–8 Feb-
ruary 1942." Vol. 1 (typescript). N.d. U.S. Army Military History Institute.
Chynoweth, Brig. Gen. Bradford G. "The 61st Division P.A. and the Visayan
Force—World War II" (typescript). December 31, 1947. U.S. Army Military
History Institute.
Fellows, Maj. Richard W. "Philippine Air Depot." March Field, California,
May 18, 1943. In Edmonds Collection, Albert F. Simpson Historical Re-
search Center.
Grover, Col. O. L. "Narrative of the Activities of the 24th Pursuit Group in
the Philippine Islands." Brisbane, Australia, October 7, 1942. In Edmonds
Collection, Albert F. Simpson Historical Research Center.
Headquarters, Far East Air Force. "Summary of Activities, 8 December 1941–

24 February 1942." [Ca. 1942]. In Brereton Collection, Dwight D. Eisenhower Library, Abilene, Kans.

"History and Approximate Diary of 3rd Battalion, 45th Infantry PS during the Philippines Campaign (December 8, 1941–April 9, 1942)." In Chunn notebooks, RG 407, Box 1443.

"History, Visayan-Mindanao Force." N.d.

Lester, Capt. John E. "Air Corps in the War." [Ca. 1945]. In U.S. Army Military History Institute.

Montgomery, Capt. Robert D. "Battle of Agloloma, Bataan, P.I., January 1942, Regarding Company A, 803rd Engineering Battalion." Tampa, Fla." June 24, 1946.

————. "Brief History (Stations, Records, and Events), Company A, 803rd Engineering Battalion (AVN)" Tampa, Fla., June 21, 1946.

"19th Bomb Group Diary." N.d. In Edmonds Collection, Albert F. Simpson Historical Research Center.

"Patrol Wing 10 Diary." N.d. In Naval Historical Center, Washington Navy Yard.

Sanders, Maj. Cecil M. "The Operations of the 57th Infantry (PS) (Philippine Division) at Anyasan and Silaiim Points, Bataan, P.I., 2 February–13 February 1942 (Philippine Islands Campaign)." Fort Benning, Ga. Infantry School, 1950.

"16th Naval District War Diary." N.d.

Sutherland, Maj. Gen. Richard M. "Brief Summary of Activities in the Office of the Chief of Staff, Headquarters, U.S. Army Forces in the Far East, 8:58 AM December 8, 1941 to 11:00 PM, February 22, 1942." In RG-2, USAFFE, MacArthur Memorial archives.

USAFFE. "Diary, General Douglas MacArthur, Commanding General, United States Army Forces in the Far East." In MacArthur Memorial archives.

"War Diary of the *Sanuki Maru*" (December, 1941–April, 1942) (in Japanese). In Naval Historical Center.

PERSONAL NARRATIVES

Bowers, Glenn. January 9, 1979, to author.

Bradford, William R. "Final Mission of the Bamboo Fleet." N.d.

Bradley, Hardy. April 18, 1983, to author.

Brown, James E. April 10, 1978, to author.

Crosby, Stephen H., Jr. 1945. (disavowed by Crosby)

Ellis, Herbert S. 1979, to author.

Ernst, Norman L. March 6, 1980, to author.

Fossey, W. James. June 14, 1978, to author.

Krieger, Andrew E. [Ca. 1943].

McGuire, Omar. August 23, 1982, to author.

"Reminiscences of Lt. Col. Howard W. Brown." SRH -045, August 10, 1945. Washington, D.C.: Signal Security Agency. In RG 457, National Archives.

Roland, Orville. August 21 and September 17, 1980, to author.

Sheppard, William A., and Edwin B. Gilmore. November 1, 1944–February 1, 1945.

Stanford, Ken. July, 1978, to author.
Stinson, Lloyd. June 8, 1978, to author.
Thorne, Henry G., Jr. September 16, 1947.
Wang, Chih. N.d.
White, Jesse. December 29, 1977, to author.
Wright, William R. "Philippine Notes." N.d.
———. [Ca. 1979].

PERSONAL DIARIES AND JOURNALS

Anabuki, Satoshi.
Arhutick, Leo.
Bell, Gilmer M.
Brodine, Baron "Barney."
Brownewell, John L.
Campbell, Alexander. Notebook.
Cappelletti, Francis M.
Collier, James V. Notebooks.
Denby, Arthur L.
Elsmore, Ray T.
Erickson, Edward.
Fairfield, William A.
Geer, John H.
Gerrity, Thomas. (published
  —see below)
Gies, Carl Parker.

Glover, Wilson. Notebook.
Hart, Thomas. Personal papers.
Hennon, William J.
Hough, Richard D.
Keator, Randall.
Lathrop, Leslie T.
McAfee, James B.
Mallonee, Richard C.
Montgomery, William H.
Obert, David L.
Posten, John.
Powell, William H.
Rowe, William M.
Sharp, William F. Notebook.
Steele, Donald.
Stewart, William N.

PHILIPPINE DEPARTMENT AND USAFFE MEMORANDA (CHRONOLOGICAL)

George, Col. H. H., to Commanding General, USAFFE. August 14, 1941.
Clagett, Brig. Gen. H. B., Commanding Officer, Air Force, USAFFE, to Commanding General, USAFFE. Subject: "Study of Air Force for United States Army Forces in the Far East." September 11, 1941.
George, Col. H. H., to Engineer, Philippine Department. October 9, 1941.
Headquarters, Air Force, USAFFE, to All Post, Group and Separate Squadron Commanders. Subject: "Preparation for Emergency." November 10, 1941.
Headquarters, Far East Air Force, to Commanding Officers, 5th Interceptor Command, 5th Bomber Command. Far East Air Service Command, and 2nd Observation Squadron. Subject: "Readiness Status of Far East Air Force." November 28, 1941.
Headquarters, USAFFE, to Commanding General, North Luzon Force, Fort Stotsenburg. Subject: "Defense of the Philippines." December 3, 1941.
Manzano, Lt. Col. December 13, 1941.
"Report Received from Major Fertig," Department Engineer. December 14, 1941.
Engineer, USAFFE, to Commanding General, FEAF. December 16, 1941.
C/S, USAFFE, to Commanding General, Visayas-Mindanao Force. December 16, 1941.

Brereton, Maj. Gen., Commanding General FEAF. "Air Estimate of Situation."
    December 22, 1941.
Richardson, 1st Lt. James D., 803 Aviation Engineers, to Engineer, USAFFE.
    December 26, 1941.
Mamerow, Capt. J. R., Adj. Gen. 5th Interceptor Command, "Aircraft Status,"
    to Commanding General, USAFFE, December 31, 1941.
Casey, Maj. Gen. Hugh J., Engineer, USAFFE, to C/S, USAFFE. Subject: "Engi-
    neer Operations, Weekly Period Ending Jan. 17, 1942, Jan. 24, 1942, Jan. 31,
    1942."
Funk, Col. Arnold J., Asst. G-3, Advance Echelon, USAFFE to G-3, USAFFE.
    January 11, 1942.
Marshall, Lt. Col. Floyd J., Asst. C/S, G-1, Headquarters, Philippine Depart-
    ment in the Field, to G-3, USAFFE. January 12, 1942.
Headquarters, FEAF. "Payment of Per Diem to Fliers." January 16, 1942.
Traywick, Lt. Col. J. T., Jr., Asst. G-3, Advance Echelon, USAFFE, to G-3.
    January 29, 1942.
Air Base Headquarters, Del Monte, to Gen. George, February 2, 1942.
"Inspection of Lt. Delamore." February 6, 1942.
Casey, Maj. Gen. Hugh H., Engineer, to FEAF. Memo No. 121. February 14,
    1942.
Rockwell, Rear Adm. Francis W., Commandant, 16th Naval District, to Com-
    manding General, USAFFE. March 1, 1942.
Eads, Maj. Harold. 5th Interceptor Command, to C/S, USAFFE. March 3, 1942.
Air Officer, USAFFE, to C/S, USAFFE. March 14, 1942.
"Inspection of FEAF Units." March 28, 1942.
Seals, Brig. Gen. Carl H., to Col. Lawrence Churchill. March 29, 1942.
Beebe, Brig. Gen. Lewis C., to Commanding Officer, FEAF. April 2, 1942.
Romulo, Col. Carlos, to C/S, SWPA. May 5, 1942.

USAFFE REPORTS, JOURNALS, AND BULLETINS

Bell, Col. Gilmer M., G-3, 71st Division. "G-3 Report." January–February, 1942.
Fifth Interceptor Command. "S-3 Report." January–April, 1942.
Nelson, Col. Frank, G-3, I Philippine Corps. "G-3 Report." February, 1942.
USAFFE. "G-2 Information Bulletin." December, 1941–February, 1942.
———. "G-2 Journal." December, 1941–February, 1942.
———. "G-3 Information Bulletin." December, 1941–February, 1942.
———. "G-3 Periodic Report." January, 1942.

MILITARY MEDAL CITATIONS

Distinguished Flying Cross
    Brownewell, John
    Franks, Perry
    Sneed, Charles
Distinguished Service Cross
    Church, Russel
    Dale, Jack

    Gies, Carl
    Wagner, Boyd
Purple Heart
    Wagner, Boyd D.
Silver Star
    Brownewell, John
    Cowgill, John

RADIOGRAMS

AGWAR to Philippine Department. December 14, 1940.

AGWAR to USAFFE. August 12, November 27, and December 23, 1941.

Beebe, Brig. Gen. Lewis, to 9 M N. March 14, 1942.

Elsmore, Col. Ray, to Brig. Gen. H. H. George. February 20, 1942.

Gregg, Col. K. J., to Brig. Gen. Lewis Beebe. March 14, 1942.

MacArthur, Gen. Douglas, to Col. Lawrence Churchill, April 7, 1942.

MacArthur, Gen. Douglas, to Brig. Gen. Bradford G. Chynoweth. February 19, 1942.

MacArthur, Gen. Douglas, to Col. William P. Morse. January 5, 1942.

MacArthur, Gen. Douglas, to Maj. Gen. Jonathan Wainwright. April 8, 21, and 30, 1942.

Marquat, Brig. Gen. William F., to Commanding General, Harbor Defenses of Manila and Subic Bays. December 5, 1941.

Philippine Department to AGWAR. December 23, 1940; January 9, March 6, April 19, and May 10, 1941.

Sharp, Brig. Gen. William F., Commanding General, Visayan-Mindanao Force, to Commanding General, USAFFE. December 20, 1941.

USAFFE to AGWAR. December 28, 1941.

Wainwright, Maj. Gen. Jonathan, to Gen. Douglas MacArthur. April 5, 1942.

INTERNAL USAFFE MESSAGES

G-3, I Corps, to Col. Constant L. Irwin, G-3, USAFFE. February 7, 1942.

George, Brig. Gen. H. H., to Col. Constant L. Irwin, G-3, USAFFE. February 7, 1942.

Irwin, Col. Constant L., G-3, USAFFE, to 5th Interceptor Command. February 8, 1942.

Irwin, Col. Constant L., G-3, USAFFE, to G-3, I Corps. February 8, 1942.

GENERAL, FIELD, AND SPECIAL ORDERS

Air Base Headquarters., Selfridge Field, Michigan. Special Orders No. 124, October 23, 1940.

5th Interceptor Command. Special Orders No. 1, December 31, 1941.

Headquarters, Allied Air Force S.W. Pacific Area. Special Orders No. 5, May 6, 1942.

Headquarters, 71st Division and South Sub-Sector. Field Order No. 2, February 25, 1942.

USAFFE. Field Order No. 2, January 7, 1942.

USAFFE. General Orders No. 1, September 16, 1941; No. 21, February 7, 1942; No. 40, March 13, 1942.

USAFFE. Special Orders No. 66, March 11, 1942.

TRANSLATIONS OF INTERCEPTED JAPANESE NAVAL MESSAGES
(RG 457, BOXES 162–63)

SRN 129,733, December 11, 1941.   SRN 129,842, December 14, 1941.

SRN 129,751, December 12, 1941.   SRN 129,868, December 16, 1941.

SRN 129,912, December 18, 1941.   SRN 130,314, December 27, 1941.
SRN 129,961, December 20, 1941.   SRN 130,625, January 6, 1942.
SRN 130,013, December 22, 1941.   SRN 131,025, January 16, 1942.
SRN 130,076, December 22, 1941.   SRN 132,001, February 3, 1942.

OTHER ITEMS

Aircraft History Cards for P-26As, P-35s, P-40Bs, P-40Es, and A-27s. Washington, D.C.: National Air and Space Museum.

Aircraft Status Report. November, 1940–November, 1941 (monthly). Philippine Department.

Basic Aircraft Machine Guns, Cal. 50, T36, and T25E3 (M3). Technical Manual TM 9-219. Washington, D.C.: War Department, April 5, 1945.

Bradford, William K. Flight Log.

Dale, Jack. Certificates to Richard W. Fellows. March 1, 1943.

Feallock, William. Certificate to Richard W. Fellows. March 8, 1943.

Fixed Aerial and Ground Gunnery. Technical Manual 1-273. Washington, D.C.: War Department, December 15, 1942.

Gerow, Brig. Gen. Leonard T., War Plans Division, to Secretary of War. Memorandum. October 2, 1941.

Grover, Col. O. L. "List of Air Corps Officers in the Philippines." Brisbane, August 22, 1942.

———. "Roster of the 24th Pursuit Group as of December 8, 1941." [1943?].

Headquarters, Air Force Combat Command, to Maj. Gen. Henry H. Arnold. Memorandum. October 1, 1941.

Identification of Japanese Aircraft. Basic Field Manual 30-38. Washington, D.C.: War Department, March 10, 1941.

The Imperial Japanese Navy in World War II. Japanese Monograph No. 116. Tokyo: General Headquarters, Far East Command, Military History Section, n.d.

Mahony, Grant. Individual Flight Record, December, 1941.

Operational Situation of the Japanese Navy in the Philippines Invasion Operations, December 1941. Japanese Monograph No. 80. Tokyo: Headquarters, Army Forces Far East, Military History Section, n.d.

Philippines Air Operations Record — Phase One. Japanese Monograph No. 11. Tokyo: Headquarters, Army Forces Far East, Military History Section, February, 1952.

"Pilots Manual for the Curtiss P-40 Warhawk." N.d.

"Report of Death" (AGO Form 52-1). War Department, Adjutant General's Office. Various, for individual deceased 24th Pursuit Group officers.

"Roster of Officers." Headquarters, 24th Pursuit Group, March 7, 1942.

Rowe, William M. Individual Flight Record, May–November, 1941.

Technical Radiogram. Wright Field, October 14, 1941.

Wagner, Boyd D. Memo to Headquarters, Pursuit Section, Northeast Area, Townsville, Queensland, May 11, 1942.

MAGAZINE AND NEWSPAPER ARTICLES

Alcorn, John S. "The Grim Reapers," *American Aviation Historical Society Journal* 20, no. 1 (Spring, 1975): 6–15.

Army and Navy Legion of Valor, March 9, 1943.

Bartsch, William H. "Good God Almighty, Yonder They Come!" *Fighter Pilots in Aerial Combat* (Costa Mesa, Calif.), no. 12 (Spring 1984): 4–9.

―――. "We Are Doomed at the Start." *American Aviation Historical Society Journal* 29, no. 2 (Summer, 1984): 141–47.

Birrn, Roland. "A War Diary." *Air Power Historian* 3, no. 4 (October, 1956): 195–202; 4, no. 1 (January, 1957): 40–45; 4, no. 2 (April, 1957): 98–103.

Boghosian, S. Samuel. "The One Man Pursuit Force." *Air Force Magazine,* September, 1973, pp. 94–98.

Cool, Capt. Paul. "Adventure over―and on―the Pacific." *Detroit Free Press,* October 25, 1942.

Durdin, F. Tillman. "Philippine Raid 'a Picnic'; Hope for Offensive Bounds." *New York Times.* April 17, 1942, pp. 1–2.

Fellows, Richard W. "Last Flight into Bataan." *Daedalus Flyer,* Winter, 1984, pp. 22–24.

Futrell, Robert F. "Air Hostilities in the Philippines, 8 December 1941." *Air University Review* (Maxwell Air Force Base, Ala.), January–February, 1965, pp. 33–45.

Gerrity, Lt. Tom. "Bataan Diary." *Los Angeles Times,* June 21–26, 1942.

Goldblith, Samuel A. "The 803rd Engineers in the Philippine Defense." *Military Engineer,* August, 1942, pp. 323–25.

Gordon, John, IV. "The Navy's Infantry on Bataan." *U.S. Naval Institute Proceedings,* March, 1985, pp. 64–69.

Groves, Patricia. "No Joy in Java." *R/C Sportsman,* March, 1977, pp. 29–34, 51.

―――. "Not Exactly First Class", *R/C Sportsman,* February, 1977.

Hileman, Millard, "698th Ordnance." *The Quan* (McKees Rocks, PA), November, 1981, pp. 7, 15.

Hoogaboom, William F. "Action Report: Bataan." *Marine Corps Gazette,* April, 1946, pp. 25–33.

Hoyt, Brig. Gen. Ross G. "The P-26A." *Air Force Magazine,* January, 1977, pp. 60–61.

Hucker, Robert. "Sam Marett, Forgotten Fighter." *Air Classics,* July, 1977, pp. 90–92, 113–14.

Hurd, Charles. "MacArthur Breaks Attack in Bataan." *New York Times,* February 12, 1942.

Manila Bulletin. 1936, 1941.

Manila Tribune. April–December, 1941.

Miza, Masami. "Meritorious Deeds of the Secret Reconnoitering Unit That Became the Shadow Strength of the Zero Fighter Squadron" (in Japanese). *Maru* (Tokyo), February, 1962, pp. 126–29.

Moore, J. James. "How Buzz Wagner Fought, Escaped Japs Revealed on Eve of Hero's Funeral." *Pittsburgh Sun-Telegraph*, January 10, 1943, pp. 1, 10.

Nichols News (Manila). April–November, 1941.

Philippine Herald (Manila). April, 1941.

Prickett, William F. "The Naval Battalion on Bataan." *U.S. Naval Institute Proceedings*, November, 1960, pp. 72–81.

Risedorph, Gene. "Last Flight into Corregidor." *Daedalus Flyer*, Summer, 1983, pp. 26–28.

Schedler, Dean. "The Last Plane from Bataan: A Reporter Tells of Island-to-Island Escape." *San Francisco Chronicle*, May 10, 1942.

Stevens, Will. "Captain Grattan Mahony, Most Chased Pilot in the Far East." *Vallejo Times Herald* (Vallejo, CA), March 1, 1942.

Teats, Maj. Edward C. "Turn of the Tide." *Philadelphia Enquirer*, December 31, 1942–January 18, 1943.

Tebbutt, Geoffrey. "U.S. Raid on Davao Masked by Jungle." *New York Times*, February 12, 1942, p. 6.

Tolley, Kemp. "The Sailormen-Riflemen of Bataan." *Military Journal* 2, no. 3 (Winter, 1978/79): 48–49.

"U.S. Bataan Pilots Pick Off Their Foe." *New York Times*, February 1, 1942.

"U.S. to Defend Philippines, Selfridge Field Fliers to Go." *Detroit News*, October 23, 1940.

Ushijima, Yasushi. "Japanese Warhawk." *American Aviation Historical Society Journal*, Summer, 1975, pp. 89–93.

Villamor, Jesus. "Farewell to Bataan." *Kislap Graphic* (Manila), August 20, 1958, pp. 12–13, 36.

———. "Suicide Mission." *Kislap Graphic* (Manila), August 13, 1958, pp. 14, 40–41.

Wagner, Boyd. "Boyd Wagner's Story: America's First Ace Tells How He Shot Down First Two Planes." *Life*, December 29, 1941, pp. 36–37.

Weller, George. "Luck to the Fighters." *Military Affairs*, Spring, 1945, pp. 33–62.

BOOKS AND CHAPTERS IN BOOKS

American Battle Monuments Commission. *Register of World War II Dead*. Washington, D.C.: American Battle Monuments Commission, n.d.

Beck, John J. *MacArthur and Wainwright: Sacrifice of the Philippines*. Albuquerque: University of New Mexico Press, 1974.

Belote, James H., and William B. Belote. *Corregidor: The Saga of a Fortress*. New York: Harper and Row, 1967.

Boeicho Kenshujo Senshishitsu (Japanese Defense Agency, War History Section). *Navy Attack Operations against the Philippines and Malaya* (in Japanese). *Senshi Sosho* 24. Tokyo: Asagumo, 1969.

———. *Southern Attack Army Air Operations* (in Japanese). *Senshi Sosho* 34. Tokyo: Asagumo, 1970.

Brereton, Lewis H. *The Brereton Diaries*. New York: William Morrow, 1946.

Brown, David. *Carrier Operations in World War II*. Vol. 2. Annapolis, Md.: Naval Institute Press, 1974.

Bulkley, Robert, Jr. *At Close Quarters: PT Boats in the United States Navy.* Washington, D.C.: GPO, 1962.

Charles, Roland W. *Troopships of World War II.* Washington, D.C.: Army Transport Association, 1947.

Cohen, Stan. *Wings to the Orient.* Missoula, Mont.: Pictorial Histories Publishing, 1985.

Dull. Paul S. *A Battle History of the Imperial Japanese Navy (1941–1945).* Annapolis, Md.: Naval Institute Press, 1978.

Dyess, William E. *The Dyess Story.* New York: G. P. Putnam's Sons, 1944.

Edmonds, Walter D. *They Fought with What They Had.* Boston: Little Brown, 1951.

Francillon, René. *Japanese Aircraft of the Pacific War.* London: Putnam, 1970.

Grashio, Samuel C., and Bernard Norling. *Return to Freedom.* Tulsa: MCN Press, 1982.

Ind, Allison. *Bataan: The Judgment Seat.* New York: Macmillan, 1944.

Izawa, Yasuho, and Ikuhiko Hata. *Japanese Army Fighter Units* (in Japanese). Tokyo: Airview, 1973.

_____. *Japanese Navy Fighter Units* (in Japanese). Tokyo: Airview, 1971.

Kenney, George. *The Saga of Pappy Gunn.* New York: Duell, Sloan and Pierce, 1959.

Knox, Donald. *Death March.* New York: Harcourt Brace Jovanovich, 1981.

Lee, Clark. *They Call It Pacific.* New York: Viking Press, 1943.

McGee, John H. *Rice and Salt.* San Antonio, Tex.: Naylor, 1962.

McGlothlin, Frank E. *Barksdale to Bataan: History of the 48th Materiel Squadron, October 1940–April 1942.* Covington, La.: privately published, 1984.

Mayborn, Mitch, and Peter M. Bowers. *Stearman Guidebook.* (Dallas, Tex.: Flying Enterprise Publications, 1973.

Messimer, Dwight. *In the Hands of Fate.* Annapolis, Md.: Naval Institute Press, 1985.

Miller, Ernest B. *Bataan Uncensored.* Long Prairie, Minn.: Hart Publications, 1949.

Mingos, Howard. *American Heroes of the War in the Air.* New York: Lanciar Publishers, 1943.

Monaghan, Forbes. *Under the Red Sun.* New York: Declan X. McMullen, 1946.

Mori, Shiro. *Kaigun Sentokitai (Navy Fighter Groups)* (in Japanese). Vol. 1, *Kaisen Zenya* (Night before outbreak of war). Tokyo: R. Shuppan, 1979.

Morton, Louis. *The Fall of the Philippines.* Washington, D.C.: Office of the Chief of Military History, U.S. Army, 1953.

_____. *Strategy and Command.* Washington, D.C.: Office of the Chief of Military History, U.S. Army, 1962.

Noyer, William L. *Mactan, Ship of Destiny.* Fresno, Calif.: Rainbow Press, 1979.

Philippine Air Force. *Fifty Years Philippine Air Force.* Manila: Philippine Air Force, 1971.

Reynolds, Robert. *Of Rice and Men.* Philadelphia: Dorrance, 1947.

Romulo, Carlos. *I Saw the Fall of the Philippines.* New York: Doubleday Doran, 1943.

Sakai, Saburo. *Ohzora no Samurai (Samurai of the Skies)* (in Japanese). Tokyo: Kojinsha, 1967).

Santos, Enrique B. *Trails in Philippine Skies.* Manila: Philippine Airlines, 1981.

Schultz, Duane. *Hero of Bataan.* New York: St. Martins, 1981.

Scott, Robert L. *Damned to Glory.* New York: Scribners, 1944. See especially chapter 2, "Subic Bay," pp. 88–104; chapter 3, "One-Man War of Cebu," pp. 105–15; and chapter 8, "Psychopathic Case," pp. 148–53.

Shimada, Koichi. "The Opening Air Offensive against the Philippines." In *The Japanese Navy in World War II,* edited by David C. Evans, pp. 71–104. Annapolis, Md.: Naval Institute Press, 1986.

Thompson, George R., Dixie R. Harris, Pauline M. Oakes, and Dulaney Terrett. *The Signal Corps: The Test (December 1941 to July 1943).* Washington, D.C.: GPO, 1957.

Toland, John. *But Not in Shame.* New York: Random House, 1961.

Underbrink, Robert L. *Destination Corregidor.* Annapolis, Md.: Naval Institute Press, 1971.

Valencia, Jerry. *Knights of the Sky.* San Diego, Calif.: Reed Enterprises, 1980. See especially "I. B. Jack Donalson," pp. 87–104.

Villamor, Jesus A. *They Never Surrendered.* Quezon City, Philippines: Vera-Reyes, 1982.

War Department. *Army Register, 1942.* Washington, D.C.: War Department, 1943.

Williams, Ted. *Rogues of Bataan.* New York: Carlton Press, 1979.

Wilmott, H. P. *Empires in the Balance.* Annapolis, Md.: Naval Institute Press, 1982.

Winter, William. *Warplanes of All Nations.* New York: Thomas Y. Crowell, 1943.

Yokoyama, Tamotsu. *Ah Zero Sen Ichidai (Oh, My Life in the Zero Fighter)* (in Japanese). Tokyo: Kojinsha, 1969).

Index

(Page numbers of illustrations italicized)

Doomed at the Start was composed into type on a Compugraphic digital phototypesetter in nine and one-half point Trump with two and one-half points of spacing between the lines. Trump was also selected for display. The book was designed by Jim Billingsley, typeset by Metricomp, Inc., printed offset by Thomson-Shore, Inc., and bound by John H. Dekker & Sons, Inc. The paper on which this book is printed carries acid-free characteristics for an effective life of at least three hundred years.

TEXAS A&M UNIVERSITY PRESS : COLLEGE STATION